A Legal Geography of

Yugoslavia's

Disintegration

A Legal Geography of

Yugoslavia's

Disintegration

ANA S. TRBOVICH

OXFORD
UNIVERSITY PRESS

OXFORD
UNIVERSITY PRESS

Oxford University Press, Inc., publishes works that further Oxford University's
objective of excellence in research, scholarship, and education.

Copyright © 2008 by Oxford University Press, Inc.
Published by Oxford University Press, Inc.
198 Madison Avenue, New York, New York 10016

Oxford is a registered trade mark of Oxford University Press
Oceana is a registered trade mark of Oxford University Press, Inc.

Library of Congress Control Number: 2007925251

ISBN 978-0-19-533343-5 (clothbound)

Note to Readers:

This publication is designed to provide accurate and authoritative information in regard to the subject matter covered. It is based upon sources believed to be accurate and reliable and is intended to be current as of the time it was
written. It is sold with the understanding that the publisher is not engaged in rendering legal, accounting, or other
professional services. If legal advice or other expert assistance is required, the services of a competent professional
person should be sought. Also, to confirm that the information has not been affected or changed by recent developments, traditional legal research techniques should be used, including checking primary sources where appropriate.

(Based on the Declaration of Principles jointly adopted by a Committee of the
American Bar Association and a Committee of Publishers and Associations.)

> You may order this or any other Oxford University Press publication
> by visiting the Oxford University Press website at www.oup.com

Table of Contents

Acknowledgements

This book is principally a product of my doctoral work at the Fletcher School of Law and Diplomacy, guided by Hurst Hannum, guru of self-determination and especially its fair distribution, Alan K. Henrikson, faithful disciple of Sir Harold Nicolson who fortified in me the love for the art of diplomacy and Alfred P. Rubin, who taught me the subtle difference between law and morality. An unofficial but ever present advisor was Professor Peter Radan from Australia, as well as other faculty from Tufts and Harvard, my two Bostonian almae mater, and other eminent scholars, most notably Susan Woodward. The Associate Dean of the Kennedy School of Government Joe McCarthy and his family, Professor Bill Moomaw from the Fletcher School, John Jenke from Tufts University, Dushan T. Batakovich and Milan St. Protich from the Institute for Balkan Studies in Serbia and the historian Slobodan G. Markovich were especially supportive. This book has been further enriched by my encounters with fellow students, academics, diplomats and politicians from the Balkans and other parts of the globe, several of whom have been directly quoted in the book and many of whom became my friends in the process, sharing an aspiration that the future would be one of building rather than destroying bridges. Harvard's Kokkalis Program for Southeastern Europe, skillfully led by Dimitris Keridis and Elaine Papoulias, is responsible for providing me with an opportunity to gain some of these invaluable experiences while studying at the Kennedy School of Government. Finally, it is my parents who encouraged me to pursue freedom by education, and my spouse and children, as well as my brothers and my wonderful extended family, who endured this effort with me. This is but a small opportunity for me to thank them all for all they have given to me, dedicating this work to all the children of the former Yugoslavia with hope that history would serve future peace.

A Note on Transliteration of Names

Diacritic marks were used for names in languages whose official script is based on the Roman alphabet. In the case of the Serbian language, where the official script is based on the Serbian Cyrillic alphabet, featuring thirty sounds and an equal number of letters, the traditional, phonetic transliteration into English was employed. However, it should be noted that Roman alphabet has also been in public use as a script for the Serbian language since the creation of Yugoslavia, particularly since 1960s, which resulted in two additional types of transliteration for Serbian language—transliteration using Roman alphabet with diacritic marks and transliteration using Roman alphabet without diacritic marks (the latter became common in the Western media since 1990s and is thus termed "recent Yugoslav"; *see* table below[1]*)*. To diminish the created confusion, personal and geographic Serbian names in all forms of transliteration are listed in the Index. The author also denotes in the text two different types of English spelling for names that have become known to the wider English speaking audience in Roman alphabet without diacritic marks rather than in the traditional phonetic transliteration. Phonetic transliteration was not applied to names of those modern Serbian authors quoted in this book who have used other types of transliteration for their works published in English.

Serbian Cyrillic letters	TRANSLITERATION			
	Roman alphabet with diacritic marks	Roman alphabet without diacritic marks ("Recent Yugoslav")	English phonetic	Guide to pronunciation
А	A	A	A	A, as 'a' in Amsterdam
Б	B	B	B	B, as 'b' in Belgium

---

[1]   Table adapted from Slobodan G. Markovich, *British Perceptions of Serbia and the Balkans, 1903-1906* (Paris: Dialogue Association, 2000); Stevan K. Pavlowitch, *Anglo-Russian Rivalry in Serbia, 1837-1839;The Mission of Colonel Hedges* (Paris; The Hague: Mouton &Co, 1961) and Leften S. Stavrianos, *The Balkans since 1453* (London: Hurst, 2000).

Serbian Cyrillic letters	TRANSLITERATION			
	Roman alphabet with diacritic marks	**Roman alphabet without diacritic marks ("Recent Yugoslav")**	**English phonetic**	**Guide to pronunciation**
В	V	V	V	V, as 'v' in **V**ienna
Г	G	G	G	G, as 'g' in **G**ambia
Д	D	D	D	D, as 'd' in **D**enmark
Ђ	Đ	Dj	Dy	Dy, as 'd y' in woul**d** **y**ou, close to the phonetic dj (џ), but softer
Е	E	E	E	E, as 'e' in **E**cuador
Ж	Ž	Z	Zh	Zh, as 's' in lei**s**ure
З	Z	Z	Z	Z, as 'z' in **Z**ambia
И	I	I	I	I, as 'i' in **I**ndia
Ј	J	J	Y	Y, as 'y' in **Y**ugoslavia
К	K	K	K	K, as 'k' in **K**enya
Л	L	L	L	L, as 'l' in **L**atvia
Љ	Lj	Lj	Ly	Ly, as 'l' in the British pronunciation of 'revolution'
М	M	M	M	M, as 'm' in **M**orocco
Н	N	N	N	N, as 'n' in **N**orway
Њ	Nj	Nj	Ny	Ny, as 'n' in **n**ew
О	O	O	O	O, as 'o' in **O**ntario
П	P	P	P	P, as 'p' in **P**oland
Р	R	R	R	R, as 'r' in **R**ussia
С	S	S	S	S, as 's' in **S**amoa
Т	T	T	T	T, as 't' in **T**ogo
Ћ	Ć	C	Ch	Ch, as 'c' in Italian pronunciation of '**c**iao,' simitlar to 'ч', but softer
У	U	U	U	U, as 'oo' in l**oo**k
Ф	F	F	F	F, as 'f' in **F**inland
Х	H	H	H	H, as 'h' in **H**olland
Ц	C	C	Ts	Ts, as 'ts' in ca**ts**
Ч	Č	C	Ch	Ch, as 'ch' in **Ch**ad
Џ	Dž	Dz	Dj	Dj as 'j' in **J**apan
Ш	Š	S	Sh	Sh, as 'sh' in **sh**are

CHAPTER 1

Legal Context of Yugoslavia's Disintegration: Sovereignty and Self-Determination of Peoples

1.1. Introduction

The tale of the break-up of the former Yugoslavia is one of context, a merging of historical events and a political compromise of two cardinal legal principles—sovereignty and self-determination of peoples. The primary aim of the present study is to assess how the international response to the Yugoslav constitutional crisis, violently erupting in 1991, impacted the development of the elusive principle of people's right to self-determination and its relationship to sovereignty.

Notably, by recognizing the right to independence of the former Yugoslav republics, the international community effectively recognized the right to secession in the case of Yugoslavia's disintegration. This policy represents an almost complete reversal of post-World War II practice,[1] which generally prohibited secession[2] and encouraged settlement of ethnic conflicts within the borders of an existing state. In the case of Yugoslavia, the fundamental principle of territorial integrity,[3] which lies at the basis of international law, appears to have been undermined.

---

[1]   One exception is the case of Bangladesh, which seceded from Pakistan in 1971. See below.

[2]   The term "secession" as used here does not include the decolonization process that took place after Second World War. It refers to entities breaking away from within internationally recognized states.

[3]   U.N. Charter, Article 2 (4): "All members shall refrain in their international relations from the threat or use of force against the territorial integrity or political independence of any state, or in any other manner inconsistent with the Purposes of the United Nations."

Moreover, the international policy in the former Yugoslavia permitted secession along internal boundaries of the Communist republics, even though these boundaries were of an administrative nature, devised by the Communist leadership of Yugoslavia after the Second World War. As a consequence, Slovenes, Croats, and Macedonians[4] created their nation-states, and the Bosnian Muslims achieved the secession of Bosnia-Herzegovina, which they increasingly came to dominate. At the same time, the Serbs residing within the republics of Croatia and Bosnia-Herzegovina, or Croats from Bosnia and Herzegovina, were not granted a corresponding right to self-determination.

In 1991, the rump Yugoslav government did not oppose the secession of Slovenes and Croats as peoples, but the inclusion of Serbian-populated areas[5] in the seceding states. The Serbs insisted that the Croats could peacefully fulfill their right to self-determination by leaving Yugoslavia—but only if they allowed the Serbs to exercise the same right by staying in Yugoslavia within the territory which they already inhabited. Croatian territorial demands, however, included the entire territory of the Socialist Republic of Croatia,[6] and the two opposing interpretations of the right to self-determination by the Serbs and the Croats soon led to war.

The reason behind the international rejection of the Serbian desire to secede with Serbian-populated territories from SR Croatia and SR Bosnia-Herzegovina was that the international community chose to interpret the right of self-determination as referring to a chosen *territory* rather than to a *people*. This was contrary to the legal definition,[7] which stipulates that peoples and not territories possess the ability to determine their status. Therefore, it appears that not only had the international community given primacy to the principle of self-determination of peoples over that of territorial integrity, but also that it selectively interpreted and applied the principle of self-determination in the case of the former Yugoslavia. The genesis behind this policy decision lies in the history of Yugoslavia's disintegration, occurring in conjunction with larger global developments, such as the end of the Cold War and the reunification of Germany. In order to determine the impact of the international policy toward the Yugoslav crisis, one must first

---

4   Here denotes the inhabitants of the Former Yugoslav Republic of Macedonia (T.F.Y.R.O.M.), internationally recognized as Macedonia by many states.

5   Slovenia's territory, with a negligible Serb minority, was not disputed.

6   All the former Yugoslav republics were termed Socialist Republics.

7   U.N. Charter, Article 1(2). For more, *see* below.

outline the evolution and the present meaning of the two legal principles in question, representing twin pillars of a modern state: sovereignty and self-determination of peoples.

1.2. Sovereignty—Evolution of Legal Meaning and Practice

The principle of sovereign equality and its corollary principles of territorial integrity and non-intervention constitute the basis of international law according to the Charter of the United Nations.[8] International law is the law governing relations among states, and the international legal system would not function if states were not considered equal before law. The international political system, in turn, would be destabilized if law did not protect a defined territory, the cardinal characteristic of a state. For this reason, the principle of territorial integrity is enshrined in all major legal documents. The U.N. Charter directs states to refrain from "the threat or use of force against the territorial integrity or political independence of any state"[9] and opposes intervention by the United Nations itself in "matters which are essentially within the domestic jurisdiction of any state."[10]

Despite its political importance or perhaps because of it, the term "sovereignty" remains without a definition upon which international jurists would agree. Yet, while there is no accord on the definition of sovereignty, it is universally agreed that: "only states can be sovereign."[11] As proclaimed by the International Court of Justice, sovereignty is the "totality of international rights and duties recognized by international law" as residing in an independent territorial unit—the state.[12]

The legal principle of sovereignty evolved with the modern notion of international law as separate from ethics and theology. Prior to the establishment of this principle, the prevailing Western view was that the world was one community,

---

8   Ibid., Articles 2(4), 2(7).

9   Ibid., Article 2(4).

10   Ibid., Article 2(7).

11   Hurst Hannum, *Autonomy, Sovereignty, and Self-Determination: The Accommodation of Conflicting Rights*, Rev. ed. (Philadelphia: University of Pennsylvania Press, 1996), 15.

12   Reparation for Injuries suffered in the Service of the United Nations, Advisory Opinion, ICJ Reports 1949, 174, 180.

ruled by natural law. Christian kings were considered to derive their power directly from God, with the strongest among them claiming to be the ruler of the entire world. Many philosophers contested this view, but it was Jean Bodin who first saw a need for a new category of law[13]—international law—as a system of maintaining balance between separate territorial units that became known as "states." Bodin declared in *De la république*, in 1576, that "since the Roman Emperors were never lords of as much as a thirtieth part of the world, and since the Empire of Germany does not form a tenth part of the territories of the Empire of Rome," the continuing claim that the Emperor of his day was lord of all the world was preposterous.[14]

The principle of sovereignty and the positivist approach to international law that emphasizes states' consent and, consequently, a treaty as the main legal *modus operandi* were put in practice almost a century later with the Peace of Westphalia.[15] The Peace of Westphalia signals "the end of the divine law, religious and dynastic conceptions . . . [and] its replacement with the notion that the political world is organized into 'states', whose relations with each other are secular, not based on the acceptance of any particular religious writings or institutions as the source of authority or substantive rule of law."[16]

By the early nineteenth century, sovereignty became the central principle in European foreign policy. Hinsley identifies the Congress of Vienna as "the first modern international political settlement . . . which, as well as giving first expression to the principle of free navigation on international rivers and laying down the rules which still regulate the ranks of diplomatic envoys, determined the frontiers of nearly every state in Europe, gave every signatory the right to uphold its terms, and was regarded as a single instrument, no part of which could be infringed without invalidating the rest."[17]

---

[13] Francis H. Hinsley, *Sovereignty* (New York: Basic Books, 1966), 180.

[14] Ibid., 179-80.

[15] Peace Treaties of Westphalia [Peace Treaty between the Holy Roman Emperor and the King of France and their respective Allies], October 24, 1648 (accessed January 14, 2002); available from http://www.yale.edu/lawweb/avalon/westphal.htm.

[16] Alfred P. Rubin, *Ethics and Authority in International Law*, ed. James Crawford, Cambridge Studies in International and Comparative Law (Cambridge: Cambridge University Press, 1997), 18.

[17] Hinsley, *Sovereignty*, 207. Note: The author mistakenly refers to the "Congress of Vicuna," but the substance of the quote relates to the Congress of Vienna [General Treaty between Great Britain, Austria, France, Portugal, Prussia, Russia, Spain, and Sweden, signed June 9, 1815, article 1, reproduced in Edward Cecil Hertslet, *The Map of Europe by Treaty* (1875), 208.]

The acceptance of legal sovereignty, however, did not automatically entail a full respect of another state's territorial integrity, since the right to make war was considered an essential part of sovereignty. Even today, when extrapolated from the historical context, sovereignty reduces to "a principle of political supremacy" and a sovereign state to a "political unit in which the authorities have a monopoly of legal force."[18]

The dilemma of whether to limit state sovereignty by an international system to avert war is still current. It was first perceived by Immanuel Kant, who

in the 1780s and 1790s, spelling out clearly the message that peace could now be founded only on self-imposed improvement in the conduct of the independent sovereign state, was the first to add to it, on the basis of some insight into the history and nature of the community and the state, both a warning and a ground for optimism.[19]

In an attempt to reach a political compromise to this dilemma, the U.N. Charter strictly defines any exceptions[20] to the principles that are the cornerstones of sovereignty—territorial integrity and non-intervention in the internal affairs of a state. Deviation from these fundamental norms can be justified only for reasons of self-defense[21] and "threat to the peace, breach of the peace or act of aggression,"[22] but exclusively through either a collective intervention by a recognized international organization or by U.N. members following a specific resolution.[23] Nonetheless, one should note that U.N. Charter provisions are not always followed and that their interpretation is at times overextended. This trend may continue, judging by the increasing influence of natural law advocates and proponents of the so-called humanitarian interventions based on unclear guidelines. Many publicists have also called for an explicit right of secession in certain instances, namely in the case of extreme oppression.[24] The root of their argument can be

---

[18] James Mayall, *Nationalism and International Society*, Cambridge Studies in International Relations, 10 (Cambridge, England; New York: Cambridge University Press, 1990), 36.

[19] Hinsley, *Sovereignty*, 212-13.

[20] U.N. Charter, Article 2(7).

[21] Ibid., Article 51.

[22] Ibid., Article 39.

[23] Individual military action is permitted without a specific Security Council resolution only in case of self-defense, in the period before Security Council takes a decision. *See* Article 51, U.N. Charter.

[24] *See* the discussion below.

found in the basic requirement of a democracy to be ruled by the people, which is where sovereignty meets self-determination.

With the American and the French Revolutions, popular sovereignty has become the sole legitimate foundation of a modern state for most of the world. Such sovereignty derived from the will of the people has led to the establishment of both the principle of territorial integrity and the principle of self-determination. Modern democracies attempt to balance these two principles, relinquishing their sovereignty internally for the sake of democratic government, and externally for the sake of peace and prosperity. As the then U.N. Secretary-General Boutros Boutros-Ghali declared: "The time of absolute and exclusive sovereignty . . . has passed; its theory was never matched by reality."[25]

At the same time, states tend to be more conservative than legal publicists, for the simple reason that their survival is threatened when sovereignty is challenged. While sovereignty and independence are often questioned, they continue to be the building blocks of the international system. In international law as in international practice, sovereignty remains the essential, compulsory qualification for full membership in the international community. Therefore, the main question is not whether the principle of territorial integrity or the self-determination of people would prevail, but how the two limit each other.

1.3. Principle of Self-Determination—Evolution of Legal Meaning and Practice

The principle of self-determination is closely tied to the concepts of "nationalism" and the "nation-state," which were born in the late eighteenth and early nineteenth centuries, creating modern states in Europe. The definition of a nation, however, has remained contentious, containing both objective and subjective characteristics, as defined by James Kellas:

> A nation is a group of people who feel themselves to be a community bound together by ties of history, culture, and common ancestry. Nations have 'objective' characteristics which may include a territory, a language, a religion,

---

[25] An Agenda for Peace, Report of the Secretary-General to the Security Council, U.N. Doc. A/47/277-S/24111 (1992), paragraph 17.

or common descent (though not all of these are always present), and 'subjective' characteristics, essentially a people's awareness of its nationality and affection for it.[26]

There is a mental process involved in nationalism, which is why the subjective component to the definition of a nation is as important as the so-called objective characteristics. As Benedict Anderson suggests, the members of even the smallest nation can never know most of their fellow nationals, "yet in the minds of each lives the image of their communion."[27] Walker Connor also stresses the importance of belief rather than actual historical fact when defining a nation as a "grouping of people who *believe* they are ancestrally related . . . ; the largest grouping that shares such a belief."[28]

In the early phase of nationalism, the principle of self-determination applied only to those nations that were perceived as viable—culturally and certainly economically.[29] In practice this meant that national movements were expected to be movements for national unification or expansion, and that there existed a threshold level in terms of size and population as a necessary requirement for state creation.

This "threshold principle" was abandoned in the second phase of nationalism (1880-1914), when any body of people considering themselves a nation might claim the right to self-determination, which then implied a right to a separate sovereign independent state for their territory. Ethnicity and language became central, increasingly the decisive or even the only criteria of potential nationhood.[30] Rather than following the union, as in the case of early nation-states of France or Italy, where language became standardized after the formation of these states, the criteria of ethnicity and language now had to precede the creation of a nation-state, as exemplified by Germany. Still, military power remained the most dominant criterion in practice. More powerful states agglomerated territory, while larger states and empires continued to homogenize different ethnic groups.

---

26 James G. Kellas, *The Politics of Nationalism and Ethnicity* (New York: St. Martin's Press, 1991), 2.

27 Benedict R. O'G Anderson, *Imagined Communities: Reflections on the Origin and Spread of Nationalism* (London: Verso, 1983), 15.

28 Walker Connor, "From Tribe to Nation," *History of European Ideas* 13 (1991), 5-18: 6 [Emphasis sic].

29 Eric J. Hobsbawm, *Nations and Nationalism since 1780: Programme, Myth, Reality* (Cambridge, England; New York: Cambridge University Press, 1990), 32.

30 Ibid., 102.

In East-Central Europe, the romantic, Germanic model of ethnicities in search of a state prevailed over the so-called classical model of civic self-determination associated with the creation of France or Italy.[31] In 1848, the spokesperson of Austro-Hungarian Serbs thus defined the nation as "a race which possesses its own language, customs and culture and enough consciousness to preserve them."[32] In a dispute with Louis Kossuth, the leader of the Hungarian revolution, the Serbian spokesperson diplomatically claimed that "one nation can live under several governments, and again, several nations can form a single state," although Kossuth quickly countered that each nation must also have its own government.[33]

Ernest Gellner warns of the danger posed by this romantic nationalism, which he perceives in intolerance towards other nations:

> Some people romanticise their real or supposed ancestral community, and at the same time oppose ethnic prejudice and wish to be fair to everyone. But you can't really have it both ways. The cozy old community *was* ethnocentric, and if you wish to love and perpetuate it as it truly was, prejudice against outsiders must be part of the romantic package-deal. The trouble about the Nazis was that they were only too consistent on this point.[34]

The sheer number of nations precludes the possibility for all to possess a separate nation-state. One's quest for independence thus necessarily renders another nation's existence vulnerable. The incompatibility of the romantic theory of self-determination with the principle of sovereignty is the subject of much study. At the same time, the classical theory of self-determination, which is consistent with principle of territorial integrity since it takes place within the confines of a state, is principally praised as democratic and progressive. Political scientists and jurists rarely admit that civic nationalism can sometimes conveniently serve as a veil for cultural assimilation.[35]

---

[31] Arguably, civic nationalism thrived in France and Italy because it occurred at an earlier historical period, when the notion of ethnicity was not very developed. For more, *see* Walker Connor, "From Tribe to Nation," *History of European Ideas* 13 (1991), 5-18. Note: Connor also notes that American immigrants "regularly identified themselves in terms of locale, region, province, and the like" and refers to current Croats describing themselves as Dalmatian, Istrian or Slavonian but not as Croat (14).

[32] Cited in Carlile A. Macartney, *National States and National Minorities*, Royal Institute of International Affairs (London: Oxford University Press H. Milford, 1934), 117.

[33] Ibid.

[34] Ernest Gellner, *Culture, Identity, and Politics* (Cambridge: Cambridge University Press, 1987), 88.

[35] *See* the discussion below, particularly pages 41-50.

Every people has a right to choose the sovereignty under which they shall live[36]

(Woodrow Wilson)

The genesis of the modern principle of self-determination originates in the democratic ideals of Woodrow Wilson, enunciated in his Fourteen Points concerning the new composition of Europe after the First World War. The key to the understanding of Wilson's conception of self-determination is the fact that for him it was entirely a corollary of democratic theory,[37] leading to a spread of democracy across the globe and the stabilization of the world order. Self-determination, as conceived by Wilson "was an imprecise amalgam of several strands of thought, some long associated in his mind with the notion of 'self-government,' others newly hatched as a result of wartime developments, but all imbued with a general spirit of democracy."[38]

Wilson's democratic goals set high standards for the world emerging out of one of the bloodiest wars. Unfortunately, his ideas were too progressive for the period, with many politicians perceiving them as naive. Indeed, while most world leaders agreed that a practice of agglomerating empires must stop and that self-government should be granted to more nations, they denied the universal applicability of this principle. Criticism came even from Wilson's own staff. Robert Lansing found self-determination to be a mere restatement of the phrase "consent of the governed," and he considered both of these phrases to be "unsusceptible of universal application."[39] He further described the principle as one that "appeals strongly to man's innate sense of moral right and to his conception of natural justice, but which, when the attempt is made to apply it in every case, becomes a source of political instability and domestic disorder and not infrequently a cause of rebellion."[40] Finally, Lansing claims that Wilson himself has "in the negotiations at Paris and in the formulation of the foreign policy of the United States . . . by his acts denied the existence of the right other than as the expression of a moral precept, as something to be desired, but generally unattainable in the lives of nations."[41]

---

[36] U.S. Congressional Record, May 27, 1916, Volume 53, Part 9, 8854.

[37] Alfred Cobban, *The Nation State and National Self-Determination*, rev. ed. (London: Collins, 1969), 63.

[38] Woodrow Wilson, cited in Michla Pomerance, *Self-Determination in Law and Practice: The New Doctrine in the United Nations* (The Hague; Boston: M. Nijhoff, 1982), 1.

[39] Robert Lansing, *The Peace Negotiations: A Personal Narrative* (1921), 96.

[40] Ibid., 102.

[41] Ibid., 98.

Charles Webster's and Sydney Herbert's appraisal was also negative: "The solution to one set of minority problems might involve the creation of another set, with the dismal prospect of the commencement of a fresh cycle of conflict, revolt, and war."[42]

In practice, the Great Powers wished to retain their influence in various smaller states, and to continue the exploitation of their respective colonies, which is why they decided to preserve control over which territory will be granted independence. They certainly could not conceive of the right to self-determination applying to their own territory and even considered preserving an enemy's empire for strategic reasons. Wilson himself had originally planned to retain the Austro-Hungarian Empire as a bulwark against German or Communist expansion, granting only minority rights to various nations within the Empire, as stipulated by Point 10 of his Fourteen Points: "The peoples of Austria-Hungary . . . should be accorded the freest opportunity of autonomous development. . . . " A similar fate was initially decided for the bulk of the Ottoman Empire as well, according to Point 12:

> The Turkish portions of the present Ottoman Empire should be assured a secure sovereignty, but the other nationalities which are now under Turkish rule should be assured an undoubted security of life and an absolutely unmolested opportunity of autonomous development.

In contrast, the Polish-Americans successfully lobbied for an independent Poland: "An independent Polish state should be erected which should include the territories inhabited by indisputably Polish populations" (Point 13).[43] The dissolution of both the Austro-Hungarian and the Ottoman Empires was inevitable, however. As Asbjørn Eide concludes,

> The end of World War I was, in many ways, the victory of nineteenth-century nationalism in Central and Eastern Europe over empires which had held power over *European* nations, but most colonial empires remained intact.[44]

---

[42]   Charles K. Webster and Sydney Herbert, *The League of Nations in Theory and Practice* (London: G. Allen & Unwin, 1933), 206.

[43]   Woodrow Wilson, *The Messages and Papers of Woodrow Wilson*, ed. Albert Shaw (New York: The Review of Reviews Corporation, 1924), 468-70.

[44]   Asbjørn Eide, "In Search of Constructive Alternatives to Secession," in *Modern Law of Self-Determination*, ed. Christian Tomuschat, Developments in International Law (Dordrecht; Boston: M. Nijhoff Publishers, 1993), 149-50.

In the process of real-power politics, the principle of self-determination was left out of the League of Nations Covenants and applied only to the defeated states and the chosen new states. The famous Article 10[45] of the draft Covenant, which represented Wilson's attempt to compromise the principle of territorial integrity by merging it with the principle of self-determination, was reduced to the preservation of territorial integrity "as against external aggression."[46] In other words, following the Peace settlement at Versailles, the law remained what it had been before—a right of revolution. Similarly, Wilson's rhetoric largely stayed in the realm of idealism. Yet, although the principle of self-determination was used to delimit post-World War I borders when they coincided with other political interests—that is, the principle was used only selectively and never against the winners—it is to Wilson's credit that the principle was put in practice for the first time to redraw the political map of Europe:

> Two trends coincided during that war: the break-up of European empires through nationalist struggle, and the advancement of democracy. Nationalism and democracy were intertwined. Encouragement of these two trends, which appeared to be almost Siamese twins, were linked in the rhetoric by Western powers, and particularly by President Woodrow Wilson, in an ambiguous way when shaping the political platform on which the war was fought and the plans for the post-war settlements were built.[47]

Wilson's vision of self-determination for peoples has lived on. After the Second World War, the attempts to create a consistent set of legal principles and a sound international legal order became more fervent among the leading world governments, and the principle of self-determination entered the first article of the United Nations Charter. Nevertheless, the vague formulation indicates that its

---

45   "The Contracting Powers unite in guaranteeing to each other political independence and territorial integrity; but it is understood between them that such territorial readjustments, if any, as may in the future become necessary by reason of changes in present racial conditions and aspirations or present social and political relationships, pursuant to the principle of self-determination, and also such territorial readjustments as may in the judgment of three fourths of the Delegates be demanded by the welfare and manifest interest of the peoples concerned, may be effected, if agreeable to those peoples; and that territorial changes may in equity involve material compensation. The Contracting Powers accept without reservation the principle that the peace of the world is superior in importance to every question of political jurisdiction or boundary." Cited in David Hunter Miller, *The Drafting of the Covenant*, 2 vols. (New York: Putnam, 1928), vol. 2, 12-13.

46   Article 10, The Covenant of the League of Nations (Including Amendments adopted to December, 1924).

47   Eide, "In Search of Constructive Alternatives to Secession," 149.

political component as a selectively applied *principle* was still stronger than its use as a legal *right*:

> The purposes of the United Nations are:
>
> . . . 2. To develop friendly relations among nations based on respect for the *principle of* equal rights *and self-determination of peoples*, and to take other appropriate measures to strengthen world peace . . . [emphasis added].

The principle of self-determination was also included in Article 55 of the Charter, but again in the context of developing "friendly relations among states" and in conjunction with the principle of "equal rights . . . of peoples." Three years later, however, in the 1948 Universal Declaration of Human Rights,[48] a reference to self-determination was omitted, even though there was a preambular reference to developing friendly relations between nations, thereby creating another inconsistency in the development of this principle.

The right to self-determination appeared in the context of human rights in the International Covenant on Civil and Political Rights (Civil Rights Covenant)[49] and in the International Covenant on Economic, Social and Cultural Rights (Economic Rights Covenant),[50] which were adopted by the U.N. General Assembly in 1966 and entered into force a decade later. Common Article 1 in both Covenants states:

> All peoples have the right of self-determination. By virtue of their right they freely determine their political status and freely pursue their economic, social and cultural development.

In fact, this is still the only right of peoples to be incorporated explicitly and separately into a binding legal instrument under the aegis of the United Nations,[51] even if the two covenants avoid any clarification of what is a people and refer to

---

[48] U.N. General Assembly Resolution 217 A (III), December 10, 1948.

[49] U.N. General Assembly Resolution 2200 (XXI), December 16, 1966. The Civil Rights Covenant entered into force on March 23, 1976.

[50] U.N. General Assembly Resolution 2200 (XXI), December 16, 1966. The Economic Rights Covenant entered into force on January 3, 1976.

[51] David Makinson, "Rights of Peoples: Point of View of a Logician," in *The Rights of Peoples*, ed. James Crawford (Oxford, England; New York: Clarendon Press; Oxford University Press, 1988), 73.

the process of decolonization, which represented the primary context of the application of this right.

Under Article 40 of the Civil Rights Covenant, states are required to submit periodic reports on their implementation of the rights guaranteed under the Covenant to the Human Rights Committee. Unfortunately, "most countries either have not specifically addressed Article 1 or have done so in such general terms that nothing was added to an understanding of its content."[52]

The interpretation of the subject of self-determination, termed "peoples" in this document varied among states, depending on their respective national interests. For instance, India made a reservation to Article 1 of the Covenant restricting its application only to "the peoples under foreign domination" and not to "sovereign independent States or to a section of a people or nation," which according to India is the "essence of national integrity."[53] Britain also made an ambiguous declaration regarding the right of peoples, arguing that obligations under the U.N. Charter, particularly those relating to the territorial integrity of states, would prevail in their policy.[54] The Soviet representative doubted the application of this right within its proper state arrangement, stating that it was "inconceivable that a republic would want to secede, since there was a solid and unshakable bond uniting all the peoples and nations of the State."[55] At the same time, Jordan expressed the so-called internal application of "the principle of self-determination [as] a continuous process [that] does not end with the declaration of independence."[56]

U.N. member states were not able to reach an agreement on the exact meaning of the right to self-determination. The Human Rights Committee later issued "general comments" concerning some provisions of the Covenant, but its general comment on Article 1[57] was not published until 1984, and it still did not clarify the meaning of "self-determination."[58] Some Committee members suggested that the

---

[52] Hannum, *Autonomy, Sovereignty, and Self-Determination: The Accommodation of Conflicting Rights*, 41.

[53] Declarations, India, U.N. General Assembly Resolution 2200 (XXI), December 16, 1966.

[54] Declarations, United Kingdom, U.N. General Assembly Resolution 2200 (XXI), December 16, 1966.

[55] Statement by the representative of U.S.S.R. to the Human Rights Committee, 42 U.N. GAOR, Supp. (No. 40), U.N. Doc. A/42/40 (1987), 106.

[56] Jordan, art. 40 Covenant on Civil and Political Rights (CCPR) Report, U.N. Doc. CCPR/C/1/Add.55 (1981), 2.

[57] General Comment 12, paragraph 6, the Human Rights Committee, adopted by the Committee at its 516th meeting on April 12, 1984, and reprinted in Manfred Nowak, *U.N. Covenant on Civil and Political Rights: CCPR Commentary* (Kehl am Rhein: N P Engel, 1993), 856-7.

[58] Hannum, *Autonomy, Sovereignty, and Self-Determination*, 42.

concept of self-determination was not limited to the colonial context, but the lack of consensus made it impossible once more to define with more precision the extent of the right.[59]

No one could decide who "peoples" were. As Sir Ivor Jennings remarked in 1956: "On the surface it seemed reasonable: let the People decide. It was in fact ridiculous because the people cannot decide until someone decides who are the people."[60] Even Robert Lansing, Woodrow Wilson's principal aide, wondered whether the unit contemplated by Wilson was "a race, a territorial area or a community."[61] The question has not been resolved to this day, because it touches at the heart of the old debate of which principle is primary—territorial integrity or self-determination of peoples. The U.N. General Assembly has not given guidance for the reconciliation of these conflicting principles. Instead, as Pomerance argues, "It has simply restated the problems, while incidentally furnishing political ammunition for states to continue the debate with regard to specific cases."[62]

The Declaration on Friendly Relations and Co-operation among States in accordance with the Charter of the United Nations (Declaration on Friendly Relations), adopted by the U.N. General Assembly in October 1970, is equally ambiguous and contradictory, proclaiming:

> Nothing in the foregoing paragraphs shall be construed as authorizing or encouraging any action which would dismember or impair, totally or in part, *the territorial integrity or political unity of sovereign and independent States conducting themselves in compliance with the principle of equal rights and self-determination of peoples* as described above and thus possessed of a government representing the whole people belonging to the territory without distinction as to race, creed or colour. [63]

While insisting on territorial integrity, the Declaration on Friendly Relations introduces a qualification: the territorial integrity of only those States "conducting

---

59 Ibid., 44.

60 Ivor W. Jennings, *The Approach to Self-Government* (Cambridge: Cambridge University Press, 1956), 56.

61 Robert Lansing, "Self-Determination," *Saturday Evening Post*, April 9, 1921, 7, cited in Pomerance, *Self-Determination in Law and Practice*, 2.

62 Pomerance, *Self-Determination in Law and Practice*, 43.

63 U.N. General Assembly Resolution 2625 (XXV), October 24, 1970 [Emphasis added].

themselves in compliance with the principle of equal rights and self-determination" would be protected. Yet even this qualification is problematic, since it includes undefined legal wording such as "the whole people."

Peter Radan offers a more liberal interpretation of the Declaration, concluding that "the propositions that emerge from an analysis of paragraph 7 are, first, that a people is not defined as the entire population of a state, and, second, that in the definition of a people is included a group defined as a nation," which is why "if groups are subjected to discrimination they are entitled to secede."[64] According to Radan, the Declaration on Friendly Relations provides for "a right to 'representative government.'"[65] To back his assertion, Radan finds examples of interchangeable use of the words "race" and "nation," implying that the term "racial" in the Declaration on Friendly Relations also includes "ethnic" discrimination.

Although I agree that the Declaration on Friendly Relations has extended the moral right of self-determination, stipulating that it could provide for the "establishment of a sovereign and independent State, the free association or integration with an independent State or the emergence into any other political status freely determined by a people,"[66] I would favor a more conservative interpretation. First, it is difficult to equate racial discrimination with ethnic discrimination. Antonio Cassese, for instance, instead deduces that the Declaration on Friendly Relations restricts the right of "internal" self-determination to peoples under racist regimes.[67] Likewise, Jean Salmon notes: "nothing is said about other criteria of discrimination such as political opinion."[68] After analyzing various U.N. General Assembly resolutions, he concludes that the significance of "peoples" is contained in what he terms the "exclusive trilogy":

    a)   peoples under colonial domination (principally non self-governing territories and territories placed under trusteeship system);

---

64   Peter Radan, *The Break-up of Yugoslavia and International Law*, Routledge Studies in International Law (London, New York: Routledge, 2002), 52.

65   Ibid., 53.

66   U.N. General Assembly Resolution 2625 (XXV), October 24, 1970.

67   Antonio Cassese, "The Helsinki Declaration and Self-Determination," in *Human Rights, International Law and the Helsinki Accord*, ed. Thomas Buergenthal (New York: Universe Books, 1977), 90.

68   Jean Salmon, "Internal Aspects of the Right to Self-Determination: Towards a Democratic Legitimacy Principle?," in *Modern Law of Self-Determination*, ed. Christian Tomuschat, Developments in International Law (Dordrecht; Boston: M. Nijhoff Publishers, 1993), 268.

b) peoples subject to alien occupation; and
c) peoples under racist regimes.[69]

Second, the Declaration on Friendly Relations, like any resolution adopted by the General Assembly, does not have the same law-making capability as a convention or another type of treaty. This is probably why "no application of that provision was ever made by a U.N. organ."[70]

Donald Horowitz also argues for a restrictive reading of the Declaration on Friendly relations, insisting that the document must be viewed in its historical context. The adoption of the Declaration followed Biafra's failed war of secession from Nigeria in which the Nigerian government purportedly committed grave war crimes. According to Horowitz, the fact that Biafra was not recognized in a situation that could be described as extreme oppression invalidates such interpretation of the Declaration.[71] Yet one could also contest Horowitz's opinion and argue that the Declaration on Friendly Relations represented a departure from such policy. While the non-discrimination qualification may be weak and unclear, its presence is sufficient to shake the resolute commentary of Mr. Héctor Gros Espiell, Special U.N. Rapporteur, that the relevant statements on territorial integrity in the Declaration on Friendly Relations and the Declaration on Colonialism imply "non-recognition of the right of secession."[72] The Declaration can be cited as a step, even if just a small step, towards greater respect for human rights:

> The innovation of the declaration rests in its implicit acceptance of limitations upon the deference to be accorded to the territorial integrity of States—limitations arising from the States' duty to provide a democratic government and protection for basic human rights.[73]

---

[69] Ibid., 256.

[70] Ibid., 268.

[71] Donald L. Horowitz, "A Right to Secede?," *Secession and Self-Determination*, eds. Stephen Macedo and Allen Buchanan, Nomos XLV: Yearbook of the American Society for Political and Legal Philosophy (New York, London: New York University Press, 2003), 50-76: 61-62. For more on this issue, *see* Thomas D. Musgrave, *Self-Determination and National Minorities* (Oxford: Clarendon Press, 1997), 195-199.

[72] Héctor Gros Espiell, Special Rapporteur, Implementation of United Nations Resolutions Relating to the Right of Peoples under Colonial and Alien Domination to Self-Determination, Study for the Sub-Commission on Prevention of Discrimination and Protection of Minorities of the Commission on Human Rights, U.N. Doc. E/CNA/Sub.2/390 (and Corr. 1 and Add. 1), June 22, 1977, 17, paragraph 74); 1978 Gros Espiell Report 1 (U.N. Doc. E/CNA/Sub.2/405, June 20, 1978), 38, paragraph 85).

[73] Buchheit, *Secession: The Legitimacy of Self-Determination*, 94.

In contrast to the provision relating to self-determination, the support for territorial integrity and non-intervention is direct and unequivocal:

> No State or group of States has the right to intervene, directly or indirectly, for any reason whatever, in the internal or external affairs of any other State. Consequently, armed intervention and all other forms of interference or attempted threats against the personality of the State or against its political, economic and cultural elements, are in violation of international law. [74]

Yet even this provision is followed by a vague proclamation, which indirectly involves the right to self-determination: "the use of force to deprive peoples of their national identity" is said to constitute "a violation of [people's] inalienable rights and of the principle of non-intervention."[75]

Another ambiguous statement concerning the principles of self-determination and territorial integrity may be found in the Consensus Definition of Aggression, which declares in its preamble that it is "the duty of States not to use armed force to *deprive peoples of their right to self-determination*, freedom and independence, or to *disrupt territorial integrity*."[76]

In 1996, the Committee on the Elimination of Racial Discrimination (CERD)[77]/ U.N. Office of the High Commissioner for Human Rights issued a general recommendation on the right to self-determination distinguishing between the "internal aspect" of this right, which obliges governments "to represent the *whole population* without distinction as to race, color, descent or national or ethnic origin" and the "external aspect of self-determination," which "implies that all peoples have the right to determine freely their political status and their place in the international community based upon the principle of equal rights and *exemplified* by the liberation of peoples from colonialism and by the prohibition to subject peoples to alien subjugation, domination and exploitation."[78] The term "exemplified" in this text again introduced ambivalence by emphasizing but not

---

[74]   U.N. General Assembly Resolution 2625 (XXV), October 24, 1970.

[75]   Ibid.

[76]   U.N. General Assembly Resolution 3314 (XXIX), December 14, 1974 [Emphasis added].

[77]   CERD is the body of independent experts that monitors implementation of the Convention on the Elimination of All Forms of Racial Discrimination by its State Parties. *See also* page 45.

[78]   Office of the High Commissioner for Human Rights, *General Recommendation No. 21: Right to self-determination*, August 23, 1996 [Emphasis added].

limiting the instances when the external right to self-determination could be applied.

Michla Pomerance describes the U.N. General Assembly declarations and pronouncements concerning the two important principles as "a shopping mart or sales catalogue," a conflicting package of principles "presented without any indication of how a desirable balance might be struck between them."[79] To search for a balance in practice, one first needs to analyze the expression of self-determination and the limiting power of its counterpart, the principle of territorial integrity, primarily through the process of decolonization, but also in the cases of secession and the so-called internal formulations of self-determination, such as autonomy, minority rights, or human rights.

1.3.1. Decolonization

In 1960, two important U.N. General Assembly resolutions (1514[80] and 1541[81]) were adopted,[82] but despite their references to the self-determination of "all peoples," in practice the right of self-determination was limited to colonial situations or colonial "peoples."[83] Nevertheless, General Assembly Resolution 1514, Declaration on the Granting of Independence to Colonial Countries and Peoples, although not a legally binding document in itself, "formed the foundation stone of what may be called the "New U.N. Law of Self-Determination."[84] It established a theoretical basis for further, universal development of this principle both in law and politics, producing a revolutionary impact through "an attempt to *revise* the Charter in a binding manner."[85]

---

[79]   Pomerance, *Self-Determination in Law and Practice: The New Doctrine in the United Nations*, 46.

[80]   U.N. General Assembly Resolution 1514 (XV), December 14, 1960 (also called Declaration on Colonialism).

[81]   U.N. General Assembly Resolution 1541 (XV), December 15, 1960.

[82]   U.N. General Assembly Resolution 1514 (XV) was adopted unanimously, by 89 votes to none, with nine abstentions (Australia, Belgium, Dominican Republic, France, Portugal, Spain, Union of South Africa, United Kingdom, and United States). U.N. General Assembly Resolution 1541 (XV) was adopted by roll-call vote of 69 to 2 (Portugal, Union of South Africa), with 21 abstentions (Albania, Australia, Belgium, Bulgaria, Byelorussian SSR, China, Czechoslovakia, Dominican Republic, France, Hungary, Italy, Luxembourg, Netherlands, New Zealand, Poland, Romania, Spain, Ukrainian SSR, USSR, United Kingdom and United States).

[83]   Hannum, *Autonomy, Sovereignty, and Self-Determination: The Accommodation of Conflicting Rights*, 46.

[84]   Pomerance, *Self-Determination in Law and Practice*, 12.

[85]   Ibid., 11.

While the UNGA Resolution 1541 is less forceful and more restrained in tone in relation to the urgency of proceeding with decolonization, Declaration 1514 employed strong, derogatory language in relation to colonialism, hoping to render illegal what most statesmen considered immoral. Most directly, it proclaimed that "subjection of peoples to alien subjugation, domination and exploitation constitutes a denial of fundamental human rights, is contrary to the Charter of the United Nations and is an impediment to the promotion of world peace and co-operation."[86] The Declaration on Colonialism promoted the *principle* of self-determination into a *"right* to self-determination,"[87] equating this right with "complete independence."[88] Although the Declaration recalls the U.N. Charter at several instances,[89] the policy it advocates is in fact contrary to the Charter's emphasis on gradual and progressive development toward increased self-government, taking into account "the particular circumstances of each territory."[90] According to the UN's founding document, colonial rule is not deemed an impediment to the maintenance of peace, as long as it is exercised in such a manner as to "further international peace and security."[91] For these reasons, most jurists, including Jennings, view Resolution 1514 as an "essentially . . . political document."[92] Some, like Rigo Sureda, are even bolder, describing Resolution 1514 as an opposition not simply to colonialism but especially to European colonialism: "the definition of colonialism as subjugation to alien rule [has depended] not on whether the ruler is alien, but on whether in being alien . . . [he] is also European."[93]

Overall, the U.N. Declaration on Colonialism (UNGA Resolution 1514) has compounded the ambiguity concerning the relations between the principles of self-determination of peoples and territorial integrity. Despite its more liberal

---

[86]   U.N. General Assembly Resolution 1514 (XV), December 14, 1960, Paragraph 1

[87]   Ibid., Paragraph 2 [Emphasis added].

[88]   U.N. General Assembly Resolution 1514 (XV), December 14, 1960, Paragraph 4

[89]   Ibid., Preamble, Paragraph 1, Paragraph 6 and Paragraph 7

[90]   Articles 73 and 76, U.N. Charter

[91]   Ibid.

[92]   Robert Y. Jennings, *The Acquisition of Territory in International Law* (Manchester: Manchester University Press, 1963), 83.

[93]   A.Rigo Sureda, *The Evolution of the Right of Self-Determination: A Study of United Nations Practice* (Leiden, AW Sijthoff, 1973), 16.

interpretation of self-determination as a right, the Declaration also affirms the primacy of the principle of territorial integrity:

> Any attempt aimed at the partial or total disruption of the national unity and the territorial integrity of a country is incompatible with the purposes and principles with the Charter of the United Nations.[94]

The subsequent paragraph of the Declaration is more vague, inviting all States to observe the Charter of the United Nations, the Universal Declaration of Human Rights, and the Declaration on Colonialism "on the basis of . . . respect for the sovereign rights of all peoples and their territorial integrity."[95] Pomerance presents two differing interpretations of these provisions. The first view "maintains that the sole aim of paragraphs 6 and 7 was to prevent future attempts to disrupt the territorial integrity of the newly independent or emergent States, and that *past* territorial claims were not protected."[96] The second interpretation, on the other hand, finds no time limit to the claims to territorial integrity, considering any reversion to former sovereignty both legally and morally justifiable.

According to Pomerance,[97] the Court and the individual opinions in the Western Sahara case do not appear to exclude either approach to the "territorial integrity issue," although in the specific case of Western Sahara, the overwhelming majority of the Court did not find merit in the Moroccan and Mauritanian claims to reversion of sovereignty.[98] The U.N. equally rejected Guatemala's claim to Belize[99] and Iraq's to Kuwait.[100] In contrast, the General Assembly cited paragraph 6 in support of the Spanish claim to Gibraltar[101] and made no objections to Goa's incorporation into India in 1952 and Ifni's into Morocco in 1969.

---

[94] U.N. General Assembly Resolution 1514 (XV), December 14, 1960, Paragraph 6.

[95] Ibid., Paragraph 7.

[96] Pomerance, *Self-Determination in Law and Practice: The New Doctrine in the United Nations*, 44.

[97] Ibid.

[98] Western Sahara, Advisory Opinion, ICJ Reports 1975, 12.

[99] U.N. General Assembly Resolution 35/20, November 11, 1980.

[100] U.N. Security Council Resolution 660, August 2, 1990, U.N. Security Council Resolution 661, August 6, 1990.

[101] U.N. General Assembly Resolution 2353 (XXII), December 19, 1967.

Other inconsistencies in U.N. practice relating to colonialism are also notable. For instance, the U.N. permitted parts of previous colonial units to determine their future separately in several cases. Ruanda-Urundi achieved independence[102] in two separate states, Rwanda and Burundi, dominated respectively by Hutus and Tutsis (and accompanied by reciprocal massacres to be repeated later). British Cameroons were also divided. The northern region became part of Nigeria and southern of French Cameroon.[103] Gilbert and Ellice islands split into two independent states—Kiribati and Tuvalu,[104] while the Northern Marianas[105] divided from Micronesia, becoming a part of the United States.[106]

At the same time, other colonies were not allowed to determine their future status separately. Thus, the General Assembly did not permit the British Togoland to be divided into four plebiscite units, which resulted in the southern districts' unwilling incorporation into Ghana.[107] An even more contentious case is that of the island of Mayotte, where the majority of the population in several referenda consistently rejected the option of joining the rest of the Comoros archipelago in an independent state, preferring to remain associated with France. However, France was unable to convince the majority of the General Assembly to support Mayotte's secession. Instead, the Assembly passed several resolutions emphasizing the need to respect the national unity and territorial integrity of the Comoros.[108]

---

[102] U.N. General Assembly Resolution 1746 (XVI), June 27, 1962.

[103] U.N. General Assembly Resolution 1608 (XV), April 21, 1961.

[104] U.N. General Assembly Resolution 3288 (XXIX), December 13, 1974, U.N. General Assembly Resolution 3433 (XXX), December 9, 1975.

[105] Repertory of Practice of United Nations Organs Supplement No. 7, Volume V, Article 76.

[106] Pomerance, *Self-Determination in Law and Practice: The New Doctrine in the United Nations*, 19.

[107] U.N. General Assembly Resolution 944 (X), December 15, 1955, U.N. General Assembly Resolution 1044 (XI), December 13, 1956.

[108] U.N. General Assembly Resolution 3161 (XXVIII), December 14, 1973, U.N. General Assembly Resolution 3291 (XXIX), December 13, 1974, U.N. General Assembly Resolution 31/4, October 21, 1976, U.N. General Assembly Resolution 32/7, November 1, 1977, U.N. General Assembly Resolution 34/69, December 6, 1979, U.N. General Assembly Resolution 35/43, November 28, 1980, U.N. General Assembly Resolution 36/105, December 10, 1981, U.N. General Assembly Resolution 37/65, December 3, 1982, U.N. General Assembly Resolution 38/13, November 21, 1983, U.N. General Assembly Resolution 39/48, December 11, 1984, U.N. General Assembly Resolution 40/62, December 9, 1985, U.N. General Assembly Resolution 41/30, November 3, 1986, U.N. General Assembly Resolution 42/17, November 11, 1987, U.N. General Assembly Resolution 43/14, October 26, 1988, U.N. General Assembly Resolution 44/9, October 18, 1989, U.N. General Assembly Resolution 45/11, November 1, 1990, U.N. General Assembly Resolution 46/9, October 16, 1991, U.N. General Assembly Resolution 47/9, October 27, 1992, and U.N. General Assembly Resolution 48/56, December 13, 1993.

The discussion over the right of the Mayotte population to self-determination is indicative of the practical difficulties in applying the principle of self-determination in conjunction with that of territorial integrity. France was appalled that the territorial principle would take precedence over "liberty," especially since the original boundaries were set by alien conquest. This interpretation startled various African states, namely Tanzania and Kenya, which were concerned over the implications of any liberal interpretation of self-determination.[109] Indeed, most state boundaries were formed by conquest, and these boundaries once internationally recognized are no less sacrosanct.

The U.N. also lacked consistency in applying referenda to assess the desires of the population, the most extreme case being that of West Irian.[110] Instead of applying the "one man, one vote" rule, there was no general plebiscite. Indonesia proceeded to adopt its own *musjawarah* system for all the elections, and they were decided by Regional Councils specially enlarged by the addition of three kinds of representatives: regional, directly elected representatives; organizational or functional representatives; and "traditional" (i.e., tribal) representatives. U.N. participation was insignificant. The end result was the formal integration of West Irian with Indonesia.[111] Indonesia's strategic value similarly delayed East Timor's exercise of right to self-determination via referendum until 1999.[112]

It appears that political interests usually prevail over law in practice, a conclusion that is also applicable to cases of secession and other expressions of self-determination: "the specific identity of the claimants—*whose* territorial integrity is pitted against *whose* self-determination—remains a crucial, if not the critical factor."[113]

---

[109] Ibid., 30-31.

[110] U.N. General Assembly Resolution 2504 (XXIV), November 20, 1969.

[111] Ibid., 33.

[112] S/RES/384, December 22, 1975, S/RES/389, April 22, 1976, S/RES/1236, May 7, 1999, S/RES/1246, June 11, 1999, S/RES/1257, August 3, 1999, S/RES/1262, August 27, 1999, S/RES/1264, September 15, 1999, S/RES/1272, October 22, 1999, U.N. General Assembly Resolution 3485 (XXX), December 12, 1975, U.N. General Assembly Resolution 31/53, December 1, 1976, U.N. General Assembly Resolution 32/34, November 28, 1977, U.N. General Assembly Resolution 33/39, December 13, 1978, U.N. General Assembly Resolution 34/40, November 21, 1979, U.N. General Assembly Resolution **35/27,** November 11, 1980, U.N. General Assembly Resolution 36/50, November 24, 1981, U.N. General Assembly Resolution 37/30, November 23, 1982, U.N. General Assembly Resolution 54/194, February 17, 2000.

[113] Ibid., 44.

1.3.2. Secession

Secession is the process by which a people seeks to attain its own nation-state or to join with another already established state with its own territorial homeland, established on a historic and/or demographic basis.[114] Most secessions are ethnic, representing "a movement which generates ethnic consensus in its community along geographical lines, on a territorial basis."[115] Some secessions are termed irredentism, stemming from territorial claims made by one sovereign state to land within another, again usually supported by historical and/or ethnic arguments.[116] The name is derived from the Italian *irridenta,* meaning "unredeemed," and originally implying the territories of Trente, Dalmatia, Trieste, and Fiume, which, although culturally Italian, remained under Austro-Hungarian or Swiss rule and were thus *unredeemed* after the unification of Italy itself.[117] It is important to note here that secession is not the only expression of self-determination. It is, nevertheless, its best known and most extreme expression.

The standard for the practice of states in the field of self-determination as it relates to secession was set immediately after the Second World War, in the decision over the *Aaland Islands* case involving the Swedish islanders' desire to secede from Finland and join Sweden at the time of Finland's separation from Russia.

The Commission of Jurists, appointed by the League of Nations Council to inquire into the justiciability of the case, denied the existence of self-determination as a legal right:

> Although the principle of self-determination plays an important part in modern political thought, especially since the Great War, it must be pointed out that there is no mention of it in the covenant of the League of Nations. The recognition of this principle in a certain number of international treaties

---

[114] Alternatively, James Crawford defines secession as "the creation of a State by the use or threat of force without the consent of the former sovereign." James Crawford, *The Creation of States in International Law,* 2nd ed. (Oxford: Clarendon Press, 2006), 375.

[115] Abeysinghe M. Navaratna-Bandara, *The Management of Ethnic Secessionist Conflict; the Big Neighbor Syndrome* (Aldershot: Dartmouth Publishing Company, 1995), 2.

[116] Some scholars, such as Thomas Ambrosio, do not include irredentism within the definition of secession, differentiating irredentism from secession as a state-initiated rather than a group-led movement [*see* Thomas Ambrosio, *Irredentism: Ethnic Conflict and International Politics* (Westport, CT: Praeger Publishers, 2001), 2]. In my opinion this distinction tends to be blurred in practice.

[117] Mayall, *Nationalism and International Society,* 57. Note: Interestingly, most of this territory became part of the former Yugoslavia, presently found in the independent state of Croatia.

cannot be considered as sufficient to put it upon the same footing as a positive rule of the Law of Nations.[118]

It then absolutely condemned any secessionist attempts, placing the principle of territorial integrity above the principle of self-determination and the issue of secession in the realm of domestic politics:

> [T]he grant or refusal of the right to a population of determining its own political fate by plebiscite or by some other method, is, exclusively, an attribute of the sovereignty of every State which is definitely constituted. [119]

The Commission of Rapporteurs, later appointed to investigate the merits of the islanders' claim firmly concurred:

> Is it possible to admit as an absolute rule that a minority of the population of a State, which is definitely constituted and perfectly capable of fulfilling its duties as such, has the right of separating itself from her in order to be incorporated in another State or to declare its independence? The answer can only be in the negative. To concede to minorities, either of language or religion, or to any fractions of a population the right of withdrawing from the community to which they belong, because it is their wish or their good pleasure, would be to destroy order and stability within States and to inaugurate anarchy in international life; it would be to uphold a theory incompatible with the very idea of the State as a territorial and political unity.[120]

Subsequently, the *Aaland Islands* decision has been frequently cited for its absolute denial of the right of secession. This approach has been disputed by Radan, who insists that the importance of the *Aaland Islands* dispute lies in the deliberations of the Commission of Jurists, concluding that the principle of national

---

[118] Report of the International Committee of Jurists entrusted by the Council of the League of Nations with the task of giving an advisory opinion upon the legal aspects of the Aaland Islands question. *League of Nations Official Journal*, Special Supplement No. 3 (Oct. 1920), 5.

[119] Ibid.

[120] The Aaland Islands Question, Report presented to the Council of the League by the Commission of Rapporteurs, League of Nations Doc. B.7.21/68/106 (1921), 27.

self-determination, squared with other principles, applies in revolutionary situations:[121]

> New aspirations of certain sectors of the nation, which are sometimes based on old traditions or on a common language and civilization, may come to the surface and produce effects which must be taken into account in the interests of the internal and external peace of nations. The principle recognising the rights of peoples to determine their political fate may be applied in various ways: the most important of these are, on the one hand the formation of an independent State, and on the other hand the right of choice between two existing States. . . . The principle that nations must have the right to self-determination is not the only one to be taken into account. Even though it be regarded as the most important of the principles governing the formation of States, geographical, economic and other similar considerations may put obstacles in the way of its complete recognition.[122]

Hurst Hannum[123] and Michla Pomerance[124] further remark that the Aaland Island Case could possibly be viewed as permitting secession in case of "a manifest and continued abuse of sovereign power to the detriment of a section of the population of a State,"[125] to which the Commission of Jurists refused to provide a clear answer, insisting that the issue remained within domestic jurisdiction.[126]

Nonetheless, it is important to note that the Commission of Rapporteurs affirmed that oppression could be the exceptional factor permitting a minority to secede as a "last resort when the state lacks either the will or the power to enact and apply just and effective guarantees of religious, linguistic, and social freedom."[127] Finland was effectively forced to offer guarantees in the form of the Law of Autonomy of May 7, 1920. The guarantees were deemed sufficient in the case of the Aaland

---

[121]   Radan, *The Break-up of Yugoslavia and International Law*, 30.

[122]   The Aaland Islands Question: Report of the Committee of Jurists, *League of Nations Official Journal*, Special Supplement No. 3 (October 1920), 6.

[123]   Hannum, *Autonomy, Sovereignty, and Self-Determination: The Accommodation of Conflicting Rights*, 471.

[124]   Pomerance, *Self-Determination in Law and Practice: The New Doctrine in the United Nations*, 7.

[125]   The Aaland Islands Question: Report of the Committee of Jurists, League of Nations, Official Journal, Special Supplement No. 3 (October 1920)

[126]   Note: The justiciability of the case was based on the view that Finland was not considered a fully constituted state at the time.

[127]   The Aaland Islands Question, Report presented to the Council of the League by the Commission of Rapporteurs, League of Nations Doc. B.7.21/68/106 (1921), 28.

Islands, with the Commission of Rapporteurs adding several recommendations to improve the proposed legislation.[128] It is a fact, however, that this part of the case did not receive much attention, which has instead been cited almost exclusively as evidence of legal opprobrium of secession. The main application of the right to self-determination after the Second World War was limited to decolonization.

The legal limit on secession was enforced through the maxim *pacta sunt servanda*, which translated to the principles of sovereignty and territorial integrity. The principle of self-determination was applied in conjunction with these two principles in the post-World War II period, forbidding any external changes in borders. Legal sources and practice generally tended to confirm that the right to secession did not exist in cases that did not relate to decolonization, just as it did not apply to ethnic groups within decolonized states. As Dietrich Murswiek remarks, "It was exactly in those resolutions in which the General Assembly of the United Nations emphasized the right of peoples freely to determine their political status that it denied firmly a right of secession."[129]

Most jurists warned that the advisory opinions of the International Court of Justice between 1960 and 1990 should be read in the context of decolonization and Cold War politics. This includes the relevant decisions in the Namibia Advisory Opinion[130] and the Western Sahara Advisory Opinion,[131] which named self-determination a right rather than a political principle, but while considering issues relating to Non-Self Governing territories. The statements pronounced at the time support such view. In 1952, Eleanor Roosevelt, the U.S. representative to the United Nations, denied that the principle of self-determination included the right to secession:

> Does self-determination mean the right of secession? Does self-determination constitute a right of fragmentation or a justification for the fragmentation of states?

---

[128] The Aaland Island Question: Report Submitted to the Council of the League of Nations by the Commission of Rapporteurs (1921) League Doc. B7.21/68/106, 28. Agreed Guarantees for the Autonomy and Swedish Character of the Aaland Islands were annexed to the League Council Resolution of June 24, 1921, and a Convention on Demilitarization and Neutralization of the Aaland Islands agreed on October 20, 1921. For more, *see* Lauri Hannikainen and Frank Horn, eds. *Autonomy and Demilitarisation: The Aaland Islands in a Changing Europe* (The Hague: Kluwer Law International, 1997).

[129] Dietrich Murswiek, "The Issue of a Right of Secession," in *Modern Law of Self-Determination*, ed. Christian Tomuschat, *Developments in International Law* (Dordrecht; Boston: M. Nijhoff Publishers, 1993), 23.

[130] Namibia Case, Advisory Opinion, ICJ Reports 1971, 16.

[131] Western Sahara, Advisory Opinion, ICJ Reports 1975, 12.

> Does self-determination mean the right of a people to sever association with another power regardless of the economic effect upon both parties, regardless of the effect upon their internal stability and their external security, regardless of the effect upon their neighbors or the international community? Obviously not.[132]

In 1970, the then Secretary-General of the United Nations, Mr. U. Thant, similarly declared:

> As far as the question of secession of a particular section of a Member State is concerned, the United Nations attitude is unequivocal. As an international organisation, the United Nations has never accepted and does not accept and I do not believe it will ever accept a principle of secession of a part of its Member State.[133]

Prior to Yugoslavia's disintegration, the right of self-determination, outside colonial situations and the case of Bangladesh, was reduced to internal solutions. Moreover, even Bangladesh, which seceded from Pakistan in 1971, could not be cited as a precedent for the right of secession. Instead, as Heraclides suggests, this particular case could be used to reinforce the previous interpretation of the principle of self-determination, since the seceding East Pakistanis were in fact a majority in Pakistan: "[The secession of Bangladesh] happens to fit well with the very essence of the principle: that it applies only and exclusively to majorities."[134] Knight concurs with this interpretation, stating that only a majority opinion, entailing "the free choice of the majority of the total population of the State out of whose territory the new State was to be carved, and not just the sub-State minority who sought separation"[135] could prevail over the principle of territorial integrity.

Majority rule is the very essence of the definition of the principle of self-determination, according to Rosalyn Higgins: "Self-determination refers to the right of

---

[132] (1952) Department of State Bulletin 917, 919

[133] *United Nations Monthly Chronicle*, no. 2 (February 1970), p. 36

[134] Alexis Heraclides, *The Self-Determination of Minorities in International Politics* (London; Portland, Or.: F. Cass, 1991), 24.

[135] David B. Knight, "Rethinking Territory, Sovereignty, and Identities," in *Reordering the World: Geopolitical Perspectives on the Twenty-First Century*, ed. George J. Demko and William B. Wood (Boulder, Colo.: Westview Press, 1999), 218-19.

the majority within a generally accepted political unit to the exercise of power."[136] Such interpretation contrasts starkly with Cobban's liberal view, depicting self-determination as a "belief that each nation has a right to constitute an independent state and determine its own government."[137] Allen Buchanan sides with the more conservative position, attesting that the principle of self-determination represents "one of the least possible justifications" for secession.[138]

Once former African colonies became independent states, they fully endorsed this view, despite the fact that decolonization often produced contrary results, splitting single peoples between different states and bundling distinct peoples into a single state. The Charter of the Organization of African Unity (OAU)[139] thus declares that member states will "safeguard and consolidate the hard-won independence as well as the sovereignty and territorial integrity of our states,"[140] while one of the purposes of the Organization is "to defend their sovereignty, their territorial integrity, and independence."[141]

Notably, Article 3 of the Charter further provides that members "solemnly affirm and declare their adherence" to the principles of "non-interference in the internal affairs of States" and "respect for the sovereignty and territorial integrity of each State and for its inalienable right to independent existence." The declarations in the OAU Charter on the inviolability of territorial integrity have been reinforced by the 1964 OAU Resolution on Border Disputes by which all OAU members "pledged themselves to respect the borders existing on their achievement of national independence,"[142] and by the 1967 OAU Resolution on the Situation in

---

[136] Rosalyn Higgins, *The Development of International Law through the Political Organs of the United Nations* (London, New York, Toronto: Oxford University Press, 1963), 104.

[137] Cobban, *The Nation State and National Self-Determination*, 39.

[138] Allen Buchanan, "The Morality of Secession," in *The Rights of Minority Cultures*, ed. Will Kymlicka (Oxford, New York: Oxford University Press, 1995), 350.

[139] Charter of the Organization of African Unity, 479 U.N.T.S. 39, entered into force Sept. 13, 1963. Please note that the Organization of African Unity became African Unity at the Durban Summit, July 9, 2002 [The Durban Declaration in Tribute to the Organization of African Unity and on the Launching of the African Union, ASS/AU/Decl. 2 (I)].

[140] Preamble, Charter of the Organization of African Unity, 479 U.N.T.S. 39, entered into force Sept. 13, 1963.

[141] Article II, Charter of the Organization of African Unity, 479 U.N.T.S. 39, entered into force Sept. 13, 1963.

[142] OAU Assembly Resolution, Border Disputes among African States, paragraph 2 [AHG/Res. 16(1), First Ordinary Session, Cairo, July 17-21, 1964].

Nigeria, in which the membership of the OAU declared its "condemnation of secession in any Member States."[143]

Secessionist movements were excluded from a right to seek and be given support "despite their claim that in substance their situation is not different from institutionalized domination and exploitation by aliens."[144] Such a distinction between decolonization and secession is purely political in the opinion of Lee Buchheit:

> One searches in vain . . . for any principled justification of why a colonial people wishing to cast off the domination of its governors has every moral and legal right to do so, but a manifestly distinguishable minority . . . must forever remain without the scope of the principle of self-determination.[145]

The artificial division between the processes of decolonization and secession, which effectively ties the right to self-determination to a territory and not to a people, stems from the desire to uphold the stability of the international legal order whose subjects are states and not peoples. As Hannum deduces:

> Africa may simply be more honest than the rest of the world in admitting that self-determination of the state has replaced the theoretical self-determination of peoples that, if taken to its logical conclusion, could result in some instances in secession.[146]

In practice, independence could be granted only once and exclusively to a colony, because once it became a state, secession was forbidden: "whenever a state has come into being, the ethnic communities within that state are legally debarred from asserting themselves as people."[147] David Knight has argued that the "rule" of granting the right to self-determination but once to "a people" within any

---

143 OAU Assembly Resolution OAU Assembly Resolution, Border Disputes among African States, paragraph 2 [AHG/Res. 51(4), Fourth Ordinary Session, Kinshasa, September 11-14, 1967].

144 Mayall, *Nationalism and International Society*, 56.

145 Buchheit, *Secession: The Legitimacy of Self-Determination*, 17.

146 Hannum, *Autonomy, Sovereignty, and Self-Determination: The Accommodation of Conflicting Rights*, 47.

147 Christian Tomuschat, "Self-Determination in a Post-Colonial World," in *Modern Law of Self-Determination*, ed. Christian Tomuschat, Developments in International Law (Dordrecht; Boston: M. Nijhoff Publishers, 1993), 16.

territory originates from the principle's restriction "by two dominating, overriding principles—sovereignty and territorial integrity."[148]

In 1992, however, the United Nations' Educational, Scientific and Cultural Organization (UNESCO) provided a different statement to the U.N. Sub-Commission on the Prevention of Discrimination and Protection of Minorities, declaring that self-determination "is not confined to a right to be enjoyed by formerly colonized peoples. It is not a right to be enjoyed once only and thereafter to be forever lost."[149] Furthermore, in 1998, the Supreme Court of Canada, deliberating on the hypothetical secession attempt by the province of Quebec, also recognized the right of self-determination as a general principle of international law, which may be extended to secession outside the colonial context in certain circumstances, overruling the principle of territorial integrity.[150] Numerous jurists have formed the opinion that extreme abuse of human rights warrants secession. Otto Kimminich, for instance, resolutely declares: "Contrary to the beliefs of those who want to preserve oppressive systems, the use of the right of self-determination is not limited to single use."[151] Other publicists, like Hannum, do not explicitly legalize secession, but argue that, "where persistent denial of the opportunity for participation occurs, the population concerned may ultimately have recourse to the principle of self-determination in order to ensure *meaningful participation* in the society in which it lives."[152] Crawford also suggests that international law could be developed to allow the right to self-determination to be applied in cases of extreme misgovernance, that is, in situations that could be described as *carence de souveraineté*.[153]

Various nongovernmental organizations have advocated a more liberal right of self-determination for decades. For instance, the 1976 Universal Declaration

---

148 Knight, "Rethinking Territory, Sovereignty, and Identities," 218-19.

149 U.N. doc. E/CN.4/Sub.2/1992/6, paragraph 3(d).

150 According to the Canadian Supreme Court a right to external self-determination is generated "in situations of former colonies; where a people is oppressed, as for example under foreign military occupation; or where a definable group is denied meaningful access to government to pursue their political, economic, social and cultural development." The Reference re: Secession of Quebec (1998) 2 S.C.R. 217, 161 DLR (4th) 385 (paragraph 138). For more, *see* Chapter 4: *International Recognition of the (Former) Yugoslav Republics.*

151 Otto Kimminich, "The Issue of a Right of Secession," in *Modern Law of Self-Determination*, ed. Christian Tomuschat, Developments in International Law (Dordrecht; Boston: M. Nijhoff Publishers, 1993), 90.

152 Hannum, *Autonomy, Sovereignty, and Self-Determination*, 115-16 [Emphasis added].

153 Crawford, *The Creation of States in International Law*, 2nd ed, 111, 126-127.

of the Rights of Peoples, adopted at a non-governmental meeting in Algiers, argues that

> Every people has the right to have a democratic government representing all the citizens without distinction as to race, sex, belief or colour, and capable of ensuring effective respect for the human rights and fundamental freedoms for all.
>
> . . .
>
> . . . Any people whose fundamental rights are seriously disregarded has the right to enforce them, . . . even, in the last resort, by the use of force. . . .
>
> . . .
>
> . . . These rights [of minorities] shall be exercised with due respect for the legitimate interests of the community as a whole and cannot authorise impairing the territorial integrity and political unity of the State, provided the State acts in accordance with all the principles set forth in this Declaration.[154]

Hannum suggests that the Algiers Declaration implicitly supports the right of a minority group to secede from the larger political entity if its human rights are denied, by qualifying the respect for territorial integrity with the following provision: "provided the State acts in accordance with all the principles set forth in this Declaration."[155] Nevertheless, while this declaration applies moral pressure on states to develop the right to self-determination, it carries scant legal value.

States tend to be more supportive of the principle of territorial integrity, which is also evident in constitutional law. Very few post-1915 constitutions recognized a right of secession in certain circumstances and even then these provisions were unclear and failed in practice.[156] Three such constitutions ended with the

---

[154] Universal Declaration of the Rights of Peoples, Algiers, July 4, 1976.

[155] Hannum, *Autonomy, Sovereignty, and Self-Determination*, 116.

[156] The constitution of the Soviet Union granted under its Article 72 "the right freely to secede" to each Union Republic but it did not grant a corresponding right to autonomous units. Still, even the republics were not allowed to apply the right in practice, as experienced by Georgia and other Union Republics in the early days of the Russian Revolution. The Yugoslav constitution was less permissive in both writing and intended application, stipulating that self-determination includes secession but insisting that territorial revisions may be possible only with the consent of all six republics and autonomous provinces. Finally, there was an ingredient of ideology in both constitutions, noted by Lenin: "While recognizing equality and an equal right to a nation state, [the proleteriat] attaches supreme value to the alliance of the proleterians of all nations, and evaluates every national demand, every national separation, from the angle of the

disintegration of the state—those of Yugoslavia, the Soviet Union and Ethiopia—while the provision relating to secession[157] in the Burmese constitution was removed in 1974, despite the complex rules of procedure that would have rendered that right almost impossible to apply in any case.[158]

Following Eritrean secession, the Ethiopian government made another attempt to legally allow for secession, but this time providing clear instructions as to how this right may be exercised. Its 1994 Constitution explicitly allows for secession[159] in the following circumstances:

(a) where the demand for secession is approved by a two thirds (2/3rds) majority of the legislature of the nation, nationality or people concerned.
(b) where the Federal Government within three years upon receipt of the decision of the legislature of the nation, nationality or people demanding secession, organises a referendum for the nation, nationality or people demanding secession.
(c) where the demand for secession is supported by a simple majority vote in the referendum.

---

class struggle of the workers." Vladimir Ilyich Lenin, "The Right of Nations to Self-Determination," *Lenin Collected* Works 20, 393-453, first published in April-June, 1914 in *Posveshcheniye*: Nos. 4, 5, and 6. Online Version: Lenin Internet Archive (marxists.org) 2000.

[157] Constitution of the Union of Burma, September 24, 1947, Chapter X: "Right of Secession":

201. Save as otherwise expressly provided in this Constitution or in any Act of Parliament made under section 199, every State shall have the right to secede from the Union in accordance with the conditions hereinafter prescribed.

202. The right of secession shall not be exercised within ten years from the date on which this Constitution comes into operation.

203. (1) Any State wishing to exercise the right of secession shall have a resolution to that effect passed by its State Council. No such resolution shall be deemed to have been passed unless not less than two-thirds of the total number of members of the State Council concerned have voted in its favour.

(2) The Head of the State concerned shall notify the President of any such resolution passed by the Council and shall send him a copy of such resolution certified by the Chairman of the Council by which it was passed.

204. The President shall thereupon order a plebiscite to be taken for the purpose of ascertaining the will of the people of the State concerned.

205. The President shall appoint a Plebiscite Commission consisting an equal number of members representing the Union and the State concerned in order to supervise the plebiscite.

206. Subject to the provisions of this Chapter, all matter relating to the exercise of the right of secession shall be regulated by law.

[158] Constitution of the Socialist Republic of the Union of Burma, January 3, 1974.

[159] "Every nation, nationality or people in Ethiopia shall have the unrestricted right to self determination up to secession." Article 39, paragraph 1, Constitution of Ethiopia, December 8, 1994.

(d) where the Federal Government transfers power to the parliament of the nation, nationality or people which has opted for secession.

(e) where property is partitioned in accordance with the law.[160]

Entities with a right to secession are listed in Article 47.1, but without limitation: "The nations, nationalities and peoples within the states provided under Sub-Article (1) of this Article shall have the right to establish, at any time, a state of their own."[161] The drafters of the Constitution have not forgotten to define the term "nation, nationality and people," which they describe as "a community" with the following characteristics:

> People having a common culture reflecting considerable uniformity or similarity of custom, a common language, belief in a common bond and identity, and a common consciousness the majority of whom live within a common territory.[162]

The Ethiopian Constitution simultaneously provides for liberal minority rights, possibly with an underlining goal to avoid secessionist attempts.[163]

Similarly, the Constitution of St. Kitts and Nevis guarantees the right of Nevis to secede from the federation, should a two-thirds majority of the island's population vote for independence in a local referendum.[164] On August 10, 1998, a referendum on Nevis to separate from Saint Kitts had 2,427 votes in favor and 1,498 against, falling short of the two-thirds majority needed.

The reason why the new Ethiopian constitution and the 1983 Constitution of St. Kitts and Nevis tend to be exceptions and that states have been reluctant to allow even a limited right to secession, is that they fear that once started it could proceed infinitely, creating instability and an increasing number of ethnic conflicts. The specter of Pandora's box was unfortunately real in the case of the former

---

[160] Article 39, paragraph 1, Constitution of Ethiopia, December 8, 1994.

[161] Article 47, paragraph 2, Constitution of Ethiopia, December 8, 1994.

[162] Article 39, paragraph 5, Constitution of Ethiopia, December 8, 1994.

[163] Article 39, paragraph 5.1-5.4, Constitution of Ethiopia, December 8, 1994.

[164] Section 113 (1) of the constitution states: "The Nevis Island Legislature may provide that the island of Nevis shall cease to be federated with the island of Saint Christopher and accordingly that this Constitution shall no longer have effect in the island of Nevis." For more *see* *The Federation of Saint Christopher and Nevis Constitutional Order of 1983* (accessed February 4, 2007); available from http://pdba.georgetown.edu/Constitutions/Kitts/kitts83.html.

Yugoslavia, further increasing states' fear of secession, ironically also termed Balkanization:

> There are many important reasons why self-determination should hence-forth remain forever confined to colonial entities. If it is to return to its original sense as primarily a right to secession it could precipitate seces-sionist claims ad absurdum, which would leave hardly any existing state intact. The result could be chaotic.[165]

Buchheit has elaborated on the possible negative effects of secession. In addition to legal arguments against secession, he added the following arguments to the fear of Balkanization:

- the fear of indefinite divisibility, because very few states are ethnically homogeneous, and often neither are the secessionist territories them-selves;
- the fear of the effect such a right could have on the democratic system, by providing a minority with an opportunity for constant blackmail—threatening to secede if there is no conformity with its wishes;
- the danger of giving birth to non-viable and particularly small entities which would rely on extensive international aid;
- the fear of trapped minorities within the seceding state who presumably cannot themselves secede in their turn;
- the fear of 'stranded majorities' in cases where the seceding territory is economically or strategically crucial to the original state.[166]

Publicists have taken opposing positions with regard to constitutionalizing seces-sion. Daniel Weinstock, for instance, favors the development of a constitutional right to secede, accompanied by an elaborate procedure that would allow "a stable, significant majority . . . but which will make it more difficult or more costly for would-be secessionists to engage in secessionist politics when such conditions are not in place."[167] In Weinstock's opinion, a constitutional right to secede would

---

[165] Heraclides, *The Self-Determination of Minorities in International Politics*, 27.

[166] Buchheit, *Secession: The Legitimacy of Self-Determination*. Note: Buchheit's view is here summarized by Heraclides, *The Self-Determination of Minorities in International Politics*, 28.

[167] Daniel Weinstock, "Constitutionalizing the Right to Secede," *Journal of Political Philosophy* 9, No. 2 (2001), 182-203: 196-197.

have two primary benefits. First, it would reduce the possibility of secession by taking away one of the principal sources of dissatisfaction that national minorities tend to have with the state to which they belong, "namely that it denies them the status that would allow them to decide for themselves whether to stay or to go." Second, it would provide "a way of controlling a process which would otherwise happen anyway in a much less manageable, and potentially more destructive manner."[168]

On the other hand, Cass Sunstein points out that "the mere existence of a secession right would fuel secessionist impulses—making the claim for cession more credible, and more frequent."[169] Sunstein insists that constitutionalizing the right to secede would:

> increase the risks of ethnic and factional struggle; reduce the prospects for compromise and deliberation in government; raise dramatically the stakes of day-to-day political decisions; introduce irrelevant and illegitimate considerations into those decisions; create dangers of blackmail, strategic behavior, and exploitation; and, most generally, endanger the prospects for long-term self-governance.[170]

In my opinion, a constitutional right to secede could reap the benefits outlined by Weinstock and avoid the dangers realistically depicted by Sunstein if the procedure were carefully outlined.[171] Another caveat that I would add is the need for the Government to respect the country's Constitution in all regards. If the government infringes on its Constitution in any domain, the authority commanded by the clause on secession will also erode and by it the government's ability to legally control the process of secession.

---

[168] Ibid., 202.

[169] Cass R. Sunstein, "Should Constitutions Protect the Right to Secede? A Reply to Weinstock," *Journal of Political Philosophy* 9, No. 3 (2001), 350-355: 355.

[170] Cass R. Sunstein, *Designing Democracy, What Constitutions Do* (New York: Oxford University Press, 2001), 95.

[171] This view is also shared by Wayne Norman: "If secessionist politics is going to happen anyway, it is better that it take place within the rule of law—especially if a well-formulated secession clause actually takes away incentives to engage in secessionist politics." Wayne Norman, "Domesticating Secession," *Secession and Self-Determination*, eds. Stephen Macedo and Allen Buchanan, Nomos XLV: Yearbook of the American Society for Political and Legal Philosophy (New York, London: New York University Press, 2003), 193-237: 210.

States, espousing the conservative position, have not taken the challenge of legal-izing secession, instead generally obstructing the development of the principle of self-determination into a universal principle by leaving the main component of its definition—"peoples"—unclear. The political implications of the principle of self-determination have resulted in its ambiguous legal formulation. As Hannum notes:

> Perhaps no contemporary norm of international law has been so vigorously promoted or widely accepted as the right of all peoples to self-determination. Yet the meaning and content of that right remain as vague and imprecise as when they were enunciated by President Woodrow Wilson and others at Versailles.[172]

At the same time, Buchanan argues that "the moral appeal of the principle of self-determination depends precisely upon its vagueness,"[173] with those claiming the "right" to self-determination conveniently becoming oblivious to the fact that self-determination need not mean full sovereignty. Such realistic interpretation by Buchanan has led Patrick Thornberry to criticize any development of the right of secession:

> For most groups, secession is an unrealizable dream and international principles purporting to promote secession are counterproductive: they threaten governments and deflect attention from more fruitful approaches to group protection.[174]

Many other human rights and minority rights advocates have also focused on non-secessionist expressions of the principle of self-determination, returning to Wilson's vision of promoting democracy through self-determination.[175]

As elaborated above, such application of the principle of self-determination has generally been state practice. Even the International Court of Justice in the Western Sahara Advisory Opinion avoided mentioning independence, while clearly

---

[172] Hannum, *Autonomy, Sovereignty, and Self-Determination: The Accommodation of Conflicting Rights*, 27.

[173] Buchanan, "The Morality of Secession," 352.

[174] Patrick Thornberry, "The Democratic or Internal Aspects of Self-Determination with Some Remarks on Federalism," in *Modern Law of Self-Determination*, ed. Christian Tomuschat, *Developments in International Law* (Dordrecht; Boston: M. Nijhoff Publishers, 1993), 118-19.

[175] *See* the discussion below.

defining self-determination as the need to pay regard to the freely expressed will of peoples.[176] The Court further recognized that "the right of self-determination leaves the General Assembly a measure of discretion with respect to the forms and procedures by which that right is to be realized."[177]

The non-secessionist forms of self-determination such as human rights and group rights have developed at a rapid pace since the Second World War. They have particularly progressed over the past two decades in the sphere of the Council of Europe and the European Union (E.U.), which is pertinent for the former Yugoslavia, all of whose past members have become members of the Council of Europe and who aspire to join the European Union.

1.3.3. Minority Rights

Legally, minorities are not peoples, except in the ambiguous area of internal self-determination, described by Pomerance as "the selection of the desired system of government."[178] Cassese similarly defines the internal right to self-determination, adding that a people should not only be able to elect but also keep the government of its choice.[179]

Judge Higgins of the International Court of Justice has denied minorities' right to self-determination, claiming that "'peoples' is to be understood in the sense of *all* the peoples of a given territory," which is why "minorities as such do not have a right to self-determination."[180] This view has been criticized by numerous jurists and countered by the 1998 decision of the Supreme Court of Canada, which has postulated that "it was clear that a people may include only a portion of the population of an existing state," further suggesting that the French-speaking population of Quebec shared many of the characteristics, such as a common language and culture, which would be considered in determining whether a specific group was a people.[181]

---

[176] Western Sahara, Advisory Opinion, ICJ Reports 1975, paragraph 59; and see, generally, paragraphs 54-59, 162.

[177] Ibid., paragraph 12.

[178] Pomerance, *Self-Determination in Law and Practice: The New Doctrine in the United Nations*, 37.

[179] Cassese, "The Helsinki Declaration and Self-Determination," 89.

[180] Rosalyn Higgins, *Problems and Process, International Law and How We Use It* (Oxford: Clarendon Press, 1994), 124.

[181] *Reference re: Secession of Quebec* (1998) 161 DLR (4th) 437, paragraphs 124-125.

This dividing line—whether real or imaginary—between peoples, "the holders of a political right of self-determination" and minorities, "essentially the holders only of cultural rights,"[182] causes most secessionist conflicts. An examination of the evolution of the rights of minorities may thus allow for a deeper understanding of the secessionist demands, possibly providing insights on how to settle ethnic conflicts within the existing boundaries of a state.

There has been no universally accepted definition of "a minority." Even the 1992 U.N. Declaration on the Rights of Persons Belonging to National or Ethnic, Religious and Linguistic Minorities[183] did not produce a definition, but simply prefaced "minority" with the adjectives "national or ethnic, religious and linguistic." A common-sense definition would be: "one of a numerically smaller, non-dominant group distinguished by shared ethnic, racial, religious, or linguistic attributes."[184] A minority right, in turn, could be termed as the right to self-preservation—containing both the physical and the cultural component: "two collective rights are accorded by general international law to every minority anywhere: the right to physical existence and the right to preserve a separate identity."[185]

It is history that reiterates the importance of collective rights. The past record has been shameful, with the Jewish and the Armenian genocide representing some of the most tragic examples. People care deeply about culture because it is an essential part of identity that is based on "belonging, not . . . achievement."[186] This feeling is so strong that people are ready to sacrifice not only their individual freedom, but also their own lives to rescue their historic heritage and preserve their ethnicity. As Avishai Margalit and Joseph Raz argue, lack of respect for a culture threatens the dignity and self-respect of its members:

> Individual dignity and self-respect require that the groups, membership of which contributes to one's sense of identity, be generally respected and not be made subject of ridicule, hatred, discrimination, or persecution.[187]

---

[182] Christian Tomuschat, ed., *Modern Law of Self-Determination*, Developments in International Law 16 (Dordrecht; Boston: M. Nijhoff Publishers, 1993), 15.

[183] U.N. General Assembly Resolution 47/135, December 8, 1992.

[184] Hannum, *Autonomy, Sovereignty, and Self-Determination: The Accommodation of Conflicting Rights*, 50.

[185] Yoram Dinstein, "Collective Human Rights of Peoples and Minorities," *International and Comparative Law Quarterly*, no. 102 (1976): 118.

[186] Avishai Margalit and Joseph Raz, "National Self-Determination," in *The Rights of Minority Cultures*, ed. Will Kymlicka (Oxford, New York: Oxford University Press, 1995), 84.

[187] Ibid., 87.

Minorities became endangered with the rise of the nation-state, which established majority rule. As Carlile Macartney asserts: "The troubles of our day arise out of the modern conception of the national state: out of the identification of the political ideals of all the inhabitants of the state with the national-cultural ideals of the majority in it."[188] Further modernization of the state, while strengthening majority rule, has also stimulated the movement for the enhancement of minority rights.

> The real turn of the minorities came when the power of the nobles was broken, and the process of systematic centralization began. The unified national institutions which now came into being were, naturally modeled on those of the majority, and the minorities were required to bring their own customs into line.[189]

International protection of minorities can be traced to The Peace of Augsburg in 1555[190] and the Treaty of Westphalia in 1648, which granted certain religious liberties.[191] The Congress of Vienna in 1815[192] and the 1878 Treaty of Berlin[193] also provided for some protection of minorities,[194] but a more comprehensive policy in this field arrived only with the formation of League of Nations and the adoption of the "minority treaties" at the end of the First World War.

The policy of minority protection was imposed on a few select states, not binding any of the Great Powers. The protections included religion, language, and cultural

---

188 Macartney, *National States and National Minorities*, 450.

189 Ibid., 40.

190 Janusz Symonides, "A Protective Framework," *UNESCO Courier*, June 1993, 44.

191 *See* Peace Treaty between the Holy Roman Emperor and the King of France and their respective Allies [Peace Treaties of Westphalia] October 24, 1648 (accessed March 12, 2001); available from http://www.yale.edu/lawweb/avalon/westphal.htm.

192 The Congress of Vienna represents an instance of first formal recognition of "national" rights; "the Poles, who are respective subjects of Russia, Austria, and Prussia, shall obtain a Representation and National Institutions, regulated according to the degree of political consideration, that each of the Governments to which they belong shall judge expedient and proper to grant them." General Treaty between Great Britain, Austria, France, Portugal, Prussia, Russia, Spain, and Sweden, signed June 9, 1815, article 1, reproduced in Edward Cecil Hertslet, *The Map of Europe by Treaty* (1875), 208.

193 Treaty Between Great Britain, Austria-Hungary, France, Germany, Italy, Russia and Turkey. (Berlin), July 13, 1878, 153 CTS 171-191.

194 *See*, for instance, Article XLIV, Treaty Between Great Britain, Austria-Hungary, France, Germany, Italy, Russia and Turkey (Treaty of Berlin), July 13, 1878: "In Romania the difference of religious creeds and confessions shall not be alleged against any person as a ground for exclusion or incapacity in matters relating to the enjoyment of civil or political rights, admission to public employments, functions, and honors, or the exercise of the various professions and industries, in any locality whatsoever."

activities,[195] not implying any broader political autonomy except in the special cases of Danzig, Memel, and Upper Silesia.[196] The Great Powers had an exclusive right to decide on the implementation of the right to self-determination.

The system of minority treaties imposed after the First World War was inefficient, because minorities did not possess *locus standi* before the Council and could not argue their case before the League in person. The submitted petitions were rarely taken up—"a total of 521 petitions were received during the period from 1929 to 1939, of which 225 were non-receivable."[197] In the last year (1939), only four petitions were received, three of which were rejected for non-receivability. The decline in petitions "reflected the decline of the minorities treaties regime itself."[198]

The League's Permanent Court of International Justice (PCIJ) did make several pronouncements where states violated the principle of equality, most famously in the case of *German Settlers in Poland*[199] and the *Minority Schools in Albania*.[200] Unfortunately, in most cases when nations came into conflict with the state, peoples moved, and boundaries did not. After the First World War, there was a transfer of Greek and Turkish populations, and after the Second World War, Germans were expelled from most Eastern European states. Certain bilateral treaties on minority protection, such as the treaty between Austria and Italy concerning the region of South Tyrol,[201] or the treaty between Italy and Yugoslavia concerning the Free Territory of Trieste,[202] were negotiated after the Second World War, but they were short-lived. Yugoslavia, then still called the Kingdom of Serbs, Croats and Slovenes, at the time refused to provide minority protection for the Romanians of the Timok Valley or for the Italians of the Dalmatian Coast, but accepted

---

[195] *See*, for instance, Article 8, Treaty between the Principal Allied and Associated Powers and the Serb-Croat-Slovene State [Yugoslav Minorities Treaty] (St. Germain-en-Laye, September 10, 1919, entered into force on July 16, 1920): "Serb-Croat-Slovene nationals who belong to racial, religious or linguistic minorities shall enjoy the same treatment and security in law and in fact as the other Serb-Croat-Slovene nationals. In particular they shall have an equal right to establish, manage and control at their own expense charitable, religious and social institutions, schools and other educational establishments, with the right to use their own language and to exercise their religion freely therein."

[196] The Peace Treaty of Versailles, June 28, 1919 (*see* especially Sections VII, VIII, X and XI).

[197] Jones, 614

[198] Musgrave, *Self-Determination and National Minorities*, 55.

[199] (1923) PCIJ Reports, Series B, No. 6.

[200] (1935) PCIJ Reports, Series A/B, No. 64.

[201] Treaty of Gruber-De Gasperi, September 1946.

[202] Treaty of Peace with Italy, Paris, February 10, 1947; Treaty Of Osimo, 1975

"to allow her Mussulmans to regulate questions of family law and personal status in accordance with their own usage, to assure the nomination of a Reiss-Ul-Ulema, and to protect mosques, cemeteries etc., recognize and give facilities to existing wakfs, and to allow the establishment of new foundations of this sort."[203]

According to Will Kymlicka, both liberal individualism and socialist internationalism have led to a denial of the rights of minority cultures, "exacerbated by an ethnocentric denigration of smaller cultures, and a belief that progress requires assimilating them into larger cultures."[204] Kymlicka quotes John Stewart Mill and Friedrich Engels to prove his assertion. Mill praises the assimilation of "an inferior and more backward portion of the human race," giving the example of the Bretons acquiring French nationality or the Welsh and Scots becoming members of the British nation.[205] Engels speaks in even more derogatory terms of smaller nations, calling them "ethnic trash" whose existence is "a protest against a great historical revolution."[206] Ephraim Nimni summarizes Engels's approach as follows: "State centralization and national unification with the consequent assimilation of small national communities was the only viable path to social progress."[207] Yet Eric J. Hobsbawm warns us that any criticism of this belief would be "sheer anachronism,"[208] since it represented the dominant view of the nineteenth century. In conclusion therefore, it was the ethnocentric nationalism rather than ideology that prevented earlier development of minority rights.[209]

The U.N. Charter contains no provision specifically addressing the issue of minority rights, emphasizing (individual) human rights and the collective right of all "peoples" to self-determination.[210] The Universal Declaration of Human Rights adopted by the U.N. General Assembly in 1948[211] makes no specific mention of

---

203 Macartney, *National States and National Minorities*, 248-252.

204 Will Kymlicka, ed., *The Rights of Minority Cultures* (Oxford, New York: Oxford University Press, 1995), 5.

205 John Stewart Mill, "Considerations on Representative Government," in *Utilitarianism, on Liberty, Considerations on Representative Government*, ed. H.B. Acton (London: J.M. Dent and Sons, 1972), 395.

206 Friedrich Engels, "Hungary and Panslavism," in *Marx and Engels, the Russian Menace in Europe*, ed. Paul Blackstock and Bert Hoselitz (Glencoe: Free Press, 1952).

207 Ephraim Nimni, "Marx, Engels, and the National Question," in *The Rights of Minority Cultures*, ed. Will Kymlicka (Oxford, New York: Oxford University Press, 1995), 61.

208 Eric J. Hobsbawm, *Nations and Nationalism since 1780: Programme, Myth and Reality*, Cambridge: Cambridge University Press, 1990, p.35

209 *See* Kymlicka, ed., Introduction, *The Rights of Minority Cultures*, 6.

210 Hannum, *Autonomy, Sovereignty, and Self-Determination*, 57.

211 U.N. General Assembly Resolution 217 A (III), December 10, 1948.

minority rights, either, reflecting the general view that this matter falls within the jurisdiction of each state.

Indeed, the minorities article was not even included in a draft declaration, since the Human Rights Commission voted down this provision beforehand, even though its wording was rather weak:

> In States inhabited by well defined ethnic, linguistic or religious groups which are clearly distinguished from the rest of the population and which want to be accorded differential treatment, persons belonging to such groups shall have the right as far as is compatible with public order and security to establish and maintain their schools and cultural or religious institutions, and to use their own language and script in the press, in public assembly, and before the courts and other authorities of the States, if they so choose.[212]

This article was brought to life half a century later as the Council of Europe Parliamentary Assembly Recommendation on the Rights of Minorities.[213]

A spokesperson for Yugoslavia argued that minorities must be protected against the danger of "losing their national character," insisting that the individual could not enjoy human rights in any meaningful sense unless adequate recognition were given to the ethnic collectivity of which he was an integral part.[214] In view of later disintegration, it is ironic that Yugoslavia was always at the forefront of minority rights protection and that the proposal for the inclusion of the principle of self-determination in the U.N. Universal Declaration of Human Rights, which was rejected, and in the International Covenants on Social and Political Rights, which was accepted thanks to the support of African, Asian, and Latin American states and despite opposition from the colonial countries of France, the United Kingdom, and Belgium, came at the request of the former Soviet Union.[215]

While the Soviet Union supported minority rights, the United States took the lead of the countries opposing special minority rights, joined by most Latin American,

---

[212] U.N. Doc E/CN.4/SR.52, 9.

[213] Recommendation 1134 (1990) on the Rights of Minorities, *Council of Europe, Parliamentary Assembly,* 1 October 1990 (14th Sitting).

[214] OR-GA, First Session, Part II, Summary Record of the Joint First and Sixth Committees, November 25, 1946, 9.

[215] For more, *see* Musgrave, *Self-Determination and National Minorities,* 67; Antonio Cassese "The Self-Determination of Peoples," *The International Bill of Rights: the Covenant on Civil and Political Rights,* ed. Louis Henkin (New York: Columbia University Press, 1981), 92.

Western European, and British Commonwealth states.[216] These so-called immigration countries claimed not to have minorities, and that since minorities did not represent a universal problem such a provision should not be included in the Declaration.[217]

Physical but not cultural preservation for minorities was established by the Convention on the Prevention and Punishment of the Crime of Genocide, which was adopted in 1948 and came into force in 1951.[218] The Convention's Article 2 protects "a national, ethnic, racial or religious group" from genocide.

In 1960, UNESCO adopted the Convention Against Discrimination in Education,[219] recognizing the rights of members of national minorities to maintenance of their own schools and the use or teaching of their own language. Still, even this convention had a limiting clause, rendering its proclamation effective only as permitted by the educational policy of the State:

> It is essential to recognize the right of members of national minorities to carry on their own educational activities, including the maintenance of schools and, *depending on the educational policy of each State*, the use or the teaching of their own language.[220]

The 1989 Convention on the Rights of the Child,[221] which was unanimously adopted and since ratified by 193 countries,[222] also speaks to education. Article 29 directs the education of the child to "the development of respect for the child's

---

216 Inis L. Claude, *National Minorities; an International Problem* (New York: Greenwood Press, 1969), 166.

217 Thornberry, *International Law and the Rights of Minorities*, 136. Note: France also claimed not to have minorities in its later reservation to the Article 27 of the Covenant on Civil and Political Rights: "Article 2 (of the French Constitution) declares that France shall be a Republic, indivisible, secular, democratic and social. It shall ensure the equality of all citizens before the law, without distinction . . . of origin, race, or religion. It shall respect all beliefs. Since the basic principles of public law prohibit distinction between citizens on grounds of origin, race or religion, France is a country in which there are no minorities and, as stated in the declaration made by France, Article 27 is not applicable so far as the Republic is concerned." CCPR/C/22/Add.2.

218 U.N. General Assembly Resolution 260 (III), December 9, 1948, entered into force on January 12, 1951.

219 General Conference of the United Nations Educational, Scientific and Cultural Organization, Convention Against Discrimination in Education, adopted on December 14, 1960, entered into force on May 22, 1962.

220 Ibid., Article 5(c) [Emphasis mine].

221 U.N. General Assembly Resolution 44/25, November 20, 1989, entered into force September 2, 1990, in accordance with article 49.

222 United States and Somalia have not ratified this Convention.

parents, his or her own cultural identity, for the national values of the country in which the child is living, the country from which he or she may originate and for civilizations different from his or her own."[223] The Convention also encourages tolerance of diversity: "The preparation of the child for responsible life in a free society, in the spirit of understanding, peace, tolerance, equality of sexes, and friendship among all peoples, ethnic, national and religious groups and persons of indigenous origins."[224]

The only legal document that specifically addresses the issue of minority rights is Article 27 of the 1966 Civil Rights Covenant. In fact, this is the only U.N. treaty provision on minority group rights after almost fifty years:

> In those States in which ethnic, religious or linguistic minorities exist, persons belonging to such minorities shall not be denied the right, in community with the other members of the group, to enjoy their own culture, to profess and practice their own religion, or to use their own language.[225]

The wording of the article "persons belonging to minorities" reflects a prevalent individualistic orientation regarding minority rights. This article does not address political rights either.

In an effort to create a more effective legislation dealing with minority rights, the United Nations established a Sub-Commission on Prevention of Discrimination and Protection of Minorities, which subsequently suggested a preparation of a Declaration of the Rights of Minorities. Yugoslavia submitted a draft of such Declaration to the Commission in 1979. That draft was revised and resubmitted in 1981 and passed to a Commission's working group, which never reached a consensus on the definition of a minority.

Finally, in 1992, the General Assembly adopted the Declaration on the Rights of Persons belonging to National or Ethnic, Religious or Linguistic Minorities.[226] This declaration affirms a positive obligation upon states to protect the minorities

---

[223] U.N. General Assembly Resolution 44/25, November 20, 1989, entered into force September 2, 1990, in accordance with article 49, Article 29 (c).

[224] Ibid., Article 29 (d).

[225] U.N. General Assembly Resolution 2200 (XXI), December 16, 1966. The Civil Rights Covenant entered into force on March 23, 1976.

[226] U.N. General Assembly Resolution 47/135, December 8, 1992.

by encouraging conditions in which the minorities can maintain and further develop their identity,[227] "except where specific practices are in violation of national law and contrary to international standards."[228] Moreover, the Declaration addresses minority participation in the political and economic life of the state:

> . . . 2. Persons belonging to minorities have the right to participate effec-tively in cultural, religious, social, economic and public life.
> 3. Persons belonging to minorities have the right to participate effectively in decisions on the national and, where appropriate, regional level concern-ing the minority to which they belong or the regions in which they live, in a manner not incompatible with national legislation. . . . [229]

The only exception to individualist orientation is Article 1 of this Declaration:

> States shall protect the existence and the national or ethnic, cultural, reli-gious and linguistic identity of minorities within their respective territo-ries, and shall encourage conditions for the promotion of that identity.[230]

Other U.N. legal instruments regarding minorities' protection include the International Convention on the Elimination of All Forms of Racial Discrimination,[231] which entered into force in 1969 and has been ratified by 173 states, and a Declaration on the Elimination of All Forms of Intolerance and Discrimination Based on Religion or Belief, adopted by the U.N. General Assembly in 1981.[232]

Furthermore, rights of minorities are protected under more general human rights provisions. Individual rights of property and contract, for instance, can be used to create group rights that can afford communities a significant degree of control over land and natural resources.[233] Indirect minority protection is provided

---

[227]   Ibid., Article 1.
[228]   Ibid., Article 4.
[229]   Ibid, Article 2.
[230]   Ibid., Article 1.
[231]   U.N. General Assembly Resolution 2106 (XX), December 21, 1965.
[232]   U.N. General Assembly Resolution 36/55, November 25, 1981.
[233]   Buchanan, "The Morality of Secession," 359.

through legislation supporting democratization. One example is Article 21, paragraph 3, of the Universal Declaration of Human Rights, which declares:

> The will of the people shall be the basis of the authority of government; this will shall be expressed in periodic and genuine elections which shall be by universal and equal suffrage and shall be held by secret vote or by equivalent free voting procedures.[234]

Similarly, various articles of the Civil Rights Covenant[235] refer to the concept of "democratic society," providing for equality before courts and tribunals (Article 14), the right to peaceful assembly (Article 21), the right to freedom of association (Article 22), and the right to freedom of expression (Article 19).

Salmon insists that democracy made "a breakthrough *as a legal concept*"[236] in the early nineties. Even though there is not full agreement on this point, one can still assert with confidence that the principle of democracy has received significantly greater legal attention since the end of the Cold War. The first important document in this regard, as Salmon notes, was produced by the Conference on Security and Cooperation in Europe (CSCE)[237] on June 29, 1990, concluding a Copenhagen Meeting of the Conference on Human Dimension.[238] The text unequivocally declares that "democracy is an inherent element of the rule of law" (Article 1, paragraph 3), and elaborates on various rights that are imperative for the functioning of a democracy and thus ensure that the will of the people serves as the basis of the authority of government" (Article 1, paragraph 7). Another two significant documents are the 1991 Charter of Paris for a New Europe[239] and the

---

[234] U.N. General Assembly Resolution 217 A (III), December 10, 1948.

[235] U.N. General Assembly Resolution 2200 (XXI), December 16, 1966. The Civil Rights Covenant entered into force on March 23, 1976.

[236] Salmon, "Internal Aspects of the Right to Self-Determination: Towards a Democratic Legitimacy Principle?" 270 [Emphasis added].

[237] On January 1, 1995, CSCE was transformed into the Organization of Security and Cooperation in Europe (OSCE). Strengthening the CSCE, Budapest Decisions, Towards a Genuine Partnership in a New Era, Conference for Security and Co-operation in Europe, 1994 Summit, Budapest, December 5-6, 1994.

[238] Document of the Copenhagen Meeting of the Conference on the Human Dimension, Conference for Security and Co-Operation in Europe, Second Conference on the Human Dimension of the CSCE, Copenhagen, 5–29 June 1990.

[239] Conference for Security and Co-operation in Europe, Charter of Paris for a New Europe, 1990 Summit, Paris, November 21, 1990.

1993 Vienna Declaration and Programme of Action.[240] The Vienna Declaration was adopted by consensus following a World Conference on Human Rights, in which all U.N. Member States and many non-governmental organizations participated. Section 1 noted that " . . . the denial of the right of self-determination . . . [was] a violation of human rights . . . " and expanded on the definition of representative government in the 1970 Friendly Relations Declaration by describing those States acting in compliance with self-determination as having " . . . a government representing the whole people belonging to the territory *without distinction of any kind*."[241] Other sources linking human rights and democracy include the declarations of the 1994 International Conference on Population and Development held in Cairo,[242] the 1995 World Summit for Social Development held in Copenhagen,[243] and of the Fourth World Conference on Women organized in Beijing the same year.[244]

A particularly important aspect of democracy for the application of the principle of self-determination is the right to popular participation, since "to be self-determining in the larger society requires a measure of political power, and this means becoming involved in the political processes of the nation."[245] Despite numerous declarations, however, the content of this right remains vague. Expressed in Article 21 of the Universal Declaration of Human Rights[246] and in Article 25 of the Covenant on Civil and Political Rights,[247] it "should be interpreted as implying more than simple majority rule through the electoral process."[248] In many respects this right reflects the internal aspect of self-determination, fundamental to both political democracy and economic development.

---

[240] Vienna Declaration and Programme of Action, the World Conference on Human Rights, June 25, 1993.

[241] Ibid., Section I.2 [Emphasis added].

[242] Programme of Action of the United Nations International Conference on Population and Development, Cairo, September 5-13, 1994.

[243] Copenhagen Declaration on Social Development, and the Programme of Action of the World Summit for Social Development, Copenhagen, March 1995.

[244] Beijing Declaration and Platform for Action, Forth World Conference on Women, Beijing 1995.

[245] Chandran Kukathas, "Are There Any Cultural Rights?" in *The Rights of Minority Cultures*, ed. Will Kymlicka (Oxford, New York: Oxford University Press, 1995), 235.

[246] U.N. General Assembly Resolution 217 A (III), December 10, 1948.

[247] "Every citizen shall have the right and the opportunity, without any of the distinctions mentioned in Article 2 and without unreasonable restrictions: (a) To take part in the conduct of public affairs, directly or through freely chosen representatives; (b) To vote and to be elected at genuine periodic elections which shall be by universal and equal suffrage and shall be held by secret ballot guaranteeing the free expression of the will of the electors; (c) To have access, on general terms of equality, to public service in his country."

[248] Hannum, *Autonomy, Sovereignty, and Self-Determination*, 113.

A 1985 study prepared by the Secretary-General on Popular Participation,[249] upon the request of the Commission on Human Rights, concluded that this right has not yet been specifically included in universal human rights instruments, but that "the essential components of the right to effective participation in the political and economic decision-making processes of government are guaranteed through related rights and freedoms."[250] In 1994 the U.N. Security Council authorized a U.N.-led, multinational military intervention in Haiti for the express purpose of restoring "the legitimately elected President," who had been deposed in a coup.[251] Yet this has been the only such action thus far that received international endorsement and also one that has not succeeded in ending the violence and bringing Haiti the benefits of a peaceful democracy.

More specific provisions on democratic governance exist in constitutional law. One of the favored political formulations tends to be consociationalism or power sharing. According to this system:

> [E]ach group is guaranteed a place in the cabinet, which therefore becomes a 'grand coalition', as well as a degree of proportionality in other areas of the political and bureaucratic process. Moreover, minority groups have a veto over certain basic issues that affect their vital interests.[252]

However, this system could potentially become undemocratic and corrupt since it "requires someone to decide what the relevant groups are, and who belongs to which group."[253] On a positive note, this system gives groups greater influence within the central legislature rather than giving national minorities more power to govern themselves separate and apart from the central legislature.[254] It is a better system than the system of overrepresentation, by which groups tend to be allotted more political positions than gained in a direct election. Unlike overrepresentation, power-sharing systems guarantee representation, autonomy, and,

---

[249] Study by the Secretary-General on Popular Participation, U.N. Doc. E/CN.4/1985/10 (1985).

[250] Ibid., 115.

[251] U.N. Security Council Resolution 940 (1994).

[252] Kymlicka, ed., *The Rights of Minority Cultures*, 176.

[253] Ibid.

[254] Will Kymlicka, "Introduction," in *The Rights of Minority Cultures*, ed. Will Kymlicka (Oxford, New York: Oxford University Press, 1995), 17.

in cases of need, the use of the minority veto.[255] Indeed, many such regulations could be developed to ensure adequate political representation of the minorities, from separate electoral roles to formal recognition of minority language interests in the Cabinet.[256]

In practice, specific minority provisions have proven to be more effective than the more general human rights provisions, defying the classical "assumption . . . that group rights would be taken care of automatically as the result of the protection of the rights of individuals."[257] Some interests simply cannot be reduced to the interests of the individual, which is why indirect protection—provided through the basic civil and political rights to all individuals regardless of group membership—is often insufficient. The non-discrimination model, dominating the international law particularly since Second World War, needs to be replaced by more substantive rights for minorities.

Others disagree, including Jeremy Waldron, who defends the "cosmopolitan alternative" and the right of people to choose aspects of diverse cultures instead of preserving their own:

> [W]e need culture, but we do not need cultural integrity. Since none of us needs a homogenous cultural framework or the integrity of a particular set of meanings, none of us needs to be immersed in one of the small-scale communities.[258]

Kymlicka maintains that Waldron does not understand minorities' strong need to preserve their culture and thereupon engage in cultural exchange. I agree with Kymlicka's arguments, considering that cultural preservation and the "cosmopolitan alternative" need not be mutually exclusive. This is the essence of the complexity of minority rights—the relationship between minority rights and individual

---

255 Arend Lijphart, "Self-Determination Versus Pre-Determination of Ethnic Minorities in Power-Sharing Systems," in *The Rights of Minority Cultures*, ed. Will Kymlicka (Oxford, New York: Oxford University Press, 1995), 286.

256 *See* Claire Palley, Constitutional Law and Minorities, Minority Rights Group Report, No. 36 (1978).

257 Ian Brownlie, "The Rights of Peoples in Modern International Law," in *The Rights of Peoples*, ed. James Crawford (Oxford, England; New York: Clarendon Press; Oxford University Press, 1988), 2.

258 Jeremy Waldron, "Minority Cultures and the Cosmopolitan Alternative," in *The Rights of Minority Cultures*, ed. Will Kymlicka (Oxford, New York: Oxford University Press, 1995), 108.

rights. As affirmed by Leslie Green, "minority rights are more dense than they appear. People have rights as members of a minority group, but members of the minority have rights as individuals *and* sometimes also as members of an internal minority."[259] Kymlicka correctly interprets Green's liberal argument, which essentially merges group and individual rights: "Just as minority cultures should be protected from pressure to assimilate to the majority culture, so internal subgroups should not be forced to comply with the traditional norms and practices of the group."[260] Indeed, there is an inherent danger that individual rights may be obliterated through the exclusive application of minority rights:

> Basing liberalism on tolerance abandons the traditional liberal concern with individual freedom of choice, and threatens to condemn individuals or subgroups within minority cultures to traditional roles that may be unsatisfying and indeed oppressive.[261]

There may be divisions between subgroups within the larger community, as there are usually divisions between elites and masses, which may have different interests, and these should be allowed to surface. When protecting group rights, one must remember that it is the rights and wants of the group that one is protecting rather than a certain group condition locked in time. As Chandran Kukathas reminds us, groups are "mutable historical formations—associations of individuals—whose claims are open to ethical evaluation [which] must, ultimately, consider how actual individuals have been or might be affected, rather than interests of the group in the abstract."[262] Finally, individuals must have a freedom to leave the group, a freedom that is provided through a tolerant, democratic society:

> The most important condition which makes possible a substantive freedom to exit from a community is the existence of a wider society that is open to individuals wishing to leave their local groups.[263]

All of these challenges have faced the European Union in a multiple form, an organization that has achieved the most advanced transnational legislation

---

[259] Leslie Green, "Internal Minorities and Their Rights," in *The Rights of Minority Cultures*, ed. Will Kymlicka (Oxford, New York: Oxford University Press, 1995), 269.

[260] Kymlicka, "Introduction," 15.

[261] Ibid.

[262] Kukathas, "Are There Any Cultural Rights?," 234.

[263] Ibid., 252.

concerning the protection of minority right and human rights, both of which are forms of exercising self-determination.

The Council of Europe adopted a Charter for Protection of Regional and Minority Languages[264] in 1992 and a Framework Convention for the Protection of National Minorities[265] in 1995, ratified by thirty-eight states so far.[266] Like the U.N. Declaration on the Rights of Minorities, the latter document switches from "protection of national minorities" (Article 1) to "every person belonging to a national minority" in subsequent articles. The reason for such inconsistency in legal documents regarding the protection of minorities is again political, creating a precarious balance between individual and group rights. The European Framework Convention for the Protection of National Minorities is nevertheless a progressive document, addressing many relevant issues beyond the so-called traditional, basic minority provisions for language, education, and religion. Furthermore, the creation of the Office of the OSCE High Commissioner on National Minorities in 1992 has made a significant contribution in resolving conflicts involving minority rights, such as the conflict in Macedonia.[267]

1.3.4. Human Rights Regime in Europe

European human rights legislation has also been boosted since the adoption of the European Convention on Human Rights and Fundamental Freedoms[268] in November 1950, which has since been ratified by forty-five states. While providing no explicit guarantee of rights to minorities, the Convention's Article 14 prohibits discrimination on the basis of "association with a national minority." It further stipulates that "the enjoyment of rights and freedoms as set forth in this Convention shall be secured without discrimination on any ground such as sex, race, colour, language, religion, political or other opinion, national or social origin, association with a national minority, property, birth or other status."

---

[264] ETS no: 148, 05/11/1992, in force 01/03/1998.

[265] ETS no: 157, 01/02/1995, in force 01/02/1998.

[266] Status as of September 17, 2004.

[267] The mission of the High Commissioner on National minorities is "to identify and seek early resolution of ethnic tensions that might endanger peace, stability or friendly relations between OSCE participating States." For more see http://www.osce.org/hcnm/, accessed on November 18, 2005. Note: One could also argue that the High Comissioner failed in important issues like bringing the Kosovo problem to policy-makers attention before the Kosovo Albanians took up arms in 1998.

[268] ETS no. 005, 04/11/1950, in force 03/09/1953.

The provisions relating to non-discrimination do not imply positive action on behalf of states, as seen in the Belgium Linguistics Case.[269]

The European Union Charter of Fundamental Rights, officially proclaimed at the Nice summit of the E.U. member states in December 2000,[270] goes a step further. It not only provides for the equality before the law of all people (Article 20) and prohibits discrimination on any ground (Article 21), but it also directly requests "the Union" to "respect cultural, religious and linguistic diversity" (Article 22). Notably, this Charter remains of declaratory character, still lacking an appropriate enforcement mechanism.[271]

Nevertheless, in the last two decades, many important human rights provisions have become enshrined in the basic documents of the European Union. The Treaty on European Union (also called the Maastricht Treaty) lists the development and consolidation of "democracy and the rule of law, and respect for human rights and fundamental freedoms" as one of the objectives of the Union's Common Foreign and Security Policy.[272] The subsequent Treaty of Amsterdam, which came into force on May 1, 1999,[273] adds a new Article 6 to the Treaty of the European Union, asserting that the Union "is founded on the principles of liberty, democracy, respect for human rights and fundamental freedoms, and the rule of law, principles which are common to the Member States." Moreover, the Treaty of Amsterdam warns that Member States violating these principles in a "serious and persistent" manner may risk the suspension of some membership

---

[269]   Case Relating to Certain Aspects of the Laws on the Use of Languages in Education in Belgium Merits, European Court of Human Rights A, No. 6, Judgment of July 23, 1968.

[270]   European Union Charter of Fundamental Rights, as signed and proclaimed by the Presidents of the European Parliament, the Council and the Commission at the European Council meeting in Nice on December 7, 2000, Official Journal of the European Communities 2000/C 364/01, December 18, 2000 (entry into force November 1, 1993).

[271]   At the Nice Summit, the European Council concluded:

"The European Council would like to see the Charter disseminated as widely as possible amongst the Union's citizens. In accordance with the Cologne conclusions, the question of the Charter's force will be considered later." European Council, Conclusions of the Presidency, Nice, December 7-10, 2000 (accessed May 4, 2003); available from http://www.europarl.eu.int/summits/nice2_en.htm. The E.U. intention has been to incorporate the text into its revised treaty (Constitution of the European Union), but the reform of the European Union has been stalled for other reasons. For more, *see* Chapter 7: *Conclusion: Former Yugoslavia's European Integration.*

[272]   Treaty on European Union (Treaty of Maastricht), Title V, Article J.1, February 7, 1992.

[273]   Treaty of Amsterdam amending the Treaty on European Union, the Treaties establishing the European Communities and related Acts, Official Journal C 340, November 10, 1997, entered into force on May 1, 1999.

rights.[274] Such a provision gives greater legal effect to declarations adopted by the European Council, namely the Declaration on Human Rights of June 1991,[275] which, *inter alia,* seeks "universal respect for human rights," or the November 1991 Resolution on Human Rights, Democracy and Development,[276] which sets the guidelines, procedures and priorities for improving the consistency and cohesion of development initiatives.[277] The European Union resolve is affirmed in the Declaration on the occasion of the fiftieth anniversary of the Universal Declaration of Human Rights, which states that the E.U. policies in the field of human rights must be "continued and, when necessary strengthened and improved."[278] The declaration includes six practical steps that aim to strengthen the E.U's human rights policy.[279]

The 2000 E.U. Charter of Fundamental Rights represents an attempt to synchronize the Union's internal and external human rights policy. Since the early 1990s—and

---

[274] Ibid., Article F.1.

[275] Declaration on Human Rights, Conclusions of the Luxembourg European Council, June 29, 1991.

[276] Resolution on Human Rights, Democracy and Development, Council and Member States, meeting within the Council, November 28, 1991.

[277] Ibid., paragraph 10.1: "The Community and its Member States will explicitly introduce the consideration of human rights as an element of their relations with developing countries; human rights clauses will be inserted in future cooperation agreements. Regular discussions on human rights and democracy will be held, within the framework of development cooperation, with the aim of seeking improvements."

[278] Declaration of the European Union on the occasion of the 50th anniversary of the Universal Declaration on Human Rights, Vienna, December 10, 1998.

[279] Ibid., B. IV:

1. enhance the capacity to jointly assess the human rights situation in the world by closer co-ordination and otherwise ensure that all pertinent means for action are available within the framework of the Union, including through the possible publication of an annual EU human rights report;

2. further develop cooperation in the field of human rights, such as education and training activities, in coordination with other relevant organisations, and ensure the continuation of the Human Rights Masters Programme organised by fifteen European universities;

3. reflect on the usefulness of convening a periodic human rights discussion forum with the participation of EU institutions as well as representatives of academic institutions and NGOs;

4. strengthen the capacities to respond to international operational requirements in the field of human rights and democratisation, such as through the possible establishment of a common roster of European human rights and democracy experts, for human rights field operations and electoral assistance and monitoring;

5. foster the development and consolidation of democracy and the rule of law and respect for human rights and fundamental freedoms in third countries, in particular through working towards the earliest possible adoption of the draft regulations, currently under consideration in the EU framework, on the implementation of co-operation operations;

6. ensure all means to achieve the coherent realisation of these goals, including through the consideration of strengthening relevant EU structures.

consistently since 1995—the European Union has included a so-called human rights clause in its bilateral trade and co-operation agreements with third countries, including the association agreements signed with aspiring members. In May 2003, the European Commission provided the latest in a series of communications with a goal of achieving even greater consistency and effectiveness of its human rights and democratization policy, this time focusing on E.U.'s Mediterranean Partners.[280] In addition to posing the promotion of human rights and democracy as a condition for E.U. membership or simply trade with the E.U. member states, the Union directly funds various programs that enhance human rights and democracy in third countries. The European Initiative for Democracy and Human Rights, created in 1994 by the European Parliament in order to promote and support human rights and democracy in third countries, had four thematic priorities for 2002-2004:

(a) Support to strengthen democratization, good governance and the rule of law
(b) Activities to supporting abolition of the Death Penalty
(c) Support for the fight against torture and impunity, international tribunals and criminal court
(d) Combating racism and xenophobia and discrimination against minorities.[281]

As a part of this initiative, in June 2002 the E.U. launched a series of eight regional Human Rights Workshops across the world. The promotion of human rights outside the European Union has become the organization's official policy. Accordingly, "the EU will ensure that the issue of human rights, democracy and the rule of law will be included in all future meetings and discussions with third countries at all levels."[282]

To enhance the effectiveness of human rights legislation, in May 1990 eighteen members of Council of Europe established the European Commission for Democracy Through Law—the Venice Commission, whose field of action is defined as "the

---

[280] Communication from the Commission to the Council and the European Parliament, "Reinvigorating EU Actions on Human Rights and Democratisation with Mediterranean Partners; Strategic Guidelines," Brussels, 21.05.2003, COM (2003) 294 final.

[281] Commission Staff Working Document: European Initiative For Democracy And Human Rights Programming Document 2002-2004, December 20, 2001, 5.

[282] European Union guidelines on Human rights dialogues, Council of the European Union, December 13, 2001.

A LEGAL GEOGRAPHY OF YUGOSLAVIA'S DISINTEGRATION

guarantees offered by law in the service of democracy."[283] As of February 2002, non-European states can also be members of the Venice Commission,[284] which has since grown into an independent legal think-tank with the following objectives:

- strengthening the understanding of the legal systems of the participating states, notably with a view to bringing these systems closer;
- promoting the rule of law and democracy;
- examining the problems raised by the working of democratic institutions and their reinforcement and development.[285]

The Venice Commission acts as an advisory body on constitutional and other relevant human rights matters, supplying opinions upon request of the Committee of Ministers, the Parliamentary Assembly, the Congress of Local and Regional Authorities of Europe, the Secretary General, or a state or international organization or body participating in the work of the Commission. In official jargon, the Venice Commission:

contributes to the dissemination of the European constitutional heritage, based on the continent's fundamental legal values while continuing to provide 'constitutional first-aid' to individual states. The Venice Commission also plays a unique and unrivalled role in crisis management and conflict prevention through constitution building and advice.[286]

The Venice Commission continues to be supported by the Council of Europe, an organization encompassing most European states, which has been at the forefront of promoting democracy and human rights since its foundation in 1949.

---

[283] Statute of the European Commission for Democracy through Law, Appendix to Resolution (90) 6, On a Partial Agreement Establishing the European Commission for Democracy through Law (adopted by the Committee of Ministers on May 10, 1990 at its 86th Session), Article 1.

[284] All Council of Europe member states are members of the Venice Commission; in addition, Kyrgyzstan joined the commission in 2004. Belarus is an associate member, while Argentina, Canada, the Holy See, Israel, Japan, Kazakhstan, the Republic of Korea, Mexico, the United States and Uruguay are observers. South Africa has a special co-operation status similar to that of the observers. The European Commission and OSCE/ODIHR participate in the plenary sessions of the Commission. For more, see http://www. venice.coe.int/site/main/presentation_E.asp?MenuL=E.

[285] Statute: Resolution (2002)3: Revised Statute of the European Commission for Democracy through Law (adopted by the Committee of Ministers on February 21, 2002 at the 784th meeting of the Ministers' Deputies), Article 1.

[286] Venice Commission Internet Presentation (accessed October 10, 2005); available from http://www.venice. coe.int/site/main/presentation_E.asp?MenuL=E.

The Council's Statute[287] reaffirms in the second paragraph of its preamble the signatory states' "devotion to the spiritual and moral values which are the common heritage of their peoples and the true source of individual freedom, political liberty and the rule of law, principles which form the basis of all genuine democracy." Article 3 of the Statute requires that "every Member . . . must accept the principles of the rule of law and of the enjoyment by all persons within its jurisdiction of human rights and fundamental freedoms." The Council of Europe possesses two bodies that apply its provisions in practice—the Human Rights Commission and Court, which Alfred Rubin praises as rare "outstanding examples" where states agreed to an institutional structure "that would actually implement agreed human rights principles."[288]

The E.U. minority and human rights texts and instruments are of utmost importance because they have advanced the effectiveness of minority and human rights protection in practice, weakening the moral justification for more extreme forms of self-determination such as secession.

1.3.5. Two Ends of a Spectrum?

The principles of sovereignty and self-determination of peoples are usually depicted as two ends of a spectrum, since sovereignty encompasses the right to preserve the territorial status quo, whereas the principle of self-determination is at least potentially aimed at territorial change. The preceding presentation has sought to establish that the two principles need not be mutually exclusive. In a modern state, both the principle of sovereignty and the principle of self-determination of peoples are based on the will of the people—or democratic governance. As Thornberry suggests:

> It is possible to read self-determination as mandating neither secession nor the artificial homogeneity of States but as a potential synthesis of respect and mutual concert between whole societies and their component groups that finds expression through the discourse and practice of human rights.[289]

On the other hand, many publicists question whether minority and human rights are in fact a part of the rights of peoples or a complementary set of rights.

---

[287] CETS 001, Statute of the Council of Europe, London, May 5, 1949.

[288] Rubin, *Ethics and Authority in International Law*, 170-71.

[289] Thornberry, "The Democratic or Internal Aspects of Self-Determination with Some Remarks on Federalism," 138.

A Legal Geography of Yugoslavia's Disintegration

Both sides could be argued according to the existing legal literature. As Hannum remarks, "neither the European nor the American convention on human rights includes specific recognition of the right of self-determination,"[290] while the African Charter on Human and People's Rights refers to it quite liberally:

1. All peoples shall have the right to existence. They shall have the unquestionable and inalienable right to self-determination. They shall freely determine their political status and shall pursue their economic and social development according to the policy they have freely chosen.
2. Colonized or oppressed peoples shall have the right to free themselves from the bonds of domination by resorting to any means recognized by the international community.
3. All peoples shall have the right to the assistance of the States Parties to the present Charter in their liberation struggle against foreign domination, be it political, economic or cultural.[291]

Moreover, it is important to note that, while it may be politically popular to speak of human rights, their implementation has been largely inadequate. Human rights often remain just moral statements without evolving into full legal rights, since a right "involves the capacity in the holder of the right, at his or her discretion to call on the public enforcement institutions of the law to act."[292] The problem with international human rights in relation to self-determination may be found in the nature of international law, which does not recognize "peoples" as its subject. As Kimminich argues, "the right of self-determination occupies 'a unique position' in international law 'because it is attributed to an entity which is not a legal person in international law.'"[293]

Indeed, when extrapolated from the rhetoric, the right to self-determination has in practice been strictly limited:

> UN and state practice since 1960 recognizes only a very limited right to 1) external self-determination, defined as the right to freedom from a former

---

[290] Hannum, *Autonomy, Sovereignty, and Self-Determination*, 44.

[291] Article 20, African [Banjul] Charter on Human and Peoples' Rights, adopted June 27, 1981, OAU Doc. CAB/LEG/67/3 rev. 5, 21 I.L.M. 58 (1982), entered into force October 21, 1986.

[292] Rubin, *Ethics and Authority in International Law*, 31. Rubin bases his definition on work by Wesley Hohfeld, who analyzes the legal meaning of right. *See* Wesley Hohfeld, *Fundamental Legal Concepts* (New Haven, CT: Yale University Press, 1923), particularly 6-10.

[293] Kimminich, "The Issue of a Right of Secession," 86.

colonial power, and 2) internal self-determination, defined as independence of the whole state's population from foreign intervention or influence.[294]

This is also the view of Antonio Cassese, who concludes that Civil and Economic Rights Covenants[295] have supplemented the U.N. Charter's references to self-determination as a principle that speaks to democratic governance: " . . . there is no self-determination without democratic decision-making."[296] Cassese deduces that the object of self-determination "can only mean the entire population in independent States or States yet to achieve independence and populations living under foreign occupation," specifically excluding the applicability of the right to minorities.[297] As discussed above, this is not the position taken by the Supreme Court of Canada.

Publicists like Crawford and Cassese[298] have praised the universality of the principle of self-determination as established by the Covenants' Article 1, which according to them ended the restricted application of the principle to colonial situations. Yet the most fervent debate centers on the criteria under which external right to self-determination may be exercised. In a realistic assessment, Buchheit admits to the possibility of a secessionist interpretation of the covenants but finds states to be overwhelmingly disinclined towards such application of the principle:

> The virulence of the debate over the inclusion of *any* reference to self-determination in these instruments, combined with the uneasiness aroused by the separatist implications of the article in many delegates who were generally in favor of inclusion, leads to the belief that article 1 of the covenants appears in spite of its possible secessionist interpretation, rather than as a confirmation of that interpretation.[299]

---

[294] Hannum, *Autonomy, Sovereignty, and Self-Determination*, 49.

[295] U.N. General Assembly Resolution 2200 (XXI), December 16, 1966. The Civil Rights Covenant entered into force on March 23, 1976; U.N. General Assembly Resolution 2200 (XXI), December 16, 1966. The Economic Rights Covenant entered into force on January 3, 1976.

[296] Antonio Cassese, *Self-Determination of Peoples: A Legal Reappraisal* (Cambridge: Cambridge University Press, 1995), 5.

[297] Ibid.

[298] James Crawford, "Outside the Colonial Context," in William J. Macartney, ed. *Self-Determination in the Commonwealth* (Aberdeen: Aberdeen University Press, 1998), 5-6; Cassese, *Self-Determination of Peoples*, 48-52.

[299] Buchheit, *Secession: The Legitimacy of Self-Determination*, 83-84.

Despite the ambiguity surrounding the implementation of the principle of self-determination, the preceding analysis of the development of the right to self-determination demonstrates significant progress in defining and applying minority and human rights. At the same time, a wider scope for implementing the external right to self-determination has been precluded by real-politik considerations, with genuine interest for the stability of the international legal order. Here one has to stress that the arguments of "liberals" or "rectificatory liberals" like Buchanan tend to be based on moral arguments that are difficult to translate into equitable, practical legal norms.[300] Indeed, texts that allow for exceptions to the general prohibition of change of international frontiers, such as the Declaration on Friendly Relations, do so in the vaguest of language and thus with questionable legal application. In conclusion, the right to self-determination can be interpreted only as an "internal" rather than an "external" right in law, except in the cases of decolonization and the special cases of Bangladesh and the former Yugoslavia—unless the latter is perceived as a precedent.

State practice in the period preceding Yugoslavia's disintegration has been loyal to Wilson's vision of self-determination, applying the principle as one that speaks to democracy as a method of government rather than independence for each ethnic group—when the principle coincided with strategic political interests. As Buchheit concludes, political opportunism has represented the one undisputed criterion:

> Perhaps the only certain lesson to be derived from a study of State practice with reference to secessionist self-determination is that, given the present absence of any indisputable rule of international law, a State's response to a particular situation will most often be determined solely by its own political interests.[301]

Only international recognition, itself a political act, can render a secession successful, since secession is "neither legal nor illegal in international law, but a legally neutral act the consequences of which are regulated internationally."[302]

---

[300] Harry Beran proposes the most radical liberal theory of secession. Assuming that the fundamental liberal value is individual autonomy, Beran argues that anyone may leave a state and that the right to secession rests with the majority population of a state, regardless of the underpinning reasons for secession. *See* Harry Beran, "A Liberal Theory of Secession," *Political Studies* 78 (1984): 21-31.

[301] Buchheit, *Secession: The Legitimacy of Self-Determination*, 105.

[302] Crawford, *The Creation of States in International Law*, 2nd ed, 390.

Crawford correctly deduces that while international law recognizes the principle of self-determination, this is not a universally applicable legal right. Instead, "it applies as a matter of right only after the unit of self-determination has been determined."[303] While admitting that this process is principally a matter of political choice, Crawford has identified the following units of self-determination:

(a) trust and mandated territories, and territories treated as non-self-governing under Chapter XI of the Charter;
(b) States, excluding for the purposes of the self-determination rule those parts of States which are themselves self-determination units as defined;
(c) other territories forming distinct political-geographical areas, whose inhabitants are arbitrarily excluded from any share in the government either of the region or of the State to which they belong, with the result that the territory becomes in effect, with respect to the reminder of the State, non-self-governing; and
(d) any other territories or situations to which self-determination is applied by the parties as an appropriate solution.[304]

This analysis would imply that, outside the colonial context, secession is possible only "when inhabitants are arbitrarily excluded from any share in the government either of the region or of the State to which they belong," as noted in section (c) above. Considering the difficulty of assessing this status,[305] Radan's argument that "the territorial definition of a 'people' renders secession illegal and flies in the face of the generally accepted view in international law that secession is neither legal nor illegal"[306] is also convincing, but only if this territorial definition has not been extended to "include the population of a federal unit of an internationally recognised and independent state" which he in fact suggests has occurred as a consequence of the international policies toward Yugoslavia's break-up in the 1990s.[307]

---

303 James Crawford, *The Creation of States in International Law* (Oxford: Clarendon Press, 1979), 101. Crawford further insists that the right to self-determination continues to be "a *lex obscura* . . . an intensely contested concept in relation to virtually every case where it is invoked." James Crawford, "The Right to Self-Determination in International Law: Its Development and Future," *People's Rights*, ed. Philip Alston (New York: Oxford University Press, 2001), 7-68: 38.

304 Crawford, *The Creation of States in International Law*, 2nd ed, 127.

305 Furthermore, as Robert Ewin suggests, "the secessionists must be able to point to injustice that they suffered before and to ensure that nobody, including those who don't want to secede, suffers after the secession." Robert Ewin, "Peoples and Political Obligation," *Macquarie Law Journal* 3 (2003), 28.

306 Radan, *The Break-up of Yugoslavia and International Law*, 4.

307 Ibid.

Additionally, the increasing acceptance of minority rights and human rights as expressions of self-determination has also contributed to the application of the principle as originally written—pertaining to a people rather than to a territory.

States have arguably exploited the ambiguity of the legal meaning of a "people" to the advantage of the ruling authority, generally opposing secession and other potentially separatist forms of self-determination. Until recently, they have strongly resisted the development of minority and human rights and continue to be watchful of any negative repercussions. Nonetheless, while governments worldwide continue to manipulate human rights jargon for political purposes, many have also understood that a certain degree of devolution of sovereignty may actually serve to protect their territorial integrity. As Thornberry reminds us, "self-determination and minority rights are locked in a relationship which is part of the architecture of the nation State, since whenever a State is forged, the result is the creation of minorities."[308]

In practice, the minority-majority conflict reduces to issues such as language, education, access to government civil service or control over natural resources, which are all facets of a representative government and which can frequently be solved by devolving power to the local level. General human rights and minority rights provisions may be adequate in most cases, while in others a more elaborate political autonomy may be necessary. As Tomuschat advocates:

> If self-determination were complemented by a hitherto missing dimension of political autonomy, or if it went as far as federal statehood within a given State, the rigidity of the sharp line which divides peoples, the holders of a political right of self-determination, and minorities, essentially the holders only of cultural rights, would be lost.[309]

Following this line of argument, Kirsten Porter suggests that minority rights can be protected and promoted within a system that grants non-territorial autonomy to national minorities while maintaining the administrative unity of a multi-national state.[310] One of the first such proposed models was devised in 1902 by

---

[308] Thornberry, *International Law and the Rights of Minorities*, 13.

[309] Tomuschat, "Self-Determination in a Post-Colonial World," 15.

[310] For more, *see* Kirsten Porter, "Realisation of National Minority Rights," *Macquarie Law Journal* 3 (2003), 51-72.

Karl Renner and Otto Bauer, Austrian politicians and scholars who believed that a national-cultural autonomy could alleviate ethnic tensions within Austria-Hungary.[311] In considering the development of self-determination today, scholars such as Jonathan Schell are returning to the models that provide for concurrent expression of multiple cultural identities within one state:

> Self-determination . . . must yield to self-determinations and selves-deter-mination—that is, to permission for more than one nation to find expression within the border of a single state and to permission for individuals and groups to claim multiple identities.[312]

Although states tend to be reluctant to approve new rules which might threaten their existence, it appears to be increasingly in their interest to develop the right of self-determination, establishing criteria for the lawfulness and legitimacy of challenges to the unity of a State, which will judge the legality of the claims for separate statehood or federal statehood or simple autonomy. If minority rights were adequately addressed internally, any request for independence would be unwarranted.

Nonetheless, despite strong optimism expressed by some legal and political experts that the scope of the right of self-determination is evolving in this direction, a long time period may be necessary to reach consensus over such a controversial issue. In the meantime, the role of the state, although declining, will continue to be paramount, buttressed by prevailing legal and political skepticism over the principle of self-determination, as expressed by Crawford in the 1970s:

> Self-determination as a legal right or principle would represent a significant erosion of the principle of sovereignty. It is a dynamic principle which, if consistently applied, could bring about significant changes in the political geography of the world. It is an overtly political principle, which raises important questions about the nature of international law and the justiciability of political disputes. And, for our purposes, it would be a most

---

[311] *See* Ephraim Nimni, ed., *National Cultural Autonomy and its Contemporary Critics* (New York: Routledge, 2005); Stéphane Pierre-Caps, "Karl Renner et l'Etat Multinationale: Contribution Juridique á la Solution d'Imbroglios Politiques Contemporains," *Droit et Société* 27 (1994), 421-441; Tibor Várady, "Collective Minority Rights and Problems in their Legal Protection: The Example of Yugoslavia," *East European Politics and Societies* 6 (1992), 260, 271.

[312] Jonathan Schell, "The Unconquerable World," *Harper's Magazine* 306 (2003), 53.

significant exception to the traditional notion that the creation of States is a matter of fact and not of law.[313]

The following analysis of Yugoslavia's disintegration, set in the special context of administrative (internal) boundaries, aims to discern the role of this conflict in the evolution of the right of self-determination.

---

[313] Crawford, *Creation of States in International Law,* 1st ed, 85.

Pre-1914 Administrative Boundaries and the Birth of Yugoslavia

2.1. Introduction

The Yugoslav civil wars of the 1990s were, like most wars, wars for territory. The internal war became international with the recognition of the seceding republics in 1992. The act of recognition did not put a halt to the strife, principally because those nations that felt aggrieved by this act, namely Serbs, (Bosnian) Croats, and increasingly, ethnic Albanians, questioned the legitimacy of the new international borders.[1]

Although many borders worldwide are questioned, the importance of the Yugoslav case lies in the fact that for the first time, outside the colonial context or a negotiated internal agreement, the international community recognized as international those boundaries that until then had served as administrative, internal boundaries of a country.[2] The legal aspects of the Yugoslav wars center around one key question: can internal administrative boundaries serve as a *legal* basis for secession? To answer this question, it is necessary to define the notion of administrative boundaries by analyzing the territorial division of Yugoslavia since its creation

---

[1] The term "legitimacy" is here used in the meaning defined by Thomas Franck as "a property of a rule or rule-making institution which itself exerts a pull toward compliance on those addressed normatively because those addressed believe that the rule or institution has come into being and operates in accordance with generally accepted principles of right process." Thomas M. Franck, *The Power of Legitimacy Among Nations* (New York, Oxford: Oxford University Press, 1990), 25.

[2] The terms "administrative" and "internal" are used intercheangeably in this book to depict the non-international boundaries of a state.

in 1918. To shed further light on the legal and political consequences of this division, the relevant pre-1918 historical context relating to administrative division will also be provided.

A survey of evolution and eventual transformation of the internal division into international frontiers will also allow us to determine the (perceived) difference between these two types of boundaries. More importantly, it will aid us in explaining why this difference causes wars, and why nations, when calling upon the principle of self-determination, overwhelmingly still seek *international* borders rather than *internal* boundaries for themselves.

2.2. The Nineteenth-Century Geography of Nationalism

In the nineteenth century many European nations became politically conscious of their "nationhood," which became one of the factors in the crumbling of the two great empires in Central-East Europe—the Habsburg and the Ottoman Empire—at the beginning of the next century. Historians have termed this issue the Eastern Question, a question of filling up the vacuum created by the gradual erosion of the Ottoman rule in Eastern Europe.[3] The Eastern Question involved not only the repositioning of the Balkan states (especially Greece, Serbia, Bulgaria, and Romania) but also of Russia and the Habsburg Empire, leading to Great Power rivalries and resulting in the First World War.

The peoples of the future Yugoslavia, most notably Croats, Serbs, and Slovenes,[4] matured as nations during this period. They strove for greater independence not only by resisting foreign rule but also by means of diplomacy and cooperation with nations who shared their aspirations either out of idealism or out of interest. The Great Powers, however, chiefly decided their fate. The year 1878 provides the

---

[3] *See* John Marriott, *The Eastern Question* (Oxford: Clarendon Press, 1917); M. S. Anderson, *The Eastern Question, 1774-1923* (New York: Macmillan, 1966).

[4] This book will mainly focus on the Croats and the Serbs as the representatives of diverging national interests whose relationship is at the core of Yugoslavia's birth and disintegration. Some information will be provided regarding the Slovenes, as a corollary to the Croat position, and about the Bosnian Muslims, an important factor in Serb-Croat relations. The development of a Macedonian, Montenegrin and Albanian national identity will be briefly elaborated to construct the full context to the unfolding of the Yugoslav conflict.

most vivid example, when the borders of the South-Slav peoples shifted drastically two times in four months as a consequence of diverging interests of the
Great Powers.[5]

2.3. Development of Serb National Movement until 1914

Modern Serbian history[6] dates to 1804, when the First Serbian Insurrection
against the Ottomans began, born out of the desire for national emancipation.[7]
This was the first national uprising against the Ottomans among the peoples of

---

[5]   In March 1878, Russia, having defeated the Ottomans, attempted to resolve the Eastern Question to her
advantage by the terms of the Treaty of San Stefano (March 3, 1878). The agreement with the Ottomans
provided Russia with overwhelming influence in the Balkans, including the much-desired outlet to the
warm seas via a Greater Bulgaria, *de facto* a Russian protectorate that included the regions of Macedonia,
Western Thrace, a portion of Albania, and a district of Serbia. Russia also awarded full recognition to
Serbia, erstwhile an autonomous principality within the Ottoman Empire (reduced in the East by the
Treaty of San Stefano to the advantage of Bulgaria) and Montenegro (almost tripled in size). In July 1878,
the Congress of Berlin, attended by Germany, Austria-Hungary, Russia, Britain, France, Italy and Turkey,
revised the Treaty of San Stefano, exploiting the fact that Russia, although victorious against the Ottomans,
was exhausted by the war and at the verge of bankruptcy. Bulgaria, which to this day celebrates the day
the Treaty of San Stefano was signed as its national day, was reduced, most of its extended
territory having been returned to the Ottomans to counter Russia's increasing influence in the Balkans.
The Congress of Berlin did recognize an independent Serbia and an independent Montenegro, within
borders that suited the Great Powers, which were then impersonated by the Concert of Europe. It also
granted Austria-Hungary the right to occupy Bosnia-Herzegovina and to control the allegedly independent Montenegrin port of Bar [Treaty between Great Britain, Austria-Hungary, France, Germany, Italy,
Russia and Turkey, July 13, 1878, 153 CTS 171-191].

[6]   The history of Serb statehood is very rich, with the first Serbian dynasty established in the eighth century.
It is not recounted here for the purpose of brevity. For more information *see* Dušan T. Bataković, ed.,
Histoire du Peuple Serbe (Lausanne: L'Age d'Homme, 2005).

[7]   The First Serbian Uprising has also been called the "Serbian National Revolution." Brutally crushed by the
Ottomans in 1813, it sparked the Second Serbian Uprising in 1815, which led to Serbia's semi-independ-
ence from the Ottomans in 1817, formalized in 1829 by the Peace of Adrianople and hatti-sharifs of 1829,
1830, and 1833. Pressured by Russia, the Sultan then granted Serbia the right to internal autonomy and
its governor a hereditary title of prince, but continued to oblige Serbia to pledge a fixed yearly tribute to
the Porte. Prior to the uprisings, the rights of the vassal Serbia were regulated by various decrees.
See Wayne Vucinich, ed. *The First Serbian Uprising 1804-1813* (Boulder, New York: Columbia University
Press, 1982); Leopold von Ranke, *History of Servia and the Servian Revolution* (London: Benn, 1848).
Please also note that "the Serbian elite raised the issue of national rights and territorial autonomy as early
as 1790, at the eccleastical-national diet held in Temesvar (present-day Romania) and attended by 75
representatives of the aristocracy, high clergy and officer corps." Dushan T. Batakovich, "A Balkan-Style
French Revolution? The 1804 Serbian Uprising in European Perspective," *Balcanica* XXXVI (Belgrade:
Institute for Balkan Studies, 2006), 113-129.

Southeast Europe, followed by the Greek Revolution of 1821. Moreover, amongst the conquered Slavs of the future Yugoslavia, only Serbs managed to create an independent state in 1878.[8] Montenegro, which had never been completely subjugated by the Ottomans, was also then recognized.[9] At the same time, these two states did not encompass all the territories where Serbs lived. Until 1912, more than half of the Serb population lived under the Ottoman and the Austro-Hungarian reign.[10]

Despite the current revisionist claims by those favoring a non-Serb Montenegrin identity, it is a historical fact that the aspirations of the Montenegrins in the late nineteenth century mirrored those of other Serbs—unification and independence of Serb-inhabited lands. The greatest Montenegrin poet, Prince-bishop Petar Petrovich Nyegosh, was the leading Serb national figure in the nineteenth century, instrumental in codifying the Kosovo myth as the central theme of the Serbian national movement.[11] The Petrovich Nyegosh dynasty, which ruled over Montenegro, even made a brief attempt to take over the role of the Serb leader and unifier, but Montenegro's small size and weak economy ultimately led to the recognition of the primacy of the Karageorgevich dynasty ruling out of Belgrade. Montenegrins had Serbian identity but they were also proud of their state, especially in the area around Tsetinye, the capital of the Kingdom of Montenegro. A sense of distinct statehood was strong enough to breed strong autonomist sentiments in a portion of Montenegro's population following the 1918 unification with Serbia and the imminent disappearance of the Montenegrin state.[12]

---

[8]   Treaty of Berlin, July 13, 1878, 153 CTS 171-191 (Article 34).

[9]   Treaty of Berlin, July 13, 1878, 153 CTS 171-191 (Article 26).

[10]   Slavenko Terzić, "The Right to Self-Determination and the Serbian Question" in *The Serbian Question in the Balkans; Geographical and Historical Aspects*, ed. Bratislav Atanacković (Belgrade: Faculty of Geography, University of Belgrade, 1995), 40. *See also* Dimitrije Djordjevic, *Les revolutions nationales des peuples balkaniques* (Belgrade: Institut d'Histoire, 1965).

[11]   *See* below.

[12]   *See* John D Treadway, *The Falcon and the Eagle, Montenegro and Austria-Hungary, 1908-1914* (West Lafayette: Purdue University Press, 1983), 16-18, 201, 210. The *Encyclopaedia Britannica* of 1914 describes Montenegrins as belonging to the "Serb race." Sir Donald Mackenzie Wallace, Prince Kropotkin, C. Mijatovich and J.D. Bourchier, *A Short History of Russia and the Balkan States*; reproduced from the 11th edition of the *Encyclopaedia Britannica* (London: The *Encyclopaedia Britannica* Company, 1914), 121, 126. According to Pawlovitch, Montenegrin "rulers considered themselves Serb, were generally supportive of a 'Serb' cause and willing to cooperate with Serbia, but nevertheless gave priority to their own territorial objectives." Stevan K. Pawlovitch, *A History of the Balkans 1804-1945* (London and New York: Longman, 1999), 108.

In the nineteenth century, the Serbian national identity had fully developed. The Serbs possessed awareness about their long history and tradition, great medieval civilization, and cultural unity, regardless of the fact that they lived under different imperial administrations. Three elements, interwoven with the legacy of the medieval Serb Nemanyich dynasty, were imperative in the forging of Serb national identity and its conservation during long periods of foreign domination—the Serbian Orthodox Church, the symbolism of Kosovo, and the Serbian language.

The identification of the Serbian Orthodox Church with the Serbian nation is deeply rooted in the national consciousness. The medieval rulers of the Serbs were closely identified with the Serbian Church and its struggle for autonomy. Following the Byzantine tradition, members of the Serb Nemanyich dynasty founded monasteries, some became monks and achieved sainthood, and in 1219 the pious St. Sava, son of Stephan Nemanya, became the first archbishop of an autocephalous Serbian church, freed from the jurisdiction of the Greek-led Archbishopric of Ohrid. The Church's independence was extinguished soon after 1459, when the Ottomans conquered Serbia. The Serbian (Christian Orthodox) Church, under the name of the Patriarchate of Pech, re-emerged a century later (1557), after an intervention by the influential Ottoman vizier of Serbian origin, Mehmed Pasha Sokollu (Sokolovich), who extended the Church's jurisdiction, bringing almost the entire Serbian nation under its wing.[13] The church was essential to Serbian identity as the only surviving Serbian institution during a long period of foreign rule and thus a form of a surrogate Serb state. Christian Orthodoxy has been one of the main Serbian traits, though there has been an important Catholic Serb minority, mainly in Dalmatia.[14] In addition, many Christian Serbs converted to Islam under the Ottomans, particularly in Bosnia and Herzegovina.

Oral folk traditions constituted another element nurturing Serbian national culture and reassurance that the nation would rise against its oppressors. A national

---

[13] Naturally, Sokolovich was Muslim, but three of the first four patriarchs of the re-established Serbian Orthodox Church—Patriarchate of Pech, in Kosovo and Metohia, were drawn from his family (the first patriarch was his brother, the Serb Orthodox monk Makariye Sokolovich). See Fred Singleton, *A Short History of the Yugoslav Peoples* (Cambridge: Cambridge University Press, 1985), 44; Radovan Samardjitch, *Mehmed Sokolovitch* (Lausanne: L'Age d'Homme, 1994); Ђоко Слијепчевић, *Историја српске православне цркве*, том 1, БИГЗ, Београд 1991 [Dyoko Sliyepchevich, *History of the Serbian Orthodox Church*, vol. 1, Belgrade, 1991], 306, 318-319.

[14] *See* below.

hero of epic songs, the legendary Marko Kralyevich, is "an embodiment of all that the Serbs wanted to believe of themselves—his heroism, his gentleness, his respect for the religious and social customs of his people, his 'machismo,' even his cruelty, but above all his fierce opposition to the Turks and his intense national pride."[15] The real Marko Kralyevich died fighting as an Ottoman vassal.

While Serb epic poetry also appealed to other Slav peoples of the Balkans, the Kosovo legends kept the spark of Serbian national consciousness alive for centuries, which burst into flame with Karageorge's[16] revolt against the Ottoman Turks in 1804. Legends of the Battle of Kosovo (June 15/28, 1389) dominated Serbian literature and art before the twentieth century. Historians observe that neither Serbs nor Turks won the battle, while both the Serbian ruler and the Ottoman Sultan died in its course. However, the Ottoman conquest of Serbia followed,[17] indicating that this battle represented a long-term loss for the Serbs. The Serbs have nonetheless celebrated the Battle of Kosovo as a symbol of their resistance to foreign occupation, of national unity, and ultimate sacrifice for homeland (Serbdom) and Heavenly Kingdom.[18] Prior to Ottoman occupation, the Serbs had reached their zenith under Dushan the Great (1331-1355), who was crowned "Emperor of the Serbs, Greeks and Bulgars."[19]

---

[15] Singleton, *A Short History of the Yugoslav Peoples*, 45.

[16] George Petrovich known as Karageorge was the leader of the First Serbian Insurrection and the founder of the Serb Karageorgevich dynasty. For more, *see* Zeljan E. Suster, *Historical Dictionary of the Federal Republic of Yugoslavia; European Historical Dictionaries No. 29* (Lanham, MD/London: Scarecrow Press, 1999), 154.

[17] Serbia lost independence only in 1459, but the Battle of Kosovo was perceived as crucial to the establishment of the 500 years of Ottoman domination over Serbia. One should stress that, in the thirteenth and fourteenth centuries, the capital city of the Serbian Kingdom and the seat of the Serbian Orthodox Patriarch were, respectively, Prizren and Pech, two cities in the modern day territory of Kosovo and Metohia.

[18] The Battle of Kosovo took place on St. Vitus' day (*Vidovdan*). The day of the Kosovo anniversary was chosen by the heir apparent to the Habsburg throne for a state visit to the occupied Sarayevo in 1914, when he was assassinated by a local Serb activist, Gavrilo Printsip, marking the beginning of the First World War. June 28 was also chosen by the ruler of the Kingdom of Serbs, Croats and Slovenes as the day on which to promulgate the Vidovdan constitution in 1921. Aware of this symbolism, Stalin chose this date to announce the expulsion of the Yugoslav Communist Party from the Cominforn in 1948.

The anniversary of the Battle of Kosovo has been honored by other nations as well. In June 1918, five months before the end of the First World War, the United States recognized it as a day of special commemoration in honor of Serbia and all other oppressed peoples fighting in the Great War. Prior to that, in 1916, a nationwide tribute to Serbia was arranged in Britain to celebrate the anniversary of Kosovo. For more information on these celebrations, *see* Thomas A. Emmert, "The Kosovo Legacy," in *Kosovo*, ed. Basil W.R. Jenkins (Alahambra, CA: The Kosovo Charity Fund, 1992), 55-57.

[19] Cited in Frits W. Hondius, *The Yugoslav Community of Nations* (Hague: Mouton, 1968), 20.

The most ardent collector of Serb oral tradition was Vuk Karadjich (1787-1864), reflecting the ideas of European early Romanticism. Notably, he was also the reformer and founder of the modern Serbian language, building on the work of other Serb linguists and philosophers, Sava Mrkaly (1783-1833); Luka Milovanov (1784-1828); and Dositey Obradovich (1742-1811), the latter a representative of European rationalism. Karadjich solidified Serbian culture, spreading and popularizing the national awakening. He also broadened the definition of Serbdom to embrace all who spoke this language, which according to him was a Serbian national heritage.[20] This idea reappeared in the formation of the first Yugoslavia, but failed in practice because a common language was not a sufficient trait to unite the Serbs, Croats and Muslims in one nation. Moreover, the majority of Croats had strongly rejected Karadjich's linguistic theory of national identity, perceiving Karadjich as a Serb nationalist.

In 1844, an unofficial plan of Serbian foreign policy was forged, inspired by a leading Polish émigré in France, Count Adam Jerzi Czartoryski, and his Balkan agent, Frantisek Zach, who wrote the first draft of this document. Iliya Garashanin (1812-1874), Serbian statesman and politician then serving as Minister of the Interior, personally endorsed a somewhat revised plan of Zach in a then-secret[21] document known as *Nachertaniye* ("Draft"). Like many of his contemporaries, Garashanin accepted that Serbia's national mission was to complete the task of national and social liberation initiated by the Serbian insurrections of 1804 and 1815. The frontiers of the state needed to be extended to encompass all areas where Serbs lived, according to the most famous paragraph of *Nachertaniye*:

> The significance and the foundation of the Serbian politics is that it not be limited to its present borders, but that it strives to embrace all Serb peoples surrounding it.[22]

---

20   Mihailo Crnobrnja, *The Yugoslav Drama* (Montreal: McGill-Queen's University Press, 1992), 37.

21   The Serbian public was not aware of the existence of the document until 1888 and of its contents until the beginning of the twentieth century. *See* Radosh Lyushich, «Илија Гарашанин о српској државности» [Iliya Garashanin on Serb Statehood] in *Гарашанин; сусрети и виђења 2001* [Garashanin; meetings and perceptions 2001], ed. Zoran Konstantinovich and Slobodan Pavichevich (Kraguyevats: Yefimia, 2002), 99.

22   "Nachertaniye of Iliya Garashanin," reprinted in Belgrade 1991, 15 [Translation mine]. English copy produced in Paul N. Hehn, "The Origins of Modern Pan-Serbism—the 1844 Nacertanije of Ilija Garasanin: An Analysis and Translation," *East European Quarterly* IX, No. 2 (Summer 1975).

Following Karadjich's lead, Garashanin defined the Serb national boundaries as linguistic and cultural, rather than exclusively ethnic or religious. However, the *Nachertaniye* also advocated historical borders, especially towards the South.

Nachertaniye was a national program created after the famous national programs in Europe demanding national liberation and union in nation-states, pursuant to similar processes in Germany or Italy. In fact, that same year the project of a Greater Greece—*Megali Idea*—was published.[23] Both the Serbian and the Greek national programs were based on the principle of inalienable historic right, in agreement with the national ideologies in Europe at the time. Serbian political parties followed this ideology within and without the princedoms, future kingdoms of Serbia and Montenegro, which is comparable to the application of "internal" and "external" right to self-determination. The most influential Serbian party, the National Radical Party, in its 1881 program thus declared the following two goals for future state organization: "internally people's prosperity and freedom, and externally state independence and freedom and unification of the remaining parts of Serbdom."[24]

Later historiography, mainly of Croat origin, has accused Garashanin of extreme Serb nationalism.[25] Yet the reading of the actual text suggests a different conclusion. The section titled "The Policy of Servia towards Bosnia, Hercegovina, Montenegro, and Northern Albania" states that "one of the main points which should be set forth is the principle of complete freedom of religion established by law" and that "every effort should be made to protect the Bosnians and other Slavs and to render them every means of assistance." *Nachertaniye* further declares:

> it would be advisable to print a short and general history of Bosnia, in which the names of several men of the Mohammedan faith and their renowned deeds would be included. It is recommended that this history be written in the spirit of the Slavic people.

---

23 Milan St. Protich, *Успон и пад српске идеје* [Rise and Fall of the Serbian Idea] (Belgrade: Institute for Balkan Studies, 1995), 68.

24 *Samouprava* (Self-Government), no. 1, January 8, 1881 [Translation mine].

25 *See, for instance*, Mirko Valentić, "Koncepcija Garašaninovog 'Načertanija' (1844)," *Historijski pregled* VII (Zagreb, 1961).

Garashanin was a pragmatic statesman who realized that "only through alliance with other surrounding peoples can she [Serbia] solve her future problems."[26] While Garashanin certainly envisioned a Serb-led kingdom, at the same time this was to be a democratic South-Slav union. According to Slobodan Yovanovich, Garashanin was one of the first statesmen to conceptualize the idea "Balkans to the Balkan peoples."[27]

In practice, union of free Serbs with the Serbs under foreign rule remained the Serbs' ultimate goal. Whether this union would be achieved independently or in union with other Slav peoples was yet to be determined. Garashanin was aware that the implementation of his policy program would not begin immediately but that it provided an important strategic vision.

Four years after the *Nachertaniye* was written, the Slavs (mainly Serbs) living in the Habsburg province of South Hungary (Voivodina)[28] allied themselves with Vienna not only to counteract the Hungarian revolutionaries, but primarily to protect their rights from the Hungarian denial of Serb identity. Their struggle was aided by the Kingdom of Serbia in an action organized by Garashanin, as well as by Serbs from other parts of the Habsburg Empire. However, to their disappointment, the Voivodina Serbs were not granted territorial autonomy by Vienna in return, but just another imperial patent reconfirming their previous privileges.[29]

---

[26]   Nachertaniye, Appendix.

[27]   Slobodan Yovanovich, *Политичке и правне расправе* I-III [Political and legal discussions I-III] (Reprinted in Belgrade: BIGZ, 1990, orig. 1908), 352.

[28]   Voivodina (Војводина) is the Serbian word for duchy. The province's original historic name is the Dutchy of Serbia, shortened to Serbian Voivodina and then just Voivodina upon its incorporation into Serbia when the attribute "Serbian" was no longer necessary.

[29]   The Serbs moved from southern Serbia (mainly Kosovo) to Voivodina in great numbers in 1690 to escape Ottoman retaliation, whose army they fought together with the Austrians. The migration to Voivodina was initiated by an Invitational manifest (so-called *Literae invitatorie*) issued by the Habsburg Emperor Leopold I to all the Christians of the Balkans on April 6, 1690. Special privileges were granted to Serbs in Voivodina by Leopold I on August 21, 1690, December 11, 1690, August 20, 1691 and March 4, 1695, confirmed by decrees in 1698 and 1699, as well as with each change of the ruler (Joseph I on August 7, 1706, Charles VI on April 10, 1715 and Maria Theresa on April 24, 1743). These privileges, allowing for church and school autonomy (including free choice of church patriarch and military ruler—duke), exemption from 10 percent tax imposed by the Catholic Church, and guarantees of personal and property rights, were limited in times of peace (under pressure from the Catholic Church and Hungarian authorities) and extended in times of crisis since the Voivodina Serbs rendered military services to the Austrian rulers. For more information *see* Vasiliye Dj. Krestich, *Грађа о Србима у Хрватској и Славонији (1848-1914)* [Documents on Serbs in Croatia and Slavonia (1848-1914)] (Belgrade: BIGZ, 1995), 88-112.

The "Duchy of Serbia and Temes Banat," established on November 18, 1849, was not a separate federal unit as such but a separate administrative district with church and school autonomy. Under Hungarian pressure even this status was abolished on December 27, 1860, with Voivodina becoming fully incorporated into Hungary. In 1868, the Hungarian authorities renewed the church and school autonomy for Voivodina Serbs, but in a limited scope, to abolish it once again in 1912. The extensive limitation of privileges, beginning with the act of 1860, stimulated political organization of the Voivodina Serbs, who gradually became the leaders of Serb political action in the Habsburg Empire.

Serbia successfully liberated its Southern territory (Old Serbia[30] and Slavic Macedonia) from the Ottoman Turks in the First Balkan War (1912-1913) but then fought a Second Balkan War to determine her boundaries in relation to other Balkan states, primarily Bulgaria, which resulted in the Treaty of Bucharest of August 10, 1913.[31] During that period the Serbian government made no overt attempts to undermine the Austro-Hungarian rule, aware that Serbia was not strong enough to fight the Empire on her own. However, the relations with Austria-Hungary became increasingly strained, especially after 1908 when the Dual Monarchy annexed Bosnia-Herzegovina, whose relative majority population at that time was Serb.[32] Perceiving the Serbs as the greatest threat to the Empire's integrity[33] and an obstacle to its expansion to the East (*Drang nach Osten*), the Habsburgs used the assassination of the Archduke Franz Ferdinand in Sarayevo in 1914 as a pretext for the punitive war against Serbia.[34]

According to Yovanovich, in Serbia at the turn of the twentieth century "the strongest idea-force was nationalism," which he identifies as a positive force that contributed to Serbia's state building:

> The people needed independent statehood in order to liberate themselves from the Turks; the dynasty needed a strong state power for its security;

---

[30] Old Serbia is a geographic region that was the core of medieval Serbia, including Rashka, Kosovo, and Metohia, as well as the northwest of today's Slavic Macedonia, including towns of Veles and Tetovo.

[31] Treaty of Bucharest, August 10, 1913, 218 CTS 322-337.

[32] *See* Dimitrije Djordjevic, "The Serbs as an Integrating and Disintegrating Factor," *Austrian History Yearbook* 3, No. 2 (1967), 48-82: 72-74.

[33] Samuel R. Williamson, Jr, *Austria-Hungary and the Origins of the First World War* (London: Macmillan, 1991), 103.

[34] For more, *see* Andrej Mitrović, *Prodor na Balkan. Srbija u planovima Nemacke i Austro-Ugarske 1908-1918* [A Foray to the Balkans; Serbia in the plans of Germany and Austria-Hungary] (Belgrade: Nolit, 1983).

the parties needed a constitutional and parliamentary state system in order to govern. Feeding itself on the components of nationalism, dynastism, partyism, the state idea grew stronger.[35]

As a result, the early twentieth century saw Serbia as a relatively modern and functional parliamentary monarchy. The 1903 Constitution (revised 1888 Constitution) reinaugurated a democratic regime, with strong guarantees for political and human rights, building upon the 1838 Constitution, which enforced a separation of executive and judicial power; the 1869 Constitution, which strengthened the role of the National Assembly; and the 1888 Constitution, which granted the National Assembly complete control over the budget, establishing a parliamentary regime.[36] Public administration reform and a professional civil service were important building blocks of a modern Serb state, with many civil servants coming from the ranks of Austro-Hungarian Serbs. By the First World War, almost universal male suffrage had existed for at least a generation in Serbia (since the Constitution of 1869) and social rights equalled if not exceeded those of West-European states; working time was limited and workers enjoyed a right to strike.

As remarked by John Allcock, "measured by the standard of the existence of representative institutions alone, Serbia [of that period] should be considered the most 'advanced' of all the South Slav lands."[37] This is not to say that Serbia lacked non-democratic elements. Notably, in 1903 a secret society largely composed of military officers murdered the autocratic King Alexander Obrenovich and Queen Draga, considering the couple to be a political embarrassment to Serbia and an

---

[35] Slobodan Yovanovich, *Влада Александра Обреновића* [The Government of Alexander Obrenovich] Vol. 2 (1897-1903) (Belgrade, BIGZ, 1990, 1st ed. 1931), 374. Note: The Obrenovich dynasty ruled in 1815-1842 and 1858-1903, and the Karageorgevich dynasty in 1842-1858 and 1903-1945. The two rival dynasties were both native, Serb. Prince Milosh Obrenovich organized the 1817 assassination of Karageorge. An arbitrary ruler, Milosh was forced to abdicate in 1839. He was succeeded by two of his sons, Milan (who ruled only several weeks) and Michael, who ruled for three years. In 1842 Karageorge's son, Alexander (1806–85), acceded to the throne, but was deposed in 1858, when the Obrenovich dynasty was reinstalled and Prince Milosh came to the throne for the second time. Prince Michael Obrenovich (1825–68), Milosh's youngest son, engineered a total Ottoman withdrawal from Serbia in 1867. However, after he was assassinated in 1868, his first cousin Milan (1854–1901) was elected to be Prince of Serbia (King from 1882) and ruled until 1889 when he abdicated in favor of his son Alexander, the last ruler of the Obrenovich dynasty (1889-1903).

[36] *See* Slobodan Yovanovich, *Политичке и правне расправе I-III* [Political and legal discussions I-III] (Reprinted in Belgrade: BIGZ, 1990, orig. 1908), 20-35.

[37] John B. Allcock, *Explaining Yugoslavia* (New York: Columbia University Press, 2000), 263.

obstacle to her democratization. Still, the subsequent Serb ruler, King Peter I Karageorgevich, was a true constitutional monarch, who had in his youth translated John Stuart Mill's essay *On Liberty* into Serbian.[38] In the nineteenth century Serbia created a modern army and a civilian bureaucracy, making a unique achievement in what was to become Yugoslavia, that of building the framework for a modern state.[39]

2.3.1. Kosovo and Metohia prior to the First World War[40]

Kosovo and Metohia represent the cradle of Serb civilization and the heart of Serb nation-building, most famously symbolized by the Kosovo legends woven over the Battle of Kosovo of 1389.[41] The better known is the etymology of the name of the northern area, Kosovo, as a field of blackbirds in Serbian. However the southwestern area, Metohia, is more telling of the tradition, stemming from the Greek word for "church property." Powerful Serb rulers of the fourteenth and fifteenth centuries had endowed the many important Serb Christian Orthodox monasteries and churches in Metohia with the surrounding land, including entire villages. The two areas, which previously formed parts of different Ottoman administrative units, merged into one only in 1945, and have been known since 1968 as "Kosovo and Metohia," or just "Kosovo," to regain the full name in the Serbian Constitution of 1990.

Serb tribes populated Kosovo and Metohia in the seventh century. From the late twelfth to the late fourteenth century, this was the center of the Serbian state, covered by the fortresses and royal courts of the Serbian rulers and their nobility in the north (Kosovo), and holding the seat of the Serb Patriarchate in Pech (Metohia). The Serbs formed a majority in this predominantly rural region, while the

---

[38] Grandson of Karageorge Petrovich, the leader of the First Serbian Insurrection against the Ottomans, King Peter I was a modest person and a patriot, Serb and European, having fought with the French army against the Germans and wounded in 1870, as well as taking part in the 1876 Serb uprising against the Ottomans in Bosnia-Herzegovina.

[39] *See* John R. Lampe, *Yugoslavia as History. Twice There Was a Country* (Cambridge, New York: Cambridge University Press, 1996), 46-55.

[40] *See* Dušan T. Bataković, "Twentieth-Century Kosovo-Metohija: Migrations, Nationalism, and Communism," *Journal of the North American Society for Serbian Studies* 13(2): 1-23, 1999; Miranda Vickers, *Between Serb and Albanian; A History of Kosovo* (New York: Columbia University Press, 1998).

[41] *See* page 70 above.

Albanians, who were a nomadic, cattle-breeding people, lived in the isolated mountainous area of Metohia, bordering Albania.[42]

Present-day Kosovo Albanians relate a different history. According to their romantic national view, Albanians are the only descendents of ancient Illyrians, who populated the Balkan Peninsula, including the region of Kosovo and Metohia, long before the Slavs. The nationalist Albanians consider themselves as the only indigenous population of Kosovo and Serbs as intruders.[43] However, there is no verifiable historical evidence that Albanians derive their origin from Illyrians. Nor is there evidence of historical Albanian presence in Kosovo, either in form of toponyms or relicts until late thirteenth century. Historians agree only that Albanians represent an autochthonous group, different from the Slavs, which lived in the same region as the Slavs, as well as other ethnic groups.[44] In 1455, Albanians made up four to five percent of the total population of present-day Kosovo.[45]

Over time, the majority of Albanians became Islamicized and therefore a privileged grouping in the Ottoman Empire that strengthened the Sultan's rule in the Balkans. The Christian Serbs, as explained above, took advantage of the Ottoman millet system under the restored independence of the Serbian Orthodox Church, under the name of the Patriarchate of Pech, Metohia. However, they were also forced to migrate north in great numbers, either out of fear or as a result of direct expulsion, leading to greater settlements of the predominantly Muslim Albanians in Kosovo and Metohia.[46] In addition, many Christian Serbs in the region were forced to adopt Islam, entering the Muslim Albanian clans and changing identity after several generations to eventually declare themselves Muslim Albanians.[47]

---

[42] At the time Albania was not an independent country. Albania gained independence only in 1912 and even then as an international protectorate.

[43] For more, *see* Stephanie Schwadner-Seivers and Bernd J. Fischer, eds. *Albanian Identities: Myth and History* (London: Hurst & Company, 2002); Arshi Pipa and Sami Repishti, eds., *Studies on Kosova* (Boulder, CO: East European Monographs, 1984).

[44] For more, *see* Peter Bartl, *Albanien; Vom Mittelalter bis zur Gegenwart* [Albanians: From Middle Ages to the Present] (Regensburg, 1995), translated to Serbian by Lyubinka Milenkovich (Belgrade: Clio, 2001), 16-18.

[45] Ibid, 59.

[46] The expulsions of Serbs were a result of retribution for their support of the Habsburgs against the Ottomans.

[47] Jovan Cvijic (Yovan Tsviyich) asserts that tribes of northern Albania are of mixed Albano-Serb origin, related to the Serb tribes of Montenegro. As an example Cvijic gives the case of the Albanian national hero Skanderbeg whose Serbo-Albanian origin is well known. Jovan Cvijic, "The Geographical Distribution of the Balkan Peoples," *The Geographical Review* V, No. 5 (May 1918), 345-361: 350. *See also* Natalie Clayer,

By 1912, when Kosovo was freed from the Ottoman rule in the First Balkan War and became once again a part of Serbia, while Metohia was absorbed by Montenegro, this area was approximately equally ethnically divided between Serbs and non-Serbs (Albanians, Turks, etc).[48] With the exception of foreign occupation during the First and Second World Wars, Kosovo and Metohia has been an integral part of Serbia thereafter.[49]

Serbs and Albanians fought on opposite sides and therefore against each other during the Serb uprisings against the Ottoman rule and in the First World War. The fate of the region interested the Great Powers, notably the Ottomans, Italy, and Austria-Hungary, which intervened at various points in time, usually inciting greater conflict among the Serbs and Albanians in Kosovo-Metohia. A stark example of such interference is contained in the 1904 letter of the Austrian Foreign Minister Goluchowski to the Austro-Hungarian Ambassador in Constantinople (present-day Istanbul), in which he delineates the following policy:

> Above all, we should intercede for the autonomous arrangement for Albania, which would embrace all the predominantly Albanian populated districts of the Vilayets of Kosovo and Monastir, erecting a stronger wall against the advance of the Serbian elements.[50]

As explained above, any strengthening of the Serbian state was then perceived as the key danger to the Austro-Hungarian Empire and an obstacle to its projection to the Southeast, towards the Greek port of Thessalonica. The most tangible

---

Aux origins du nationalisme albanais; la naissance d'une nation majoritairement musulmane en Europe (Paris: Editions Karthala, 2007).

[48] Dusan T. Batakovic, *The Kosovo Chronicles* (Belgrade: Plato 1992), 135-136, based on Austrian and Serb census results: Haus Hof und Staats Archiv, Wien, Politisches Archiv XII, k. 272 Nationaliteten und Religionskarte der Vilajete Kosovo, Salonika, Scutari Janina und Monastir, 1903; Ivan Kosancic, *Novopazarski sandzak* [Sanjak of Novi Pazar] (Belgrade, 1912), 16-18; Jevto Dedijer, "Stara Srbija; geografska i etnografska slika" [Old Serbia; Geographic and Ethnographic Picture], *Srpski knjizevni glasnik* XXIX (1912), 674-699.

[49] For an analysis of Serbian policies towards Albanians from 1804 to 1939, *see* Djordje Stefanovic, "Seeing the Albanians through Serbian Eyes: The Inventors of the Tradition of Intolerance and Their Critics," *European History Quarterly* 35, no 3, 465-492 (1995).

[50] Original: "Wir müßten daher vor allem für eine autonome Ausgestaltung Albaniens eintreten, in das alle überwiegend mit Albanesen bevölkerten Districte der Vilajete von Kossovo und Monastir einzubeziehen wäre gegen das Vordringen des serbischen Elements ein starker Wall errichtet." Letter of Austrian Foreign Minister Goluchowski to the Austro-Hungarian Ambassador Calice in Constantinople, December 31, 1904, printed in *Documents from the Vienna Archives*, Book II (1904), edited by Andrija Radenich (Belgrade: Historical Institute, 1973), 717-718 [Translation mine].

result of this Austro-Hungarian policy was the creation of an independent Albania in 1912.[51]

Prior to that period, Albanians had been developing a literary culture. The first books in the Albanian language, published by 1555, were religious, Catholic books, distributed in the area today known as the Northern Albania. The first Albanian authors from the fourteenth and the fifteenth century, who all lived and worked in Italy, had used the Latin script[52] and there were also several Albanian authors who lived in the Ottoman Empire and wrote in Turkish, Arabic, and Persian.[53] The first literary Albanian book appeared in Italy in 1685.[54] Unlike most other European nations, the Albanians cannot recall a tradition of statehood stemming from the Middle Ages. Albanian national pride instead centers on George Castriotti (Gjerg Kastrioti) Skanderbeg (1405-1468) of Serbian-Greek-Albanian origin, who organized uprisings against the Ottomans in 1443-1468.[55]

Albanian author Stavro Skendi considers the end of the nineteenth century as the time when the Albanian national awakening occured, principally in response to the decline of the Ottoman Empire, which had generally rendered the Albanians privileged and therefore complacent.[56] The most important event that demonstrated the readiness of the Albanian elite to fight for what they considered to be Albanian territory but that the Treaty of San Stefano of March 1878 had allocated to Serbia, Montenegro, and Greece,[57] is the meeting of the Albanian League on June 10, 1878 in Prizren. The Albanian League was created by forty-three Albanians who urged their fellow nationals both to take up arms and to appeal to the representatives of the Great Powers summoned at the Congress of Berlin to grant them an autonomous Albanian region formed of four different vilayets,

---

[51] According to Penguin Atlas: "Albanians … hadn't fought for their freedom or even asked for it: the country owed its exisence to Turkey's inability to defend it and Austria's determination that it shouldn't become Serbian." Colin McEvedy, *The Penguin Atlas of Recent History (Europe since 1815)* (Penguin, 1982).
[52] Peter Bartl, *Albanien; Vom Mittelalter bis zur Gegenwart* [Albanians: From Middle Ages to the Present] (Regensburg, 1995), translated to Serbian by Lyubinka Milenkovich (Belgrade: Clio, 2001), 83-86.
[53] Ibid., 90.
[54] Ibid., 86.
[55] Harry Hodgkinson, *Scanderbeg: From Ottoman Captive to Albanian Hero*, 2nd ed. (I.B. Tauris, Centre for Albanian Studies, 2005).
[56] Stavro Skendi, *The Albanian National Awakening 1878-1912* (Princeton, NJ: Princeton University Press, 1967).
[57] *See* footnote 5.

including the vilayet of Kosovo. The Albanian League was not united, with some members requesting independence and others autonomy within the Ottoman Empire.[58]

As in the case of Italy, the true forging of a national identity among Albanians followed the creation of the national state. As underscored by Pawlovitch, as late as 1922 "the country was not yet a united one; few saw themselves first and foremost as Albanians,"[59] while Stark Draper claims that the Albanian national feeling fully developed only after the Second World War.[60]

2.4. Development of Slovene National Movement until 1914

Slovene nationalism was confined to the Slovene territory, Carinthia,[61] which had been a province under Habsburg domination since the thirteenth century and only briefly existed as an independent state in the eighth century, when it came under foreign rule that lasted until the formation of the Kingdom of Serbs, Croats, and Slovenes in 1918.

Slovene nationalism was just nascent in the nineteenth century, and like Serb nationalism it romantically focused on culture—language, literature and songs.[62] The instigators of Slovene renaissance were Bartholomeus (Jernej) Kopitar (1780-1844), who published a Slovene grammar book in 1808 and reformed the Slovene language, and Anton Linhart, who wrote the first history of the Slovenes from a national point of view, founded modern Slovene theatre and was actively engaged in Slovene education reform.[63]

---

[58] Peter Bartl, *Albanien; Vom Mittelalter bis zur Gegenwart* [Albanians: From Middle Ages to the Present] (Regensburg, 1995), translated to Serbian by Lyubinka Milenkovich (Belgrade: Clio, 2001), 95-95.

[59] Stevan K. Pawlovitch, *A History of the Balkans 1804-1945* (London and New York: Longman, 1999), 234.

[60] Stark Draper, "The Conceptualization of an Albanian Nation," *Ethnic and Racial Studies* 20, no. 1, January 1997.

[61] Slovenes also lived in other Austro-Hungarian administrative areas where they were a significant minority, namely in Carniola, Styria, Gorica, Istria, and Trieste, and many became Germanized. *See* Fran Zwitter "The Slovenes and the Habsburg Monarchy" *Austrian History Yearbook* 3, No. 2 (1967), 159-188: 159.

[62] According to Peter Radan, the evolution of Serb, Croat and Slovene nationalism in the nineteenth century was influenced by the romantic nationalist ideas of Johann Gottfried Herder (1744-1803) and Johann Gottlieb Fichte (1762-1814). Peter Radan, *The Break-up of Yugoslavia and International Law*, Routledge Studies in International Law (London, New York: Routledge, 2002), 12-15.

[63] *See* Michael B. Petrovich, "The Rise of Modern Slovenian Historiography," *Journal of Central European Affairs* 22 (1963), 440-467, 459-467 and Rado L. Lencek, "The Enlightenment's Interest in

Yet unlike the Serbs, the Slovenes, who were small in number and of the same faith as their rulers, enjoyed a relatively fair treatment under the Habsburgs, who ruled more liberally than the Ottomans, and they were under no threat of Magyarization. As a result, the Slovenes had no national program of liberation. They did not seek independence but demanded more autonomy within the Austro-Hungarian Empire and this only towards the end of the nineteenth century.[64] Some Slovenes fought as volunteers with the Serb army in the First World War but most remained loyal to the Dual Monarchy, which the Slovene historians explain by fear caused by a delicate geographic position of little Slovenia surrounded by Austria, Hungary and Italy.[65]

Allcock strongly refutes any claims to long-standing traditions of Slovene political democracy. His research demonstrates that under the Franchise Act of 1873 only an estimated 5.9 percent of the population enjoyed the right to vote and that the Reichsrat (Austrian Parliament) "never saw more than one ethnic Slovene representative between 1867 and 1907."[66] The only political activity was manifest at the local level, which is not insignificant. However, even political representation via political parties did not lead to democratization or greater nation building among the Slovenes. The representatives of the most important Slovene party, the Slovene's People Party, "tended to be somewhat illiberal and clerically oriented Catholics, with a pronounced loyalty to Vienna, which frequently brought them into conflict even with other Slav parties."[67]

2.5. Development of the Croat National Movement and Croat-Serb Relations until 1914

As in the case of the Serbs and the Slovenes, language and literature became the building blocks of Croat national consciousness in the nineteenth century. Ljudevit Gaj (1809-1872) led this language reform, modifying the Latin alphabet

---

Languages and the National Revival of the South Slavs" *Canadian Revue of Studies in Nationalism* 10 (1983), 111-134.

[64] Fran Zwitter "The Slovenes and the Habsburg Monarchy" *Austrian History Yearbook* 3, No. 2 (1967), 159-188: 166-167.

[65] *See, for instance,* Vekoslav Buchar, *Политичка историја Словеначке* [The Political History of Slovenia] (Belgrade: Politika AD, 1939), 67.

[66] Allcock, *Explaining* Yugoslavia, 252-253.

[67] Ibid., 254.

to partially conform to the rule "one sound, one letter," established for the Cyrillic alphabet by Vuk Karadjich. Gaj also adopted the shtokavian dialect of the Serbian language as the Croat literary dialect.[68] His reform was an essential part of the so-called Illyrian movement, resisting attempts from Budapest to Magyarize the Croats and entertaining the idea of a common "Illyrian" (that is, South Slav) state. Serbs, including Garashanin, mistrusted Ljudevit Gaj and therefore questioned the authenticity of the Illyrian movement, having discovered that Gaj also acted as a spy for the Viennese authorities.[69]

In contrast to Slovene and Serb nationalism, which mainly relates to people, Croat nationalism principally relates to territory, a policy which has over time become the root of competing claims between the two nations that inhabit present-day Croatia—the Croats and the Serbs:

> While Serbian nationalism was fashioned so as to appeal to the minds and hearts of all Serbian people, regardless of where they lived, Croatian nationalism, largely legalistic, was predicated on territorial claims, without taking account of who lived in these territories.[70]

Consequently, to explain the development of Croat nationalism and its goals[71], a more detailed study of former Austro-Hungarian provinces that form the present-day Croatia is required, followed by a brief survey of Bosnia's history, another territory of competing claims between the Croats and the Serbs.

---

[68] For more, see Zeljan E. Suster, *Historical Dictionary of the Federal Republic of Yugoslavia; European Historical Dictionaries No. 29* (Lanham, MD/London: Scarecrow Press, 1999), 118-119.

[69] *See* Vasiliye Dj Krestich, Знаменити Срби о Хрватима [Eminent Serbs on Croats] (Novi Sad: Prometey, 1999), 18-19.

[70] Zarko Bilbija, "The Serbs and Yugoslavia" in *The Serbs and their National Interest*, eds. Norma von Ragenfeld-Feldman and Dusan T. Batakovic (San Francisko: Serbian Unity Congress, 1997), 96-97.

[71] One of the most eminent Croat historians, Vjekoslav Klaić, writing an extensive Croat history published between 1899 and 1911 and reprinted in 1975, thus wrote the history of the regions where Croats lived (not necessarily as a majority) in which the history of foreign rulers and their policy is a dominant trait, as is the life of various Croat nobles [*see* Vjekoslav Klaić, *Povijest Hrvata; od najstarijih vremena do svršetka XIX stoljeća* [History of Croats from the earliest times to end of 19th century] (Zagreb: Nakladni Zavod Matice Hrvatske, 1975)]. Later Croat historians strongly emphasized those elements that attested to various rights granted to Croats by foreign rulers, alleging that these rights amounted to uninterrupted Croat "statehood."

2.5.1. Croats and Serbs in Austro-Hungarian Provinces of Dalmatia, Krayina, Croatia and Slavonia

Historically, "Croatia" has been an amorphous geographic concept, with significant changes in size and ownership of sovereignty. It existed as a small independent state in the Middle Ages,[72] but it was absorbed by the Austro-Hungarian Empire following the death of the last Croatian king in a battle against the Hungarians in 1097. Croatia became one of many provinces, administratively linked with the province of Slavonia, most of which forms part of present-day Croatia. A third formerly Habsburg province that also forms part of present-day Croatia, but which has historically been more autonomous than the original province of Croatia or the province of Slavonia, is Dalmatia. Austrians ruled Dalmatia, while Hungary administered Croatia and Slavonia in the Empire. Finally, the fourth region whose territory has been incorporated in today's Croatia is (Voyna) Krayina or the Military Frontier, ruled by the Austrians until 1881 when it was placed under Hungarian auspices.[73]

Dalmatia certainly enjoyed the largest degree of autonomy in the Austro-Hungarian Empire. It entered the Habsburg monarchy much later than the other South-Slav provinces, as a result of the Congress of Vienna in 1815, when it was taken from Napoleonic France. Indeed, Dalmatia retained a distinctive character during most of its history, not unifying with the other Austro-Hungarian provinces inhabited by South-Slavs until the formation of the Kingdom of Serbs, Croats, and Slovenes more than a hundred years after the Habsburg conquest (1918). As Allcock has clarified, "Although Croats had tended to include Dalmatia within their understanding of the historical 'Croat lands', these had long been Venetian possessions." Moreover, the Ragusan Republic (Dubrovnik) had retained relative independence until 1808. By the Treaty of Campo Formio (1797), Venice ceded Dalmatia to Austria and, following the intervening Napoleonic period, Austrian control was reasserted in 1815.[74]

---

[72]   Medieval Croatia reached its peak under the reign of Tomislav (910-928), who proclaimed himself king in 924.

[73]   The peninsula of Istria is sometimes studied as a separate, fifth region although most historians tend to group Istria with Dalmatia.

[74]   Allcock, *Explaining* Yugoslavia, 255.

In 1874 Dalmatia's population was mostly made up of Croats and Serbs, with a small Italian minority, which nevertheless had significant cultural influence.[75] The exact proportions of Serbs and Croats cannot be precisely determined. Historians at the time made estimates based on language and religion, and while language was considered to be one and the same, there was also a large number of Roman Catholic Serbs in Dalmatia.[76]

Serbs lived mostly in the south of Dalmatia, in the Bay of Kotor, and in Dubrovnik. They were also to be found in the towns of Zadar and Shibenik and in the hinterland of northern Dalmatia.[77] The Serb presence in Dalmatia and its hinterland is centuries old. In addition to some older historical documents, living witnesses of Serb presence are the Serbian Christian Orthodox monasteries of Krupa (built in 1317) and Krka (built in 1350). A brief account of economic, cultural, scientific, and political influence of the Dubrovnik Serbs is an illustrative example of the significant Serb presence in southern Dalmatia:

> For many centuries Dubrovnik traded with its Orthodox hinterland and received immigrants therefrom. The most renown inhabitants of Dubrovnik, Ivan Gundulic, poet (1583-1638) and Rudjer Boskovic, scientist and philosopher (1713-1787), famous in the European circles, were of the Serbian origin . . . . In 1890, the Serbian Party won the municipal election in Dubrovnik. They got votes of the Orthodox Serbs and of the Catholic Serbs as well. In Ston, on the Peljesac peninsula, St. Sava founded an eparchy in 1219.[78]

---

[75]   According to one historian, Rade Petrovich, "89 percent of the population of Dalmatia spoke only Serbo-Croatian in 1874; about 8 percent spoke both Serbo-Croatian and Italian; 3 percent spoke only Italian" (Rade Petrović, *Nacionalno pitanje u Dalmaciji u XIX stoljeću* [National question in Dalmatia in XIX Century] [Sarajevo: Svjetlost, and Zagreb: Prosvjeta, 1982], 17-18; cited in Nicholas J. Miller, *Between Nation and State* [Pittsburgh: University of Pittsburgh Press, 1997], 29). For more, *see* Vasilije Krestić, *History of the Serbs in Croatia and Slavonia 1848-1914*, trans. Margot and Boško Milosavljević (Belgrade: BIGZ, 1997).

[76]   For more information on Roman Catholic Serbs *see* Lazo M. Kostich, *Католички Срби* [Catholic Serbs] (Toronto: St. Sava Serb Cultural Club, 1963) and Ivan Stojanović, *Povjest Dubrovačke Republike* [The History of the Republic of Dubrovnik], orig. written in German by Ivan Hristijan v. Engel (Dubrovnik: Srpske Dubrovačke Štamparije A. Pasarića, 1903).

[77]   Serbs began to settle in the coastal city of Rijeka only after the Second World War, following the expulsion of most of its Italian inhabitants by the Yugoslav Communist authorities.

[78]   Jovan Ilić, "The Serbs in the Former SR Croatia" in *The Serbian Question in the Balkans; Geographical and Historical Aspects*, ed. Bratislav Atanacković (Belgrade: Faculty of Geography, University of Belgrade, 1995), 307-348: 317.

Three nations therefore claimed this region—Serbs, Croats, and Italians. Yet one should note that prior to and during the Habsburg reign, many Dalmatians identified themselves simply as Dalmatians or Slavs, rather than Serbs, Croats, or Italians.[79]

Krayina[80] is the region established by Vienna in the 1520s as a military frontier zone between the Habsburg and the Ottoman Empires, on empty land bordering the provinces of Dalmatia, Croatia, and Slavonia to the West and Bosnia-Herzegovina on the East. The people who came to inhabit this region, predominantly Serbs, fought for the Habsburgs to defend them against the Ottomans. [81] In return, they enjoyed a large degree of autonomy that included independent schooling and an autonomous church. Slavo-Serbian (the language that predates the current version of the Serbian language) was used as a language of instruction and Serb Orthodox clerics oversaw schools in Krayina. It was the *Statuta Valachorum*,[82] a decree issued by Emperor Ferdinand II in 1630, that placed Krayina under direct rule by Vienna, removing the jurisdiction of the local Croatian Diet and effectively creating a separate region at the expense of the Croatia-Slavonia province. Internal organization of the Krayina was based on local autonomy, with courts for each of three captaincies, elected for yearlong terms by the elders of each district. This civil government and courts were in charge of all civil penalties, with military courts limited to corporal punishment and that only for members of the military. The Statute also elaborated military requirements: a minimum of six thousand soldiers was required to gather within

---

[79] As late as 1860, a Dalmatian politician reported no more than seven pro-Slavic politicians in Dalmatia, further noting that several of these declared themselves as Slavo-Dalmatians, also considering Dalmatians to be a separate ethnic group. For more, *see* Josip Vrandečić, "Nacionalne ideologije u Dalmaciji u 19. stoljeću" [National ideologies in Dalmatia in the 19th century] in Dušan Gamser, Igor Graovac and Olivera Milosavljević, eds., *Dijalog povjesničara-istoričara* [Dialogue of historians 4] (Zagreb: Friedrich Naumann Stiftung, 2001).

[80] Military Border or Frontier in English; Militärgrenze in German.

[81] For one of the earliest autochthonous demographic accounts of Krayina, *see* Spyridon Yovich, *Ethnographic Picture of the Military Border in Slavonia*, 2nd ed., orig. 1835 [Етнографска слика Славонске војне границе] (Belgrade: Chigoya shtampa, 2004), especially 43-48.

[82] The legislation had the same name and purpose as the law of 1467-8, by which the Ottomans granted privileges to Serbs in vassal Serbia. However the Austro-Hungarian law granted more extensive rights, at once creating an autonomous region and an effective military system defending their Empire. The integral text of the *Statuta Valachorum*, proclaimed on October 5, 1630, is reproduced in Latin, Serbian and German in Dinko Davidov, *Српске привилегије* [Serbian Privileges] (Novi Sad, Belgrade: Matitsa Srpska, Institute for Balkan Studies, Svetovi, 1994), 145-147.

three hours of any alarm. Krayina inhabitants were exempt from various land and protection taxes imposed on others.[83]

Upon the creation of Krayina, Croatian noblemen demanded that their levy power be extended to this area. In the eighteenth century, the Croatian representatives in the Hungarian parliament even requested "the enactment of laws and regulations which would make life impossible for the Serbian people and for the Orthodox Church,"[84] such as to prevent the organization of Serbian high schools, the building of Serb Orthodox churches, and so on. However, Vienna rejected these demands, needing the Krayina manpower to fight the Ottoman onslaught. In turn, the inhabitants of Krayina were extremely loyal to the Habsburgs, regarding them as the guarantors of their privileged status. According to Gunther Rothenberg:

> At the time when serfdom and subservience to feudal lords were still the general rule, [they] regarded themselves as free tenants of the emperor who were far superior to ordinary peasants.[85]

However, the Austrians tended to overlook local derogations to privileges at a time of a low war danger. The Catholic Church used these opportunities to forcefully convert the residents of the Military Frontier:

> As long as the service of the Orthodox Grenzer were needed, their religion was respected; but when the need had passed the throne did nothing to restrain the efforts of the Catholic hierarchy, which, with the zealous collaboration of the military, attempted forcibly to convert the Orthodox or at least to coerce them to accept the Uniat rites.[86]

Despite the forced conversions and the taxing demands of the Croat noblemen, the Serbs and the Croats generally lived peacefully in the Krayina, where Serbs were a majority.[87] The Krayina Serbs also enjoyed good relations with other

---

83 Miller, *Between Nation and State*, 10-11.

84 Edmond Paris, *Genocide in Satellite Croatia; A Record of Racial and Religious Prosecutions and Massacres* (Chicago: American Institute for Balkan Affairs, 1961), 11.

85 Gunther E. Rothenberg, *The Military Border in Croatia, 1740-1881* (Chicago: University of Chicago Press, 1966), 9.

86 Ibid., 29.

87 *See* Drago Roksandić, *Srbi u Hrvatskoj* [Serbs in Croatia] (Zagreb: Vjesnik, 1991), 55-70.

Habsburg provinces where Croats formed the majority—Croatia, Slavonia, and Dalmatia. Serious scholars have therefore refuted the postulated "age-old antagonisms" between Serbs and Croats.[88]

The Croats of *Croatia-Slavonia* enjoyed a limited political autonomy from the Habsburgs since their official incorporation into the Austro-Hungarian Monarchy in 1102. However, many present-day Croat historians find the position of Croatia's subservience to Hungary in the Habsburg Empire impossible to accept, because it testifies to the loss of Croatian statehood in the Middle Ages. Contrary to the established scholarly evidence, they tend to describe the Croat position within the Dual Monarchy as a voluntary sharing of power and a personal union between Croatia and Hungary:

> In the early Middle Ages Croatia entered into something of a commonwealth with Hungary.[89]

Some Croat historians go beyond this explanation and depict Croatia as one of the three states that comprised the Habsburg Empire that was according to them in name only a "Dual" Monarchy.[90] Historical legalism based on continuity of the Croat state[91] is characteristic of Croatian historiography,[92] and it follows in many

---

[88] *See*, for instance, Lampe, *Yugoslavia as History*, 30.

[89] Stephen Gazi, *A History of Croatia* (New York: Barnes & Noble Books, 1993), ix.
A document titled *Pacta Conventa* that was supposedly signed in 1102 but not saved was claimed by leading Croatian historians to be a contract stipulating personal union of Hungary and Croatia. However, even if its autheticity were accepted, the document still would not represent anything more than a contract between the feudal ruler of Croatia, Hungarian King Koloman, and his Croatian vassals, i.e. it would not be perceived as an inter-state agreement in domain of public international law. Marko Kostrenčić, s. v. "Pacta conventa," *Enciklopedija Jugoslavije* (Zagreb, 1955), 404; Nada Kalić, "Pacta conventa ili tobožnji ugovor izmedu plemstva dvanaestoro plemena i kralja Kolomana 1102. godine" [*Pacta conventa* or the alleged contract between twelve tribes and king Koloman of 1102], *Historijski pregled* 2 (1960).

[90] *See, for instance*, Milan Vladisavljević, *Hrvatska autonomija pod Austro-Ugarskom* [Croatian autonomy under Austria-Hungary] (Belgrade: Politika AD, 1939).

[91] *See also* Emilio Pallua, "A Survey of the Constitutional History of the Kingdom of Dalmatia, Croatia, and Slavonia" *Canadian-American Slavic Studies* 24 (1990), 129-154.

[92] Croatian-American and Austrian-American historians Charles and Barbara Jelavich share the Croat viewpoint that Croatia and Hungary "remained as separate kingdoms united through the crown." Rather then having been conquered, Croats had, according to this view, "elected the ruler of Hungary as their monarch" in 1102, and, by the same reasoning, in 1527 "after the defeat of Hungary by the Turks, Croatia elected the Habsburg emperor as her king." *See* Charles and Barbara Jelavich, *The Establishment of the Balkan National States, 1804-1920* (Seattle, London: University of Washington Press, 1993; 1st edition 1986), 247.

aspects, and is a reaction to, similar Hungarian designs. Croatian historical legalism was rejected by the Hungarian and other historians such as Hondius who viewed it as "a complex and national malaise [of the Croats]."[93] Nevertheless it is important to emphasize the firm belief of most Croats in its factuality since nationhood tends to be based on belief rather than reality.[94] The belief in the idea that Croatian statehood had never been extinguished contributed to the emergence of modern Croat national consciousness in the nineteenth century, with a goal of reunification of the alleged Triune Kingdom of the Middle Ages (Croatia, Dalmatia, and Slavonia).

An undisputable fact is that the Habsburg rule was less oppressive than the Ottoman, sharing the Roman Catholic religion and cultural views with the Croats, who retained the institutions of a parliament and a governor (*ban*), who was nevertheless selected by Vienna or Budapest, which also had full control of the provinces' finances.[95] Nonetheless, as observed by Singleton, dominant Croat families did not display any strong national feelings, Croat or Hungarian:

> They were more concerned with the consolidation of their estates and with the expansion of their personal power. Two of the leading families, the Zrinski and the Frankopani, held land in both Croatia-Slavonia region and Hungary and moved freely between their lands.[96]

However, an era of centralization and Magyarization ensuing in the late nineteenth century placed Croatia-Slavonia under direct Budapest rule:

> The railways were being constructed as an integral part of the Hungarian railway system. Also, Hungarian flags, emblems, coats of arms, and inscriptions were being erected everywhere.[97]

---

[93] Hondius, *The Yugoslav Community of Nations*, 20

[94] *See* Benedict R. O'G Anderson, *Imagined Communities: Reflections on the Origin and Spread of Nationalism* (London: Verso, 1983); Maria N. Todorova, *Imagining the Balkans* (Oxford, New York: Oxford University Press, 1997).

[95] Charles Jelavich, "The Croatian Problem in the Habsburg Empire in the Nineteenth Century" *Austrian History Yearbook* 3, No. 2 (1967), 83-115: 100.

[96] Singleton, *A Short History of the Yugoslav Peoples*, 55-56.

[97] Aleksa Djilas, *The Contested Country; Yugoslav Unity and Communist Revolution*, 1919-1953 (Cambridge: Harvard University Press, 1991), 31.

Nationalist Croats from Croatia and Slavonia developed an increasing animosity towards the Hungarians, whom they then viewed as oppressors, while others remained loyal to Budapest.

It was not until the nineteenth century that the provinces of Croatia and Slavonia had a first governor of Croatian origin, Josip Jelačić, previously a mid-ranking Austrian military official. Jelačić entertained a good relationship with the Habsburg Serbs. He referred to the "Croat and Serbian People" in his proclamations, and declared on September 7, 1848: "Religious differences make no barriers between brothers in social or public life. We proclaim full equality [between Croats and Serbs]."[98]

When the Hungarians begun to demand greater rights from the Austrian Habsburgs, the Croats and the Serbs in the Empire, led by Ban Jelačić, fought fervently on the Austrian side. Croats, who were under Hungarian rule in the Empire, resisted Magyarisation and hoped to obtain greater rights from the Austrian emperor. The Krayina Serbs supported the Croats not only because of Jelačić's fair treatment of both Serbs and Croats, but also because the Hungarians had begun encroaching on the Austrian rule in Krayina. Finally, the Hungarians had directed their Magyarisation policy not just against Croats but also against Serbs and other ethnic groups in provinces under their rule. A key factor in forging a Croato-Serb military coalition against the Hungarians was the uprising of the Voivodina Serbs (then a part of Southern Hungary) against the Hungarian authorities during the 1848-49 revolution.[99] The Krayina Serbs demanded that Jelačić provide their brethren with military aid. The Serb Patriarch Joseph Rayachich, who had consecrated Jelačić as a ban, seconded this demand.[100] Although the Croat-Serb army then delivered a serious blow to the Hungarian forces, they lost the battle. The Hungarian revolution was quelled by Russian troops who aided the Austrian crown, bound by the Holy Alliance.[101]

---

[98] Cited in Branko Vincic, "History of Serbs in Croatia," *Krayina; Tragedy of a People* (Hamilton, ON: Canadian-Serbian Council, 1998), 41.

[99] *See* above.

[100] Rothenberg, *The Military Border in Croatia, 1740-1881*, 151. Note: "Joseph Rayachich" is also spelled as "Josif Rajačić."

[101] Article 2 of the Holy Alliance Treaty, signed on September 26, 1815 by the sovereigns of Austria, Prussia, and Russia, stipulated that "the sole principle of force, whether between the said Governments or between their Subjects, shall be that of doing each other reciprocal service, and of testifying by unalterable good will the mutual affection with which they ought to be animated, to consider themselves all as members of one and the same Christian nation." Edward Cecil Hertslet, *The Map of Europe by Treaty* (London, 1875) (accessed February 10, 2005); available from http://www.napoleonseries.org/reference/diplomatic/alliance.cfm.

The good relations between the Serbs and the Croats in the Habsburg Empire were further strengthened in 1867, when the Croatian Diet declared that the Serbian and the Croatian nations and their languages were equal.[102] However this decision was not always respected. Notably, the first Croat teachers' general assembly in 1871 concluded that teaching was to be conducted in Croatian only.[103] Perhaps this change in attitude came as a result of the 1868 Croato-Hungarian agreement (*Nagodba*).[104] The agreement dealing with Croato-Hungarian relations was a consequence of the Austro-Hungarian Compromise of 1867, which had turned the Habsburg Monarchy into a Dual Monarchy, now placing the province of Croatia-Slavonia completely in the sphere of Hungary.

The Croato-Hungarian agreement delineated Croatian autonomy within Hungary with Croatian as the official language. Yet it stressed in the first article that Hungary and the provinces of Croatia, Slavonia and Dalmatia formed "one and the same political community,"[105] with Budapest retaining control over the choice of governor, finances, and the most important port, Fiume (Rijeka). While Croats placed their hopes on this agreement, perceiving it as a document apt to strengthen their rights within the Empire, Hungarians considered it a first step in Croatia's transformation into an integral part of Hungary. Hungarian and other foreign historians, including those writing in that period,[106] constantly emphasized the limits to Croatia's autonomy within Hungary, while Croatian historians tended to exaggerate its scope.[107] Notably, just as Hungarians wanted to render Croats a Hungarian "political nation," Croats preferred to view the Serbs as "political Croats," a view that Serbs fiercely rejected.[108] This issue formed the core of Croato-Serb

---

[102] *Saborski spisi sabora kraljevinah Dalmacije, Hrvatske i Slavonije od godine 1865-1867* [Parliamentary Acts of the Parliament of the Kingdoms of Dalmatia, Croatia and Slavonia 1865-1857] (Zagreb, 1900), 308.

[103] Decision cited in Vasiliye Dj. Krestich, *Из историје Срба и српско-хрватских* односа [From the History of Serbs and Serb-Croat Relations] (Belgrade: BIGZ, 1994), 210-211.

[104] Integral text of the political compromise between Croatia and Hungary of November 18, 1868, reproduced in François Rodolphe, *Les Constitutions Modernes-Recueil des constitutions en vigueur dans les divers Etats d'Europe, d'Amérique et du monde civilisé* (Paris: Challamel, 1910), Vol. I, 505, and in Snezana Trifunovska, *Yugoslavia through Documents from its Creation to its Dissolution* (Dordrecht: Martinus Nijhoff, 1994), 50-58.

[105] Ibid., translation mine. Original text: "La Hongrie et la Croatie, Slavonie et Dalmatie forment une seule et même communauté politique . . . "

[106] *See*, for instance, Percy Alden, ed., *Hungary of Today* (London: Fawside House, 1909), 394.

[107] *See*, for instance, Gazi, *A History of Croatia*, ix.

[108] *See* Tihomir Cipek, "Oblikovanje hrvatskoga nacionalnog identiteta. Primordijalni identitetski kod u ranoj hrvatskoj političkoj misli" [Shaping of Croatian national identity. Primordial identity code in early Croatian political thought] in *Dijalog povjesničara-istoričara* [Dialogue of historians 4],

antagonism, which developed as Croatian nationalism ripened in the second half of the nineteenth century.

Consequently, Croatia's frustrations regarding its position in the Austro-Hungarian monarchy were not placated with the *Nagodba*. Thirteen years later (1881), after the occupation of Bosnia-Herzegovina in 1878 diminished the importance of Krayina's role in defending the Empire's borders to the East, the Habsburgs dissolved the Krayina province under great pressure from Hungary, incorporating it into Croatia-Slavonia. Since then, the Serbs became an important factor in the Croato-Hungarian conflict:

> With the new lands, Croatia added 61 percent more territory and 663,000 more people, of which 55 percent were Serbs. This simple transfer of land and people from one jurisdiction to another upset the equilibrium of Croatian politics by inserting a non-Croatian element into what had been a largely Croatian land. By 1910, Orthodox Serbs made up approximately 25 percent of [Croatia-Slavonia's] population.[109]

While the majority of the Serbs living in the Austro-Hungarian Empire were peasants, some were also bankers and wealthy landowners. In 1897, Serbian farmers' collectives began to be formed in the Austro-Hungarian Empire, providing small-scale aid in the form of seeds, feed, educational materials, and classes to Serbian peasants. Linking all the collectives was the Serbian bank and the influential Serbian Economic Society and its newspaper, *The Tradesman* (*Привредник*), seated in Zagreb. Started in 1888, it was devoted to economic education and general advancement of Serbs, who dominated Croatia's economy until 1914.[110]

The Matitsa Srpska, a Serbian scholarly and cultural organization, was founded in Budapest in 1826, but subsequently transferred to Novi Sad, Voivodina, the hub

---

eds. Dušan Gamser, Igor Graovac, and Olivera Milosavljević (Zagreb: Friedrich Naumann Stiftung, 2001); Mirjana Gross and Agneza Szabo, *Prema hrvatskome gradjanskom društvu. Društveni razvoj u civilnoj Hrvatskoj i Slavoniji šezdesetih i sedamdesetih godina 19. stoljeća* [Towards a Croat Civil Society. Social Development in Civil Croatia and Slavonia in 1860s and 1870s] (Zagreb, 1992), 129-157.

[109] Miller, *Between Nation and State*, 18. Importantly, Serbs constituted absolute majority in more than a dozen towns and a relative majority in many more. *See* "Popis zitelja od 31.prosinca 1910. u Kraljevinama Hrvatskoj i Slavoniji" [Census of December 31, 1910, in the Kingdoms of Croatia and Slavonia] in *Publikacije Kr.zemaljskog statističkog ureda u Zagrebu*, LXIII (Zagreb, 1914), 50-51.

[110] All these organizations were founded by members of the Serbian Independent Party.

of Serb publishing activities. However, while promoting Serb interests, the Serb banks, cultural institutions, and party organizations also "served to segregate Serbs from their neighbors and inculcate an insular sense of community."[111]

Anxious about the termination of Krayina in 1881, the Serbs received reassurances from Emperor Francis Joseph that "all measures have been taken to place [the inhabitants of Krayina] on equal status with all other inhabitants of [Habsburg] lands of the Hungarian crown."[112] In return for the preservation of their previous privileges, the Serbs opted for loyalty to the Hungarian governor of Croatia-Slavonia, Count Charles Khuen-Herdervary (1882-1903). Khuen-Herdervary began a divide-and-rule policy in the region by granting greater privileges to the Serbs. In directly placing the Hungarian government rather than the Croatian Diet in the service of Serbian interests, Khuen-Hedervary drew Serbs into the Hungarian, rather than Croatian, administrative context. In 1887 and 1888, the Parliament passed two laws, one legalizing the use of the Serbian language and Cyrillic alphabet, and the other assuring the existence of Serbian Orthodox schools in districts where Serbs were a majority.[113] Many Serbs were dissatisfied with the scope of these laws, which they believed to be less generous than the privileges granted to Serbs in 1868, emphasizing religious and cultural rather than national rights.[114] The 1887-1888 legislation was imprecise and it did not apply to the entire territory of the Serb-inhabited provinces. For instance, the 1887 "Law regulating the activities of the Eastern Greek Church and the use of Cyrillic" stipulated that the Cyrillic alphabet could be used in court proceedings "there where Serbs lived in greater numbers."[115]

Count Khuen-Hedervary's actions generated a strong Croatian opposition. He was portrayed as a tyrant in Croatian historiography, although "during the entire twenty years of his rule exactly one man was shot."[116] The Croatian nationalism

---

[111] Miller, *Between Nation and State*, 24.

[112] Document cited in Rothenberg, *The Military Border in Croatia, 1740-1881*, 192.

[113] Miller, *Between Nation and State*, 37.

[114] *See* Zharko Miladinovich, *Тумач повластица, закона, уредаба и других наређења српске народне црквене автономије у Угарској, Хрватској и Славонији* [Interpretation of privileges, laws, decrees and other orders of the Serb national church autonomy in Hungary, Croatia and Slavonia] (Novi Sad, 1897), 100-101.

[115] Article 3, Law regulating the activities of the Eastern Greek Church and the use of Cyrillic, adopted on May 14, 1887, produced in Krestich, *Documents on Serbs in Croatia and Slavonia*, 89

[116] Hondius, *The Yugoslav Community of Nations*, 71.

that developed very timidly in resistance to the Hungarian rule, aiming at the unification of Croatia, Slavonia, the Military Frontier (Krayina), Dalmatia and Bosnia and Herzegovina into a single state according to a national program drafted by Yanko Drashkovich in 1832,[117] was rapidly enhanced by Khuen-Hedervary's actions—and directed against the Serbs who agreed to the ban's concessions in a desire to preserve their own culture represented by the Christian Orthodox faith and the Cyrillic alphabet. As elucidated by Miller:

> Serbs' behavior in Croatia was rooted in their fear of losing their collective identity. They were conscious of their history and proud that they had maintained their identity through centuries of Ottoman and Habsburg administration. . . . [They] could do nothing but accept Khuen-Hedervary's patronage, given the attitude of the most popular Croatian political parties and their leaders.[118]

It became a policy of Croatian politics to resist the granting of any recognition to Serbian institutions and cultural identity without previous acceptance by Serbs of the concept that the only "political nation" in Croatia was the Croatian.[119] This policy was advocated by the extreme nationalist Ante Starčević (1823-1896) and the Croatian Party of Rights.

Starčević, like many other Croat intellectuals, believed that Croatian statehood had never been extinguished, but that "the Croatian state" had merely been ruled by foreigners. According to him, this state encompassed all the Illyrian provinces of the Roman Empire, and was inhabited exclusively by Croats. Starčević not only denied any claim to Serbian nationhood, but even argued that members of the medieval Serbian Nemanyich dynasty had been the "purest-blooded Croats."[120]

Starčević had turned fiercely anti-Serb when he failed to obtain the post of Professor at the University in Belgrade, and since that time had regarded Serbs as an inferior race amidst the Croats that was either to abandon its national consciousness and become Croat, or to be exterminated. Not only did Starčević

---

[117] *See* Gazi, *A History of Croatia,* 179

[118] Miller, *Between Nation and State,* 42.

[119] Ibid.

[120] Dennison Rusinow, *The Yugoslav Experiment 1948-1974* (London: C.Hurst and company, 1977), 13.

launch the slogan "The Serbs are a breed fit only for the slaughterhouse,"[121] but he also claimed Slovenes as ethnic Croats. He aspired to a Greater Croatia that would encompass Slovenia, the provinces of Croatia, Slavonia, Dalmatia, and Krayina, as well as Bosnia and Herzegovina. In brief, Starčević was "the progenitor of extreme Croatian nationalism, which sought to suppress and perhaps even to exterminate all those who had a different national consciousness."[122] Yet despite overwhelming historic evidence to the contrary, modern Croat historians have identified Starčević as one of most eminent Croatian liberals, enlightened by the ideals of the French revolution and committed to democracy and the rule of law.[123]

Another ideology that emanated from Croatian resistance to Magyarization was the Croat version of Yugoslavism, which foresaw a union of South Slavs into one, highly federalized region based on alleged "historic rights." The goal was not independence but autonomy in the form of a separate federal unit dominated by Croats. The champion of this ideology was Bishop Josip Juraj Strossmayer, who had also briefly contemplated unification of the South-Slav lands of the Dual Monarchy with Serbia in the mid-1860s.

Serb politics in the Austro-Hungarian Empire at the beginning of the twentieth century were divided between those supporting cooperation with the Croats (the Independents), and those who supported some cooperation but insisted on forming an entity separate from the Croats in the future and joining with the Kingdom of Serbia (the Radicals).

The Independent Serbian party (which later became the Serbian National Independent party) was founded in August 1881 as the first Serbian opposition party in Croatia, demanding Serbian church and school autonomy, budgetary support for Serbian institutions in Croatia, equality of the Cyrillic with the Latin alphabet, the right to display the Serbian flag, and revision of an agreement with Hungary.[124] From late 1902 on, the party's leader, Svetozar Pribichevich, was the most active and influential Serbian politician in Croatia. Born in Kostaynitsa in

---

[121] Paris, *Genocide in Satellite Croatia*, 11.

[122] Djilas, *The Contested Country*, 106-7.

[123] *See* Pavo Barišić, "Ante Starčević (1823-1896)" in *Liberalna misao u Hrvatskoj* [Liberal Idea in Croatia], eds. Andrea Feldman, Vladimir Stipetić and Franjo Zenko (Zagreb: Friedrich Naumann Stiftung, 2000), 105-120.

[124] Miller, *Between Nation and State*, 38.

Krayina, he was brought up in such a way as "to have deep devotion toward the Serbian national idea and fully uncritical love towards Serbia, Montenegro and Russia."[125] His party advocated a broader version of Serbdom seeing Serbs as part of a larger, Serbo-Croatian nation.

A more vocal party, the *Serbian National Radical Party*, came into force in 1887. It was not active in the entire province of Croatia-Slavonia, which then also included Krayina, but based its political activity on the privileges granted to Serbs by the earlier Habsburg monarchs. The party goal was to extend the Serbian church and school autonomy to the political realm, building a basis for Serb territorial autonomy beyond Voivodina. According to the Radicals' Autonomy Program of 1897, Serbs should seek "the right of autonomy not only in the church/ school and property/financial [fields] but also in the political arena."[126] The Radicals based their claim on the set of privileges granted by Habsburg Emperor Leopold I in 1690, refusing the changes brought about by the subsequent Croato-Hungarian agreement. As portrayed by Miller, the *Serbian Radical Party* led by Yasha Tomich "represented a tried and true version of Serbianness: that the Serbian community was [Christian] Orthodox, isolated, threatened with assimilation, and needful of vigilance."[127] The Serb vigilance developed in response to aggressive Magyarization and rising Croatian denial of Serbian identity in the Empire.

In September 1902, *Srbobran* (Serb-Defender), a newspaper published by the *Independent Serbian* party, reprinted an article titled "Serbs and Croats" from the Serbian Literary Herald (*Српски књижевни гласник*), the leading literary journal in the Kingdom of Serbia. This article by Nikola Stoyanovich, a young Serb student from Bosnia and future member of the Yugoslav Committee, argued that the Serbs, having a stronger culture, would eventually culturally absorb the Croats. It caused a great uproar among the Croats, whose extremists protested in Zagreb, looting and destroying many Serbian banks and businesses.[128] The extent of the violence shocked the Serbs in the Empire.[129]

---

[125] Ibid., 47.

[126] Cited in Miller, *Between Nation and State*, 40.

[127] Ibid., 51.

[128] Ibid., 52-54.

[129] *See* correspondence of Serb notables describing the 1902 riots, reproduced in Krestich, *Documents on Serbs in Croatia and Slavonia*, 333-337.

Three years after this incident, however, a group of enlightened Serbs and Croats formed an official political coalition, realizing that Magyarisation threatened them both and that the Viennese authorities did not support a further federalization of the Empire. Thus, at the turn of the century, a politics of Croato-Serb cooperation prevailed, born out of the 1897 unification of the Croat and Serb youth organizations into the United Croatian and Serbian Youth. The youth leaders later formed parties that entered into a Serbo-Croatian government coalition, reflecting Pribichevich's belief that: "the Serbo-Croatian conflict cannot be considered a national question, because Serbs and Croats are not two different nations but parts of one and the same nation."[130]

One of the goals of the Croato-Serb coalition was unification of Dalmatia with Croatia-Slavonia, with the purpose of strengthening the struggle against the Austro-Hungarian dominance. Concerned about the previous nationalist Croatian policy, the Serbs joined the Coalition under one important condition, contained in the Zadar Resolution:

> Concerning the demands of our brother Croats for the reincorporation of
> Dalmatia to Croatia and Slavonia . . . the Serbian parties are prepared to
> [support this] if the Croatian side . . . bindingly recognizes the equality of
> the Serbian nation with the Croatian.[131]

On November 14, 1905, the parliamentary club of the Croatian Party and the club of the Serbian National party signed a declaration in the Dalmatian parliament to that effect, stating that, "the Croats and Serbs are one people, equal to one another." The two parliamentary clubs further agreed to interchangeably use Serbian and Croatian language and flags, to allow for Serbian culture and history to be aptly represented in education and for judicial use of Cyrillic script when cases are filed in that script.[132] This agreement was a corner stone of a coalition that was

---

[130] Svetozar Pribičević, "Misao vodilja Srba i Hrvata" [Guiding Thought of Serbs and Croats] in Jovan Banjanin et al., *Narodna misao* (Zagreb: Dionička tiskara, 1897), 50.

[131] *Stenografički zapisnici sabora Kraljevine Hrvatske, Slavonije i Dalmacije (1901-1906)* [Stenographic Minutes of the Parliament of the Kingdom of Croatia, Slavonia and Dalmatia] (Zagreb: Tisak kraljevske zemaljske tiskare, 1903), v.5, pt. 2, 966, cited in Miller, *Between Nation and State*, 83.

[132] Minutes of the meeting in Zadar on November 14, 1905. printed as a document "Agreement with the Croats" (Sporazum sa Hrvatima) by the Serb Dubrovnik printing house, kept in the Archives of the Serbian Academy of Arts and Sciences, dr F. Nikich's fund, number 14.528; reprinted in Krestich, *Documents on Serbs in Croatia and Slavonia*, 422-424.

announced a month later, becoming a significant factor in Croatia-Slavonia after the elections of May 1906.

In 1909 Ban Rauch of Croatia-Slavonia attempted to dismantle the Croato-Serbian political coalition by trying fifty-three Serbs (mostly supporters of the Serbian Independent party) for alleged high treason of encouraging Serbian nationalism aiming to destroy the Empire. It was evident that this trial was purely political, and Rauch failed to dismantle the Coalition. At the same time the trial demonstrated the existence of a strong Serbian national consciousness in the Austro-Hungarian Empire, even if it could not prove its subversive nature.

Aleksa Djilas explains how the Croatian-Serbian Coalition successfully joined the Croatian and the Serbian interests:

> The Yugoslavism of the Croatian-Serbian Coalition was made possible by its emphasis on liberal-democratic political institutions and on the universal right of nations to self-determination. Arguments for political legitimacy had moved away from the irreconcilable Croatian and Serbian national ideologies based on historical memories. The coalition opposed the participation of clergy in political affairs and held that religious beliefs and values were the private concern of the individual. This separation of the churches from politics helped to remove an important obstacle to Croatian and Serbian cooperation and unity.[133]

Nevertheless, the Serbian Radicals rapidly abandoned the Coalition, claiming that Serbian interests could not be forwarded in conjunction with the interests of the Croats in the Austro-Hungarian Empire, and that Serbs should strive for autonomy from both the Habsburgs and the Croats.

Even the Serbian Independents had important disagreements with the Croatian political parties. One of these involved a strong opposition to the annexation of Bosnia. Although the Independents considered that Bosnia should become part of the Kingdom of Serbia, they were only able to protest against the Austro-Hungarian annexation only indirectly, objecting that it "was carried out against

---

[133]   Djilas, *The Contested Country*, 34-35.

the precedent of the Berlin agreement . . . [and that] the people of Bosnia and Herzegovina were not consulted."[134]

Although party politics and parliamentary action significantly matured in the nineteenth-century provinces of Croatia-Slavonia and Dalmatia, Allcock concludes that: "as in Slovenia, the political class . . . was extremely small." The difference was that some Croat nobility survived, and that "Croats had not been marginalized within the urban middle strata to the same extent as had the Slovenes."[135] Yet, the electorate amounted to less than 2 percent of the population, 50-60 percent of which were state officials. The new electoral law of 1910 increased the number of eligible voters to only 8 percent.[136] Seton-Watson also observed a lack of democracy in the Croatia of that period (Croatia-Slavonia province): Public voting and tax qualification, which was extremely high for so poor a country, made "freedom of election" in Croatia a mere farce.[137]

The Austro-Hungarian Croats and Serbs entered the twentieth century with their respective national consciousness fully awakened, but with different and ever-more opposing national goals. A comprehensive but highly uncritical *Croatian History*, originally published in five volumes between 1899 and 1911, thus speaks about the Croatian struggle for nationhood and "reunification of Croatian lands," ignoring Serbian interests and even their presence.[138] The ensuing world wars and civil wars brought the Croato-Serb conflict to the fore.

2.6. Bosnia and Herzegovina prior to 1914

At the 1878 Congress of Berlin, the provinces of Bosnia and Herzegovina were given a special status in the no-man's land of dualism, as an imperial possession administered by the Austro-Hungarian Empire.[139] In 1879, Bosnia and Herzegovina were 18 percent Roman Catholic, 38 percent Muslim and 43 percent Serbian

---

[134] Miller, *Between Nation and State*, 124.

[135] Allcock, *Explaining* Yugoslavia, 255.

[136] Charles Jelavich, "The Croatian Problem in the Habsburg Empire in the Nineteenth Century," *Austrian History Yearbook* 3, No. 2 (1967), 83-115: 99.

[137] R.W. Seton-Watson, *The Southern Slav Question* (London, 1911), 104-5.

[138] Vjekoslav Klaić, *Povijest Hrvata* [Croatian History] I-V, 2nd ed. (Zagreb: Nakladni zavod Matice Hrvatske, 1975).

[139] Treaty of Berlin, July 13, 1878, 153 CTS 171-191 (Article 25).

Christian Orthodox.[140] The three groups were intermixed, although many areas within Bosnia and Herzegovina, including sections of larger towns, were nationally homogenous. The Serb Christian Orthodox population predominated in the countryside, while the Muslim Slav portion of the population dominated the urban areas, having been given economic and political privileges after converting to Islam during Ottoman occupation.

Prior to Ottoman occupation, the four religious denominations in Bosnia and Herzegovina were: Roman Catholic, Serbian Christian Orthodox, Jewish,[141] and so-called Bogomile (considered a heretic version of Christianity by the Orthodox and the Catholics[142]). The provinces of Bosnia and Herzegovina at times belonged to either Serb or Croat territory, partially or wholly. Its rulers changed their religious denomination according to interest. Culturally and numerically, however, the Serbs as a nation dominated Bosnia from the early Middle Ages until the late twentieth century, which is well documented.[143] The oldest written document in the Serbian language (and its Cyrillic script) is the Trade Treaty signed by Kulin, the Bosnian ban (governor), and the people of Dubrovnik in 1189,[144] while the most renowned medieval ruler of Bosnia, Tvrtko I Kotromanich (1353-1391), was as a descendant of the Serb Nemanyich dynasty crowned in the Serbian monastery of Milesheva over the tomb of St. Sava in 1377, with words "I, Stephan Tvrtko, King of Serbs, Bosnia and the Littoral was given this throne of the Serbian rulers, my ancestors, by God." To Serbs from Serbia, his enthronement did not represent outside rule but just another move of the seat of the Serbian state.

---

140   Miller, *Between Nation and State*, 30.

141   "The centuries-old community of Sephardim, numbering approximately 2,000 in 1878, grew to 4,985 as reported in the 1910 census.... A community of Ashkenazim grew from only a few families at the beginning of the [Austro-Hungarian] occupation to 1,412 in 1910." Robert J. Donia, "Fin-de-Siècle Sarajevo: the Habsburg transformation of an Ottoman town," *Austrian History Yearbook*, January 2002. For more *see* Todor Kruševac, "Društvene promene kod bosanskih jevreja za austrijskog vremena" [Social change among Bosnian Jews in Austrian times], in *Spomenica, 400 godina od dolaska Jevreja u Bosnu i Hercegovinu* [Commemoration of the four-hundredth anniversary of the arrival of the Jews to Bosnia-Herzegovina], ed. Samuel Kamhi (Sarajevo, 1966), 71-97.

142   Bogomilism may be defined as a Gnostic dualistic sect, the synthesis of Armenian Pailicianism and the local Slavonic Church reform movement in Bulgaria and Bosnia-Herzegovina between 950 and 1396 and in the Byzantine Empire between 1018 and 1186. For more, *see* L.P. Brockett, *The Bogomils of Bulgaria and Bosnia; the Early Protestants of the East* (Philadelphia: American Baptist Publication Society, 1879).

143   See Dusan T. Batakovic, *The Serbs of Bosnia & Herzegovina: History and Politics* (Paris: Dialogue, 1996).

144   Ilić, "The Serbs in the Former SR Croatia" in *The Serbian Question in the Balkans*, 317.

Herzegovina, a region encompassing southeastern areas of Bosnia and northeastern areas of ancient Montenegro (Zeta), had been established since the fifteenth century as an autonomous Serbian region. In 1448, Stefan Vukchich Kosacha of Hum, to assert his independence, dropped his title of *Voivoda* (duke) of Bosnia, which reflected his subordination to the Bosnian king, taking the title of "Herzog (duke) of Hum and the Littoral." The following year he further adapted the title to "Herzog of St. Sava," after the Serbian saint whose relics lay at the Serbian Monastery of Milesheva on Herzeg's lands until they were burned by Ottomans in Belgrade in 1594.[145] His lands became known as Herzegovina and are today called Old Herzegovina since parts of these lands are no longer in Bosnia but in present-day Montenegro and Serbia.

Following Ottoman occupation, many of the Muslim rulers admitted to their Serbian origin. For instance, Sali-pasha, the mutesharif of Pech (a town in the Serbian province of Kosovo and Metohia), who was born in the Bosnian town of Tuzla, told Yovan Tsviyich (Jovan Cvijic), famous Serbian geographer, in 1900 that he was of "Serbian blood" and that "he was looking after Serbian monasteries." Another famous example is, above-mentioned, Bayo Sokolovich, a Christian Orthodox Serb from Vishegrad, who was taken as a child to Istanbul as human levy imposed on the Christians in the Ottoman Empire to become Sokollu Mehmed Pasha. He advanced through his education to a high post in the Ottoman administration, and he was eventually appointed Grand Vizier, holding the highest administrative office in the Ottoman Empire below the Sultan.[146] In addition to performing the important role of restituting the independent Serbian Orthodox Church,[147] Sokolovich built a bridge in his hometown, later made famous by the Nobel-award winning Serbian novelist Ivo Andrich. The main symbolism of this bridge was that it connected the Serbs of Bosnia with the Serbs in Serbia.[148]

---

[145]   Robert J. Donia and John V.A. Fine, Jr., *Bosnia and Herzegovina; A Tradition Betrayed* (New York: Columbia University Press, 1994), 33-34

[146]   Ibid., 45. *See also* footnote 13 above.

[147]   *See* above.

[148]   There is much historic evidence to prove the predominantly Serbian origin of Muslims who converted to Islam during the long reign of the Ottoman Empire. After the Second World War almost the entire Muslim intelligentsia in Bosnia-Herzegovina declared itself as Serbian. A famous writer Mesha Selimovich (1910-1982) left a testimonial declaration to the Serbian Academy of Arts and Sciences in order to put a stop to further debate on his origin. He then declared himself a Serb, precisely locating the home of his ancestors and dedicating all his work to the Serbian Academy of Arts and Sciences. Mesha Selimovich's testimonial statement has been reprinted in Batakovic, ed., *Histoire du Peuple Serbe*, 367. For more on Sokolovich and other famous Serb Muslims from Bosnia *see* Milenko M. Vukichevich, Знаменити Срби муслимани [Eminent Serb Muslims], 2nd ed. (Belgrade: NNK, 1998; orig. 1906).

The idea that the Muslims of Bosnia and Herzegovina were not newcomers or converts but an indigenous, separate grouping, was encouraged by the Austrians after they had occupied Bosnia and Herzegovina in 1878. By leaning on local Muslims, they aimed to "reduce the influence of the local Serbs—at the time, both the largest and the most articulate, nationally-aware ethnic community in Bosnia."[149] While the Serbs in Bosnia and Hezegovina strove for a union with Serbia, the Croats, whose national sentiment had fully awoken only in the nineteenth century, supported the Austrian rule, hoping that this province would merge with the province of Croatia-Slavonia.[150] Bosnia's Muslim community aspired to a more autonomous status within the Ottoman Empire, allying with the Serbs until 1910 in their resistance to the Austrian rule.[151]

The leaders of the Serbian community in the town of Mostar presented their first petition to the Austrian authorities in 1881, protesting a law introducing conscription in Bosnia.[152] This was followed by the 1882 peasant uprising, which was a failed attempt to prevent occupation by armed resistance. The Serb political movement spread in late 1890s to all major regions of Bosnia and Herzegovina. The Serbs circulated petitions, negotiated with the government, published a newspaper, *Serbian Word* (*Српска ријеч*),[153] and held meetings to rally support in various towns. After much struggle their efforts produced an agreement with the government, and in September 1905 the regime promulgated a statute providing for the autonomy of Serbian church and school communities throughout Bosnia.[154]

Note: Authors of Croat origin sometimes dispute this position, further claiming that the Bosnian Serb origin is non-Slavic: "Most of the present-day Serbs in Bosnia and Hercegovina descend from the medieval, non-Slavic Vlachs." "Ethnic and Religious History of Bosnia and Hercegovina," ed. Francis H. Eterovich and Christopher Spalatin, eds. *Croatia; Land, People, Culture* (Toronto: University of Toronto Press, 1970), 386.

[149] Donia and Fine, *Bosnia and Herzegovina; A Tradition Betrayed*, 36.

[150] For more *see* Tomislav Kraljačić, *Kalajev rezim u Bosni i Hercegovini (1882-1903)* [The Kállay Regime in Bosnia and Hercegovina (1882-1903)] (Sarajevo: Veselin Masleša, 1987).

[151] For more *see* Nusret Šehić, *Autonomni pokret Muslimana za vrijeme austrougarske uprave u Bosni i Hercegovini* [The Autonomy Movement of Muslims during Austro-Hungarian Administration in Bosnia-Herzegovina] (Sarajevo, 1980); Milorad Ekmečić, *Bosanski ustanak 1875-1878* [Bosnian Uprising 1875-1878] (Sarajevo: Veselin Masleša, 1973), 120-132.

[152] Hamdija Kapidžić, *Hercegovački ustanak 1882. godine* [The Herzegovinian Uprising of 1882] (Sarajevo, 1973).

[153] *See* Vladimir Chorovich, *Политичке прилике у Босни и Херцеговини* [Political situation in Bosnia and Herzegovina] (Belgrade: Politika AD, 1939), 38.

[154] Donia and Fine, *Bosnia and Herzegovina; A Tradition Betrayed*, 101-102.

Austrian systematic suppression of Serbian national feeling and an attempt to create "a Bosnian nation" through cultural and other policies had failed.[155]

In October 1907, encouraged by a liberalized Austrian stance toward political expression, Serbian activists created the *Serbian National Organization* (SNO), which won all seats allocated to the Serbs in the Parliament convening in 1910. Its political program asserted that Bosnia and Herzegovina were Serbian lands and that the majority of Bosnian Muslims were Serbs by nationality who had embraced Islam.[156] SNO entered a coalition with the leading Muslim landlords in the Parliament, which lasted only one year. The Muslim party suspected that Serbian nationalists had instigated the peasant uprising against the landlords (who were mainly Muslim) and entered a coalition with the Croats lasting until the First World War (1914).[157] Different organizations from Serbia covertly helped the Serbs from Bosnia and Herzegovina, particularly after the provinces' official annexation by Austria-Hungary in 1908.

During the war, in October 1914, the government in the Croatia-Slavonia province restricted the use of the Serbian Cyrillic script and, in January 1915, banned it completely from public use, while in Bosnia Serb high schools were closed and thousands of civilian Serbs imprisoned or forcefully moved. At the same time, the Austro-Hungarian government distributed weaponry to the Bosnian Croats and Muslims, who were considered loyal to the Dual Monarchy.[158] The three groups, Bosnian Muslims, Croats, and Serbs, thus entered the First World War politically divided. The Serbs, who were always a majority, or at least a relative majority, in Bosnia, considered it to be a Serb land.[159] The Croats aspired to Bosnian territory

---

[155] The Austrians tried to suppress the use of Serbian Cyrillic script, banned magazines from Serbia and in March 1905 they forbid the distribution of the book *History of the Serbian People*.

[156] Donia and Fine, *Bosnia and Herzegovina; A Tradition Betrayed*, 109.

[157] Ibid.

[158] Batakovic, ed., *Histoire du Peuple Serbe*, 253-4. *See also* Lampe, *Yugoslavia as History*, 106-107. Lampe emphasizes the role played by Austro-Hungarian General of Croatian origin, Stephan Freiherr Sarkotić von Lovčen, in mobilizing Bosnian Croats and Muslims to persecute Serb civilians in Bosnia, and calls the Muslim-Croat massacre of Serb civilians in Focha "the first incidence of active 'ethnic cleansing' in Bosnia-Herzegovina." For more on Sarkotić *see* Richard B. Spence, "General Stephan Freiherr Sarkotić von Lovčen and Croatian Nationalism," *Canadian Review of Studies in Nationalism* 17, 1-2 (1990), 147-55.

[159] Aspirations to liberate Bosnia from foreign rule have been a constant among the Serbs, including the leader of the First Serbian Insurrection, Karageorge, who bore a seal bearing the inscription "With the mercy of God, George Petrovich, [in the name] of all the people of Serbia and Bosnia." Cited in Misha Glenny, *The Balkans; Nationalism, War, and the Great Powers, 1804-1999* (New York: Penguin Books, 1999), 13.

because it was in certain periods considered a part of their short-lived medieval kingdom and geo-strategically beneficial (Croatia-Slavonia is shaped like a crescent, with Bosnia in the middle). The Bosnian Muslims were for centuries a privileged religious group that wished to retain its status.

2.7. The Macedonian Question

Macedonia is a region occupying an important strategic location in the middle of the Balkan Peninsula, immersed in the Greek Byzantium, Bulgarian, and Serbian states, alternatively, before the Ottoman conquest. According to one of the most objective historical accounts, produced by Stevan Pavlowitch, in Macedonia of the nineteenth century, "the majority spoke South Slav variations that ranged from established Serbian to established Bulgarian, and felt no strong identity."[160] In the mid-nineteenth century the identity of Macedonian Slavs was primarily religious, not national. They were Christian Orthodox, as opposed to Muslims, and not particularly affiliated to any ethnic group. However, by the end of the same century four ethnic groups started to compete to attract the Christians of Macedonia and this competition embodied "the Macedonian Question."[161] In addition to strong Hellenic elements that gained popularity among Balkan Christian Orthodox elites throughout the Balkans in early stages of the national movements, Bulgarian propaganda proved also to be very strong since the 1870s, when the separate church organization (Egzarchate) was established.[162] The Serbian and the Romanian propaganda apparatuses were intensified in the 1890s through the school system. By the end of the century the Bulgarian propaganda, acting through the Egzarchate and the church-led schools, proved to be the most successful and for this reason most of foreign observers regarded Macedonian Slavs as Bulgarians at the beginning of the twentieth century. The incorporation of the so-called Vardar Macedonia to Serbia after the Balkan Wars gave advantage to Serbian propaganda. The Serbian community was strong in the northwest parts of Slavic Macedonia, while its eastern part was pro-Bulgarian. The Bulgarian occupation of Slavic Macedonia during the Second World War accentuated these pro-Bulgarian elements, partly as a result of the expulsion of about 140,000 Serbs

---

[160] Stevan K. Pavlowitch, *Serbia; The History behind the Name* (London: Hurst & Company, 2002), 78.

[161] For more on conflicting claims to Macedonian nationality, *see* Loring M. Danforth, *The Macedonian Conflict; Ethnic Nationalism in a Transnational World* (Princeton, NJ: Princeton University Press, 1997).

[162] For more, see Georges Castellan, *Histoire des Balkans XIVe-XXe siècle* (Paris: Fayard, 1991), 350-351.

from this area.[163] A distinct Macedonian identity was encouraged and fully institutionalized only in Tito's Yugoslavia.

Indeed, although the Bulgarians, Serbs, Greeks and Romanians traditionally competed for the region based on historic, ethnic, and linguistic claims, and although one could trace some elements of Bulgarian-sponsored Macedonian identity to the nineteenth century, the Macedonian national feeling at a wider, popular level had not fully formed until after the Second World War, under the Communist framework. Even the failed Ilinden uprising against the Ottomans in 1903 could not be defined as a Macedonian national uprising, having been organized by a Bulgarian-sponsored and Vlach-led secret organization. Macedonian-conscious elite is not apparent before the twentieth century. Krste P. Missirkov's 1903 book *On Macedonian Matters*[164] could be regarded as one of the first Macedonian national programs, albeit receiving popular support only several decades later.[165]

2.8. The Birth of Yugoslavia

The Kingdom of Serbs, Croats, and Slovenes[166] was formed in the aftermath of the First World War, on December 1, 1918, changing its name to "the Kingdom of Yugoslavia" (meaning "Kingdom of South Slavs") in 1929 in order to symbolically reflect the union of South Slav peoples (but not including Bulgarians) into a single state.[167]

---

[163]   Dusan T. Batakovic, *Yougoslavie. Nations, religions, idéologies* (Lausanne: L'Age d'Homme, 1994), 267.

[164]   Krste P. Missirkov, *On Macedonian Matters*, translated by Alan McConnell (Skopje: Macedonian Review Editions, 1974, orig. 1903).

[165]   Contradicting this view, Andrew Rossos asserts that the Macedonian nationalism had "existed illegally" since the first quarter of the nineteenth century, "recognized neither by the theocratic Ottoman state nor by the two established Orthodox churches in the empire" and denied by the neighboring nations, Bulgarians, Greeks and Serbs. *See* Andrew Rossos, "*The British Foreign Office and Macedonian National Identity, 1918-1941*," *Slavic Review* 53, No. 2 (Summer, 1994), 369-394.

[166]   Bulgarians did not enter the new union of the South Slavs, while the Slav Macedonians and the Muslim Slavs were not considered as nations at the time.

[167]   Yugoslavia later changed its name five times. In 1945 it was called the "Democratic Federal Yugoslavia," and then the "Federal People's Republic of Yugoslavia," becoming the "Socialist Federal Republic of Yugoslavia" in 1963, the "Federal Republic of Yugoslavia" in 1992, and finally the "State Union of Serbia and Montenegro" in 2003, fully disintegrating in 2006 when Montenegro and Serbia became independent states.

Only Serbia and Montenegro enjoyed the status of an independent state in the period immediately before the First World War. The rest of the new Yugoslavi state became composed of the South-Slav portion of the crumbled Austro-Hungarian Empire. The provinces of Dalmatia and Slovenia were ruled by Austria, while Banat and Bachka belonged to Hungary. Croatia, together with the provinces of Srem and Slavonia, and incorporating Krayina as of 1881, was also part of Hungary with special autonomy. The provinces of Bosnia and Herzegovina, which had been administered jointly by Vienna and Budapest since 1878, were annexed to the Dual Monarchy in 1908. The amplitude of the previous disunion of the new South Slav conglomerate is demonstrated by the fact that this was the first time that Dalmatia became a part of a state shared by other South-Slavs since medieval times.

Hailed as a spontaneous union by the South Slav peoples freed from foreign yoke, the creation of the first Yugoslavia was in fact largely imposed by external factors. Croats and Slovenes came out of the First World War as losers, having fought on the side of the Austro-Hungarian Empire. The Serbs, on the other hand, had fought on the side of the victorious Allies. Even among the Serbs from Austria-Hungary, there was, by a vast majority, a declining allegiance to the Empire. Faced with Austro-Hungarian disintegration, the Slovenes feared a new German influence and the Croats Italian occupation of Dalmatia. To Serbs, Yugoslavia was the safest way to unite the geographically dispersed nation[168] in one state. To Croats and Slovenes, it provided the means of avoiding a new submission to a foreign power and paying hefty war reparations, while in parallel becoming an equal partner in a state for the first time since the early Middle Ages.

The Serbian war aims were outlined in three declarations—two Nish Declarations and the Corfu Declaration. The Serbian National Assembly adopted two Nish Declarations on December 7, 1914 and August 23, 1915. The second Nish declaration clarified the first in that the goal of the war effort was no longer "liberation and unification of all our captive brethren Serbs, Croats and Slovenes"[169] but

---

[168] According to the 1921 census, the percentage of Serbs in the total population was 98.4 percent in Serbia (within the borders before the Balkan wars of 1912), 43.9 percent in Bosnia and Herzegovina, 30 percent in Banat, Bachka, and Baranya (parts of Voivodina), 24.1 percent in Croatia (Croatia-Proper and Slavonia) and 17 percent in Dalmatia. *See* Branislav Gligorijević, "Unutrašnje (administrativne) granice Jugoslavije izmedju dva svetska rata 1918-1941" [Internal (Administrative) Boundaries of Yugoslavia between two World Wars 1918-1941], *The History of 20th Century* X, no 1-2 (1992), 22.

[169] "Niška Deklaracija" [Nish Declaration], December 7, 1914, in Branko Petranović and Momčilo Zečević, eds., *Jugoslavija 1918-1984, Zbirka dokumenata* [Yugoslavia 1918-1984; Collection of documents] (Belgrade: Rad, 1985), 22.

"freedom and unification of the Serbo-Croat-Slovenian people."[170] Interestingly, a Slovenian historian, Vekoslav Buchar, recounts how the addition of the Slovenians as a group to be liberated came only after an intervention (that is, lobbying) by a Slovene activist Niko Županić, who resided in Serbia.[171] The first time that the war aims were officially proclaimed, in the public announcement made by Prince Regent Alexander on August 4, 1914, all the South-Slav inhabited regions of the Dual Monarchy were listed except the Slovene region.[172]

During the war, the Government of the Kingdom of Serbia negotiated the pillars of the new South Slav state with the self-declared representatives of Austro-Hungarian South Slavs or the Belgrade-sponsored Yugoslav Committee, presided by a Dalmatian Croat, Ante Trumbić. Although the Committee was established in May 1915, the idea for the creation of the Yugoslav Committee originally came from Pashich in October 1914. Alex Dragnich suggests that the delay was caused by Trumbić's hesitation. Trumbić was simultaneously negotiating an independent Croatia but reverted to Yugoslavism at the news of the Allies' secret territorial promises of relegating Dalmatian coast to Italy.[173] Contrary to Pashich's idea, the Yugoslav Committee purported to represent all South Slavs, rather than just the émigré community. Its members were mainly exiled Croatian and Slovene politicians and intellectuals from Austria-Hungary, but also included several influential Serbs from the Dual Monarchy. Since its foundation, the Yugoslav Committee sought cooperation with the Serb authorities in Belgrade, realizing that this was the only possible means of achieving their goal—South Slavs freed from foreign reign and united in one federalized state in which the three nations—Serbs, Croats, and Slovenes—then hailed as three tribes of the same nation, would be equal.[174]

---

[170] "Zakljucak tajne sednice Narodne skupstine Kraljevine Srbije" [Conclusions of the secret session of the National Assembly of the Kingdom of Serbia], December 23, 1914, in Petranović and Zečević, eds., *Yugoslavia 1918-1984; Collection of Documents*, 24.

[171] *See* Buchar, *The Political History of Slovenia*, 62-64.

[172] Announcement produced in Nikola Stoyanovich, *Србија и југословенско уједињење* [Serbia and the Yugoslav Union] (Belgrade: Politika AD, 1939), 8.

[173] Alex N. Dragnich, *Serbia, Nikola Pasic and Yugoslavia* (New Brunswick: Rutgers University Press, 1974), 113-114. *See* footnote 179.

[174] *See* Gale Stokes, "The Role of the Yugoslav Committee in the Formation of Yugoslavia" in Dimitrije Djordjevic, ed., *The Creation of Yugoslavia 1914-1918* (Santa Barbara: Clio Books, 1980), 51-71: 53-54; Michael Boro Petrovich, *A History of Modern Serbia, 1804-1918* (New York: Harcourt Brace Jovanovich, 1976), 630-632; Milada Paulova, *Jugoslavenski odbor; povijest jugoslavenske emigracije za Svjetskog rata od 1914.-1915.* [Yugoslav Committee; the History of the Yugoslav Emigration during the World War, 1914-1915] (Zagreb: Prosvjeta, 1925); Ante Mandić, *Fragmenti za historiju ujedinjenja* [Fragments for the History of Unification] (Zagreb: JAZU, 1956).

However, throughout the war, relations between the Serbian government and the Yugoslav Committee were strained. The Yugoslav Committee saw itself as an equal partner to the Serb government, which it was not in reality. Pashich was further irritated by statements made by the committee's members regarding the country's future external borders, which he considered detrimental to the common cause if made at time of war.

The Serb government and the Yugoslav Committee, however, were able to agree on a common goal, signing the Corfu Declaration on 20 July 1917,[175] which Pashich had generally regarded as a declaration of solemn political goals rather than a legally binding document. In its Preamble, the Corfu Declaration stressed that Serbs, Croats and Slovenes were "a three-named people that [was] one and the same by blood, spoken and written language, sentiment of unity, continuity and wholeness of territory, where it lived undivided."[176] The Corfu Declaration had fourteen points, like the famous Wilson's Declaration, adopted several months later. It provided for equality of the three nations, specifically mentioning freedom of religion (Point 7), free use of flags and emblems (Point 4), national name (Point 5) and script (Latin and Cyrillic, Point 6). Notably the Corfu Declaration stipulated that the new country would be a monarchy, headed by the Serb Karageorgevich dynasty (Point 1), called "the Kingdom of Serbs, Croats and Slovenes" (Point 2). The internal organization would be decided by the new Constitution, to be adopted by a "Constitutional Assembly" directly elected by a secret ballot (Point 14). The Corfu Declaration remained ambiguous when stipulating that Constitutional Assembly would decide by a "numerically qualified majority" (Point 14). However, the unitary preference for a new state was hinted by another provision in Point 14, which stated that the future administrative units of the country would be "marked with natural, social and economic conditions."[177]

---

[175] "Krfska deklaracija" [Corfu Declaration], July 20, 1917, in Petranović and Zečević, eds., *Yugoslavia 1918-1984; Collection of Documents*, 51-53. An English translation of the Corfu Declaration is found in Trifunovska, *Yugoslavia Through Documents From Its Creation to its Dissolution*, 141-142. Note: Several days after the signing of the Corfu Declaration, this document was officially espoused by the Montenegrin Committee for National Unity, established in March 1917 in Paris. "Deklaracija Crnogorskog odbora za narodno ujedinjenje" [Declaration of the Montenegrin Committee for National Unity], August 11, 1917, in Petranović and Zečević (eds), *Yugoslavia 1918-1984, Collection of documents*, 54.

[176] Corfu Declaration, July 20, 1917.

[177] Ibid., 53.

The Yugoslav Committee strongly supported the Corfu Declaration, alarmed by the news of the secret Treaty of London of April 26, 1915[178] between the Allies (Britain, France, Russia) and Italy, by which Italy was promised significant Habsburg territory along the Adriatic coastline in return for switching to the Allies' side in the war.[179] In addition, the Yugoslav Committee needed to affirm its authority as a representative of the Austro-Hungarian South Slavs, contended by fellow politicians still loyal to the Dual Monarchy. Indeed, the South Slav members of the Austrian parliament had established a Yugoslav Club just two months earlier, on May 29, 1917. On May 30, they, with the notable exception of Serbian members of parliament, adopted what became known as the May Declaration, demanding "unification of all lands in the Monarchy, inhabited by Slovenes, Croats and Serbs, into one, autonomous state body, free from foreign rule and founded on democracy, *under the scepter of the Habsburg-Lorraine dynasty.*"[180] Unlike the Yugoslav Committee, the Yugoslav club had a mandate, having been directly elected by the people. Moreover, the Croatian Party of Rights and three Slovene parties officially espoused the May Declaration.[181] The Yugoslav Committee needed the authority provided by the Declaration of Corfu, which represented an agreement with the official Serb government.

The Corfu Declaration represented a compromise for the Serbian government, derived principally as a result of the Russian Revolution of March 1917, which

---

[178]   Treaty of London, April 26, 1915, 221 CTS 56-63.

[179]   The details of the Treaty of London were made publicly known only in February 1917, when published by the Bolshevik newspaper *Izvestija* (cited in Hondius, *The Yugoslav Community of Nations*, 83). However, the essence of the treaty's provisions was widely known in diplomatic circles soon after the treaty was signed. By the London treaty, Serbia's allies, Britain, France and Russia promised Italy large areas of Austro-Hungarian territory, mainly along the northern Adriatic. Excerpts of the Treaty of London have been reproduced in Petranović and Zečević, eds., *Yugoslavia 1918-1984; Collection of Documents*, 39-41. *See also* Dragoljub R. Zivojinovic, *America, Italy, and the Birth of Yugoslavia 1917-19* (Boulder CO: East European Quarterly, 1972); Milan Marjanović, *Londonski ugovor iz godine 1915.* [The 1915 Treaty of London] (Zagreb: JAZU, 1960).

[180]   The May Declaration is produced in Buchar, *The Political History of Slovenia* [Translation and emphasis mine], and in Petranović and Zečević, eds., *Yugoslavia 1918-1984; Collection of Documents*, 68-69.

Although the May Declaration is often cited as a proof of loyalty to the Austro-Hungarian Empire, other historians argue this was a brave move on the part of the South Slav members of parliament, who were not in a position to openly call for South Slav Union in the form of a new state, but that it was evident that such a union automatically implied the disintegration of the Austro-Hungarian Empire. *See, for instance,* Hondius, *The Yugoslav Community of Nations*, 126.

[181]   *See* Deklaracija Starčićeve stranke prava [Declaration of Starčević's Party of Rights], June 5, 1917 and Izjava vodja slovenackih stranaka [Statement of leaders of Slovene Parties], September 15, 1917 in Petranović and Zečević, eds., *Yugoslavia 1918-1984; Collection of Documents*, 70-71.

implied the loss of Serbia's principal ally. By signing on to this declaration, the Serb government effectively forgave the territorial promises of an enlarged Serbia offered by Britain's Foreign Secretary, Sir Edward Grey, in August 1915.[182] Mussolini was particularly furious at the news of the Corfu Declaration, declaring, "With the Corfu Declaration, Serbia lost Italy's friendly arm."[183] One of the key historical questions here, vital for the understanding of future developments, is why Serbia, a winner of the First World War, which already existed as a rump kingdom recognized by Congress of Berlin in 1878, did not establish an enlarged state of its own in 1918.

First, although President Wilson promoted the principle of self-determination, he did not advocate the break-up of the Austro-Hungarian Empire, and his Fourteen Principles, announced on January 8, 1918, included only "autonomous development" rather than independence for the South Slavs (Point 10). At the same time Point 11 (the Balkans paragraph) stipulated the withdrawal of all Central Powers' troops from Serbia and Montenegro, free access to the sea for Serbia, further advocating that "the relations of the several Balkan states to one another [be] determined by friendly counsel along historically established lines of allegiance and nationality."[184]

Second, once the Great Powers accepted the disintegration of the Austro-Hungarian Empire in mid-1918, they feared that further disintegration would not be easy to control and that it would pose a bad example to areas within their own states that aspired towards greater independence. At the same time, a new multinational state appeared to be a suitable replacement for its predecessor in the European balance of power system.

Third, the neighboring states hoped to take advantage of the end of the Dual Monarchy to enlarge their own territories. The most fervent was Italy, which

---

[182] Serbia was offered all of Bosnia-Herzegovina, large parts of present-day Croatia, including the southern part of the Dalmatian coast. At the same time, Serbia was asked to relegate a large portion of the Slav Macedonia to Bulgaria. For more, see Dragovan Šepić, *Italija, saveznici i jugoslavensko pitanje 1914-1918* [Italy, the Allies and the Yugoslav Question, 1914-1918] (Zagreb: Školska knjiga, 1970).

[183] Edoardo Susmel and Duilio Susmel, eds. "Il patto di Corfu," *Opera omnia di Benito Mussolini* IX (Florence, La Fenice, 1951), 104-107. Note: Mussolini was not then in power.

[184] President Woodrow Wilson's Fourteen Points, January 8, 1918, Delivered in Joint Session, U.S. Congress; (accessed May 4, 2005); available from http://www.lib.byu.edu/~rdh/wwi/1918/14points.html.

yearned for the entire coast of Dalmatia.[185] Hungary and Bulgaria also posed irredentist claims against the territory of the future Yugoslavia.[186] Italians had even intervened to challenge the right of South Slavs to liberation:

> In the Allies' reply of January 1917 to President Wilson's Peace Note, the Great Powers included, along with other aims, a demand for 'the liberation of Italians, of Slavs, of Roumanians, and of Czecho-Slovaks from foreign domination.' The original reference to 'Southern Slavs' by which the Allies implied Serbia's hope of gaining Bosnia, Herzegovina, and Dalmatia, was changed by the Italians "who did not want to encourage the Serbs."[187]

To counteract these claims, Serbia joined forces with other South Slavs. The British secret offer of August 1915 was no longer an option, having been annulled at the Paris Peace Conference, based on the first of President Woodrow Wilson's Fourteen Points, which prohibited secret agreements.[188]

During the war and thereafter, the union of all Serbs in one state remained the consistent goal of the Serbs. The reason that they chose a common state with the Slovenes and the Croats, rather than a carving of a Greater Serbia from the territories inhabited by the Serbs in the former Austro-Hungarian Empire, was that without unequivocal support from the Great Powers this was the only option that avoided further conflict. Deprived of Russian support, the Serbs chose Yugoslavia as a more peaceful means of achieving national union. More than half of the Serb adult male population had vanished in the First World War,[189] and the Serbian army, although still strong, preferred a stop to further human sacrifices. Furthermore, this was a time when Wilsonian ideals of peace and unity among

---

[185] See Enes Milak, *Italija i Jugoslavija 1931-1937* [Italy and Yugoslavia 1931-1937] (Belgrade: Institut za savremenu istoriju, 1987).

[186] One of the reasons why the Serbian government hesitatated to endorse the London Treaty is that this agreement, while providing significant territorial gains to Serbia formerly in Austro-Hungarian possession, also stipulated that Serbia cede its claims over Macedonia to Bulgaria. For more, see, Ivo Lederer, *Yugoslavia at the Paris Peace Conference; A Study in Frontiermaking* (New Haven: Yale University Press, 1963), 16-25.

[187] Alfred Cobban, *The National State and National Self-Determination* (New York: Thomas Y. Crowell, rev. ed., 1969), 53.

[188] Protich, *Rise and Fall of the Serbian Idea*, 204.

[189] About 55 percent of adult males and 25 percent of the total population of Serbia died in the First World War. Cited in William Dorich, "Epilogue" in *Kosovo* (Alhambra, CA: Kosovo Charity Fund, 1992), 175. At the Peace Conference in Paris, the Serbs documented the loss of 1,247,000 people—845,000 civilians and 402,000 soldiers. *See* Lampe, *Yugoslavia as History*, 107 and Batakovic, *Yougoslavie*, 140.

nations were becoming highly popular in Europe, and many Serb politicians embraced this vision with enthusiasm. One of the enthusiastic Yugoslavists was the Prince Regent Alexander himself, who had instructed Pashich in 1915 to reject the Serb enlargement offered by the British diplomacy, an act which later Serb historians, "with the benefit of hindsight," have termed "a great tragedy for the Serb nation."[190]

Without a common state Serbs could hope for certain territorial gains, but it was unlikely that they would achieve a complete national union.[191] In a South Slav union they would share their sovereignty with others, but their entire nation would be in one state. Moreover, the Serbs strongly believed that they could become the anchor of that future state, based on their relative size and economic strength. They hoped to follow the path of countries like France or Italy, which had unified their states in this manner in the previous two centuries. France, in particular, openly backed "a unitary Yugoslav state on the pattern of Italy or Poland," fearing that a federal arrangement would be divisive and weak.[192]

Yet although the Serbian negotiating position over the internal arrangement of the new state was significantly stronger than that of Slovenes or Croats, the Serbs, by and large, did not misuse their position. They demanded a constitutional, democratic, and parliamentary monarchy with the Serb Karageorgevich dynasty at the head, but they did not ask for any privileged status or any veto power, as had Prussia, for example, when unifying Germany.[193] At the same time, the achieved internal division of the new state was not a reasoned compromise. Croat and Slovene Habsburg-type federalists had to accept a centralized, unitary system of governance, because the Serbs extended parliamentary democracy to the semi-feudal milieu of the South-Slav portions of the Austro-Hungarian Empire,

---

[190] Alex N. Dragnich, "Nikola Pasic" in *The Serbs and their Leaders in the Twentieth Century*, eds. Peter Radan and Aleksandar Pavkovic (Aldershot: Ashgate, 1997), 47.

[191] Some historians claim otherwise:

"The costly victory in the First World War, in which one third of the Serbian population perished, gave the Serbs a sense of pride and confidence that if Yugoslavia were not realized they were sure that a "Great Serbia" would be, through the acquisition of the South Slav provinces which were wholly or preponderantly Serbian. It is understandable that the Serbian representatives should be apprehensive about losing something they had (Serbia) for something tenuous and beset with deep-seated internal problems (Yugoslavia)." Wayne Vucinich, "The Formation of Yugoslavia," *Creation of Yugoslavia 1914-1918*, 200-201.

[192] Lampe, *Yugoslavia as History*, 108.

[193] Alex N. Dragnich, "The Serbian Government, the Army, and the Unification of Yugoslavs," *Creation of Yugoslavia 1914-1918*, 43.

committing a significant sacrifice in human and material resources for the creation of the common state.

Although the Corfu Declaration was indeed a declaration and thus not a legally binding document, many of its provisions were put in practice upon the formation of the Kingdom of Serbs, Croats and Slovenes after the war. In the meantime, rumors circulated that Pashich had betrayed the aims of the Declaration, seeking a greater Serbia. Dragnich argues that these rumors emanated from several sources (Austro-Hungarian, Italian, Yugoslav Committee members, and perhaps even Pashich's Serbian political opponents), but that they had no ground in reality. While it is true that Pashich had instructed the Serbian diplomatic representatives in London and Washington at the end of 1917 to find out the intentions of the Allies regarding the fate of Bosnia and Herzegovina, this was done with the aim of clarifying Wilson and Lloyd George's vague statements regarding this area and not with the aim of seeking an enlarged Serbia.[194]

On the contrary, Pashich publicly proclaimed his support for the right to self-determination just one month before the formation of the first Yugoslavia, in an interview with Reuters in October 1918:

> Serbia regards it as her duty to liberate the Serbs, Croats and Slovenes. Once freed, they will enjoy the right of free disposition, that is to say, the right to declare themselves either in favor of uniting with Serbia on the basis of the *Declaration of Corfu* or, if they so wish, of constituting themselves into small States as in the distant past. Not only do we not wish to pursue an imperialistic policy, but we do not desire to limit in any fashion the rights of Croats and Slovenes to their self-determination; nor to insist upon the *Declaration of Corfu*, if it does not correspond to their own desires.[195]

At this time, Pashich also stated: "Corfu Declaration is a proof that Serbia and Serbs do not desire a dominant position in the future community."[196] He also

---

[194] Pashich explained his intentions in a telegram to the Serb minister (i.e. ambassador) to the United States. *See* Dragnich, *Serbia, Nikola Pasic and Yugoslavia*, 128-129. For more, see Comte Sforza, *Pachitch et l'Union des Yougoslaves* (Paris: Gallimard, 1938).

[195] *La Serbie*, October 28, 1918, cited in Ivo Lederer, *Yugoslavia at the Paris Peace Conference; A Study in Frontiermaking* (New Haven: Yale University Press, 1963), 41-42. Also printed in *The Times* and *Morning Post* for October 17, 1918, cited in Dragnich, *Serbia, Nikola Pasic and Yugoslavia*, 132.

[196] Izjava N. Pašića listu "Morning Post" [Statement of N. Pashich to the Morning Post], October 17, 1918, in Petranović and Zečević, eds., *Yugoslavia 1918-1984; Collection of Documents*, 59 [translation mine].

explained that the creation of a federal state was not seriously considered because determination of borders among the Yugoslav nations would be a difficult process, involving the resettling of populations that lived intermixed with one another.[197]

According to Dragnich, it was Trumbić who was a strong Croatian nationalist, but dared not voice Croatian aspirations for independence for fear of "Croatia" being left under Austria-Hungary, and reduced in size.[198]

As the tide of war turned to Serbia's advantage in 1918 and it became evident that the Dual Monarchy would not survive, the May Declaration became irrelevant. Most of the Austro-Hungarian South Slavs opted for unification with Serbia. For some this was a prime goal and for others a compromise, preferred to Italian or other foreign rule. On October 6, 1918, the National Council of Slovenes, Croats and Serbs[199] was founded, declaring itself to be the political representative of the South Slavs of Austria-Hungary,[200] with the aim of establishment of a state unifying all Slovenes, Croats, and Serbs, irrespective of current administrative and state boundaries, "led by the great ideas of national self-determination and democracy."[201] The establishment of the National Council of Slovenes, Croats and Serbs followed that of the National Council for Slovenia and Istria of August 17, 1918.[202]

On October 29, 1918, the National Council of Slovenes, Croats and Serbs proclaimed itself the government of the new state of Serbs, Croats and Slovenes.[203] Its decision followed that of the Croatian Diet, which had on that day declared

---

[197] Ibid.

[198] Dragnich, *Serbia, Nikola Pasic and Yugoslavia*, 120.

[199] "Saopštenje o osnivanju Narodnog Vijeća Slovenaca, Hrvata i Srba" [Announcement on the establishment of the National Council of Slovenes, Croats and Serbs], October 6, 1918, in Petranović and Zečević, eds., *Yugoslavia 1918-1984; Collection of Documents*, 83. An English translation is found in Trifunovska, *Yugoslavia Through Documents From Its Creation to its Dissolution*, 144.

[200] "Sastav i pravilnik Narodnog Vijeća Slovenaca, Hrvata i Srba" [Composition and Statute of the National Council of Slovenes, Croats and Serbs], Article 1, 5-6, October 8, 1918, in Petranović and Zečević, eds., *Yugoslavia 1918-1984; Collection of Documents*, 83-84. An English translation is found in Trifunovska, *Yugoslavia Through Documents From Its Creation to its Dissolution*, 145.

[201] "Objava Narodnog Vijeća SHS" [Announcement of the National Council of Serbs, Croats and Slovenes], October 19, 1918, in Petranović and Zečević, eds., *Yugoslavia 1918-1984; Collection of Documents*, 86-87 [translation mine].

[202] "Narodni svet za Sloveniju i Istru" [National Council for Slovenia and Istria], August 17, 1918, in Petranovic and Zecevic, eds., *Yugoslavia 1918-1984; Collection of Documents*, 82.

[203] On November 1, 1918, the National Council appointed the Yugoslav Committee as representative of the State of Slovenes, Croats and Serbs in international relations.

the end of "state-legal relations and connections" between the Triune Kingdom of Croatia, Slavonia and Dalmatia (which allegedly existed in the Middle Ages) and the Kingdom of Hungary and the Austrian Empire (Article I), and proclaimed this territory to be part of the (still not established) State of the Slovenes, Croats and Serbs, independent of Hungary and Austria (Article 2).[204] Significantly, the Croatian Diet based its decision "on the basis of the complete right of people's self-determination which is now recognized by all warring parties" (Article 1). On November 3, 1918, the National Council requested but never obtained recognition from the governments of France, Great Britain, the USA, and Italy. On November 8, 1918, only Serbia recognized the new *government* but not the *state*.[205] The same day Pashich sent a note to the Serbian diplomatic representatives in Paris, London, and Washington asking them to seek recognition for the National Council. Again the word "government" was used, not "state." Moreover Pashich stated that the National Council would be considered "a *government* of Yugoslavs on the territory of the former Austro-Hungarian Monarchy *until the definitive constitution of a single state of Serbs, Croats and Slovenes*."[206] Protich explains the Serbian act of recognition as "a sign of generosity towards a party whose status was, in the least, questionable."[207]

At the same time, the Serbian government did not consider the National Council to be on equal footing as negotiators of the internal organization of the new state. Pashich signed a declaration to that effect at the Geneva conference of November 9, 1918 (Geneva Declaration),[208] principally as a result of pressure stemming from the Serbian opposition parties. Nonetheless, a unified front was

---

[204] "Proglasenje Države Slovenaca, Hrvata i Srba" [Proclamation of the state of Slovenes, Croats and Serbs,] October 29, 1918, in Petranović and Zečević, eds., *Yugoslavia 1918-1984; Collection of Documents*, 88-89. An English translation is found in Trifunovska, *Yugoslavia Through Documents From Its Creation to its Dissolution*, 147-148.

[205] "N Pašic—A Korošecu," November 8, 1918, in Petranović and Zečević, eds., *Yugoslavia 1918-1984; Collection of Documents*, 96-97. An English translation is found in Trifunovska, *Yugoslavia Through Documents*, at 148-149.

[206] Dispatch of Pashich to the accredited ministers (ambassadors) of the Kingdom of Serbia in Paris, London, Washington and Rome, Geneva, November 8, 1918; reproduced in Petranovic and Zecevic, eds., *Yugoslavia 1918-1984; Collection of Documents*, 234 [translation and emphasis mine].

[207] Protich, *Rise and Fall of the Serbian Idea*, 210.

[208] For a text of the Geneva Declaration of November 9, 1918, see Ferdo Šišic, *Dokumenti o postanku Kraljevine Srba, Hrvata i Slovenaca, 1914-1919* [Documents on the Creation of Kingdom of Serbs, Croats and Slovenes] (Zagreb, 1920), 236-238 or Petranović and Zečević, eds., *Yugoslavia 1918-1984; Collection of Documents*, 104-105.

needed to demonstrate the impossibility of survival of the Austro-Hungarian Monarchy.[209] As Pashich explained to Stoyan Protich, the acting head of the Serbian cabinet, in a long telegram:

> under the pressure of events I was faced with the alternative: yield at the expense of Serbia's reputation and my own or take upon myself the curse of the people because with our disunity we wrecked the unity of our people.[210]

The Geneva Declaration refuted the Declaration of Corfu by failing to affirm that the new state would be a consititutional monarchy led by the Karageorgevich dynasty, proposing instead that a "common ministry of Serbs, Croats and Sloveness," be composed of three members of the Serb government and three members of the National Council of Serbs, Croats and Sloveness, with a purpose of negotiating a new state arrangement and other relevant issues until the adoption of a new Constitution. The Serb Prince Regent refused to sanction Pashich's signature to the Geneva Declaration and Pashich's cabinet resigned.[211] In Zagreb, Svetozar Pribichevich, the leader of Serbs from Austria-Hungary, also opposed the agreement. The end result was that neither the Serb government nor the National Council accepted the ill-fated Geneva Declaration, a document that remained a draft proposal without legal effect.[212]

It is important to note that the State of the Slovenes, Croats and Serbs was not formed for the sake of creating an independent state, but with a goal of establishing a representative body that would act on the unification of the Slav provinces of the Austro-Hungarian Empire with the Kingdom of Serbia. This is most clear in the decision of the Dalmatian National Council of November 16, 1918, declaring that the province of Dalmatia would unilaterally join the Kingdom of Serbia in the absence of overall unification.[213] As Hondius has pointed out, "the regional national councils were already threatening to join Serbia on their own accord."[214]

---

[209] Batakovic, ed., *Histoire du Peuple Serbe*, 275 and Dragnich, *Serbia, Nikola Pasic and Yugoslavia*, 122-134.

[210] Dragnich, *Serbia, Nikola Pasic and Yugoslavia*, 124.

[211] Hondius, *The Yugoslav Community of Nations*, 88. Stojan Protich's letter of resignation of November 11, 1918 is produced in Petranovic and Zecevic, eds., *Yugoslavia 1918-1984; Collection of Documents*, 106.

[212] *See* Protich, *Rise and Fall of the Serbian Idea*, 186-192.

[213] Cited in Milorad Ekmečić, *Stvaranje Jugoslavije 1790-1918* [Creation of Yugoslavia 1790-1918], Vol 2 (Belgrade: Prosveta, 1989), 820.

[214] Hondius, *The Yugoslav Community of Nations*, 89.

The process of establishing a joint government in the formerly Habsburg South Slav provinces was rushed, not entirely democratic and not entirely successful. While the Croatian Diet adopted a resolution to this end, it had jurisdiction over only two provinces—Croatia and Slavonia. The Slovenes elected a government only in October 1918, but indirectly—from the ranks of the Slovene People's Party and the National Progressive Party. In the provinces of Bosnia and Herzegovina, "the executive authority" became the National Council of Serbs, Croats and Slovenes for Bosnia and Herzegovina, also established only on October 20, 1918 from of the ranks of political parties that were also represented in the National Council in Zagreb.[215] While both the Slovene and the Bosnian national councils initially placed themselves under the jurisdiction of the National Council in Zagreb they did so solely with the purpose of entrusting one body to perform the process of unification with Serbia. That the Zagreb government was not a full-fledged government is also supported by a decision of the Voivodina assembly (then incorporating the provinces of Bachka, Banat and Baranya) of November 25, 1918, to directly merge with the Kingdom of Serbia, which was instantly accepted by Serbia.[216] The Kingdom of Montenegro also decided to unite with Serbia unilaterally and prior to the creation of the South-Slav state,[217] as did the forty-eight of the fifty four municipalities in Bosnia.[218] In Montenegro, the Great National Assembly also voted for Montenegro's unification with Serbia on November 13, 1918, reflecting the wishes of the majority population that elected the pro-unification delegates a month prior to this decision. The Assembly

---

[215] Peter Radan, *Self-Determination, Uti Possidetis and Post-Secession International Borders: The Case of Yugoslavia*, Unpublished Doctoral Dissertation, University of Sydney, 1998, paragraph 5026.

[216] "Odluka Velike Narodne Skupštine Vojvodine" [Decision of the Great National Assembly of Voivodina], November 25, 1918, in Petranović and Zečević, eds., *Yugoslavia 1918-1984; Collection of Documents*, 112.

[217] This is not the first attempt of union. In March 1914, the Montenegrin king Nicholas in a personal letter to King Peter offered a financial and diplomatic union of Montenegro with Serbia. However, Serbia could not accept the offer due to strong Austro-Hungarian opposition. The Austro-Hungarians closely monitored Serbia-Montenegro relations. An example is a discovery made by their secret service of a military agreement between Serbia and Montenegro drafted in June 1903 calling for joint action in case of Austro-Hungarian occupation of Kosovo. *See Documents from the Vienna Archives*, Book II (1904), edited by Andriya Radenich (Belgrade: Historical Institute, 1973), 61-62. *See also* Ilija Przhich, Спољашња политика Србије (1804-1914) [Serbia's Foreign Policy (1804-1914)] (Belgrade: Politika AD, 1939), 160-161.

[218] Hamdija Kapidžić, "Pokušaj ujedinjenja Bosne i Hercegovine sa Srbijom u novembru 1918" [Attempt of unification of Bosnia and Herzegovina with Serbia in November 1918] in *Bosna i Hercegovina pod austrougarskom upravom* [Bosnia and Herzegovina under the Austrio-Hungarian rule] (Sarajevo: Svjetlost, 1968); "Narodno vijeće u Banjaluci—Vojvodi S. Stepanoviću" [National Council in Banya Luka] to Duke S. Stepanovich, November 27, 1918, in Petranović and Zečević, eds., *Yugoslavia 1918-1984; Collection of Documents*, 115.

simultaneously dethroned the Montenegrin King Nicholas I and the Petrovich Nyegosh dynasty, accepting the rule of the Karageorgevich dynasty:[219]

> ... Montenegro unites with its brother Serbia into a single State under the dynasty of Karadjordjevic and, thus united, enters the common fatherland of our threefold people of Serbs, Croats and Slovenes. ...

> ... The Serbian people in Montenegro is of one blood, speaks one language and has the same aspirations, is of the same religion and has the same customs as the people that lives in Serbia and other Serbian lands.[220]

However, even in Montenegro the question of unification was not posed directly to the population and very few delegates were opposed to the achieved terms of unification.[221] At the same time, the population of the Habsburg Carinthia region, the only province in which a direct vote was taken on the question of unification as a result of the Paris Conference, said 'no' to a Yugoslavia on October 10, 1920. Although two-thirds of the population was Slovene, only 41 percent of the total population in Carinthia desired a common South Slav State, which means that a significant number of Slovenes, like the Austrians of the region, desired to be part of Austria.[222] Some deduce from this plebiscite result that the majority of Slovenes, and perhaps even Croats, were of this opinion. Others believe that the Yugoslav movement was dominant among all South Slav peoples. No matter what the prevailing ideology, it is clear that the perceptions of the goal of the common Slav State were different among its component nations, as reflected in the ensuing argument over the constitution.

In Bosnia and Herzegovina, the National Council had, upon constitution, declared itself for union of all Yugoslav peoples, inviting Serbia's Fieldmarshall Stepa Stepanovich to liberate them from the Habsburgs.[223] On November 23, 1918,

---

[219]   "Odluka Velike Narodne Skupštine Srpskog naroda u Crnoj Gori" [Decision of the Great Serb National Assembly in Montenegro], November 13, 1918, in Petranović and Zečević, eds., *Yugoslavia 1918-1984; Collection of Documents*, 113-115.

[220]   Cited in Hondius, *The Yugoslav Community of Nations*, 89.

[221]   On the Montenegrin assembly decision for unification see Dimitrije Dimo Vujović, *Podgorička Skupština 1918* [Podgoritsa Assembly 1918] (Zagreb: Školska knjiga, 1989), esp. 101-119; Jovan R Bojović, ed., *Podgorička Skupština 1918* (Gornji Milanovac: Dečje novine, 1989).

[222]   Thomas M Barker, *The Slovene Minority in Carinthia*, East European Monographs (Boulder, 1984), 164-165.

[223]   Stoyanovich, *Serbia and the Yugoslav Union*, 66.

the Central Committee of the National Council in Zagreb proclaimed the unification of the State of Slovenes, Croats and Serbs with Serbia and Montenegro[224] and
elected an implementing Committee. This Committee had little leverage when it
arrived to Belgrade on November 28, 1918. Members of the National Council of
Serbs, Croats and Slovenes were aware that the majority of the population they
claimed to represent would no longer stand behind them if unification with Serbia
were not achieved. Some of their nominally subordinate councils had already undermined their authority by deciding to join Serbia directly, such as the National Council
of Voivodina and the majority of Bosnian municipalities as outlined above.

Late on 1 December 1918, the head of the delegation, Ante Pavelić (who was not
the same Pavelić who later founded the Nazi Ustasha movement in Croatia)
appeared before the Prince Regent Alexander and read an address that referred to
a single state under the reign of the Serb monarch. At the occasion, Prince-Regent
Alexander Karageorgevich proclaimed the Kingdom of Serbs, Croats and
Slovenes,[225] and this was the only proclamation producing legal effect. After all, the
provisional Zagreb Council and the Belgrade government were not equal partners.
On 16 December 1918, the Serbian National Assembly declared to be "happy in
being able to give its political confirmation to the accomplished fact of the political
union of the Serbs, Croats and Slovenes" but with one important caution:

> It trusts that the State frontiers will be drawn in such a way as not to impair
> our right of national self-determination and it expects the Government to
> defend this right to the uttermost.[226]

In recognizing the Kingdom of Serbs, Croats and Slovenes, the Great Powers obligated the new state to guarantee language and religious rights, as well as other

---

[224] "Proclamation by the National Council of the Unification of the State of Slovenes, Croats and Serbs with
the Kingdom of Serbia and Montenegro," November 23, 1918, in Trifunovska, *Yugoslavia Through
Documents From Its Creation to its Dissolution*, 151-153.

[225] "Adresa izaslanstva Narodnog Vijeća SHS Prestolonasledniku Aleksandru i njegov odgovor" [Address of
the delegation of the National Council of SCS to the Prince Regent Alexander and his response],
1 December 1918, in Petranović and Zečević, eds., *Yugoslavia 1918-1984; Collection of Documents*,
121-124. An English translation is found in Trifunovska, *Yugoslavia Through Documents From Its Creation
to its Dissolution*, 157-160.

[226] Official proclamation of the union of the Kingdom of Serbia and Montenegro with the state of the
Slovenes, Croats and Serbs, adopted by the National Assembly of Serbia at its 98th ordinary sitting,
Belgrade, 16 December 1918, reproduced in Ferdo Sisic, *Abridged Political History of Rieka (Fiume)*
(Paris, 1919), Appendix, LXXXII.

group rights, both for the three constituent nations and for "nationals who belong to racial, religious or linguistic minorities."[227]

The "new state" relied in the main on the legislation of the Kingdom of Serbia prior to the adoption of the new constitution in 1921. Whether the Kingdom of Serbs, Croats and Slovenes, formed in December 1918, is a new state or a continuation of the Kingdom of Serbia, is a question that has troubled many jurists. Slobodan Yovanovich argues that by international law, the Kingdom of Serbs, Croats and Slovenes is a continuation of the previous Serbian state, since only Serbia existed as a state to which remnants of the Austro-Hungarian Empire were joined, succeeding to all contracts and treaties of the Kingdom of Serbia.[228] However, Yovanovich also insists that by constitutional law, this was a new state, which had new state symbols, and to which a new constitution applied (once adopted in 1921), making no reference to the previous constitution. Others disagree with Yovanovich, who, although a respected lawyer, was also an ardent yugophile and thus biased in that respect. They argue that there was constitutional continuity since the new constitution of the Kingdom of Serbs, Croats and Slovenes was based on the liberal 1903 Serbian constitution and the Serbian Parliament was the only body to officially ratify the unification of the Kingdom of Serbia with the South Slav parts of the Austro-Hungarian Empire. Another argument in favor of those who claim the continuity of the Serbian state is that the Austro-Hungarian Slavs did not join at once but the region of Voivodina united with the Kingdom of Serbia several days earlier.[229] Montenegro also joined the Kingdom of Serbia prior to the December act of unification. Finally, the new common state of South Slavs was ruled by the same monarchy, the Serbian Karageorgevich dynasty.

---

[227] Articles 7-11, Treaty of Peace between the Principal Allied and Associated Powers and the Serb-Croat-Slovene State [Yugoslav Minorities Treaty], Saint-Germain-en-Laye, 10 September 1919, entry into force 16 July 1920, *American Journal of International Law*, Supplement, Vol. XIV (1920), 333.

[228] Slobodan Yovanovich, *Политичке и правне расправе* I-III [Political and legal discussions I-III] (Reprinted in Belgrade: BIGZ, 1990, orig. 1908), 381-399.

[229] Ibid., 388-399.

Yugoslavias' Administrative Boundaries (1918-1991)

3.1. First Administrative Division of the South Slav Union: Thirty-three Districts (1921-1929)

The joining of the South Slavic peoples represented both a unique historical moment and a significant government challenge.[1] Serbs, Croats, and Slovenes lived under six different administrations before the formation of the Kingdom of Serbs, Croats and Slovenes (later named Yugoslavia) in 1918.[2] Due to different experiences of government, these nations disagreed on an internal organization of their new country. Opposing views were held by the Serbs, who argued for a unitary state with strong local government at the lowest levels (municipalities) based on the French model, and the Slovenes and Croats, who preferred a federal arrangement that delegated more powers to larger federal units formed upon a predominantly ethnic principle based on the Austro-Hungarian model. At the same time not all Croats preferred a federal arrangement. The Dalmatian regional government, for instance, "longing for strong support against the Italians—wanted a centralized State."[3]

The magnitude of these differences was evident from the onset. The very day the Kingdom of Serbs, Croats and Slovenes was founded, the parliament undertook a heated debate concerning this issue. The difficulty lay in the ambiguity of the Declaration of Corfu. Point 13 of the Declaration, stipulating the creation of autonomies based on "natural, social and economic" conditions, could be

---

[1]   See Chapter 2: *Pre-1914 Administrative Boundaries and the Birth of Yugoslavia.*

[2]   Laza Marković, *Jugoslovenska država i hrvatsko pitanje (1914-1929)* [The Yugoslav state and the Croatian question (1914-1929)] (Zagreb: Komisiona naklada, 1935), 192.

[3]   Frits W. Hondius, *The Yugoslav Community of Nations* (Hague: Mouton, 1968), 89.

interpreted both as a provision for creating administrative districts and as an argument for a federated state.[4] The Corfu Declaration also failed to determine the majority needed for the adoption of a constitution more precisely than "qualified."

In February 1921, the commission appointed by Stoyan Protich[5], the Minister for Preparation of the Constitutional Assembly, drafted a constitution that was based mostly on the Belgian Constitution because of its famed progressiveness and provisions relating to municipal and district government that were not included in the previous constitution of the Kingdom of Serbia. These provisions were later further amended according to the Dutch and English formulae, where the self-government system had been more broadly based and more strongly developed.[6] Moreover, the constitutional commission analyzed the previous administrative procedures and systems in different parts of Yugoslavia, concluding that a centralist system existed throughout Austria-Hungary and that even in the province of Croatia-Slavonia, where decentralization in some areas was allowed, the power lay with the governor (*ban*).[7]

In the end, the constitutional committee did not specify an administrative division of the state[8] and Protich created his own draft. In Article 4 of his draft constitution, Protich delineated the division of the Kingdom of Serbs, Croats and Slovenians first into provinces and districts, and then further into smaller administrative units.[9] He named nine regions that would gain the status of provinces in this proposal, following certain historic lines (Serbia, Croatia, Bosnia-Herzegovina, Dalmatia, Slovenia, Montenegro, Macedonia, Banat, and Srem), which stirred a strong parliamentary debate. Protich's draft constitution was

---

4   Marković, *The Yugoslav state and the Croatian question*, 59.

5   The Commission's five members were leading experts, representing different political ideas and all three nations, Serbs, Croats, and Slovenes.

6   Stoyan Protich, *Nacrt Ustava* [Draft Constitution] (Beograd: Dositeja Obradovica, 1920), vi.

     It is evident that Protich undertook a comparative study of administrative arrangements in the more advanced countries because he provides extensive footnotes regarding the system of Belgium, Holland and Italy, which are divided into nine, eleven and sixteen districts respectively.

7   Alex N. Dragnich, *Serbia, Nikola Pasic and Yugoslavia* (New Brunswick: Rutgers University Press, 1974), 148-149.

8   Marković, *The Yugoslav state and the Croatian question*, 69.

9   "Ustavni nacrt Stojana Protića" [Draft Constitution by Stoyan Protich], in Branko Petranović and Momčilo Zečević, eds., *Jugoslavija 1918-1984, Zbirka dokumenata* [Yugoslavia 1918-1984; Collection of documents] (Belgrade: Rad, 1985), 166.

opposed both by the (Serb) Democratic Party and by members of his own (Serb) Radical Party, who believed that it catered to separatist tendencies while dividing the Serbs into different administrative units. The Croats, who preferred a greater Croatian unit, encompassing Dalmatia and additional territory from other provinces, also opposed it.[10] Protich, who attempted to create a compromise between the separatists and the unitarists, eventually resigned.[11]

Although the rift between the federalists (most Croats and Slovenes) and the unionists (Serbs) at first appeared unbridgeable, a unitary constitution was voted on June 28, 1921[12] by 223 out of 419 deputies, including members of a minor Slovene party (the Slovene Peasant Party), and Muslim parties from Bosnia and Herzegovina and Southern Serbia and Macedonia (the Yugoslav Muslim Organization and the South Muslim Organization, respectively). The Croatian Community Party and the Slovenian People's Party voted against it while the Croatian Peasant Party had boycotted the National Assembly, proceeding to draft a constitution for an independent state to be named the Neutral Peasant Republic of Croatia.[13]

---

[10] See Dragnich, *Serbia, Nikola Pasic and Yugoslavia*, 149.

[11] According to a document discovered by Protich's grandson, historian Milan St. Protich, Stoyan Protich saw great economic loss for Serbia in entering a unitary state arrangement. By doing so, Serbia relinquished the right to significant war reparations that would have boosted and modernized the Serb economy. In addition, by allowing the exchange of the strong Serbian dinar for the Austrian crown, whose value was "less than the value of the paper on which it was printed" Serbia further weakened its economy. Stoyan Protich argued that Serbia's economic development would have drawn the former Austro-Hungarian territories into Serbia's sphere faster than a unitary constitution. However, the Serb government, again led by Pashich, did not share his opinion. *See* Protich, *Rise and Fall of the Serbian Idea*, 254-256.

The current Croatian historians, on the other hand, point to their economic loss in losing the trade arrangement previously enjoyed with the Austrian state, due to economic policy dominated by Belgrade in the new state. *See* Mira Kolar-Dimitrijević, "Privredne veze izmedju Austrije i sjeverne Hrvatske od 1918. do 1925" [Economic ties between Austria and North Croatia] in *Historijski zbornik* XLV, No. 1 (Zagreb, 1992), 1-374: 57-88.

[12] *Službene novine Kraljevine Srba, Hrvata i Slovenaca*, No. 142a, June 28, 1921. The 1921 Constitution is reprinted in Dusan Mrdjenović, ed., *Ustavi i Vlade Kneževine Srbije, Kraljevine Srbije, Kraljevine SHS i Kraljevine Jugoslavije (1835-1941)* [Constitutions and Governments of the Duchy of Serbia, Kingdom of Serbia, Kingdom of Serbs, Croats and Slovenes and Kingdom of Yugoslavia (1835-1941) (Belgrade: Nova Knjiga, 1988) and in Branko Petranović and Momčilo Zečević (eds), *Jugoslovenski federalizam, ideje i stvarnost, Tematska zbirka dokumenata* [Yugoslav federalism, ideas and reality; Thematic collection of documents] *Vol. 1*, 1914-1943 (Belgrade: Prosveta, 1987), 127-140. An English translation is reprinted in Howard Lee McBain & Lindsay Rogers, *The New Constitutions of Europe*, Doubleday (New York: Page & Co, 1922), 348-378.

[13] Peter Radan, *Self-Determination, Uti Possidetis and Post-Secession International Borders: The Case of Yugoslavia*, Unpublished Doctoral Dissertation, University of Sydney, 1998, paragraph 5038.

Stjepan Radić, who led the Croatian People's Party, was the most vocal separatist, calling for secession of Croatia from Yugoslavia.[14] This was consistent with his post-World War I standpoint, when he produced the only dissenting voice against the decision of the Central Committee of the National Council to proceed with South Slav unification.[15] In 1922, Radić succeeded in gathering three Croatian parties into one Croatian block, which requested a sovereign status for Croatia, within or outside Yugoslavia, from the Great Powers at a meeting in Genoa.[16] He considered the creation of the Kingdom of 1918 to be illegal as it was achieved without the consent (ratification) of the Croatian Diet.[17] As Radan explains, the fact that the new Constitution made no provision for the Croatian Diet implied to Radić "a deprivation for Croatia of historic rights and meant that Croats were worse off within Yugoslavia than they had been within the Austro-Hungarian Empire."[18] Later Radić compromised and became a Minister of Education in the Yugoslav government, stating, "We do not pose any state legal requests nor do we plan to do so."[19] In 1927, he even entered into a coalition with Pribichevich, formerly the leader of integral Yugoslavism, turned federalist.[20]

---

[14] Importantly, although Radić was a Croat nationalist, he was not fervently anti-Serb. He hoped to incorporate Serbs as obedient citizens of an independent Croatia, but without depriving them of certain limited rights. In early 1903, he wrote that Croats should recognize the Serb name and allow free use of the Serb flag and Cyrillic script while the Serbs should recognize Croatia as their homeland. *See* Bogdan Krizman, *Korespondencija Stjepana Radića 1885-1918* [Correspondence of Stjepan Radić 1885-1918] (Zagreb, 1972), book 1, 406-7.

[15] Radić publicly denounced the Central Committee's decision, stating that the only acceptable option for the Croats was to seek south Slav political cooperation in the form of a confederated republic. He made a futile last minute bid to enlist the support of the Czechs to establish a single central European state comprised of Croat, Slovak and Czech territories of the former Habsburg Empire and to be called Burgenland. *See* Radan, Unpublished Doctoral Dissertation, paragraph 5029.

[16] "Memorandum Hrvatskog bloka medjunarodnoj konferenciji u Djenovi" [Memorandum of Croatian Bloc to the International Conference in Genoa], March 25, 1922, in Petranović and Zečević, eds., *Yugoslavia 1918-1984; Collection of Documents*, 197.

[17] Srdjan Trifkovic, "The First Yugoslavia and Origins of Croatian Separatism" *East European Quarterly* 26 (1992), 345-370: 352-353; George W. Cesarich, "Yugoslavia was Created against the Will of the Croatian People" in Antun F. Bonifacic and Clement S. Mihanovich, eds., *The Croatian Nation in its Struggle for Freedom and Independence* (Chicago: "Croatia" Cultural Publishing Center, 1955), 192-211, at 207, 209.

[18] Radan, Unpublished Doctoral Dissertation, paragraph 5041.

[19] "Izjava S. Radića o prihvatanju monarhije i centralizma" [Statement by S. Radić on accepting monarchy and centralism], April 1925, reprinted in Petranović and Zečević, eds., *Yugoslavia 1918-1984; Collection of Documents*, 207.

[20] Sporadic imprisonment of Radić and other Croat secessionists in the period between 1918 and 1921 is seen by present Croat historians as systematic greater Serbian repression. *See* Bosiljka Janjatović, "Progoni triju političkih grupacija u Hrvatskoj (1918-1921)" [Persecution of three political groupings in Croatia] in *Historijski zbornik* XLV, No. 1 (Zagreb, 1992), 1-374: 89-104.

At the same time, the other major national groups,[21] the Slovenes and Slavic Muslims, were not actively engaged in the political struggle between the Serbs and Croats. Instead they exploited the Serbo-Croat differences to become over-represented in the administration and gain a disproportional amount of political power. The Slovenes, enjoying a distinct language from Serbian/Croatian, achieved *de facto* self-rule in their region while the Slavic Muslims enjoyed special cultural and economic privileges.

The 1921 Constitution established a district (*oblast*) as the basic political, economic, and administrative unit in Yugoslavia (Article 95). By a ministerial decree, the Kingdom was divided into 33 districts as the broadest territorial units.[22] This was the first administrative division of Yugoslavia. All ensuing territorial divisions were also termed "administrative," both in documents and in the names on maps. The 1922 legislation was based on Article 25 of the Constitution, which limited the size of each district to no more than 800,000 citizens. The size limit was imposed to preclude any division on the ethnic principle, while attempting to achieve economic and administrative efficiency. A leading Serbian legal analyst at the time concluded that this appeared to be the most effective size for a self-governing district, and that those who argued for federalism with larger units argued for political and psychological reasons rather than administrative and economic reasons.[23]

Some deviations from this general rule were made, establishing the districts so as to conform to boundaries of the previous provinces, namely in Bosnia and Herzegovina. This was partly done out of concessions made to the leading, pro-Serb Muslim party for voting the unitary constitution.[24] Similarly, the district

---

[21] "The aspirations of other national groups [not Serbs, Croats and Slovenes] were either suppressed or of marginal interest to central state authorities. Into this category fell the Magyars of the Voivodina region and the Albanians in Kosovo. The Macedonians were of some concern in that Macedonian separatism was advocated by the Internal Macedonian Revolutionary Organisation (IMRO), which was funded and supported by Bulgaria who saw the Macedonians as Bulgarians. However, the Macedonian problem was largely an international matter concerned with resisting Bulgarian irredentism." Radan, Unpublished Doctoral Dissertation, paragraph, 5035.

[22] "Uredba o podeli zemlje na oblasti" [Decree on dividing state into districts], April 26, 1922, Official Gazette of the Kingdom of Serbs, Croats and Slovenes, no 92, April 28, 1922, reprinted in Petranović and Zečević, eds., *Yugoslavia 1918-1984; Collection of Documents*, 184-185.

[23] Marković, *The Yugoslav state and the Croatian question*, 211.

[24] Article 135 of the 1921 constitution required the division to be completely within the framework of Bosnia-Herzegovina's historical boundaries as originally established during the Ottoman occupation of that region. *See* Branko Z. Milojevic, "The Kingdom of Serbs, Croats, and Slovenes: Administrative

boundaries on the territory of the pre-war Serbia followed largely those of prior administrative units. Perhaps this is the reason why the commercial and industrial handbook of the 1928 Yugoslavia, prepared by the United States government, lists its geographic regions as: "Slovenia, Croatia-Slavonia, Dalmatia, Bosnia-Herzegovina, Montenegro, Voivodina, Macedonia and Serbia."[25]

While not enjoying any special privileges set by law, the Serbs as the largest ethnic group dominated the new state by the very factor of their size. According to the 1921 census,[26] the percentage of Serbs in the total population was 98.4 percent in Serbia (within the borders before the Balkan wars), 43.9 percent in Bosnia-Herzegovina, 30 percent in Banat, Bachka and Baranya (parts of Voivodina), 24.1 percent in Croatia-Slavonia and 17 percent in Dalmatia. Serbs also dominated the top administrative and diplomatic positions, particularly in the beginning, partly because the other nations were under foreign rule prior to 1918.[27] This also explains the fact that "the Slovenes and Croats were well represented in the lower and middle ranks of the bureaucracy."[28] Nevertheless, the unitary arrangement caused insecurity within the other groups who considered that a federated system would allow for a better national balance. To Serbs a unitary system was preferred since it was democratic and any division on ethnic principle would not be possible in practice. As Pashich argued in Corfu and later in the Yugoslav National Assembly in 1923,

> We can go into a federation, but we can also, and this is more natural, go into an undivided state. For a federation, we would first of all need to divide up: the Croats to themselves, the Slovenes to themselves, and the Serbs to themselves. Only then could we draw boundaries and create a federation . . .

Divisions in Relation to Natural Regions," *Geographical Review* 15 (1925), 82, cited in Peter Radan, *The Break-up of Yugoslavia and International Law*, Routledge Studies in International Law (London, New York: Routledge, 2002), 138.

[25]   Kenneth S. Patton, *Kingdom of Serbs, Croats and Slovenes (Yugoslavia): A Commercial and Industrial Handbook* (Washington, DC: U. S. Government Printing Office, 1928), 1.

[26]   Reprinted in Branislav Gligorijević, "Unutrašnje (administrativne) granice Jugoslavije izmedju dva svetska rata 1918-1941" [Internal (administrative) boundaries of Yugoslavia between two world wars 1918-1941] *The History of 20th Century* X, no 1-2 (1992): 22.

[27]   As a result of the public administration reform instigated by King Alexander (*inter alia*, in 1844, he introduced a Civil Code, adapted from Austrian law) and a great number of top civil servants educated in France in the late nineteenth century for the purpose of joining the administration, the Serb civil service became highly professional. *See* Hondius, *The Yugoslav Community of Nations*, 55.

[28]   Dragnich, *Serbia, Nikola Pasic and Yugoslavia*, 160.

but when we began to draw boundaries on the map, we saw that it was impossible. [29]

Until 1929, Yugoslavia was a parliamentary democracy, dominated by the Radical party of Nikola Pashich. However, on June 20, 1928, after an ethnically-motivated dispute, a deputy from Montenegro, Punisha Rachich, shot and killed two Croat deputies in the assembly. Stjepan Radić was also wounded and later died on August 8, 1928. This event prompted King Alexander Karageorgevich to dissolve the National Assembly and nullify the Constitution on January 6, 1929, with a stated goal of preserving the unity of the state and its peoples.[30] This was soon followed by a period termed by Dragnich as "guided democracy,"[31] based on the Constitution promulgated by the King on September 3, 1931, in which the legislative authority was shared between the King and the Parliament. This was a step back in terms of democracy, with the parliamentary monarchy replaced by a constitutional monarchy.

3.2. Banovinas (1929-1939)

In October 1929, the anational character of the internal administrative system was reinforced. Nine *banovinas* (provinces) were established, with Belgrade becoming a separate administrative area under the direct rule and supervision of the Minister of Internal Affairs of the Kingdom.[32] These nine provinces were the following: banovina of Drava, with headquarters in Ljubljana; banovina of Sava, with headquarters in Zagreb; banovina of Vrbas, with headquarters in Banja Luka; banovina Primorska, with headquarters in Split; banovina of Drina, with headquarters in Sarajevo; banovina of Zeta, with headquarters in Cetinje; banovina of Dunav (Danube), with headquarters in Novi Sad; banovina of Morava, with headquarters in Nish; and banovina of Vardar, with headquarters in Skoplje. These provinces were not primarily defined by ethnic or historical considerations,

---

29   *Spomenica Nikole P. Pasica* [In memory of Nikola P. Pashich] (Belgrade, 1926), 110.

30   "Proklamacija Kralja Aleksandra" [Proclamation of King Alexander], January 6, 1929, in Petranović and Zečević, eds., *Yugoslavia 1918-1984; Collection of Documents*, 262. An English translation is found in Trifunovska, *Yugoslavia Through Documents From Its Creation to its Dissolution*, 190-191.

31   Alex N. Dragnich, *The First Yugoslavia, Search For a Viable Political System* (Hoover Institution Press, Stanford, 1983), 86.

32   "Zakon o nazivu i podeli Kraljevine na upravna područja" [Law on name and division of Kingdom into administrative areas], Article 2, October 3, 1929, in Petranović and Zečević, eds., *Yugoslavia 1918-1984; Collection of Documents*, 265.

deriving their shape and names from the geographic surroundings (rivers or sea) based on the French model.

King Alexander hoped that regional division would preserve regional traditions while building national unity. To assert this view, the same law changed the name of the state, which officially became the Kingdom of Yugoslavia on October 3, 1929.[33] The subsequent 1931 Constitution,[34] promulgated by King Alexander, who thereby ended the personal rule, preserved the system of banovinas (Article 83) and detailed boundary delimitation among these provinces. The *banovine* were termed "self-governing units" (Article 84), as they were granted certain legal competences (Article 90) and headed by the governor (*ban*). However, the King appointed the governor (Article 85) and the central government supervised the banovina legislation (Article 92).

In addition to the internal reorganization of the state, King Alexander's public administration reform included fighting against corruption and other reformist, European-minded initiatives. The accompanying political reform was highlighted by the prohibition of nationalist parties, soon to be followed by the banning of all political parties. This was opposed by most Serbs, who perceived the king's policies to be abrogating their political and civil liberties, and by the Croats, who interpreted the suppression of nationalism as a mask for Serb hegemonism.[35] The most nationalist elements reacted violently. In October 1934, a Bulgarian assassin sponsored by Mussolini and Hungarian authorities and working for the Croatian and Macedonian/Bulgarian separatist organizations (the *Ustasha* and *IMRO*, respectively)[36] murdered King Alexander during his state visit to France.[37]

---

[33]   Ibid., Article 1.

[34]   Constitution of the Kingdom of Yugoslavia, September 3, 1931, *Official Gazette of Yugoslavia* no 207/1931; relevant excerpts reproduced in Petranović and Zečević, eds., *Yugoslav federalism, ideas and reality*, Vol. 1, 1914-1943, 306-311.

[35]   *See* Radan, *The Break-up of Yugoslavia and International Law*, 141.

[36]   "Italy and, to a lesser extent, Hungary were complicit in the assassination of Aleksandar by their support and financing of the *Ustasha* movement. Yugoslavia brought charges against Hungary before the League of Nations in November 1934. France, at that time seeking rapprochement with Italy, was able to prevent Yugoslavia bringing charges against Italy. The League's investigation, headed by Anthony Eden, found that some Hungarian officials may have had some connection with the activities of the assassins." Radan, Unpublished Doctoral Dissertation, paragraph 5053, footnote 1313.

[37]   The French foreign minister, Louis Barthou, was also murdered at the time.

The Regency Council, headed by Alexander's first cousin Prince Paul[38] took over the reign. Prince Paul focused on resolving the Serb-Croat conflict, fearing that further aggravation of this problem could be exploited by Nazi Germany, which pressured Yugoslavia to join its ranks following the Austrian Auschluss in 1938. The end result was the Agreement of August 23, 1939, negotiated between Prince Paul's government, led by Dragisha Tsvetkovich (Cvetković), and the leader of the Croatian Peasant Party, Vladko Maček.[39]

This agreement was also a result of British support for the Croatians, which culminated with the resignation of the Serbian Prime Minister, Milan Stoyadinovich, in February 1939 and his confinement to Mauritius by the British authorities. Stoyadinovich's efforts to isolate the Croat separatists were thus nullified. Three years earlier, in 1935, Stoyadinovich had formed a coalition of the former (Serbian) Radical Party with the leading Slovene party (Slovene People's Party) and the leading Bosnian Muslim party (Yugoslav Muslim Organization), called the Yugoslav Radical Union,[40] which strove to enhance the rule of the local rather than regional authorities. He had also negotiated an agreement of cooperation with Italy, signed in Belgrade in March 1937 and strengthened by a statement of commitment of the Italian government to dismantle the Ustasha (Croat Fascist) organization in Italy.[41]

3.3. Banovina Hrvatska (1939-1941)

The Tsvetkovich-Maček Agreement, redrafted into a "Decree on Banovina Hrvatska (Croatian Province)" on August 26, 1939,[42] aimed to revive the Croatian assembly (Article 4). The king would share the legislative competence with this assembly in matters relating to "agriculture, commerce, industry, forests and mines, public works, social welfare, health, education, physical culture, justice

---

[38] Peter, Alexander's eldest son was a minor.

[39] The text of the "Cvetković-Maček Agreement" (1939) is reproduced in Petranović and Zečević, eds., *Yugoslav federalism, ideas and reality,* Vol. 1, 1914-1943, 508-510.

[40] The text of the Decision on establishing the Yugoslav Radical Union [Odluka o stvaranju JRZ], September 5, 1935, is produced in Petranović and Zečević, eds., *Yugoslav federalism, ideas and reality,* Vol. 1, 1914-1943, 347-348.

[41] Protich, *Rise and Fall of the Serbian Idea,* 321-325. *See also* Dr Milan Stoyadinovitch, *La Yougoslavie entre les deux guerres; ni le pacte, ni la guerre* (Paris: Nouvelles Editions Latines, 1979).

[42] "Uredba o Banovini Hrvatskoj" [Decree on Banovina Hrvatska], Official Gazette of the Kingdom of Yugoslavia, August 26, 1939, in Petranović and Zečević, eds., *Yugoslav federalism, ideas and reality,* Vol. 1, 1914-1943, 514-516.

and internal administration" (Article 2). Executive authority remained in the hands of a governor, who was appointed by the Crown and responsible to the Crown and a new Croatian assembly (Articles 4 and 8). All other matters remained in the realm of the central government (Article 2). Importantly, the Tsvetkovich-Maček Agreement reiterated the equality of Serbs, Croats, and Slovenes within the Croatian province, as well as the equality of major religious denominations (Article 3).

The territory of the new Croatian province became defined by Article 1, which listed the Savska and Primorska Banovina as well as the districts of Dubrovnik, Shid, Ilok, Brchko, Gradachats, Derventa, Travnik, and Foynitsa. However, according to the Tsvetkovich-Maček Agreement, the precise boundaries and a definitive regulation of legislative competencies of the Croatian province were to be determined in the future reorganization of the state (Article 4).

The temporary character of the Agreement was stressed by the fact that it was not ratified in the National Assembly but promulgated by royal decree. Moreover, the legal basis used for the decree was questionable. Although Article 116 of the 1931 Constitution allowed the king to rule by decree in certain emergency situations,[43] it did not authorize constitutional reform, which was the *de facto* effect of the Agreement.[44]

Banovina Hrvatska was created in a provisional agreement out of three provinces, with the six remaining provinces keeping the purely geographic, non-ethnic names and character, which immediately stirred nationalism on behalf of other Yugoslav ethnic groups who demanded their "own" provinces. The main grievance was that, although the Province of Croatia encompassed most of the Croatian population (both Dalmatia and parts of Bosnia were included in one, Croat-dominated system of governance for the first time in history), it also included a large part of the Serbian population and territory. Even though one could

---

[43] "[I]n case of war, mobilization, upheaval and revolt, which would call in question the legal order and the security of the state, or when public interest is generally endangered to such an extent" (Excerpt of Article 116, *Constitution of Yugoslavia*, September 3, 1931)

[44] For more *see* Mirjana Stefanovski, "Pitanje pravne valjanosti Uredbe o Banovini Hrvatskoj" [Question of legal validity of the Decree on Banovina Hrvatska] in Dragaš Denković and Jovica Trkulja (eds), *Pravna i politička misao Mihaila Ilića* [Legal and political thought of Mihailo Ilich] (Belgrade: Pravni fakultet Univerziteta u Beogradu, 1995), 306-317.

interpret this move as emphasizing the division for purely administrative reasons, the name indicated otherwise.

The provisory nature of the agreement, confirmed by a brief decree promulgated the following day stipulating that another royal decree could "reunify [the provinces] and . . . modify their territorial scope,"[45] enabled its acceptance by the non-Croat Yugoslav nations. However, as it became immediately clear that it would be difficult to delineate boundaries where populations were intermixed or to "extract" non-Croat territory out of the newly created province, the 847,000 Serbs residing in "Banovina Hrvatska" also reacted by means of a petition. They demanded that the territories where they were the dominant ethnic group be excluded from the new province.[46] The Serb Cultural Club, established in Belgrade in 1937 upon an initiative of non-party intellectuals led by Slobodan Yovanovich, created a project in 1940 ("Acts Concerning the Organization of Serbian Lands") that called for a unification of the remaining provinces—Vrbaska, Drinska, Dunavska, Moravska, Zetska, and Vardarska into a region called "Serbian lands" with a capital in Skoplje, present-day Macedonia, and seats in Sarajevo, Tsetinye, Novi Sad, and Nish, where autonomous authorities would be established.[47] The Serbs supported the potential creation of a Slovene banovina out of Savska banovina, but it was not possible for Slavic Muslims to create a separate province, nor was that considered as legitimate as the demands of the Serbs or the Croats at the time when the Slavic Muslims were a religious rather than an ethnic affiliation. The Croats, not wishing to relinquish any of the newly-gained territory, championed double standards in the future reorganization of the state:

> What the Croat leaders sought was the ascertainment of Croatian territory by application of nationalist and historical criteria, but the division of the rest of Yugoslavia by the application of geographic criteria.[48]

---

[45]   Decree of the Regency Council of Yugoslavia extending the Decree of August 26, 1939, regarding the Banovina of Croatia to other Banovinas, Belgrade, August 27, 1939, reproduced in British and Foreign State Papers 143, 734 and in Trifunovska, *Yugoslavia through Documents From Its Creation to its Dissolution*, 201.

[46]   Momčilo Zečević, "Ideoloske osnove jugoslovenskih unutrasnjih razgranicenja" [The ideological basis for the internal boundary delimitation], *The History of 20ᵗʰCentury* X, no 1-2 (1992): 177.

[47]   Nacrt uredbe o organizaciji srpske zemlje [Draft Decree on the Organization of Serbian Land], 1940, in Petranović and Zečević, eds., *Yugoslav federalism, ideas and reality*, Vol. 1, 1914-1943, 569-70. *See also* Momčilo Zečević, "The ideological basis for the internal boundary delimitation," 177.

[48]   Radan, *The Break-up of Yugoslavia and International Law*, 142.

Although the more extreme Croat elements, the Ustasha, preferred immediate independence,[49] Maček's party opted for compromise, in great part because of outside considerations.[50] According to Ivo Banac, Croatian politics of this period were "illiberal and indifferent to issues of liberal democracy and human rights; it did not strive to democratization of the Yugoslav state but its federalization, or destruction."[51]

The experience of Banovina Hrvatska demonstrated how a territorial solution to one national question in Yugoslavia could be imposed only to the detriment of another group's national question. Instead of reducing interethnic tensions, the Agreement reinforced a deep, seething crisis in Yugoslavia's governance. Its resolution was precluded by the Second World War, which replaced politics by violence—a civil war between the Serbs and the Croats.

3.4. Yugoslavia during the Second World War and the Formation of the Federalist People's Republic of Yugoslavia (1941-1945)

A pro-Allied military coup was organized on March 27, 1941 in Belgrade, toppling the government that had previously signed an accord with the Axis powers, and installing King Alexander's son Peter, still a minor, on the throne.[52] This event was immediately followed by a German-led Axis invasion of Yugoslavia, launched on April 6, 1941. The occupying Axis powers divided Yugoslavia during the war.

---

[49] It appears that most Croats shared the sentiments of the Ustasha, which is reflected in their warm reception of the invading German troops two years later (April 1941). *See* Vladko Macek, *In the Struggle for Freedom* (University Park: State University Press, 1957), 230.

[50] In secret negotiations with Italy, Maček arrived at a preliminary agreement in March 1939. According to this agreement, Italy would finance Croat insurrection against Yugoslavia with a goal of establishing "an independent Croat state in union with Italy." Nevertheless, Maček, fearing the impact of the outbreak of the Second World War, chose to compromise in his negotiations with Cvetkovich.

Count Ciano, Mussolini's aid who negotiated with Maček's emissaries, records in his diary the details of the negotiation of the secret Croat-Italian agreement in March 1939. Relevant excerpts are reproduced in Petranović and Zečević, eds., *Yugoslavia 1918-1984; Collection of Documents*, 355-357.

[51] Ivo Banac, "Glavni pravci hrvatske povijesti u dvadesetom stoljecu" ["Main trends of the Croatian history in the twentieth century"] in in *Liberalna misao u Hrvatskoj* [Liberal Idea in Croatia], eds. Andrea Feldman, Vladimir Stipetić and Franjo Zenko (Zagreb: Friedrich Naumann Stiftung, 2000), LIX [Translation mine].

[52] For a discussion of factors that led to the coup *see* Jacob B. Hoptner, *Yugoslavia in Crisis, 1934-1941* (New York: Columbia University Press, 1962), 255-256, and Macek, *In the Struggle for Freedom*, 220.

The political rift among the Yugoslav peoples transformed itself into a military battle on opposing sides. Croats overwhelmingly sided with the Nazis, while the Serbs and many Slovenes and Bosnian Muslims fought on the side of the Allies. The resulting civil war between the Croats and the Serbs was particularly vicious, with the Croatian Ustasha regime committing genocide against the Serbian population, an act that would have permanent repercussions on Serb-Croat relations.[53]

At the same time, a civil war was also conducted among the two Serb-dominant resistance movements based on ideology.[54] The first resistance movement to emerge, known as the Chetniks,[55] was led by General Dragolyub-Drazha Mihailovich. At first it was composed mainly of members of the former Yugoslav army, which is why it was officially called "the Yugoslav army in the homeland." Initially, the aim was to restore the pre-war monarchy and unitary state structure,[56]

---

[53]   The Nuremberg Tribunal described the acts of Ustasha Croats as constituting genocide [Thomas D. Musgrave, *Self-Determination and National Minorities* (Oxford: Clarendon Press, 1997), 230]. For more *see* Menachem Shelah, "Genocide in Satellite Croatia During the Second World War" in Michael Berenbaum, ed., *A Mosaic of Victims, Non-Jews Persecuted and Murdered by the Nazis* (New York: New York University Press, 1990), 74-79; Jozo Tomasevich, *War and Revolution in Yugoslavia, 1941-1945; Occupation and Collaboration* (Stanford: Stanford University Press, 1975), particularly 380-415. Note: The Croatian policy of genocide was also directed against smaller Jewish and Roma communities in the region, as well as against a small number of Croat dissidents.

[54]   Milan St. Protich insists that this was not a war of Serbs against Serbs but Serbs against Communists, regardless of the ethnicity of the Communists. Protich, *Rise and Fall of the Serbian Idea*, 339.

[55]   At the time this movement was in fact called "Drazhinovtsi," stemming from their leader's first name, while several autonomous pro-Monarchy military groups took the name of Chetniks. These were not under direct rule of Drazha Mihailovich but leaders called "dukes." Some of these units collaborated with the Italians, which in time compromised their resistance. One "duke" was liquidated by Drazha's men because of his cooperation with the Germans, and so were several local leaders who murdered civilians and robbed the peasants. *See* Dušan T. Bataković, ed., *Histoire du Peuple Serbe* (Lausanne: L'Age d'Homme, 2005), 320-323 and Hondius, *The Yugoslav Community of Nations*, 188-189.

At the same time, it appears that there was an actual agreement of cooperation between the Partisans and the Germans, signed in March 1943, aimed both against Drazha's troops and against the Allies, in case they landed in the Balkans, which was expected. Protich believes that this may be part of the answer as to why the British switched sides and came to support the Partisans; they wished to remove the Partisans from the German or the Soviet sphere. *See* John R. Lampe, *Yugoslavia as History. Twice There Was a Country* (Cambridge, New York: Cambridge University Press, 1996), 216; Walter R. Roberts, *Tito, Mihailović, and the Allies, 1941-1945* (New Brunswick, NJ: Rutgers University Press, 1973; reprint. Durham, NC: Duke University Press, 1987), 106-112; Jean-Christophe Buisson, *Héros trahi par les alliés; le général Mihailović 1893-1946* (Paris: Perrin, 1999).

[56]   Jozo Tomasevich, *War and Revolution in Yugoslavia, 1941-1945: The Chetniks*, 166-178; Milan Vesovic and Kosta Nikolic, *Ujedinjene srpske zemlje, Ravnogorski nacionalni program* [United Serb lands; National program of Ravna Gora] (Belgrade: Vreme Knjige, 1996), 33-55.

but it changed towards the end of the war (Ba Congress of January 1944) to accepting a federated structure, albeit with a dominant Serb unit.[57] The Chetniks were
predominantly Serb but also included other Yugoslavs, such as Slovenes.[58]

The Communist Party of Yugoslavia (CPY)[59] was headed by Josip Broz Tito, who
was asked by Stalin to instigate the second resistance movement in Yugoslavia—
the Partisans—two weeks after the Nazis had attacked the USSR. Although Tito
personally was of Croat and partly Slovene origin,[60] the Partisan movement
attracted mostly Serbs, initially coming from those areas of the country where the
Croat Fascists were committing genocide.[61] Other ethnic groups in time were also
drawn to the movement as a result of the Partisan policy of "brotherhood and
unity," a declared equitable treatment of all national groups. The Partisans introduced the Leninist concept of national self-determination into their political program,[62] relying on patriotic and nationalist sentiments to enhance their following.
Always practical, the Communist Party of Yugoslavia now favored a reunited

---

[57] The Ba resolutions are reprinted in Petranović and Zečević, eds., *Yugoslav federalism, ideas and reality,* Vol.
1, 1914-1943, 817-821.

[58] *See* Aleksandar Bajt, *Bermanov dosje* [Berman's File] (Ljubljana: Mladinska knjiga, 1999).

[59] The CPY cooperated with *IMRO* (Internal Macedonian Revolutionary Organization) during the early
1920s and with the Croat *Ustasha* and Albanian separatists in Kosovo in the early 1930s. Following an
incident on August 2, 1921 when a young communist assassinated Milorad Drashkovich, the Yugoslav
Minister of the Interior, the CPY was declared illegal under the Yugoslav State Security Act of 1921. For
more *see* Singleton, *A Short History of the Yugoslav Peoples,* 194-195; Ivan Avakumovic, *History of the
Communist Party of Yugoslavia* I (Aberdeen: University of Aberdeen Press, 1964), 107-108; Aleksa Djilas,
The Contested Country; Yugoslav Unity and Communist Revolution, 1919-1953 (Cambridge: Harvard
University Press, 1991), 83-89; Paul Shoup, *Communism and the Yugoslav National Question* (New York:
Columbia University Press, 1968), 32-39.

[60] According to his official biography, Tito was a locksmith by profession and a Communist activist across
Europe.

[61] Tito confirmed the predominance of Serbs in the Partisan movement during the first year of the resistance in an article he authored in December 1942, and recognized the need of the Partisans to attract
support from other national groups: Josip Broz Tito, "The National Question in Yugoslavia in the Light of
the National Liberation War" in Fabijan Trgo, ed., *The National Liberation War and Revolution in
Yugoslavia (1941-1945); Selected Documents* (Belgrade: Military History Institute of the Yugoslav People's
Army, 1982), 394-402, at 401-402. In Bosnia-Herzegovina, the major theater of the Partisan struggle,
Serbs remained the majority within the ranks of the Partisans until the end of the war: Attila Hoare, "The
People's Liberation Movement in Bosnia and Hercegovina, 1941-45: What did it mean to fight for a Multi-
National State?" *Nationalism & Ethnic Politics* 2 (1996), 415-445: 418. According to British intelligence,
Serbs formed three quarters of the Partisan army until after the middle of 1943: James Gow, "After the
Flood: Literature on the Context, Causes and Course of the Yugoslav War—Reflections and Refractions"
Slavonic & East European Review 75 (1997), 446-484: 450.

[62] Walker Connor, *The National Question in Marxist-Leninist Theory and Strategy* (Princeton: Princeton
University Press, 1984), 155-156.

but federated Yugoslavia, having supported in the past both a centralist state with a single, Yugoslav nationality[63] and the dismemberment of Yugoslavia.[64]

The Partisan appeal to nationalism characterizes the 1942 speech by Tito in which he said:

> Here in Bosnia, you men of Serbia and Montenegro, are fighting all enemies, and will continue to do so for this is at the same time a struggle for the freedom of the Serbian and Montenegrin peoples. And tomorrow, when the time comes—and I assure you, comrades, that time is not far off—you will march again into Serbia, Montenegro . . . to liberate your people.[65]

Many Serbs joined the Partisans without complete understanding of their political and ideological goals, even naively believing that after the war there would be no currency, tax or any other levies. They had no knowledge of the real situation in the Soviet Union, which for them still symbolized "Mother Russia," protector of Christian Orthodox Slavs.[66] Unlike the Chetniks, who had a defensive strategy, hoping to avoid draconian German retributions on the civilian population in Serbia,[67] the Partisans had an offensive strategy, with less care for the enormous collateral loss of life. As the Partisans were presented by Allied missions as a more significant force, the Allies, who had originally supported the Chetniks, switched their allegiance in 1943.[68]

---

63 Rezolucija o nacionalnom pitanju [Resolution on the National Question], 1924, reprinted in Petranović and Zečević, eds., *Yugoslavia 1918-1984; Collection of Documents*, 237-242.

64 Two important decisions of the Fifth Congress of the Commintern in 1924 were the following:
". . . . 2) Serbs, Croats, and Slovenes are three different peoples. The theory of a unique three-named people of Serbs, Croats and Slovenes is just a mask for the greater Serb imperialism. . . .
7) . . . The general declaration regarding the right to self-determination, stressed by the CPY, must be expressed in the form of separating Croatia and Slovenia and Macedonia from Yugoslavia and creating independent republics" [Translation mine]. Cited in Bataković, ed., *Histoire du Peuple Serbe*, 291.

65 Connor, *National Question in Marxist-Leninist Theory and Strategy*, 155.

66 Bataković, ed., *Histoire du peuple serbe*, 322-3.

67 One hundred hostages were executed for one dead German officer and 50 hostages for one soldier, resulting in massacres, including an incident in the town of Kraguyevats where children were gathered from schools and executed together with the adults. *See* Singleton, *A Short History of the Yugoslav Peoples*, 194-195.

68 On Allied policies toward the Yugoslav resistance movements *see* Mark C. Wheeler, *Britain and the War for Yugoslavia, 1940-1943*, East European Monographs (Boulder, 1980); M. Deroc, *British Special Operations Explored, Yugoslavia in Turmoil 1941-1943 and the British Response*, East European Monographs (Boulder: 1988); Voyislav G. Pavlovich, *Од монархије до републике; САД и Југославија (1941-1945)* [From Monarchy to a Republic; USA and Yugoslavia (1941-1945)] (Belgrade: Clio/Glas srpski, 1998).

The third mass movement in Yugoslavia, the Croat Ustasha, sided with the German and Italian Nazis. This extremist national Croat movement became the foundation for Nazi rule in the so-called Independent State of Croatia.[69] The bloody four-year war period (1941–1945) represented the first time that the Croats had had their own state since the Middle Ages. However this state was independent in name only, having been established by the Italians and Germans as a puppet regime. The territory of Nazi Croatia roughly corresponded to the territories of the present-day Croatia and Bosnia-Herzegovina, with the addition of the region of Srem in Voivodina (Serbia).

Ante Pavelić and Gustav Perčec had established the Ustasha movement in 1929, with the goal of achieving Croatian independence through terrorism and armed struggle. Prior to the Second World War, the Ustasha enjoyed the backing of some sections of the Croat population, with the vast majority of Croats supporting the Croatian Peasant Party. In Croatia, the roots of the Ustasha movement were found in the writing of Ante Starčević, as elaborated above.[70] Starčević's son-in-law, a successful lawyer, Josip Frank, who defined the Croat identity strictly in terms of Serbophobia, carried on Starčević's ideology. Frank opposed any cooperation between the Croats and the Serbs.

> Skillful in using nationalist slogans and radicalizing the people, he became in the first decade of the [twentieth] century a leading anti-Serbian demagogue and the instigator of the persecution of Serbs in Croatia.[71]

His followers were called Frankovci, and they were the most fervent participants of the Ustasha movement.

> Their nationalist ideology was rudimentary. Many of these peasants hated Serbs in an irrational, intuitive way that had much of its basis in folk memory. It was a kind of proto-fascist sentiment and would prove a fertile ground for fascist ideology.[72]

---

[69] It was actually Italy that appointed the Ustasha leader, Ante Pavelić, to head the Croat government, in return for guarantees that Dalmatia would be relinquished to Italy, but the *de facto* ruler of Croatia was a German emissary of the Reich, von Horstenau. An Italian Duke from the Savoy dynasty was offered the Croatian crown but he refused the offer in disdain.

[70] Djilas, *The Contested Country*, 117.

[71] Ibid., 108.

[72] Ibid., 110.

At the same time, the followers of the Ustasha movement believed that Slavic Muslims were Croats, a view that was also shared by many moderates such as Vlatko Maček.[73] This Ustasha stance was reflected in Ante Pavelić's statement of July 1938:

> It is not permissible to speak of Bosnia and Herzegovina as if they were countries in their own right or to distinguish the Muslims from the Croatian nation, because Bosnia is the heart of the Croatian state, and the Muslim tribes, a part of the Croatian nation.[74]

In the Nazi Croatia, capital punishment was rendered mandatory for all those who in any way offended "the honor and vital interests of the Croatian people" or who even "by attempt" threatened the Croatian state. The deliberate imprecision of the crucial terms of this law was intended to provide the Ustasha with a framework that would allow the murder of political opponents and members of minority groups.[75] The Ustasha aimed to destroy all Serbian national marks, pursuing a strategy similar to that which the Nazi Germans had developed against the Jews.[76] The brutal persecution of Serbs took the form of large-scale massacres, both in concentration camps and by a direct slaughter of villages. The fate of the Serbs in Croatia was defined by a policy declared by Mile Budak, Minister of Education in the Nazi Croatia, on July 22, 1941: "One third of the Serbs we shall kill, one third of the Serbs we shall displace, and one third we shall convert to Catholicism and thus assimilate into Croats."[77] Milovan Žanić, Minister of the Legislative Council

---

[73] Vlatko Maček, who negotiated the creation of Banovina Hrvatska in 1936, stated in 1936: "The Croatian Peasant Party, as the political organization of the entire Croatian nation, considers the Bosnian Muslims the purest part of the Croatian nation, by origin, by history, and by dialect." Cited in David Atlagić, *Nacija, nacionalno pitanje i odnosi medju narodima Jugoslavije* [Nation, national question and relations among Yugoslav nations] (Belgrade: Radnički univerzitet "Djuro Salaj," 1964), 8.

[74] Atlagić, *Nation, national question and relations among Yugoslav nations*, 8.

[75] Djilas, *The Contested Country*, 116-117.

[76] "Their fanatical persecution of Serbian Orthodox priests was inspired by the fact that the Serbian Orthodox religion was part of the Serbian national identity, and the Serbian Orthodox church a defender of Serbian national interests. . . . Villages whose names contained words or expressions that were associated with the Serbian nationality or religion, or were considered to be more typical of the Serbian vocabulary than of the Croatian, were given new names. Use of the Cyrillic alphabet was banned. In addition, Serbs' movement was limited, they were no longer allowed to live in certain residential areas, and they had to wear a blue band with the letter *P* (for *Pravoslavac*, Orthodox) on their right arm." Djilas, *The Contested Country*, 118.

[77] *Speech of July 22, 1941*. Cited in Vladimir Dedijer, *The Yugoslav Auschwitz and the Vatican* (Prometheus, 1988), 141.

and another close collaborator to Pavelić, was the first to use the term "cleansing" in the Balkans, proclaiming on May 2, 1941:

> This country can only be a Croatian country, and there is no method that we would hesitate to use in order to make it truly Croatian and *cleanse* it of Serbs, who have for centuries endangered us and who will endanger us again if they are given the opportunity.[78]

One of the most disconcerting characteristics of the Ustasha regime was the explicit and implicit support of some sections of the Catholic Church for the conversions and even murders of Serbs, Jews, and Roma.[79] Even the German Nazis were appalled by the extent of the Croat Ustasha crimes, and intrigued by their fascination with Catholicism, which a German newspaper called "an extraordinary ecclesiastical struggle."[80] The reason why Catholicism played a crucial role in Croat nationalism was that their nationalism developed in opposition to Serbs, and that religion embodied the main difference between the Croats and the Serbs, who possessed similar ethnic characteristics and spoke the same (at least very similar) language.

While the number of Serbs killed in order to "cleanse" the Croatian state is violently debated among Croat and other historians (estimates range from 10,000 to

---

[78] *Novi List*, June 3, 1941, cited in Djilas, *The Contested Country*, 120. [italics mine] According to Richard West, Viktor Gutic, Prefect of Western Bosnia, Franciscan preacher, was also "one of the first on record to use the term 'cleansing' (in Serbo-Croat 'čišćenje,' pronounced cheesh-chen-ye) to mean the elimination of Serbs or Orthodox Christians from the [Independent State of Croatia]," a term that "later became the semi-official euphemism, occurring constantly in the documents of the administration." Richard West, *Tito and the Rise and Fall of Yugoslavia* (London: Sinclair-Stevenson, 1994), 93.

[79] *See* Jonathan, Steinberg, "The Roman Catholic Church and Genocide in Croatia, 1941-1945," *Christianity and Judaism*, ed. Diana Wood (London: Blackwell Publishers, 1992), 463-480; Stella Alexander, "Croatia: The Catholic Church and Clergy, 1919-1945," *Catholics, the State, and the European Radical Right, 1919-1945*, ed. Richard J. Wolff and Jörg K. Hoensch (New York: Columbia University Press, 1987), 31-66; Menachem Shelah, "The Catholic Church in Croatia, the Vatican and the Murder of the Croatian Jews," *Holocaust and Genocide Studies* 4, No. 3 (1989), 323-339; Mark Biondich, "Religion and Nation in Wartime Croatia: Reflections on the Ustasha Policy of Forced Religious Conversions, 1941-192, *Slavonic and East European Review* 83, No. 1 (January 2005), 71-116; Marco Aurelio Rivelli, *L'Arcivescovo del genocidio* [Archbishop of Genocide] (Milano: Kaos Edizioni, 1999); West, *Tito and the Rise and Fall of Yugoslavia*; Paris, *Genocide in Satellite Croatia*, 63; John Corwell, *Hitler's Pope; The Secret History of Pius XII* (New York: Penguin Group, 1999), 256-260

[80] *Die Zeitung*, Berlin, April 2, 1944, cited in Paris, *Genocide in Satellite Croatia*, 69.

750,000 victims of the Ustasha death camps alone[81]), it is indisputable that the Croatian puppet state, with the tacit or open knowledge of its citizens of Croat nationality, attempted to wipe out the Serbs.[82] The Croatian genocide against the Serbs, symbolized by the largest and most horrific Jasenovac (Yasenovats) concentration camp, has deeply resided in the minds of Serbs since the Second World War, strongly reinforcing their sense of vulnerability and the fear of loss of national identity developed during the foreign rule of the Austro-Hungarians and the Ottomans.

The issue of Croatian genocide was not properly examined in the aftermath of the Second World War, allegedly in order to avoid deep political divisions between the nations who were to live in brotherhood and unity in Tito's new Yugoslavia.[83] For the same reason, the genocide against the Serbs had never received sufficient internal or international attention. At the same time, the Communist historiography tended to equate the systematic, extensive Croat crimes against the Serbs with sporadic, though also indiscriminatory and criminal, retributions of the Chetniks over Bosnian Muslims (region of Focha in 1942-1943).[84] Croat historiography[85] has also tended to equate the Ustasha and Chetnik crimes with the Communist

---

[81] "The greatest genocide during the Second World War, in proportion to a nation's population, took place, not in Nazi Germany but in the Nazi-created puppet state of Croatia. There in the years 1941-1945, some 750,000 Serbs, 60,000 Jews and 26,000 Gypsies—men, women and children—perished in a gigantic holocaust." Paris, *Genocide in Satellite Croatia*, 9. The *Encyclopedia of the Holocaust* states that 600,000 people were killed in the largest concentration camp, Jasenovac. Robert Rozett and Shmuel Spector, eds., *The Encyclopedia of the Holocaust* 2 (Yad Vashem and The Jerusalem Publishing House and Facts On File, 2000), 739: entry: "Jasenovac." The number of casualties has been a matter of fierce debates among historians and other experts. Later estimations of casualties are much smaller than the original ones. Kočović's demographic analysis identifies the total number of casualties among Serbs (including Montenegrins) during World War II in all areas of Yugoslavia to be 537,000. The highest casualties were among Serbs in Croatia where every sixth Serb was killed and among Serbs in Bosnia where every seventh Serb was killed. Bogoljub Kočović, *Žrtve Drugog svetskog rata u Jugoslaviji* [Victims of the Second World War in Yugoslavia] (Sarajevo: Svjetlost, 1990), 86, 97.

[82] Nicholas J. Miller, *Between Nation and State* (Pittsburgh: University of Pittsburgh Press, 1997), 171.

[83] The Communists covered up much of the Croat Nazi crime. An example is a memorial of a mass crime in the town of Blagaj that does not refer to the nationality of the victims while evasively describing the perpetrators as "fashists." See Bataković, ed., *Histoire du Peuple Serbe*, 317.

[84] See Georges Castellan, *Histoire des Balkans XIVe-XXe siècle* (Paris: Fayard, 1991).One should note that a portion of the Bosnian Muslims took part in the war on behalf of Nazis. For more *see* George Lepre, *Himmler's Bosnian Division; The Waffen-SS Handschar Division 1943-1945* (Atlgen, PA:Schiffer, 1997).

[85] Present-day Croat historians, including the late Croat president Franjo Tudjman, largely underestimate the number of Ustasha victims. In addition, they list Croats among the concentration camp victims to render the ethnic origin less relevant, although the number of dissident Croats is relatively small. Franjo Tudjman, *Bespuća povijesne zbiljnosti: Rasprava o povijesti i filosofiji zlosilje* [Impasses of historical reality: A discussion of the history and philosophy of malevolent power], 2nd ed. (Zagreb: Matica Hrvatska, 1989).

executions of the Ustasha at the end of the war (1945).[86] The Yugoslav Communist leadership naturally denied these crimes, suppressing any debate over these important issues that had to be resolved to rebuild trust among the peoples of Yugoslavia. The creation of the second Yugoslavia in 1945 certainly was not the logical consequence of the ethnic strife occurring during the Second World War.

Ironically, the Partisan movement that eventually led to a federated state and a state arrangement that was not favored by the Serbs had succeeded chiefly due to the Serb effort, with other Yugoslav nations largely allying with the Nazis during the war or entertaining more narrow regional loyalties. The Croatian Communists were the least active in the Partisan movement and even Tito reprimanded them for their lack of military effort during the war and their mistreatment of Serbs.[87] In the Kosovo area, the local communists (and nationalists) were hostile to the Partisans and the Partisans prevailed only after a ruthless suppression of the 1944-1945 Albanian revolt.[88]

Before describing the new state arrangement, it is of value to ascertain whether the Second Yugoslavia represents a continuation of the First Yugoslavia or a new state. While many jurists assert that this was the same state with a new government, others claim that the change in the government was so substantive[89] that it created a new state, symbolized by the new name. A Democratic Federative Yugoslavia was promulgated on March 7, 1945 by a "provisory government," to be renamed the Federative People's Republic of Yugoslavia in 1946 and the Socialist Federative Republic of Yugoslavia (SFRY) in 1963. The latter is a weaker argument, as exemplified by the French revolution, which substantially changed the government of France but did not create a new country. Moreover, on November 1, 1944, less than a week following the liberation of the Yugoslav capital, the Communist-led Partisans, represented by Tito, had concluded an agreement with the royal-government-in exile, represented by its Prime Minister, Dr. Ivan Šubašić

---

[86] The Communists also executed many Serbs, members of Chetnik units as well as civilians, usually the most prominent individuals in various towns (teachers, businesspeople, priests). For more on "Red terror" *see* below.

[87] For a detailed account of the Yugoslav Partisan Movement *see* Shoup, *Communism and the Yugoslav National Question*, 68.

[88] Elez Biberaj, *Albania, A Socialist Maverick* (Boulder: Westview Press, 1990), 114-116; Branko Petranović, *Srbija u drugom svetskom ratu, 1939-1945* [Serbia in the Second World War] (Belgrade: Vojna štamparija, 1992), 552-61; Shoup, *Communism and the Yugoslav National Question*, 104-11.

[89] Essentially, monarchy was abolished (and exiled) and Communist rule installed. Note: The Karageorgevich family, led by Prince Alexander II, returned permanently to Serbia in 2001, following change of regime. Constitutional monarchy was not reinstituted but Serbia became once again a parliamentary democracy.

"in realization of the need to preserve the forms of legal continuity of the new state, particularly for purposes of international recognition."[90]

No matter what the conclusion, an undisputed fact is that the Communist Yugoslavia represented a drastically different state structure and a discontinuation of the previous state with regard to the founding principles. Communism replaced the elements of nationalism and democracy. The party and the state merged and Yugoslavia's constitutions consequently did not pose legal authority. The legal principles of self-determination, federalism, and minority rights acquired a distorted meaning in the Yugoslav framework.

3.5. The Communist Federal Arrangement

To attract other nations, the Communist Party of Yugoslavia (CPY), which was the organizational force behind the liberation struggle, allowed the formation of regional units, which became the basis of the ensuing division of Yugoslavia into six republics (Slovenia, Croatia, Bosnia and Herzegovina, Serbia, Montenegro, and Macedonia) and two autonomous provinces within Serbia (Voivodina and Kosovo and Metohia).

In the 1940s, the CPY also possessed an ambition to create a Balkan Federation,[91] having in mind Albania, Bulgaria, and possibly Greece, an idea that dated to the early twentieth century.[92] Due to a failed Communist insurgency in Greece, Bulgaria's resistance to the idea, and Yugoslavia's expulsion from the Cominform in 1948, this project failed.

The genesis of a federated Yugoslavia was instigated by the "Decision about the formation of Yugoslavia on the federal principle," adopted at the Second Session

---

[90] Michael Boro Petrovich, "The Central Government of Yugoslavia," *Political Science Quarterly* 62, No. 4 (1947), 504-530: 508.

[91] On the proposed Balkan Federation *see* Christopher Binns, "Federalism, Nationalism and Socialism in Yugoslavia," in Murray Forsyth (ed), *Federalism and Nationalism*, (Leicester: Leicester University Press, 1989), 115-146: 125-128; Branko Petranović, *Balkanska Federacija 1943-1948* [Balkan Federation 1943-1948] (Šabac: IKP Zaslon, 1991).

[92] Bulgaria and Serbia had previously made attempts to create a certain type of a union, establishing a customs union and a secret military agreement on March 30, 1904. However their interests diverged thereafter, partly due to overlapping territorial claims (mainly regarding Macedonia) and partly due to the Austro-Hungarian pressure and actions. For more on the Austro-Hungarian perspective of Serb-Bulgarian relations, *see Documents from the Vienna Archives*, Book II (1904), ed. Andriya Radenich (Belgrade: Historical Institute, 1973), particularly 337-343, 415-416, 425-426, 450-452, and 565-567.

of the Anti-Fascist Council of the National Liberation of Yugoslavia (AVNOJ).[93] AVNOJ convened in the medieval Bosnian capital of Jajce (Yaytse) on November 29 and 30, 1943, in the presence of 143 out of 250 "elected" delegates, as well as the representatives of the Anglo-American army mission. It represented a self-declared government, which decided by a means of acclamation, that is, spontaneous applause as a sign of general approval, without voting, which Protich sarcastically describes as "unknown to the tradition of modern democracies."[94]

The Anti-Fascist Council proclaimed a united federated state of Yugoslavia, and even named its new republics, but it did not discuss the precise boundaries of the federal units, in order to avoid political disagreements during war. AVNOJ also recognized five constituent nations to be the Serbs, Croats, Slovenes, Macedonians, and Montenegrins,[95] while granting "full national rights" to the national minorities in Yugoslavia.[96] Bosnian Muslims were considered to be a religious denomination at the time. The Partisan leadership initially planned to render Bosnia-Herzegovina a province within Serbia,[97] but decided on a separate republic

---

[93] On November 27, 1942, the first AVNOJ Congress convened in the town of Bihach in Bosnia, declaring itself the legitimate representative of the Yugoslav peoples. "Rezolucija o organizaciji AVNOJ" [Resolution on the organization of AVNOJ], November 27, 1942, in Petranović and Zečević, eds., *Yugoslav federalism, ideas and reality,* Vol. 1, 1914-1943, 722-733, Point 1, at 727. English translation is found in Trgo, ed., *The National Liberation War and Revolution in Yugoslavia (1941-1945)*, 389-390.

Radan provides the following overview: "At its third Congress, held in Belgrade on August 7-9, 1945, AVNOJ was renamed the Provisional National Assembly. Furthermore, a number of members of the 1938 National Assembly of the Kingdom of Yugoslavia, together with representatives of six other political parties and certain prominent individuals, were co-opted as additional members of the new Provisional National Assembly. On August 21, 1945 the Provisional National Assembly passed a Law on the Constituent Assembly for the purposes of electing a Constituent Assembly to prepare a new constitution for Yugoslavia. The Constituent Assembly was to consist of two chambers, namely the Assembly of Nationalities and the Federal Assembly. The election for a new Constituent Assembly "in which a spirit of competition was conspicuously lacking," was held on November 11, 1945, resulting in an overwhelming victory for the Popular Front, headed by the CPY. The Popular Front received 88.69 percent of votes cast in the election for the Assembly of Nationalities and 90.48 percent of the votes cast in the election for the Federal Assembly." Radan, Unpublished Doctoral Dissertation, paragraph 5069.

For more information on AVNOJ, *see* Rusinow, *The Yugoslav Experiment 1948-1974*, 2.

[94] Protich, *Rise and Fall of the Serbian Idea*, 348.

[95] "Odluka o izgradnji Jugoslavije na federativnom principu, "Decision on Constructing Yugoslavia Upon a Federal Principle, November 20, 1943, Point 2, reproduced in Petranović and Zečević, eds., *Yugoslavia 1918-1984; Collection of Documents*, 546.

[96] Ibid., Point 4.

[97] Branko M Pecelj, "Constitutional Characteristics of the Socialist Republic of Bosnia and Herzegovina" *Review of the Study Centre for Jugoslav Affairs* 5 (1965), 328-338: 330.

at the second Congress of AVNOJ[98] "partly due to the probability of Serbo-Croat tensions if the original plan were to proceed, and partly because Bosnia-Herzegovina had been a stronghold of the Partisan movement during the Second World War."[99] The Bosnian case was an exception to the unwritten rule that republics were each a homeland to one predominant national group. Since several groups inhabited Bosnia—two nations and three religious affiliations—and the Serbs, who were pre-dominant in another republic, Serbia, represented a relative majority, the guiding principle for creating a separate republic there was not national but territorial. Over time, the Communists granted more privileges to the Bosnian Muslims, including the status of a nation. As the British historian Nora Beloff has explained:

> Anomalously, as a Party member may not practice religion, the Moslem members of the Central Committee in Bosnia had to call themselves Moslem atheists: a contradiction in terms.
>
> Conscious of the religious realities, however, the Titoists did their best to appease practicing Moslems. Their seminaries were generously endowed, their theologians treated as respected members of the academic commu-nity, and their publications received generous allocations of paper, ena-bling them to publish 100,000 copies of their religious books.
>
> Further, whereas for the building of churches, permits were generally refused (in Belgrade the vast half-finished Cathedral of St Sava, intended by the monarchy to be the centre of Serb Orthodoxy, remains a physical reminder of atheist supremacy), there were no obstacles to the construc-tion in Bosnia of about 800 new mosques, mainly paid for by Middle Eastern benefactors. Also, in foreign policy solidarity with the Moslems was demonstrated by the consistent support given by Tito and his succes-sors to the PLO and all anti-Israel Arab states.[100]

The exact process of the formation of the internal Yugoslav boundaries, and which factors were used to determine them, were never revealed. For instance, "the first

---

[98] "Odluka Drugog zasedanja Antifašističkog Vijeća narodnog oslobodjenja Jugoslavije o izgradnji Jugoslavije na federativnom principu" [Decision of the Second AVNOJ Session on Constructing Yugoslavia Upon a Federal Principle], November 29, 1943, in Petranović and Zečević, eds., *Yugoslav federalism, ideas and reality*, Vol. 1, 1914-1943, 800-801. An English translation is found in Trgo, ed., *The National Liberation War and Revolution in Yugoslavia (1941-1945)*, 585-586.

[99] Radan, Unpublished Doctoral Dissertation, paragraph 5075.

[100] Nora Beloff, *Tito's Flawed Legacy: Yugoslavia and the West, 1939-84* (London: Victor Gollancz, ltd., 1985), 215.

map with borders of federal units was published in 1945, yet the documentation which was used for the drafting of this map has not been preserved."[101] The archives contain no data on this matter, either, which indicates that the relevant documents have either been lost or willfully destroyed, the latter being more probable. At the same time, "the manner in which these borders appear and were accepted, would indicate that they were decided in party circles or in a narrow circle of highest rank close to Tito."[102] The decision was made towards the end of the war, which is why these boundaries have also been called the "AVNOJ boundaries."

Considering the secrecy surrounding the political decision on internal boundary formation, it is not surprising that the legal delimitation of various republics and provinces took place only indirectly—through a process of constitutional amendments after the war in the form of laws concerning territorial organization of the respective republics. In this manner, all federal units established their boundaries by the end of 1947.[103]

Some smaller changes to the inter-republican boundaries were made immediately after the reconstitution of Yugoslavia. One important boundary modification was implemented regarding the region of Srem, a part of Voivodina that was partitioned between the republic of Serbia and the republic of Croatia. This is a unique case, where an inter-republican commission was formed for the purposes of boundary delimitation, and where boundaries were drawn mainly on ethnic rather than purely historic lines.[104] Nevertheless, a closer study of the division of Srem reveals that political considerations dominated the Communist decision-making even in this case.

The original decision of the committee to confirm the status of Srem as a part of Voivodina, made by the Central Committee of the Communist Party in July 1943, was stalled for nine months. In a final decision, Croats did not cede a part of Srem, under the explanation that the majority of its population

---

[101] Miodrag Zečević and Bogdan Lekić, *Frontiers and Internal Territorial Division of Yugoslavia* (Belgrade: Ministry of Information of the Republic of Serbia, 1991), 23.

[102] Ibid., 17.

[103] Ibid., 22.

[104] Interview, Milovan Djilas, "Srbi ne vode pravedan rat" [Serbs are not waging a just war], *Danas* (Zagreb), November 12, 1991, 39.

were Croat.[105] The fact that such a population structure was the result of the just-committed Croatian genocide against the Serbs, which included a policy of populating the area with Croats during the Ustasha regime and counting an ethnic group of Bunyevtsi as Croats,[106] was not taken into account.

Generally, the boundaries of the Yugoslav republics were based on a historical rather than purely ethnic principle, in that they relied on the Austro-Hungarian and Ottoman administrative divisions, past international treaties, and the banovina system of the first Yugoslavia. They were roughly determined at a meeting of the AVNOJ Presidency on 24 February 1945:

> Slovenia is taken in the borders of the former Dravska *banovina;* Croatia in the borders of the former Savska *banovina* with 13 districts of the former Primorska *banovina* and the Dubrovnik district of the former Zetska *banovina;* Bosnia-Hercegovina in the borders specified in the Berlin agreement; Serbia in the borders before the Balkan wars with districts taken from Bulgaria in the Treaty of Versailles; Macedonia—Yugoslav territories south of Kacanik and Ristovac; Montenegro in the borders before the Balkan wars with the Berane and Kotor districts and Plav and Gusinje.[107]

A combination of historical divisions was used and additionally adapted in order to satisfy the national demands of most Yugoslav nations. The Slovenes gained the territory they claimed under the Austro-Hungarians, which in 1922 comprised two districts and in 1929 made up the Dravska banovina, slightly enlarged by a part of the Istrian peninsula ceded by Italy to Yugoslavia after the Second World War. The boundaries of Bosnia-Herzegovina were those established at the Congress of Berlin in 1878,[46] which had since been largely maintained, with the exception of the 1921 unitary system of governance and the creation of the Croatian *banovina* in 1939. In the case of Macedonia, boundaries approximated the claims of early Macedonian nationalists to Macedonian territory within the confines of Yugoslavia. The boundaries of Montenegro resembled those of the Montenegrin state prior to its entry into the First World War. A slight reduction

---

[105] Ljubodrag Dimić, "Nekoliko dokumenata o privremenoj administrativnoj granici izmedju jugoslovenskih republika Srbije i Hrvatske" [Several documents on the temporary administrative boundary between the Yugoslav republics, Serbia and Croatia], *History of 20th Century* X, no 1-2 (1992), 232.

[106] Ibid., 233.

[107] Cited in Kosta Cavoski, *Na rubovima srpstva; Srpsko pitanje danas* [On the edges of Serbdom; Serbian question today] (Belgrade: Tersit, 1995), 25.

of these boundaries was compensated for by the addition of the Kotor district, which, prior to the First World War, had been part of Dalmatia, ruled by the Habsburgs from Vienna. In the case of Croatia, the administrative boundaries approximated those of the provinces of Croatia, Slavonia, Krayina, and Dalmatia, now joined for the first time in one administrative unit. To that was added Baranya, which had as part of Voivodina joined Serbia prior to the formation of Yugoslavia, and the greater part of the Istrian peninsula gained from Italy after the Second World War, from which the Communists expelled Italians en masse. The Communist Republic of Croatia thus included within its territory the majority Serb region of Krayina. At the same time, not all Croats resided within the new republic. Serbia had a small Croatian minority while Croats made up part of the population of Bosnia and Herzegovina.[108] In the case of Serbia, the creation of the Republic of Macedonia reduced its boundaries in the south from those with which it entered the First World War. In the Northern Serbian province of Voivodina, which had formed part of Serbia since November 1918, the Serbs became a majority as a result of Communist expulsion of the German minority and resettlement of Serbs from other areas, including Kosovo and Macedonia. Finally, a significant portion of Serbs resided in other federal units, namely Bosnia (as a relative majority) and Croatia (as one of two constitutive nations next to Croats).[109]

The choice of federal units was a highly contentious point in determining the new administrational arrangement. Many areas within Yugoslavia, in addition to the six proposed republics, qualified for autonomous territorial organization. Voivodina, Slavonia, Sandjak, Kosovo, Boka, Herzegovina, Krayina, Dalmatia, Istria, Dubrovnik, and probably Carniola and Styria in Slovenia met the conditions for various forms of autonomy. All tendencies of this nature were suppressed in these areas, except in Kosovo which became an autonomous region and Voivodina, which became an autonomous province within Serbia (1946).

Towards the end of the war, when Dalmatia demanded autonomy based on its historical autonomy and the relative autonomy of the Dalmatian Partisan movement, Tito intervened personally in favor of the party leadership of Croatia,

---

[108] According to the 1948 census, Bosnia and Herzegovina was composed of Serbs (44.2 percent), Muslims (30.7 percent), Croats (23.9 percent). Source: *Statistical Yearbook of Yugoslavia 1991* (Belgrade: Federal statistics bureau, 1992).

[109] *See* later discussion and footnote 129.

impeding Dalmatia's bid for autonomy status.[110] Since then, Dalmatia had been strongly dominated by the Croats from the Croatia-Slavonia province.

Another plan rejected by Croatian Communists and by Tito was one proposed during the war by Mosha Piyade,[111] a member of the Central Committee of the CPY, together with some other Serbian Communists, for an autonomous region of Serbs in Croatia (Krayina). The party explanation for this rejection was that "toward the end of the war and immediately afterward the CPY was fighting to gain the support of the Croatian masses and considered that the creation of a Serbian autonomous region would have been unpopular with them."[112] Milovan Djilas recollects that Piyade's plan, backed by a mass on statistics on population, was received with embarrassment by the Communist leadership:

> Everyone was silent, perplexed. I think I saw dejection even in Tito's face; perhaps as a Croat he found it awkward to oppose the idea. . . . I was the first to come out against Pijade's proposal; the segregated territory was unnatural, lacking a center of viability, and moreover provided fuel for Croatian nationalism. Kardelj immediately agreed. . . . Rankovic squelched [Pijade] by remarking that the Serbs and Croats were not so different that the Serbs and Croats had to be divided.[113]

Djilas concluded that creating a Serb autonomous unit within Croatia was not a viable option, amounting to "splitting the Croatian nation and preventing its free development."[114]

Serbia was "split" however, not at the AVNOJ session but by the provisions of the 1946 constitution, which established the autonomous *province* of Voivodina and the autonomous *region* of Kosovo-Metohia[115] within the republic of Serbia (Article 2).[116]

---

[110] Zečević and Lekić, *Frontiers and Internal Territorial Division of Yugoslavia*, 20.

[111] Prior to World War II, Piyade was a wall painter.

[112] Djilas, *The Contested Country*, 172.

[113] Milovan Djilas, *Wartime* (London: Martin Secker & Warburg, 1977), 356.

[114] Cited in Vojislav Kostunica, "The Constitution and the Federal States" in Dennison Rusinow, ed., *Yugoslavia, A Fractured Federalism* (Washington, DC: The Wilson Center Press, 1988), 78-92: 92.

[115] The 1963 Constitution referred to Kosovo and Metohia as a province, shortening the name to just Kosovo in 1968.

[116] [Emphasis added.] Note: The 1946 Constitution allowed for establishment of additional republics and autonomous provinces and regions, as acts within the jurisdiction of the federal government (Article 44).

The significant presence of a minority population was a purported criterion for the creation of these provinces in Serbia. However while in Voivodina the Serbs represented a relative majority (Hungarians were the most significant minority);[117] the regions of some other republics with a population ethnically different from those to whom the republic nominally belonged, such as the Serb Krayina or Italian-dominant Istria in present day Croatia, could never obtain autonomous status.[118] An even more indicative example is that of the Albanian-dominant Western Macedonia, which was not granted autonomy, in contrast to Kosovo-Metohia, where the significant number of Albanians was a key reason for autonomy status. Importantly, Kosovo-Metohia, unlike Western Macedonia, also represented the cradle of Serb culture and history. It is evident that a combination of historical and national criteria, used to establish autonomous units within republics, applied solely to Serbia. Moreover, in Serbia the criteria were selectively implemented, as Voivodina failed to meet the ethnic criteria.

Yugoslavia's Communist leadership rejected comparisons between the two provinces created in Serbia and the regions in other republics that could also potentially be turned into autonomous provinces, by differentiating between the "constituting nations" of Yugoslavia and the "nationalities."[119] Slovenes, Serbs, Croats, Macedonians, Montenegrins, and later also Bosnian Muslims enjoyed the status of constituent nations. According to the Communist rhetoric, each of these constituent nations had a home republic, and therefore could not obtain autonomy status in another republic despite significant presence there.

Although the Constitution specifically provided for equality of constituent and other nations (Article 245, 1974 Constitution), non-constituent nations were legally less than a nation. They were even called by a diminutive term, "nationality" (*narodnost*). This term was a Communist invention. It had a different meaning than the better-known legal term, "minority," and it did not signify "one's citizenship" in the Yugoslav context. The Yugoslav nationalities were those ethnic

---

At the same time, the constitution of a republic decided "the scope of the autonomy of autonomous provinces and autonomous regions" (Article 103).

[117] According to the 1952 census, Serbs accounted for 50.8 percent and Hungarians for 25.5 percent. In 1991, the Serbs accounted for 57.1 percent and the Hungarians for 16.9 percent. Source: *The Serbian Question in the Balkans* (Belgrade: University of Belgrade, 1995).

[118] Dragoljub Popovic, *Short Essays on Serbian Constitutional Problems* (Belgrade: Center for Serbian Studies, 1997), 17-18.

[119] Atlagić, *Nation, National Question and Relations among Yugoslav Nations*, 31.

groups that had a national homeland outside Yugoslavia and therefore did not enjoy a right to a republic, despite the fact that some, like the Albanians, were numerically larger than certain constituent nations (the Montenegrins). This is not to say that nationalities were more oppressed by the Communist leadership than the constituent nations. On the contrary, the Albanians and the Hungarians gained an elaborate autonomy status. Furthermore, there was a policy of "protected nationalities," which allowed for numerous (minority) rights.[120] However, even if we accept the Communist logic for granting republic and autonomous status to various nations and nationalities, respectively, we must acknowledge that it utterly fails to explain why the Albanians in Western Macedonia did not obtain autonomy status similar to that of Albanians in Serbia (Kosovo and Metohia).

A more plausible explanation is to be found in the Communist theory, which regarded the numerically and historically dominant nation as the oppressor that had to be confined. In Yugoslavia this nation was Serb,[121] in Czechoslovakia Czech, and in the Soviet Union Russian.[122] The general disrespect for the contribution of Serbs in the fight against Nazi occupiers became evident as soon as Partisans re-entered Serbia in 1944. The Partisans ignored the fact that the Serbs constituted the majority of their troops and that Serb Chetniks, whom the Partisans labeled as traitors, also fought against the Nazis. Upon entering Belgrade on November 7, 1944, Milovan Djilas, acting in the capacity of a Partisan General, declared that the Serbian nation should "by a ruthless fight against the foreign enemy and its domestic servants repay [the other nations of Yugoslavia] the debt accrued during three and a half years of bloody war for the liberation of

---

[120] The Yugoslav nationalities policy recognized many "protected nationalities" (narodnosti), such as Albanians, Hungarians, Turks, Slovaks, Bulgarians, Romanians, Ruthenes/Ukrainians, Czechs, and Italians, amounting to 2,200,000 persons or 10.8 percent of the total population in 1971. Yugoslavia's record on national rights in the period 1969-81 was commendable for all groups except Gypsies. Sabrina Ramet, *Nationalism and Federalism in Yugoslavia (1962-1991)* (Bloomington: Indiana University Press, 1992), 54. The Yugoslav Constitution rendered unconstitutional and a criminal offence "propagating or practicing national inequality and any incitement of national, racial or religious hatred and intolerance" (Article 170/3 of the 1974 SFRY Constitution, Article 187, Constitution of Socialist Autonomous Province of Kosovo, Belgrade 1974).

[121] Nora Beloff calls this attitude "an eagerness to humble an over-mighty Serbia" Beloff, *Tito's Flawed Legacy*, 192.

[122] Viktor Knapp, "Socialist Federation—A Legal Means to the Solution of the Nationality Problem: A Comparative Study," *Michigan Law Review* 82 (1984), 1213-1228: 1214-1215.

the Serbian nation."[123] When describing the first Yugoslav constitution, Edvard Kardelj, a Slovene who was Tito's close associate and the principal interpreter of Yugoslav Communist ideology[124], declares overtly: "The old system of hegemonistic greater-Serb cliques upheld by reactionary anti-national Croat, Slovene and other influences has been done away with." He further says:

> Our peoples have signed their act of unification with their blood and have put the principles of self-determination and equality of rights into practice by building up the federal units and the united federative state community. In this way they have created all the conditions necessary for the liquidation of the nationality problem which constantly shook and undermined the old Yugoslavia.[125]

The end result was that the Serbs felt particularly aggrieved by the internal divisions, while the others, namely Croats, alleged that these internal divisions were but a mask for the renewed Greater Serbian hegemony. The changes in the status of internal boundaries, eventually leading to a high level of decentralization, reassured the nationalist[126] Croats and worried the nationalist Serbs.

The situation in Yugoslavia at the end of the war was further complicated by the fact that Yugoslav Partisans simultaneously with introducing a new regime conducted a campaign of "Red terror" that first affected Serbia in the autumn of 1944 and then to a lesser extent also Croatia and Slovenia in the spring of 1945, causing hundreds of thousands to perish. Harsh reprisals against civilians were conducted in Belgrade in the autumn of 1944 (approximately 10,000 perished), but also against fugitive Croatian, Slovene, and some Serbian troops, as well as civilians of all nationalities at the end of the war. Yugoslavia's Albanians, who rebelled against the Partisans in late 1944, were also the subject of Red terror in the winter of 1944–1945, as well as Italians in Dalmatia and Istria and ethic Germans in

---

123 Slobodan G. Marković, "Josip Broz—upotreba naučnih ustanova u Srbiji za deifikaciju jugoslovenskog diktatora" [Josip Broz—the Use of Scientific Institutions in Serbia for the Deification of the Yugoslav Dictator], *Hereticus* III (2005), No. 1, 33.

124 Prior to World War II, Kardelj was an elementary school teacher.

125 Edvard Kardelj, *Main Characteristics of the Constitution of the Federative People's Republic of Yugoslavia*, Speech broadcast by Radio Belgrade on December 5, 1945, and published by the Office of Information attached to the Government of the Federative People's Republic of Yugoslavia, Belgrade 1947, 26-27.

126 The term "nationalist" is not used in a negative context, but to differentiate from purely Communist, i.e. non-national ideology.

Voivodina.[127] The Communist reprisals created additional mistrust among different Yugoslav peoples. For many émigré Croats, the place of veneration became Bleiburg, a small town at the border between Slovenia and Austria, where thousands of Croats were summarily executed in May 1945. Importantly, Croatian nationalists, including future Croat president Franjo Tudjman, viewed this reprisal as a deed of Serbian and not Yugoslav communists.[128] The Red terror helped Communists to eliminate opposition and to gradually cement their power, but it also contributed to inter-ethnic tensions.

Considering that it was the Serbs who again came out of the war on the side of the victors, having endured a heavy loss of human life, this time in large part as a result of a civil war, including genocide by their co-patriots, the Croats, who for the second time fought a war on the losing side, Serb acceptance of the new state arrangement is even more difficult to understand than their loyalty to a continued Yugoslavia. There are several reasons why the Serbs, instead of forming a strong Serb state, opted for a federated Yugoslavia under a Communist veil.

First, as in the post-World War I period, the geographical dispersal of the Serb population rendered the creation of an all-inclusive Serb unit impossible without at least partially infringing on territories of other ethnic groups, which would have created additional conflicts. About 27 percent of Serbs lived outside the Republic of Serbia[129] and almost 40 percent outside Serbia proper (not including the two provinces).

Second, and more importantly, in the post-World War II period many Serbs, especially outside Serbia, had gradually accepted Communism, rejecting Serb and espousing Yugoslav nationalism. Importantly, these Communist Serbs represented the majority of the new leadership, with the pre-war, non-Communist elite

---

[127]   Dimitrije Djordjevic estimates in his memoirs the death toll to be several tens of thousands for Serbia and Bosnia. Milan Trešnjić, a major in the Partisan army secret service, estimated the death toll in Belgrade alone to be around ten thousand. Total casualties of the Red terror among Yugoslavs executed during the "liberation" of Yugoslavia, in 1944-1945 was significantly higher. According to Michael Lees it is about 250,000. Ljubo Sirc, former Partisan and later professor of political economy at Glasgow University, estimated a higher figure of 300,000. John R. Lampe puts the figure at around 100,000 in the period 1945-46. For more, *see* Slobodan G, Marković, "Communist 'Liberation' and new Order in Belgrade," *The South Slav Journal* 24, No. 3-4 (Autumn-Winter 2003), 12-13.

[128]   Tudjman, *Impasses of historical reality*.

[129]   Montenegrins are not counted as Serbs in this figure. Note: Similarly, at that time 22 percent of Croatian Yugoslav population lived outside Croatia. Figures cited in Djilas, *The Contested Country*, 3.

either killed or forced to emigrate. It was only in the 1970s and 1980s that some of the former high-ranking Serb Communists became voices of dissent with regard to the internal organization of the Yugoslav state.

Third, although the Communist movement led by Josip Broz Tito represented an imposed unifying element, the establishment of the Second Yugoslavia was not a result of a mass popular movement of brotherhood and unity, as asserted by the Communist historiography. The role of the Great Powers was once again crucial. The countries that became "the Western Bloc" in the new post-World War II balance of power arrangement supported the Yugoslav Communist leadership in fear that Yugoslavia would otherwise be utterly dominated by the Soviet Union. Consequently, the restoration of an independent Serbian state was discouraged, a stance that was aided by the fact that the Serb elite were largely purged, allowing (Serb) Communists to put ideology before national interests. Furthermore, the Western countries believed that a federated arrangement in Yugoslavia would instill a democratic rule. As Beloff explains, "To the West, the word federation had a reassuringly democratic and liberal connotation.[130] Yugoslavia was chosen as the buffer state in the Cold War. The fate of the Yugoslav peoples, as a state where the influence of the West and the East would be equally divided, was decided over dinner between Churchill and Stalin on October 9, 1944, in Moscow. It was written on a half-sheet of paper: 50–50 percent.[131]

Finally, the Communist leadership consistently insisted on the administrative nature of the internal boundaries. Although publicly propagating federalism, the Communist Party of Yugoslavia planned to remain the sole power center, granting no substantive authority to the republics, which appealed to Communist Serbs.

The Slovenes and the Croats gradually accepted Communism and Tito's second Yugoslavia for the same reasons they entered the first Yugoslavia—as losers of another war who could become prey to the surrounding nations if they opted to create their own mini-states. Moreover, many of those who opposed Communism were eliminated in the Red terror at the end of the war in May 1945. Still, like the Serbs, they grumbled about territorial deprivation. The Croats, for instance,

---

[130] Beloff, *Tito's Flawed Legacy*, 193.

[131] Winston Churchill, *The Second World War* (Abridged with an Epilogue on the Years 1945-1957), Book IV, "Triumph and Tragedy: 1943-1945" (London: Cassell, 1959), 852-853.

while generally satisfied, complained about a 40-kilometer (25-mile) strip along the Adriatic coast that was carved out of Dalmatia to extend the region of Herzegovina.[132]

It also important to note here that administrative boundaries created by the Yugoslav Communist leadership in 1945 incurred changes thereafter. For instance, the Autonomous Province of Kosovo and Metohia became enlarged in 1959, when the village of Leshak from Central Serbia was added to the municipality of Leposavich in Kosovo and Metohia in a process of reorganization of smaller administrative units—districts and municipalities.[133]

3.6. The Changing Geography of Yugoslavia's Constitutions

The first Yugoslav Constitution was promulgated on January 31, 1946, asserting self-determination as the founding principle of the new state. Article 1 stipulated:

> The Federative People's Republic of Yugoslavia is a federal peoples' state, republican in form, a community of peoples equal in rights who, on the basis of their right to self-determination, *including the right of secession*, have expressed their will to live together in a federative state. [134]

This provision was reiterated in all Yugoslav constitutions, having first appeared in the brief AVNOJ Decision.[135] It was further complemented by Article 4 of the 1946 Constitution providing that "National minorities in Yugoslavia will be secured with all the national rights," and which also stems from AVNOJ.

---

[132]   Beloff, *Tito's Flawed Legacy*, 192.

[133]   *See* Law on territories of municipalities and districts in the People's Republic of Serbia, *Official Gazette of People's Republic of Serbia*, 51/1959, and Law on territories of municipalities and districts in the People's Republic of Serbia, *Official Gazette of People's Republic of Serbia*, 56/1955.

[134]   Constitution of the Federal Peoples' Republic of Yugoslavia, 1946, *Official Gazette of FPRY*, 10/1946. An English translation of the 1946 Constitution is reprinted in Robert J Kerner, ed., *Yugoslavia* (Berkeley: University of California Press, 1949), 487-512 [Italics mine].

[135]   "Odluka Drugog zasedanja Antifašističkog Vijeća narodnog oslobodjenja Jugoslavije o izgradnji Jugoslavije na federativnom principu" [Decision of the Second Session of AVNOJ on the construction of Yugoslavia upon the federal principle], November 29, 1943, in Petranović and Zečević, eds., *Yugoslav federalism, ideas and reality*, Vol. 1, 1914-1943, 800-801. English translation is found in Trgo, ed., *The National Liberation War and Revolution in Yugoslavia (1941-1945)*, 585-586.

The principle of sovereignty was also stressed in the Article immediately following the provision for self-determination (Article 2), intertwined with the federal principle:

> In order for the principle of sovereignty of the peoples of Yugoslavia to be implemented, for Yugoslavia to represent a true homeland of all its peoples and never again become a domain of any hegemonistic clique, Yugoslavia is forming, and will be formed on the principle of federalism, which will assure a full equality of Serbs, Croats, Slovenians, Macedonians and Montenegrins, that is, of the peoples of Serbia, Croatia, Slovenia, Macedonia, Montenegro and Bosnia and Herzegovina.

The principles of sovereignty and self-determination had a specific meaning in Communist Yugoslavia. First, sovereignty was granted simultaneously to the federal units and to the founding peoples (Articles 9 and 10). The principle therefore could not be applied to any separate part of the Yugoslav territory (including the respective republics), but only to the state of Yugoslavia as a whole.

Similarly, the prevailing communist ideology called for a different interpretation of the definition of national self-determination in Yugoslav law. First, as explained above, the legal definition of peoples had two variants in Communist Yugoslavia: constituent nations and nationalities. The Yugoslav constitutions did not grant an explicit right to nationalities to "self-determination, including the right to secession." This right was reserved to constituent nations. Second, Lenin had set the standard for the Communist perception of national self-determination as the first phase of Communist establishment, a step leading to international proliferation of workers' class struggle:

> While recognizing equality and an equal right to a nation state, [the proleteriat] attaches supreme value to the alliance of the proletarians of all nations, and evaluates every national demand, every national separation, *from the angle* of the class struggle of the workers.[136]

The Slovene ideologue Edvard Kardelj provided a specifically Yugoslav definition for a nation as "a specific community of peoples arising on the basis of the social

---

[136] Vladimir Ilyich Lenin, "The Right of Nations to Self-Determination," *The Nationalism Reader*, ed. Omar Dahbour and Micheline R. Ishay (New Jersey: Humanities Press, 1995), 210.

division of labor in the epoch of capitalism, in a compact territory and within the framework of a common language and close ethnic and cultural similarity in general."[137] As Kardelj elaborated at that time, a nation could not disappear until objective socio-economic development was reached, providing for economic equality of nations.[138]

Therefore, the principle of self-determination was considered to be a right that has already been consummated by the peoples of Yugoslavia when they joined a Communist Yugoslavia, rendering this process irreversible.[139] Secession of various republics was permitted (Article 1), but a change in the boundaries required consent of all the other republics (Articles 12, 44), annulling the application of the right to secession in practice.

The internal boundaries and the external borders of the Yugoslav state were considered sacrosanct because they were based on the Partisan struggle. As elaborated by Milovan Djilas in a statement made before the National Assembly on January 17, 1946, the Constitution was simply:

> . . . the great achievement of [Yugoslav Communist] struggle up to the present, as one of the conclusive acts of that struggle, an act which gives final form on a legal basis to the programme, which we put forward at Jajce in 1943.[140]

Notably, despite this elaborate reasoning, Tito had initially opposed granting the republics the right to self-determination, fearful of future secessionist movements. As Aleksa Djilas has explained,

> [Tito's] apprehension was primarily caused by the extremism and crimes of the Ustashas during the war. He finally consented when he was reminded that such a right was part of the program of the CPY before the war, that the Comintern advocated it, and that it had roots in the traditions of most European socialist parties.[141]

---

[137] Shoup, *Communism and the Yugoslav National Question*, 203.

[138] Atlagić, *Nation, national question and relations among Yugoslav nations*, 34.

[139] Djilas, *The Contested Country*, 167.

[140] Statement made by Milovan Djilas in the National Assembly (Belgrade: Office of Information attached to the Government of the Federative People's Republic of Yugoslavia, 1947), 7-8.

[141] Djilas, *The Contested Country*, 167.

In practice, as with the 1936 Soviet Constitution,[142] which served as a model for this first post-World War II Yugoslav Constitution, the liberal provisions relating to self-determination amounted to a façade of a centrally organized state. The Yugoslav Constitution was just slightly more faithful to practice, by explicitly not granting the republics the right to an independent foreign policy and independent armed forces. In contrast, the Soviet Constitution provided its republics with such a right, but did not apply the right in practice (any challenge to the integrity of the USSR constituted high treason, punishable by death). However, while the Soviet Union's legal definitions approached its practice over time, the Yugoslav constitutional law became increasingly ambiguous, allowing for different interpretations.

The 1946 Constitution provided for symbolic Soviet-type federalism, with the real power remaining in the hands of a centralized Communist Party of Yugoslavia.

---

[142] The Union of Soviet Socialist Republics (USSR) represented a federation of fifteen Union republics. Union republics were organized on a national basis, with each republic encompassing the territory inhabited by one or more national groups. The larger union republics were further subdivided into regions, territories, and autonomous republics. The territories of the largest and most important nationalities that also bordered on foreign states were designated as union-republics, while the smaller national groups (most of whom resided within the borders of the Russian Republic) were provided for in a hierarchy of administrative units called autonomous republics, autonomous regions, and autonomous areas. (Autonomous areas were known as national areas in the constitutions adopted prior to 1977.)

The Soviet Union Republics enjoyed a constitutional right to secede from the USSR at will, as well as a right to maintain direct relations with foreign states. Yet, the right to secession, guaranteed by Article 72 of the 1977 Constitution, was partly emasculated by Article 73, notably clauses 2 and 4. These clauses stipulated that the highest bodies of the USSR state authority had the right both to "determination of the state boundaries of the USSR" and "settlement of other matters of All-Union importance." This additional article did not feature in the first USSR Constitution, in which the right of secession was most clearly formulated. The legal practice was to ignore the boundaries and independent competencies of federal and autonomous republics.

The decentralization of the Soviet Union slightly advanced only after the death of Stalin in 1953, which ended the so-called "cult of the individual." Since the XX Party Congress in 1956 the Soviet republics have gained both more executive and legislative power. Legislative power in the fields of criminal and common law had especially increased since 1957. The same year, the administration of the entire industry came into the hands of the republics. Authority devolved to the bureaucratic subsystems, such as the military, factory managers, or jurists, without a viable conflict resolution mechanism, becoming one of the factors of the USSR's disintegration. *See* Harold J. Berman and John B. Quigley, eds., *Basic Laws on the Structure of the Soviet State* (Cambridge: Harvard University Press, 1969), xvii-xviii; "Federation, Defederation and Refederation: from the Soviet Union to Russian Statehood," *Federalism: The Multiethnic Challenge* (London: Longman Group, 1995), 158; Gordon B. Smith, ed., *Public Policy and Administration in the Soviet Union* (New York: Praeger Publishers, 1980), 5, 145; *Karakter i funkcije federacije u procesu konstituisanja samoupravnog društva* (Beograd: Institut za političke studije VSPN, 1968), 49, 120-121.; Reneo Lukic and Allen Lynch, *Europe from the Balkans to the Urals; The Disintegration of Yugoslavia and the Soviet Union* (New York: Sipri, Oxford University Press, 1996).

According to Shoup, this was the prevailing attitude of the new Yugoslav leadership: The war and revolution provided [Yugoslavia] with a new generation of cadres whose first loyalty was to the CPY and its essentially unitary approach to the nationality problem.[143]

Consequently, once Tito broke with Stalin in 1948 and Yugoslavia became isolated from the rest of the Communist bloc, the Yugoslavs were in need of inventing a model that was different from Stalin's stern centralism but that simultaneously did not lead to decentralization. The end product was termed "workers' self-management," a failed Yugoslav communist construction that purported to radically change the concept of economic progress.

According to the evasive Yugoslav communist rhetoric, "the concept of self-management federalism resulted in a multinational federation which ideologically emulates the concept of the working class."[144] The declared goal of the Yugoslav model was to grant more power to the workers through a system of workers' councils. Any strengthening of the republics as opposed to the self-managed enterprises was depicted as an unintended consequence that the system would try to limit. This model was enshrined in the Basic Law on Workers Self-Management, enacted on June 27, 1950,[145] leading to the Fundamental Constitutional Law of January 13, 1953,[146] which *de facto* created a new constitution.

Edvard Kardelj claimed that the 1953 constitutional changes combated any hegemonization of the country, while preventing the application of the principle of self-determination for "reactionary and anti-socialist aims that undermine friendships or spread hatred among peoples, impeding their natural cooperation."[147]

---

[143] Shoup, *Communism and the Yugoslav National Question*, 91-92.

[144] Vesna Popovski, "Yugoslavia: Politics, Federation, Nation," *Public Policy and Administration in the Soviet Union* (New York: Praeger Publishers, 1980), 190.

[145] "Osnovni zakon o upravljanju državnim privrednim poduzećima i višim privrednim udruženjima od strane radnih kolektiva" [Framework law on the management of public economic enterprises and higher economic associations by the work collectives], June 27, 1950, in Branko Petranović and Čedomir Štrbac, eds., *Istorija socialističke Jugoslavije* [History of Socialist Yugoslavia], Documents I, Vol. 2 (Belgrade: Radnička štampa, 1977), 325-331.

[146] "Ustavni zakon o osnovama društvenog i političkog uredjenja Federativne Narodne Republike Jugoslavije i saveznih organa vlasti" [Constitutional law on the foundations of social and political regulation of the Federal People's Republic of Yugoslavia and the federal authorities], January 13, 1953, *Official Gazette of FPRY*, 3/1953.

[147] Edvard Kardelj, "Prednacrt Ustava FSRL" [Draft Constitution of SFRY], *Komunist* (1962), 127 [Translation mine].

Self-determination was perceived as a means of creating a common Yugoslav nationality, officially introduced in late 1950s, following the Novi Sad language agreement of 1954. This agreement proclaimed that Serbs, Croats and Montenegrins shared a single language[148] and culture, implying to a certain extent that these groups constituted one nation.[149]

The pro-Yugoslav feeling was strongly encouraged.[150] Often speaking in simplified fashion, Tito used the example of culture to explain that the decentralization carried out by the new constitutional structure had political limits. In a 1962 speech, he called "closing of culture into republic frames" to be absolutely detrimental to the peoples' interest. "Our life needs to develop in Yugoslav dimensions," he proclaimed.[151] Prominent Serb writer and party member Dobritsa Chosich supported Tito at the time, writing:

> Let us declare ourselves in favour of Yugoslavism as a form of internationalisation, as a socialist community of equal and free peoples without any national privileges whatsoever. . . . Yugoslavism is a part of the historically inevitable process of the integration of the world.[152]

As Shoup has remarked, the Yugoslav people generally tended to look optimistically into the future and felt that they were contributing to the shaping of the modern world.[153]

However, in the 1960s it became pointedly clear that the Partisan movement and its Communist ideology did not succeed in suppressing the nationalist sentiments. The more economically advanced republics of Slovenia and Croatia

---

[148] Conclusions of the Novi Sad Agreement, December 1954, reproduced in Petranović and Zečević, eds., *Yugoslav federalism, ideas and reality,* Vol. 1, 1914-1943, 734-736. *Note*: Croatian and Serbian linguistically differ as much as British and American English.

[149] Steven L Burg, "Ethnic Conflict and the Federalization of Socialist Yugoslavia: The Serbo-Croat Conflict" *Publius: The Journal of Federalism* 7 (1977), 119-143: 122.

[150] For more on the Yugoslavism policy, *see* Aleksandar Pavkovic, "Multiculturalism as a prelude to state fragmentation: the case of Yugoslavia," *Journal of Southern Europe and the Balkans* 3, No. 2 (2001).

[151] Edvard Kardelj, "Draft Constitution of SFRY," 140 [Translation mine]. Original: "Na primjer, ja smatram da je apolutno štetno ako bismo našu kulturu, naš kulturni život zatvorili u republičke okvire. Naš kulturni život treba da se razvija u jugoslovenskim razmjerama."

[152] Cited in Lawrence R Godtfredsen, *Federalism and Yugoslav Political Integration* (Unpublished Doctoral Dissertation, Tufts University, 1973), 308.

[153] Shoup, *Communism and the Yugoslav National Question,* 263.

demanded greater control over economic resources. They desired a larger share in the decision-making process and a smaller share of the economic burden, reflected in their subsidization of the poorer Yugoslav regions, such as Kosovo-Metohia. At the same time, the less prosperous regions protested that their low economic productivity was partly a consequence of the Communist planning policy that moved all the industry from Serbia westwards after the war, transforming the eastern parts of the country largely into producers of raw materials.[154] Moreover, the Krayina Serbs expressed a quiet but growing discontent with the lack of investment there, rendering Krayina into the least developed part of Communist Croatia.

To respond to increased national tensions, the CPY leadership reversed course. Instead of further centralization aimed at developing workers' self-management, the new constitution, adopted on April 7, 1963,[155] provided a first significant step towards decentralization of the state. Integral Yugoslavism, first attempted by King Alexander in the 1930s, was once again effectively rejected. The new Constitution provided for a new interpretation of the Yugoslav federation as a "community of nations."[156]

In addition to greater freedom to regulate their own internal constitutional and organizational structures, the Republic obtained extended legislative competence, increasing their leverage in relation to the federal government. The right of national self-determination, including the right to secession, was restored (Introductory Part, Section I),[157] and so was the Chamber of Nationalities.

---

[154] "In the first years after the war, new factories from Serbia were moved to Slovenia (which, according to official interpretation, had a more developed industry and working class) and, in return, dilapidated machinery from Slovenia were granted to Serbia. A part of Serb industry was moved to Bosnia after 1948, mainly for strategic reasons (fear of Soviet attack)." Bataković, ed., *Histoire du Peuple Serbe*, 348 [Translation mine].

[155] Constitution of the Socialist Federalist Republic of Yugoslavia, April 7, 1963, *Official Gazette of SFRY*, 14/1963.

[156] Ibid.

[157] "The peoples of Yugoslavia, on the basis of the right to every people to self-determination, including the right to secession, on the basis of their common struggle and their will freely declared in the People's Liberation War and Socialist Revolution, and in accordance with their historical aspirations, aware that the further consolidation of their brotherhood and unity is to their common interest, have united in a federal republic of a free and equal peoples and nationalities and have founded a socialist federal community of the working people. . . . "

At the same time, the 1963 Constitution clarified, and thereby strengthened, the provision of the 1946 Constitution that rendered secession impossible without an overall agreement on the borders of a seceding territory. It declared that any changes to republic boundaries required an agreement among the assemblies of the relevant republics (Article 109).

Constitutional decentralization was accompanied by a decentralization within the League of Yugoslav Communists (LCY). The process was initiated in 1968, when the republican congresses of the LCY were for the first time held before the all-Yugoslav Congress.[158] Edvard Kardelj, a theoretician of Yugoslavism who had strongly rejected more narrow nationalisms in the past,[159] moved to the Slovene capital, Ljubljana. He now purported that the goal of the 1963 Constitution was to "protect the peoples of Yugoslavia and their Republics from all hegemony, violation of national rights, economic exploitation, inroads into their culture and language and into their independent national life in general."[160]

A decentralization of LCY was made possible by the ousting of one of the most prominent Serbian Communists, Alexander Rankovich,[161] in 1966. Head of the secret police, Organizational Secretary of the League of Communists in control of cadres, and *de facto* leader of the Serbian Communist party, Rankovich was even considered to be Tito's successor.[162] Rankovich opposed further reform to the economy, considering that liberalization would harm the interests of the under-developed regions. Ironically, he became accused of economic nationalism and the republics gained further economic independence after his dismissal. Simultaneously, the republican parties obtained significantly more power, now controlling the delegates sent to the federal government. Subsequently, political career no longer lay with the federal but the republican party and government. Furthermore, the secret police was decentralized and there was also partial

---

[158] Vesna Popovski, "Yugoslavia: Politics, Federation, Nation," 189.

[159] "In nationalistic manifestations there is expressed everything that is reactionary, ideologically backward, or momentarily disorientating in our social life." Cited in Shoup, *Communism and the Yugoslav National Question*, 205.

[160] Edvard Kardelj, "Draft Constitution of SFRY," 120.

[161] Prior to World War II, Rankovich was a tailor apprentice.

[162] Steven L Burg, *Conflict and Cohesion in Socialist Yugoslavia, Political Decision Making Since 1966* (Princeton: Princeton University Press, 1983), 27-30. There is no evidence of Rankovich's nationalist outlook. *See* Shoup, *Communism and the Yugoslav National Question*, 213. *See also* Nenad V. Petrovic, "The Fall of Aleksandar Rankovic" *Review of the Study Centre for Yugoslav Affairs* I, No 6 (1967), 533-551. Petrovic portrays Rankovich as a scapegoat for failed Communist economic reforms.

territorial division of the Yugoslav People's Army with the creation of supplementary territorial forces in 1969, partly inspired by the Soviet invasion of Czechoslovakia in 1968.

Although some perceive the onset of the LCY decentralization in 1968 as a trigger for the effective overall Yugoslav decentralization, others cite an earlier date, referring to the delegation of control over the economy from the federal organs to the republics that took place in the early 1950s. According to Sabrina Ramet, a direct consequence of these changes was that "by 1965, the federal government no longer had any direct means of control over enterprises."[163] Autarchic tendencies had developed as each republic sought to develop its economic independence, even if it compromised the benefits of a free market. As related by Ramet, "Unnecessary duplications of services as well as productive capability occurred, although the interests of the federal government and of the country at large suffered."[164]

Decentralization of the party and of economic policy led to the development of Yugoslav federalism in practice. These changes came to be reflected in the amendments to the 1963 Constitution, adopted on June 30, 1971.[165] The most important of these amendments changed Article 39, requiring the consent of the federal units (or of their appropriate organs) before the Federal Assembly could adopt the Yugoslav social plan or other laws affecting the Yugoslav economy. In other words, each Yugoslav republic acquired veto power over a range of issues.

Once these constitutional changes were implemented, the Yugoslav federalism progressively became a "contract and participant inter-republican system," in which decision-making power emanated from the periphery rather than the center.[166] The jurisdiction of the federal government was confined to defense, foreign affairs, foreign trade, and the unity of the economic and social system. The devolution of power to the republics was accompanied by changes in the tax system, restricting the direct taxation powers of the federal government to customs and administrative fees. The federal government came to depend on the republics for the greater part of its financing.

---

[163] Ramet, *Nationalism and Federalism in Yugoslavia* (1962-1991), 71.
[164] Ibid.
[165] *Official Gazette of SFRY*, 29/1971.
[166] Ramet, *Nationalism and Federalism in Yugoslavia* (1962-1991), 67.

Although substantial, the constitutional changes of 1971 did not stifle the out-
bursts of nationalism. This time, language sparked the conflict. While most
linguists asserted that Serbo-Croatian was one language, Croatian nationalists
claimed otherwise. They aimed to differentiate the Croatian language from Serbian
(Serbo-Croatian) in order to strengthen their sense of a separate identity.

In 1971, a massive Croat national uprising, termed "Maspok" (short for "mass
movement") or the "Croatian Spring," was mounted, demanding an independent
Croatian literary language. "Maspok" posed the greatest danger to Yugoslavia's
integrity since 1941, having received wide support among the Croats. Importantly,
recognition of a separate Croat language was not the only goal of Croat nationalists. It was accompanied by insistence on exclusive use of Croatian in Croatia's
schools, press, and official communications,[167] which implied eviction of the
Serbian language from Croatia. The Croat nationalists further attempted to
declare Croatia to be the national state of the Croats only,[168] and to reassert that
this state represented a continuation of the medieval Croat kingdom. Tito, who
led the Yugoslav Communist apparatus unchallenged, rejected these requests.
Tito quickly suppressed the Croatian Spring, purging Croatia's Communist party
and other republic institutions.[169] The Yugoslav Communist leadership also
replaced a great portion of the police in Croatia with Serbs, which inadvertently
contributed to the gradual rise of ethnic conflict in the republic of Croatia.

Concurrently, Tito, who was of Croat origin and did not wish to appear unfair to
his compatriots, suppressed Serb intellectuals who rose in response to Croatian
demands, which had directly infringed on Serb rights. The Serb nationalists
requested that Croatia's Serb population (about 15 percent) be educated in their
own language[170] and that the Belgrade media use the Cyrillic script.

---

[167] Ibid., 102; Hondius, *The Yugoslav Community of Nations*, 326-328; Dennison Rusinow, *The Yugoslav Experiment 1948-1974* (London: C Hurst & Co, 1997), 224-225.

[168] Ramet, *Nationalism and Federalism in Yugoslavia (1962-1991)*, 111-115.

[169] For more on the Croatian Spring *see* Burg, *Conflict and Cohesion in Socialist Yugoslavia, Political Decision Making Since 1966*, 27-30. 98-135; Ante Cuvalo, *The Croatian National Movement, 1966-1972*, East European Monographs (New York, 1990); Miko Tripalo, *Hrvatsko proljece* [Croatian Spring] (Zagreb: Globus, 1990); Jovan Kesar, Djuro Bilbija and Nenad Stefanović, *Geneza maspoka u Hrvatskoj* [Genesis of Maspok in Croatia] (Belgrade: Knjizevne novine, 1990).

[170] Burg, "Ethnic Conflict and the Federalization of Socialist Yugoslavia: The Serbo-Croat Conflict," 119-143, 127-128; Hondius, *The Yugoslav Community of Nations*, 326-328; Rusinow, *The Yugoslav Experiment 1948-1974*, 224-225.

The most outspoken was a Serb writer, Dobritsa Chosich, erstwhile a proponent of Yugoslavism as one of the most prominent Serb Communists. Like his Slovene counterpart Edvard Kardelj, Chosich was also transformed into a nationalist. However, while Kardelj came to espouse decentralization, Chosich had consistently opposed it, particularly with regard to Kosovo-Metohia. Dobritsa Chosich came to represent what I would term a "Communist nationalist." Normally an oxymoron, this term describes someone who genuinely believes in the benefits of Communism, centralized in the firm hands of a party leadership, but who also has nationalist sentiments. Ironically, Chosich became known as a Communist dissident as a result of his criticism of the decentralization process. He was expelled from the LCY in 1968.

Mihailo Dyurich, a professor of law at Belgrade University, was another vociferous representative of Serb discontent. His argument was that constitutional devolution of power by means of the 1971 amendments rendered Serbs the most disadvantaged of Yugoslavia's constituent nations and that the republic boundaries had to be adjusted if they were to be regarded as national borders.[171]

Although Tito suppressed the Croat and Serb nationalists in 1971, he was aware that Yugoslavia's future was seriously threatened, which is why he subsequently focused on strengthening the party system. Tito's unquestioned authority allowed him to continue to make the most important decisions and to preserve Yugoslavia. At the same time, Tito allowed further concessions to the nationalist demands, enshrined in the provisions of the 1974 Constitution.[172] By granting the federal sub-units (republics and provinces) a veto power over most federal legislation, the 1974 Constitution provided for a *de facto* confederated constitutional system in Yugoslavia, albeit not fully implemented during Tito's reign. Tito remained the supreme decision-maker.[173]

The Constitution of 1963 limited the presidency of Yugoslavia to two tenures for any one person. Tito was specifically exempted from this provision by the same

---

[171] Mihailo Djurić, "Smišljene smutnje" [Devised confusions], *Anali pravnog fakulteta u Beogradu* XIX, No. 3 (1971), 230-233.

[172] Constitution of the Socialist Federalist Republic of Yugoslavia, 1974, *Official Gazette of SFRY*, 9/1974.

[173] "In reality, the party blanketed the entire country and no federal unit had the right either to tamper with the constantly changing rules and decrees regulating the Titoist version of self-management . . . or to give any encouragement to private enterprise or to Western forms of economic and political freedom. Beloff, *Tito's Flawed Legacy*, 196

article. Thus he became a *de facto* president for life in 1963, which was formalized in the Constitution of 1974. In the same year the tenth congress of LCY elected Josip Broz Tito to be its president without restrictions in terms of the duration of his tenure. Thus he became what some authors termed an uncrowned monarch[174] or a republican constitutional monarch.[175] Tito apparently made a compromise. He secured monarchical powers until his death at the federal level and in return allowed republican nomenclatures to widen their power and to develop mini states.

The 1974 constitution acquired a contractual structure. Any amendment required a two-thirds majority of both chambers of the Federal Assembly (the Federal Chamber and the Chamber of Republics and Provinces[176]), and adoption by all of the six republics and two provincial assemblies (Articles 398-403). At the same time, the constitutions of the federal units no longer had to be in accordance with the federal constitution. The only demand was that they could not be contrary to the federal constitution.

The composition of delegates to chambers of the Federal Assembly was rendered proportional to the federal unit. Each republic had the same number of delegates and the two provinces a lesser but mutually equal number of delegates (Articles 291-292). Prior to the constitutional amendments in 1988, the delegates were representatives of self-management and socio-political organizations, but thereafter they were to be directly elected.

Apart from this vital transformation in the balance of various republics and the federal organs, the 1974 Constitution embodied a set of further legal paradoxes. The constitution stipulated a simultaneous equality of rights for member republics and an inequality in liabilities (federal budget contribution, number of army conscripts, etc.)—or equality of citizens in terms of liabilities (tax payment, army service) and a great inequality in rights concerning decision-making in the

---

[174] Kosta Cavoski, *Half a Century of Distorted Constitutionality in Yugoslavia* (Belgrade: Centre for Serbian Studies, 1997), 14.

[175] Slobodan G. Markovich, "Two Centuries of Convergence or Divergence between Serbia and Western Europe," in S. G. Markovich, E. B. Weaver and V. Pavlovic (eds.), *Challenges to New Democracies in the Balkans* (Belgrade: Cigoja Press, 2004), 114.

[176] Successor to the Chamber of Nationalities, which had no real decision-making power.

On Federal Assembly in the previous period, *see* Edvard Kardelj, *The New Yugoslav Federal Assembly* (Belgrade: Mladost, 1964), 62.

most important federal organs—both houses of the SFRY Parliament, the SFRY Presidency and the Yugoslav Constitutional Court.[177]

The 1974 Yugoslav Constitution has often been described as one of the longest and most complicated world constitutions. In addition to escalating nationalism, the reason for creating such an ambiguous, contradictory, and inefficient constitutional arrangement for Yugoslavia was the so-called inheritance question or the problem of Tito's succession. Tito safeguarded his power so strongly, that he fashioned a system in which any conflict resolution among the republics called for his personal intervention.

Article 333 of the 1974 Constitution declared Tito to be the President of Yugoslavia "without temporal limitation of the mandate." After his death, according to Articles 313-332 of the Constitution, Tito was to be replaced by a nine-person rotating presidency based on the idea of parity, with each of the federal units allocated one seat, plus, *ex officio*, the President of the LCY (Article 321). This system of collective government was first adopted in the 1971 amendments. However the presidency was then envisaged to be even larger, with more seats allocated to a republic (three) than to a province (two).

In brief, the Constitution of 1974 did not settle the inheritance question but bypassed it.[178] It is the constitutional shaping of such an idea that transformed the Yugoslav state of that time into a confederation, where the Communist nomenclature became the bearer of sovereignty in each of the republics.

Ramet praises the decentralization provided by the 1974 Constitution, claiming that it led to improved inter-republican cooperation, particularly in the forum provided by the Federal Assembly and its Chamber of Republics and Provinces,[179] which was proclaimed "the highest organ of government within the framework of the rights and responsibilities of the federation" (Article 282). However, an indisputable fact is that the need for unanimity in adopting legislation led to an increasing use of temporary measures, brought about as a result of the mediation

---

[177] Miodrag Jovicic, ed., *Osnovi novog ustavnog uredjenja Jugoslavije* [Foundations of the constitutional regulation of Yugoslavia] (Belgrade: SANU, 1990), 29.

[178] Even though the office of vice-president had been previously introduced (in 1963), it was abolished four years later.

[179] Ramet, *Nationalism and Federalism in Yugoslavia* (1962-1991), 65.

of the collective presidency, in force after Tito's death in 1980, and other government institutions (Article 356).[180]

The 1974 Constitution, while completing the process of decentralization in terms
of political and economic power, strengthened those provisions that referred
to the country's sovereignty. With ample ambiguity, SFRY was described as
"a federal state, as a state community of voluntarily united peoples and their
socialist republics, as well as socialist autonomous provinces" (Article 1). However,
Article 3 is more direct, stating that this was "a state founded upon sovereignty of
peoples" and not upon sovereignty of member republics and provinces.

This was in line with changes made to the Constitution of the Socialist Republic of
Croatia with the aim of equating the Croats and the Serbs as the constituent peoples
of the republic, thereby rectifying the relevant provisions of the 1963 Constitution.[181]
Similarly, in Bosnia-Herzegovina, the Serbs, Croats, and Muslims were defined as
the constituent peoples of that republic. Muslims were officially recognized as a
constituent nation in 1971 when the regular Yugoslav census was taken.

At the same time, the central leadership rejected the Serb and Croat demands that
the internal boundaries be altered to more closely resemble national boundaries.[182] Instead, the 1974 Constitution strengthened the internal boundaries of the
country. Article 5 expanded the stipulation of the 1963 constitution that required
consent for changes in internal boundaries to all the federal subunits, thereby
including the two autonomous provinces.

Like the republics, the two autonomous provinces had gained a greater degree of
autonomy both from the federal and the republic organs with each amendment
to the constitution, culminating with the Constitution of 1974. Furthermore, the
1974 Constitution had created both a legal and a practical contradiction by

---

[180] Julie Mostov, "Democracy and Decisionmaking" in Dennison Rusinow (ed), *Yugoslavia, A Fractured
Federation* (Washington, DC: The Wilson Center Press, 1988), 105-119: 108-109.

[181] Initially, Article 1 of the 1963 Croatian Constitution stipulated that Croatia was established "in common
struggle with the *other nations of Yugoslavia*," which was changed into "in common struggle with the
Serbian nation and the nationalities in Croatia and and with the other nations and nationalities in
Yugoslavia" [italics added]. Cited in *Hrvatski Tjednik* [Croatian Weekly], September 10, 1971, 1 and in
Ramet, *Nationalism and Federalism in Yugoslavia (1962-1991)*, 112-113.

[182] Steven L Burg, "Republican and Provincial Constitution Making in Yugoslav Politics," *Publius: The Journal
of Federalism* 12 (1982), 135.

declaring the provinces to be simultaneously federal units and a part of the territory of the Republic of Serbia, which itself was a federal unit. The provinces
were proclaimed "a constitutive element of the federation," which transferred
certain elements of statehood to them, implicitly depriving the Republic of Serbia
from exercising these powers on the territory of the provinces.[183] This abnormal
condition *de facto* created two parallel constitutional arrangements in Serbia. The
republic constitution nominally applied to its entire territory, but in practice it
was only relevant to Serbia proper without the northern and southern province.[184]
The provinces obtained the same legal status as the republics and consequently
enjoyed distinct legislative bodies and separate legal systems, as well as their own
executive organs, Supreme Courts, National Banks, Attorneys General, and so on.[185]

Moreover, while the autonomous provinces could independently amend their
constitutions, Serbia could not amend the republic constitution without the consent
of the autonomous provinces (Article 427 of the Constitution of Serbia, 1974).

As a result of such a conflicting legal system, which rendered the republic government hostage to its provinces, the decision-making procedure in Serbia often
resulted in deadlocks. The resentment of Serb intellectual dissidents increased,
but it was contained during Tito's rule when the LCY still had a leading role in
governing Yugoslavia.

Tito addressed the question of the administrative division at the very onset of the
new Yugoslav federation. On May 12, 1945, in a speech to the Founding Congress
of the Communist Party of Serbia, he related his vision of the administrative
arrangement of Yugoslavia:

> Various elements, former accountants and writers, say that Tito and the
> communists tore Serbia into pieces. Serbia is in Yugoslavia, and we do not plan
> to create countries within Yugoslavia that will go to war with each other.

---

[183] Pavle Nikolic, "Socijalisticke autonomne pokrajine i novi ustav" [Socialist autonomous provinces and the
new Constitution], in *Osnovi novog ustavnog uredjenja Jugoslavije* [Foundations of the new Yugoslav
constitutional order], ed. Miodrag Jovicic (Belgrade: SANU, 1990), 55.

[184] Milivoj Draskovic, "Specificnost ustavnog polozaja SR Srbije" [Specificity of the constitutional position of
SR Serbia]i in *Osnovi novog ustavnog uredjenja* Jugoslavije [Foundations of the new constitutional regulation of Yugoslavia], ed. Miodrag Jovicic (Belgrade: SANU, 1990), 74.

[185] Popovic, *Short Essays on Serbian Constitutional Problems*, 18.

If Bosnia and Herzegovina is sovereign, if they have their own federal unit, then we haven't dismembered Serbia but created happier Serbs in Bosnia, as happy as the Croats and Muslims are. *It is simply a question of administrative division.* I do not want there to be dividing borders in Yugoslavia. As I have said a hundred times, I want borders to be those that will unite our peoples.[186]

Although one cannot verify the candor of Tito's sentiments, his speech, as the supreme leader of Yugoslavia, certainly represents an official deliberation of the Yugoslav administrative boundaries. The people of Yugoslavia were constantly reassured that the internal division of the country would never be used in such a manner as to transform the created federal units into sovereign states.

As explained by Yosipovich, a Yugoslav jurist writing in 1963,

The term administrative, that is the administrative-territorial unit, was used in laws and other texts in 1952. Since then, the term community was used more frequently, and currently the term *socio-political community* is in use.[187]

In brief, the Communist component of internal boundaries was emphasized. The Yugoslav peoples were repeatedly told that the internal boundaries served exclusively administrative purposes. At the same time, the decentralization process made the purported administrative boundaries more real over time, albeit intertwined in an increasingly complex constitutional arrangement.

External factors contributed to Yugoslavia's integrity. In the Cold War framework, Yugoslavia enjoyed the "non-aligned" position, benefiting from vast economic aid from the West.[188] As Beloff elucidates:

The system would have collapsed under the weight of its own extravagance had the Yugoslav leadership not suddenly been showered with manna from heaven, in the form of apparently limitless supplies of petro-dollars.[189]

---

[186] "Iz govora Generalnog Sekretara KPJ JB Tita na osnivackom kongresu KP Srbije" [From the speech of the General Secretary of the CPY Josip Broz Tito at the Founding Congress of the Communist Party of Serbia], May 8, 1945 (Belgrade, 1972), 213 [Emphasis added]; also printed in Petranović and Zečević, eds., *Yugoslav federalism, ideas and reality,* Vol. 1, 1914-1943, 159.

[187] Dushan Yosipovich, *Принципи политичко-територијалне поделе у Југославији* [Principles of political-cal-teritorial division in Yugoslavia] (Belgrade: Rad, 1963), 4.

[188] Cold War policy will not be discussed in greater detail in this book.

[189] Beloff, *Tito's Flawed Legacy,* 199.

A LEGAL GEOGRAPHY OF YUGOSLAVIA'S DISINTEGRATION

At the same time, mismanagement of foreign aid exacerbated the economic situation in the country. According to the Yugoslav economist Mihailo Crnobrnja, the political will to implement serious changes, such as those proposed by the 1983 Kreigher Commission, made up of eminent politicians and experts from all the Yugoslav republics and autonomous provinces, was missing. Crnobrnja also criticizes the industrialized nations that provided aid to Yugoslavia. They reprogrammed the past debt and granted further loans to Yugoslavia in the 1980s without conditioning their assistance with a need to apply market-oriented reforms.[190] The end result was a worsened economic situation in Yugoslavia, combined with the reluctance of the international community to support true reforms in the late 1980s:

> Having burned their fingers with Yugoslavia on the occasion of the stabilization program, the West would understandably be reluctant and cautious in its assistance on the next occasion, when a true and deeper reform would be taking place.[191]

The lack of authoritative leadership following Tito's death in 1980, compounded by a declining economy burdened with a massive foreign debt, unleashed the forces of nationalism, represented in inter-republican rivalries. As Crnobrnja explains, "Rather than blaming systemic causes for poor economic performance, because that would have involved self-criticism as well, the popular line became that others were to blame."[192]

Open rivalries became possible with the departure of Yugoslavia's dictator and the crumbling of the Communist system, a process that was simultaneously taking place in all Eastern Europe and the Soviet Union, inducing an end to the Cold War. After all, with all the privileges of a non-aligned country, Yugoslavia was still a Communist state, where Tito simultaneously held positions as head of government, of the army, and of the party, in "a classic case of the dictatorship of the proletariat, as enunciated by Lenin and as practiced by Stalin in the Soviet Union."[193] In this system the state was also the party. Significantly, towards the

---

[190] Mihailo Crnobrnja, *The Yugoslav Drama*, 2nd edition (Montreal: McGill-Queen's University Press, 1996), particularly 84-88.

[191] Ibid., 86.

[192] Ibid., 88.

[193] Singleton, *A Short History of the Yugoslav Peoples*, 211.

end of his life, in 1978, Tito admitted: "There is no Yugoslavia. . . . There is no party any more."[194]

* * *

The national awakening of the Yugoslav peoples in the nineteenth century was a reflection, a ripple of a greater European movement. However, instead of establishing nation-states, Slovenes, Croats, and Serbs created a joint, multinational state in 1918. In addition to an indigenous movement for unification, outside powers played a prominent role in this process. The South Slav remnants of the two great empires—the Austro-Hungarian and the Ottoman, with the exception of Bulgaria, and the addition of the small Serb state of Montenegro, became anchored onto the Kingdom of Serbia, transforming it into a new state.

The internal arrangement of the First Yugoslavia changed several times in a relatively short period (1918-1941), never to the satisfaction of all of its constituents. During the two World Wars, Yugoslavia's peoples were, for the most part, each other's enemies.

The post-World War II, Communist Yugoslavia represented a starkly different state context, where principles of nationalism and democracy became invalidated by the new ideology. While the internal divisions of the state were relatively constant in Tito's Yugoslavia, their legal significance was not. Constitutional changes produced an ever-more complicated and dysfunctional arrangement, most vividly represented by the 1974 Constitution. Yugoslavia's unifying element was Tito's dictatorial rule and the Cold War framework that called for a status quo.

In the early 1990s, the aims of the reawakened nationalists with respect to the shared Yugoslav territory once again diverged. To be more precise, they contradicted each other with regard to territorial division, repeating the scenario produced in this historical overview on more than one occasion. The Serb drive for centralized state structure, as a practical means of maintaining their geographically dispersed nation in one state, once again stood in blatant contrast to the generally separatist national policy of some other Yugoslav ethnic groups, namely the Slovenes, the Croats, and the Albanians, who saw Yugoslavia as a transitional phase towards full national independence.

---

[194]   Jasper Ridley, *Tito, A Biography* (London: Constable, 1994), 409.

The (Self-) Determination of the Yugoslav Peoples

4.1. Introduction

In assessing the application of the right to self-determination in the case of the former Yugoslavia, one must first turn to the peoples of Yugoslavia and ask what was their (self-) determination, that is, what did they want? This question is treacherously simple. It requires a definition of the "peoples of Yugoslavia," which can be set only arbitrarily, since the legal interpretation of peoples with regard to the right to self-determination is vague.[1]

The Constitution of the Socialist Federalist Republic of Yugoslavia (SFRY) limits "the right to self-determination, including secession" to six Yugoslav constituent peoples/nations:[2] Slovenes, Croats, Muslims, Serbs, Montenegrins and Macedonians (Article 1). Yugoslav "nationalities," the largest of which were the Albanians, did not enjoy the constitutional right to self-determination, including the right to secession (to be effected by means of constitutional amendments). As explained earlier,[3] Yugoslav constitutional law treated only the six constituent nations as "peoples" in the legal sense. The Arbitration Commission, set up by the European Community in 1991 to provide legal advice in the framework of the International peace conference on Yugoslavia, acted inconsistently in this matter, failing to provide a different definition of "the people" in terms of title to right to self-determination.[4]

---

[1] See Chapter 1: *Legal Context of Yugoslavia's Disintegration: Sovereignty and Self-Determination of Peoples.* Please also note that this book does not aim to explain the cause of the war in the former Yugoslavia since this is not of direct relevance.

[2] The term "narod" [народ] in Serbo-Croatian denotes both "a people" and "a nation."

[3] See Chapter 3: *Yugoslavias' Administrative Boundaries (1918-1991).*

[4] For more, *see* Chapter 5: *International Recognition of the (Former) Yugoslav Republics.*

Another problem lies in determining the will of the peoples in essentially undemocratic regimes, such as Serbia or Croatia of 1990s, or in multinational entities such as Bosnia and Herzegovina where one ethnic group (Bosnian Muslims, also termed Bosniak), while waging war against the other two ethnic groups, often claimed to represent the entire population. Moreover, the assumption that elites represent the public or that the official statements reflect honest opinions is imperfect, if the only one available.

Finally, adjectives assigned to various "peoples" have morally strengthened their "right" to self-determination and influenced the formulation of the recognition policy, which ultimately rendered constitutionally illegal secessions successful. This practice had been initiated by the late 1980s, when outside commentators divided the key actors into the (Communist) conservatives—that is, those who were less prone to change—and the (market-oriented) liberals, who were open to change. The Serbs were generally labelled as the conservatives and the Croats and Slovenes as the liberals. However, if the change is defined as reforms rendering Yugoslavia into a functional market/state, then these labels could easily be reversed. As Susan Woodward argues:

> Those whose views might seem more liberal and Western were in fact the most conservative about change, the most antireform, and the most nationalistic. They insisted on exclusive priority to what they defined as the national interests (and therefore national rights) of their republic.[5]

Woodward stresses that the Yugoslav economy differed from that of other East European countries because it had participated in Western markets (1965 full member of World Trade Organization predecessor, the General Agreement on Tariffs and Trade; 1971 associate member of the European Community; 1979 member of the European Free Trade Association) and was decentralized; therefore "it was not the central government or the poorer areas that had political and economic privileges to protect, but rather the republican politicians, especially those in the wealthier and more western regions."[6]

A most poignant example is when, in June 1985, the Slovene and the Croatian republican parliaments rejected three laws dealing with the reform of foreign

---

[5] Susan L. Woodward, *Balkan Tragedy; Chaos and Dissolution after the Cold War* (Washington, D.C.: The Brookings Institution, 1995), 61.

[6] Ibid.

economic relations, which, *inter alia*, proposed to end the stalemate in federal decision-making by introducing majority rule. The Slovenes and the Croats acted against measures proposed by the International Monetary Fund,[7] at the time strongly opposing the economic model that allowed the European Union member states to achieve faster growth.

Nevertheless, political compromises continued to be made within Yugoslavia. In October 1988, the League of Communists of Yugoslavia (LCY) central committee "in a deal that omitted or modified all amendments to the federal constitution that Slovenia found objectionable . . . approved the Serbian parliament's revisions, reducing to provincial status what Serbia claimed was the *de facto* republican status of the two provinces."[8] This decision at the federal level paved the way for Serbia's effective if not *de jure* revocation of Kosovo's autonomy.[9]

However only a year later, with the end of the Cold War and the subsequent unleashing of nationalism throughout Eastern Europe, the Slovenes made the first direct steps towards Yugoslavia's dismemberment. The process of constitutional revisions, originally aimed at enhancing the joint state's efficiency,[10] was reversed.[11]

4.2. Slovenia's Bypass to the European Union via Secession

On September 27, 1989, the Slovenian Assembly adopted provisions requiring the assembly's agreement before federal authorities could intervene in Slovenian affairs as a result of any alleged "emergency" situation within the republic (Amendment LXIII), thereby appropriating legal powers that the SFRY Constitution

---

[7] *See* Woodward, *Balkan Tragedy*, 74.

[8] Ibid., 94.

[9] *See* pages 232-236 below.

[10] On November 25, 1988, the Yugoslav Assembly adopted Amendments IX-XLVII to the SFRY Constitution, mainly removing the inefficient provisions of the failed Yugoslav "self-management" economic model. Based on these amendments the republics had the obligation to align their constitutions.

[11] According to Robert M. Hayden: "It became clear in 1989, however, that constitutional proposals being put forth and adopted first in Slovenia and then a year later in Croatia were meant to ensure that there would be no workable state." Robert M. Hayden, *Blueprints for a House Divided; The Constitutional Logic of the Yugoslav Conflicts* (Ann Arbor: The University of Michigan Press, 2000), xii.

vested in the federal authorities (the SFRY Presidency).[12] The Slovenes argued that this was a preventive measure,[13] taken in reaction to the federal presidency's declaration of emergency measures for the Serbian province Kosovo and Metohia[14] earlier that year.

Asserting the right to "defend the republic's position and right" by undertaking measures against federal acts that infringed on the rights of Slovenia, including invalidation of such acts,[15] the Slovenes indirectly invoked the nullification doctrine,[16] upon which two important building blocks of the future Slovene state were founded. The first was the *de facto* creation of the Slovene National Army via Constitutional Law for the implementation of Amendment XCVI to the Slovene Constitution and the Constitutional Law for the implementation of Amendments XCVI and XCVII to the Slovene Constitution in the field of National Defense, which elevated the authority of the territorial defense forces[17] of Slovenia, while simultaneously providing that Slovene recruits will no longer serve in the Yugoslav National Army, "unless the recruit so requests."[18] Secondly, by Amendment XCIX, the Slovenes proclaimed the right to independently maintain relations with other states and international organizations, the right that was in the first instance used

---

[12]　*See* Articles 313, 329 and 330 of the SFRY Constitution and "The Opinion of the Yugoslav Constitutional Court on the Contradiction of Amendments IX-XC to the Slovene Constitution with SFRY Constitution" [Мишљење Уставног суда Југославије о супротности амандмана IX-XC на устав СР Словеније с уставом СФРЈ], January 18, 1990, *SFRY Official Gazette [Службени лист СФРЈ]*, February 23, 1990, vol. 46, no. 10.

[13]　*Danas*, Vol. 8, No, 389 (1989), p. 12.

[14]　The issue of Kosovo riots is to be discussed in Chapter 6 of this book, *Changing Borders by Force*.

[15]　Amendments XLVI and LXII.

[16]　The nullification doctrine, pronounced at a time of South Carolina's attempted secession from the United States in 1830s, "was based on the theory that the Union is a voluntary compact of states and that the federal government has no right to exercise powers not specifically assigned to it by the U.S. Constitution." [*The Columbia Electronic Encyclopedia*, 6th ed., entry: nullification (New York: Columbia University Press, 2005)] However, the federal authorities prevailed in asserting their supremacy. For more, *see* C. S. Boucher, *The Nullification Controversy in South Carolina* (1916, repr. 1968); C. M. Wiltse, *John C. Calhoun: Nullifier, 1829–1839* (1949); W. W. Freehling, ed., *The Nullification Era* (1967); M. D. Peterson, *Olive Branch and Sword: The Compromise of 1833* (1982).

[17]　Territorial defense forces were created under Tito's 1969 defense review and "designed to present a systematically organized, prolonged, guerrilla resistance to any invader," with the primary aim of avoiding a replica of the 1968 USSR's invasion of Czechoslovakia. Territorial defense forces, including weaponry, had been under republican authority, financed from republican, local, and enterprise revenues. *See* Woodward, *Balkan Tragedy*, 26.

[18]　Amendments to the Constitution of SR Slovenia, *Uradni list Republike Slovenije* [Official Gazette of the Republic of Slovenia], numbers 37/90, 4/91, 10/91.

to campaign for recognition of Slovene independence. The Yugoslav Constitutional Court declared these provisions to be "contrary to the SFRY Constitution."[19]

However, the Slovenes deemed both these and all future acts towards secession[20] legally justifiable on the basis of Amendment X, giving the Republic of Slovenia the formal right to secede from Yugoslavia.[21] The Slovene interpretation of this Amendment was that the application of the right to secession was to be exclusively regulated by the Slovene National Assembly by a process delineated in Amendment LXXII to the Slovene Constitution, which was also declared unconstitutional by the Yugoslav Constitutional Court.

While affirming the Slovene right to self-determination, including secession, the SFRY Constitutional Court stressed that this right was to be equally enjoyed by all the Yugoslav (constituent) "peoples and their socialist republics." In the reasoning of the Court, the process relating to the application of "the right to self-determination, including secession" affected not only Slovenia but all parts of Yugoslavia, invoking questions of the composition of the SFRY and its borders, internal material, and other relations, SFRY's position as a member of the international

---

19   Мишљење Уставног суда Југославије о супротности амандмана IX-XC на устав СР Словеније с уставом СФРЈ [The Opinion of the Yugoslav Constitutional Court on the Contradiction of Amendments IX-XC to the Slovene Constitution with SFRY Constitution], January 18, 1990, *SFRY Official Gazette*, February 23, 1990, vol. 46, no. 10, 593; Мишљење Уставног суда Југославије о супротности уставног закона за спровођење уставних амандмана XCVI и XCVII на устав Републике Словеније у области народне одбране са уставом СФРЈ [The Opinion of the Yugoslav Constitutional Court on the Contradiction of Constitutional Law for the Implementation of Constitutional Amendments XCVI and XCVII to the Slovene Constitution in the field of national defense with SFRY Constitution], October 2, 1991, and "The Opinion of the Yugoslav Constitutional Court on the Contradiction of Constitutional Amendment XCIX to the Slovene Constitution with SFRY Constitution" [Мишљење Уставног суда Југославије о супротности уставног амандмана XCIX на устав Републике Словеније с Уставом СФРЈ], October 2, 1991, in Milovan Buzadjich, *Сецесија бивших југословенских републике у светлости одлука Уставног суда Југославије; Збирка докумената с уводном расправом* [Secession of former Yugoslav republics in light of decisions of the Yugoslav Constitutional Court; Collection of Documents with Introductory Discussion] (Belgrade: Official Gazette of SRY, 1994), 77-88. *Note:* The Constitutional Court of Yugoslavia, while interpreting the constitutional right of self-determination, reiterated that this issue resided within its direct jurisdiction, and that it was therefore the only institution that could provide its valid interpretation.

20   On July 2, 1990, the Slovenian Assembly adopted a Declaration on the Sovereignty of the Republic of Slovenia, and on October 5, 1990 the Slovenian Assembly enacted amendments that invalidated all of Yugoslav constitutional legislation inconsistent with the Slovenian Constitution, placing the Slovene (republican) Constitution above the Yugoslav (federal) Constitution in all areas.

21   Amendment X provided for the "complete and undeniable right" to "self-determination, including the right to secession."

community and rights, material and other obligations determined by international agreements.

In the opinion of the Court, the Slovene people could not act unilaterally but only in agreement with all Yugoslav nations and republics. Their right to self-determination could only be realized "in a manner determined by the SFRY Constitution." In practice, considering that the Yugoslav Constitution did not provide any mechanism for the implementation of the right to secession, this process would take the form of constitutional amendments, based on a negotiated agreement of all the constituent nations, since any change in republican boundaries required consent of all federal units [Articles 5(1) and 5(3) of the SFRY Constitution] while the SFRY Assembly decided on any changes to the (external) SFRY borders [Articles 283(4) and 285(6)]. Although the Court did not implicitly call for constitutional amendments as a means of realizing the right to secession in its decisions on the 1989 Slovene amendments, it did do so when adjudicating the constitutionality of certain provisions of the Law on Plebiscite on Sovereignty and Independence of the Republic of Slovenia:

> The Assembly of the Republic of Slovenia cannot adopt acts and undertake measures . . . that lead to independence and dissociation of the Republic of Slovenia from [the SFRY] until the SFRY Constitution is amended, pursuant to the procedure determined therein, that is, until the procedure for negotiating the future inter-republican relations is unanimously determined on the basis of the SFRY Constitution.[22]

In conclusion, the Constitutional Court of Yugoslavia unequivocally ruled that it is the Yugoslav Federal Assembly that decides on any changes of internal state boundaries, upon obtaining consent of all the republics and provinces. Unilateral secessionist acts were not permitted according to the Yugoslav Constitution. A legally applied right to secession required constitutional amendments achieved by a negotiated agreement of all the constituent nations.

---

[22] "Одлука о оцењивању уставности одредаба чл. 4 и чл. 10 Закона о плебисциту о самосталности и независности Републике Словенија" [Decision on Evaluating the Constitutionality of the Provisions of Articles 4 and 10 of the Law on Plebiscite on the Sovereignty and Independence of the Republic of Slovenia], January 10, 1991, *Службени гласник СФРЈ* [Official Gazette of SFRY], November 7, 1991, in Buzadjich, *Secession of former Yugoslav republics in light of decisions of the Yugoslav Constitutional Court,* 95-97.

In a number of deliberations, the Yugoslav Constitutional Court concluded that all republics, with the exception of Montenegro, had violated the federal constitution in their 1988/89 amendments that had the goal of aligning the republican constitutions with the 1988 amendments to the federal constitution. However, these violations were mainly technical, with serious deviation from the letter and the spirit of the SFRY Constitution made only by Slovenia. As a consequence of the Court's rulings, on March 27, 1990, the Yugoslav federal assembly passed, by majority vote, a resolution mandating that the provisions of republican and provincial constitutions that had been determined by the court to be contrary to the federal constitution must be brought into agreement with the latter document within three months.[23]

The Slovenes did not abide by the Yugoslav Constitutional Court's decisions. They challenged the court's competence in this matter based on procedural reasons.[24] According to the Yugoslav Constitution (Article 378[25]), the Constitutional Court of Yugoslavia could be asked for "an opinion" on constitutionality of legal acts, but it was instead asked for a judgment ("a decision"). The Court accepted the request but issued an opinion, remaining within its constitutionally granted jurisdiction.

The purpose of the semantic differentiation (the use of the words "opinion" and "not contrary to" when adjudicating higher legal acts of the republics, compared to the words "decision" and "in conformity with," when ruling on regulations) in the Yugoslav constitutional system was to limit the executive authority of the Constitutional Court with the goal of inducing political compromise deemed necessary in a multiethnic state. As Milovan Buzadjich, the president of the Yugoslav Constitutional Court at the time of pronounced opinions on the constitutionality of Slovene and other 1989/1990 amendments to the SFRY Constitution, explains, when the Court finds certain republican or provincial laws contrary to federal legislation, a political agreement of the SFRY National Assembly and republic and provincial assemblies is required to bring legal effect to the Court's

---

23 Hayden, *Blueprints for a House Divided*, 46.

24 Outlined in "Separate Opinion of Judges Ivan Kristan and Radko Močivnik to The Opinion of the Yugoslav Constitutional Court on the Contradiction of Amendments IX-XC to the Slovene Constitution with SFRY Constitution," reprinted in Buzadjich, *Secession of former Yugoslav republics in light of decisions of the Yugoslav Constitutional Court*, 77-79.

25 SFRY Constitution, Article 378: "The Constitutional Court of Yugoslavia gives its opinion to the Assembly of the SFRY as to whether a republican or provincial constitution is contrary to the Constitution of the SFRY."

ruling.[26] However, the Slovenes chose to reinterpret the realm of legal compromise as a right of the Slovenian Assembly to enact amendments exclusively of other Yugoslav institutions. As enunciated by Miran Potrč, the president of the Slovenian Assembly and its Constitutional Commission, "not one federal authority has the authority to participate with its advice in the procedure for amending the republican constitution" while the opinion of the Yugoslav Constitutional court on this matter "had no legal effect."[27]

In defying the decisions of the Yugoslav Constitutional Court on a procedural basis, the Slovenes indirectly refuted the substance of the matter as well. The court's scope of jurisdiction was based on Article 206 of the SFRY Constitution, which specified that "republican constitutions and provincial constitutions may not be contrary to" the constitution of the Socialist Federal Republic of Yugoslavia (SFRY), and Article 207 (as amended on November 25, 1988), which provides that "republican and provincial laws and other regulations . . . may not be contrary to federal laws." Although the phrase "not contrary" does not clearly set the hierarchy of the Yugoslav constitutional system, Hayden maintains that any ambiguity is resolvable using the necessary logic of a federal system:

> [T]he provisions of the federal constitution must override conflicting provisions in the constitutions of constituent units of the federation. If this rule were not to hold, then the federal constitution would become literally meaningless, since its provisions could be overridden, and hence effectively repealed, by any of the constituent parts of the federation.[28]

If the federal constitution were not paramount, as elaborated in the most famous American constitutional decision, *Marbury v. Madison* (1803),[29] it could also be amended by unilateral action of its constituents.

However, the Slovenes were not the only ones to question the supremacy of federal authorities. One could argue that all the republican political decision makers

---

26 For more, *see* Buzadjich, *Secession of former Yugoslav republics in light of decisions of the Yugoslav Constitutional Court*, 16-21.

27 *Borba* daily newspaper, September 28, 1989, 1.

28 Hayden, *Blueprints for a House Divided*, 39.

29 "Certainly all those who have framed written constitutions contemplate them as forming the fundamental and paramount law of the nation, and consequently the theory of every such government must be, that an act of the legislature repugnant to the constitution is void." U.S. Supreme Court, Marbury v. Madison, 5 U.S. 137 (1803).

ignored the federal judicial decisions by not taking steps towards ensuring their execution or by later enacting amendments that resembled those made by Slovenia in September 1989. At the time, the President of the Constitutional Court admitted that the refusal of the republics to comply with the court order illustrated "the domination of the political over the legal sectors."[30]

In retrospect, insufficient support for the Court's decisions within Yugoslavia as well as by the international community could be viewed as a missed opportunity for conflict resolution, especially since the Court acknowledged the existence of a legal path to secession and called for negotiations, as did the Canadian Supreme Court several years later (1998), using strikingly similar reasoning.[31] In rendering this decision, the Yugoslav Constitutional Law disregarded the Communist interpretation of the right to self-determination as the right that was used once and for all in the (re)creation of Yugoslavia after the Second World War.[32]

According to the Yugoslav Constitutional Court President, Milovan Buzadjich, the reason why the ruling on the Slovene amendments spoke of the right to self-determination of peoples *and* republics of Yugoslavia is that in case the peoples decided to secede, all republics would need to agree on any changes of frontiers.[33] Indeed, as Radan emphasizes, "nothing in the 1974 Constitution explicitly tied the rights of self-determination and secession to the republics."[34] Yet, instead of espousing the call made by the Yugoslav Constitutional Court for amendments to the constitution to outline the procedure for eventual secession as a framework for negotiating a peaceful resolution of the Yugoslav conflict, the international actors later supported the Slovene interpretation of the constitutionally granted "right to self-determination, including secession."

Since in the Communist context the state and the party were one, the Slovenes undertook first political action regarding future Yugoslav "reform" at the Extraordinary Fourteenth Congress of the League of Communists of Yugoslavia (LCY)

---

30   D. Shtrbats, "The Court Assesses and Rules," *Politika: The International Weekly*, April 14-21, 1990, 3.

31   *Reference re: Secession of Quebec* [1998] 2 SCR 217. For more detail, see Chapter 1: *Legal Context of Yugoslavia's Disintegration: Sovereignty and Self-Determination of Peoples.*

32   *See* Chapter 3: *Yugoslavias' Administrative Boundaries (1918-1991).*

33   Author's Interview with Milovan Buzadjich, Belgrade, August 24, 2005.

34   *See* Peter Radan, "The Legal Regulation of Secession: Lessons from Yugoslavia," Paper presented at the International conference on Legal and Political Solutions to Disputes over Sovereignty—From Kosovo to Quebec, held at Belgrade University, July 7-10, 2005.

in January 1990. The Slovene representatives proposed that the LCY be transformed into a union of "independent and free republican communist parties"—a "League of Leagues." Their proposal to "confederalize" the LCY failed to obtain a congress majority.

At the time, Serbia's president Slobodan Miloshevich[35] accused all those who proposed the decentralization of LCY of calling for a "war among Yugoslav communists . . . and a war among Yugoslav nations."[36] The Slovene Communists, followed by the Croatian delegation, abandoned the Congress, effectively dismantling the LCY.[37] The Slovene Communist leader Milan Kučan then remarked: "When we left, the party ceased to exist."[38]

In republic elections across Yugoslavia in 1990, victory went to parties with nationalist platforms, led by (former) communists,[39] with the exception of Bosnia-Herzegovina where three nationalist parties, representing the Muslims, Serbs, and Croats, governed in a trilateral power-sharing arrangement.[40] However, although on the surface the anti-nationalist, pro-Yugoslav parties gained only marginal support throughout Yugoslavia, a significant part of the electorate, and Serbian voters in particular, both within and outside Serbia voted precisely in this manner. Glenny stresses that in Serbia, Miloshevich's party gained only 48 percent of the votes despite the fact that the opposition had "no money, very little access to the media and a catastrophic lack of experience."[41] In other words, the Miloshevich regime, even at the apex of its political power, did not reflect the majority public opinion, while the Croatian Serb electorate, for instance, overwhelmingly voted for the (Croat/civic) Communists rather than for the Serb

---

[35] Often spelled as Milosevic in English.

[36] *Associated Press Report*, January 21, 1990.

[37] "Extraordinary LCY Congress," *BBC Summary of World Broadcasts*, EE/0675/C/1, January 30, 1990.

[38] *Washington Post*, February 4, 1990, A01.

[39] Milan Kučan, the former leader of the Slovene League of Communists received 44 percent of the vote in the first round and 58 percent in the second. The government was formed by a coalition of parties with a pro-independence platform, which jointly held 55 percent of the vote but individually taking 3.5 percent to 13 percent of the electorate. The largest party in the coalition received fewer votes than the Communist party alone. In Croatia, the Croatian Democratic Union won 41.5 percent of the vote and the League of Communists in alliance with smaller left-wing parties 37 percent of the vote. The government was formed as a grand coalition of all but the Serbian Democratic party.

[40] For more on republican elections and results, *see* Woodward, *Balkan Tragedy*, 119-123.

[41] Misha Glenny, *The Fall of Yugoslavia; The Third Balkan War*, 3rd rev. ed. (New York: Penguin Books, 1996), 41.

national party (Serbian Democratic Party),[42] in hopes that their vote would buttress the integrity of Yugoslavia. The nationalists in Croatia and Slovenia also found a respectable opponent in the "national" Communist parties of their own.[43]

The newly elected republican leaders met in a series of summits in the first half of 1991.[44] However, no agreement could be reached between Croats and Slovenes, officially calling for a confederation, and Serbs, demanding a centralized federal state, despite compromise-seeking proposals by the presidents of Bosnia-Herzegovina and Macedonia, who feared the possibility of a military conflict in a multiethnic environment.

While these summits were still under way, Slovenia and Croatia announced their intention to secede from Yugoslavia no later than June 26, 1991. According to Misha Glenny:

> Slovenia, which was bound to Yugoslavia by markets but less by blood or by political inclination, was unable to disguise its impatience with the idea of any Yugoslavia even before these talks were really under way.[45]

Prior to seceding, Slovenia had delivered on its election promises by stopping the bulk of its payments to the Federal Fund for Underdeveloped Regions and, as explained above, by legislating that military duty be performed only on Slovene territory, ignoring the decision of the Yugoslav Constitutional Court that such provisions were unconstitutional and therefore illegal.

The Slovene leadership claimed legality of action based on the result of a plebiscite, held on December 23, 1990, with a question "Should the Republic of Slovenia become an autonomous and independent state?" In a turnout of 93.2 percent of the electorate, it passed with 88.5 percent.[46]

---

[42] This is shown by the victory of the League of Communists of Croatia in majority Serb municipalities.

[43] The Croat nationalists, represented by the Croatian Democratic Union (HDZ), usurped all power thanks to the majority electoral system. For election results in Croatia and Slovenia, *see* note 39.

[44] For a summary of these summit meetings *see* "Discussions Between the President or Presidents of the Presidencies of the Yugoslav Republics," in *Yugoslav Survey* 32, no. 2 (1991), 32-38; Momir Bulatović, *Pravila ćutanja; istiniti politički triler sa poznatim završetkom* [Rules of Silence; A True Political Thriller with a Familiar Ending] (Belgrade: Narodna knjiga, 2004), 24-42.

[45] Glenny, *The Fall of Yugoslavia*, 86.

[46] *See* Woodward, *Balkan Tragedy*, 139.

In the opinion of the Slovene Secretary for International Cooperation and future Minister of Foreign Affairs, Dimitrij Rupel, this result gave the Slovene Parliament "a mandate to take the necessary measures, within a six-month period, to establish the statehood of the Republic of Slovenia and enter into negotiations on future relations with the other Yugoslav republics."[47] This is the inverse procedure from one advocated by the Yugoslav Constitutional Court or the Canadian Supreme Court, which stipulate that negotiations be conducted as a means of arriving at a consensual realization of the right of secession.

On October 4, 1990, the day before the Slovene Parliament created a unilaterally imposed *de facto* confederation by rendering the Slovene Constitution a higher act than the SFRY Constitution and a month before holding a plebiscite on secession, the Croat and Slovene leadership presented a joint proposal for restructuring Yugoslavia into a confederation, along the model of the European Community,[48] elaborated by Slovene State Secretary Rupel:

> We advocate solutions similar to the Benelux countries and the European Community . . . The confederal organization of Yugoslavia means that all the Yugoslav states are its legal successors. In this context, we invoke the Vienna Convention on the succession of states in light of international agreements. All international agreements referring solely to Slovene territory will be passed to the Republic of Slovenia. In view of all the other bilateral and multilateral international agreements, Slovenia is prepared to reach agreement with the other party on their continued validity. As far as international borders are concerned, Slovenia advocates the consistent respect for the principles of the Helsinki Final Act on the inviolability of the existing borders in Europe. With regard to the border between the Yugoslav states, Slovenia resolutely opts for the validity and immutability of the existing borders, with the provision that this issue will have to be regulated by an international agreement.[49]

---

[47] Dimitrij Rupel, "Slovenia and the World," *Review of International Affairs* XLII (Belgrade, February 5, 1991), 13.

[48] "A confederal model among the south Slavic states," *Review of International Affairs* 41, no. 973 (Belgrade, October 1990), 11.

[49] Rupel, "Slovenia and the World," *Review of International Affairs*, 13.

The Croat-Slovene proposal, titled "Model of a Confederacy in Yugoslavia,"[50] amounted to an alliance of independent states that would be looser than the European Community (now European Union), with separate diplomatic missions abroad, separate defense forces, and weak common institutions. The benefits of the model included a common market, a customs union, and the possibility of joint projects and cooperation in areas such as environmental protection, but the lack of enforcement mechanisms rendered these benefits a nullity. According to Hayden, that the proposed model "was actually never more than a constitutional sham, adoption of which would have simply ratified the demise of the country"[51] is most evident from the Transitional and Concluding Provisions providing for an easy exit from the "common state":

2. After the agreement would be in force for ten "(or five?)" years, or at any time after that, the states members would, at the request of any of them, consult among themselves concerning the revision of the agreement or the dissolution of the confederacy.
3. Depending on the further development of European integration, the states members of the confederacy may, before the period envisioned, individually or together, by individual decision or that of the council of ministers, leave or dissolve the confederacy and seek acceptance in the European community.[52]

In a similar vein, the Slovenes, while declaring themselves positively towards the proposal made by the Bosnian and Macedonian leaders for a reformed confederal Yugoslavia,[53] which included the option that the joint agreement could be revised every five or ten years (Part VI), refused even functions such as joint defense, proposing instead "joint command" of separate armed forces[54] that would be difficult to apply in practice. In an interview given in 2000, the Slovene president Milan Kučan openly stated that the Bosnian/Macedonian proposal could only have been a "time schedule for the disassociation of the country that could

---

50   For a detailed analysis of the "Model of a Confederacy in Yugoslavia," *see* Hayden, *Blueprints for a House Divided*, 53-65.
51   Ibid., 17.
52   Cited in Ibid., 60.
53   Izetbegovic-Gligorov Platform, printed in English in *Focus*, Special Issue, January 14, 1992, 82-86.
54   Kiro Gligorov, "Podela zivog mesa" [Dividing Living Flesh], Interview, "Witnesses of Yugoslavia's Disintegration," *Radio Free Europe* (accessed February 5, 2005); available from http://www.danas.org/svjedoci/html/Kiro_Gligorov.html.

possibly prevent a conflict, even war," and "a shield for Slovenia to terminate its transition period and prepare everything for the independence in June 1991."[55]

The declaratory nature of the Slovene support for a confederate arrangement is also shown by the Slovene refusal "even to consider the EC [European Community] proposal[56] for a customs union and any other post-Yugoslav economic relations among the former republics that would require recreating what it had fought against since 1985-87; that there be no administrative apparatus or institutions in common."[57] The Slovene representatives strongly believed that their interest lay in acting internationally "as an equal among equals, as an international-legal entity" and that its independence was "an instrument for its inclusion as an equal member of the European community of nations and states."[58] However, the sentiment of the Slovene people appears to have been more nuanced. According to the opinion polls, the majority of Slovenes, and in fact the majority of all Yugoslav citizens, favored some type of a common structure among Yugoslav peoples.[59]

In simple terms, the Slovene interest in independence was chiefly economic. The Slovene ethnos lived compactly and very few Slovenes resided in other Yugoslav republics. Speaking a Slavic language different from Serbo-Croatian, the Slovenes developed their culture in the Yugoslav framework, taking full advantage of the Communist parole of promotion of diversity.[60] This important policy of the Communist Yugoslavia to suppress nationalism of nations deemed threatening to its integrity, namely the Serbs but also Croats, while facilitating development of "nationhood" for those nations who entered the twentieth century without full national development, such as the Slovenes, and even "recognizing" and thus creating new nations such as the Macedonians and the (Bosnian) Muslims, is often overlooked by outside commentators. The Slovenes, however, are appreciative of

---

[55] Milan Kučan, "Otpor Srboslaviji" [Resisting Serboslavia], Interview, "Witnesses of Yugoslavia's Disintegration," *Radio Free Europe* (accessed February 5, 2005); available from <http://www.danas.org/svjedoci/html/Milan_Kucan.html>.

[56] Refers to EC's Brussels draft treaty convention written by EC civil servants in autumn 1991.

[57] Woodward, *Balkan Tragedy*, 181-182.

[58] Rupel, "Slovenia and the World," *Review of International Affairs*, 13.

[59] *See* Hayden, *Blueprints for a House Divided*, 64.

[60] So watchful were the Slovenes of their cultural autonomy within Yugoslavia that the Slovenian Writers Association blocked educational reform proposed in 1983 by Yugoslav authorities to enhance the common learning base of the Yugoslavs by rendering the curriculum 50 percent federal (Yugoslav) and 50 percent republican. *See* Andrew Baruch Wachtel, *Making a Nation, Breaking a Nation: Literature and Cultural Politics in Yugoslavia* (Stanford: Stanford University Press, 1998), 184-189.

this period. According to Carol Rogel, as part of Yugoslavia, Slovenes were afforded realpolitik advantages, as well as cultural and spiritual benefits of union with other Southern Slavs.[61]

The Slovenes also benefited from the westward move of industry by Tito in the post-World War II period, which, combined with generally hardworking and entrepreneurial population, access to low-cost raw materials from other Yugoslav republics, and proximity to Western markets, resulted in stronger economic growth compared to other parts of Yugoslavia. When the Yugoslav economy entered a crisis in 1980s, the Slovenes were not willing to take a disproportional share of the burden to compensate for the less productive republics. They preferred a more speedy entrance in the European economic market. Dimitrij Rupel explained this position:

> Slovenia is not leaving Yugoslavia to become an island in Europe; it is not leaving because of egotism or because it wants to behave like a spoilt child, but because it is impossible to get into Europe with Yugoslavia. This point was proven when Yugoslavia applied for membership of the Council of Europe, the European Free Trade Association, OECD, etc. They received the Hungarians, the Czechs and the Slovaks and they are now in the process of receiving the Poles. We Slovenes feel like captives in Yugoslavia.[62]

The Slovenes wanted to leave Yugoslavia so as not to be "a perpetual minority" but simultaneously took steps to join the European Union. According to a Slovene analyst, Peter Vodopivec,

> [T]he main argument against Yugoslavia . . . was that the Slovenes, as a small people in a system operating on majority voting principles, were fated to be a perpetual minority. As such they did not have any chance of realizing their national political ideas and pursuing their interests.[63]

---

[61] Carole Rogel, "In the Beginning: the Slovenes from the Seventh Century to 1945," in Jill Benderly and Evan Kraft, eds., *Independent Slovenia; Origins, Movements, Prospects* (London: Macmillan Press, 1994), 3-21: 3-4.

[62] "Rupel on Slovenia's foreign policy," *Tanjug* (Belgrade), April 24, 1991, in FBIS-EEU-91-081, April 26, 1991, 39.

[63] Peter Vodopivec, "Seven Decades of Unconfronted Incongruities: The Slovenes and Yugoslavia" in Jill Benderly and Evan Kraft, eds. *Independent Slovenia; Origins, Movements, Prospects* (London: Macmillan Press, 1994), 42.

Cultural and linguistic preparation for independence was delineated in the Slovene National Program, published in the Slovene weekly *Nova revija* in February 1987.[64] To differentiate themselves further from other Yugoslav ethnic groups and to buttress their demand for independence, the Slovenes stressed their interest in human rights. In November 1989, that is, only a year after concurring to the abolition of autonomous provinces in Serbia, they refused the association of Serbs and Montenegrins from Kosovo the right to assemble and hold a "meeting for truth," supporting the Kosovo Albanians. The Serbian government (veiled in the Socialist Alliance of Working People, an organization of the Serbian Communist party) in turn responded with economic measures, calling for a boycott of Slovene goods in Serbia, later secretly approved by the Serbian parliament.

In the late 1980s, the Slovenes were very active in civic initiatives, which were at times anti-military and anti-state, or at least perceived to be so, leading to clashes with the federal government. Notably, in the spring of 1988, three Slovene journalists were tried by the military and convicted for publishing military secrets, resulting in large protests in Slovenia.[65] However, as elaborated above, the Slovene determination was rooted in economic considerations.

On June 24, 1991, Slovenia proclaimed independence,[66] defining a mechanism for its legal implementation by the Law on the Enforcement of the Constitutional Act on the Autonomy and Independence of the Republic on Slovenia. The next day, the Slovene Assembly adopted a Declaration of Independence, formally stating that Slovenia was "no longer . . . a part of the Socialist Federalist Republic of Yugoslavia."[67] Article II of the new Slovene "Constitutional Charter" specified that its international borders would be the same as those existing within "hitherto SFRY."[68] A Slovene professor of law, Bojko Bučar, argued that any boundary

---

[64] "Contributions to the Slovenian National Program," *Nova Revija*, no. 57, February 1987.

[65] *See* Woodward, *Balkan Tragedy*, 95. Ironically, one of the anti-military activists, Janez Janša, later became the Slovene Minister of Defense.

[66] Constitutional Charter on the Autonomy and Independence of the Republic on Slovenia, June 24, 1991, printed in English in *Focus*, Special Issue, January 14, 1992, 97-99, at 98.

[67] Slovenia's Declaration of Independence, June 24, 1991, printed in English in *Focus*, Special Issue, January 14, 1992, 92-96.

[68] Constitutional Charter on the Autonomy and Independence of the Republic of Slovenia, June 24, 1991, printed in English in *Focus*, Special Issue, January 14, 1992, 97-99: 98.

dispute in Yugoslavia should be resolved according to international law, specifically referring to *uti possidetis*, the Charter of the Organization of African Unity and the Helsinki Final Act.[69]

The Yugoslav Constitutional Court declared these acts unconstitutional and annulled the Slovene Constitutional Charter.[70] Since the Court asserted that Slovenia was legally an integral part of Yugoslavia and since all the Yugoslav constituent nations enjoyed equal rights throughout Yugoslavia, there was no legal recourse to challenge the provisions of the new Slovene Constitution that specifically granted rights to "the Italian and Hungarian national communities" (Article III), but not to Serbs, Croats, or any other (former) Yugoslav peoples. Almost seventy thousand people (nearly 30 percent of the non-Slovene citizens of the SFRY who were domiciled in Slovenia in 1991) were deprived of Slovene citizenship and relevant property rights as a result of this legal anomaly when Slovenia became internationally recognized.[71] In 1992, one-fourth of these people (about 18,300 former SFRY citizens) became known as "the erased," as they were removed from the Slovenian population registry. Their destiny remains unresolved.[72]

4.3. The Croat Call for Democracy and Claim to Territory

The Croat determination, like the Slovene, envisaged secession. However, the Croats claimed that the force behind their attempt to secede was not Croatian but Serbian nationalism. They simultaneously explained that the unitary Yugoslavia was doomed to failure simply because Croats and Serbs were "very different." While proposing a "federation" of Yugoslav states, the Croat nationalist leader,

---

[69]   Bojko Bučar, "Medjunarodni aspekti jugoslovenske reforme i osamostaljenja Slovenije" [International aspects of the Yugoslav reform and the Autonomy of Slovenia], *Medjunarodna Politika*, no. 988 (June 1991), 4. For more on *uti possidetis, see* Chapter 5: *International Recognition of the (former) Yugoslav Republics.*

[70]   Одлука о оцењивању уставности Основне уставне повеље о самосталности и независности Републике Словеније [Decision on Evaluating the Constitutional Charter on the Autonomy and Independence of the Republic of Slovenia], October 16, 1991, *Official Gazette of SFRY*, December 13, 1991, vol. 47, no. 89, 1422; Одлука о оцењивању уставности Уставног закона за спровођење Основне уставне повеље о самосталности и независности Републике Словеније [Decision on Evaluating the Law on Enforcement of the Constitutional Charter on the Autonomy and Independence of the Republic on Slovenia], October 16, 1991, *Official Gazette of SFRY*, December 13, 1991, vol. 47, no. 89, p. 1427.

[71]   Hayden, *Blueprints for a House Divided*, 78.

[72]   *See* Amnesty International Report: *Slovenia, 2005* (accessed September 6, 2005); available from http://web.amnesty.org/report2005/svn-summary-eng.

Franjo Tudjman, also openly stated that Croatia "will have closer ties with Germany than with any other country."[73]

The Croat leadership engaged in an active public relations campaign, projecting an image of a nation that wanted to break with Communism and "rejoin" the Western world and its values. According to this campaign, the primary goal of the Croat determination was democracy.[74] Yet what the Croats claimed was territory, not only of the Socialist Republic of Croatia, but also parts of the Socialist Republic of Bosnia and Herzegovina (the most extreme nationalists also claimed parts of Serbia and Montenegro):

> Echoing a widely held Croatian perspective, Tudjman suggested that the Croatians and Moslems (who in his view were mainly Islamicized Croats) living in Bosnia-Hercegovina be included in the new affirmation of Croatian sovereignty. Moreover, he implied that this perspective might eventually involve certain adjustments in the territorial boundaries between the existing units of the presently constituted Yugoslav state. "Croatia and Bosnia," Tudjman would remark in an interview shortly after the election, "constitute a geographical and political unity, and have always formed a joint state in history."[75]

Nonetheless, there was a dichotomy between Tudjman's open discourse at home and his speeches that were mindful of foreign audience. At the official proclamation of the new Croatian Constitution, for instance, Tudjman was careful to stress Croatia's disinterest in the change of republican boundaries, aware that he could not insist on Croatia's recognition within these boundaries while seeking change in Bosnia's boundaries:

> Although the Republic of Croatia has many reasons to be dissatisfied with the existing borders, we accept the status quo, being aware that today is not

---

[73] A complete statement from *FBIS-EEU*, April 26, 1990, p. 81, reads:
"The Serbs either want a Greater Serbia or a unitary Yugoslavia. Contrary to this we are demanding either a Yugoslav confederation or separation. . . . Croatians and Serbs do not only have different historic characteristics: they also belong to different cultures. Therefore any attempt to create a unitary Yugoslavia is doomed to fail. The future new federation of states must guarantee a high degree of independence both for the Serbs and the Croatians. . . . According to our tradition we are closely linked with central Europe and with Germany. . . . Croatia will have closer ties with Germany than with any other country."

[74] "All we Croatians want is democracy" was the title of a professionally prepared opinion editorial by Croat leader Franjo Tudjman, published in the *New York Times*, June 30, 1990.

[75] *FBIS-EEU*, May 8, 1990, 57 and *Kurier*, May 10, 1990, 5.

the time for changing borders in Europe, because the international community will not accept such alterations.[76]

Yet in practice, the so-called historic rights, which laid claims on (at least) portions of Bosnia, constituted the platform for the Croat request for independence, combined with a call to end alleged Serb hegemonism:

> Croatian sovereignty means above all that we restore Croatian legitimacy. In the last 45 years Croatism has not only been exposed to pressure but also to persecution. . . . Streets and squares named after Croatian kings were changed. Croatian children were not allowed to sing innocent Croatian songs. Look at who the editors of radio, television, and newspapers are. . . . [W]e cannot agree with there being 40 percent Serbs in the government of Croatia, and 61 percent in the trade unions administration, when 11 percent of the total population is Serb. Nor can we agree with there being 6 1/2 Serbs among the seven chief editors on television (because one of them is half Croatian and half Serb).[77]

While it is a fact that Serbs were over-represented in the police and some other government organs in proportion to their demographic status in the republic of Croatia, this stemmed in part from a significantly larger Serb participation in the Partisan movement on this territory and in part from the 1971 Communist purge of the police forces to counteract the Croat national movement.[78] Another contributing factor was the lower economic status of Serbs in Croatia, forcing them to choose employment in the police. At the same time, the Serbs did not dominate any of the important republic structures. For instance, only once was there a Serb president of the Croatian Parliament (Yovo Ugrchich, 1982-1983), a president of the Council of Communists of Croatia (Stanko Stoychevich) and a secretary for internal affairs for the Republic of Croatia (Urosh Sliyepchevich). Simultaneously the key decision-maker in all Yugoslavia was a Croat (and partly Slovene)—Josip Broz Tito.

---

[76] "We stand before a great historic test," A speech delivered by Franjo Tudjman at the session of the Sabor of the Republic of Croatia on the occasion of the promulgation of the Constitution of the Republic," Zagreb, December 13, 1990, *The Constitution of the Republic of Croatia*, Prepared by Lj. Veljković (1991), 7, reproduced in Trifunovska, *Yugoslavia Through Documents*, 237-250: 245.

[77] *FBIS-EEU*, April 24, 1990, 66.

[78] *See* Chapter 3: *Yugoslavias' Administrative Boundaries*.

Croat nationalism was suppressed by the Communist regime, but not less so than Serb nationalism, including Serb cultural endeavors in Croatia. The Serb institutions in Croatia, formed at the end of the Second World War, had quickly disappeared. The Serbian singing society Obilich (*Обилић,* founded in October 1944) was incorporated into a new Serbo-Croatian singing federation, and the Museum of Serbs in Croatia (founded in 1947) was transformed into a depart-ment at the Historic Museum of Croatia in 1952 and closed in 1967. The Serbian cultural and educational society "Education" (*Просвјета,* founded in November 1944), remained the sole organization promoting Serbian identity and culture in Croatia until its closure in 1972.[79] It was closed precisely as an act of parity follow-ing the suppression of the 1971 Croatian nationalist movement. Yet despite evi-dence to the contrary, the Croats still perceived the Serbs as having hegemony.[80] This view strengthened the Croats' desire to leave the common state and fed their nationalist fervor, particularly because the definition of a Croat often equaled "not Serb."

This also explains why extremist Croat nationalism is both reflected and rooted in the attempted revision of history. The Croats have always resented the rights granted to Serbs in Croatia, and most especially Krayina's historic separate exist-ence. Croat historians have claimed that Krayina's settlers were not Serbs but "Vlachs,"[81] and some have even postulated that it was the Croats who established

---

[79] See Ratko Bubalo, "Stanje ljudskih i državljanskih prava u Hrvatskoj" [The State of Human Rights and Citizenship Rights in Croatia], *Srbi u Hrvatskoj* [Serbs in Croatia], ed. Ivo Banac (Zagreb: Helsinki Committee for Human Rights in Croatia, 1998), 40, and Momčilo Kosović, "Srpske političke, privredne i kulturne ustanove poslije Drugog svetskog rata" [Serbian Political, Business and Cultural Institutions After World War II], in *Republika Srpska Krajina* [Republic of Serbian Krayina] (Belgrade: Radnička štampa, 1996), 367-377. Note: Prosvjeta was reestablished as a Serbian cultural society in 1993 but the Croatian government still has not returned the society's premises and other property confiscated by the Communist regime. For more, *see* http://www.skdprosvjeta.com.

[80] In the address to the Croatian Assembly, on the occasion of the adoption of the new Croatian Constitution, the Croat President Franjo Tudjman argued that "the new democratic authorities in Croatia are being imperiled by the dogmatic-communist, Yugoslav-unitaristic and Greater Serbian-hegemonistic forces, unified in their intolerance towards any Croatian national or state-building idea." Franjo Tudjman, "We find ourselves before a great historical test," Statement at the Occasion of the Ceremonial Proclamation of the Constitution of the Republic of Croatia in the Croatian Assembly on December 22, 1990, *Izvješća Hrvatskoga sabora* [Proceedings of the Croatian Assembly], number 15, December 22, 1990.

[81] While all Orthodox settlers were indeed called Vlachs by the Habsburg authorities, and some truly were Vlachs and different from the Serbs, the majority were Serbian and even the Vlachs assimilated into Serbs by the nineteenth century. As Nicholas Miller explains, "the term Vlach became a weapon in the war to devalue Serbian claims to territory and history in Croatia." For more, *see* Nicholas J. Miller, *Between Nation and State; Serbian Politics in Croatia before the First World War* (Pittsburgh, PA: University of Pittsburgh Press, 1997), 5.

Krayina.[82] The Nazi Croat Ustasha further claimed that the First Yugoslavia was formed by forceful annexation of Croat lands by the Serbs.[83] Nevertheless, the most disturbing attempted revision of history occurred in the late 1980s and early 1990s, promulgated by the new Croat leader Franjo Tudjman, former Communist general and military historian, who, like Tito, stayed on as president "for life," albeit just of Croatia. At the opening meeting of the Peace Conference on Yugoslavia in the Hague on November 5, 1991, Tudjman stated, "During World War II, the victims of the Croatian people were not lesser than the victims of the Serbian people,"[84] reiterating his previous allegations that the crimes against Serbs (as well as against Jews) in the World War II period have been exaggerated.[85]

The Catholic Church in Croatia, which has strong influence among Croats, also refused to acknowledge the World War II genocide against mainly Serbs, but also Jews, Roma and anti-fascists in Nazi Croatia, stating in its official journal as late as 1998, "They write and talk about a genocide that did not occur."[86] In 2003, on his first trip to the Serb part of Bosnia (Republic of Srpska), Pope John Paul II offered an apology for the first time, asking Serbs "to forgive wrongs committed by the Catholic Church in World War II."[87] Tudjman had offered an apology to

---

[82] "Owing to the continuing Turkish menace, the Croatians decided to establish a permanent defense organization. Thus a military organization of a new and original type, called Vojna Krajina (Military Frontier Zone) was born. Most of the Croatian people lived under it until 1881, and it has left deep traces on the Croatian people and their way of living." Ivan Babich, "Military History," in *Croatia; Land, People, Culture*, Vol. I, eds. Francis H. Eterovich and Christopher Spalatin (Toronto: University of Toronto Press, 1964), 136.

[83] When requesting military aid against the Serbs from the Italian government, the Croat puppet government argued: "The Croats have maintained their national identity and state independence through the centuries in a more or less clear form until the end of the world war. In 1918 Serbia, aided by Western democracies, completely eradicated any state or national identity by annexing our territory and holding the Croat nation under the hegemony of Belgrade." *Croatian Appeal to the Italian Foreign Minister*, June 1940 (DDI, 9, VI, number 848) cited in Srdja Trifkovic, *Ustasha; Croatian Separatism and European Politics, 1929-1945* (London: The Lord Byron Foundation for Balkan Studies, 1998), 317.

[84] Cited in Radovan Samardzic, ed., *Sistem neistina o zločinima genocida 1991-1993. godine* [System of untruths regarding crimes of genocide in 1991-1993] (Belgrade: Serbian Academy of Arts and Sciences, 1994), 27.

[85] In his book *Impasses of historical reality*, published in 1989, just a year before winning Croat republic elections, Tudjman attests that no more than 30,000 or 40,000 Serb and other people, including Jews and Roma, were murdered by the Ustasha. Franjo Tudjman, *Bespuća povijesne zbilnosti: Rasprava o povijesti i filosofiji zlosilje* [Impasses of historical reality: A discussion of the history and philosophy of malevolent power], 2nd ed. (Zagreb: Matica Hrvatska, 1989). For more reliable sources on Ustasha's World War II victims, see Chapter 3: *Yugoslavias' Administrative Boundaries*.

[86] *Glas Koncila*, number 31 (Zagreb, July 31, 1998), cited in Samardzic, ed., *System of untruths regarding genocide crimes of 1991-1993*, 23 [Translation mine].

[87] "Pope calls for healing," *Reuters*, June 23, 2003.

B'nai B'rith for putting the number of Jews killed in the Holocaust at one million instead of six million in his book, and for stating "Thank God, my wife is neither a Serb nor a Jew" during his 1990 campaign trail,[88] but he never apologized to the Serbs.

Instead, in 1990 Tudjman and other prominent members of his party (Croatian Democratic Union or HDZ) commemorated the so-called Croatian victims of fascism.[89] The Croatia of the 1990s[90] came to perceive the World War II Croatian puppet state as an important building block of Croatian statehood: The Ustasha movement had simply fought for national self-determination using all methods available to it at the time.[91]

The reinterpretation of World War II history in Croatia in a positive light is a consequence of distorted Communist historiography and lack of open discussion. According to Mark Biondich: "Tito's regime had its own version of the [Second World] war in which all peoples of Yugoslavia, including Croats, participated in the heroic struggle against fascism."[92] Furthermore, admitting that Croats committed severe crimes against Serbs during that period clashed with the dogma of Croats being a victimized nation:

> Well after 1945, the Croat nationalist memory of the Second World War continued to be nurtured on the perception that Croats had since 1918 repeatedly been victimized by Serbs, whether in royalist or Communist Yugoslavia.[93]

---

[88]   David Binder, "Franjo Tudjman: Ex-Communist General Who Led Croatia's Secession, Is Dead at 77," *New York Times*, December 11, 1999.

[89]   Dinko Sakić, the commander of the notorious World War II Jasenovac concentration camp, was present at this event and others held pictures of Ante Pavelić, the Ustasha leader.

[90]   Most Croats share Tudjman's glorification of the so-called Independent State of Croatia (NDH), according to a 1997 opinion poll published by the Croatian weekly *Globus* [Article from *Globus* reprinted in *Naš Glas*, Zagreb, October 1997, 7]. The poll found that two thirds of Croatians view the NDH positively, and that only one third considers NDH to have been a Nazi state. According to the same poll, more than 80 percent of the Croatian citizens believe that NDH brought about "liberation from Greater Serbian dictatorship," while 55-63 percent of Croats would not allow their child to marry a Serb or a Muslim.

[91]   Mark Biondich, "'We were defending the state': Nationalism, Myth, and Memory in Twentieth-Century Croatia," in John R. Lampe and Mark Mazower, eds. *Ideologies and National Identities; The Case of Twentieth Century Southeastern Europe* (Budapest, New York: Central European University Press, 2004), 54-82, at 67.

[92]   This view is analyzed by Biondich, "'We were defending the state': Nationalism, Myth, and Memory in Twentieth-Century Croatia," in *Ideologies and National Identities*, 66.

[93]   Ibid, 70.

Historical textbooks in Croatia as late as 2000 described NDH in a positive light, drawing what Ivo Goldstein finds to be a scandalous conclusion:

> The entire spiritual opus [literature, law, fine art etc.] is imbued with the spirit of democracy, freed from all the strings of the state bureaucracy.[94]

Reinterpretation of history was followed by a return of state emblems from that period. In early 1990s, the new Croat government adopted many of the *NDH* symbols, including the red and white checkered shield and the currency. Literary Croat was pronounced the only language of administration in Croatia and the Serbs' Cyrillic script dismissed. Several streets of the new Croatia were renamed after the Nazi Minister of Religion and Education, Mile Budak, who was one of the main propagators of the Ustasha policy of genocide against the Serbs during World War II.[95] This represented a fierce provocation to the Serbs in Croatia who lost family in Ustasha's massacres. In addition to instilling fear in the Serb citizens of Croatia, the new regime also relieved many of their employment. As Glenny vividly describes: "When the militant dogs of the HDZ were unleashed and allowed to organize purges of the state administration, Serbs throughout Croatia were shaken by the spectre of persecution."[96]

Eventually, the Croat nationalist outburst also led to violence, ironically targeted at "loyal" Croatian Serbs and preceding any violent reaction on their end:

> Even before the war began, the government was concerned to hush up nationalist-motivated crimes against its Serb population while when applying for recognition, its police and soldiers were involved in the slaughter of innocent Serbs. . . . The victims were the so-called "loyal" Serbs who had not crossed over to the JNA [Yugoslav National Army] or Krajina Serbs. These urban Serbs were among the greatest victims of the war, whose plight, however, is one of the least well known. Tens of thousands were hounded from their homes in the big cities either through direct intimidation, expulsion or through the pervasive climate of fear.[97]

---

94   Cited in Ivo Goldstein, "O udžbenicima u Hrvatskoj" [On textbooks in Croatia], in *Dijalog povjesničara-istoričara 3* [Dialogue of historians 3], eds. Dušan Gamser, Igor Graovac, and Olivera Milosavljević (Zagreb: Friedrich Naumann Stiftung, 2001), 19.

95   *See* Hayden, *Blueprints for a House Divided*, 70

96   Glenny, *The Fall of Yugoslavia*, 13.

97   Ibid.,123.

The more moderate Croat politicians like Stipe Mesić,[98] the last president of the former Yugoslavia and the current president of Croatia, stipulated a different means of handling the Serb minority—via Croatian demographic revival. In a book titled "How we destroyed Yugoslavia,"[99] he stated that one of Croatia's goals was to "undertake everything possible to enable a rapid return of Croatian people from the diaspora into the home country, and simultaneously stimulate a demographic revival."[100]

In conclusion, Croat self-determination, as represented by the Croatian government, translated not only to the claim to the territory of the Socialist Republic of Croatia and (parts of) Bosnia and Herzegovina, but also to the negation of Serb ethnicity and relevant rights on the same territory. In addition to irrational motivation, the latter could also be described by pure geopolitics: the Serb-majority region in Krayina is the central communications junction between the Croatian capital and the littoral region.

Support for independence was overwhelming among Croats. On May 19, 1991, 93 percent of the 83.6 percent of the Croatian electorate who chose to vote circled "yes" to the ambiguous referendum question: "Do you agree that the Republic of Croatia as a sovereign and independent state, which guarantees cultural autonomy and all civil rights to Serbs and members of other nationalities in Croatia, may enter into an alliance with other republics?" In this manner, they wished to fulfill the "historical right of the Croatian nation to full state sovereignty," based on the "inalienable . . . right of the Croatian nation to self-determination and state sovereignty," as determined by the Preamble to the 1990 Croatian Constitution.[101] The overwhelming majority of Croats denied the same

---

[98] The term "moderate" is relative here. In the early 1990s even Mesić engaged in inflammatory nationalist speeches, stating that the Croats "won a victory on April 10th" (when the fascist Independent State of Croatia was formed) "as well as in 1945" (when the anti-fascists prevailed and the Socialist Republic of Croatia was formed), as well as that Croatia needs to apologize to no one for the Jasenovac concentration camp (i.e. the World War II genocide of Serbs). A video clip and transcript of this speech are available at http://www.index.hr/clanak.aspx?id=334481 (accessed March 4, 2007).

[99] This is the actual translation of the title. The official translation of the book's English version is "The demise of Yugoslavia."

[100] Stipe Mesić, *Kako smo srušili Jugoslaviju: politički memoari posljednjeg predsjednika* Predsjedništva SFRJ [How We Destroyed Yugoslavia: Political Memoirs of the Last President of Yugoslavia] (Zagreb: Globus International, 1992), ix.

[101] *Ustav Republike Hrvatske* [Constitution of the Republic of Croatia], *Izvješća Hrvatskoga sabora* [Proceedings of the Croatian Assembly, number 15, December 22, 1990. *Note:* Legal documents relating to Croatia's secession from Yugoslavia are examined in more detail later in this work.

"historical" and "inalienable" right to fellow Serbs living in Croatia. Most Serbs from Croatia boycotted the referendum, holding their own plebiscite a week earlier to approve the decision to join the Republic of Serbia (as the region of Krayina) and to remain within Yugoslavia.[102]

4.4. The Serbs: Rights of a Constituent Nation

The general Serb position was enshrined in the Memorandum of the Serbian Academy of Sciences and Arts entitled "On Current Social Questions in Our Country" (the Memorandum), composed in 1986 and leaked to the press in its draft form.[103] Although its authors claim that the Memorandum was "never signed by anyone, not even by the members of the Committee which wrote it, for the simple reason that it had been stolen before it was even completed,"[104] the vision and the policy prescribed in the text were fully espoused by the Serb authorities.

While the (draft) Memorandum became notorious as a document envisioning an expansionist Greater Serbia, this assertion is not entirely correct. Just a single phrase of the (draft) Memorandum could be interpreted as a cause for concern by other Yugoslav nations, but exclusively due to its ambiguity. After noting that "all of the nations within Yugoslavia must be given the opportunity to express their wants and intentions," and that "Discussions and agreements in this vein must precede an examination of the Constitution," the Memorandum asserts: "Naturally, Serbia must not take a passive stand in all this, waiting to hear what others will say, as she has done so often in the past."

Otherwise, the Memorandum passionately describes the Serbs' grievances against the Communist regime, depicting the Serbs as its greatest victims, who need to re-establish their rights. It condemns the decentralization process that reached its peak with the 1974 Constitution and calls for a change of Constitution that would reinstall the post-World War II centralized federalism for both political and economic reasons. The Memorandum openly demands full reintegration of

---

[102] For more on Croatia's independence movement in early 1990s, *see* Marcus Tanner, *Croatia; A Nation forged in War* (New Haven and London: Yale University Press, 1997).

[103] Published in *Vechernye novosti*, Belgrade evening newspaper, on September 24, 1986. An English translation of the Memorandum is found in Kosta Mihailovich and Vasiliye Krestich, *Memorandum of the Serbian Academy of Sciences and Arts; Answers to Criticisms* (Belgrade: Serbian Academy of Arts and Sciences, 1995), 95-140.

[104] Mihailovich and Krestich, *Memorandum of the Serbian Academy of Sciences and Arts; Answers to Criticisms*, 89.

the two Serbian autonomous provinces, Voivodina and Kosovo and Metohia, into Serbia. The authors of the Memorandum here use inflammatory language, calling the Albanian expulsions of Serbs "a genocide" and ignoring the Serb expulsions of Albanians at other points in the past.[105] According to Lampe, the Memorandum thus provided "ammunition for Miloshevich's nationalist campaign,"[106] and "played a part in [Yugoslavia's] disintegration in a similar fashion as Croat President Tudjman's writings on "injustices he saw inflicted on Croatia since the First World War."[107]

Nonetheless, although Serb complaints are strongly voiced in the Memorandum, the text makes no mention of Greater Serbia, advocating instead constitutional changes that would transform Yugoslavia into "a productive, enlightened, and democratic society, capable of living from our own labor and creativity and able to make a contribution to the world community." The Serbian preference for Yugoslavia is here based on the same arguments that led the Serbs to form the First and the Second Yugoslavia, aptly summarized in the 1991 Declaration on the Peaceful Settlement of the Yugoslav Crisis and against Civil War and Violence, adopted by the Serbian Assembly:

> [T]he preservation of Yugoslavia is of special importance to the Serb people, for it would enable it to stay together and to realize its legitimate

---

[105] The percentage of Serbs in the ethnic structure of Kosovo rapidly dwindled in the Communist era, particularly in the period between 1961, when it amounted to 27.4 percent, and 1981, when it was 13.3 percent (15 percent with Montenegrin Serbs), according to the official census, with Albanians constituting about 77 percent in the total population of Kosovo and Metohia. Several factors contributed to this shift. The most important is the birthrate, the highest in Europe for Kosovo Albanians [in 1985 it reached 2.5 percent, more than three times the Yugoslav average; *see* Branko Horvat, *Kosovsko pitanje* [The Kosovo Question] (Zagreb: Globus, 1988), 130]. Another factor is uncontrolled mass immigration from Albania. The third factor is a decision of the Communist authorities, which by a decree of March 6, 1945 officially prohibited the return of over 60,000 Serbs who had settled in Kosovo in the interwar period. At the same time, over 75,000 Albanians from Albania, settled in Kosovo by the Italian authorities during the Second World War, remained on the property of Serb interwar settlers. Only a small number of Serbs succeeded in retrieving their property after the 1949 break with Albania. A fourth factor relates to harassment of Kosovo Serbs by their Albanian neighbors, frequently reported by the *New York Times*, particularly in the early 1980s. However, the latter does not constitute "genocide." It is also important to note that tens of thousands of Albanians, together with Turks and other Ottoman Muslims also fled Kosovo when the Ottoman Empire disintegrated. For more, *see* Dušan T. Bataković, ed., *Histoire du Peuple Serbe* (Lausanne: L'Age d'Homme), 2005.

[106] John R. Lampe, *Yugoslavia as History. Twice there was a country* (Cambridge, New York: Cambridge University Press, 1996), 6.

[107] Franjo Tudjman, *Bespuća povijesne zbilnosti: Rasprava o povijesti i filosofiji zlosilje* [Impasses of historical reality: A discussion of the history and philosophy of malevolent power], 2nd ed. (Zagreb: Matica Hrvatska, 1989).

---

national interests. Since it is the historical right and the necessity of the Serb people to live in one democratic state, it must be taken into consideration by every proposal to solve the Yugoslav crisis.[108]

It is little known that many proposals presented in the Memorandum, particularly regarding the relationship of Serbia's republic and provincial authorities, stem from the "Blue Book," drafted in 1977 by an expert committee[109] summoned by the Serbian Presidency, but published only in 1990,[110] having been shelved by a majority vote of the Presidency of the Central Committee of the Yugoslav League of Communists. Several committee members who vehemently opposed the Blue Book were of Serbian ethnicity,[111] but considered any strengthening of the economic and political system of the Republic of Serbia to be against their Communist and Yugoslav ideals.[112]

The substance of the draft Memorandum (1990) focuses on economic problems. The document stresses that: "Serbia's economy has been subject to unfair terms of trade" but concludes its analysis with optimistic, compromise-seeking recommendations:

> It follows from this analysis that political democratization and infusion of new blood, genuine self-determination and equality for all members of all the Yugoslav nations, including the Serbs, full exercise of human, civil, and economic and social rights, and consistent streamlining of the Yugoslav

---

[108] Article 7, Declaration on the Peaceful Settlement of the Yugoslav Crisis and against Civil War and Violence, April 2, 1991, printed in English in *Focus*, Special Issue, January 14, 1992, 52.

[109] Members of the expert committee were: prof. dr Naydan Pashich (Member of the Presidency of the Serbian League of Communists), prof. dr Miodrag Zechevich, prof. dr Radoslav Ratkovich, Velya Markovich, Milivoye Drashkovich and Nikola Stanich. Edvard Kardelj's suggestions were also included in the final draft of the Blue Book. *See* Radoslav Ratkovich, "Plava knjiga—anatomija jedne misterije" [Blue Book—Anatomy of a Mystery], Interview in *Kako je razvlašćivana Jugoslavija* [How Yugoslavia Became Deprived of Authority], *Intervju*, special edition, October 10, 1988, 80.

[110] Integral text of the Blue Book in Serbian is printed in Mirko Djekic, *Upotreba Srbije; optuzbe i priznanje Draze Markovica* [Making Use of Serbia; Accusations and Avowal of Drazha Markovich], (Belgrade: Beseda 1990), 123-174.

[111] The greatest opponents of the Blue Book were Milosh Minich, Zhivan Vasilyevich, and Mirko Popovich. For more, *see* Slavoljub Djukic, *Kako se dogodio vodja* [How a Leader was Born] (Belgrade: Filip Visnjic, 1992), 246-247.

[112] For more, *see* Ratkovich, "Blue Book—Anatomy of a Mystery," *Intervju*, 80; Dragoslav Markovich, Diskontinuitet [Discontinuity], Interview, "Witnesses of Yugoslavia's Disintegration," *Radio Free Europe* (accessed February 5, 2005); available from http://www.danas.org/svjedoci/html/Dragoslav_Markovic.html.

political system and development policy are those indispensable prerequisites without which recovery from the present crisis in Yugoslav society could not even be imagined.

The Memorandum's main line of argument, proposing a more centralized economic system, is in full agreement with the recommendations for reform of the Yugoslav economy made by the International Monetary Fund and other international economic institutions at the time.[113]

In brief, most Serbs were prepared to support a reformed Yugoslavia as a peaceful solution to the looming crisis, provided the reform entailed the political integration of Serbia's provinces and addressed other Serb grievances described in the draft Memorandum. Serbian resentment of past Communist policies became personified in Tito. The majority became anti-Tito rather than anti-Yugoslav. It was Tito who, according to the majority opinion, attempted to weaken the Serbs by "republicanizing" Yugoslavia, dividing Serbia into three parts (central Serbia and two provinces), and accentuating differences between Montenegrin and other Serbs, while enlarging the Croat territories wherever possible and allowing the Croats to hegemonize the regions of Dalmatia, Istria, and Krajina that historically possessed a distinct identity. Similarly, the Serb elite claimed that Tito's recognition of a Muslim nationality weakened their position in Bosnia-Herzegovina. Finally, Serb politicians asserted that Tito attempted to economically weaken the Serbian-populated territory by concentrating the industry in the western parts of Yugoslavia and transforming Serbia into a producer of raw materials.[114]

While it is difficult to prove that Tito intended to weaken the Serbian position by design, and while other Yugoslav nations have their own grievances towards Tito's regime and the 1974 Constitution,[115] a weaker Serbia was its indisputable consequence. The 1974 constitutional charter left three million Serbs (one third of the total Serb population in SFRY) outside their home republic. The immediate question that arises is why the Serbs had not protested more strongly when the policies

---

[113] For more, *see* Woodward, *Balkan Tragedy*, 59; Paul Shoup, "Crisis and Reform in Yugoslavia," in *Telos* no 79 (1989), 129-147: 132-135.

[114] For more, *see* Chapter 3: *Yugoslavias' Administrative Boundaries (1918-1991)*.

[115] "Survey data show that dissatisfaction with the constitution of 1974 was quite high among all regions and ethnic groups in the country but especially among the Serbs in Serbia proper. Sergije Pegan, "Politicki system" [Political System], in Drasko Grbic (ed.), *Jugosloveni o drustvenoj krizi (istrazivanje javnog mnjenja, 1985. godine)* [Yugoslavs on Crisis of the Society (Public Opinion Research in 1985)] (Belgrade: Komunist, 1989), pp. 61-63

that they perceived as detrimental to their interests were devised and implemented. One answer lies in the genuine Serbian belief in Communism and their conception of Yugoslavism as an identity that was higher than their national identity. As Zarko Bilbija explains:

> The reason why Tito could proceed with impunity against the Serbs was because he had many of them on his side. They became willing suppressors of their own nation. Some because they refused to surrender the idea of Yugoslavism, others because they joined the Communist movement and became internationalists.[116]

For the same reason, the Serbs were the least prepared of the Yugoslavs for the disintegration of Yugoslavia. According to Bilbija:

> They had become so denationalized by this time that they directed their greatest efforts toward the salvation of Yugoslavia and its Communist regime rather than toward the protection of their own people who were being assaulted from all sides by their Yugo-Slav compatriots.[117]

As explained in the previous chapter, the Serb elite projected a vision of national communism, normally an oxymoron. This vision is also reflected in the Memorandum. Yugoslavia was strongly preferred to a Greater Serbia. At the same time, to the Serb leadership a reformed Yugoslavia did imply a stronger Serbia and improved Serb rights throughout Yugoslavia. The Serbian proposal for restructuring of the common state, entitled "A Concept for the Constitutional System of Yugoslavia on a Federal Basis,"[118] and presented in October 1990, claimed to espouse the model of a "modern federation." The proposal was framed as a set of principles, elaborated in documents that were considered, but not adopted, by the Yugoslav Presidency in March 1991.

Based on these texts, the Serbian leadership advocated, *inter alia*, federal elections based on the principle "one man, one vote" throughout Yugoslavia. Importantly,

---

[116] Zarko Bilbija, "The Serbs and Yugoslavia," in *The Serbs and their National Interest*, eds. Norma von Ragenfeld-Feldman and Dusan T. Batakovic (San Francisco: Serbian Unity Congress, 1997), 99.

[117] Ibid., 101.

[118] "Predstavništvo SFRJ dostavilo Skupštini koncept federativnog uredjenja Jugoslavije" [The SFRY Presidency submitted a Concept of Federal Arrangement of Yugoslavia to the Assembly], reprinted in *Borba*, October 18, 1990, 2.

the proposal also stipulated that a simple majority would suffice to determine the will of a people, but that plebiscites should be conducted in all parts of the country and not just at the level of republics. Such a process is reminiscent of the creation of the Jura canton in Switzerland in 1978 by a cascade of popular votes at three levels—the Jura region, districts, and communes, arriving at a territorial division deemed acceptable to all parties.[119] However, the right to express one's self-determination by a way of a plebiscite would be limited to the constituent nations according to the Serb proposal. In this way, the secession of Kosovo, even if allowing further cessions of Serb-dominated parts of this province, would effectively be precluded because Albanians did not enjoy the status of a constituent nation. All parts of Yugoslavia not voting for secession would remain in Yugoslavia and the Federal Assembly would determine the thus established the territorial division of Yugoslavia. This proposal confirms that Serbs were not opposed to the secession of other Yugoslav nations wishing to do so, with the exception of the Albanian minority, but only within the confines of their ethnic boundaries.

The Slovenes and the Croats rejected the Serbian proposal immediately, feeling threatened by any reforms that would lead to conceding authority to the federal government, or that would allow for a more significant Serbian influence based on population size.[120] To them, the only acceptable solution would be "one unit, one vote," with all republics enjoying equal rights, including the right to veto, with minimal joint state functions, as elaborated above.

In August 1991, when the secession of Slovenia and Croatia was well under way, the Serb leadership invited the Bosnian and Montenegrin leaders to a joint meeting to consider another proposal, later termed "the Belgrade Initiative,"[121] aimed at reforming now rump Yugoslavia. The President of the Bosnian Presidency and the Bosnian Muslim leader Alija Izetbegovic (Aliya Izetbegovich) rejected the invitation, claiming that all republican representatives should participate in its consideration. However, the President of the Bosnian National Assembly, a Bosnian Serb, took part in the talks and signed on to the proposal. The text of

---

[119] For more, *see* Pierre Boillat, *Jura, naissance d'un etat—Aux sources du droit et des institutions jurassiennes* [Jura, Birth of a State—At the Source of Jurassian Law and Institutions] (Lausanne : Editions Payot, 1989).

[120] In 1981, the Serbs constituted the largest ethnic group in Yugoslavia (36 percent of the total population), but approximately 3 million of the over 8.1 million Serbs living in the country resided outside the Republic of Serbia, including its two provinces.

[121] Printed in English in *Focus*, Special Issue, January 14, 1992, 115-117.

the Belgrade Initiative was subsequently submitted to all Yugoslav republics, the federal presidency, and the federal assembly, albeit without producing an agreement.[122]

The Belgrade Initiative reiterates the commitment to preserving Yugoslavia (Article 1), "based on equality of the republics and peoples" (Article 2), which resembles the compromising ambiguity of the 1974 Constitution. Furthermore, the document, although briefly listing four "common interests of the equal republics and peoples of Yugoslavia" (Article 3), comprises the most important state functions in these four interests, *de facto* creating a federal state. One marked departure from the past Yugoslav Constitution is found in insistence on "the broadest political and social liberties and rights of citizens, on a multi-party parliamentary system, on a market economy and on guarantees for and freedom and equality of all types of ownership" (Article 3). The Serbian effort to produce a new text as a departing point for further negotiations is evidence of an adjustment of the Serbian position, allowing room for compromise, but possibly insufficiently great for the other groups.

While negotiating the future of Yugoslavia, the leadership of the Republic of Serbia simultaneously focused on the key symbol of (perceived) injustice made to Serbs by the Tito-dictated Yugoslav internal organization: the fate of the Serbs of Kosovo-Metohia. By publicly promising to the Kosovo Serbs "Nobody, either now or in the future, has the right to beat you" in a speech made on April 24, 1987, the leader of the League of Communists of Serbia who later became the Serb president, Slobodan Miloshevich, officially espoused nationalism. Emerging from a meeting of angry Kosovo Serbs who were complaining of harassment at the hand of the local ethnic Albanian-dominated authorities, Miloshevich further stated:

> First I want to tell you comrades, that you should stay here. This is your country, these are your houses, your fields and gardens, your memories. You are not going to abandon your land because life is hard, because you are oppressed by injustice and humiliation. It has never been a characteristic of the Serbian and Montenegrin people to retreat in the face of obstacles, to demobilize when they should fight, to become demoralized when things are difficult. You should stay here, both for your ancestors and your descendants.

---

[122] For more, *see* Ibid., 115.

But I do not suggest you stay here suffering and enduring a situation with which you are not satisfied. On the contrary! It should be changed, together with all progressive people here, in Serbia and in Yugoslavia. . . . Yugoslavia does not exist without Kosovo! . . . Yugoslavia and Serbia are not going to give up Kosovo![123]

Acting out of opportunism, Miloshevich's turn to nationalism[124] only followed the trend unraveling amidst the collapsing Cold War system. In an attempt to secure his rule over Serbia, Miloshevich also chose to ignore and even block the federal authorities when he deemed them challenging to his own authority or aims. A pertinent example is Serbia and Montenegro's refusal to endorse the Croatian representative, Stipe Mesić, as the president of the federal presidency, out of fear that he might take steps to undermine Yugoslavia, which he in fact reported to have done when leaving the post,[125] later even publishing a book "How We Destroyed Yugoslavia."[126] Following this principle, the new Serbian Constitution, enacted in September 1990, partly undermines the federal Constitution with the following provision:

If acts of the agencies of the Federation or acts of the agencies of another republic, in contravention of the rights and duties it has under the Constitution of the Socialist Federal Republic of Yugoslavia, violate the equality of the Republic of Serbia or in any other way threaten its interests, without providing for compensation, the republic agencies shall issue acts to protect the interests of the Republic of Serbia.[127]

---

[123]   Slavoljub Djukic, *Izmedju slave i anateme: Politicka biografija Slobodana Milosevica* [Between Glory and Anathema: Political Biography of Slobodan Milosevic] (Belgrade, 1994), 49. *See also* the 1995 BBC video documentary: *Yugoslavia: Death of a Nation*, part 1.

Note: Although the Slovenes and the Croats had already entertained plans to secede from Yugoslavia, which had been publicly avowed in Croatia since 1971, Miloshevich's speech in Kosovo is often inappropriately described as the trigger of Yugoslavia's disintegration: "As Milosevic whipped up Serb nationalist fervour, the idea that the other states were better off on their own took root. The disintegration of Yugoslavia had begun." Ian Oliver, *War and Peace in The Balkans; The Diplomacy of Conflict in the Former Yugoslavia* (London: I.B. Tauris, 2005), 7.

[124]   Several weeks prior to this event, Miloshevich had described nationalism as an obstacle to development, declaring, "We communists must do everything in our power to eliminate consequences of nationalist and separatist behavior of contra-revolutionary forces." Slobodan Miloshevich, *Године расплета* [Years of Unraveling] (Belgrade: BIGZ, 1989), 143.

[125]   Stipe Mesić, Address to the Croatian Assembly, December 8, 1991.

[126]   Mesić, *How We Destroyed Yugoslavia.*

[127]   Article 135, Constitution of the Republic of Serbia, 1990.

One of three principal authors of the 1990 Serbian Constitution, Ratko Markovich, claims that these provisions were drafted to take account of the political realities, "so that Serbia would not become a legally decapitated state as a result of external factors (in case of successful secession of other Yugoslav republics)."[128] Precisely not to appear disrespectful to the Federal constitution and state, the same Article 135 also provides:

> The rights and duties vested under the present Constitution in the Republic of Serbia, which is part of the Socialist Federal Republic Yugoslavia, violate the equal terms of the federal constitution are to be exercised in the Federation, shall be enforced in accordance with the federal constitution.[129]

Although Markovich maintains that Slobodan Miloshevich did not have a role in the drafting of the 1989 Amendments to the Serbian Constitution nor in the new, 1990 Serbian Constitution, which were instead politically coordinated by Borisav Yovich, Markovich attests that "Miloshevich politically paved the way to the Constitution's legal solutions,"[130] the most significant of which related to a changed status of the autonomous provinces.[131]

At the same time, unlike other newly adopted constitutions of the (former) Yugoslav republics, the Serbian Constitution of 1990 opted for civic rather than ethnic national determination, as "the democratic state of all citizens living within it" (Article 1), where "sovereignty belongs to all citizens of the republic" (Article 2). Only the Preamble to the 1990 Constitution speaks of the Serbian people's determination to "create a democratic State of the Serbian people."

Indeed, Miloshevich openly faltered in his support of a revamped, if geographically smaller, Yugoslavia on only one occasion, during the March 1991 riots in Belgrade, when the Serbian democratic forces demanded a change of regime. Failing to obtain the Yugoslav presidency's majority approval for imposing a state of emergency, the president of Yugoslavia of Serbian origin, Borisav Yovich,

---

[128] Author's Interview with Ratko Markovich, Professor of Constitutional Law at the University of Belgrade and one of key authors of the 1990 Serbian Constitution, Zlatibor, Serbia, July 24, 2005.

[129] Article 135, Constitution of the Republic of Serbia, 1990.

[130] Author's Interview with Ratko Markovich, Professor of Constitutional Law at the University of Belgrade and one of key authors of the 1990 Serbian Constitution, Zlatibor, Serbia, July 24, 2005.

[131] Discussed in more detail later in this book.

resigned. Although Yovich quickly withdrew the resignation, Miloshevich delivered an emotional speech broadcast on state television on March 16, 1991:

> Yugoslavia has entered into the final phase of its agony. The Presidency of the Socialist Federalist Republic of Yugoslavia and its powers, which in reality do not exist, has since last night finally expired. . . . The Republic of Serbia will no longer recognize a single decision of the Presidency under the existing circumstances because it would be illegal.[132]

While Miloshevich never officially relinquished his preference for a (rump) Yugoslavia from then on, Serb public opinion became ever more varied and disunited. As aptly described by Aleksandar Pavkovic:

> While in the 1980s some liberals called for a liberal and democratic unification of the Serbs in one state, other liberals opposed any such project on grounds that it could not be carried out without the consent of other national groups in the former Yugoslavia.[133]

However, the Serb intellectual dissidents found no partner in other former Yugoslav republics in their attempts to democratically reform Yugoslavia[134] or to later mediate a peaceful resolution of the looming military conflict.[135] Similarly, democrat government officials, such as the Serbian-American businessman Milan Panich, failed to attract the support of other ethnic groups inhabiting Serbia with grievances against the Miloshevich regime, namely the Albanians, in overturning

---

[132] *FBIS-EEU,* March 18, 1991, 47.

[133] Aleksandar Pavkovic, "Review Article: The Origins of Contemporary Serb Nationalism: Yet Another Case of trahison des clercs?" in *The Slavonic and East European Review* 82, no. 1 (January 2004), 86.

[134] According to Jasna Dragovich-Soso, as reviewed by Pavkovic, "all attempts by Belgrade dissidents to establish a common dissident organizations with their Slovene counterparts for the defence of freedom of thought and speech met with failure. . . . [B]y the mid-1980s the Slovene dissidents concluded that Yugoslavia no longer offered a framework for their political action and their focus likewise shifted to a nationalist program for Slovenia's independence." Pavkovic, "Review Article: The Origins of Contemporary Serb Nationalism: Yet Another Case of trahison des clercs?" 87.

[135] Glenny recounts the failure of the conference of parliamentary parties of Yugoslavia in summer 1990, organized by the "Democratic Party in Serbia" in Sarajevo, when the Croat and Bosnian representatives demonstrated a complete lack of good will to even discuss issues at stake, demanding a translation of the discussion to Croatian and Bosnian, which is comparable to "somebody from Glasgow requesting that a Londoner's speech be translated into Scottish English." For more, *see* Glenny, *The Fall of Yugoslavia,* 146.

this regime to pursue a more democratic policy of resolving the ethnic conflict reflected in overlapping territorial claims.[136]

4.4.1. Krayina's Trapped Minority

Ethnic Structure

According to the official 1991 census, just over 12 percent of the population of the Socialist Republic of Croatia declared themselves Serbs.[137] Of the hundred municipalities in SR Croatia, there were several where Serbs had an overwhelming majority (Donyi Lapats 98 percent; Knin 88.5 percent; Dvor na Uni 85 percent). There were thirteen municipalities in which the Serbs had either an absolute or a relative majority of the population, such as in Pakrats, with 46 percent Serbs and 36 percent Croats. There were also many municipalities in which the Croats had a relative majority and the Serbs a significant minority. The best known such example is the town of Vukovar (44 percent Croat and 37.5 percent Serb). Finally, almost one-third of the Serbs were scattered in relatively small groups in a number of Croatian towns where they represented less than 10 percent of the population.[138]

Serbs were a majority in the Krayina region. In total, the share of the territory where the Serbian population represented majority was larger than the Serbian participation in SR Croatia's population. Two reasons for such a demographic structure are that a great portion of the Serb population died in the Second World War, while many also emigrated during the Communist period, both to more developed, fertile regions such as Voivodina and to the urban centers in Yugoslavia and abroad, mainly for economic reasons.

---

[136] According to exit polls Panich was close to victory (polls showed both Miloshevich and Panich receiving about 47 percent of the vote. Official tallies claimed that Miloshevich received 55 percent and Panich only 34 percent of the vote. The Albanian vote for Panich would have made the rigging of elections very difficult. For more on this election, *see* Douglas E. Schoen, "How Milosevic Stole the Election," *New York Times Magazine*, February 14, 1993, 40.

[137] Nevertheless, this figure must be reassessed, considering the unreliability of censuses in Yugoslavia, particularly in 1991, when the nationalist Croatian party undertook the census after just winning the elections. Apart from irregularities in the conducting and the reporting of the census, there were certainly also a high number of Serbs who declared themselves as Yugoslavs, non-declared or even declared themselves as Croats, particularly if living in urban areas of Croatia, fearing possible Croat reprisals.

[138] Mihailo Crnobrnja, *The Yugoslav Drama* (Montreal: McGill-Queen's University Press, 1992), 25.

Political organization

The first Serb rally in Krayina took place on February 27, 1989, as the Serbs in the town of Knin demonstrated in solidarity with the Serbs from Kosovo and Metohia. The protest was provoked by the decision of the Union of Croatian Syndicates to open a charity fund for the Albanian strikers at a Kosovo mine of "Stari trg," whom the Serbs viewed as political rather than economic protestors. The Serb demonstrators carried Yugoslav flags and pictures of Josip Broz Tito, singing Yugoslav-themed songs in addition to traditional Serbian songs. Croatian television then chose to emphasize the more national Serbian characteristics of the rally, failing to report on its Yugoslav elements, which in fact dominated the scene.[139] The second large rally in Knin took place on February 2, 1990, this time explicitly called "For Yugoslavia" to remove any possible doubt regarding the position of Krayina Serbs on the future of the common state.

Yovan Rashkovich (Jovan Raskovic) became the first leader of Krayina Serbs in the early 1990s as the President of the Serbian Democratic Party (SDS),[140] founded in Knin in February 1990. A respected psychiatrist by profession, Rashkovich has explained that Serbs have a different relationship towards Yugoslavia than other Yugoslav peoples,[141] as a consequence of different history and demographic composition within Yugoslavia. Serbs generally regarded themselves as both Serb and Yugoslav, and since this identification was strong, it was difficult for the Serbs in Croatia to additionally formulate their identity as Croats. The Croats generally fail to understand this phenomenon, because, for the majority, their affiliation to Yugoslavia was never strong.

The Serbs inhabiting the former Yugoslav republic of Croatia desired a continuation of Yugoslavia and cultural autonomy for Krayina as a part of any future constitutional reform. However, if Yugoslavia were to become a confederation, they requested territorial autonomy for Krayina. As Yovan Rashkovich has elaborated:

> If Yugoslavia remains a federal union, then we will propagate and be satisfied with a cultural and national autonomy, which means that we want to freely pronounce our Serbian name, to publish Serbian newspapers,

---

139 Srdjan Radulovich, *Sudbina Krajine* [The Fate of Krayina] (Belgrade: Dan Graf, 1996), 11-12.

140 SDS became the leading party of the Serbian people on the territory of (former) SR Croatia.

141 Yovan Rashkovich, *Луда земља* [An Insane Country] (Belgrade: Akvarijus, 1990), 157.

to have an official right to use the Serbian language, that Cyrillic script is in public use wherever the Serbs are a majority, and to have our Serbian television. If Yugoslavia becomes a confederation, then things change. In that case we will also declare a territorial autonomy. Clearly, this will also occur in the case that there is no confederal Yugoslavia.

Rashkovich alerted the new nationalist Croat government that any attempt on their behalf to secede from Yugoslavia would be countered by a Serbian demand for the region of Krayina to remain in Yugoslavia: "If the Croatian people want their own state, then the Serbs will decide their own fate." Rashkovich added that if Croatia seceded from Yugoslavia, Serbs from SR Croatia would try to attach themselves to Serbia.[142]

In the early to mid-1990, the Serbs in Croatia exhibited no signs of separatism, instead demonstrating concern for basic language and educational rights, which would translate into general minority rights. In the 1990 parliamentary election in Croatia, they overwhelmingly gave their vote to the Party of Croatian Communists, with Serb Democratic Party receiving only 13.5 percent of the Serb vote.[143]

However, on July 25, 1990, as the Croatian Assembly adopted amendments to the Croatian Constitution[144] without consulting with Serb representatives, the Serbs created an ad hoc National Assembly, which proclaimed the Autonomy of the Serbs in Croatia pending upon a future referendum.[145] The right to self-determination features prominently in this document:

> The Serbian people gives itself the right to, on historical territories bound by the current borders of Croatia, determine with whom it shall live, in which regime it shall live, and how it will associate itself with other peoples in Yugoslavia.
>
>   . . .

---

[142] Cited in Crnobrnja, *The Yugoslav Drama*, 237.

[143] For an analysis of this election, *see* Valhre P. Gagnon, Jr, *The Myth of Ethnic War: Serbia and Croatia in the 1990s* (Ithaca, N.Y.: Cornell University Press, 2004), 138-140.

[144] *See above.*

[145] Declaration of Sovereignty and Autonomy of the Serb People in Croatia [Deklaracija o suverenosti i autonomiji srpskog naroda u Hrvatskoj] in Radulovich, *The Fate of Krayina*, 123-4.

Based on its sovereignty, the Serbian people in Croatia has the right to autonomy. The content of the autonomy shall depend on the federal or confederal arrangement of Yugoslavia.[146]

On August 19 and September 2, 1990, the Serbs conducted a referendum on autonomy within Croatia, defying a ban by Zagreb authorities. The referendum took place only in those towns where the Serbs were a majority, namely the region of Krayina. Officially, 756,781 Serbs took part in this plebiscite.[147] Of this total, it is said, 756,549 voted for Serbian autonomy, 172 voted against, and 60 ballots were invalid.[148] On September 30, 1990, another Declaration of Serb Autonomy was proclaimed.[149]

At the time of the referendum, the Krayina Serb leader, Rashkovich, clarified the Serb position: "We do not want an autonomy that aims to create a Serbian state in Croatia; we want a cultural autonomy."[150] As Rashkovich reiterated, it was "up to the Croatian parliament, HDZ and Dr. Franjo Tudjman to make the move."[151]

Rashkovich met with the Croat president Tudjman to share these views, asking that Serb representatives be involved in the drafting of any future amendments to the Constitution of the Socialist Republic of Croatia. The Serb leader took a conciliatory, compromise-seeking position, claiming that he was aware that Croats and Serbs had to cooperate with each other.[152] This need was made even greater by the fact that, while half of the Serbs in SR Croatia resided in the majority Serb region of Krayina, another half resided in the majority Croat areas, such as the capital town of Zagreb. However, as cited above, Rashkovich also avowed that

---

[146] Ibid., 123 [translation mine].

[147] Note: Provided this number is correct, the Serb participation in Croatian population was not 12 but 18 percent, which would confirm the assumption that most of the declared "Yugoslavs" were Serbs.

[148] Mile Dakic, *Srpska Krajina; Istorijski temelji i nastanak* [Serbian Krayina: Historical Foundations and Creation] (Knin: Iskra, 1994), 52.

[149] *See* Ibid., 52-3.

[150] Radulovich, *The Fate of Krayina*, 22. *See also* Glenny, *The Fall of Yugoslavia*, 19.

[151] Rashkovich, *An Insane Country*, 250-1.

[152] The transcript of talks between Franjo Tudjman and Yovan Rashkovich (Zagreb, July 1990), which were recorded, was subsequently printed in the Croatian weekly *Danas*; reproduced in Velyko Djurich Mishina, ed. *Република Српска Крајина; Десет година послије* [Republic of Serbian Krayina; Ten years later] (Belgrade, Dobra volya, 2005), 281-290.

Croatian secession from Yugoslavia would be followed by a secession of the Serb regions from Croatia.[153]

As the ruling Croatian party (Croatian Democratic Community—HDZ) proceeded with the adoption of the new Croatian Constitution alone, the Krayina Serbs, represented by the Serbian National Council of Krayina, rushed to proclaim the formation of the Serbian Autonomous Region of Krayina (SAO Krayina) on December 21, 1990, a day before the adoption of the new Croatian Constitution that relegated the Serbs from a constituent nation to a minority. The statute declared that "SAO Krayina is a form of territorial autonomy within the Republic of Croatia."[154] Another two autonomous districts were established soon thereafter: an autonomous district of Slavonia, Baranya, and Western Srem, and an autonomous district of Western Slavonia.[155]

The new Croatian Constitution, enacted on December 22, 1990, alienated the Serbs by referring to them as one of Croatia's minorities and thereby stripping the Serbs of the equality with the Croats they had enjoyed in the previous constitutions. Articles 1 and 2 of the previous Croatian Constitution had stipulated the following:

1. The Croatian nation, in harmony with its historical aspirations in common struggle with the *Serbian nation*[156] and nationalities in Yugoslavia, realized, in the national liberation war and in the socialist revolution, its own national state—the Socialist Republic of Croatia—and, proceeding from the right of self-determination, including even the right of secession, in the free expression of its own will and in order to protect its national independence and freedom, to build socialism and advance multifaceted social and national development, conscious that the further strengthening of the fraternity and unity of the nations and nationalities of Yugoslavia was in their common interest, voluntarily united with the other nations and nationalities in the Socialist Federated Republic of Yugoslavia.

---

[153] R. Dmitrovich, "Повратак Крајине: Хрватска и њен нови Устав" [Krayina's Return: Croatia and its new Constitution] *Nin*, no. 208620, December 1990, 13.

[154] Dakich, *Serbian Krayina: Historical Foundations and Creation*, 52-53.

[155] Ibid., 52.

[156] The Serbian word "narod"(*народ*) may be translated both as "nation" and "people."

2. The Socialist Republic of Croatia is the sovereign national state of the *Croatian nation*, the state of the *Serbian nation in Croatia*, and the state of the nationalities that live in it.

Instead of this formulation, the Croatia of 1990 became "the national state of the Croat nation and the state of the members of other nations and minorities who are its citizens: Serbs, Muslims, Slovenes, Czechs, Slovaks, Italians, Hungarians, Jews and others," on the basis of "the right of the Croatian nation to self-determination and state sovereignty."[157] Article 2 of the new Croatian Constitution also envisaged:

> The Republic of Croatia can either enter into or secede from union with other states. In this case the Republic of Croatia has the sovereign right to decide the amount of power to be relinquished.[158]

By this provision, the Croats attempted to "legalize" their secession from Yugoslavia, more explicitly than the Slovenes but certainly following the Slovene example.

As previously explained, the symbols of the newly proclaimed state, such as the checkered flag, to the Croats represented tradition, while to the Serbs, they were reminiscent of the Nazi Croat state of World War II that used these symbols, arousing fear of a renewed pogrom.

Croatian actions, rather than instigation from Serbia, represented the key reason for Serb resistance. Serbs from Croatia reacted to the Croatian government's acts, a pattern most evident in Krayina's proclamation of a disassociation from Croatia on February 28, 1991, one week after Croatia's declared disassociation from Yugoslavia.[159]

---

[157] Part I (Historical Foundations), *Constitution of the Republic of Croatia*, 1990. Note: Constitutional decision on the sovereignty and independence of the Republic of Croatia, Zagreb, June 25, 1991, also proceeded from "the inalienable, inconsumable, indivisible and untransferable right of the Croatian nation to self-determination, including the right of disassociation and association with other nations and States, and from the sovereignty of the Republic of Croatia rested in all its citizens." Reproduced in A.P. Blaustein and G.H. Flanz, eds. *Constitutions of the Countries of the World*, Release 92-3, Issued May 1992, and in Snezana Trifunovska, *Yugoslavia Through Documents From Its Creation to its Dissolution* (Dordrecht: Martinus Nijhoff, 1994), 299-301: 299.

[158] Ustav Republike Hrvatske [Constitution of the Republic of Croatia], Izvjesca Hrvatskoga sabora [Proceedingss of the Croatian Assembly], number 15, December 22, 1990, 17.

[159] Resolution of the Croatian Assembly, February 21, 1991.

SAO Krayina's Resolution reiterates Krayina Serbs' commitment to a (rump) Yugoslavia:

> SAO Krayina remains in a state of Yugoslavia, that is in a common state with the Republic of Serbia and Montenegro, as well as with the Serbian people in the Republic of Bosnia and Herzegovina and other peoples and republics that accept a common state.[160]

Importantly, the Resolution's Preamble refers to the right of self-determination, confirmed by the August 1990 referendum, and it stresses that Serbs outside the Kingdom of Serbia joined Yugoslavia in 1918 "as a people." The argument that it was the people that formed Yugoslavia and not republics is further emphasized by the use of the term "disassociation" in the title of the resolution. In this Resolution, the Serbs of SR Croatia also recognize "the rights of the Croat people to separate from the Yugoslav state," however, "within the bounds of their ethnic space" (Article 3). The Serbs consented to Croatian secession but without the territory that the Serbs dominated both historically and demographically, whose boundaries were no less historical than the administrative boundaries of SR Croatia.

The Serbs of SR Croatia acted independently of Republic of Serbia leadership (aka Slobodan Miloshevich) in the first phase of the conflict. Yovan Rashkovich, the first leader of the Krayina Serbs, was a staunch anti-Communist, who ideologically opposed Miloshevich, even openly supporting Miloshevich's opposition, the Democratic Party. Rashkovich believed that Serbs in Croatia had to be independent of Serbia in their negotiations with the Zagreb authorities. As the conflict in Croatia radicalized, sparked by the adoption of the new Croatian Constitution, Rashkovich was ousted by a more militant leader, Milan Babich, who allied himself closely with Miloshevich. Babich expressed the following viewpoint:

> Serbs in Croatia believed that Miloshevich was the true representative of the Serbian people and that he would not betray the interests of any part of the Serb nation in Yugoslavia. We don't need mediators between the

---

[160] Article 1, Resolution on the disassociation of the Republic of Croatia and SAO Krajina, February 28, 1991. This Resolution was later formalized by a decision of SAO Krayina to separate from Croatia and remain within Yugoslavia: Odluka o odvajanju od Republike Hrvatske [Resolution on the disassociation of the Republic of Croatia and SAO Krajina], March 18, 1991, in Dakich, *Serbian Krayina: Historical Foundations and Creation*, 21-22.

government and Krajina to resolve the political relations in Croatia, but the Serb people should act united through its representatives in resolving the political crisis and interethnic relations in Yugoslavia, and I believe that Miloshevich is an authentic representative of the Serb nation in Yugoslavia.[161]

On April 1, 1991, following a Croat attack on the majority Serb town of Plitvitse (Plitvice), Babich decided to fully shift from Rashkovich's policy and declare Krayina's union with Serbia.[162] Even Miloshevich was surprised by Babich's decision, and he never accepted Krayina's union with Serbia, which was in line of his official policy of agitating for a reformed Yugoslavia rather than a Greater Serbia. As a result, the Krayina leadership rephrased the plebiscite question, originally planning to assess Krayina people's desire to join Serbia. In a plebiscite held on May 12, 1991, the Serbs of SR Croatia overwhelmingly voted in favor of SAO Krayina *remaining in Yugoslavia*.[163]

However, Babich simultaneously took steps to institutionalize SAO Krayina. On April 30, 1991, the SAO Krayina National Assembly was constituted and Milan Babich elected President.[164] After an utter disappointment with Belgrade, SAO Krayina and the Bosnian Serb Republic declared a union on October 31, 1992,[165] but this declaration also remained a dead letter because of Miloshevich's disapproval.[166]

On June 25, 1991 Croatia formally declared independence,[167] referring to the "inalienable, inconsumable, indivisible and nontransferable right of the Croatian people to self-determination, including the right of disassociation." This right was tested at the May referendum. The fact that the Serbs from Croatia boycotted this

---

161 *See* Radulovich, *The Fate of Krayina*, 28.

162 Odluka o prisajedinjenju SAO Krajine Republici Srbiji [Decision on Joining of SAO Krayina with Serbia], April 1, 1991, in Radulovich, *The Fate of Krayina*, 133.

163 Radulovich, *The Fate of Krayina*, 30-31 [Emphasis added].

164 Dakich, *Serbian Krayina: Historical Foundations and Creation*, 54.

165 The text of the so-called Prijedor Declaration, named after the town where it was adopted, is produced in Serbian language in Rayko Kuzmanovich, Конститутивне акти Републике Српске [Constitutional Acts of the Republic of Srpska] (Banja Luka: Glas srpski, 1994), 135-138.

166 Radulovich, *The Fate of Krayina*, 30-31.

167 The Croatian Assembly adopted a Constitutional Decision on the Sovereignty and Independence of the Republic of Croatia and a Declaration on the Establishment of the Sovereign and Independent Republic of Croatia, published in the *Official Gazette of the Republic of Croatia*, no. 31/91 and reproduced in English in Trifunovska, *Yugoslavia through Documents*, 299-304.

referendum and voted "to remain in Yugoslavia" at an independently organized plebiscite during the same period had no impact on the Croatian government. Incredibly, Stipe Mesić has claimed that "about 70 percent of Serbs from Croatia"[168] had answered positively to the referendum on the independence of Croatia. Such claims were a part of a later official Croat explanation that it was Serbs from outside Croatia that created the conflict in Croatia.

The demands of Serbs in Croatia grew with each Croatian step towards independence. The conflict over rights quickly transformed itself into a conflict over territory. The Croats, like the Slovenes, declared their administrative boundaries as the new international borders in their new constitutional acts. These documents were declared unconstitutional and void by the Yugoslav Constitutional Court,[169] which reiterated the following:

> Even though the procedure for realizing the right to self-determination, including the right to secession, is not determined by the SFRY Constitution, this does not imply that his right could be realized on the basis of unilateral acts on self-determination and secession. Not a single people, or a republican assembly, could decide on the realization of that right by a unilateral act before the procedure and conditions under which this right could be realized is determined."[170]

However, an EC sponsored legal advisory body, termed the Arbitration Committee, produced a different legal opinion.[171] On December 17, 1991, the European Community adopted a Declaration on Yugoslavia,[172] which rendered Croatia's

---

[168] Mesić, *How We Destroyed Yugoslavia*, xiii.

[169] Одлука о оцењивању уставности Уставне одлуке о сувk ности и самосталности Републике Хрватске [Decision on Evaluating the Constitutionality of the Constitutional Decision on the Sovereignty and Independence of the Republic of Croatia], October 16, 1991, in Buzadjich, *Secession of former Yugoslav republics in light of decisions of the Yugoslav Constitutional Court*, 156-159; Одлука о оцењивању уставности Декларације о проглашењу суверене и самосталне Републике Хрватске [Decision on Evaluating the Constitutionality of the Declaration on the Establishment of the Sovereign and Independent Republic of Croatia], November 13, 1991, in Buzadjich, *Secession of former Yugoslav republics in light of decisions of the Yugoslav Constitutional Court*, 159-162.

[170] Одлука о оцењивању уставности Уставне одлуке о сувk ности и самосталности Републике Хрватске [Decision on Evaluating the Constitutionality of the Constitutional Decision on the Sovereignty and Independence of the Republic of Croatia], October 16, 1991, in Buzadjich, *Secession of former Yugoslav republics in light of decisions of the Yugoslav Constitutional Court*, 158.

[171] For more, *see* Chapter 5: *International Recognition of the (former) Yugoslav Republics*.

[172] Printed in English in *Focus*, Special Issue, January 14, 1992, 251-252.

recognition of independence, within the administrative boundaries of Communist Yugoslavia, imminent. Three days later, on December 19, 1991, the three "Serbian autonomous districts" in Croatia merged and proclaimed the Republic of Serb Krayina an independent state.[173] The Constitution of the Republic of Serb Krayina in a way represented an inverse of the Constitution of the Republic of Croatia promulgated a year earlier. It declared the newly formed Serb state "a nation state of the Serb nation and the state of all citizens living in Krayina" (Article 1) and based its claim to statehood upon the right to self-determination. Importantly, the Constitution of the Republic of Serb Krayina recognized the other Yugoslav people's right to self-determination, requesting the same for the people of Krayina:

> We recognize the sovereign right of every nation including the nation of Slovenes and the nation of Croats to choose its own destiny and establish its own state. We Serbs, the people of Krayina, hereby retain the same rights for ourselves. (Preamble: Basic Principles)[174]

A plebiscite on the determination of the people of Krayina followed two and a half years later, when the physical conflict stabilized. On June 19–20, 1993, 98.6 percent of the voters in the ballot (93.8 percent of the total number of voters) voted for the independent Republic of Serb Krayina and its union with the Serb Republic and other Serbian lands.[175]

Since the Croats hoped to secede from Yugoslavia with the entire territory of the Republic of Croatia, including the Serb region of Krayina, this political conflict turned into a physical conflict over territory. It was termed a "log revolution" because Serbs begin erecting wood barricades in Krayina in the summer of 1990, as the Croats attempted to take control over the police stations and any weapons in the region.[176] Milan Martich, a police inspector from Knin, then became a

---

[173]   Dakich, *Serbian Krayina: Historical Foundations and Creation*, 56-7.

[174]   Printed in English in Slobodan Yarchevich, *Република Српска Крајина; државна докумената* [Republic of Serb Krayina; State Documents] (Belgrade: Miroslav, 2005), 139-140

[175]   It is important to note that the ethnic balance in the region had shifted by 1993. Many Croats had either fled or been expelled from Krayina, while many Serbs fled there from majority-Croat towns, again either out of fear or actual harassment. Since Serbs were a majority in the Krayina even prior to the conflict, this means that the result of the referendum would have been unchanged, but that the popular support for Krayina's independence probably would not have been as overwhelming.

[176]   As explained later in the text, the Yugoslav People's Army was not the sole source of military power. Each Yugoslav republic had territorial defense forces, set up to provide guerilla resistance in case of attack.

prominent figure among the Serbs, having refused to accept new Croatian uniforms marked with what Serbs viewed as Nazi Croatia symbols.[177]

The first open clashes took place in the spring of 1991. Although the Croatian government has widely claimed that the war was caused by "Serb aggression," Zlatko Kramarić, the former Croat mayor of Osijek in Slavonia, later avowed that Croatian forces made the first attack. The target was the village of Borovo Selo in Slavonia, a region bordering Serbia, on May 2, 1991, as well as the village of Tenya (Tenja) in the beginning of July.[178] Many civilians were killed in these attacks, as confirmed by a testimony given by Miro Bajramović, former sub-commander of the Croatian special police forces, to the Croatian independent weekly, *The Feral Tribune*, on September 1, 1997.[179]

Before the war began, both the Croat government and the Serbs from Krayina armed themselves clandestinely, drawing from the supplies of the Yugoslav People's Army (YPA) and the Territorial defense forces as well as by importing weapons from abroad.[180] Similarly, the Slovene authorities had planned for a separate Slovenian army for a full year before the war erupted.[181]

4.5. The Role of the Yugoslav People's Army

In 1991, at the outbreak of hostilities both in Slovenia and in Krayina, the Yugoslav People's Army attempted to fulfil its role of guarding the integrity of Yugoslavia professionally:

> The task assigned to the YPA by the federal presidency in early 1991 was similar to that of a peacekeeping force—separation of forces, disarming

---

[177] Radulovich, *The Fate of Krayina*, 17.

[178] Zlatko Kramarić. Interview to "Slobodna Dalmacija" [Free Dalmatia; regional, previously independent newspaper]; cited in Radovan Samardjich, ed., *Sistem neistina o zlocinima genocida 1991-1993. godine* [System of untruths regarding genocide crimes of 1991-1993] (Belgrade: Serbian Academy of Arts and Sciences, 1994), 332. After the war, Miro Bajramović, erstwhile subcommander of the Croatian special police, confessed to government-orchestrated attacks on Serb civilians in Slavonia in 1991: "Miro Bajramović's Confession," *Feral Tribune* (Split, Croatia), September 1, 1997; Chris Hedges, "Croatian's Confession Describes Torture and Killing on Vast Scale," *New York Times*, September 5, 1997.

[179] *Feral Tribune*, Split, Croatia, September 1, 1997.

[180] In January 1991, Belgrade television showed a documentary, secretly filmed by the Yugoslav counterintelligence, which revealed illegal Croatian arms imports from Hungary.

[181] *See* Mihailo Crnobrnja, *The Yugoslav Drama* (Montreal: McGill-Queen's University Press, 1992), 152.

paramilitaries, and a holding action until political talks could resume—and there is evidence that it was attempting to do just that long into 1991.[182]

With the disintegration of the League of Communists of Yugoslavia, the YPA was the only organization capable of completing this task, which is why in April 1990, the Yugoslav Minister of Defense Velyko Kadiyevich (Veljko Kadijevic) had "declared openly that the army was prepared to defend the territorial integrity of Yugoslavia with all means necessary."[183] Kadiyevich later argued that the general staff had no choice but to act, for if it "had refused to execute its part of the task of the political decisions of the Parliament of the SFRY, then that could be the end of the army in the worst possible way."[184]

On June 25, 1991, when the Slovene Assembly declared independence and the Slovene police overtook the customs posts, the Yugoslav federal government adopted the Decision on the Direct Insurance of the Implementation of Federal Legislation on Crossing of the State Border on the Territory of the Republic of Slovenia.[185] However, the YPA military operation in Slovenia was limited, resulting in a few deaths.[186] The federal authorities ordered the Yugoslav army to retreat from Slovenia[187] as a part of the European Community-mediated agreement of July 7, 1991 (the so-called Brioni Declaration[188]). The YPA respected this decision as well as the decision of the federal authorities of May 6, 1991 not to impose a state of emergency in Croatia, despite such a request from the Army. Significantly, the YPA also refused to intervene in Slovenia at the urging of only one part of the Yugoslav presidency (the Serbs), when the Yugoslav Constitutional Court declared the Slovene 1989 amendments unconstitutional.[189]

---

[182]   Woodward, *Balkan Tragedy*, 391.

[183]   Ibid., 136.

[184]   Veljko Kadijević, *Moje vidjenje raspada: vojska bez države* [My Views of the Break-Up: Army Without the Country] (Belgrade: Politika, 1993), 122-23.

[185]   Decision on the Direct Insurance of the Implementation of Federal Legislation on Crossing of the State Boundary on the Territory of the Republic of Slovenia, *Official Gazette of the SFRY*, no 47, 1991; printed in English in *Focus*, Special Issue, January 14, 1992, 88.

[186]   For more, *see* Glenny, *The Fall of Yugoslavia*, 95-97 and Woodward, *Balkan Tragedy*, 166-170.

[187]   Одлука о премештању јединица ЈНА са територије Републике Словеније у друге делове СФРЈ [Decision of the SFRY Presidency regarding Transfer of Yugoslav People Army Units from the territory of Slovenia to other parts of the SFRY], published in Buzadjich, *Secession of former Yugoslav republics in light of decisions of the Yugoslav Constitutional Court*, 234-235.

[188]   Yugoslav-EC Joint Declaration, July 8, 1991, printed in English in *Focus*, Special Issue, January 14, 1992, 110-114.

[189]   Borisav Yovich, *Последњи дани СФРЈ* [The Last Days of SFRY] (Belgrade: Politika, 1995), 28, 41.

Two reasons are often cited to explain the YPA's failure to protect Yugoslav integrity. One is that the army was unprepared for popular resistance and the other that a political deal was broken between the Slovene and the Serb president. Susan Woodward suggests a different interpretation, finding the cause in "the rapidity with which the conflict had evolved, the absence of policy for such a contingency, and the general confusion over appropriate action when political disintegration creates doubt about constitutionality and legality."[190] The fact that the Presidency's decision to retreat the army from Slovenia was not published in the Official Gazette of SFRY precluded the Yugoslav Constitutional Court from deciding on its constitutionality. The court nevertheless submitted its opinion to the Yugoslav Assembly, pursuant to Article 376 of the Yugoslav Constitution, asserting that the Presidency's decision was contrary to various provisions of the SFRY Constitution, particularly relating to provisions of safeguarding the country's territorial integrity. Importantly, the Federal Government's Decision to "transfer" Yugoslav forces included the following Point 9: "This decision does not prejudge the future regulation of relations in Yugoslavia, nor does it bring into question its territorial entirety."[191]

As the conflict in Croatia intensified, the YPA disintegrated along national lines. This process was facilitated by the existence of the civilian militia, the territorial defense forces.[192] The ethnic conflict in Croatia resulted in vast destruction, war crimes, numerous displaced persons of all ethnicities, and finally in an exodus of most of the Serbian population from Croatia.[193]

4.6. The Partition of Bosnia-Herzegovina

Ethnic Structure

SR Bosnia-Herzegovina portrayed a more complicated national landscape than Croatia, because of the intense ethnic mix of the population. Furthermore, the third nation living with Serbs and Croats in Bosnia were the Muslims, claimed by

---

[190] Woodward, *Balkan Tragedy*, 167.

[191] Decision of the SFRY Presidency regarding Transfer of Yugoslav People Army Units from the territory of Slovenia to other parts of the SFRY, published in Buzadjich, *Secession of former Yugoslav republics in light of decisions of the Yugoslav Constitutional Court*, 234-235.

[192] *See* footnote 17.

[193] For more, *see* Chapter 6: *Changing Borders by Force* and Chapter 7: *Conclusion: Former Yugoslavia's European Integration*.

both the Serbs and the Croats to be a part of their respective nation,[194] but declaring themselves a distinct nation.

In 1981, the Serbian population share in the total population of Bosnia and Herzegovina was 32 percent, while the Serbian households[195] owned 51.4 percent of the land. The Muslim population share was 39.5 percent, and their households owned 27.3 percent of the land, while the Croats represented 18.4 percent of the Bosnian population, and owned 17.3 percent of the land in Bosnia and Herzegovina.[196] For historic reasons elaborated earlier in this work, the Serbs, living mainly in the rural areas, owned a much larger share of the total land than was proportional to their demographic participation.

According to the 1991 census, Bosnia-Herzegovina had around 4,365,000 inhabitants. Of that number almost 43.7 percent declared themselves Muslims, 31.4 percent Serbs, and just over 17 percent Croats. The rest belonged to other nationalities, including 5.5 percent declared Yugoslavs. In 1991, the Serbs owned around 64 percent of the land in Bosnia and Herzegovina.[197]

The disparity between ethnic structure and land ownership, as well as a clear demographic shift to the advantage of one ethnic group, the Bosnian Muslims, fuelled the later struggle for territory. The percentage of Serbs in Bosnia had been much higher, at a steady 43-44 percent of the population from the end of the nineteenth century until 1961,[198] when it suddenly dropped due to the high birth

---

[194] Bosnian Muslim leader Alia Izetbegovic recounts how the Croat leader Franjo Tudjman once told him not to create a Muslim party, since "Croats and Muslims in Bosnia and Herzegovina are one people. Muslims are Croats and feel that way." Alija Izetbegovic, *Sjećanja; autobiografski zapis* [Memoirs; autobiographic script] (Sarajevo: TKD Sahinpasic, 2001), 82 [Translation mine]. Original text: "Gospodine Izetbegoviću, nemojte stvarati neku muslimansku stranku, to je potpuno pogrešna stvar, jer su Hrvati i Muslimani u BiH jedan narod. Muslimani su Hrvati i osjećaju se tako."

[195] Heads of households declared as Serbian.

[196] Milena Spasovski, Dragica Živković and Milomir Stepić, "The Ethnic Structure of the Population in Bosnia and Herzegovina" in *The Serbian Question in the Balkans; Geographical and Historical Aspects*, ed. Bratislav Atanacković (Belgrade: Faculty of Geography, University of Belgrade, 1995), 263-306, at 295. The analysis is based on the official Yugoslav census of March 31, 1981, which is taken as the last reliable population census by professional demographers, considering that the conflict had already erupted at the time of the 1991 census. *See also* Steven L. Burg and Paul S. Shoup, *The War in Bosnia-Herzegovina: Ethnic Conflict and International Intervention* (New York: M. E. Sharp Inc., 1999), 26-28.

[197] For an overview of the past population censuses for Bosnia and Herzegovina, *see* Kuzmanovich, *Constitutional Acts of the Republic of Srpska*, 24.

[198] Ibid.

rate among the Muslims compared to a very low birth rate among the other two peoples, as well as due to the higher rate of emigration among Serbs and Croats, both to other parts of Yugoslavia as well as to seek employment abroad.

Political Organization

The Bosnian Muslims were the first of the three dominant ethnic groups in Bosnia and Herzegovina to organize a political party along national lines by founding the "Party of Democratic Action" (SDA) on May 26, 1990. Misha Glenny argues that as a consequence of this act "Alija Izetbegovic and the Moslem leadership . . . bear a historic responsibility for the breakdown of the consensus between the three Bosnian communities."[199] The Serbs and the Croats of Bosnia and Herzegovina rushed to organize their own national parties in time for the first multiparty elections in November 1990. The Serbian Democratic Party (SDS) was established on July 27, 1990 and the Croat Democratic Union (HDZ) on September 6, 1990. The people of Bosnia and Herzegovina overwhelmingly voted along national lines, which led to a trilateral government that shared authority in proportion to demographic strength.[200] Based on this arrangement, a Bosnian Muslim headed the collective presidency composed of all ethnic groups, a Bosnian Serb became the President of the National Assembly and a Bosnian Croat was appointed prime minister. Ethnic power-sharing was also reflected in the local self-government. However, sharing did not imply joint ethnic cooperation but cooperation by ethnic division, whereby the dominant ethnic group governed a municipality exclusively of other two ethnic groups.[201] As Burg and Shoup underscore, "None of the three nationalist parties in Bosnia was committed to the notion of a civil society."[202]

A delicate multiethnic balance in Bosnia was maintained by an important agreement that legislation dealing with the status of any of the three constituent peoples could be passed only by consensus. This agreement was imprinted in the amendments to the Bosnian constitution of July 1990. Amendment LIX declared Bosnia to be "a democratic sovereign state of equal citizens, the nations of Bosnia

---

[199] Glenny, *The Fall of Yugoslavia*, 149.

[200] For election results, *see* Hayden, *Blueprints for a House Divided*, 91-92.

[201] For more, *see* Robert M. Hayden, "Constitutional Nationalism and the Logic of the Wars in Yugoslavia," *Problems of Post-Communism* 43, no. 5 (1996) and Robert M. Hayden, "Constitutional Nationalism in the Formerly Yugoslav Republics," *Slavic Review* 51 (1992).

[202] Burg and Shoup, *War in Bosnia-Herzegovina*, 12.

and Herzegovina—Muslims, Serbs and Croats and members of other nationalities who live within it," while Amendment LXI guaranteed "proportional representation of the nations and nationalities of Bosnia and Herzegovina" in governmental institutions. Amendment LXX created a "Council for Questions of the Establishment of Equality of the Nations and Nationalities of Bosnia and Herzegovina" in the parliament. A proportional composition of the Council, a requirement of agreement of its members "from the ranks of all the nations and nationalities" to approve an issue, and a further requirement of a two-thirds majority of the parliament to pass the relevant legislative provisions provided for a triple safeguard of national equality in Bosnia and Herzegovina, guaranteed by the republic's constitution.

Using these guarantees, the Serb political representatives successfully rejected the Bosnian Muslim proposal of January 30, 1991 that the National Assembly adopt a Declaration of State Sovereignty and Indivisibility of the Republic of Bosnia and Herzegovina, and the subsequent Muslim-Croat proposal to declare the supremacy of republican over federal legislation. However, on October 14, 1991, despite Serb objections, the Bosnian Muslim and the Bosnian Croat parties (SDA and HDZ) submitted a "Memorandum on the Sovereignty of Bosnia-Herzegovina to the National Assembly."[203]

The proposed Memorandum declared the republic a sovereign and independent state within its existing boundaries and rejected "the Belgrade Initiative" to form a new federation of nations (peoples) and republics choosing to remain within Yugoslavia.[204] The Bosnian Muslim and the Bosnian Croat parliamentary representatives conditioned their support for the Yugoslav federal government by participation of all federal units in the meetings of the federal presidency and the federal assembly (Article 2). They also argued that Bosnia and Herzegovina "would not accept any constitutional solutions for a future Yugoslav community which would not include both Serbia and Croatia" (Article 3). Such a proposal could be viewed as hypocritical since it was made at the time when the Croatian independence appeared imminent (six days earlier Croatia decided to break all state-legal ties with Yugoslavia, to which the Memorandum indirectly refers in

---

[203] Memorandum on the Sovereignty of Bosnia-Herzegovina to the National Assembly, *Official Gazette of the Socialist Republic of Bosnia and Herzegovina*, 32/91; printed in English in *Focus*, Special Issue, January 14, 1992, 182-183.

[204] *See* the discussion above.

Article 1). Alternatively, it could be perceived as a weak effort to preserve Yugoslavia, which would be more difficult to elaborate.

The Serb parliamentary representatives (SDS) in turn submitted a competing resolution that did not condition participation in Yugoslav structures by activity of all federal units. However, the SDS-sponsored "Resolution on the Position of Socialist Republic of Bosnia and Herzegovina in Resolving the Yugoslav crisis"[205] simultaneously provided that were Croatia to secede, this would initiate a "mechanism . . . for realizing the right to self-determination, including the right to secession, of the peoples of Bosnia and Herzegovina (Muslims, Serbs, and Croats) who no longer wish to remain in such a federal state and wish to establish their own states or join other internationally recognized states" (Article 4). Importantly the SDS proposal further specified that this "mechanism" would be "agreed upon through a special act on a plebiscite of the constituent peoples of Bosnia-Herzegovina" and that "the results of the plebiscite [would] be established for each nation separately, for the republic as a whole, and on the territorial principle (settlement, neighborhood community and commune)" (Article 4), which is again reminiscent of the case of establishment of the Jura canton in Switzerland.[206]

Since the Bosnian Muslims and the Bosnian Croats proceeded to discuss the Memorandum on the Sovereignty of Bosnia-Herzegovina in the National Assembly, ignoring Serb constitutional rights to prevent its submission to the National Assembly, the Serbian members of the parliament overwhelmingly boycotted this discussion. The Bosnian Muslims and the Bosnian Croats exploited the Serb boycott of the National Assembly in order to adopt the Memorandum on October 15, 1991 by a majority vote of delegates present.[207]

On January 24, 1992, during a marathon session of the National Assembly of Bosnia and Herzegovina, the three dominant ethnic groups came close to agreeing on a political-territorial reorganization of Bosnia. The Muslim leader, Alija Izetbegovic, rejected the compromise achieved by members of his own party and instead called for a vote on the resolution to hold a plebiscite. Izetbegovic had

---

[205] Resolution on the Position of Socialist Republic of Bosnia and Herzegovina in Resolving the Yugoslav crisis; printed in English in *Focus*, Special Issue, January 14, 1992, 183-184.

[206] *See* discussion above at page 200.

[207] The Yugoslav Constitutional Court could not adjudicate the constitutionality of this act for procedural reasons related to political situation (at least eight members of the Court had to agree). *See* Buzadjich, *Secession of former Yugoslav republics in light of decisions of the Yugoslav Constitutional Court*, 51.

hoped to achieve a unitary Bosnian state with the help of international recognition based on a majority vote of all citizens, regardless of the constitutional provisions. Although the seventeen-hour long session was adjourned at 3.30 a.m. on January 25, 1992 by the President of the National Assembly (of Serbian ethnicity), who announced its continuation at 10.00 a.m. the same day, the Bosnian Muslim and the Bosnian Croat delegates met an hour later and approved the resolution to hold a plebiscite on February 29–March 1, 1992, with a question: "Are you for a sovereign and independent Bosnia and Herzegovina, a state of equal citizens, nations of Bosnia and Herzegovina—Muslims, Serbs, Croats, and other nations that live in it?" According to official results, an overwhelming 99.4 percent of the voters answered positively to the question. However, only 63.4 percent of the voting population went to the polls, with the Serbs boycotting the plebiscite. The Serbs had organized a plebiscite on November 9-10, 1991, when, allegedly, 1,350,000 million Bosnian citizens, or 96.4 percent of those who took part in the vote, voted for a sovereign Serb state that could be a part of Serbia or Yugoslavia.[208]

Both the vote on the Memorandum on the Sovereignty of Bosnia-Herzegovina and the vote on the plebiscite were "of dubious legality" and certainly unconstitutional as they did not respect the guarantees of national equality outlined above.[209] However the European Community, as in the cases of Slovenia and Croatia, ignored the Yugoslav constitutional provisions. Subsequently, Bosnia and Herzegovina entered into a violent ethnic conflict. The level of violence stemmed from the conflicting positions of the three dominant ethnic groups, whose "right to self-determination" could be realized only to the detriment of at least one of the other two groups.

The Bosnian Muslims initially supported two options—Bosnia in a continued state of Yugoslavia (federal or confederal) that included both Croatia and Serbia, or Bosnia's secession from Yugoslavia and its constitution as a unitary state.[210] They were the largest single ethnic group in Bosnia, with favorable future demographic

---

[208] Kuzmanovich, *Constitutional Acts of the Republic of Srpska*, 12.

[209] For more, *see* Hayden, *Blueprints for a House Divided*, 92-97and Burg and Shoup, *War in Bosnia-Herzegovina*, 79.

[210] The Bosnian Muslims envisaged an independent Bosnia as "a centralized, unitary State, arranged into a number of regions possessing merely administrative functions." International Conference on the former Yugoslavia, *Report of the Co-Chairmen on the Progress in Developing a Constitution for Bosnia and Herzegovina*, October 27, 1991, 4.

prospects, which would allow them to increasingly dominate an independent Bosnian state. Indeed, when addressing Muslim audiences abroad, the Bosnian Muslim leader Izetbegovic "spoke with great feeling about the need of the Muslim nation in Bosnia to have its own state."[211] Since the Bosnian Muslims generally lived dispersed across Bosnian territory, they deemed the division of Bosnia unacceptable for the same reasons that Serbs deemed the division of Yugoslavia unacceptable. If Bosnia were partitioned, Bosnian Muslims would no longer live in one state. The Bosnian Muslims therefore had an inverse position towards Bosnia as opposed to Yugoslavia. In 1991, the Bosnian Muslim "Platform for the Future Yugoslav Community,"[212] also supported by the Macedonian republic leadership, proposed that Yugoslavia be reorganized into a confederacy where the republics had veto power on all federal legislation.

The Bosnian Muslim party that won the majority support of the Bosnian Muslims in the 1990 elections, the SDA, represented a more militant and religiously nationalist option, led by Alija Izetbegovic, who spent eight years in prison under the communists for Islamic fundamentalist beliefs.[213] A more moderate and secular Bosnian Muslim Party, the Moslem Bosniak Organization (MBO), split from the SDA two months before the elections. Its leader, Adil Zulfikarpasic (Zulfikarpashich), prior to 1990 had lived for twenty years in Switzerland. Unlike Izetbegovic, Zulfikarpasic was open to negotiating a reformed Yugoslav state and had come to an agreement with the Serbian leadership that was denounced by Izetbegovic.[214]

---

[211] Burg and Shoup, *War in Bosnia-Herzegovina*, 67; Alija Izetbegović, *Odabrani govori, pisma, izjave, intervjui* [Selected speeches, letters, statements, interviews] (Zagreb: Prvo muslimansko Dioničko društvo, 1995), 102.

[212] Platform for the Future Yugoslav Community, published in *Borba* on June 4, 1991; the English text is available in *Review of International Affairs*, October 20, 1990. See Hayden, "Bosnia's Internal War and the International Criminal Tribunal," *Fletcher Forum of World Affairs* 22, no. 1: 45-63, 1998.

[213] Izetbegovic authored *The Islamic Declaration*, published in 1970 and reprinted in 1990, as a blueprint for a Muslim-dominated state of Bosnia and Herzegovina. In 1946, the Yugoslav Communist authorities sentenced Izetbegovic to three years in prison for his 'pan-Islamic' activities; that is, alleged attempts to create an independent Islamic state, and a further fourteen years (of which he served just over five) in 1983 for writing the Islamic Declaration.

[214] Zoran Jelicic, "History's Witness: Adil Zulfikarpashich," *Vreme News Digest Agency* No 168, December 12, 1994; *See also* Lenard J. Cohen, *Broken Bonds; Yugoslavia's Disintegration and Balkan Politics in Transition*, 2nd ed. (Boulder: Westview Press, 1995), 241; BBCSWB, August 6, 1991, Part 2 (Eastern Europe), C.1 Special Supplement, p. EE/1143/B/1, and BBCSWB, September 2, 1991, Part 2 (Eastern Europe), C.1 Special Supplement, p. EE/1166/B/1.

Another Bosnian Muslim faction was led by Fikret Abdich. The differences between Abdich and Izetbegovic over war aims and strategy became so stark that Abdich's faction proclaimed the Autonomous Province of Western Bosnia in the north-west Bosnia on September 27, 1993. Although initially hoping to gain recognition as a separate administrative unit within Bosnia, "on the basis of equitable decision-making," this unit was transformed into the Republic of Western Bosnia towards the end of the Bosnian war on July 26, 1995. This self-proclaimed statelet lasted only a week, collapsing after the Croat "liberation" of the Krayina because the Bosnian Muslims of this region cooperated closely with the Serbs, jointly fighting the other Bosnian Muslims.[215] This phenomenon is a witness to mixed loyalties among the Bosnian Muslims, a consequence of the incomplete nation-building process.

In July 1990, the Izetbegovic-led SDA launched a branch of their party in the Sandzak, a predominantly Moslem area that divided Serbia and Montenegro. At the time, Izetbegovic argued that: "should Serbia and Montenegro decide to unify in some future new federation or confederation, the Moslems of the Sandzak would demand both cultural and political autonomy."[216] In July 1991, Izetbegovic visited Turkey to request Bosnia-Herzegovina's admission to the Organization of Islamic States and made additional visits to major Islamic states without consultation with other members of the Bosnian presidency.[217]

As Slovenia's and Croatia's secession appeared likely to succeed, Izetbegovic expressed preparedness of the Bosnian Muslims to fight for independence with arms:

> If the threat that Slovenia and Croatia leave Yugoslavia is carried out, Bosnia will not remain in a rump Yugoslavia. Bosnia does not accept to remain in a Greater Serbia and to be its part. . . . If need be, (Bosnian) Muslims will defend Bosnia with arms.[218]

---

[215] For more on the Republic of Western Bosnia, *see* Brendan O'Shea, *Crisis at Bihac: Bosnia's Bloody Battlefield* (Phoenix Mill: Sutton Publishing, 1998).

[216] Cohen, *Broken Bonds*, 144.

[217] Laura Silber and Alan Little, *Yugoslavia: Death of a Nation*, revised and updated edition (New York: Penguin Books, 1997), 213.

[218] Izetbegovic, *Memoirs*, 82 [Translation mine]. Original text: "Ako se ostvare prijetnje da Slovenija i Hrvatska izadju iz Jugoslavije, Bosna neće ostati u krnjoj Jugoslaviji. Bosna ne prihvata da ostane u velikoj Srbiji i da bude njen dio. [. . .] Ako zatreba Muslimani će oružjem braniti Bosnu."

Misha Glenny has criticized the provocative policy-making of the Bosnian Muslim leadership:

> [Bosnian Muslims] coaxed their people into a war for which they were criminally unprepared, and at times have both consciously and unconsciously allowed the mass slaughter of their own in the hope of receiving weapons from the West so that they might fulfil their political agenda.[219]

Other analysts, such as Paul Mojzes, have also asserted that a claimed goal of a multiethnic Bosnian state was but a mask for a narrow nationalist agenda:

> [T]he claim that they went to battle for a multiethnic, multireligious state continued to be made for the benefit of the international community, but an increased number of them turned into purely Islamic units defending a Muslim nationalist ideology.[220]

The Bosnian Croats opted for secession, but not as a goal in itself. They aspired to ultimately rejoin the Croats in Croatia, either by merging the two new states of Croatia and Bosnia, or, if that was not possible, by seceding for the second time, now from Bosnia. Although Bosnia and Herzegovina was ethnically mixed, Bosnian Croats tended to concentrate in Western Herzegovina, and there were also many other areas with a majority Serb population. In other words, if Bosnia were to be divided according to ethnic dominance of various settlements, Bosnian Muslims would be most disadvantaged since they, for historical reasons, resided in larger towns across Bosnia. This is why the Bosnian Muslim leaders rejected the first peace plan proposed for the cantonization of Bosnia that was genuinely supported by both the Bosnian Croats and the Bosnian Serbs, because it would allow them self-rule in areas they dominated and prevent Bosnian Muslim domination of the state.[221]

In line with their view of Bosnian independence as a first step towards subsequent Bosnian partition, the Bosnian Croats established the Croat Community of

---

[219] Glenny, *The Fall of Yugoslavia*, 183.

[220] Paul Mojzes, "The Camouflaged Role of Religion in the War in Bosnia and Herzegovina" in *Religion and the War in Bosnia*, ed. Paul Mojzes (Atlanta: Scholars Press, 1998), 95.

[221] According to Glenny, "The Bosnian Croats supported the cantonization of Bosnia as envisaged by the Lisbon agreement of March, 18, 1992, as whole-heartedly as Radovan Karadzic." Glenny, *The Fall of Yugoslavia*, 192. For more on various peace proposals for Bosnia, *see* Chapter 6: *Changing Borders by Force*.

Herzeg-Bosnia and the Croat Community in the Sava Valley in northeastern Bosnia in November 1991, just weeks after voting in favor of the sovereignty declaration in the Bosnian Assembly. On July 3, 1992, the Bosnian Croats proclaimed the state of Herzeg-Bosnia, which had been operating *de facto* since September-October 1991.[222] This action fully reflected the public statement made at the time by the Croat president Tudjman, the undisputed leader of all Croats, that "the solution to an all-out war in the crumbling Yugoslavia was the division of BiH [Bosnia and Herzegovina] between Croatia and Serbia."[223] Kiro Gligorov, the Macedonian leader, later recounted how Tudjman showed him a detailed map of how Bosnia should be divided between Serbs and Croats, leaving a small portion for Bosnian Muslims as well.[224] To Tudjman this represented a compromise position, since he, as explained above, like many nationalist Croats shared the belief that the "Muslim population [was] overwhelmingly of Croatian origin."[225] Partition of Bosnia, whether by cantonization or otherwise, was the first step in the realization of Croatian self-determination, whose goal was a nation-state of all Croats.

A month after the outbreak of war in Bosnia the leaders of Bosnian Serbs (Radovan Karadjic) and Croats (Mate Boban) met in Austria and agreed in principle on a division of Bosnia which would give the Croats 20 percent of the territory, the Serbs 65 percent of the territory and the Moslems 15 percent. The agreement failed because there was no agreement as to who would control the town of Mostar.[226]

As a result, the Bosnian Muslims and the Bosnian Croats created an unusual alliance of two ethnic groups with incompatible war aims. As explained by Glenny:

> Alija Izetbegovic's war aim was the restoration of a unitary state with a relatively centralized government in Sarajevo. This was always incompatible

---

[222] The Bosnian Croats even adopted the currency of the neighboring Croatia. For more, *see* Glenny, *The Fall of Yugoslavia*, 157.

[223] Cited in Ibid., 149.

[224] Kiro Gligorov, "Podela živog mesa" [Dividing Living Flesh], Interview, "Witnesses of Yugoslavia's Disintegration," Radio Free Europe (accessed February 5, 2005); available from http://www.danas.org/svjedoci/html/Kiro_Gligorov.html.

[225] Franjo Tudjman, *Nacionalno pitanje u suvremenoj Evropi* [National Question in Contemporary Europe], 2nd ed. (Munchen-Barcelona: Knjižica Hrvatske Revije, 1982), 140.

[226] For more, *see* Glenny, *The Fall of Yugoslavia*, 193. Croat President Tudjman and Serb President Miloshevich also met on at least two occasions to discuss partition of Bosnia. For more, *see* Burg and Shoup, *War in Bosnia-Herzegovina*, 104.

with the war aims of the Croats, but neither side could realize their aims without first establishing Bosnia's independence from Yugoslavia.[227]

The Bosnian Muslims had two more important reasons to ally with the Croats: tens of thousands of displaced Bosnian Muslims resided in Croatia and all illegal weapon supplies to Bosnia came through Croatia.[228]

Unlike the Serbs in SR Croatia who claimed a right to a part of this republic's territory (the region of Krayina), the Serbs in SR Bosnia-Herzegovina asserted at least an equal right to all of Bosnia as the Bosnian Muslims and Croats, if not a greater right derived from historic legacy.[229] The Bosnian Serbs' first preference was for Bosnia to remain in Yugoslavia, because then the Serbian nation would not be divided into different states, and the increasing Bosnian Muslim demographic dominance in Bosnia-Herzegovina would be diluted.

The position of the Bosnian Serbs was articulated by their political leader, Radovan Karadjich:

> Serbs, Croats and Muslims can no longer live together. Just as the Croats and Muslims didn't want to live in a united Yugoslavia, so we don't want to live in their states. You can't keep a dog and a cat in a box together. Either they would always be quarreling and fighting or they would have to stop being what they are.[230]

Alarmed by demographic trends and the Bosnian Muslim fundamentalism heralded by the Bosnian Muslim leader Izetbegovic, the Bosnian Serbs feared a loss of national identity, which in turn fueled their own nationalism.[231] On April 26, 1991, reacting to the Muslim-Croat proposal for a sovereignty declaration in January 1991, the Bosnian Serbs established the "Community of Bosnian Krayina," consisting of fourteen Serb-controlled municipalities. As the Muslims and Croats

---

[227] Ibid.

[228] Ibid., 195.

[229] The Serb historic legacy to Bosnia is contested by Bosnian Muslims and Bosnian Croats. For more, see Chapter 2: *Pre-1914 Administrative Boundaries and the Birth of Yugoslavia.*

[230] Cited in *Unfinished Peace; Report of the International Commission on the Balkans* (Washington: Carnegie Endowment for International Peace, 1996), 16.

[231] For a more elaborate study of the rise of ethnic nationalism in the former Yugoslavia see Hayden, *Blueprints for a House Divided*; Aleksandar Pavkovic, *Fragmentation of Yugoslavia; Nationalism and War in the Balkans*, 2nd ed. (London: Palgrave Macmillan, 2000).

took further steps to effect Bosnia's secession from Yugoslavia, the Bosnian Serbs responded by creating four Serbian Autonomous Districts in Bosnia in September 1991. As delineated above, this action was concurrent with similar endeavors by the Bosnian Croats.[232]

Hoping to prevent Bosnia's international *recognition* and "to defend their freedom, sovereignty, status of a constituent people, dignity and future,"[233] the Bosnian Serbs proclaimed a separate republic on January 9, 1992.[234] They officially declared independence only on April 7, 1992, the day after the European Community recognized Bosnia and Herzegovina as an independent state. Although their goal was "to remain" in a (rump) Yugoslavia, their action was now viewed as secessionist.

On October 24, 1992, in preparation for their own secession from Bosnia in case Bosnia were to secede from Yugoslavia,[235] the Serb representatives first proclaimed the Assembly of the Serb People in Bosnia and Herzegovina and declared the will of the Serb people of Bosnia and Herzegovina to remain in Yugoslavia.[236] Several days later, on February 28, 1992, the Bosnian Serb Assembly enacted the Constitution of the Bosnian Serb Republic (named the Republic of Serb People in Bosnia-Herzegovina upon formation in January 1991 and renamed the Bosnian Serb republic or the Republic of Srpska in August 1992, after Bosnia's international recognition).[237] Like the seceding Slovenes, Croats, or Bosnian Muslims, the Bosnian Serbs legally justified their right to secession by referring to "the inalienable and nontransferable, natural right . . . to self-determination."[238] As stipulated by the new Slovene and Croat constitutions, the Serb republic would also be a national state ("a state of the Serb people," Article 1). However, unlike Croatia and Slovenia, the Bosnian Serb republic would not be a newly independent state but a part of the Yugoslav federation (Article 3).

---

[232] For more, *see* Burg and Shoup, *War in Bosnia-Herzegovina*, 73-74.

[233] Preamble to the Declaration on Proclamation of the Republic of Serbian People in Bosnia Herzegovina, January 9, 1992.

[234] Integral text of the Declaration on Proclamation of the Republic of Serbian People in Bosnia Herzegovina is printed in Serbian in Kuzmanovich, *Constitutional Acts of the Republic of Srpska*, 123-129.

[235] On October 15, 1991, the Bosnian National Assembly unconstitutionally adopted the Memorandum on the Sovereignty of Bosnia-Herzegovina. *See* page 220 above.

[236] Kuzmanovich, *Constitutional Acts of the Republic of Srpska*, 19-23.

[237] Integral text reproduced in Serbian language in Kuzmanovich, *Constitutional Acts of the Republic of Srpska*, 73-110.

[238] Preamble to the Constitution of the Serb Republic, 1992.

The Constitution of the Serb Republic was the first to recognize a need for close relations among the Bosnian constituent nations. Its Article 4 provided that Republika Srpska "could enter into communities with state entities established by other constituent nations of Bosnia and Herzegovina," which was later to be emulated by the Bosnia-Herzegovina Constitution, negotiated as an end to the military conflict, but referring to the possibility of special relations of Bosnia with Croatia and Serbia, respectively. The boundaries of the Serb republic were defined as Serb majority areas as well as those regions where the Serbs became a minority as the result of genocide (Article 2), referring to the Croat Ustasha genocide against the Serbs during the Second World War.

The Croats and the Muslims fought with the Serbs and with each other for their piece of Bosnian territory. While negotiating over various peace proposals, they argued over maps, invoking various principles such as demography, history, legal title, geo-strategic, or economic considerations, but ethnic maps tended to dominate.[239] In the 1992-1995 period, the peoples of Bosnia and Herzegovina experienced one of the most gruesome and bloody wars that resulted in a high number of deaths and massive population movements.[240]

4.7. Macedonian Cohabitation

Macedonian[241] authorities also opted for "a national state of the Macedonian people" in 1989, amending their previous Constitution that had declared Macedonia "a state of the Macedonian people and the Albanian and Turkish minorities." According to the 1991 census these minorities accounted for 21 percent and 4.8 percent, respectively, while Macedonians comprised 64.6 percent of

---

[239] Susan Woodward also stresses the importance of economic assets, citing Karadjic's claim to "the rights of national sovereignty over 64 percent of Bosnian territory where (he said) Bosnian Serb households held legal title to land and farms," and a Serb complaint that the proposed Vance-Owen peace plan deprived them "of energy sources and industrial plants." For more, *see* Woodward, *Balkan Tragedy*, 212, 270.

[240] For more on the ethnic conflict and war crimes in Bosnia during 1992-1995, *see* Xavier Bougarel, *Bosnie; Anatomie d'un conflit* (Paris: La Découverte, 1996).

[241] The Slavs in Macedonia have developed a distinct Macedonian ethnicity mainly within the Yugoslav Communist framework, which institutionalized the "Macedonian literary language" and sponsored the establishment of a separate "Macedonian Orthodox Church" in 1967. In the past, both the Serbs and the Bulgarians have claimed Macedonians as part of their own national being—and territory. In the recent conflict, Serbs were quick to recognize Macedonian separate statehood, while the Bulgarians stalled the recognition of a separate Macedonian language until 1999. The Serbian Orthodox Church does not recognize the Macedonian Orthodox Church but this conflict is principally ecclesiastical and not ethnic in nature.

the total population of Macedonia. As in Bosnia, the demographic trends predicted a rapidly changing population structure, with an increase of the (Muslim) Albanian population and a decrease of the Macedonian share in the total population.[242] Another parallel to Bosnia was the resemblance of the 1990 elections to the population census, bringing a coalition of nationalist parties to power, albeit with a significant vote also going to the reformed Communists.

The secession of Macedonia from Yugoslavia took place more quietly than that of Croatia and Slovenia. Until its announced exit from the SFRY on January 25, 1991, by way of a Declaration on the Sovereignty of the Socialist Republic of Macedonia,[243] Macedonia had adopted significantly fewer legal acts that nullified the federal constitution and other federal acts.

In seceding from Yugoslavia, however, Macedonia followed the path of Croatia and Slovenia, basing this process on the "right to self-determination, including secession" (Article 1 of the Declaration) and invalidating the supremacy of the SFRY Constitution (Articles 2 and 5). At the same time, the Macedonian leadership probably had a greater interest in preserving Yugoslavia than Croatia or Slovenia, mainly as a way of buttressing its fragile internal ethnic balance. For this reason the Macedonian Declaration on the Sovereignty specified that Macedonia would proceed to independence only if the "relations among the sovereign republics in SFRY are not resolved by consensus and democratically, and in a manner that does not infringe on the sovereignty of the Republic [of Macedonia]" (Article 7).[244] As in the cases of Slovenia and Croatia, the Yugoslav Constitutional Court ruled unconstitutional the provisions of the Macedonian Declaration on Sovereignty that invoked nullification of federal constitution (Articles 2 and 5).[245]

---

[242] Kyril Drezov, lecturer in the Politics of South-east Europe at Keele University in United Kingdom, speaks of "demographic explosion" of the Albanians, which, combined with the "close to negative" Slav Macedonian birth rate, is likely to lead to Macedonian Albanians forming "as much as 40 per cent of the entire Macedonian population" within a generation. Kyril Drezov, "Collateral Damage: The Impact on Macedonia of the Kosovo War," *Kosovo: The Politics of Delusion*, eds. Michael Waller, Kyril Drezov and Bülent Gökay (London; Portland, OR: Frank Cass, 2001), 60.

[243] Integral text published in Buzadjich, *Secession of former Yugoslav republics in light of decisions of the Yugoslav Constitutional Court*, 260-261.

[244] Ibid.

[245] Одлука о оцењивању уставности Декларације о суверености Социјалистичке Републике Македоније [Decision on Evaluating the Constitutionality of the Declaration on Sovereignty of the Socialist Republic of Macedonia], January 28, 1991, *Official Gazette of SFRY*, no 35/91, reprinted in Buzadjich, *Secession of former Yugoslav republics in light of decisions of the Yugoslav Constitutional Court*, 229-231.

Upon Slovenian and Croat declarations on independence, Macedonians organized a plebiscite, held on September 8, 1991. The question, positively answered by 95.26 percent of those who voted, reflects the Macedonian determination for Yugoslav confederation: "Are you in favor of a sovereign and autonomous Macedonia with the right to join a future alliance of sovereign states of Yugoslavia?" However, this was the expression of the Macedonian Slavs, with Macedonian Albanians boycotting the plebiscite.

Like the Croats of Bosnia, Macedonia's Albanians preferred a partition of Macedonia by means of autonomy status and a subsequent merging of the majority Albanian Western Macedonia with other Albanian-populated areas. On January 11 and 12, 1992, Macedonia's Albanians organized a separate plebiscite to buttress their demand for territorial and political autonomy. They also demanded the status of a constituent nation,[246] which they hoped would grant them the right to secession.

Catering to its minorities, the Macedonian Assembly inserted guarantees in the new Constitution, enacted on September 17, 1991, "providing a full citizens' equality and permanent cohabitation of the Macedonian people with . . . [the] nationalities living in the Republic of Macedonia."[247] The principle of cohabitation is also reflected in the establishment of "a Council for Interethnic Relations" in the National Assembly, composed of the president of the assembly and "two members each from the ranks of the Macedonians, Albanians, Turks, Vlachs and Romanies, as well as two members from the ranks of other nationalities in Macedonia" (Article 78). Notably, neither the Bulgarian nor the Serb minority of Macedonia was specified in this document.

Hoping to prevent violence, the international community provided peacekeeping troops. U.N. peacekeepers were deployed in Macedonia based on Security Council Resolution 795 (1992) of December 11, 1992, to be replaced by a NATO-supervised mission in March 1999. Although a violent conflict did erupt in 2001, international mediation successfully settled it by applying the decentralization policy that diffused maximum rights to the local level and thus diminished the

---

[246] Derek Hall, *Albania and the Albanians* (London: Pinter Reference, 1994), 212.

[247] Preamble, Constitution of SR Macedonia, November 17, 1991 (accessed July 7, 2005); available from http://www.b-info.com/places/Macedonia/republic/Constitution.shtml.

appeal of secession.[248] Yet the two main communities, Macedonian Slavs and the Macedonian Albanians "live largely segregated from each other."[249]

On January 6, 1992, in order to alleviate Greek apprehensions over potential Macedonian territorial claims to parts of Greece, Macedonia further amended the Constitution to assert that it had "no territorial pretensions against neighboring states" (Amendment I) and that its boundaries could be changed only "in accordance with the Constitution and on the principle of free will, as well in accordance with generally accepted international norms." (Amendment II). Despite several mediation attempts since this period, the conflict over the name of Macedonia continues to trouble Greek-Macedonian relations.

4.8. Kosovo's Albanians: Rights of a Nationality

Unlike in Macedonia, in the Serbian province of Kosovo and Metohia, Albanians were a majority.[250] Furthermore, Kosovo enjoyed the status of an autonomous province that translated to the *de facto* status of a republic, as explained in the previous Chapter. Since such a position created deadlocks in Serbian decision-making procedure and was considered unjust by most Serbs, aggravated by the systemic discrimination against Kosovo Serbs under Tito's regime,[251] the Serbian president Slobodan Miloshevich curtailed Kosovo's autonomy. This took place in a legal if not fully democratic fashion, by Amendments to Serbia's Constitution of March 29, 1989.[252] The provincial governments in Voivodina and Kosovo, dominated by Miloshevich's cronies, consented to these amendments, adopted by the Serbian National Assembly. In another undemocratic but tenuously legal act, the Serbian Assembly suspended and assumed all powers of Kosovo's Assembly and Executive Council on June 26, 1990, invoking a technicality, but responding to increased Albanian political mobilization.[253]

---

248 For more *see* Chapter 7: *Conclusion: Former Yugoslavia's European Integration.*

249 Drezov, "Collateral Damage: The Impact on Macedonia of the Kosovo War," 60.

250 According to the 1991 census, Albanians accounted for 81.6 percent of the total population of Kosovo and Metohia. *See also* footnote 105.

251 Marina Blagojevic, "The Migration of Serbs from Kosovo during the 1970s and 1980s: Trauma and/or Catharsis" in Nebojsa Popov, ed., *The Road to War in Serbia: Trauma and Catharsis* (Budapest: Central European University Press, 2000), 224-230. *See also* footnote 105.

252 Amendments to the Constitution of the Republic of Serbia, *Official Gazette of the Socialist Republic of Serbia*, 11/1989.

253 For more *see* Cohen, *Broken Bonds*, 122-123.

The new Serbian Constitution, enacted on September 28, 1990,[254] returned the original name to the southern Serbian province, contained in the 1963 Yugoslav Constitution: "the Autonomous Province of Kosovo and Metohia," stipulating that the two Serbian autonomous provinces are "forms of territorial autonomy" (Article 6). The competence of the autonomous provinces is significantly limited (Articles 108-112), with Article 112 clearly specifying the supremacy of the republic over provincial authority:

> If an agency of an autonomous province, despite a warning of the corresponding republic agency, fails to execute a decision or a general enactment of the autonomous province, the republic agency may provide for its direct execution.

As a consequence, as Dr. Markovich explains:

> In the [1990] constitutional order of Serbia there still are autonomous provinces, but now as units of territorial autonomy, such as the provinces in Italy, and autonomous communities in Spain, in other words—without state functions.[255]

Miloshevich at the time specifically noted that these changes were not made with a view of creating a Greater Serbia. Instead, according to him, Serbia only wished to be in "an equitable position with other republics,"[256] not stifled by internal deadlocks in decision making.

Kosovo's Albanians resented these changes and challenged their legitimacy, while simultaneously recalling rights granted to them by the at least equally, and arguably more, undemocratic Communist dictatorship. The Albanians of Kosovo and Metohia demanded that Kosovo become a republic, a request that first openly emerged in the 1960s, highlighted in the 1968 demonstrations by Albanian students. Tito granted such status to Kosovo Albanians in all but name by the subsequent amendments to the Yugoslav Constitution, enshrined in the

---

[254] Constitution of the Republic of Serbia, *Official Gazette of the Republic of Serbia*, 1/1990.

[255] Ratko Markovich, "The Constitution of the Republic of Serbia," Text published in the official Internet presentation of the Government of Serbia in 1995 (accessed June 6, 2005); available from http://www.serbia-info.com/facts/constitution.html.

[256] Miloshevich, *Years of Unraveling*, 298.

1974 Yugoslav Constitution. In practice, Albanians dominated the Kosovo local authority:

> Albanian language and culture became predominant in administration, education, and the media, aided by hundreds of teachers brought in from Albania. By 1978, Albanians comprised two thirds of the provincial party membership and occupied most leading party and state positions. Police and security organs were said to be three-quarters Albanian.[257]

Nonetheless, in March 1981, ten months after Tito's death, the Kosovo Albanians rioted again, in an action that began as a student protest over poor food in the student cafeteria but gained a national character several days later. They demanded constituent nation status for themselves and a republic status for the autonomous province of Kosovo. Kosovo Albanian nationalists also envisioned enlargement of Kosovo to parts of Western Macedonia and their subsequent union with Albania.[258] Yugoslav federal authorities violently suppressed these demonstrations, in an act supported by all the republics. It should be noted, however, that ethnic Albanians continued to enjoy relatively extensive minority rights and that the president of Yugoslavia between May 1986 and May 1987 (the head of the collective presidency of Yugoslavia rotated on an annual basis) was an ethnic Albanian from Kosovo, Sinan Hasani.

In the midst of the 1989/90 Yugoslav constitutional crisis, Kosovo's Albanians, like Macedonia's Albanians, reiterated their demand for the status of a constituent nation with the accompanying right to secession. Taking cues from the Slovenes, and to symbolically mark their request for equal rights, the Albanian members of the Kosovo's Assembly met outside the Assembly and proclaimed Kosovo an independent unit within Yugoslavia, equal to other Yugoslav republics, on the

---

[257] Louis Sell, *Slobodan Milosevic and the Destruction of Yugoslavia* (Durham and London: Duke University Press, 2002), 76.

[258] As Bechir Hoti, then the Kosovo Albanian Executive Secretary of the Communist Party of Kosovo, told the *New York Times* in 1982: "The Albanian nationalists have a two point platform.... [F]irst to establish what they call an ethnically clean Albanian republic and then merger with Albania to form a greater Albania." Marwin Howe, "Exodus of Serbians stirs Province in Yugoslavia," *New York Times*, July 12, 1982, A8. For more on the Kosovo riots *see* Aleksandar Pavkovic, *The Fragmentation of Yugoslavia; Nationalism in a Multinational State* (London: Palgrave Macmillan, 1997), 86-87. Pedro Ramet, "Kosovo and the Limits of Yugoslav Socialist Patriotism" (1989) 16 *Canadian Review of Studies in Nationalism* 227-250; Arishi Pipa, "The Political Situation of the Albanians in Yugoslavia, With Particular Attention to the Kosovo Problem: A Critical Approach" (1989) 23 *East European Quarterly* 159-181; Miranda Vickers, *Between Serb and Albanian, A History of Kosovo*, (London: Hurst & Co, 1998), 197-217.

same day that the Slovenes issued their declaration of sovereignty, July 2, 1990. The Kosovo Albanian "Constitutional Declaration on Kosovo as a sovereign and equal unit within the federal (confederal) Yugoslavia and an equal subject to other units in the federation (confederation)"[259] described the Albanian population of Kosovo and Yugoslavia as having the status of a "nation" rather than the status granted to it by the SFRY Constitution of a nationality. In the view of the Albanians, this legally justified their declared invalidation of the March 1989 amendments to Serbia's constitution and consequential secession from Serbia.

The Yugoslav Constitutional Court ruled that the Kosovo Albanian Declaration was unconstitutional and therefore void, based on arguments similar to those in the case of the Slovene amendments, but also denying the use of the Constitutionally guaranteed right to self-determination, including secession, to the Kosovo Albanians because they were considered a minority ("a nationality") rather than a constituent nation.[260]

On July 5, 1990, the Serbian Assembly dissolved Kosovo's assembly and government, an action that was endorsed by Yugoslavia's Presidency on July 11, 1990. The dismissed Albanian delegates met in the Kosovar town of Kachanik on September 7, 1990, and issued the Kachanik Resolution, reiterating the demands made in July. However, they also "adopted" the Constitution of the Republic of Kosovo, which, referred to "the right of self-determination to the point of secession" (Preamble) and declared Kosovo "the state of the Albanian people and members of other nations and national minorities that are its citizens" (Article 1). Otherwise, the "Constitution of the Republic of Kosovo" closely resembled the new Serbian Constitution. The newly established Kosovo Assembly elected Ibrahim Rugova president of Kosovo on May 24, 1991. A plebiscite held on September 26-30, 1991 again produced results comparable to ethnic census, as the majority Kosovo Albanians overwhelmingly voted in favor of Kosovo's

---

[259] Constitutional Declaration on Kosovo as a sovereign and equal unit within the federal (confederal) Yugoslavia and an equal subject to other units in the federation (confederation), printed in Serbian in Buzadjich, *Secession of former Yugoslav republics in light of decisions of the Yugoslav Constitutional Court*, 259-260 [Translation mine].

[260] Одлука о оцењивању уставности Уставне декларације о Косову као самосталној и равноправној јединици у оквиру федерације (конфедерације) Југославије и као равноправног субјекта са осталим јединицама у федерацији (конфедерацији) [Decision on Evaluating the Constitutionality of the Constitutional Declaration on Kosovo as a Sovereign and Equal Unit within the Federal (Confederal) Yugoslavia and an Equal Subject with other Units in the Federation (Confederation), reproduced in Buzadjich, *Secession of former Yugoslav republics in light of decisions of the Yugoslav Constitutional Court*, 226-229 [Translation mine].

sovereignty and independence, as against the wishes of Serbs and other Kosovo ethnic groups.[261] On October 18, 1991, Kosovo Albanians declared Kosovo's independence and requested international recognition.

Following generally peaceful resistance in the early 1990s, Kosovo Albanians took up armed rebellion in 1996,[262] further intensified in 1998, with the aim of achieving Kosovo's independence and subsequent merging of Kosovo into a Greater Albania. The Serbian government, on the other hand, took measures to suppress Albanian resistance. As Hayden notes:

> After 1987 Kosovo was ruled by the Serbian government in the ways in which other countries govern territories in which the majority of the population rejects inclusion within the state (such as Kashmir by India or the West Bank by Israel): through the heavy hand of police and military control.[263]

The conflict in Kosovo exploded during the NATO bombing of Serbia and Montenegro in spring 1999 when the actions of the Serb militia resulted in a displacement of over 850,000 ethnic Albanians from Kosovo.[264] Since then, the violence has continued, directed against the Serbs and other non-Albanians in Kosovo.[265]

4.9. Recursive Secessions Continue

The disintegrative processes, ultimately leading to secession of four (former) Yugoslav republics (Slovenia, Croatia, Bosnia, and Macedonia), fueled movements for a greater level of autonomy, possibly including independence in other parts of Yugoslavia, as well. In the Sandjak region, the Muslims had established their own assembly to represent "all Muslims in Serbia"[266] on the same day as the

---

[261] As reported, of the 87 percent of Kosovo's eligible voters who voted, 99.87 percent voted in favor. For more, *see* Elez Biberaj, "Kosova: The Balkan Powder Keg," in P. Janke, ed. *Ethnic and Religious Conflicts: Europe and Asia* (Dartmouth: Aldershot, 1994), 12-13.

[262] The first attack took place on April 22, 1996, when masked members of the so-called Kosovo Liberation Army (the KLA) killed three young Serb civilians at a café. For more, *see* Misha Glenny, *The Balkans; Nationalism, War, and the Great Powers, 1804-1999* (New York: Penguin Books, 1999), 652-659.

[263] Hayden, *Blueprints for a House Divided*, 169.

[264] *See* Patrick Ball, *Policy or Panic? The Flight of Ethnic Albanians from Kosovo, March-May 1999* (New York: American Association for the Advancement of Science, 2000).

[265] For more, *see* subsequent chapters of this book.

[266] Woodward, *Balkan Tragedy*, 143.

Serbs in the Krayina region took part in a referendum (May 12, 1990); in Voivodina most political parties agitated for a greater level of autonomy, while Montenegro's population opted for independence in 2006.[267] These and other similar movements, such as the Croatian Italian minority demand for autonomy on the Istrian peninsula, are being resolved in a peaceful manner, with the focus on rights rather than purely territory.

* * *

The era of communism to many, including the Yugoslav peoples, represented a period when history had stopped. Vaclav Havel described this halt of history using a metaphor: "One can say that communism was a kind of anesthesia and that the society wakes up now in a state in which it was before going unconscious."[268] Unfortunately, the peoples of Yugoslavia awakened to nationalism attempting to re-carve their national territories with violence.

A Serb writer and ideologue, Dobritsa Chosich, has asserted that Slovenes and Croats had always seen Yugoslavia as a transitory means towards a nation-state of their own, recounting Kardelj's statement during their conversation at the creation of the Program of the League of Communists of Yugoslavia:

> Yugoslavia is historically a temporary institution. It is a consequence of an imperialistic era. . . . With the development of world integrationary processes . . . its peoples will enter new associations and integrations according to the civilizational or spiritual affinities. . . . Understandably, we the Slovenes will be with the Austrians and Italians and you Serbs will naturally be with the Bulgarians or Orthodox nations that are historically closer to you.[269]

Although nations have tended to rise to fight oppression, in Yugoslavia their nationalism was fed by an elaborate system of cultural, economic, political and other rights. As Peter Radan argues:

> In granting substantial cultural, social, political, economic and legal rights to various national groups within the framework of federal and sub-federal

---

[267] More in Chapter 7: *Conclusion: Former Yugoslavia's European Integration*.

[268] Quoted in Georges Mink and Jean-Charles Szurek, *Cet étrange post-communisme: rupture et transitions en Europe centrale et orientale* (Paris: La Découverte, 1992), 27 [Translation mine].

[269] Jovan Ilić, "The Balkan Geopolitical Knot and the Serbian Question," in *The Serbian Question in the Balkans*, ed. Bratislav Atanacković (Belgrade: Faculty of Geography, University of Belgrade, 1995), 17.

territorial units, Yugoslavia facilitated the nationalism, not only of the Croats, but also the Slovenes, Bosnian Muslims, Macedonians and Albanians.[270]

This line of argument is also supported by Andrew Wachtel, who concludes:

> Although it was believed that giving the various nations more autonomy would reduce centrifugal tensions within the country, this did not happen. Rather the separate nations of Yugoslavia simply demanded more and more autonomy at the expense of a rapidly weakening center.[271]

Only the Serbs, as the largest and most dispersed nation in Yugoslavia, had a vested interest in preserving the common state. Serbian demography both precluded the creation of a Serb nation-state without incurring a significant level of violence, and it implied a demoted status for a significant part of the population in case of successful secessions. Indeed, the protection of minorities becomes an essential question in the withering Yugoslavia, as a means of fulfilling the "internal" right to self-determination. Nevertheless, this issue was not resolved upon the creation of the new nation-states on the territory of the former Yugoslavia, partly due to a rushed recognition policy of the European Community, led by Austria and Germany.

---

[270] Peter Radan, *Self-Determination, Uti Possidetis and Post-Secession International Borders: The Case of Yugoslavia*, Unpublished Doctoral Dissertation, University of Sydney, 1998, paragraph 5132.

[271] Andrew Baruch Wachtel, *Making a Nation, Breaking a Nation, Literature and Cultural Politics in Yugoslavia* (Stanford: Stanford University Press, 1998), 226.

CHAPTER 5

International Recognition of the (Former) Yugoslav Republics

International intervention in Yugoslavia in the 1990s manifested itself in multiple forms, which often intertwined and complemented each other. The most important types of foreign intervention in the case of Yugoslavia have been recognition of independence, mediation, peacekeeping (including peace enforcement and peace building), military intervention, sanctions, and humanitarian assistance. For the purpose of the study of the application of the right to self-determination in the case of Yugoslavia, the following aspects of international intervention shall be explored in more detail:

(a) The recognition policy (focusing on policy formulation of the main actors, namely the European Communities—EC[1] member states and the United States of America);
(b) Mediation, with a focus on territorial settlement and people(s)' rights in Croatia and Bosnia and Herzegovina;
(c) Military intervention in Serbia and Montenegro in 1999 (termed "Kosovo intervention").

---

[1] In 1992, the European Communities (frequently called in singular, the European Community) was transformed into the European Union by the Treaty of the European Union (also known as the Treaty of Maastricht), signed on February 7, 1992, and entered into force on November 1, 1993. For an integral text of the Treaty of Maastricht, *see* http://europa.eu.int/en/record/mt/top.html.

5.1. Recognition as State-Building: Great Power Intervention

As in the past historical development[2] of the various Yugoslav peoples and their ethnic space, in the early 1990s the Great Powers[3] again actively participated not only in the recognition of new states in the Western Balkans but also in their state-building, partly by granting recognition itself.

The recognition policy was formulated in the context of the end of the Cold War and Eastern Europe's expressed desire to join the Euro-Atlantic structures, namely the European Community, the Council of Europe, and the North Atlantic Treaty Organization. At the time, it was believed that Yugoslavia, as a country that was not a part of the East Bloc[4] and that possessed the strongest ties with the West among the Eastern European countries, would be the leader in these integrative processes. In the era of large-scale European integration and an extraordinary surge in optimism about the future of international relations, the disintegration of Yugoslavia was considered an anomaly. Yet the Soviet Union faced similar problems, which is why the international community took care to avoid the creation of a negative precedent in its treatment of the Yugoslav crisis. However, the war in the Gulf, initiated by Iraq's invasion of Kuwait in August 1990, and the complex readjustment of international organizations (namely the UN, Conference for Security and Cooperation, NATO, Western European Union, etc.) to the post-Cold War challenges, thwarted the amount of international political attention available for the resolution of the Yugoslav conflict,[5] simultaneously enhancing the international preference for the status quo.

As a consequence, in the early stages of the Yugoslav conflict, the members of the international community appeared unanimous in their decision to uphold Yugoslavia's territorial integrity. The support was principally rhetorical, despite

---

2   *See* Chapter 2: *Pre-1914 Administrative Boundaries and the Birth of Yugoslavia* and Chapter 3: *Yugoslavias' Administrative Boundaries (1918-1991).*

3   Today these are the USA, the EU, NATO, and the United Nations Security Council members. The phrase "international community" usually refers to these countries.

4   Yugoslavia was a member of the Organization of Nonaligned Countries that gathered many Third World countries, which attempted to mitigate tension between East and West. The late Yugoslav president Josip Broz Tito was one of the leaders of the non-aligned movement.

5   For more on the relationship between the Yugoslav and Soviet Union disintegration, *see* Reneo Lukic and Allen Lynch, *Europe from the Balkans to the Urals; The Disintegration of Yugoslavia and the Soviet Union* (New York: Sipri, Oxford University Press, 1996), 244-5.

intelligence information that a violent conflict was imminent in the case of Yugoslavia's political collapse.[6]

On May 30 and 31, 1991, the European Community mission, led by the Chairperson of the European Council of Ministers, Jacques Santer, and the E.C. president, Jacques Delors, made one significant attempt to resolve the Yugoslav crisis within its existing *international* borders, offering economic incentives. The E.C. offered the Yugoslav leaders an economic stick by conditioning the pending Yugoslav-EC association agreement by the country remaining united, and an economic carrot by promising about $4.5 billion in aid if a political settlement were reached, as well as additional financial assistance from international financial institutions, such as the IMF, in support of Yugoslav reforms. Each of the Yugoslav republican leaders responded by reiterating their conflicting positions, analyzed earlier in this work.[7] The E.C. proposal had arrived too late, following a decade of rapidly dwindling financial assistance[8] and a concurrent rise of nationalism. Inadequate foreign support to the economic reforms in Yugoslavia, heralded by the so-called Kreigher Commission (1983-1985) and the Vrhovec Commission (1985-1986), which were composed of Yugoslav politicians and experts, had two interlinked causes: poor implementation of serious economic reforms (devised mainly by the Kreigher Commission), and the unstructured international lending policy.[9]

---

[6] The U.S. administration was kept informed by the Central Intelligence Agency. *See* Stephen Larrabee, "US Policy in the Balkans: From Containment to Strategic Reengagement" in Constantine P. Danopoulos and Kostas G. Messas, eds. *Crises in the Balkans, Views from the Participants* (Boulder: Westview Press, 1997), 275-295: 280.

[7] *See also* Lenard J. Cohen, *Broken Bonds; Yugoslavia's Disintegration and Balkan Politics in Transition,* 2nd ed. (Boulder: Westview Press, 1995), 219; British Broadcasting Company, Summary of World Broadcasts, Part 2 (Eastern Europe), June 5, 1991, EE/1090/A1.

[8] *See* Susan L. Woodward, *Balkan Tragedy; Chaos and Dissolution after the Cold War* (Washington, D.C.: The Brookings Institution, 1995), 156.

[9] In the early 1980s, over 85 percent of Yugoslavia's debt was reprogrammed, allowing commercial banks to refinance its commercial component, and facilitating additional financial assistance. However, as Mihailo Crnobrnja explains:

"There was no externally imposed design for these reforms, not was there a definition of an 'acceptable minimum' that would justify the financial aid. Neither were there any political conditions imposed other than the understanding that the aid should foster market-oriented reforms." (85)

Crnobrnja's analysis implies that Yugoslavia's reforms were mishandled by the international economic community, ultimately reducing their support when it was truly needed:

"Having burned their fingers with Yugoslavia on the occasion of the stabilization program, the West would understandably be reluctant and cautious in its assistance on the next occasion, when a true and deeper reform would be taking place." (86)

Mihailo Crnobrnja, *The Yugoslav Drama* (Montreal: McGill-Queen's University Press, 1992), 85-86.

On June 19, 1991, the Conference on Security and Cooperation in Europe (later transformed into the Organization on Security and Cooperation in Europe[10]) adopted a declaration in support of "democratic development, unity and territorial integrity of Yugoslavia," noting that "it is only for the peoples of Yugoslavia themselves to decide on the country's future" but that the "the existing constitutional disputes should be remedied . . . without recourse to the use of force and in conformity with legal and constitutional procedures."[11] The U.S. Secretary of State, James A. Baker III endorsed this declaration during his visit to Belgrade on June 21, 1991, but he also added that the United States would not accept the use of force as a legitimate means of preserving Yugoslavia.[12] The ambiguity of Secretary Baker's statement, possibly reflecting the efforts of the Albanian-American lobby that promoted the separatist goals of the Kosovo Albanians,[13] or simply asserting a strong U.S. preference for a peaceful resolution of the conflict, had the possibly inadvertent result of instilling hope to the separatists.[14]

Yet the U.S. President George Bush was unequivocal, asserting on March 28, 1991: "The United States . . . will not encourage those who would break the

---

[10] On January 1, 1995, CSCE was transformed into the Organization of Security and Cooperation in Europe (OSCE). Strengthening the CSCE, Budapest Decisions, Towards a Genuine Partnership in a New Era, Conference for Security and Co-operation in Europe, 1994 Summit, Budapest, December 5-6, 1994.

[11] Statement on the Situation in Yugoslavia, First Meeting of the CSCE Council of Ministers, Berlin, June 19-20, 1991 (accessed October 4, 2005); available from http://www.osce.org/documents/html/pdftohtml/4138_en.pdf.html.

[12] For Baker's personal account *see* James A Baker III, *The Politics of Diplomacy, Revolution, War and Peace, 1989-1992* (New York: G. P. Putnam's Sons, 1995), 478-483. For an account by the U.S. ambassador to Yugoslavia see Warren Zimmermann, *Origins of a Catastrophe, Yugoslavia and Its Destroyers—America's Last Ambassador Tells What Happened and Why* (New York: Times Books, 1996), 133-138; *see* also Thomas L. Friedman, "Baker Urges End to Yugoslav Rift," *New York Times*, June 22, 1991, A-1, and David Binder, "U.S. Deplores Moves," *New York Times*, June 26, 1991, A-7.

[13] "The powerful Albanian-American political lobby was able to contribute to two U.S. Senate fact-finding trips to Kosovo during 1990, including one led by the Senate minority leader Bob Dole. These stressed the repression of the Albanian majority and led to the Nickles Amendment to the Federal budget requiring a cut-off of American aid to Yugoslavia in May 1991 unless the State Department certified Serbia was not guilty of gross human rights violations in Kosovo. Whilst the aid package was negligible, five million dollars, more important was the commensurate requirement that the U.S. vote against any new loans in the IMF and World Bank." John Williams, *Legitimacy in International Relations and the Rise and Fall of Yugoslavia* (London: Macmillan Press, 1998), 114.

[14] According to Terret, Baker's ambiguous message convinced all parties that they enjoyed a degree of international support for their opposing political agendas. Steve Terrett, *The Dissolution of Yugoslavia and the Badinter Arbitration Commission; A Contextual Study of Peace-Making Efforts in the Post-Cold War World* (Aldershot: Ashgate Dartmouth Publishing, 2000), 70-71.

country apart."[15] Many European community member states, particularly the United Kingdom, France, and the Netherlands, also voiced a strong disapproval of the attempted secession[16] of Croatia and Slovenia from Yugoslavia.[17]

Following Baker's visit to Yugoslavia, on June 23, 1991, the E.C. Foreign Ministers declared that they would not recognize any unilateral declaration of independence by either Slovenia or Croatia.[18] Two days later, Croatia and Slovenia proceeded to do exactly that. Furthermore, the Slovenes seized the border posts, which eventually facilitated their secession by provoking a reaction from the Yugoslav People's Army,[19] which was constitutionally mandated to protect Yugoslavia's integrity.

U.S. Secretary of State James Baker has regretted the fact that the U.S. government did not have sufficient strength to condone Slovenia's and Croatia's unilateral secession. Testifying before the U.S. House of Representatives International Relations Committee on January 12, 1995, Baker stated:

> [I]t was Slovenia and Croatia who unilaterally declared independence. . . . They used force to seize their border posts. And that, indeed, triggered the civil conflict. . . . [T]he position of the United States with respect to maintaining the territorial integrity of Yugoslavia, was supported by 32 countries of the [CSCE]. Everyone supported that. And it was the right policy. And it's too bad we didn't stand up to that policy for longer than we did.[20]

---

15   George Bush Letter to the SFRY Prime Minister Ante Marković of March 28, 1991, reproduced in *Focus*, Special Issue, Belgrade, January 14, 1992, 44-5.

16   For the definition of secession, *see* Chapter 1: *Legal Context of Yugoslavia's Disintegration: Sovereignty and Self-Determination of Peoples*, 23.

17   Thomas D. Musgrave, *Self-Determination and National Minorities* (Oxford: Clarendon Press, 1997), 115-116. For more on the French policy regarding the Yugoslav conflict, *see* Ronald Tiersky, "France in New Europe," *Foreign Affairs* (Spring 1992); Alex Macleod, "French policy toward the war in the former Yugoslavia: a bid for international leadership," *International Journal* LII, No. 2 (Spring 1997).

18   *The European Report*, June 26, 1991, no. 1688, 7.

19   Susan Woodward describes this act as "the winning strategy": "If they could provoke the Yugoslav army into violent resistance of their moves toward independence and appear to be using force only in self-defense, they could trigger E.C. and U.S. support for their goal." Woodward, *Balkan Tragedy*, 165.

20   Hearing By the House International Relations Committee, Chaired by Representative Benjamin A Gilman, Witness: James Baker, Former Secretary of State, January 12, 1995, Federal News Service Transcript (Lexis/Nexis).

The Brioni Accord,[21] mediated by the European Community Ministerial Troika on July 7 and 8, 1991, settled the brief conflict between the Slovene and the Yugoslav army, initiated by the Slovene proclamation of independence and its take-over of border posts. The agreement, monitored by unarmed E.C. observers, facilitated a three-month moratorium on independence but without calling for a status quo ante. Instead, it provided that "Control of border crossings will be in the hands of Slovenian police."[22] Although the Brioni Accord specified that the Slovene police should "act in conformity with federal regulations" and that "customs duties shall remain a federal revenue," the effect of the accord was to recognize Slovenia's imminent secession. The federal troops (Yugoslav People's Army) withdrew from Slovenia but the Slovenian forces did not demobilize, ignoring this part of the accord. An appeal for urgent negotiations, beginning "no later than August 1, 1991, on all aspects of the future Yugoslavia without preconditions" was also disregarded in the main.[23] For all these reasons, the Slovene president Milan Kučan views the Brioni Accord as the "first act of Slovenia's international recognition."[24]

However, the Brioni Accords can be viewed in this light only retrospectively since the policy of delaying recognition in favor of a peaceful negotiation of the Yugoslav crisis and an overall settlement of the conflict continued to prevail over the policy of early recognition for another five months after the Brioni Accord (until mid-December 1991).[25] The agreement on cease-fire relating to the violent conflict in Croatia, negotiated on September 2, 1991, thus carried careful language. Asymmetric in form, it favored the federal state by specifying that "the Croat

---

21 Joint Declaration of the E.C. Troika and the Parties Directly Concerned with the Yugoslav Crisis (also called the Brioni Accord or the Brioni Agreement), July 7, 1991, reproduced in *Focus*, Special Issue, Belgrade, January 14, 1992, 110-112 and in Snezana Trifunovska, *Yugoslavia Through Documents From Its Creation to its Dissolution* (Dordrecht: Martinus Nijhoff, 1994), 311-315.

22 Ibid., Annex II, reproduced in *Focus*, Special Issue, Belgrade, January 14, 1992, 110-112.

23 *See* the discussion on the Peace Conference on Yugoslavia, established on August 27, 1991, 10-12.

24 Milan Kučan, "Otpor Srboslaviji" [Resisting Serboslavia], Interview, "Witnesses of Yugoslavia's Disintegration," *Radio Free Europe* (accessed February 5, 2005); available from http://www.danas.org/svjedoci/html/Milan_Kucan.html [Translation mine]; Original: "To je bio prvi akt međunarodnog priznavanja Slovenije, iako se možda to nije htelo, ali je formalno tako bilo."

25 As late as November 8, 1991, the Statement issued by the heads of state and government participating in the meeting of the North Atlantic Council in Rome stipulated: "The prospect of recognition of the independence of those republics wishing it, can only be envisaged in the framework of an overall settlement, that includes adequate guarantees for the protection of human rights and rights of national or ethnic groups within the individual republics." Europe Documents No. 1744, November 13, 1991, reproduced in Trifunovska, *Yugoslavia Through Documents*, 380-381:381.

National Guard reserve forces shall be demobilized," but that the Yugoslav People's Army merely "return to barracks."[26] Yet like many other cease fires negotiated in Croatia, it was not respected.

The rapid reverse turn in international policy towards Yugoslavia was generated by Germany, strongly supported by Austria and the Vatican.[27] However, it was the peaceful disintegration of the Soviet Union in August 1991, combined with the German leverage within the European Community, that allowed the German view to prevail. The August 1991 statement by the Austrian vice-chancellor, Erhard Busek, that "the collapse of communism in the USSR modifies the situation in Yugoslavia [in that] there is no more reason not to recognize the independence of Slovenia and Croatia"[28] strongly reflects Yugoslavia's position as a country whose geopolitical importance and therefore the need to maintain its integrity withered with the Cold War.

Germany's struggle to sway international policy towards sanctioning Slovenia's and Croatia's secession was not easy. Many states convincingly argued that the war in Yugoslavia was essentially a domestic affair,[29] leading the U.N. Security Council to hear the representative of Yugoslavia but no representative of any of the seceding republics as late as September 25, 1991.[30]

---

26   Thomas M. Franck, "Postmodern Tribalism and the Right to Secession," in *Peoples and Minorities in International Law*, eds. Catherine Brölmann, René Lefeber, and Marjoleine Zieck (Dodrecht: M. Nijhoff, 1993), 21.

27   "The Vatican openly lobbied for the independence of the two predominantly Roman Catholic republics, with decisive influence through episcopal conferences on the Bavarian wing of the ruling German party, the CSU, and hence on Kohl's CDU." Woodward, *Balkan Tragedy*, 149.

    "Think of the support of Mr. Kohl, the German Chancellor, Mr. Genscher, his deputy, the support of the Vatican and the Pope, Mr. Cossiga, the Italian President, his visit to Croatia. You should not forget the very intense communications and help offered by friendly Austria." Josip Manolic, Tudjman's close associate, FBIS_EEU-94-080, April 26, 1994, 44. *See also* Misha Glenny, *The Fall of Yugoslavia; The Third Balkan War*, 3rd rev. ed. (New York: Penguin Books, 1996), 188-192; Jean-Louis Tauran, "The Holy See and world peace: the case of former Yugoslavia," *The World Today*, July 1994, 125-128;

28   *Calendrier de la crise Yougoslave*, 15, E.C. document cited in Woodward, *Balkan Tragedy*, 178.

29   *See* Franck, "Postmodern Tribalism and the Right to Secession?" 21.

30   On September 25, 1991, UNSC adopted the Resolution 713 establishing an arms embargo in Yugoslavia, which notes that the UNSC has "heard the statement by the Foreign Minister of Yugoslavia" but mentions no other representative from Yugoslavia; UN Security Council Resolution 713 (accessed September 25, 1991); available from http://www.un.org/Docs/scres/1991/scres91.htm.

There are multiple explanations for German, Austrian, Vatican, or Belgian[31] support to Slovene and Croat secessions, ranging from the more realpolitik economic and religious interests[32] to the more altruistic espousal of the principle of self-determination, albeit selectively interpreted.[33] The German people had benefited from national self-determination in Germany's 1990 reunification, and they wanted to aid other seemingly oppressed peoples achieve the same. On July 1, 1990, the then Secretary-General of German's Christian Democratic Union (CDU), Volker Ruhe, had argued:

> We won unification through the right to self-determination. If we Germans now think that everything may remain as it is in Europe, that we may pursue a policy of the status quo without recognizing the right to self-determination of Croatia and Slovenia, we lose our moral and political credibility.[34]

In their zeal, the Germans were unable to distinguish between the different implications of the principle of self-determination in Germany compared to Slovenia and Croatia. The latter involved disintegration of a country rather than its integration and a division of another people (the Serbs), with equal rights to self-determination, if the secession were effected. A distorted prism of the Yugoslav reality was concocted in Germany by an active public relations campaigns of the Slovenes and Croats, aided by the Catholic Church and about 400,000 Croat *Gastarbeiter* ("guest workers" without permanent residence permits).[35]

---

[31]   The Belgian Prime minister Wilfred Martens encouraged E.C. members "to envisage the recognition of independence of Slovenia and Croatia. . . " *The European Report*, No. 5528, July 5, 1991.

[32]   "From the mid-1980s on, both Austria and the Vatican had pursued a strategy to increase their sphere of economic and spiritual influence in central and eastern Europe, respectively." Woodward, *Balkan Tragedy*, 148-9. For more, *see* Cohen, *Broken Bonds*, 236. Note: Claims that Germany aided Croatia because of their shared Nazi past are not convincing and they are not analyzed in this book.

[33]   *See*, for instance, Daniele Conversi, "German-Bashing and the Breakup of Yugoslavia," *The Donald W. Treadgold Papers*, Jackson School of International Studies, University of Washington, 1998.

[34]   Cited in Philip Gordon, *Die Deutsch-Französische Partnerschaft und die Atlantische Allianz* [The German-French Partnership and the Atlantic Alliance] (Bonn: Arbeitspapiere zur Internationalen Politik, no. 82, 1993), 48.

[35]   For more *see* Williams, *Legitimacy in International Relations and the Rise and Fall of Yugoslavia*, 120; Woodward, *Balkan Tragedy*, 184-5; Stipe Mesić, *Kako smo srušili Jugoslaviju: politički memoari posljednjeg predsjednika Predsjedništva SFRJ* [How We Destroyed Yugoslavia: Political Memoirs of the Last President of Yugoslavia] (Zagreb: Globus International, 1992), 75; Cohen, *Broken Bonds*, 238; Nenad Ivanković, *Bonn: druga Hrvatska fronta* [Bonn: The Second Croatian Front] (Zagreb: Mladost, 1993); Hanns W. Maull, "Germany in the Yugoslav Crisis," *Survival* 37, no.4 (Winter 1995-96), 99-130; Michael Thumann, "Between Ambition and Paralysis: Germany's Balkan Policy, 1991-1994," *The Balkans and CFSP;*

The statement of Michael Libal, who served as the head of the Southeast European Department of the German Foreign Ministry responsible for the day-to-day conduct of German policy towards the former Yugoslavia from 1991 to 1995, demonstrates that Germany had decided at the onset of the Yugoslav conflict that Serbs were its main culprits:

> Although, for the time being, I remained committed to the concept of Yugoslav unity in one form of the other, I had already come to rather definite conclusions as to where the true responsibility for the disintegration of Tito's Yugoslavia was to be found. In my view, Milosevic, Serbian hegemonism, and Serb nationalism were far more to blame for the crisis than the 'secessionist' forces, which were left no other choice than to try to escape the spectre of Serb domination.[36]

The language used by Libal, starkly resembling that of Croatian nationalists, provides compelling evidence of their successful public relations campaign. In that light, Libal does not recognize that the principle of self-determination could apply to Serbs wishing to "secede from Croatia," instead invoking the principle of territorial integrity in this case:

> According to the principle of territorial integrity, the right of the Croatian government to exercise its authority in the Serb-inhabited parts of the country was not in doubt.[37]

Although other E.C. members, namely the United Kingdom, France, and Spain continued to be opposed to recognizing the seceding (former Yugoslav) states, concerned about possible implications for their own internal cleavages,[38] the issue

---

The Views of Greece and Germany, CEPS Paper No. 59 (Brussels, July 1994); Flora Lewis, "Bavarian TV and the Balkan War," *New Perspectives Quarterly*, Vol. II, No. 3, Summer 1994, 44-47; Beverly Crawford, "Explaining Defection from International Cooperation: Germany's Unilateral Recognition of Croatia," *World Politic*. 48, No. 4 (July 1996), 482-521. Note: The Serbian community in Germany was smaller whilst the Serbian government failed to see the merits of a public campaign. Instead, the Serbian president Slobodan Miloshevich had refused audience to the U.S. Ambassador to Yugoslavia, Warren Zimmerman, for over nine months when he arrived in 1989.

[36] Michael Libal, *Limits of Persuasion; Germany and the Yugoslav Crisis, 1991-1992* (Westport, CT: Praeger Publishers, 1997), 9.

[37] Ibid., 29.

[38] For more, *see* Williams, *Legitimacy in International Relations and the Rise and Fall of Yugoslavia*, 108.

was ultimately settled by "Machiavellian horse-trading."[39] During a twelve-hour meeting of foreign ministers in Brussels during the night of December 15-16, 1991, Germany made a set of compromises on the E.C. monetary union, conceding to Britain's request to opt out of the Social Charter envisaged by the Maastricht Treaty[40] that was in the final stages of negotiation. Achieving consensus on the Maastricht Treaty was important since this enabled a vital transformation of the European Community into a three-pillar European Union (EU), expanding the organization's competences beyond a single market, onto common foreign and security policy and cooperation in justice and home affairs. Moreover, joint efforts in resolving the Yugoslav crisis represented the litmus test of EU's common foreign policy. Germany reluctantly agreed to a policy that all six republics of Yugoslavia would be eligible for recognition, while all the E.C. countries conceded to Greece's condition that a state requesting recognition should have no territorial claims against a neighboring E.C. state and not use a name that implied such claims.[41] The latter had the primary goal of preventing any possible territorial claims to Greek territory of the (former) Yugoslav republic of Macedonia.[42]

This E.C. recognition policy was officially promulgated as an agreement on principles, specified in the Declaration on the Guidelines on the European Community Recognition of New States in Eastern Europe and in the Soviet Union issued at the end of the E.C. ministerial meeting on December 17, 1991. According to this Declaration, to gain E.C. recognition, "these new States" would have to demonstrate:

a) respect for the provisions of the Charter of the United Nations and the commitments subscribed to in the Final Act of Helsinki and in the Charter of Paris, especially with regard to the rule of law, democracy and human rights;

b) guarantees for the rights of ethnic and national groups and minorities in accordance with the commitments subscribed to in the framework of the CSCE;

---

[39] Expression used by Glenny, *Fall of Yugoslavia*, 192.

[40] The Treaty on European Union, February 3, 1992, http://europa.eu.int/en/record/mt/top.html.

[41] For more about the E.C. meeting, *see* Woodward, *Balkan Tragedy*, 184; Libal, *Limits of Persuasion*, 83-5; Hans-Dietrich Genscher, *Rebuilding a House Divided: A Memoir by the Architect of Germany's Reunification* (New York: Broadway Books, 1998), 513-515; Cohen, *Broken Bonds*, 238.

[42] Many analysts have claimed that Greece's fear in this respect is unsubstantiated, but such discussion is beyond the scope of this work.

    c) respect for the inviolability of all frontiers which can only be changed by peaceful means and by common agreement;

    d) acceptance of all relevant commitments with regard to disarmament and nuclear non-proliferation as well as to security and regional stability;

    e) commitment to settle by agreement, including where appropriate by recourse to arbitration, all questions concerning State succession and regional disputes. The Community and its member States will not recognise entities which are the result of aggression. They would take account of the effects of recognition on neighbouring States.[43]

Additional conditions were mandated for the Yugoslav republics, postulated in a separate Declaration on Yugoslavia,[44] issued on the same occasion. Any republic of the Socialist Federal Republic of Yugoslavia (SFRY) could apply for E.C. recognition by December 23, 1991, provided it continued to support the U.N. mediation efforts and the EC's Conference on Yugoslavia, accepting the provisions laid down in the Draft Convention[45] of the Conference, "especially those in Chapter II on human rights of national or ethnic groups." Finally, a republic seeking recognition would have to commit to adopting constitutional and political guarantees that it had "no territorial claims on" and "would conduct no hostile propaganda activities" against a neighbouring E.C. state, thereby alleviating Greece's concern over possible Macedonian demands.[46] The Declaration on Yugoslavia stressed that these guarantees would need to be adopted "prior to recognition," rendering this condition more stringent than the provisions for human and minority rights, including the establishment of a special status for significant minorities contained

---

[43]   Declaration on the Guidelines on the European Community Recognition of New States in Eastern Europe and in the Soviet Union, December 16, 1991, reproduced in *Focus*, Special Issue, Belgrade, January 14, 1992, 249-250.

[44]   Declaration on Yugoslavia, December 17, 1991, reproduced in *Focus*, Special Issue, Belgrade, January 14, 1992, 251-252.

[45]   On October 18, 1991, the so-called Carrington Draft Convention was signed by five of the six Yugoslav republics. Serbia refused to sign the document, objecting to the key provision that a general settlement of the crisis would involve "recognition of the independence, within the existing borders, unless otherwise agreed, of those republics wishing it." Croatia signed the document but specified a number of substantial objections.

    For an integral text of the Draft Convention, *see* Arrangements for a General Settlement proposed by the Conference on Yugoslavia at the Hague, October 18, 1991, reproduced in *Focus*, Special Issue, Belgrade, January 14, 1992, 194-201.

[46]   *See* Chapter 4: *The (Self-) Determination of the Yugoslav Peoples.*

in Chapter II of the Draft Convention of the Peace Conference on Yugoslavia.[47] This reflects the influence of "political realities" on the formulation of the recognition policy, which the E.C. was forthright in admitting would be its guiding principle in granting recognition, together with "the normal standards of international practice," namely the principles of international public law of the territorial integrity (Helsinki Final Act[48]) and self-determination.[49] Such an approach confirms Lauterpacht's famous proposition, made in 1947, that recognition of states is not a matter governed by law but a question of policy.[50] At the same time jurists such as Cassese have praised the Guidelines on the European Community Recognition of New States in Eastern Europe and in the Soviet Union as "profoundly innovative . . . [even] revolutionary," because they link the criteria associated with "internal" self-determination, including minority rights, with acceptance of the legitimacy of "external" self-determination.[51]

The United States accepted the E.C. recognition policy on Yugoslavia, having granted Europe the political lead in this matter,[52] while Russia remained neutral.

---

[47]   II c) Special status: "In addition, areas in which persons belonging to a national or ethnic group form a majority, will enjoy a special status (autonomy). Such will provide for:
   a. The right to have and show the national emblems of that group;
   b. The right to a second nationality for members of that group in addition to the nationality of the republic;
   c. An education system which represents the values and needs of that group;
   d. i. A legislative body
       ii. An administrative structure, including a regional police force;
       iii. And a judiciary
   responsible for matters concerning the area which reflects the composition of the population of the area;
   e. Provisions for appropriate international monitoring
   The status set out above will apply, in particular, to the Serbs living in areas in Croatia where they form a majority.

[48]   Final Act of the Helsinki Conference on Security and Co-operation in Europe: Questions Relating to Security in Europe—Declaration on Principles Guiding Relations between Participating States, August 1, 1975, 14 ILM 1292, principle 4.

[49]   Declaration on the Guidelines on the European Community Recognition of New States in Eastern Europe and in the Soviet Union, December 16, 1991, reproduced in *Focus*, Special Issue, Belgrade, January 14, 1992, 249.

[50]   Hersch Lauterpacht, *Recognition in International Law* (Cambridge: Cambridge University. Press, 1947), 1.

[51]   Antonio Cassese, *Self-Determination of Peoples: A Legal Reappraisal* (Cambridge: Cambridge University Press, 1995), 268.

[52]   As Richard Melanson explains: "Though Secretary Baker, in a well-publicized speech in Belgrade in the spring of 1991, pleaded for Yugoslavian unity, he seemed to be aiming his remarks primarily at the Soviet republics. Moreover, he also acknowledged at about same time that 'we don't have a dog in this [i.e. Yugoslav] fight.'" Richard A. Melanson, *American Foreign Policy since the Vietnam War; The Search for Consensus from Nixon to Clinton* (New York: M.E. Sharpe, 1996), 256.

In a painfully honest appraisal of Russia's role in the Yugoslav crisis, Glenny asserts:

> Wherever possible, Moscow avoided involvement, and its support for the Serbs was usually grudging, motivated not by pan-Slavism or pan-Orthodoxy, but by its own strategic interests in Europe.[53]

A similar role was also played by China, which was mainly concerned about the implications of the Yugoslav conflict on its nationalist problems and China's international position.[54]

The United States outlined four principles guiding its policy toward the republics of Yugoslavia:

a) the United States would accept any outcome chosen peacefully, democratically, and through negotiation;
b) the United States would not recognize changes in *internal or* external borders achieved through force, intimidation, or threats;
c) the republics must be committed to resolving disputes through peaceful negotiation; and
d) the republics must be committed to respecting the human rights of all citizens, including the members of all ethnic groups.[55]

Since August 1991, the EC, joined by the U.S. government, promulgated the principle "that any change of *internal and* international borders by force [were] unacceptable"[56] The SFRY Presidency countered that "a possible recognition of

---

At the same time, Europe initially espoused this leadership position with considerable enthusiasm. Jacques Poos, Luxembourg's Foreign-Minister then famously stated: "This is the hour of Europe…not the hour of the United States," cited in Terrett, *The Dissolution of Yugoslavia and the Badinter Arbitration Commission*, 71.

53   Glenny, *Fall of Yugoslavia*, 245. For more on the Russian foreign policy towards the Balkans in this period, see Lenard J. Cohen, "Russia and the Balkans: pan-Slavism, partnership and Power," *International Journal* XLIX, no. 1 (Canadian Institute of International Affairs, Autumn 1994), 814-845; Hans-Joachim Hoppe, "Moscow and the Conflicts in Former Yugoslavia," *Aussenpolitik*, no. 3 (1997), 267-277.

54   For more, see Czeslaw Tubilewicz, "China and the Yugoslav Crisis, 1990-94: Beijing's Exercise in Dialectics, *Issues & Studies* 33, no. 4 (April 1997): 94-112.

55   Cited in Morton H. Halperin, David J. Scheffer and Patricia L. Small, eds., *Self-Determination in the New World Order* (Washington, DC: Carnegie Endowment for International Peace, 1992), 36-37. [Emphasis added]

56   Declaration on Yugoslavia, August 20, 1991, E.C. Press Release P.77/91; reproduced in Trifunovska, *Yugoslavia Through Documents*, 330.

the unilateral secessionist acts of Slovenia and Croatia would be in flagrant violation of the Charter of the United Nations, the Helsinki Act and of all international
conventions on the inviolability of borders."[57] Yet the international actors had quietly transferred the legal sanctity of international frontiers mandated by the U.N.
Charter and the Helsinki Final Act to (a federal state's) internal boundaries. The
origin of the idea is unknown, but it did feature in the unofficial program of
the Bosnian Muslim, Izetbegovic-led Party of Democratic Action, the "Public
Declaration of Forty Party Founders" published in March 1990:

> We advocate Yugoslavia's continuity as a free community of peoples, that is,
> as an alliance of states with current federal borders. In this sense, we sup-
> port the credo "Helsinki for Yugoslavia."[58]

In a resolution adopted a year later, on March 13, 1991, the European Parliament
declared "that the *constituent republics and autonomous provinces* of Yugoslavia
must have the right freely to determine their own future in a peaceful and democratic manner and on the basis of recognized international and *internal* borders."[59]
In accordance with the policy of granting the right to self-determination to the
republics, developed under manifest German influence, the E.C. also asserted an
official distinction between peoples and minorities: "The right to self-determination
of all *peoples* in Yugoslavia cannot be exercised in isolation from the interests and
rights of *ethnic minorities* within the individual Republics."[60]

In conclusion, the E.C. recognition policy, while officially supporting the
Conference on Yugoslavia, established by the E.C. on August 27, 1991[61] as an

---

57 Assessment and positions of the SFRY Presidency concerning the proclamation of the independence of
    the Republic of Croatia and Slovenia, Belgrade, October 11, 1991, *Review of International Affairs*. XLII
    (5.X-5.XI 1991), 12; reproduced in Trifunovska, *Yugoslavia Through Documents*, 353-357:354.

58 Public Declaration of Forty Party Founders, Point VI. Integral text of the Declaration reproduced in Alija
    Izetbegović, *Sjećanja; autobiografski zapis* [Memoirs; autobiographic script] (Sarajevo: TKD Sahinpašić,
    2001), 69-75: 71 [Translation mine]. Original text: "Zalažemo se za održanje Jugoslavije kao slobodne
    zajednice naroda, odnosno saveza drzava sa sadašnjim federalnim granicama. U tom smislu, podržavamo
    devizu 'Helsinki za Jugoslaviju.'"

59 Cited in Susan L. Woodward, "Redrawing Borders in a Period of Systemic Transition," in *International
    Organizations and Ethnic Conflict*, eds. Milton J. Esman and Shibley Telhani (Ithaca, NY: Cornell University
    Press, 1995), 208. [Emphasis added]

60 E.C. Declaration on the situation in Yugoslavia, adopted at the Informal meeting of Ministers for Foreign
    Affairs, Haarzuilens, October 6, 1991, UN Doc. S/23114, Annex II, reproduced in Trifunovska, *Yugoslavia
    Through Documents*, 351-352: 352 [Emphasis added].

61 E.C. Declaration on Yugoslavia of August 27, 1991, reproduced in *Focus*, Special Issue, Belgrade, January 14,
    1992, 128-129.

impartial forum for negotiations, and officially convened on September 7, 1991 in the Hague, severely undermined its founding principles. On the occasion of the ceremonial opening of the Conference of Yugoslavia, the representatives of the European Community and its member states and of Yugoslavia and its republics had declared, *inter alia*, that the outcome of the negotiations "must take into account the interests of all" and that they were "determined never to recognize changes of *any* borders which have not been brought about by peaceful means and by agreement."[62]

That Germany never regarded the peace negotiations seriously is evident from its repeated reassurances to Slovenia and Croatia that the recognition of independence was "only a matter of choosing the right moment and the right circumstances."[63] Germany did not even respect the E.C. Recognition Guidelines, announcing its decision to recognize Slovenia and Croatia as independent states on December 19, 1991.

The warnings of the dire consequences of early recognition of the seceding Yugoslav states, voiced by many high-ranking officials, were to no avail. Cyrus Vance, U.N. envoy to Yugoslavia, was seriously concerned that premature recognition would endanger the ongoing peace initiatives and he attempted to alert the German foreign minister Hans-Dietrich Genscher in December "that recognition had to be held out as a reward for a peaceful settlement. To give up that weapon before such a settlement was reached would mean more war."[64] In a similar vein, Lord Carrington, the Chairperson of the Peace Conference on Yugoslavia, implored that that early recognition of Slovenia and Croatia by the E.C. "might well be the spark that sets Bosnia-Herzegovina alight."[65] The U.S. Deputy Secretary of State, Lawrence Eagleburger, shared these concerns, warning the E.C. members on December 13, that early, separate recognition of Croatia and Slovenia would not only undermine the peace efforts but would "almost inevitably lead to greater bloodshed."[66] Finally, on December 14, 1991, in a last minute effort to prevent the

---

[62] E.C. Declaration on the Occasion of the Ceremonial Opening of the Conference on Yugoslavia, The Hague, September 7, 1991, reproduced in *Focus*, Special Issue, Belgrade, January 14, 1992, 150 [Emphasis added].

[63] A spokesman for the Slovenian Ministry of Foreign Affairs, following President Kučan's visit to Germany in early October. *FBIS-EEU*, October 10, 1991, 35.

[64] Woodward, *Balkan Tragedy*, 187-188.

[65] Letter to the Dutch foreign minister Hans van den Broek, as chair of the E.C. Troika on December 2, 1991, cited in Woodward, *Balkan Tragedy*, 184.

[66] Cited in Halperin,. Scheffer and Small, eds., *Self-Determination in the New World Order*, 35-36.

act of "early, selective and uncoordinated recognition," the U.N. Secretary General Javier Perez de Cuellar also warned the German foreign minister, Genscher, that such a policy could block U.N. peace efforts.[67]

Responding to this letter, the German Foreign Minister, Hans-Dietrich Genscher, reiterated Germany's standpoint that recognition would limit rather than escalate the violence. Genscher also attempted to legitimize the E.C. recognition policy by referring to the principle of territorial integrity (non-violability of frontiers) but applying the principle with respect to internal in addition to external borders of Yugoslavia:

> I would like to point out that according to the Treaty of Helsinki and the Paris Charter, the borders in Europe are inviolable and cannot be changed by force. Therefore, the EC has demanded that the *internal and* external borders of Yugoslavia be respected.[68]

Such novel legal interpretations were also embodied in the opinions of the advisory body attached to the Conference on Yugoslavia, which was called the Arbitration Commission, but became known as the Badinter Commission after its Chair Robert Badinter, the President of the French Constitutional Council.[69]

5.2. The Badinter Commission

Despite the name, this Arbitration commission did not have a mandate to arbitrate and could not create any binding legal decisions concerning Yugoslavia.[70]

---

67   Ibid. Note: U.N. Secretary General also addressed the Minister for Foreign Affairs of the Netherlands, which held the E.C. Presidency at the time, on December 10, 1991, warning of "explosive consequences" of early recognition. [U.N. Doc. S/23280, Annex IV].

68   Cited in Glenny, *Fall of Yugoslavia*, 190 [Emphasis added].

69   Other members of the Arbitration Commission were the president of the German Federal Constitutional Court (Roman Herzog), the president of the Italian Constitutional Court (Aldo Corasaniti), the president of the Spanish Constitutional Court (Francisco Tomas y Valiente) and the president of the Belgian Arbitration Court (Irene Pètry). The European Commission appointed the five judges. The procedure stipulated that three judges were to be nominated by the E.C. and two judges by the SFRY Presidency by unanimous consent. If the consensus were not reached the E.C. would be responsible for nominating the two remaining judges as well, which is what occurred. *See* The E.C. Declaration on Yugoslavia of August 27, 1991, reproduced in *Focus*, Special Issue, Belgrade, January 14, 1992, 128-129.

70   The Arbitration Commission did not meet the minimum requirements suggested by the International Law Commission's Model Rules on Arbitral Procedure (Article 37, Hague Convention on Peaceful Conflict Resolution, 1907), which call for an arbitration *compromis* to be established among parties,

Instead, it was considered another tool in the E.C. mediation efforts. Nevertheless, its advisory opinions have formed a basis for the E.C. recognition policy regarding Yugoslavia,[71] despite the fact that they were not followed in full and that many of the pertinent opinions were published *after* Germany had already recognized Croatia and Slovenia.

The Arbitration Commission delivered ten opinions between December 1991 and July 1992. The Badinter Commission also rendered an interlocutory decision[72] prior to its eighth opinion and another five opinions when it was reconstituted in January 1993.[73]

The EC-appointed Arbitration Commission responded to questions posed by the parties to the Conference on Yugoslavia, which were to be "transmitted" by the Chairperson of the Conference of Yugoslavia. As specified by the E.C. Declaration of September 3, 1991:

> In the framework of the Conference, the Chairman will *transmit* to the Arbitration Commission the issues submitted for arbitration and the results

---

indicating as a minimum: "(a) the undertaking to arbitrate according to which the dispute is to be submitted to the arbitrators; (b) the subject-matter of the dispute and, if possible, the points on which the parties are or are not agreed; (c) the method of constituting the tribunal and the number of arbitrators" [*General Assembly Official Records*, 13th Session, Supplement No. 9, Doc. A/3859, 5-8 (1958). Instead, the Badinter Arbitration Commission was established by what Pellet describes as "a gentleman's agreement … a concerted act without any binding legal force." See Alain Pellet, "Note sur la Commission d'arbitrage de la Conférence européenne pour la paix en Yougoslavie" [Note on the Arbitration Commission of the European Peace Conference on Yugoslavia], 37 AFDI (1991), 331. According to the E.C. Declaration, "The Commission would consider the applications and *provide advice* on whether the republics had fulfilled the requirements of the Guidelines and Declaration [Emphasis added]."

71 *See* Hurst Hannum, "Self-Determination, Yugoslavia, and Europe: Old Wine in New Bottles?" 3 *Transnational Law and Contemporary Problems* 57 (1993), 63; Paul C. Szasz "The Fragmentation of Yugoslavia," The American Society of International Law: Proceedings of the 88th Annual Meeting (April 6-9, 1994), 34.

72 The Interlocutory Decision [ILM 31 (1992), 1518] will not be discussed here as it relates to Serbia and Montenegro's challenge to the Arbitration Commission's competence to deliberate the terms of succession, which are beyond the scope of this analysis.

73 The composition was changed, with three permanent members designated by the E.C. among incumbent Presidents of Constitutional Courts of E.C. Member States or from the highest courts of those States, the fourth member designated by the President of the ICJ from among the former ICJ members or persons qualifying under Article 2 o the ICJ Statute, and the fifth member designated by the President of the European Court of Human Rights from among the Court's members. These were Robert Badinter (the President of the French Constitutional Council), Francisco Paolo Casavola (President of the Constitutional Court of Italy), Roman Herzog (President of the German Federal Constitutional Court), Elizabeth Palm (Judge of the European Court of Human Rights), Jose Maria Ruda (former President of the ICJ).

of the Commission's deliberations will be put back to the Conference through the Chairman.[74]

5.2.1. Dissolution

The first issue tackled by the Badinter Arbitration Commission was the legal definition of Yugoslavia's disintegration. Lord Carrington here overstepped his mandate by changing the question that was posed by the Serbian authorities ("Is secession a legal act from the standpoint of the United Nations Charter and other relevant rules of international law?"[75]) into "Is Yugoslavia in the process of disintegration or breaking-up"? Recalling that Croatia and other Yugoslav republics had approved the original question, Milenko Krecha, who acted as one of the key legal advisors to the Serbian government, has postulated that this act of the Conference's Chairperson transformed the Arbitration Commission into a "political advisory body, serving the chairperson of the Conference" instead of it being "an expert, advisory body of the Conference established to clarify legal issues."[76]

According to Opinion No. 1 of the Arbitration Commission of the Peace Conference on Yugoslavia (Opinion No. 1),[77] ironically handed down on November 29, 1991, the National Day of Yugoslavia, the Socialist Federalist Republic of Yugoslavia (SFRY) was "engaged in a process of dissolution." In its response, the Badinter Arbitration Commission invented a novel interpretation of a seldom-employed legal term, dissolution. Etinski has analyzed the cases that the International Law Commission had described to be characterized by the process of "dissolution" (Great Colombia, Union of Norway and Sweden, Austro-Hungarian Empire, Union of Iceland and Denmark, United Arab Republic, Mali Federation and the Federation of Rhodesia and Nyasaland (YILC 1972, vol. II, 292-295; YILC, 1976, vol. II, 150), concluding that the term applied to a composite state, "founded by the union of two or more Statxes or two or more provinces." Etinski has further emphasized that: "in all cases the dissolution means the separation of *all members* of composite states" but that "the *surviving member States are not always new*

---

74   E.C. Declaration on Yugoslavia, September 3, 1991, printed in *Focus*, Special Issue, Belgrade, January 14, 1992, 145.

75   Milenko Kreća, "Badinterova Arbitražna komisija; kritički osvrt" [Badinter's Arbitration Commission; A Critical Commentary] in *Jugoslovenski pregled [Yugoslav Review]*, Belgrade, 1993, 69.

76   Ibid., 70.

77   Opinion No. 1 of the Arbitration Commission of the Peace Conference on Yugoslavia (1992) 31 ILM 1494.

States in the sense of international law." Etinski arrives at a similar conclusion about state succession when analyzing the dismemberment of the British Empire, the French Community, the Ottoman Empire, the Netherlands Indies, or Congo's separation from Belgium.[78] Kohen further argues that the seceding republics "cannot impose on those who remain to dissolve the federation," which is why "continuity of the state can be as long as there are at least two federal entities that wish to maintain the federal structure."[79]

The Badinter Commission outlined three reasons for this finding. First, "the Republics [had] expressed their desire for independence." Second, the federal organs "no longer [met] "the criteria of participation and representativeness *inherent in a federal State*" [Emphasis added]. Third, "the authorities of the Federation *and the Republics* [had] shown themselves powerless to enforce respect for the succeeding ceasefire agreements concluded under the auspices of the European Communities or the United Nations Organization" [Emphasis added].

Using similar reasoning, in its Opinion No. 8 of July 4, 1992,[80] the Badinter Arbitration Commission found that the process of dissolution was "now complete and that the Socialist Federal Republic of Yugoslavia no longer exists." The Commission once again utterly disregarded the fact that the seceding republics had themselves referred to the right to secession, even explicitly so in their new constitutions.[81] It employed a line of argument similar to that in its first Opinion, expanded to include new developments (plebiscite on sovereignty and independence held in Bosnia in February 1992; Serbia and Montenegro constituted the Federal Republic of Yugoslavia in April 1992; Slovenia, Croatia, and Bosnia-Herzegovina received widespread international recognition and U.N. membership; U.N. Security Council Resolutions and the European Council Declaration on Yugoslavia of June 27, 1992, referred to "the former" Yugoslavia). One decisive

---

78 Rodoljub Etinski, "Has the SFR of Yugoslavia Ceased to Exist as a Subject of International Law?" in Radovan Petkovich, *International Law and the Changed Yugoslavia* (Belgrade: Institute of International Politics and Economics, 1995), 32-34.

79 Marcelo G. Kohen, "Le problème des frontières en cas de dissolution et de séparation d'états: quelles alternatives?" *Revue Belge de Droit International* 1998/1 (Brussels: Editions Bruylant), 133 [translation mine]. Original text: " . . . celles-ci ne peuvent pas imposer à ceux qui restent de dissoudre la fédération. C'est pourquoi, tant qu'il y aura au moins deux entités fédérées désireuses de garder la structure fédérale, il peut y avoir continuité de l'Etat."

80 Opinion No. 8 of the Arbitration Commission of the Peace Conference on Yugoslavia (1992) 31 ILM 1521.

81 *See* Chapter 4: *The (Self-) Determination of the Yugoslav Peoples.*

factor, outlined in Opinion No. 8, entailed the fact that the seceding states accounted for the "greater part of the territory and population" of the SFRY.[82]

In declaring Yugoslavia's "dissolution," which it used interchangeably with the term "breaking-up,"[83] the Badinter Commission described the situation of a state challenged by disintegrative processes, and did not present legal qualification for its cause. In contrast, this was the gist of the brief opinion (just over a page long), produced by the Constitutional Court of Yugoslavia on the same issue,[84] addressed to the Badinter Arbitration Commission and submitted to the Yugoslav Secretariat for Foreign Affairs on December 5, 1991—that is, a week after the Badinter Commission delivered its Opinion No. 1. The Court focused on the causes of disintegration, stressing that "One can speak of break-up, that is of the disintegration of Yugoslavia only as a consequence of unconstitutional acts of certain republics declaring sovereignty and independence."[85] The Yugoslav Constitutional Court explicitly declared that Yugoslavia was challenged by secession:

> Yugoslavia is not a contractual association of sovereign states. . . . Yugoslavia was not created as a federation of sovereign and independent states in the form of republics of the Yugoslav state community, but as a federal state of the peoples of Yugoslavia and their republics. Therefore, every republican act by which a republic is declared a sovereign and independent state is an unconstitutional change of the state structure of Yugoslavia, that is, an act of secession.[86]

The Badinter Commission made no reference to this or any other opinion issued by the Yugoslav Constitutional Court, having considered only the opinion of Stipe Mesić, the then President of the SFRY Presidency of Croat origin, produced outside the regular procedure of establishing the presidency's position.[87]

---

[82] Seceding republics accounted for about 40 percent of Yugoslavia's territory and 45 percent of its population.

[83] *See* Opinion No. 3 of the Arbitration Commission of the Peace Conference on Yugoslavia (1992) 31 ILM 1499.

[84] Response to the question of Lord Carrington about whether Yugoslavia is facing disintegration or secession, December 5, 1991, Document no 365/91, reproduced in Milovan Buzadjich, *Secession of former Yugoslav republics in light of decisions of the Yugoslav Constitutional Court; Collection of Documents with Introductory Discussion* [Сецесија бивших југословенских репиблике у светлости одлука Уставног суда Југославије; Збирка докумената с уводном расправом] (Belgrade: Official Gazette of SRY, 1994), 239-240, at 240.

[85] Ibid. [Translation mine].

[86] Ibid. [Translation mine].

[87] For this reason, Krecha claims that this was Stipe Mesić's "private opinion." Kreća, "Badinter's Arbitration Commission; A Critical Commentary," *Yugoslav Review*, 70-71.

By expressly circumventing an analysis that would inevitably lead to the same conclusion as deduced by the Yugoslav Constitutional Court, the Badinter Commission provided the E.C. with a justification for recognition that would not appear to be sanctioning secession. Although the legal validity of the Badinter Commission's ruling on Yugoslavia's dissolution could be challenged,[88] the E.C. endorsed the Commission's reasoning in support of its political decision to recognize the seceding Yugoslav republics.

Slovenia had also attempted to avoid the use of the term "secession," but for a different reason—out of concern for the term's implication regarding the process of state succession. The Slovenes instead used the term "disassociation." As the Slovene president Kučan explained in March 1991, in contrast to disassociation, "secession is the recognition that a state remains, that one part secedes, and that the part that remains determines for the other the conditions under which it can secede, the obligations it may take with it, and finally the rights that may possibly be recognized by it."[89]

Since the proclamation of dissolution and the process of succession were indeed intertwined, the international community denied the continuity of Yugoslavia in the form of two republics with such determination, Serbia and Montenegro, despite the fact that the two entities joined the first Yugoslavia as states in 1918, while the other parts of Yugoslavia represented fractions of the Austro-Hungarian and Ottoman Empire.[90] In this respect, the international community acted contrary to legal pronouncements by W.E. Hall:

> Even when an internal change takes the form of temporary dissolution, so that the State, either from social anarchy or local disruption, is momentarily unable to fulfil its international duties, personal identity remains unaffected; it is only lost when the permanent dissolution of the State is proved

---

[88]   See the discussion below.

[89]   FBIS-EEU, March 19, 1991, 51.

[90]   For more on the problem of Yugoslavia's succession, see Kreca, "Badinter's Arbitration Commission; A Critical Commentary," Yugoslav Review, 1993; David O. Lloyd, "Succession, Secession, and State Membership in the United Nations," New York University Journal of International Law and Politics 26 (1994); Etinski, "Has the SFR of Yugoslavia Ceased to Exist as a Subject of International Law?," International Law and the Changed Yugoslavia.; Konstantin Obradovich, "Problemi vezani za sukcesiju SFRJ" [Problems relating to the SFRY Succession], Medjunarodno pravo i jugoslovenska kriza [International Law and the Yugoslav Crisis], ed. Milan Shahovich (Belgrade: Institute for International Politics and Economy, 1995), 275-315.

by the erection of a fresh State, or by the continuance of anarchy so prolonged as to render reconstitution impossible or in a very high degree improbable.[91]

. . .

The identity of a State therefore is considered to subsist so long as a part of the territory which can be recognised as the essential portion through the preservation of the capital or of the original territorial nucleus, or which represents the State by the continuity of government, remains either as an independent residuum or as the core of an enlarged organization.[92]

Etinski further recalls an important decision made by the U.S. Court of Appeals in 1954,[93] reversing the 1952 ruling of the U.S. District Court on the extradition of the Nazi Croat Andrija Artuković to Yugoslavia.[94] The U.S. Court of Appeals found that the United States could extradite Artuković under the Extradition treaty concluded between the Kingdom of Serbia and the United States on 12-25 October 1901, since the Kingdom of Serbs, Croats and Slovenes was a successor to the Kingdom of Serbia, which was the "central or nucleus nation"[95] of the new state. The United States, as *amicus curiae*, made an even more explicit argument:

Evidence indicates that the State formerly known as Serbia continued as an international juridical entity upon its enlargement into the Kingdom of the Serbs, Croats, and Slovenes in 1918, and consequently the treaty rights and obligations of that State continued in force and applied to the whole of its territory.[96]

Bartos also deduces that "Yugoslavia's creation as an amalgamation of territories around the nucleus of Serbia" represents an important factor, warranting secession as "the more appropriate characterization of the situation."[97]

---

[91] William Edward Hall, *A Treatise on International Law*, 8th ed. (Oxford: Oxford University Press, 1924), 21.

[92] Ibid. *See also* Lassa F.L. Oppenheim, *International Law, A Treatise*, 4th ed. (London: A.D. Mc. Nair, 1928), 160.

[93] Ivanchevich v. Artukovic, in United States, Federal Reporter, second series, vol. 211 F2 nd., 565 (1954, Court of Appeals, 9th Circuit), *Yearbook of the International Law Commission*, 1970, vol. II, 125.

[94] Artukovic v. Boyle, in United States, Federal Supplement, vol. 107, 11, 20, note 6 (1952, District Court, Southern District, California), *Yearbook of the International Law Commission*, 1970, vol. II, 125.

[95] Cited by Marjorie M. Whiteman, *Digest of International Law*, vol. 2, 1963, 942.

[96] Ibid., 943, paragraph II.

[97] Tomas Bartos, "Uti Possidetis. Quo Vadis?" *Australian Year Book of International Law*, 18 (1997), 37-96: 75.

In defining the considerations undertaken in its ruling, the Arbitration Commission spelled out the "commonly defined" characteristics of a state without directly quoting the Montevideo Convention on the Rights and Duties of States but providing the essence of its definition.[98] The Badinter Commission proceeded to add another condition, "the government's sway over the population and the territory," which in a federal-type state implied that its federal organs ". . . represent the components of the Federation and wield effective power."

In public international law neither the loss of a state's territory nor of its population, nor lower government participation can justify declaring the end of a state. Thomas Musgrave offers several examples to support this view.[99] First, Pakistan has continued to exist as a state, preserving its seat in the UN, after losing the entire eastern part of its territory and about 57 percent of its population when Bangladesh seceded.[100] Biafra's secession from Nigeria and the conflict in Cyprus exemplify how the participation and representativeness of a state's government are not indicative of the state's continued existence or otherwise.[101] Radan on the other hand gives the example of Somalia, while Jovanovich refers to Afghanistan and Albania of the late 1990s as states whose international legal personality was not questioned despite the widespread anarchy.[102]

The Badinter Commission failed to explore the cause of the purported lack of representative government in the case of Yugoslavia, since such an exercise would also have invoked the issue of secession. Notably, the seceding republics had abandoned their positions in the federal government. Secondly, the remaining officials in the federal government did not directly represent the non-seceding

---

[98] Montevideo Convention on the Rights and Duties of States, Article 1: "The State as a person of international law should possess the following qualifications: (a) a permanent population; (b) a defined territory; (c) a government; and (d) a capacity to enter into relations with other States." 165 League of Nations Treaty Series (1933), 19. The Convention was signed at Montevideo on December 26, 1933, and entered into force on December 26, 1934.

[99] James Crawford, *The Creation of States in International Law* (Oxford: Clarendon Press, 1979), 404-405, 417; William Edward Hall, *A Treatise on International Law*, 8th edition (London: Oxford University Press, 1924), 21-22. Furthermore, the ICJ declared in the Western Sahara Case: "No rule of international law, in the view of the Court, requires the structure of the State to follow any particular pattern, as is evident from the diversity of the forms of States found in the world today." [1975] ICJ Reports 12, 43-44.

[100] Musgrave, *Self-Determination and National Minorities*, 202.

[101] Ibid., 203.

[102] Peter Radan, *The Break-up of Yugoslavia and International Law*, Routledge Studies in International Law (London, New York: Routledge, 2002), 211. Vladislav Jovanovich, "The Status of the Federal Republic of Yugoslavia in the United Nations," *Fordham International Law Journal* 21 (1998), 1726-7.

republics but all of Yugoslavia, as stipulated by the 1974 SFRY Constitution (Articles 129, 362, 397). Thirdly, the federal authorities acted as a counterpart to the United Nations, having approved the so-called Vance Plan for a peacekeeping operation in the republic of Croatia, established by the U.N. Security Council Resolution 721 of November 27, 1991. Finally, the Badinter Commission did not analyze the nature of the administrative borders in Yugoslavia, an exercise that is related to the determination of Yugoslavia's legal birth as a state, arbitrarily assumed by the Commission to be 1945. As shown by the survey of Yugoslavia's political history, the administrative borders had changed several times after 1918, based on diverse criteria, and with varying degrees of authority granted to the territories they delimited.[103] The main purpose of the administrative borders was to effectively govern the state rather than to separate territories. Therefore, as argued by the Court of Arbitration in the Dubai-Sharjah Border Arbitration:

> [O]ne cannot attribute the same value to a boundary which has been set-
> tled under a treaty, or as the result of an arbitral or judicial proceeding, in
> which independent interested Parties have had a full opportunity to present
> their arguments, as to a boundary which has been established by way of an
> administrative decision emanating from an authority which could have
> failed to take account of the Parties' views and arising from a situation of
> inherent inequality.[104]

Furthermore, the Badinter Arbitration Commission has maintained that plebi-scites on sovereignty and independence represent a significant factor contribut-ing to a state's "dissolution" and eventual extinction. Several year later, in 1998, the Supreme Court of Canada, in the advisory opinion that addressed the constitu-tionality of a hypothetical unilateral declaration of independence by Canada's province of Quebec, confirmed the traditional position of international law in this regard, stating that a plebiscite in favor of secession "in itself and without more, has no direct legal effect, and could not in itself bring about unilateral seces-sion."[105] At the same time, Canada's Supreme Court also argued that a clear majority vote in Quebec on a clear question in favor of secession would confer democratic legitimacy on the secession initiative which all of the other participants

---

[103] For more, *see* Chapter 3: *Yugoslavias' Administrative Boundaries (1918-1991)*.

[104] Dubai-Sharjah Border Arbitration (1981) 91 ILR 543, 579.

[105] *Reference re: Secession of Quebec* (1998) 161 DLR (4th) 385: 424 (paragraph 87).

in Confederation would have to recognize.[106] However, the plebiscites conducted in Yugoslavia were neither constitutional, as officially ruled by the Yugoslav Constitutional Court,[107] nor democratic in nature. They were held at a time of great political upheaval, in a region that had just initiated its transition from Communism, where people did not have access to free information and balanced debate. The ambiguity of the questions posed at the plebiscites compounded the problem, leading analysts like Peter Radan to question "whether all of those who voted 'Yes' did so with the actual desire that their republic become an independent state."[108]

At the moment, it is difficult to foresee whether the Badinter Commission's ruling on dissolution has created any new legal principle or provided evidence of state practice relating to state creation. The discussion above demonstrates that the Badinter Commission's arguments for Yugoslavia's "dissolution" or extinction can be seriously challenged, a conclusion that is underscored by the Commission's own assertion in Opinion No. 8 that Yugoslavia was "still a legal international entity"[109] when it delivered its first opinion.[110] The inconsistency of the Badinter Commission was crowned in its Opinion No. 11.[111] In this opinion, the Badinter Commission lists dates when various former Yugoslav republics became independent states (Croatia and Slovenia on 8 October 1991, Macedonia on November 17, 1991, Bosnia and Herzegovina on March 6, 1992, and Serbia and Montenegro on April 27, 1992), simultaneously postulating that the process of dissolution in Yugoslavia had begun on November 29, 1991, that is, *after* three of the new states had achieved their statehood. Both Craven and Radan maintain that this is evidence that these states arose as the result of secession.[112] For all these reasons, serious publicists like James Crawford do not espouse the Arbitration Commission's

---

[106] Ibid.

[107] *See* Chapter 4: *The (Self-) Determination of the Yugoslav Peoples.*

[108] Radan, *Break-up of Yugoslavia and International Law*, 208.

[109] Opinion No. 8 of the Arbitration Commission of the Peace Conference on Yugoslavia (1992) 31 ILM 1521: 1522.

[110] For more, *see* Matthew Craven, "The European Community Arbitration Commission on Yugoslavia," *British Yearbook of International Law* 66 (1995), 369.

[111] Opinion No. 11 of the Arbitration Commission of the Peace Conference on Yugoslavia (1992) 31 ILM 1589.

[112] Craven, "The European Community Arbitration Commission on Yugoslavia," 377; Radan, *Break-up of Yugoslavia and International Law*, 223.

ruling on Yugoslavia's dissolution but simply note that "this was the position taken by the international community."[113]

While jurists like Alain Pellet[114] praise the precedent-setting quality of the Badinter Arbitration Commission's Opinions, others, like Hurst Hannum, warn of the danger of the Commission's conclusion on dissolution as it creates a modality by which the federal units could easily secede, disrupting international stability and discouraging state decentralization:

> If a state is founded on a federal (or, presumably, confederate) principles, then it is sufficient for a constituent republic or republics to cease participating in the federal government in order to deprive the state as a whole of recognition as a state by the international community.[115]

The latter has already proven true in Yugoslavia, reflected in Croatia's unwillingness to grant autonomous status to the Serbian minority and in Serbia's suppression of Kosovo's autonomy. Even more disconcerting is Badinter's position on cease-fires, which may encourage secessionist groups to engage in hostilities and violate any negotiated cease-fires to demonstrate a frail government authority.

While the effect of the Badinter Commission's Opinion No.1 (confirmed in its later Opinion No. 8) on future cases remains uncertain, it indubitably has acted as a critical basis for additional legal experimenting in the case of Yugoslavia.

5.2.2. Self-Determination of the Serbs

The most intricate issue facing the Arbitration Commission was whether the Serbian people in Croatia and Bosnia-Herzegovina enjoyed a right to self-determination. Once again, Lord Carrington had reformulated the original question(s) posed by the Republic of Serbia: "Who is entitled to the right of self-determination from the standpoint of public international law—a nation or a federal unit? Is the right to self-determination a subjective collective right or the right of a

---

[113] James Crawford, "State Practice and International Law in relation to Secession," *The British Yearbook of International Law* 69 (1998), 85-117:92.

[114] *See* Alain Pellet, "The Opinions of the Badinter Arbitration Committee; A Second Breath for the Self-Determination of Peoples," *European Journal of International Law* 3 (1992).

[115] Hurst Hannum, "Self-Determination, Yugoslavia, and Europe: Old Wine in New Bottles?" 3 *Transnational Law and Contemporary Problems* 57 (1993), 64.

territory?" Not only did Lord Carrington focus on the issue of Serbian people's rights, but he also limited the issue to two Yugoslav republics instead of Yugoslavia as a whole. At the same time he described the Serbs in these two republics as constituent peoples of Yugoslavia, while they were also the constituent peoples of the two republics, as pronounced in their respective constitutions.[116]

In producing its Opinion No. 2,[117] delivered on January 11, 1992, the Arbitration Commission relied on the Yugoslav constitution, but only when it supported its case, as have the seceding republics in their secessionist acts.[118] As a result, a situation was created in which a constitution, instead of inducing compromise on a contentious issue, "afford[s] legitimacy to the side that in fact wishes to bring down the constitutional structure."[119]

Turning the Yugoslav Constitution upside down, the Badinter Commission concluded that "the right to self-determination must not involve changes to existing frontiers at the time of independence . . . except where the States concerned agree otherwise" and that "where there are one or more groups within a State constituting one or more ethic, religious or language communities, they have the right to recognition of their identity under international law."[120]

However, the Badinter Commission did not apply this conclusion to Yugoslavia as a whole but to its constituent republics, defining the people as an ethnic rather than a civic concept, but limiting the ethnic right to an administrative unit and effectively transferring the right from a people to a territory (republic). The Serbs could not exercise their right to self-determination in Yugoslavia but in its constituent units. According to the Badinter Arbitration Comission:

> the Serbian population in Bosnia-Herzegovina and Croatia is entitled to all the rights concerned to minorities and ethnic groups under international

---

116 *See* Chapter 4: *The (Self-) Determination of the Yugoslav Peoples.*

117 Opinion No. 2 of the Arbitration Commission of the Peace Conference on Yugoslavia (1992) 31 ILM 1497.

118 *See* Chapter 4: *The (Self-) Determination of the Yugoslav Peoples.*

119 Robert M. Hayden, *Blueprints for a House Divided; The Constitutional Logic of the Yugoslav Conflicts* (Ann Arbor: The University of Michigan Press, 2000), 13.

120 Opinion No. 2 of the Arbitration Commission of the Peace Conference on Yugoslavia (1992) 31 ILM 1497: 1498.

law *and* under the provisions of the draft Convention of the Conference on Yugoslavia of 4 November 1991. . . . and . . .

[T]he Republics must afford the members of those minorities and ethnic groups all the human rights and fundamental freedoms recognized in international law, including, where appropriate, the right to choose their *nationality*. [Emphasis added]

The Badinter Commission effectively interpreted the Yugoslav Constitution as a document that granted the right to self-determination to the republics, including a right to secession. It claimed that the provision demanding consent of all federal units for any changes in the internal borders did not apply to secession but only to changes in the territory of each republic. Such an interpretation would have been plausible if the self-determination did not refer to the Yugoslav constituent peoples (nations), rather than to the republics. It is striking that the Badinter Commission completely omits this fact from its analysis of the Yugoslav Constitution and that it does not cite the Constitution's reference to the right to self-determination. The first words of the 1974 SFRY Constitution were the following:

The peoples of Yugoslavia, stemming from the right of every people to self-determination, including the right to secession, on the basis of their freely expressed will . . . have joined together into a federal republic of free and equal peoples and nationalities. (Preamble, Basic Principles I)

The Badinter Arbitration Commission turned the Serbs from a constituent people to a minority that could potentially claim minority rights, just as had the Croatian Constitution a year before that.[121] An important effect of this transformation was that the Serbian right to self-determination could "not involve changes to existing frontiers."[122] To further support this view, the Badinter Commission invoked Article 1 of the International Human Rights Covenants, applying international law as selectively as the provisions of the Yugoslav constitution.[123]

---

[121] Ustav Republike Hrvatske [Constitution of the Republic of Croatia], *Izvješca Hrvatskoga sabora* [Proceedingss of the Croatian Assembly], number 15, December 22, 1990.

[122] Musgrave, *Self-Determination and National Minorities*, 170.

[123] In a similar vein, the Slovenes justify the assertion of Slovenian economic sovereignty in the 1989 amendments to the Slovene Constitution with a reference to article 1 of the International Covenant on Economic, Social, and Cultural Rights. Not only is such an interpretation in conflict with the

Yet the Canadian Supreme Court arrived at a different conclusion when deliberating on the right to self-determination. While failing to precisely define the holders of this right ("a people"), the Court unambiguously stated: "It is clear that 'a people' may include only a portion of the population of an existing state."[124]

Nonetheless, the Canadian Supreme Court also argued that "peoples are expected to achieve self-determination within the framework of their existing state" since the external right to self-determination (right of secession) applied only in a limited number of cases: "where 'a people' is governed as part of a colonial empire where 'a people' is subject to alien subjugation, domination or exploitation; and possibly where 'a people' is denied any meaningful exercise of its right to self-determination within the state of which it forms a part."[125]

The Badinter Arbitration Commission, by opting for a territorial application of the principle of self-determination, denied Serbs the application of the "external" right to self-determination, except within the confines of the republic where they were a majority (Republic of Serbia). This was in line with the previous decisions of the European Community that had already implicitly described the Serbs as minorities. For instance, the E.C. Declaration on the Situation in Yugoslavia of 6 October 1991 states:

> The right to self-determination of all peoples of Yugoslavia cannot be exercised in isolation from the interests and rights of ethnic minorities within the individual Republics.[126]

Moreover, the recognition of Croatia and Slovenia by Germany and several other states preceded the issuance of Opinion No. 2 of the Badinter Commission.

---

constitutional provisions for a unified Yugoslav market (articles 251 and 253 of the Yugoslav constitution), but, as discussed earlier (*see* Chapter 1: *Legal Context of Yugoslavia's Disintegration: Sovereignty and Self-Determination of Peoples*), the application of article 1 of the International Covenant on Economic, Social, and Cultural Rights is problematic due to a disagreement among states regarding its scope, with many claiming that it refers solely to the process of decolonization and with no agreement as to the definition of the bearer of this right.

124 *Reference re: Secession of Quebec* (1998) 161 DLR (4th) 437, paragraph 124.

125 Ibid., 448, paragraph 154.

126 E.C. Declaration on the Situation in Yugoslavia, October 6, 1991, reproduced in Trifunovska, *Yugoslavia Through Documents*, 351-2.

The political decision made was that the borders of the (former) Yugoslav republics were more sacrosanct than Yugoslavia's international borders and that the
"external" right to self-determination applied to Yugoslavia but not to the newly
independent states arising Yugoslavia's "dissolution." The double standards are
particularly striking because they are applied on the same territory.

Such a policy has led Serbian analysts such as the historian Branko Petranovich to
conclude:

> International actors . . . have emphasized the principle of republics (admin-
> istrative borders) and not the right of peoples to self-determination; and
> even when they quoted the latter principle, it did not apply to the Serbian
> people.[127]

Susan Lalonde has also argued that the Badinter Arbitration Commission changed
the right to self-determination of peoples into the self-determination of territory:

> As a result of the commission's analysis, the right of self-determination is
> no longer a subjective collective right but rather has become the right of
> particular units of territory.[128]

In practice, although the Badinter Commission propagated group minority rights,
including a vague right to choose a nationality and a more specific right to a special status for minorities, as elaborated in the Draft Convention of the Peace
Conference, even the internal right to self-determination did not materialize in
the main for Serbs in Croatia, for example.

Rejecting the Arbitration Commission's Opinion, The Vice-President of the
Yugoslav Presidency, Branko Kostich recalled the traditional interpretation of
this principle as one pertaining to a people rather than territory,[129] stressing that
the problem was not one of respecting the right to self-determination in principle

---

[127] Branko Petranović, *Istoričar i savremena epoha* [Historian and the Contemporary Period] (Belgrade: Vojska, 1994), 406.

[128] Suzanne Lalonde, *Determining Boundaries in a Conflicting World; The Role of Uti Possidetis* (Montreal: McGill University Press, 2002), 186

[129] "The right to self-determination and secession is the right of nations and not the right of republics." Letter by Yugoslav Presidency Vice-President to Chairman of the Conference on Yugoslavia, December 8, 1991, reproduced in *Focus*, Special Issue, Belgrade, January 14, 1992, 239-245:240.

but in territorial delimitation based on the peoples' preferences: "in Croatia, where the Serbian people has expressed itself in favour of remaining in Yugoslavia, there is a problem of territorial delimitation."[130]

The Badinter Arbitration Commission avoided the process of territorial delimitation by another selective interpretation of the Yugoslav constitution and the principles of international public law.

5.2.3. *Uti possidetis*

The third important question addressed by the Badinter Commission in Opinion No. 3,[131] delivered on January 11, 1992, involved the legal elaboration of a policy of recognizing the internal borders of Yugoslavia: "Can the internal boundaries between Croatia and Serbia and between Bosnia and Herzegovina and Serbia be regarded as frontiers in terms of public international law?"

Rendering a positive response to this question, the Badinter Commission outlined four key arguments:

> *First*—All external frontiers must be respected in line with the Principles stated in the *UN Charter* . . . [and other international instruments].
> *Second*—The boundaries between Croatia and Serbia, between Bosnia and Serbia, and possibly between other adjacent independent States, may not be altered except by agreement freely arrived at.
> *Third*—Except where otherwise agreed, the former boundaries become protected by international law. . . .
> *Fourth*—According to well established principles of international law, the alteration of existing frontiers or boundaries by force is not capable of producing any legal effect.

To justify its conclusion, the Arbitration Commission selected the second and the fourth paragraph of Article 5 of the Yugoslav Constitution, which stipulated that the Republics' territories and boundaries could not be altered without

---

[130] Letter by Yugoslav Presidency Vice-President to Chairman of the Conference on Yugoslavia, December 8, 1991, reproduced in *Focus*, Special Issue, Belgrade, January 14, 1992, 239-245:242.
[131] Opinion No. 3 of the Arbitration Commission of the Peace Conference on Yugoslavia (1992) 31 ILM 1499.

their consent.[132] The Arbitration Commission failed to remark that the fourth paragraph of the article also specified that changes of a boundary of an autonomous province also required its consent. Significantly, the Badinter Arbitration Commission ignored the provincial administrative boundaries, later rejecting an application for recognition from the Kosovo Albanian representatives.[133]

The Commission also opted to omit the provisions of paragraphs 1 and 3 of the same Article, which speak to the territorial integrity of Yugoslavia and which are violated by the Commission's ruling:

1. The territory of the [SFRY] is indivisible and consists of the territories of its socialist republics. . . .
3. A border of the SFRY cannot be altered without the consent of its republics and autonomous provinces.

Furthermore, as Radan convincingly argues, the territorial integrity of republics and the sanctity of their borders referred to in paragraphs 2 and 4 of Article 5 applied only in the context of the Yugoslav state whose own territorial integrity and borders remained in place.[134]

To further rationalize the recognition of Yugoslavia's internal borders, the Arbitration Commission referred to the legal principle of *uti possidetis juris*,[135]

---

[132] " . . . 2. A republic's territory cannot be altered without the consent of that republic and the territory of an autonomous province—without the consent of the autonomous province.

4. A boundary between republics can only be altered on the basis of their agreement, and in the case of a border of an autonomous province—on the basis of its consent" (SFRY Constitution, Article 5).

[133] "Kosovo calls for E.C. recognition," *Agence France Press*, December 24, 1991. On June 15, 1992, the E.C. declared "that frontiers can only be changed by peaceful means and [reminded] the inhabitants of Kosovo that their legitimate quest for autonomy should be dealt with in the framework of the E.C. Peace Conference." E.C. Press Statement, Luxembourg, June 15, 1992.

[134] Radan, *Break-up of Yugoslavia and International Law*, 234.

[135] This Latin phrase literary means "as you possess you shall continue to possess." For more on the evolution of the principle of *uti possidetis juris* since its use in Roman law, *see* Constantine Antonopoulos, "The Principle of Uti Possidetis Juris in Contemporary International Law," *Revue hellénique de droit international* 49 (1996), 29-88; Lalonde, *Determining Boundaries in a Conflicting World*; Tomas Bartos, "Uti Possidetis. Quo Vadis?" *Australian Year Book of International Law*, 18 (1997), 37-96. Steven R. Ratner, "Drawing a Better Line: *Uti Possidetis* and the Borders of New States," *American Journal of International Law* 90 (1996), 590-624.

invoked for the first time outside the colonial context. The Badinter Arbitration Commission claimed that this principle "though initially applied in settling decolonization issues in America and Africa, is today recognized as a general principle," quoting from the ruling by the International Court of Justice in the Frontier Dispute Case (Burkina Faso and Mali) to support its assertion:

> Nevertheless the principle is not a special rule which pertains to one specific system of international law. It is a general principle, which is logically connected with the phenomenon of the obtaining of independence, wherever it occurs. Its obvious purpose is to prevent the independence and stability of new States being endangered by fratricidal struggles. . . . [136]

Importantly, the Badinter Commission does not quote the final phrase of this paragraph: "provoked by the challenging of frontiers following the withdrawal of the administering power. A complete reading of the text would suggest that the ICJ finds *uti possidetis juris* to be a general principle, albeit limited to the realm of decolonization.

Furthermore, according to the Badinter Commission's ruling, the principle of *uti possidetis* applies "once the process [of disintegration] leads to the creation of one or more independent states." Again, the Commission does not analyze the causes of such a situation, nor does it specify that the principle of *uti possidetis juris* could be applied only in the case of "dissolution." Moreover, the Badinter Commission here contradicts itself since, as one can deduce from its Opinions 1 and 8, the SFRY still enjoyed the status of a state at the time Opinion 3 was issued, implying the pre-emptive application of the *uti possidetis* principle.

Yet Lalonde, who has scrupulously researched the role of the principle of *uti possidetis*, asserts that this is "a phantom principle, a precedent based on political reality"[137] rather than a principle that has become customary law. Lalonde refutes even the assertion made in the decision on the *Frontier Dispute Case*, that *uti possidetis* is "a firmly established principle of international law where decolonization

---

[136] Frontier Dispute Case, (1986) ICJ Reports 554 at 565 (paragraph 20).

[137] Suzanne Lalonde, "The Role of *Uti Possidetis* in Determining Boundaries: From Kosovo to Quebec," Paper presented at the International conference on Legal and Political Solutions to Disputes over Sovereignty—From Kosovo to Quebec, held at Belgrade University, July 7-10, 2005.

is concerned,"[138] stressing that "the meaning and influence to be attributed to the *uti possidetis* principle in the colonial context is not beyond doubt."[139]

Lalonde further insists that even in cases when *uti possidetis* was invoked in the colonial context, it was "applied to entities that have already achieved independence through various processes" and "only in relation to the territory each had come to control"[140] rather than as a basis for international recognition. This view is also taken by the ICJ in its deliberation on the Burkina Faso-Mali Frontier Dispute:

> International law—and consequently the principle of *uti possidetis*—applies
> to the new State (as a State) not with retroactive effect but immediately and
> from that moment onwards.[141]

However, the Badinter Arbitration Commission created a precedent by using the *uti possidetis juris* principle to select the territorial units that would become eligible for recognition. According to Craven, the Arbitration Commission used "*uti possidetis* as a tool for establishing the presumptive statehood of the entities to emerge from the dismemberment of the SFRY and to deny the autonomous Serbian Republics the benefit of that presumption."[142] Joshua Castellino and Steve Allen concur, maintaining that the Badinter application of the principle of *uti possidetis* reverses the process of self-determination: "Instead of seeking a territorial settlement for a vulnerable people, it seeks to 'settle' people within a fixed territory."[143] This is not in the spirit of the right to self-determination, as stressed by Judge Dillard's Separate Opinion in the Western Sahara Case: "[I]t is for the people to determine the fate of the territory and not the territory the fate of the people."[144]

---

138   Frontier Dispute Case, (1986) ICJ Reports 554 at 565.

139   Lalonde, *Determining Boundaries in a Conflicting World*, 190. For more on the application of the principle of *uti possidetis* in the decolonization context *see* Ibid., 24-138; *see also* Tomas Bartos, "Uti Possidetis. Quo Vadis?" *Australian Year Book of International Law*, 18 (1997), 37-96, at 43-69.

140   Lalonde, Determining Boundaries in a Conflicting World, 192.

141   Frontier Dispute Case, (1986) ICJ Reports 554, at 568, paragraph 30.

142   Craven, "The European Community Arbitration Commission on Yugoslavia," 388.

143   Joshua Castellino and Steve Allen, "The Doctrine of *Uti Possidetis*: Crystallization of Modern Post-Colonial Identity," *German Yearbook of International Law* 43 (2000), 205-226: 224. For more on the authors' critique of *uti possidetis*, see also Joshua Castellino and Steve Allen, *Title to Territory in International Law; A Temporal Analysis*, Law, Social Change and Development Series (Aldershot: Ashgate, 2003), especially 21-25.

144   Advisory Opinion of the International Court of Justice on the Western Sahara, Sep. Op. Dillard [October 16, 1975] ICJ Reports, 116.

In taking this approach, the Badinter Arbitration Commission forgave the potentially stabilizing effect of invoking the *uti possidetis juris* principle in the case of Yugoslavia, which in other cases was based on the consent of the parties to apply the principle.[145] As discussed, the federal authorities and the government of the Republic of Serbia refused to accept internalization of the administrative republican borders, while the Croatian authorities accepted such a solution only when realizing that it was necessary for achieving international recognition, otherwise preferring the borders be recarved to include portions of the neighboring Bosnia. The seceding republics had never themselves explicitly referred to the principle of *uti possidetis juris* when requesting recognition.[146] Similarly, none of the statements issued by the E.C. or its member states explicitly referred to the principle. The behavior of the seceding Yugoslav republics and the states that furnished them with international recognition leads Lalonde[147] and other jurists like Corten[148] and Radan[149] to refute claims that the principle of *uti possidetis juris* has become customary law as a result of the international recognition of Yugoslavia's seceding republics.[150] Instead, the principle was misapplied since the issue was not one of the exact location of the borderlines, as in the case of decolonization disputes, but, as Radan notes: "What was in dispute was the question of whether these lines should be future international borders."[151]

In the practical case of Quebec, the policy-makers and the jurists again clashed in their assessment as to whether the application of *uti possidetis* to recognize the Yugoslav republics within their internal borders represents a legal precedent. The report commissioned by the Government of the Canadian province of Quebec,

---

[145] *See* Louis Mortimer Bloomfield, *The British Honduras/Guatemala Dispute* (Toronto: The Carswell Company Limited, 1953), 94; Antonopoulos, "The Principle of Uti Possidetis Juris in Contemporary International Law, 44-45.

[146] *See* Barbara Delcourt, "L'application de l'uti possidetis juris au démembrement de la Yougoslavie: règle coutumière ou impératif politique?," *Revue Belge de Droit International* (Brussels: Bruylant, 1998/1), 53.

[147] Lalonde, *Determining Boundaries in a Conflicting World.*

[148] Olivier Corten, "Droit des peuples à disposer d'eux-mêmes et uti possidetis: deux faces d'une même médaille?" in Olivier Corten et al., eds. *Démembrements d'Etats et délimitations territoriales: l'uti possidetis en question(s)* (Brussels: Bruylant, 1999).

[149] Radan, *Break-up of Yugoslavia and International Law.*

[150] Such assertions are made by the following authors, among others: Nicolas Angelet, "Quelques observations sur le principe de l'uti possidetis a l'aune du cas hypothétique de la Belgique" in Olivier Corten et al., eds. *Démembrements d'Etats et délimitations territoriales:l'uti possidetis en question(s)* (Brussels: Bruylant, 1999); G. Nesi, "L'uti possidetis hors du contexte de la décolonisation: le cas de l'Europe" *AFDI* 44 (1998); and Malcolm N. Shaw, "Peoples, Territorialism and Boundaries" *European Journal of International Law* 3 (1997).

[151] Radan, *Break-up of Yugoslavia and International Law*, 233.

drafted by Alain Pellet[152] in close collaboration with four other prominent international law experts (Thomas M. Franck, Rosalyn Higgins, Malcolm N. Shaw, and Christian Tomuschat) in May 1992, concludes:

> [I]n cases of secession or dissolution of States, pre-existing administrative boundaries must be maintained to become borders of the new States and cannot be altered by the threat or use of force, be it on the part of the seceding entity or of the State from which it breaks off.[153]

Yet while this is the position taken by the Quebec authorities, defined in Bill 99 (An Act respecting the exercise of the fundamental rights and prerogatives of the Quebec people and the Quebec State), which was adopted by the Quebec provincial parliament in December 2000,[154] the same view is not shared by the Canadian federal government, other groups in Canada, or by other jurists, as noted above.

In June 2000, the Canadian federal parliament passed the Clarity Act (Bill C-20)[155] with the purpose of clarifying the Supreme Court's Reference on Secession[156] issued in August 1998. The Clarity Act specified that in any constitutional negotiations on secession the borders of Quebec, together with adequate realization of

---

[152] It probably is not a coincidence that the principal author of the Quebec Report is Alain Pellet, a professor of international law and member of the U.N. International Law Commission, who served as an international law consultant to the Badinter Commission. The Quebec report of May 1992 refers to the Badinter Commission Opinions as an important basis for their conclusions.

[153] Thomas Franck et al., *The Territorial Integrity of Quebec in the Event of the Attainment of Sovereignty* (The Quebec Report), May 8, 1992, paragraph 2.47.

[154] Article 9 of Bill 99 specified that "The territory of Québec and its boundaries cannot be altered except with the consent of the National Assembly" and that "the Government must ensure that the territorial integrity of Québec is maintained and respected." At the same time the absolute sovereignty of the Quebec parliament was enshrined in Article 13: "No other parliament or government may reduce the powers, authority, sovereignty or legitimacy of the National Assembly, or impose constraint on the democratic will of the Québec people to determine its own future."

[155] An Act to give effect to the requirement for clarity as set out in the opinion of the Supreme Court of Canada in the Quebec Secession Reference (Clarity Act), adopted on June 29, 2000.

[156] Reference re: Secession of Quebec (1998) 161 DLR (4th) 385:427. The Reference had also addressed the question of boundaries, but in vague terms, stating: "Nobody seriously suggests that our national existence, seamless in so many aspects, could be effortlessly separated along what are now the provincial boundaries of Quebec" (paragraph 96).

aboriginal and minority rights, would be a matter for negotiation [Article 3(2)].[157] The Northern Crees, living in Quebec's northern territories, have also insisted that the Quebec Bill 99 rests on fallacy because the Quebecois people do not exist, with a dangerous consequence of denying appropriate rights to the Aboriginal Peoples of Quebec:

> The key strategy in Bill 99 is the creation of a single fictitious 'Québec people' throughout the province with the right of self-determination. All aspects of this right are to be controlled by the Québec government and National Assembly. In this way, each of the Aboriginal Peoples in Québec is to be effectively denied the status of a 'People', the right to self-determination and the right to self-identification. These are grave violations of our human rights.[158]

The rhetoric of the Northern Crees of Canada is reminiscent of the complaints made by the Serbs of Bosnia who also asserted that there was no Bosnian nation and that the creation of a Bosnian nation and state turned them into a minority with a degraded status and limited rights. Moreover, Bosnia is an example where the traditional application of the *uti possidetis juris* principle was ultimately rejected. According to Bartos:

> the fundamental characteristic of retaining former boundaries was ultimately discarded in the case of Bosnia-Herzegovina since the Dayton Accords wrought a *de facto* re-partition of that entity.[159]

Finally, one should beware of the danger of confusing the function of the *uti possidetis* principle with the principle of territorial integrity. Alain Pellet has used the two principles interchangeably:

> The territorial integrity of States, this great principle of peace, indispensable to international stability, which as noted by the Committee and the

---

157 Article 3 (2): "No Minister of the Crown shall propose a constitutional amendment to effect the secession of a province from Canada unless the Government of Canada has addressed, in its negotiations, the terms of secession that are relevant in the circumstances, including the division of assets and liabilities, any changes to the borders of the province, the rights, interests and territorial claims of the Aboriginal peoples of Canada, and the protection of minority rights."

158 "Bill 99: A Sovereign Act of Dispossession, Dishonour and Disgrace," Brief of The Grand Council of the Crees (Eeyou Istchee) to the Québec National Assembly Committee on Institutions (Summary), February 1, 2000 (accessed July 7, 2005); available from http://www.gcc.ca/archive/article.php?id=101.

159 Bartos, "Uti Possidetis. Quo Vadis?" 77.

International Court of Justice, was invented in Latin America to deal with the problems of decolonisation, and then further applied in Africa has today acquired the character of a universal, and peremptory norm.[160]

Significantly, accepting the Pellet / Badinter Commission interpretation of the *uti possidetis* principle would be destabilizing to the international system as it would arbitrarily choose "the people" (those with an external right to self-determination), discouraging states from granting internal right to self-determination in form of territorial autonomy.[161] The Northern Crees identified this danger:

> The international law principle of 'territorial integrity' does not apply to provinces. However, it is still used so as to deny the James Bay Crees and other Aboriginal Peoples the right to determine our own future and that of our territories.[162]

Indeed, the principle of territorial integrity applies to international boundaries while the principle of *uti possidetis* could be implemented in demarcation of international boundaries, together with other principles in this field such as equity. In light of strong challenges to the customary application of *uti possidetis*, and dangers of selective interpretation of this principle, I would strongly concur with Lalonde's assertion that *"Uti possidetis* represents a valid option, not a binding solution imposed under the mantle of custom."[163]

---

[160] Pellet, "The Opinions of the Badinter Arbitration Committee; A Second Breath for the Self-Determination of Peoples," 180.

[161] *See* Hurst Hannum, "Rethinking Self-Determination," *Virginia Journal of International Law* 34 (1993), 39; Wildhaber, "Territorial Modifications and Breakups in Federal States" [1995] *Canadian Yearbook of International Law*, 41-43; C. Hilling, "Les frontières du Québec dans l'hypothèse de son accession a l'indépendance: pour une interprétation contemporaine de l'uti possidetis juris" in O. Corten et al., eds. *Démembrements d'Etats et délimitations territoriales: l'uti possidetis en question(s)* (Brussels: Bruylant, 1999), 239.

[162] "Bill 99: A Sovereign Act of Dispossession, Dishonour and Disgrace," Brief of The Grand Council of the Crees (Eeyou Istchee) to the Québec National Assembly Committee on Institutions (Summary), February 1, 2000 (accessed July 7, 2005); available from http://www.gcc.ca/archive/article.php?id=101.

The response of the rump Yugoslav Federal government to the Badinter Arbitration Commission's opinion on self-determination (Opinion No. 2), representing the Serbian position, arrived at the same conclusion: "the right to self-determination, including the right to seek independence or secession, could not be exercised by sub-State regions of existing States unless those regions were populated by only one 'people,' a nation." *Yugoslav Federal Presidency Position*, December 18, 1991, reprinted in Trifunovska, *Yugoslavia Through Documents*, 475-8, 481-5.

[163] Lalonde, *Determining Boundaries in a Conflicting World*, 240. Similarly Bartos concludes: *"uti possidetis* should be viewed as a starting-point or material consideration in the litigation of boundary disputes

5.3. Recognizing Slovenia, Croatia, and Bosnia and Herzegovina, and Not Recognizing Macedonia

In Opinion No. 1, the Badinter Commission declared that "the existence or disappearance of the state is a question of fact" and that "the effects of recognition by other states are purely declaratory."[164] Yet in its later opinions the Badinter Commission advised applicants for E.C. recognition on which steps to take in order to achieve statehood, using recognition as a carrot and therefore in constitutive rather than declaratory manner. Moreover, the E.C. conferred statehood onto entities that did not satisfy the traditional nor Badinter criteria.

On January 11, 1992, in examining the question of recognition, the Badinter Arbitration Commission ruled that Slovenia[165] and Macedonia[166] "satisfy the tests in the Guidelines on the Recognition of New States in Eastern Europe and in the Soviet Union and the Declaration on Yugoslavia." At the same time, the Badinter Commission found that Croatia[167] and Bosnia and Herzegovina[168] did not qualify for recognition. Croatia "met the necessary conditions for its recognition by the Member States of the European Community," albeit with one important reservation:

> the Constitutional Act of 4 December 1991 does not fully incorporate all the provisions of the draft Convention of 4 November 1991, notably those contained in Chapter II, Article 2(c), under the heading "Special status."

However, the German recognition of Croatia on December 23, 1991, extended pre-emptively precisely out of fear that the E.C. would not recognize Croatia because it did not fulfil the conditions established by the E.C. Recognition Guidelines,[169] pressured the European Community into recognizing Croatia

---

rather than an absolute rule of paramount significance." Tomas Bartos, "Uti Possidetis. Quo Vadis?" *Australian Year Book of International Law*, 18 (1997), 37-96: 96.

[164] Opinion No. 1 of the Arbitration Commission of the Peace Conference on Yugoslavia (1992) 31 ILM 1494.

[165] Opinion No. 7 of the Arbitration Commission of the Peace Conference on Yugoslavia (1992) 31 ILM 1512.

[166] Opinion No. 6 of the Arbitration Commission of the Peace Conference on Yugoslavia (1992) 31 ILM 1507.

[167] Opinion No. 5 of the Arbitration Commission of the Peace Conference on Yugoslavia (1992) 31 ILM 1503.

[168] Opinion No. 4 of the Arbitration Commission of the Peace Conference on Yugoslavia (1992) 31 ILM 1501.

[169] Beverly Crawford's compellingly argues the German unilateral action was caused "by a spiral of mistrust that emerged in international negotiations in the face of German domestic pressure for a policy of diplomatic recognition, which was itself "nourished by conflicting international norms and underdeveloped

despite the ruling of the Badinter Commission. The E.C. merely requested an official promise of the Croatian government that it would amend its Constitution. As deduced by Beverly Crawford:

> Acceptance of the conditions substituted for fulfilment of them, and the conditionality requirement was conveniently swept under the table.[170]

The acceptance of Badinter Commission conditions came in the form of a letter by the Croatian President Tudjman to Robert Badinter,[171] as the head of the Arbitration Commission. In its Opinion No. 5, the Badinter Commission notes the receipt of this letter and the fact that the Croatian President in his letter accepted the draft Convention provisions "in principle," but as quoted above, the Commission also boldly states that the implementation of these provisions was inadequate.

The substance of the Croatian president's letter was never fully implemented. Instead of revising its Constitution, as suggested by the Badinter Commission, the Croatian government proposed a constitutional law, adopted five months after the recognition, in May 1992. This law "had little legitimacy with the Croatian public and did little to dissuade Serbs from their fears of discrimination or worse."[172] Having been the most active in negotiating Croatia's recognition, Germany was notably absent in monitoring the implementation of minority rights for the Serbs in the independent Croatia.

On July 4, 1992, the Arbitration Commission declared that Croatia satisfied the conditions for recognition by the Member States of the E.C. set out in the joint statement on Yugoslavia and the Guidelines on the Recognition of New States in Eastern Europe and in the Soviet Union. Although the Badinter Commission again noted that Croatia did not fully incorporate the Carrington Convention's provisions on autonomy, this was no longer an obstacle to commending Croatia's

---

institutions for European foreign policy cooperation." *See* Beverly Crawford, "Explaining Defection from International Cooperation: Germany's Unilateral Recognition of Croatia," *World Politics* 48, No. 4 (July 1996), 482-521: 485-497.

[170] Ibid., 497.

[171] Franjo Tudjman to Robert Badinter, letter, Zagreb, January 15, 1992.

[172] Woodward, *Balkan Tragedy*, 191.

qualifications for independence.[173] In a report issued in December 1992, the U.N. Human Rights Committee was more critical:

> The Committee was concerned with the preamble to the Constitution, whereby the Republic of Croatia is defined as 'the national state of the Croat nation and a state of members of other nations and minorities.' Concern was expressed about long-standing discrimination against, and harassment of, ethnic Serbs residing within Croatia.[174]

In examining Bosnia and Herzegovina's eligibility for recognition, the Badinter Commission concluded that: "the will of its peoples of Bosnia-Herzegovina to constitute [the republic] as a sovereign and independent State cannot be held to have been fully established."[175] Nevertheless, the Commission also noted that its findings could be reviewed if a referendum "of all the citizens of [Bosnia-Herzegovina] without distinction" were held "under international supervision." The Badinter Commission indirectly proposed the government of Bosnia and Herzegovina to hold a civic referendum, which was contrary to the Constitution of Bosnia-Herzegovina that specifically states that all matters of general importance such as sovereignty and independence must be agreed upon by a consensus of the three ethnic groups: Bosnian Muslims, Croats, and Serbs.[176] This provision was required because a simple majority vote could, as a result of demographic structure, ignore the position of one of Bosnia's constituent nations, which indeed occurred with the vote on independence. In delivering this opinion, the Badinter Commission also implicitly sanctioned the unconstitutionally adopted Memorandum on the Sovereignty of Bosnia-Herzegovina to the National Assembly, which caused the distancing of the Serb representatives from the common Bosnian structures, and which a Bosnian Serb representative in the Bosnian presidency, Dr Bilyana Plavshich, identifies as the decisive moment that ultimately led to war:

> The irregularity of adopting the Memorandum [on Bosnia's Sovereignty . . .] in my opinion was the cause of the war. Shootings, bombs, . . . and other

---

173 Conference on Yugoslavia, Arbitration Commission, Observations on Croatian Constitutional Law, July 4, 1992: 92 ILR 209: 211.

174 Concluding Observations of the Human Rights Committee: Croatia, December 28, 1992, CCPR/C/79/Add.15, at 7.

175 Opinion No. 4 of the Arbitration Commission of the Peace Conference on Yugoslavia (1992) 31 ILM.

176 For more, *see* Chapter 4: *The (Self-) Determination of the Yugoslav Peoples.*

war horrors were just a consequence of this event. When a legal basis according to which the society lives and functions is lost, only a small step separates us from a violent conflict.[177]

Calling for a civic referendum in Bosnia also invokes another logical question, rhetorically posed by both ordinary people and analysts like Crnobrnja:

> Why was there neither pressure nor recommendation to hold a referendum in Yugoslavia to establish what the *citizens* of Yugoslavia, and not ethnic groups, thought about self-determination?[178]

According to Woodward, such a referendum would be equivalent to the federal elections that Slovenia prevented in December 1990 and would represent "the normal U.N. practice of a plebiscite when the fate of a people and a territory are at stake."[179]

However, once again the holder of the (external) right to self-determination was selectively chosen. The Badinter Commission noted but ignored the results of the referendum held by the Bosnian Serbs, in which they expressed their "right" to remain in Yugoslavia. Similarly, in Macedonia, the non-vote of the substantial Albanian minority was also ignored.

The European Community member states, several other European states, and Canada formally recognized Croatia and Slovenia as independent states on January 15, 1992.[180] On March 10, 1992, the E.C. and the U.S. issued a joint statement in which they declared a willingness to recognize the Republic of Bosnia and Herzegovina, and "agreed strongly to oppose any effort to undermine the stability and territorial integrity" of both of Bosnia and Herzegovina and Macedonia.[181] The United States officially recognized Bosnia and Herzegovina on April 7, 1992, noting that Bosnia and Herzegovina, Croatia and Slovenia all "meet

---

[177] Bilyana Plavshich [Biljana Plavsic], "*Witnessing*" [*Сведочим*] (Banya Luka: Trioprint, 2005), 91 [Translation mine].

[178] Crnobrnja, *Yugoslav Drama*, 200.

[179] Woodward, *Balkan Tragedy*, 191.

[180] *See* Patrick Moore, "Diplomatic Recognition of Croatia and Slovenia," *RFE/RL Research Report*, Vol. 1, No. 4, January 24, 1992.

[181] US/EC Declaration on the Recognition of the Yugoslav Republics, Brussels, March 10, 1992.

the requisite criteria for recognition," but without denoting these criteria.[182] Croatia, Slovenia and Bosnia, and Herzegovina all became members of the United Nations on May 22, 1992.[183] At the same time, the European Union did not recognize Macedonia until December 16, 1993 despite the positive opinion of the Badinter Arbitration Commission, due to Greece's objections to Macedonia's name and other state insignia.

In practice, both the United States and the European Community deviated from their own guidelines. Moreover, at the time of recognition Croatia and Bosnia-Herzegovina did not even possess the minimal legal standards for statehood as delineated by the Montevideo Convention.[184] The Croatian government had no control over approximately one-third of its territory, while the Bosnian rump government did not have control over more than two thirds of Bosnia's territory. The Bosnian Muslim leader and President of Bosnia's rump presidency Alija Izetbegovic publicly asserted at the time that Bosnia "could not protect its independence without foreign military aid."[185] Indeed, international recognition was applied in a constitutive rather than declaratory sense towards both of these republics.

Bosnia and Herzegovina's recognition again invoked the question of government representativeness. In the case of Yugoslavia as a whole, insufficient representativeness of the government was held to be a key factor in proclaiming the country's "dissolution." Yet in Bosnia, the Badinter Commission utterly ignored the issue and even contributed to the government's inadequate representativeness. As previously discussed, the sovereignty resolution and the referendum were organized unconstitutionally and without participation of one constituent people, the Bosnian Serbs. Moreover, there is a pertinent question as to who the Bosnian people are. The Yugoslav Constitution did not recognize a Bosnian identity and neither did the people of Bosnia, identifying themselves as Muslims, Croats, or

---

182 White House Press release, Washington, April 7, 1992.

183 UNSC Docs. A/46/912-S/23884, A/46/913-S/23885, A/46/921-S23971 of May 21, 1992 and UNGA Resolutions 46/236, 46/237 and 46/238, May 22, 1992.

184 The Brioni Accord, as discussed earlier, guaranteed Slovenia control of its territory. As Janez Janša, the first Slovene Minister of Defense, proudly asserts in his book on Slovene take-over of border posts and brief war against the Yugoslav People's Army "Slovenia had indeed taken control of all its territory. The key condition for international recognition had been fulfilled." Janez Janša, *The Making of the Slovenian State 1988-1992; The Collapse of Yugoslavia* (Ljubljana: Mladinska knjiga, 1994), 246.

185 *ABC News*, May 5, 1992.

Serbs in the 1990 elections. The Bosnian joint presidency had a role to represent all the ethnic groups, but the president of the presidency, Alija Izetbegovic acted otherwise, independently touring the Muslim states in 1991.[186] All factors considered, the Badinter Commission had stronger arguments to proclaim Bosnia and Herzegovina's dissolution than in the case of Yugoslavia. Instead, the European Community conferred independence onto this fledgling state.[187] The internationalization of the Bosnian crisis rendered the intervention by the federal authorities illegal. As averred by Izetbegovic, the Bosnian Muslims viewed the referendum as "crossing the Rubicon" and moving from "civil war" to the state of "aggression."[188]

5.4. Selective Morality of Secession

The key political argument for recognizing the seceding Yugoslav republics was the insistence that the federal authorities be prevented from using force to preserve Yugoslavia's territorial integrity. The European Community, while condemning all violence in Croatia, simultaneously called on the Federal Presidency to " . . . put an immediate end to the illegal use of the forces under its command."[189] The E.C. did not clarify the illegality in its reference. The Badinter Arbitration Commission avoided the issue completely and did not even deliberate on the retrieval of the Yugoslav People's Army (YPA) from Slovenia, which could have been employed as a valuable argument in declaring Yugoslavia's "dissolution."

---

[186]   Woodward, *Balkan Tragedy*, 176. Bilyana Plavshich [Biljana Plavsic], who served as one of the Serbian members of the Bosnian joint presidency, recalls that "The Presidency functioned as if it were a private company of Alija [Izetbegovic] and Ejup Ganic [Member of the Presidency]." Plavshich, *Witnessing*, 69 [Translation mine].

[187]   According to Glenny, this act "pushed Bosnia into the abyss." Glenny, *Fall of Yugoslavia*, 143. The U.S. Secretary of State Warren Christopher had also asserted that "the Germans bear a particular responsibility" for the failure of the international community to stop the bloodshed. [Cited from an interview published in *USA Today*, June 17, 1993).]

[188]   Alija Izetbegovic, "Dvije strane rubikona" [Two Sides of a Rubicon], Interview, "Witnesses of Yugoslavia's Disintegration," *Radio Free Europe* (accessed February 5, 2005); available from http://www.danas.org/svjedoci/html/Alija_Izetbegovic.html [Translation mine].

Note: The first victims of the Bosnian war were a murdered Serbian groom's father and a wounded guest at a wedding party in Sarayevo on March 1, 1991, an incident that was followed by the erection of Serb barricades in the city.

[189]   E.C. Bulletin 7/8, August 28, 1991, 107-116.

Yet a closer analysis of the use of force would reveal that the YPA responded to the indubitably illegal use of force by the secessionists. As Crnobrnja recounts, the Slovenes managed to refocus attention away from their illegal takeover of the boundaries of Yugoslavia and on the attempt at forcible dislocation of Slovenes from posts they ought not to have occupied in the first place"[190] while "Croatia decided to provoke the JNA [YPA] by blockading barracks and cutting off communal supplies to them."[191] The supporters of recognition were aware of this "winning strategy"[192] and they encouraged it.[193]

These actions were coupled with a propaganda campaign, facilitated by the YPA attacks on historical sites,[194] but well orchestrated nonetheless. According to Woodward:

> the lack of world attention to the nearly incessant bombardment of Mostar, which suffered far greater human and physical damage than Sarajevo and had at least as venerable a multicultural tradition, demonstrates the effect of such a campaign and the capacity to manage the media.[195]

In the case of Yugoslavia, YPA was presented as an occupying force—an invader, a position that ironically served the European politicians to facilitate recognition of seceding republics.[196]

---

[190] Crnobrnja, *Yugoslav Drama*, 164.

[191] Ibid., 167. As the war developed the paramilitaries were active on all sides in the conflict. *See* Crnobrnja, *Yugoslav Drama*, 169.

[192] *See* footnote 19.

[193] According to Crnobrnja, the Croatian President Tudjman made an informal visit to Bonn at the time and "came away encouraged to step up the level of confrontation with the JNA" (p. 194). Crnobrnja further states: "Though the Croats were fighting almost as hard [as the YPA] there was, on German insistence, no call nor pressure on them to stop deliberate provocations" (p. 197). Crnobrnja, *Yugoslav Drama*.

[194] "No matter if the destruction of the old town was relatively restricted, or that Croats amplified the picture of destruction by burning old tires to generate thick black clouds of smoke coming from the old walls. The *idea* of holding Dubrovnik hostage and inflicting even the smallest damage on it was unacceptable to public opinion throughout Europe and beyond." Crnobrnja, *Yugoslav Drama*, 172. Susan Woodward elaborates on the importance of a public relations campaign, effectively used by Croatian and Slovene government and later by Bosnian Muslim leadership to portray themselves as innocent victims of a Serb occupation force. Woodward, *Balkan Tragedy*, 207-209.

[195] Ibid., 235.

[196] *See, for instance*, Statement of Minister of State, United Kingdom Foreign and Commonwealth Office, December 12, 1991, 200 *House of Commons Debates*, 5th series, col 1166.

As postulated by Hannum, the E.C. policy relating to the use of force in the former Yugoslavia has led to a new, albeit inconsistent state practice, dependent primarily on political interests:

> The traditional international practice of non-intervention in civil wars has been replaced by a selective rule which prohibits some central governments (for example, Belgrade) from suppressing secession by force, accepts the use of force by others (for example, Colombo and New Dehli), and has yet to make up its mind about even more compelling cases (for example, Kurds and Tibetans).[197]

One important negative consequence of this policy, which encourages the use of force by a secessionist group to attract international attention, is that it hinders meaningful peace negotiations:

> Most of the breaches of the cease-fire were made by the Croats because their strategic interest, at that point, was international recognition, which seemed far more difficult to achieve if the fighting stopped.[198]

Williams concurs with this finding, deducing that the international policy with respect to the use of force encouraged Croats "to hold out against any possible negotiated change" while "add[ing] to the determination of the Croatian Serbs, backed by Serbia and the JNA, to bring about changes and to argue the case for the self-determination of the Croatian Serbs."[199] Similarly, the Bosnian Muslim leader, Alija Izetbegovic, reneged on the Lisbon Accord, the first peace plan proposed for Bosnia that advocated its cantonization, in view of imminent international recognition.

At the time, the German Chancellor, Helmut Kohl, claimed that recognition was the only solution to the crisis in Yugoslavia:

> If dialogue and peaceful co-existence are no longer possible, then we have to consider, especially from our understanding of the principle of

---

[197]   Hurst Hannum, "Self-Determination, Yugoslavia, and Europe: Old Wine in New Bottles?" 3 *Transnational Law and Contemporary Problems* 57 (1993), 68.

[198]   Crnobrnja, *Yugoslav Drama*, 195.

[199]   Williams, *Legitimacy in International Relations and the Rise and Fall of Yugoslavia*, 121.

self-determination, the diplomatic recognition of those republics, that no longer would like to be part of Yugoslavia.[200]

While it is always difficult to ascertain when the possibilities of peaceful conflict resolution become fully exhausted, a strong case could be made that peace negotiations were not exhausted in the case of Yugoslavia, considering that the Peace conference on Yugoslavia was just initiated when the European Community, pushed by Germany, opted for recognition.

While early recognition precluded the possibility of a political settlement based upon a readjustment of boundaries, one could also argue that an attempt at redrawing boundaries would have created myriad different problems, possibly extending beyond Yugoslavia. For instance, Hungary placed a territorial request immediately following the Brioni accord, when the prime minister of Hungary, Jószef Antall, declared: "We gave Vojvodina to Yugoslavia. If there is no more Yugoslavia, then we should get it back."[201] However, a more compelling case could still be made for making a stronger attempt at achieving a negotiated settlement. Such a settlement could even have been agreed within internal Yugoslav borders, according to the chief negotiator at the Yugoslav Peace Conference, Lord Carrington:

> I didn't speak against recognition as such, but against its timing. Croatia was recognized in the middle of the peace conference at which I got both Tudjman and Milosevic to agree to Krajina's autonomy in Croatia. Among other things, that autonomy was to include also separate police forces. The recognition was to follow only after that.[202]

In retrospect, it is regrettable that the European Commission rejected the proposal of the Dutch presidency, made on July 13, 1991, eight days after Slovenia and Croatia declared independence within their administrative boundaries,

---

[200] Deutscher Bundestag: Stengraphische Protokolle [Stenographic Minutes] 12/37, September 4, 1991: 3019. Original: "Wenn Dialog, wenn friedliches Miteinander nicht mehr möglich sind, dann stellt sich für uns, auch und gerade aus unserem Verständnis von Selbstbestimmungsrecht, die Frage, diejenigen Republiken, die nicht mehr zu Jugoslawien gehören wollen, völkerrechtilich anzuerkennen."

[201] "It could do the most harm to Vojvodina Hungarians," NÉPSZA-BAD-SÁG, July 9, 1991, in FBIS, Daily Report: East Europe, July 11, 1991, 40.
Note: Hungarians later distanced themselves from this position, but there is evidence that the Hungarians illegally sold rifles to Croatia (*see* Woodward, *Balkan Tragedy*, 219).

[202] Peter Lord Carrington, interviewed by Dragan Chichich, in Serbian weekly *NIN*, no. 2338, October 20, 1995), 12-13.

that the Yugoslav crisis be resolved by "a voluntary redrawing of internal borders," precisely to achieve consistency in the application of the right to self-determination:

> The Presidency continues to feel that it is necessary to reconcile the various principles of the Helsinki Final Act and the Charter of Paris which may apply to the situation in Yugoslavia. It considers it especially important that selective application of principles be avoided. The principle of self-determination e.g. cannot exclusively apply to the existing republics while being deemed inapplicable to national minorities.[203]

Only a negotiated settlement could have resolved the legal contradictions inherent in the SFRY Constitution, which the President of the Yugoslav Constitutional Court, Milovan Buzadjich, has compared to those in the Charter of the United Nations, stressing that: "[The Yugoslav Constitution] stipulated both the right to self-determination and the territorial integrity of the SFRY."[204]

In examining these legal intricacies, the Yugoslav Constitutional Court essentially made the same ruling as the Canadian Supreme Court several years later,[205] deducing that secession could be legally effectuated only by means of constitutional amendments. The duty to negotiate was central to the Court's opinion in both cases. The Canadian Supreme Court insisted that the seceding province had to "respect the rights of others":

> Negotiations would be necessary to address the interests of the federal government, of Quebec and the other provinces, and other participants, as well as the rights of all Canadians both within and outside Quebec.[206]

In other words, one people's right to self-determination could not be applied to the detriment of another people's right to self-determination, which is exactly what occurred in the case of Yugoslavia when this right was granted to a preselected territorial unit.

---

[203] Cited in David Owen, *Balkan Odyssey* (London: Indigo, 1996), 31-33.

[204] Buzadjich, *Secession of former Yugoslav republics in light of decisions of the Yugoslav Constitutional Court*, 12 [translation mine].

[205] "The secession of a province from Canada must be considered, in legal terms, to require an amendment to the Constitution, which perforce requires negotiation. The amendments necessary to achieve a secession could be radical and extensive . . . but this . . . does not negate their nature as amendments to the Constitution." Reference re: Secession of Quebec (1998) 161 DLR (4th) 423, paragraph 84.

[206] Reference re: Secession of Quebec (1998) 161 DLR (4th) 426, paragraph 92.

However, the judgments of the Yugoslav Constitutional Court were not given the same weight as the later judgments of the Canadian Constitutional Court, possibly because Canada, unlike the Yugoslavia of the 1990s, is a full-fledged democracy. One could deduce from this practice that the right of secession is a (subjective) moral right that overrules the Constitution in less democratic states, but only when one of the great powers takes a strong position to this effect. In this manner, an act of secession is rendered effective by the means of recognition. The Canadian Supreme Court has acknowledged such a possibility but emphasized that while international recognition could render secession successful, it would not "provide any retroactive justification for the act of secession."[207]

As late as August 1991, Hans van der Broek, the Dutch Foreign Minister had declared that "separatism is not the way ahead" and that "The right to self-determination is not an absolute, unqualified principle—its practical application needs to be squared with other principles."[208] Yet while van der Broek probably implied that the principle of territorial integrity should also be respected in order to maintain the stability of the international legal order, one could argue that it was at least equally important to apply the principle of self-determination in a more equitable fashion in order to ensure a peaceful resolution to the conflict and the stability of new boundaries. Instead, the arbitrary application of this principle created a destabilizing precedent. As elaborated by Woodward:

> The precedent set by the German manoeuvre was that the principle of self-determination could legitimately break up multinational states, that EC application of this principle was arbitrary, and that the surest way for politicians bent on independence to succeed was to instigate a defensive war and win international sympathy and then recognition.[209]

Alain Pellet, who acted as international law consultant to the Badinter Commission, has proudly asserted that the Badinter Comission "has contributed to a more precise definition of the attributes of the right to self-determination."[210] In my

---

[207] Ibid., 448, paragraph 155.

[208] Nicolas Rothwell, "EC Ready to Broker New Talks on Peace," *The Australian*, August 14, 1991, 6.

[209] *See* Woodward, *Balkan Tragedy*, 189.

[210] Pellet, "The Opinions of the Badinter Arbitration Committee; A Second Breath for the Self-Determination of Peoples," 179. Several other jurists have also endorsed certain aspects of the Badinter Arbitration Commission's Opinions. *See* Martyn Rady, "Self Determination and the Dissolution of Yugoslavia," *Ethnic and Racial Studies* 19 (1996), 387; Rein Mullerson, "The Continuity and Succession of States By Reference to the Former Soviet

opinion, the Badinter Commission attempted but failed to balance the implications of the right to self-determination with a political decision to internationalize the Yugoslav administrative republican boundaries.

Certain analysts, like Williams, have sarcastically commented that "Badinter . . . served the purpose of cloaking the political needs of the E.C. and the situation in Yugoslavia in the mantle of a semi-independent, semi-judicial procedure."[211] Others, like Marc Weller, have been even blunter in their criticism:

> Overall, the generally very brief opinions of the Commission are likely to attract considerable and probably hostile scholarly interest. They are underpinned by the shallowest legal reasoning and do not appear destined to assist the international community greatly when addressing the potentially dangerous problem of secession in the future.[212]

Terret, on the other hand, finds that the work of the Arbitration Commission could not be fairly evaluated because it was "utilised for a task for which it was not created and one with which its members were not experienced,"[213] having been originally summoned to advise on the Yugoslav constitutional crisis and therefore composed of constitutional lawyers. Moreover, the European Community has

---

USSR and Yugoslavia," *International and Comparative Law Quarterly* 42 (1993), 485-7; Gino J. Naldi, "Separatism in the Comoros: Some Legal Aspects," *Leiden Journal of International Law* 11 (1998), 249-51.

[211] Williams, *Legitimacy in International Relations and the Rise and Fall of Yugoslavia*, 130. Similarly, Barbara Delcourt concludes: "It appears that the European position, which ... favored the maintenance of internal boundaries was politically motivated and that the advisory 'jurisprudence' of the Badinter Commission has affirmed a political solution by giving it a judicial polish." Delcourt, "L'application de l'uti possidetis juris au démembrement de la Yougoslavie" *Revue Belge de Droit International*, 70-106: 91 [translation mine]. Original text: « il semble que la position européene qui a consisté à favoriser le maintien des limites internes était motivée politiquement et que la 'jurisprudence' consultative de la Commission Badinter a entériné une solution politique en lui donnant un vernis juridique. »

[212] Marc Weller, "International Law and Chaos," *Cambridge Law Journal* 52, no. 8 (1993). Other jurists, as discussed above, have also been highly critical of the Badinter Arbitration Commission, particularly with regards to the implementation of the *uti possidetis* principle (*see* supra, 33-35).

However, as Radan notes, several jurists have found the Badinter Arbitration Commission's opinions of relevance to other conflicts [Zaim M. Necatigil, *The Cyprus Question and Turkish Position in International Law*, 2ⁿᵈ edition (Oxford: Oxford University Press, 1993), 231-3; Milan Paunovic, "Serbia's Borders are Inviolable," *Review of International Affairs* 4, no. 1067, April 15, 1998), 1-4; Catriona Drew, "Independence through Devolution—Scotland, Self-determination and the Badinter Paradox," *Juridical Review*, no. 2 (1996), 161-4; John Dugard, "Secession: Is the Case of Yugoslavia a Precedent for Africa?," *African Journal of International and Comparative Law* 5 (1993), 163-75.]

[213] Terrett, *The Dissolution of Yugoslavia and the Badinter Arbitration Commission*, 181-185.

chosen to ignore the Commission's advice on constitutional issues in the case of Croatia, which, as Terret underscores, were "the only issues it was competent to rule on authoritatively."[214] The Arbitration Commission's members have not commented their deliberations or debated the issues at stake with other jurists. Notably Robert Badinter, in a personal interview with the author, refused to discuss the Opinions of the Arbitration Commission, insisting that they speak for themselves and should be analyzed on their own.[215]

As noted above, the Yugoslav Rump Presidency protested several times over the E.C. Recognition Guidelines, even seeking "support and protection of the United Nations."[216] However, arbitration by the International Court of Justice was not a valid option since Yugoslavia had not accepted the Optional Protocol to the Statute of the International Court of Justice and since only states could bring up cases before this court.[217] The rump Yugoslav government refuted the deliberations of the Badinter Arbitration Commission, emphasizing that the Badinter Commission "ignored the current constitutional and legal system of the SFRY and was inconsistent in applying the principles of public international law."[218] While the Badinter Arbitration Commission selectively applied the Yugoslav Constitution, other jurists like Bagwell have shown an utter lack of comprehension of the Yugoslav constitutional system and history, which was probably shared by many policy-makers:

> The history of the Yugoslav nation is marked by the voluntary association of the numerous *republics* into one federal state, therefore it would not be so unusual for a voluntary disassociation of the federation.[219]

---

[214] Ibid., 185.

[215] Author's Interview with Robert Badinter, Paris, November 19, 2002.

[216] Federal Presidency's Letter to Security Council President, December 19, 1991, reprinted in *Focus*, Special Issue, Belgrade, January 14, 1992, 263-265: 263.

[217] The Statute of the International Court of Justice, Article 34.1. *Note:* The European Court of Justice was not an available venue, either, since its competence was restricted to cases brought by E.C. institutions, member states or E.C. citizens and only concerning "the interpretation and application of this [EC] Treaty" (Article 164).

[218] Letter by Yugoslav Presidency Vice-President to Chairman of the Conference on Yugoslavia, December 8, 1991, reproduced in *Focus*, Special Issue, Belgrade, January 14, 1992, 239-245:239.

[219] Ben Bagwell, "Yugoslavian Constitutional Questions: Self-Determination and Secession of Member Republics," *Georgia Journal of International and Comparative Law* 21, No. 3 (1991), 520 [Emphasis mine]. Note: As seen from the historical overview, *peoples* and not republics had joined to form Yugoslavia in 1918, with republics established only in 1945, following different administrative divisions in the interwar period (districts and provinces).

This crucial misunderstanding, the notion that Yugoslavia was born by association of units that later simply disassociated from each other, has probably been critical to the endorsement of a modern application of the principle of *uti possidetis juris* and the accompanying territorial application of the principle of self-determination. Indeed, based on this historical and legal fallacy, another jurist, Daniel Kofman, concludes:

> Administrative borders bear added significance when they are constituents of a federation . . . the greater the autonomy and constitutional powers of the administrative unit, the firmer the application of *uti possidetis* should be, all else being equal.[220]

As discussed earlier, this approach has a rather dangerous consequence of discouraging constitutional flexibility. Moreover, it prevents recursive secessions only in theory, but may contribute to the aggravation of conflict in practice, ultimately leading to further partitions and exodus of population, as seen in the case of Yugoslavia.

In addition to considering alternative principles to *uti possidetis juris* in determining boundaries to resolve an ethnic conflict and promote stability, one should also contemplate a more consistent and equitable approach in the implementation of the right to self-determination. [221] Hannum, for instance, proposes the following:

> [M]inorities in a new state founded to preserve ethnic or cultural homogeneity should be granted the same rights of self-determination that were asserted by the seceding population. Legitimate self-determination can only be exercised on the basis of the consent of all involved parties, not just those who wish to separate.[222]

---

[220] Daniel Kofman, "Secession, Law and Rights: The Case of the Former Yugoslavia," *Human Rights Review* I, No. 2 (2000), 9-26:23.

[221] *See* Robert Y. Jennings, "Closing Address," *Peoples and Minorities in International Law*, eds. Catherine Brölmann, René Lefeber, and Marjoleine Zieck (Dodrecht: M. Nijhoff, 1993), 341: 346; Ratner, "Drawing a Better Line," 616-623.

[222] Hurst Hannum, "The Specter of Secession, Responding to Claims for Ethnic Self-Determination," *Foreign Affairs* 77, no. 2 (1998), 17. *See also* Thomas M. Franck, *Fairness in International Law and Institutions* (Oxford: Clarendon Press, 1995), 167.

Two important benefits could be discerned from this approach, which builds on Weinstock's proposition[223] for constitutionalizing the right to secession:

> First, the realization that some loss of territory might result if independence or even autonomy was achieved absent meaningful consensus within the territory might encourage those who favor secession to consider other, more broadly acceptable alternatives. Second, the possibility of opting out of a new state might allay the fears of those groups which, for whatever reasons, strongly oppose any change in their current status.[224]

The development of the proposed mechanism could have possibly averted the escalation of violence that followed the premature recognition. As David Owen has unwaveringly asserted:

> [T]o rule out any discussion or opportunity for compromise in order to head off war was an extraordinary decision. My view has always been that to have stuck unyieldingly to the internal boundaries of the six republics within the former Yugoslavia, . . . as being the boundaries for independent states, was a folly far greater than that of premature recognition itself.[225]

Since the use of force played a critical role in formulating such a political decision, it may be useful to study how the use of force both by the war parties and by the recognizing states in the intensified Yugoslav conflict further affected the right to self-determination and the right to territorial integrity in the case of Yugoslavia.

---

[223] *See* Chapter 1: *Legal Context of Yugoslavia's Disintegration: Sovereignty and Self-Determination of Peoples.*

[224] Hurst Hannum, *Autonomy, Sovereignty, and Self-Determination: the Accommodation of Conflicting Rights* (Philadelphia: University of Pennsylvania Press, 1996), 505.

[225] Owen, *Balkan Odyssey*, 34.

Changing Borders by Force

6.1. Introduction

Having forgone the policy of negotiating an overall settlement for the former Socialist Federal Republic of Yugoslavia (SFRY) and proceeding with the internationalization of its administrative boundaries, the international community, led by the European Community (E.C.) in conjunction with the United Nations (U.N.) and later the United States, embarked on a flurry of mediation activities among radicalized war parties. From the moment of recognition, the road to peace, already marred by violence, was constructed almost exclusively by force, both of indigenous and external origin. The force employed affected the application of the right to self-determination, translating this right to territorial autonomy in Bosnia, self-government under international supervision in Kosovo and Metohia, decentralization and group rights in Macedonia, or nominal human rights without a right to territorial autonomy in Croatia. The magnitude of force and the international evaluation of the legitimacy of the use of force by the official authorities and the insurgents became crucial to the redrafting of constitutions to mandate stronger group rights, in some cases coupled with the redrawing of boundaries—albeit within the newly independent states. Self-determination, on its own and with the exception of a general insistence on respect for human rights, was irrelevant to the international community. Self-determination gained bearing only when accompanied by insurgency and even then most states rejected its most extreme form, secession, as a possible option. International recognition of former Yugoslav republics, excused by a state of dissolution that allegedly invalidated the right to territorial integrity, was treated as an exception and not a precedent to be replicated. In the post-recognition period, different solutions to claims of self-determination were accentuated by a continuation of an inconsistent interpretation of the right to territorial integrity, rendering Bosnia's or Macedonia's external borders sacrosanct but Federal Republic of Yugoslavia (Serbia and Montenegro) borders open to change. Realpolitik and domestic policy interests of the intervening states and organizations prevailed over considerations relating to a people's right to self-determination, as they have throughout the history of this principle, but they also impacted its evolution.

6.2. Mediation

Ad hoc mediation techniques were created to deal with the Yugoslav crisis since the existing mechanisms, such as the Conference on Security and Cooperation in Europe (CSCE)[1] "Valetta Mechanism," could not be applied. The CSCE Member States, including Yugoslavia, had agreed to refer disputes to one of the various methods of pacific dispute resolution but *not* if the dispute involved "territorial integrity or national defence, title to sovereignty over held territory, or competing claims with regard to the jurisdiction over other areas . . . ".[2] The International Conference on the *former* Yugoslavia (ICFY),[3] co-chaired by the U.N. Secretary-General and the President of the European Council of Ministers, was convened in London in August 1992, and later transferred to Geneva, acting as an umbrella for the international mediation of the Yugoslav conflict until 1994, when the lead was taken first by the so-called Contact Group (representatives of France, Germany, Russia, the United Kingdom, and the United States) and several months later by the United States alone. A Statement of Principles adopted at the London Conference, "emphasiz[ing] the policy of non-recognition of territorial changes brought about by non-peaceful means, as well as the need for negotiations to ensure the respect of human rights and international humanitarian law"[4] evoked the founding principles of the Hague Conference, which had been effectively ignored. The principal negotiators, with the title of Conference co-chairmen, were people of high standing, but changed on two occasions, justifying their departure by claiming insufficient international coordination and support for their efforts.[5]

---

[1]   As noted below, on January 1, 1995, CSCE was transformed into the Organization of Security and Cooperation in Europe (OSCE). Strengthening the CSCE, Budapest Decisions, Towards a Genuine Partnership in a New Era, Conference for Security and Co-operation in Europe, 1994 Summit, Budapest, December 5-6, 1994.

[2]   Report of CSCE Experts on Peaceful Settlement of Disputes, Section XII, reprinted in (1991) 30 ILM, 382-95.

[3]   Emphasis added. Note: The wording reflected the change of policy stemming from international recognition of the seceding Yugoslav republics.

[4]   Statement of Principles adopted at the Peace Conference on Yugoslavia, 31 ILM (1992), 1533.

[5]   Lord Peter Carrington, Chairman of E.C. Peace Conference on Yugoslavia (1991-2) was replaced by Cyrus Vance, former U.S. Secretary of State who served as U.N. Secretary-General's Personal Envoy for Yugoslavia (1991-2) and Co-Chairman of the ICFY (1992-3), later to be replaced by Thorvald Stoltenberg, the former Norwegian Foreign Minister (1993-5). U.S. Assistant Secretary of State, Richard Holbrooke ultimately replaced Stoltenberg and Lord David Owen, former U.K. Foreign Secretary and Co-Chairman

The mediation activities were accompanied by humanitarian assistance,[6] peace-keeping operations—and sanctions. The economic sanctions, which played an important role in settling borders of new states emerging from the former Yugoslavia, were enforced prior to recognition of seceding republics. On November 8, 1991, at a meeting in Rome, the European Community suspended the implementation of the EC-SFRY Agreement on trade cooperation and initiated its annulment, excluded Yugoslavia from the list of beneficiaries of the General Preferential Treatment, formally suspended aid to SFRY on the basis of the PHARE pre-accession assistance program, suspended a textile agreement with SFRY, and decided to request from the U.N. Security Council the introduction of an oil embargo for Yugoslavia.[7] However, as with all future sanctions, these measures would be applied selectively, excluding those republics that "cooperate in the E.C. peace endeavors."[8] As early as December 2, 1991, the EC reestablished the preferential trade provisions and the benefits of the PHARE aid program, approving additional aid of one hundred million ECUs for all republics except Serbia and Montenegro.[9]

Imposing sanctions on the Federal Republic of Yugoslavia (FRY, comprising Serbia and Montenegro) several days after the Yugoslav People's Army (YPA) troops had withdrawn from Bosnia and not sanctioning Croatia while officially acknowledging that "elements of the Croatian Army" had not withdrawn,[10]

---

of the ICFY (1992-5) as the mediator of the Bosnian conflict, assisted by the E.U. Peace Envoy Carl Bildt, the former Swedish Minister of Foreign Affairs. Several statesmen also acted as mediators at a certain period, such as the French president François Mitterand, the Russian presidents Gorbachev and Yeltsin, the Greek Prime Minister Constantine Mitsotakis and the former U.S. President Jimmy Carter.

6   For more, see Boško Jakovljević, "Humanitarna pomoć u jugoslovenskoj krizi" [Humanitarian Assistance in the Yugoslav Crisis], *Medjunarodno pravo i jugoslovenska kriza* [International Law and the Yugoslav Crisis], ed. Milan Šahović (Belgrade: Institute for International Politics and Economy, 1995), 275-315.

7   *See* E.C. Bulletin 7.8-91 at 108, Note: The United States also suspended economic assistance to Yugoslavia on May 20, 1991. On December 6, 1991, the U.S. State Department announced the establishment of a trade embargo on Yugoslavia [announcement reproduced in Review of International Affairs (Belgrade), Vol. XLII (1.XII 1991), 30.

8   On December 2, 1991, the E.C. Council decides that sanctions are to be applied only to Serbia and Montenegro. For more *see* Obrad Račić, "Mirno rešavanje sporova i traženje rešenja za jugoslovensku krizu" [Peaceful Conflict Resolution and Seeking Solutions to the Yugoslav Crisis] *Medjunarodno pravo i jugoslovenska kriza* [International Law and the Yugoslav Crisis], ed. Milan Šahović (Belgrade: Institute for International Politics and Economy, 1995), 89-119: 102.

9   [EC] Declaration on Positive Measures, December 2, 1991, reproduced in the *Review of International Affairs* (Belgrade), Vol. XLII (1.XII 1991), 27.

10 Report of the Secretary-General Pursuant to Paragraph 4 of Security Council Resolution 752 (S/24049, May 30, 1992). The Report, saying that Belgrade does not control the Bosnian Serb members of the YPA who remained in Bosnia and formed an army of their own, but that Croatian forces have not withdrawn,

significantly diminished both the moral and the legal authority of sanctions. The duplicity of the international sanctions policy, in a practice that continued as the war escalated,[11] further produced a "significant [adverse] psychological effect in Serbia."[12]

Dimitrijević and Pejić further stress that the goals of the sanctions had been both unclear and inconstant. Aimed at first to limit the FRY's support for Bosnian Serb war aims and in this manner strengthen the fledgling Bosnian state[13] and, unofficially, to topple Slobodan Miloshevich, the sanctions later focused on pressuring Serbia to convince the Bosnian Serb leadership to renounce parts of conquered territory to settle the Bosnian conflict. However, the sanctions against the FRY persisted when Belgrade failed in its genuine attempt to influence the Bosnian Serbs to accept the Vance-Owen Peace Plan in Bosnia.[14] The sanctions policy was so unclear that two years after the enforcement of sanctions, 42.5 percent of the Serbian citizens admitted that they did not know what conditions their country had to fulfill in order to achieve at least the easing of sanctions.[15]

The only sanction officially imposed on the entire territory of the (former) Yugoslavia was the arms embargo, based on the U.N. Security Council Resolution 713 of September 25, 1991, which invoked Chapter VII of the U.N. Charter regarding the threat to international peace and security.[16] Nevertheless, the arms embargo was evaded on a large scale, which was known and tolerated by other

---

arrived an hour after the decision on the sanctions was made, as reported in "U.N. Serb report arrived to late," *The Los Angeles Times*, June 4, 1992, and "Embarrassment at U.N.," *New York Times*, June 4, 1992, A3. There have been allegations that the delay was not accidental; *see* statement made by International Action Center, (accessed April 5, 2000); available from http://www.iacenter.org/bosnia/waris.htm.

[11] The strongest wording used against Croatia appears in the Statement by the President of the Security Council of February 3, 1994 (S/PRST/1994/6), which recognizes that Croatia's incursions into Bosnia constitutes a "serious hostile act against a Member State of the United Nations" and "a violation of international law," demanding Croatia's withdrawal and threatening to "consider other serious measures" in case this does not occur, but later not acting upon this threat.

[12] Vojin Dimitrijević and Jelena Pejić, "Učinci sankcija protiv SR Jugoslavije" ["The Effects of Sanctions against the SFRY"], *Medjunarodno pravo i jugoslovenska kriza* [International Law and the Yugoslav Crisis], ed. Milan Šahović (Belgrade: Institute for International Politics and Economy, 1995), 245-274: 252,

[13] *See* David Owen, *Balkan Odyssey* (London: Indigo, 1996), 43.

[14] U.N. Security Council Resolution 820, April 17, 1993.

[15] Dimitrijević and Pejić, 255. The poll was conducted on May 21, 1994, and covered about 200 people in Serbia; published in NIN on May 27, 1994, 14.

[16] "All states shall, for the purposes of establishing peace and stability in Yugoslavia, immediately implement a general and complete embargo on all deliveries of weapons and military equipment to Yugoslavia." U.N. Security Council Resolution 713, November 25, 1991.

states and the United Nations organization.[17] As David Owen, one of the key mediators attempting to resolve the Bosnian conflict, has cynically remarked:

> The morality of the arms embargo was being discussed as a matter of high principle, while the Bosnian Muslims pretended that they had no arms, the Croatians kept very quiet about the arms they were collecting and passing on, and both were manufacturing them.[18]

While economic sanctions have received wide criticism as a policy that hurts the ordinary people but strengthens the power hold of the extremist politicians,[19] Owen has claimed that they were vital in inducing the Serbian government to cajole the Bosnian Serbs into accepting various territorial settlements on the table during the peace negotiations.[20] They certainly influenced the radical shift in official Serb policy in August 1992, when the Government of Serbia professed to be accepting "Tito's boundaries among the republics of his Socialist Yugoslavia as the official international borders between Yugoslavia and its neighbouring countries," further stating "that it has no territorial claims on any of its neighbours."[21] Indeed,

---

[17] Owen, *Balkan Odyssey*, 45, 70.

[18] Ibid., 347.

[19] The standard of living of 85 percent of the FR Yugoslavia's population dropped to the subsistence level and the mortality rate due to infectious diseases went up 214 percent [Zeljan E. Suster, *Historical Dictionary of the Federal Republic of Yugoslavia;* European Historical Dictionaries No. 29 (Lanham, MD/London: Scarecrow Press, 1999), 267]. For more on the impact of sanctions on FRY, *see* Richard Garfield, Economic Sanctions, Health and Wellbeing in Yugoslavia, 1990-2000; Report published by U.N. OCHA and UNICEF/Belgrade (New York: U.N. Office for the Coordination of Humanitarian Affairs, 2001) (accessed November 7, 2004); available from http://www.humanitarianinfo.org/sanctions/handbook/docs_handbook/Garfield_Ocha-Yug.pdf. For a reassessment of the effectiveness of sanctions policy, *see* United Nations Sub-Commission on the Promotion and Protection of Human Rights (Working Paper prepared by Mr. Marc Bossuyt), "The adverse consequences of economic sanctions on the enjoyment of human rights," June 21, 2000 (U.N. Document E/CN.4/Sub.2/2000/33).

Misha Glenny purports that sanctions "have had no perceptible impact on the ability of the Bosnian Serbs to wage war; they have strengthened Miloshevich's political position, further weakened the Serbian opposition and made life miserable for those Serbs who are not responsible for the carnage; they have enabled many decidedly undesirable characters who do not bear responsibility for the war and its unseemly prosecution in Serbia, Montenegro and elsewhere to make large sums of money; and they continue to have grave consequences for the economies of Hungary, Romania, Bulgaria, Macedonia and Greece." [Misha Glenny, *The Fall of Yugoslavia; The Third Balkan War*, 3rd rev. ed. (New York: Penguin Books, 1996), 211-212.] Dimitrijević and Pejić also deduce that sanctions had a negative effect on the democratization process in Serbia, strengthening the regime and weakening the opposition and the civil society in addition to inciting humanitarian problems. [Dimitrijević and Pejić, 245-274.]

[20] *See* Owen, *Balkan Odyssey*, 144.

[21] Letter from the Prime Minister of the Federal Republic of Yugoslavia [Milan Panich] addressed to the President of the Security Council, August 17, 1992, U.N. Doc. A/46/960—S/ 24454, Annex.

Yugoslavia formally recognized Slovenia on August 12, 1992, and expressed interest in normalizing relations with other former Yugoslav republics. The wording of the statement, namely the term "Tito's borders," strongly indicates that the Serb policy was changed under duress and that the moral authority of internationalizing inter-republican boundaries continued to be questioned.

As the Yugoslav crisis deepened, the sanctions policy was both strengthened and diversified,[22] seeking to produce a greater impact on the FRY authorities rather than afflicting its citizenry. The sanctions were eased for Serbia and Montenegro only on September 23, 1994 (U.N. Security Council Resolution 943), as a result of the FRY's repeated support for a peaceful settlement in Bosnia and the trade embargo it imposed against the Bosnian Serbs, allowing the FRY's participation in sports events and cultural exchanges, and the use of Belgrade airport and the Bar ferryboat for passenger traffic. Simultaneously, the U.N. Security Council imposed additional sanctions on the Bosnian Serb leadership, "demanding that [the Bosnian Serb] party accept [the proposed peace plan] unconditionally and in full."[23]

Following the negotiation of the Dayton Peace Agreement in Bosnia and Herzegovina, in its resolution 1022 (1995) of November 22, 1995, the Security Council indefinitely suspended the sanctions against the Federal Republic of Yugoslavia. In resolution 1074 (1996) of October 1, 1996, the Council decided to terminate sanctions against the Federal Republic of Yugoslavia and the Bosnian Serbs. Nevertheless, the so-called outer wall of international sanctions remained in force, blocking the FRY from seeking assistance from international financial institutions. On March 31, 1998, as a result of an escalated conflict in the Serbian province of Kosovo and Metohia, sanctions were re-imposed on the FRY,[24] only to be lifted following the toppling of the Miloshevich regime in Serbia in October 2000.

---

[22] In its resolution 757 (1992) of May 30, 1992, the Security Council imposed economic and other sanctions on the Federal Republic of Yugoslavia (Serbia and Montenegro), including a full trade embargo, a flight ban and the prevention of the participation of the Federal Republic of Yugoslavia in sporting and cultural events. In its resolution 787 (1992) of November 16, 1992, the Security Council stated that the transshipment through the Federal Republic of Yugoslavia of petroleum, coal, steel and other products, unless authorized on a case-by-case basis by the Sanctions Committee, would be prohibited. In resolution 820 (1993) of April 17, 1993, the Council further strengthened the sanctions against the Federal Republic of Yugoslavia by freezing all of the assets owned or controlled by the FRY authorities.

[23] In its resolution 942 (1994) of September 23, 1994, the Security Council imposed comprehensive economic and diplomatic sanctions on Bosnian Serb military forces.

[24] U.N. Security Council Resolution 1160, March 31, 1998.

As another tool with the aim of mitigating the conflict but also bringing war criminals to justice, an ad-hoc International Criminal Tribunal for Yugoslavia (ICTY) was created by a U.N. Security Resolution 827 of May 26, 1993, based on U.N. Security Council Resolution 808 of February 22, 1993.[25] Furthermore, the U.N. Commission on Human Rights appointed a Special Rapporteur to report on the human rights situation in the former Yugoslavia.[26] The first foreign military engagement, sanctions notwithstanding, came in the form of peacekeeping in the former Yugoslav republic of Croatia.

6.3. Peacekeeping: The Case of Krayina

6.3.1. The Vance Plan

Having negotiated a series of short-lived cease-fires, Cyrus Vance, serving as the U.N. Secretary-General Personal Envoy for Yugoslavia, convened a meeting in Geneva on November 23, 1991, attended by president Slobodan Miloshevich of Serbia, President Franjo Tudjman of Croatia, Secretary of State for National Defense of Yugoslavia, and Lord Carrington, then Chairmen of the European Community Conference on Yugoslavia. The parties agreed to an immediate cease-fire and a U.N. peacekeeping operation in the Republic of Croatia, subsequently initiated through the U.N. Security Council Resolution 721 of November 27, 1991. Subsequent negotiations resulted in a more comprehensive peace plan, which became known as the Vance Plan. The Vance Plan did not represent a permanent negotiated settlement but an "interim arrangement to create the conditions of peace and security required for the negotiation of an overall settlement of the Yugoslav crisis,"[27] endorsed by U.N. Security Council Resolution 724 of December 15, 1991. On January 2, 1992, the parties to the conflict signed the Implementing Accord,[28] permitting the creation of a U.N. Protection Force (UNPROFOR) for deployment in the former Yugoslav republic of Croatia.[29]

---

[25]   The work of ICTY, subject of much controversy, is generally beyond the scope of this book, but noted when relevant.

[26]   The first person charged with this task was the former Polish Prime Minister Tadeusz Mazowiecki.

[27]   Article 1, *Vance Plan*, "Concept for a United Nations Peace-Keeping Operation in Yugoslavia, as Discussed with Yugoslav Leaders by the Honourable Cyrus R. Vance, Personal Envoy of the Secretary-General and Marrack Goulding, Under-Secretary-General for Special Political Affairs," November/December 1991.

[28]   S/23239, annex (31 ILM, 1425).

[29]   The U.N. Security Council Resolution 727 sent fifty military liaison officers to Yugoslavia to help maintain a cease-fire, and Resolution 740 of February 7, 1992, raised their number to seventy-five. Finally, U.N. Security Resolution 743 of February 21, 1992, authorized an initial deployment of troops under the name "United Nations Protection Force" (UNPROFOR).

Noting that the Government of Yugoslavia had requested a peacekeeping force (S/23240), the subsequent U.N. Security Council Resolution 743 of February 21, 1992, left the legal basis of the UNPROFOR deployment vague. The Resolution did not explicitly refer to Chapters VI or VII of the U.N. Charter, but it did use the Chapter VII language, stating that "the situation in Yugoslavia continues to constitute a threat to international peace and security," and it also referred to Resolution 713, which instituted an arms embargo in Yugoslavia based on Chapter VII.

The Vance Plan called for the complete withdrawal of the Yugoslav People's Army (YPA) and other Serb military units from the republic of Croatia. It also provided for the establishment of three "UN Protected Areas" (UNPAs) in regions with significant Serb populations which had come under the effective control of the JNA or Serb troops: Eastern and Western Slavonia, and Krayina. Within the UNPAs, the plan required the complete withdrawal or demobilization of all military units, including the Croatian National Guard and army, as well as all territorial paramilitary forces. Only lightly armed police forces could remain in the Protected Areas to maintain order, and these were subject to supervision by U.N. forces to assure non-discrimination and the protection of human rights. The U.N. forces had the authority to control access to the Protected Areas, ensuring that no new military forces or equipment be introduced.

As a result of breaches of cease-fires and other organizational issues, the UNPROFOR's deployment was delayed until March 8, 1992. The initial budget granted to UNPROFOR was $250 million, instead of the $600 million estimated by the Secretary-General. By early 1993 UNPROFOR's annual costs approached $1.2 billion.[30] The financial problems of international peacekeepers were an important obstacle in resolving the Yugoslav conflict, evident both in Croatia and in other Yugoslav republics.

One of the key provisions of the Vance Plan, namely that it guarded peace await-ing the overall settlement of the Yugoslav crisis,[31] was overturned by the prema-ture recognition of Croatia. While the Krayina Serb representatives held onto the original mandate of the Vance Plan, the Croatian recognition inevitably affected

---

[30] Statement by the President of the Security Council (S/25162), January 25, 1993.

[31] According to Article 5, "Subject to the Council's agreement, the operation would remain in Yugoslavia until a negotiated settlement of the conflict was achieved." *Vance Plan*, November/December 1991.

the implementation of the peace plan, mostly by preventing the disarmament of the parties in conflict. According to the UNPROFOR Commander, Lieutenant General Satish Nambiar:

> Disarmament was not achievable as long as distrust persisted. Perhaps it could have been accomplished when the parties adopted the Vance Plan at the end of 1991, but by the time UNPROFOR was deployed, all sides had been arming in anticipation of further conflict.[32]

Demilitarization was disabled by repeated breaches of ceasefires, almost exclusively inflicted by the Croats in avoiding the repetition of the Cyprus scenario, where the U.N. peacekeepers have maintained the island's partition line for over three decades now.[33] Furthermore, the Serbs resisted demilitarization and refused to demobilize because they were aware that the Croats were arming heavily and in full knowledge and therefore tacit support of the U.N. and other important international actors.[34] As a result of a changed situation, initiated by Croatia's international recognition, the Vance Plan was adapted, with the international community progressively insisting that the solution to the conflict be found within the framework of the newly independent Croatian state.

6.3.2. Evolution of the Vance Plan: From "Pink Zones" to "Z-4" and "UNCRO"

On June 30, 1992, Security Council Resolution 762 authorized UNPROFOR to undertake monitoring functions in the so-called "pink zones." These areas were controlled by the YPA and populated largely by Serbs but were outside the agreed UNPA boundaries. The resolution requested the withdrawal of the Croatian Army and all other forces. The United Nations Civilian Police (UNCIVPOL) was engaged to monitor the existing police forces' maintenance of law and order, with particular regard to the well-being of any minority groups in the areas. European

---

[32] Interview with Lieutenant General Satish Nambiar, UNPROFOR Commander, conducted and cited by Barbara Ekwall-Uebelhart and Andrei Raevsky, *Managing Arms in Peace Processes: Croatia and Bosnia-Herzegovina* (Geneva: United Nations Institute for Disarmament Research, 1996), 33.

[33] As affirmed by Owen: "The Croatian government was understandably determined from the start to avoid a repeat of what had happened in Cyprus, with the U.N. absence entrenching the *de facto* partition of the island, and so they never abided by the ceasefire" Owen, *Balkan Odyssey*, 70.

[34] Ibid.

Community Monitoring Mission (ECMM) personnel were deployed on both sides of the lines of confrontation outside UNPAs.

On August 7, 1992, the Security Council adopted Resolution 769, which enhanced the UNPROFOR's strength and mandate to enable it to control the entry of civilians into the UNPAs and to perform immigration and customs functions at those UNPA boundaries that coincided with international borders. This was in addition to the authority given to UNPROFOR to prevent the movement of arms, ammunition and other war-like material into the UNPA. This Resolution was never fully implemented since the Krayina Serbs maintained that the Republic of Serbian Krayina as a sovereign state had the right to carry out these functions.[35]

On January 22, 1993, the Croatian army attacked the protected region, invading the Maslenitsa area. The Krayina Serbs, in turn, removed their weapons from the U.N. storage sites and mobilized a successful counterattack. The Croat action forced the UNPROFOR to utterly abandon the disarmament measures contained in its mandate. The Security Council "strongly condemned" the Croat attacks against UNPROFOR members,[36] but without any serious repercussions for the Croats. In subsequent Resolutions 807 of February 19, 1993, and 815 of March 30, 1993, the U.N. Security Council did not insist on Croatian withdrawal from the conquered/reoccupied territory nor did it impose any sanctions against Croatia. Instead, the latter resolution emphasized "its commitment to ensure the respect for the sovereignty and territorial integrity of Croatia," strengthening the UNPROFOR mandate only with respect to their own security. Significantly, this was the first U.N. Resolution regarding the conflict in Croatia to be explicitly based on Chapter VII of the U.N. Charter.

The fact that the Croatian authorities were regarded as legitimate and the Krayina Serbs as insurgents following Croatia's international recognition also resulted in a different treatment of ethnic cleansing under way. While the Serbs of Croatia were rightly admonished for expelling many Croats from the majority-Serb region of Krayina, the cleansing of numerous Serbs from other parts of Croatia occurred unnoticed. In his letter to U.S. President William Clinton, the Krayina Serb

---

35   See Slobodan Yarchevich, *Република Српска Крајина; државна документа* [Republic of Serb Krayina; State Documents] (Belgrade: Miroslav, 2005).

36   U.N. Security Council Resolution 802 of January 25, 1993.

president Goran Hadzich expressed his deep grievance concerning this matter, albeit without admitting to or stopping similar acts committed by the Serbs:

> I wish to remind you that Croatia has, from 1991 to 1993, banished 300,000 Serbs from Croat towns, and that no one took note of that, except in the report of the U.N. Secretary-General to the Security Council of 15 June 1993.[37]

In April 1993, the UNPROFOR negotiated another cease-fire agreement that stipulated the withdrawal of the Croatian troops behind the ceasefire lines preceding the incursions, the withdrawal of Serbs from the "pink zones," and the submission of Serb heavy weapons. Yet, on September 9, 1993, the Croatian army carried out another military incursion in the area called Medjak Pocket and seized three Serb villages, using aircraft to bomb Serb positions and provoking a retaliatory rocket firing, with one rocket reaching a suburb of the Croatian capital, Zagreb. Croatian forces ultimately obliged with a new cease-fire agreement, but destroyed most houses during their withdrawal, committing atrocities against the civilian population.[38]

Finally, on December 17, 1993, the Croat and Serb representatives signed the Truce Agreement mediated by UNPROFOR, agreeing to cease armed hostilities along all existing confrontation lines and open further negotiations. These negotiations resulted in a more comprehensive cease-fire agreement of March 29, 1994, which allowed for the heavy weapons disarmament. Nevertheless, since the parties could easily remove their weapons from the storage sites, their warring capabilities were not affected.

On December 2, 1994, UNPROFOR achieved further progress by facilitating an economic agreement between the Serb and Croat factions. The agreement concerned the water supply, electricity, railways, the oil pipeline, and the

---

[37] Letter from Goran Hadzich, President of the Republic of Serbian Krayina, to William Clinton, President of the United States, 1993, printed in Slobodan Yarchevich, *Република Српска Крајина; државна документа* [Republic of Serb Krayina; State Documents] (Belgrade: Miroslav, 2005), 358. Note: The Report of the Secretary General Pursuant to Security Council Resolution 743 (S/23777) of April 2, 1992, also speaks of "continuing reports of mass expulsions, and other coercion against certain communities *on both sides*" [emphasis added], and later reports also mention expulsions on both sides (e.g. S/24600). However the Security Council resolutions usually single out "Serb-controlled areas in the Republic of Croatia" as the violators (e.g. U.N.S.C. Resolution 820 of April 17, 1993).

[38] United Nations, *The United Nations and the Situation in the Former Yugoslavia, Reference Paper*, March 15, 1994, 13; Garth Pritchard, "Truth Lies Buried in Balkan Hell Holes," *The Toronto Sun*, August 12, 2001.

Zagreb-Belgrade highway.[39] Unfortunately, the climate of reconciliation was jeopardized when the Croatian Government decided, on January 12, 1995, not to agree to a continuation of UNPROFOR's mandate beyond March 1995.[40] This reflected the Croat strategy to end the peacekeeping agreement when prepared to militarily take over the Serb-held areas, which is indicated in the vaguely worded statement of the Croatian leader made two years earlier in support the UNPROFOR operation:

> The establishment of Croatian sovereignty and the peaceful reintegration of these areas are our fundamental commitments by which we will abide for *as long as possible.*[41]

Shortly following this announcement, on January 30, 1995, the "Zagreb-4" ambassadors—comprising the U.S. and Russian Ambassadors to Croatia and Ambassadors Geert Ahrens and Kai Eide of the International Conference on Former Yugoslavia, presented the "Draft agreement on the Krajina, Slavonia, Southern Baranja and Western Sirmium."[42] The so-called Z-4 Plan proposed to allow the Krayina Serbs to retain their own president, government, flag, language, radio, TV, social welfare system, and police force, and to raise their own revenue. However, the Z-4 Plan referred to only two of the five Krayina districts (one third of the Krayina territory) and guaranteed only 10 out of 148 seats in the House of Representatives (6.7 percent, compared to 12.2 percent Serb share in Croatia's total population according to the 1991 census) and one Cabinet position. Moreover, no consideration was given to amnesty, which was a major concern for the Serbs. Neither party accepted the plan but several months later, in May 1991, the Krayina Serbs agreed to negotiate their future status on the basis of the Z-4 plan.[43]

---

[39] Agreement on Economic Issues of December 2, 1994 is reproduced in Bertrand B. Ramcharan, ed., *The International Conference on the Former Yugoslavia: Official Papers* (Kluwer Law International, 1997), 467-473.

[40] Barbara Ekwall-Uebelhart and Andrei Raevsky, *Managing Arms in Peace Processes: Croatia and Bosnia-Herzegovina* (Geneva: United Nations Institute for Disarmament Research, 1996), 53.

[41] Letter from Franjo Tudjman, President of the Republic of Croatia to Boutros Boutros Ghali, Secretary General of the United Nations, September 13, 1993, reproduced in Slobodan Yarchevich, *Република Српска Крајина; државна документа* [Republic of Serb Krayina; State Documents] (Belgrade: Miroslav, 2005), 374-377: 374 [Emphasis added].

[42] One of the versions of the "Z-4 Plan" is reproduced in Srdjan Radulovic, *Sudbina Krajine* [Krayina's Destiny] (Belgrade: Dan Graf, 1996), 166-181.

[43] Laura Silber, "Explosive mood in Croatia worries UN," *The Financial Times*, May 10, 1995, 3.

On March 31, 1995, the Security Council enacted Resolution 981, which terminated UNPROFOR, and created the UN's "Operation Restore Confidence" under the so-called Stoltenberg Plan. The U.N. troops became known as UNCRO, referring to the U.N. peacekeepers for the Republic of Croatia, whose mission was based on an agreement between "the Government of Croatia and the local Serb authorities." The language describing the U.N. mission in Croatia had certainly come to reflect the international agreement over Croatia's ultimate authority in Krayina.

On August 3, 1995 talks between the Croatian government and the Krayina Serbs were held in Geneva under the auspices of the ICFY, with an agreement reached on all the main substantive points.[44] However, according to Owen, "the decision to attack had already been taken in Zagreb."[45] The planned visit of the ICFY co-chairman, Thorvald Stoltenberg, to Zagreb to continue the peace negotiations, and even a formal announcement by Krayina Serb leader Milan Babic that Serbs would accept the Z-4 plan failed to stop the Croatian onslaught:

> The Croatian attacks appeared to make a mockery of a last-ditch bid by U. N. mediator Thorvald Stoltenberg to get Croatia to respond to the first-ever Serb offer of peaceful reintegration of the lands they have held since a six-month war in 1991.[46]

6.3.3. Operations "Flash" and "Storm": The Fall of Krayina

On May 1, 1995, the Croatian Army attacked Western Slavonia ("UN Sector West") under a pretext of reopening the highway, which was previously closed due to an expressly created incident involving a Croat murdering a Serb at the gas station and a subsequent retaliatory killing of Croats by Serbs on

---

[44] At the time the ICFY co-chairman Thorvald Stoltenberg declared himself confident that an accord could be reached between the Croatian government and Krayina Serbs. See "Stoltenberg optimistic on accord between Croatia and Krajina Serbs," *Deutsche Presse-Agentur*, August 3, 1995.

[45] Owen, *Balkan Odyssey*, 328. Note: During a meeting with his senor military officials, Tudjman described the negotiations over Z-4 as "a mask." See Minutes from the meeting of the President of Croatia Franjo Tudjman with military officials on July 31, 1995, on the Croatian island of Brioni, Part I, reproduced in Velyko Djurich Mishina, ed. *Republic of Serbian Krayina; Ten years later [Република Српска Крајина; Десет година послије]* (Belgrade, Dobra volya, 2005), 312.

[46] "Croat Forces Attack Serb Rebels' Capital; Last-Ditch Talks in Geneva Fail," *Associated Press*, August 4, 1995.

the highway.[47] The war crimes accompanying the attack were aimed at terrifying the Serb population and encouraging their mass exodus.[48] About 13,200 Serbs fled Western Slavonia after the Croat attack, according to U.N. relief workers.[49] The Croatian government claimed to have liberated the area, which is inconsistent with the facts on the ground. According to Brendan O'Shea:

> In using the term 'liberated' the President [of Croatia] clearly chose to indulge in another bout of historical revisionism because had he been bothered to consult either the 1981 or the 1991 census he would have discovered that this area had always been overwhelmingly Serb since the days of Vojna Krajina.[50]

Three months later, the Croats engaged in an even more ambitious attack, that of "reoccupying" Krayina (UN Sector South). The war crimes connected to this military operation were even more extensive. According to estimates of the U.N. High Commission for Refugees (UNHCR), the International Committee of the Red Cross (ICRC), and the Commissariat for Refugees in Serbia, about 250,000 Serbs[51] fled Krayina as a result of the Croatian attack. The ICRC collected reports of 700 missing Croatian Serbs by 1998 in addition to several hundred people known to have been murdered.[52] The Croats had indiscriminately shelled the

---

47 Croat President Tudjman ordered his heads of defense and police to create an incident that could serve as a pretext for the attack on Western Slavonia, as was revealed once the minutes from the meeting became public. *See* Minutes from the meeting of the Defense and National Security Council, held in Presidential palace, April 30, 1995. Croatian General Janko Bobetko claims that the military operations Flash and Storm were prepared by December 5, 1994. For more, *see* Janko Bobetko, *Sve moje bitke* [All my battles], Zagreb: Vlastita naklada, 1996.

48 These crimes were uncovered, despite the organized attempt by the Croatian authorities to hide the evidence:

"As the Croatian army rolled into each town and village with their clean-up teams right behind them, literally washing the blood off the streets, painting white lines on the roads, erecting road signs in Latin script and clearing away all war debris before the international media were allowed into the area, the streets were empty save for a few elderly people who were either too old or sick to embark on a journey into exile." Brendan O' Shea, *Crisis at Bihac; Bosnia's Bloody Collapse* (Phoenix Mill: Sutton Publishing Limited, 1998), 207.

49 Silber, "Explosive mood in Croatia worries UN," 3.

50 O' Shea, *Crisis at Bihac*, 205.

51 The Human Rights Watch estimates that 200,000 Serbs fled. Human Rights Watch, "Croatia: Impunity for Abuses Committed during 'Operation Storm' and the Denial of the Right of Refugees to Return to the Krajina," Vol. 8, No. 13 (D), August 1996. For more, *see* Predrag R. Dragic Kijuk, "A Land Laid Waste," *Krajina; Tragedy of a People* (Hamilton, ON: Canadian-Serbian Council, 1998), 159.

52 According to Human Rights Watch, the Croatian offensive "resulted in the death of an estimated 526 Serbs, 116 of whom were reportedly civilians." Furthermore, "in the months following the August

town of Knin and targeted refugee convoys, in an action that the Croatian Defense Minister Susak later described as "incidents" that were "minor" in nature.[53] About 73 percent of the houses were completely or partially destroyed by fire and most of the remainder were vandalized, plundered, and ransacked.[54] Notably, many war crimes occurred in the aftermath of the attack, amounting to an organized campaign with the aim of preventing the return of the Serbian population to Krayina:

> Croatian soldiers have burned Serbian villages and destroyed property belonging to Serbs. As of mid-August 1995, these crimes apparently are being conducted with impunity and appear aimed at preventing the return of those Serbs who had lived in the area but who fled during the offensive. . . . Persons held in detention also were beaten and otherwise mistreated following their capture.[55]

The U.N. officials have concluded that the attacks following Operation Storm represented "a part of a systematic campaign to drive the 3,500 remaining Serbs

---

offensive, at least 150 Serb civilians were summarily executed and another 110 persons forcibly disappeared." Human Rights Watch, "Croatia: Impunity for Abuses Committed during 'Operation Storm' and the Denial of the Right of Refugees to Return to the Krajina," Vol. 8, No. 13 (D), August 1996. *Note:* Veritas, an independent research organization based in Belgrade, Serbia and Banya Luka, Bosnia, which cooperates with ICTY, has documented 1,960 Serbian victims of Operation Storm, out of which 1,205 are civilians (522 women, 12 children). In sum, Veritas estimates about 7,000 ethnic Serb victims (6,808 names have been verified thus far), while Croatian government and expert estimate around 13,500 ethnic Croat victims. To this number are to be added 1,000-1,500 soldiers of the Yugoslav People's Army, residents of other republics of different ethnicities (including Croats and Serbs), who died at the beginning of the war, mainly in Eastern Slavonia (Vukovar), bringing the total to 21,500-22,000 lost human lives in the war in Croatia. Author's Interview with Savo Shtrbats, Director of Veritas, Belgrade, December 7, 2005 (updated in March 2007). The estimated number of victims of all ethnicities in Croatia, but not including non-residents (YPA soldiers from other Yugoslav republics), was reported by *Reuters* to be 20,091 (June 19, 2001).

53 Brendan O' Shea, *Crisis at Bihac; Bosnia's Bloody Collapse* (Phoenix Mill: Sutton Publishing Limited, 1998), 227.

54 The human right abuses committed during and in the wake of Operation Storm by the Croat forces include "extrajudicial executions and disappearances; torture, including rape; a massive program of systematic house destruction; attempts at forcible expulsions and numerous incidents of maltreatment." ["Croatia: Impunity for Killings After Storm," *Amnesty International*, January 8, 1998.] U.N. has stated since late August 1995 to be in possession of evidence "that people were buried in mass graves and... killed in execution-style [John Pomfret, "U.N. Reports Mass Graves in Krajina," *Washington Post*, August 19, 1995]. To these crimes, the maltreatment of U.N. troops should be added: "Danish troops were forced to march in front of the advancing HV [Croatian Army] infantry and tanks in order to provide what essentially amounted to a human shield." See O' Shea, *Crisis at Bihac*, 226.

55 Human Rights Watch, *Civil and Political Rights in Croatia*, 1995, 16.

from the Krajina and prevent those who want to return from coming back."[56] The E.U. monitors confirmed the Croatian government's tacit consent to these criminal actions:

> The Croatian authorities made no serious effort to halt these crimes or to bring the criminals to justice, pointing to their complicity in what was in effect a campaign of 'ethnic cleansing.[57]

In March 1999, the Hague Tribunal investigators officially "concluded that the Croatian Army carried out summary executions, indiscriminate shelling of civilian populations and 'ethnic cleansing' during a 1995 assault."[58] The final effect of the Operations "Flash" and "Storm" is that "today's Croatia has become the most ethnically cleansed of all Balkan states."[59] The official census in 2001 registered 4.54 percent Serbs in Croatia—about a third of the 1991 level.[60] On January 15, 1996, in an address to the Croatian National Assembly, Croatian president Tudjman had concluded that "a successful Operation Storm resolved the principal internal problem of the Croatian state forever."[61]

---

[56]   Chris Hedges, "Arson and Death Plague Croatia," *New York Times*, September 30, 1995.

[57]   *Unfinished Peace; Report of the International Commission on the Balkans* (Washington: Carnegie Endowment for International Peace, 1996), 102.

[58]   Raymond Bonner, "War Crimes Panel Finds Croat Troops 'Cleansed' the Serbs," *New York Times*, March 21, 1999, A1. The following is the key excerpt from the indictment: "During and after Operation Storm, at all times relevant to this Amended Indictment, Ante Gotovina, with others including Ivan Cermak, Mladen Markac and President Franjo Tudman, participated in a joint criminal enterprise, the common purpose of which was the forcible and permanent removal of the Serb population from the Krajina region, including by the plunder, damage or outright destruction of the property of the Serb population, so as to discourage or prevent members of that population from returning to their homes and resuming habitation" [The International Criminal Tribunal For The Former Yugoslavia, Prosecutor v. Ante Gotovina, Case No. IT-01-45, Amended Indictment, February 19, 2004 (paragraph 7)]. Important evidence in the process is contained in the transcript from the meeting of President Tudjman with military leadership on July 31, 1995, where Tudjman describes the goal of Operation Storm as "making such blows that Serbs practically disappear" [Minutes from the meeting of the President of Croatia Franjo Tudjman with military officials on July 31, 1995 on the Croatian island of Brioni, Part I, reproduced in Velyko Djurich Mishina, ed. *Republic of Serbian Krayina; Ten years later [Република Српска Крајина; Десет година послије]* (Belgrade, Dobra volya, 2005), 312].

[59]   O' Shea, *Crisis at Bihac*, 231.

[60]   "Croatia Publishes Census Results," *RFE/RL Newsline*, Vol. 6, No. 113, Part II, June18, 2002.

[61]   Cited in George Uskokovich, ed. *Срби; избеглице, прогнаници и расељена лица крајем XX века* [Serbs; refugees, banished and displaced persons at the end of XX century] (Belgrade: University in Belgrade, 2000), 83.

However, while the United Nations and most European countries condemned the Croatian government's major offensive against separatist Croatian Serbs, the Clinton administration expressed cautious support.[62] According to news reports, U.S. Ambassador to Croatia Peter Galbraith knew in advance of Croatian military plans and "expressed his approval of Croatia's Operation Storm, which ethnically cleansed the 300,000 Serbs out of the Krajina."[63] U.S. Assistant Secretary of State Richard Holbrooke claims to the contrary that Croats acted "against American recommendations,"[64] but simultaneously quotes another U.S. diplomat, Robert Frasure, who alludes to a U.S. role in the Croatian military action: "We 'hired' these guys [the Croats] to be our junkyard dogs because we were desperate."[65] In his later memoirs, U.S. President William J. Clinton is more open, saying "I was rooting for the Croatians"[66] and admitting that the U.S. government had "authorized a private company to use retired U.S. military personnel to improve and train the Croatian army."[67] Clinton avoids mentioning the exodus of Krayina Serbs and the criminal activities of the Croat troops, instead briefly stating that the "Croatian forces took Krajina with little resistance."[68]

U.S. Ambassador to Croatia Peter Galbraith had publicly remarked that the Croatian action did not constitute ethnic cleansing as "ethnic cleansing was a specialty of the Serbs,"[69] while U.S. Assistant Secretary of State for European and Canadian Affairs Holbrooke stated that it "might be viewed as a milder version of ethnic cleansing,"[70] nonetheless referring to the operation as "a complete success."[71] Journalists reporting from the region, like Charles Krauthammer of the *Washington Post*, did not share this view, insisting: "There is either one moral standard regarding ethnic cleansing, or none. There cannot be two."[72]

---

[62] Dana Priest, "U.S. Cautiously Supports Offensive against Serbs," *Washington Post*, August 5, 1995. For more, *see* Glenny, *Fall of Yugoslavia*, 284.

[63] Robert Fisk, "Foreward" in Brendan O' Shea, *Crisis at Bihac; Bosnia's Bloody Collapse* (Phoenix Mill: Sutton Publishing Limited, 1998), xiii.

[64] Richard Holbrooke, *To End a War* (New York: Random House, 1998), 72.

[65] Ibid., 73. Other authors, such as Pavlowitch, also assert that Croats received "informal American help." Stevan K. Pavlowitch, *Serbia; The History behind the Name* (London: Hurst & Company, 2002), 215.

[66] Bill Clinton, *My Life* (New York: Vintage Books, 2005), 667.

[67] Ibid.

[68] Ibid.

[69] Glenny, *Fall of Yugoslavia*, 281.

[70] Holbrooke, *To End a War*, 160.

[71] Ibid., 72.

[72] Charles Krauthammer, "Ethnic Cleansing That's Convenient," *Washington Post*, August 15, 1995.

Holbrooke further recalls expressing to Tudjman "[his] general support for the offensive" and asking Tudjman not to attack the town of Banya Luka (Banja Luka) because it would certainly be within the Serb portion of Bosnia in any future settlement and would generate many additional refugees. Holbrooke's words "Mr. President, I urge you to go as far as you can, but not to take Banja Luka" are a testimony to, at the very least, a U.S. encouragement for Croat actions.[73]

Notably, Croatia's insurgence in Bosnia was not officially condemned as an act of outside aggression on an independent state. Neither was the Bosnian Muslim incursion into Croatia during Operation Storm, which was taken in support of ethnic Croat attack on ethnic Serbs in Croatia.[74] Throughout Holbrooke's account one idea prevails: Serbs as the bad guys need to be beaten to concede territory at the negotiating table.

Consequently, many U.S., German, and other analysts of the war in the former Yugoslavia have persistently described Croatia's action in a positive manner. Thomas Weiss, for instance, has remarked: "The West talked, but Croatia acted."[75] He further described the ethnic cleansing of Krayina almost as a side effect of the Croatian campaign:

> In an ironic twist, the largest refugee flow of the war—indeed the largest in Europe since the Soviet crushing of the Hungarian uprising in 1956— resulted from a successful Croatian military campaign.[76]

This position was probably taken for two reasons. The first is that Serbs, generally collectively equated with the regime of Slobodan Miloshevich, have been perceived as the guiltiest of the warring parties. The second critical factor is that the U.S. government, at least indirectly, assisted the Croatian military action. Retired U.S. military officers privately trained the Croatian forces, while the CIA

---

[73]   Holbrooke, *To End a War*, 160.

[74]   The Croat "recuperation" of Krayina was aided by the Bosnian Muslim 5th Corps, as subsequently avowed by the Bosnian Muslim leaders. Extracts from an interview with Brigadier Mirsad Selmanovic, Chief of Staff of Army of Bosnia and Herzegovina 5th Corps in the Sarayevo weekly political paper: *Ljiljan*, June 2, 1997 (reporter Isnan Taljic), 57-60.

[75]   Thomas G. Weiss, "Collective Spinelessness: U.N. Actions in the Former Yugoslavia," *The World and Yugoslavia's Wars*, ed. Richard H. Ullman (New York: Council on Foreign Relations, 1996), 69.

[76]   Ibid., 70.

reportedly provided crucial intelligence information.[77] The North Atlantic Treaty Organization (NATO) bombing of the Bosnian Serb positions, including command and control capabilities, which the Bosnian Serbs shared with the Krayina Serb forces, further facilitated the Croatian military action, although this was not its primary aim.[78]

Barbara Ekwall-Uebelhart and Andrei Raevsky from the United Nations Institute for Disarmament question why NATO failed to use airstrikes to protect the Krayina Serbs, an act that they had taken several weeks prior to protect the Bosnian Muslims of the Bihac area.[79] Although the UNPROFOR's role in Croatia had originally been defined as ensuring "that the areas remain demilitarized, and that all persons residing in them were protected from fear of armed attack,"[80] the U.N. forces did nothing to oppose the attack, and according to certain reports,[81] they actually complied with a Croatian order to immediately withdraw from the confrontation line.

While Ekwall-Uebelhart and Raevsky acknowledge the military weakness of the UNPROFOR, they claim that the U.N. troops could have effectively blocked the Croats' main entrance to Sector West, the Zagreb-Belgrade highway, for a certain

---

[77] *See above. Also, Jane's Intelligence Review Pointer* asserts that the main reason for the Croatian success was the reconnaissance information provided by the U.S. CIA's Gnat 750 remote-piloted vehicles, which helped the Croats identify weak points in Serb defenses. *See* Tom Ripley, "Croat Surgical Strike Successful," *Jane's Intelligence Review Pointer*, June 1995, 2. *See* also "4 Navy Jets Bomb Serb Missile Sites," *Navy Times*, August 21, 1995, 2; "Maric Aide Says NATO Led Croat Offensive," *Oslobodjenje* (Sarajevo), August 23, 1995, 4, as translated by FBIS, September 5, 1995; Chris Black, "U.S. Veterans' Aid to Croatia Elicits queries," *Boston Globe*, August 13, 1995, 12; Charlotte Eager, "Invisible United States Army Defeats Serbs," *The Observer* (UK), November 5, 1995, 25; Paul Harris, "Corporate Mercenaries with Links to Arms Sellers and the Pentagon Are Fulfilling United States Policy Aims by Proxy," *Scotland on Sunday* (U.K.), May 5, 1996, 15; Yves Goulet, "MPRI: Washington's Freelance Advisors," *Jane's Intelligence Review*, July 1, 1998, 38; and Raymond Bonner, "War Crimes Panel Finds Croat Troops 'Cleansed' the Serbs," *New York Times*, March 21, 1999, A1; John Barry and Roy Gutman, "What did the CIA know," *Newsweek*, August 27, 2001.

[78] *See* pages 326-330.

[79] Why should a counterattack against the 5th Muslim Corps in Bihac ["UN Safe Area"] trigger a NATO airstrike and a Croatian attack on Okucani ["UN Protected Area"] not do so? After all, the Croatian attack on UNPA West triggered a flow of thousands of refugees from western Slavonia which greatly contributed to the ethnic cleansing of the sector." Ekwall-Uebelhart and Raevsky, *Managing Arms in Peace* Processes, 16.

[80] Article 7, "Concept for a United Nations Peace-Keeping Operation in Yugoslavia, as Discussed with Yugoslav Leaders by the Honourable Cyrus R. Vance, Personal Envoy of the Secretary-General and Marrack Goulding, Under-Secretary-General for Special Political Affairs" [Vance Plan] (Annex III, Report of the Secretary General Pursuant to Security Council Resolution 721, S/23280, December 11, 1990).

[81] Ekwall-Uebelhart and Raevsky, *Managing Arms in Peace* Processes, 16.

time period, enabling the Serb forces to prepare a defense. In addition, these two authors inquire why the U.N. had not provided more robust forces if it is indeed true that the U.N. headquarters in Zagreb were aware of the Croats' plan to forcefully "retake" the areas for two years prior to the attack.[82] They conclude that both the lack of the UN's response and the weak defense provided by the Serbs had a political background. In addition to a certain U.S. involvement, allegations have been made that Croatian authorities acted in agreement with Miloshevich, resulting in inadequate Serb defense of the region.[83] Certainly, the Krayina Serbs were not able to defend themselves without the aid of Serbia or the Bosnian Serb forces.

The peacekeepers both in Bosnia and in Croatia, struggling with insufficient resources and an unclear mandate, had faced serious moral predicaments such as whether to counter an attack by the country's recognized government, or whether to assist the people to flee. The latter dilemma is well illustrated by a peacekeeper, Major Last:

> There were both legal and ethical issues in assisting the movement of large groups across boundaries. On one hand, some argued that we were assisting ethnic cleansing. On the other hand, perhaps we were making it easier to reach a settlement to the conflict, with the troublesome and disputed enclaves out of the way.[84]

Following Croatian military action, the U.N. Security Council adopted Resolution 1009 of August 10, 1995, which expressed concern over reported human rights violations, and

> [condemned] in the strongest terms the unacceptable acts by Croatian Government forces against personnel of the United Nations peace-keeping forces, including those which have resulted in the death of a Danish member of those forces and two Czech members.

---

[82] Ibid., 118-120.

[83] Milan Martich, then-President of the Serbian Republic of Krayina claims to have been betrayed by Miloshevich in an interview "Milošević nas je izdao" [Miloshevich betrayed us], *Vreme*, August 3, 1996, 20-21.

[84] Major D.M. Last, "Reflections from the Field: Ethical Challenges in Peacekeeping and Humanitarian Interventions," *The Fletcher Forum of World Affairs* 24, no. 1 (Spring 2000), 73-86: 80.

The resolution further called on the Croatian authorities to

> (a) respect fully the rights of the local Serb population including the rights to remain, leave or return in safety, (b) allow access to this population by international humanitarian organizations, and (c) create conditions conducive to the return of those persons who have left their homes.

Subsequently, U.N. Security Council Resolution 1919 of November 9, 1995, expressed "deep concern" over reports of human rights violations, requesting more adamantly "that the Government of the Republic of Croatia take urgent measures to put an end to violations of international humanitarian law and of human rights, and investigate all reports of such violations so that those responsible in respect of such acts be judged and punished." Croatia did not heed these demands, having already witnessed the U.N.'s ineffectiveness in enforcing such resolutions in the wake of political pressure from powerful states that approved of Croatia's actions. Serbia under Miloshevich also showed little concern for the Serb refugees."[85]

6.3.4. Reintegration of Eastern Slavonia

The fate of Eastern Slavonia, the sole part of Croatia still in the hands of Serb forces, was the only wider issue discussed during the Dayton Peace negotiations of November 1995. At the time, Miloshevich reportedly told Holbrooke that "the technical issues were really about one core question: would the Serbs have rights as a minority in eastern Slavonia." Noting the irony of Miloshevich arguing a human-rights case, Holbrooke conceded that "he had a point."[86]

As a consequence of an agreement made at Dayton, on November 12, 1995, the Government of the Republic of Croatia and "the local Serbian community" signed the Erdut Agreement.[87] The Agreement initiated a U.N. peacekeeping operation for the region with both military and civilian components, under the name "United Nations Transitional Administration for Eastern Slavonia, Baranya and

---

[85] Ilya Smilyanich, *Dalmatian Kosovo* (Belgrade: Serbian Cultural Society "Zora" and Association of Serbs from Croatia, 2006), 53.

[86] Holbrooke, *To End a War*, 238.

[87] "Basic Agreement on the Region of Eastern Slavonia, Baranya and Western Sirmium," U.N. Doc. S/1995/951, annex, reproduced in Ramcharan, *The International Conference on the Former Yugoslavia*, 487-488.

Western Sirmium" (UNTAES). The U.N. Security Council resolution 1025 of November 30, 1995, endorsed the UNTAES operation, initially for a year and then extended for another year.[88] Even though the U.N. attempted to convince the Serbian population of this region to remain thereafter, more than half of Eastern Slavonia's Serbs left in 1997, mistrusting the Croatian government.

In Croatia, a mass people transfer effectively ended the quest of the trapped Serbian minority for self-determination that would be wider in scope than basic human and minority rights.[89] At that moment, the Croatian government, as cynically remarked by Lord David Owen, readily embarked on the path to European integration:

> Croatia from 1995 will be the most ethnically pure of the former Yugoslav states and after this Tudjman will be content for it to join the EU.[90]

The only "unresolved" issue for the Croatian authorities regarded the Prevlaka peninsula, a strategic strip of land overlooking the Montenegrin Bay of Kotor, disputed by Croatia and the Federal Republic of Yugoslavia. The Prevlaka peninsula was demilitarized upon an agreement of the presidents of FRY and Croatia of September 30, 1992, endorsed by the U.N. Security Council Resolution 779 of October 6, 1992, with which the Yugoslav People's Army fully complied. U.N. peacekeepers monitored the demilitarization of the Prevlaka peninsula until December 15, 2002, when the Montenegrin and Croatian authorities concluded a final agreement on the reintegration of Prevlaka into Croatia.

---

[88]   U.N. Security Council Resolution 1037 of January 15, 1996.

[89]   According to Human Rights Watch: "Between 300,000 and 350,000 Croatian Serbs left their homes during the 1991-95 war in Croatia, mostly for Serbia and Montenegro, and Bosnia and Herzegovina. By August 2004, the government had registered 112,162 Serb returnees. The actual number of returns is significantly lower because many Croatian Serbs leave again for Serbia and Montenegro or Bosnia after only a short stay in Croatia" (accessed September 26, 2005); available from http://hrw.org/english/docs/2005/01/13/croati9857.htm.

[90]   Owen, *Balkan Odyssey*, 75. Hayden suggests that the number of Serbs in Croatia by late 1995 had been reduced to 90,000 from the 1991 figure of 570,000. Robert M. Hayden, "Constitutional Nationalism and the Logic of the Wars in Yugoslavia," *Problems of Post-Communism* 43, no. 5 (1996), 31. Cedric Thornberry, deputy head of UNPROFOR in the former Yugoslavia from 1992 to 1994 has also remarked: "But one of the most puzzling features of the Yugoslav tragedy has been the comparative lack of significance world has attached to events in the Krajina region . . . Today, through the 'ethnic cleansing' that has occurred, Croatia has become the most 'ethnically pure' state in the whole of the former Yugoslavia." Cedric Thornberry, "Saving the War Crimes Tribunal," *Foreign Policy*, no 104 (Fall 1996), 79.

6.4. Bosnia-Herzegovina: The Maps

6.4.1. The Cutileiro Plan

Just prior to Bosnia and Herzegovina's international recognition, in February and March 1992, the European Community, led by the Portuguese Foreign Minister and Secretary General of the European Union José Cutileiro, attempted to negotiate a peaceful settlement of the fuming conflict. The peace proposal, which has become known as the Cutileiro Plan (also known as Carrington-Cutileiro Plan and the Lisbon Agreement), envisaged a cantonization of Bosnia by which the country would be divided into three principal territorial units and governed by a power sharing arrangement of its three main ethnic groups, Muslims, Serbs, and Croats.[91] The three Bosnian ethnic groups had initially endorsed the Cutileiro plan at a meeting on March 18, 1992, but the Bosnian Muslims subsequently reneged on the agreement. Many analysts, including Lenard Cohen, believe that the key reason for this is their belief that the Americans would provide them with a better deal if hostilities erupted.[92] Warren Zimmerman, the U.S. ambassador to Yugoslavia at the time, denied the accusations that the U.S. government advised the Muslims to abandon the Lisbon agreement, but admitted to having asked Izetbegovic why the Muslim side had signed the Agreement if he were unhappy with it.[93]

Hayden stresses that the Lisbon Agreement was the only peace plan primarily drawn up by parties to the conflict and even briefly agreed upon by all parties.[94] Otherwise, this peace plan resembles all the subsequent peace proposals in that it accepts the partition of Bosnia to be the only means to end the violence. The core of the negotiations constantly regarded the maps. The constitutional framework was not unimportant, but it was certainly secondary.

---

[91] "Statement of Principles of March 18, 1992, for New Constitutional Arrangements for Bosnia and Herzegovina," reproduced in Ramcharan, *The International Conference on the Former Yugoslavia*, 24-28.

[92] Lenard J. Cohen, Broken Bonds; Yugoslavia's Disintegration and Balkan Politics in Transition, 2nd ed. (Boulder: Westview Press, 1995), 243.

[93] Ljiljana Smajlovic, "Interview: Warren Zimmerman," *Vreme News Digest Agency,* No. 144 (June 27, 1994).

Note: In a Letter to the Economist magazine (December 9-15, 1995), Jose Cutileiro also states: "President Izetbegovic and his aides were encouraged to scupper that deal [Lisbon Agreement] and to fight for a unitary Bosnian state by well-meaning outsiders who thought they knew better."

[94] Robert M. Hayden, *Blueprints for a House Divided; The Constitutional Logic of the Yugoslav Conflicts* (Ann Arbor: The University of Michigan Press, 2000), 100.

6.4.2. The Vance-Owen Peace Plan

The "Proposed Constitutional Structure for Bosnia and Herzegovina,"[95] published on October 28, 1992, dubbed the "Vance-Owen Peace Plan" (VOPP), aimed to design a decentralized state that relegated all authority to ten autonomous provinces or cantons (four would be under Serbian control, while six would remain under the control of Muslims and Croats), except those functions related to the maintenance of international relations. The central government's authority was restricted, further limited by international supervision. For instance, the initial version of the VOPP had stipulated that the central government would be in charge of national defense, but "supervised by an appropriate authority, designated by [the ICFY]" (art. V.A.2).[96] The roads between the provinces would also be placed under international control and a variety of courts and institutions would be charged with ensuring human rights, leading Hayden to conclude that Bosnia would be "a protectorate" and "the ultimate 'quasi-state,'" while its provinces would be "functioning states . . . without . . . international personality."[97]

In marking the provinces' borderlines, the VOPP claimed to have primarily a number of factors:

> Boundaries of the provinces [are] to be drawn so as to constitute areas as geographically coherent as possible, taking into account ethnic, geographical (i.e. natural features, such as rivers), historical, communication (i.e. the existing road and railroad networks), economic viability, and other relevant factors. (Article I.B.1)

However, the boundaries mainly followed the ethnic maps of 1981 and one ethnic group dominated each province. Comparing the VOPP with the Lisbon Agreement, Hayden maintains that it differed only in several instances, largely to the benefit of the Bosnian Croats.[98] One of the primary authors of the VOPP

---

[95] Proposed Constitutional Structure for Bosnia and Herzegovina (Vance-Owen Peace Plan), International Conference on the Former Yugoslavia, document STC/2/2, October 27, 1992.

[96] The final version of the VOPP called for progressive demilitarization. *See* Ustavni principi za Bosnu i Hercegovinu:, Article 5, printed in *Borba*, January 7, 1993, 20 and reproduced in Hayden, *Blueprints for a House Divided*, 103. The integral version of the VOPP, signed in Geneva on January 30, 1993, is reproduced in Ramcharan, *The International Conference on the Former Yugoslavia*, 249-251.

[97] Hayden, *Blueprints for a House Divided*, 103.

[98] "Vance-Owen gave the Croats everything they asked for in early 1992 except for an island of territory north of Sarajevo, and with the addition of land in Trebinje district that they had not even requested;" . . . "The Serbs received about what they would have received in March 1992; but their holdings, unlike

blames the U.S. government for blocking the proposal's acceptance by the Bosnian Muslims, once more by giving them hope that they could achieve a better deal.[99] The Bosnian Serbs voted down the agreement in the parliament,[100] although their leader had accepted the proposal under pressure from the Serbian President Miloshevich who fully endorsed the VOPP. The principal reason for the rejection was that the plan's implementation would require that the Bosnian Serbs withdraw from nearly 40 percent of their then land holdings.[101] Since the VOPP provided contiguous and large territory to the Bosnian Croats, they exited the military alliance with the Bosnian Muslims and proclaimed a "Herzeg-Bosnia" republic. Although the U.N., under the auspices of the International Conference on the former Yugoslavia, tried to implement parts of the VOPP on the Muslim-Croat-held territory, it failed because the Croats "were carving out their own areas, like the Serbs."[102]

Owen stresses that the main strength of the VOPP was in its attempt to provide solid human rights guarantees in order to counter the brutal policy of ethnic cleansing that characterized the Bosnian war. The subsequent peace plans were similar to the VOPP in scope but provided for a different territorial division that produced separate and contiguous ethnic areas and thus changed the spirit of VOPP.

6.4.3. The Union of Three Republics Plan (Owen-Stoltenberg Plan)

The Constitutional Agreement of the Union of Republics of Bosnia and Herzegovina[103] is better known as the Owen-Stoltenberg plan, although the

---

those of the Croats, were fragmented and largely not contiguous with either Yugoslavia [Serbia and Montenegro] or each other," whole the Muslim territory was contiguous but generally drawn in a way that it was not viable. Ibid., 104-105.

99 See Owen, *Balkan Odyssey*, 106-111. Susan Woodward explains that "the United States refused to support the Vance-Owen plan on the grounds that it gave insufficient land to the 'Muslims.'" Susan L. Woodward, *Balkan Tragedy; Chaos and Dissolution after the Cold War* (Washington, D.C.: The Brookings Institution, 1995), 306.

100 The Bosnian Serb authorities subsequently organized a popular referendum, which overwhelmingly rejected the VOPP.

101 Owen, *Balkan Odyssey*, 91, 133.

102 Ibid., 173.

103 Constitutional Agreement of the Union of Republics of Bosnia and Herzegovina; Appendix I to the Letter from the U.N. Secretary-General addressed to the President of the Security Council, August 20, 1993, U.N. Document S/26337 and reproduced in Ramcharan, *The International Conference on the Former Yugoslavia*, 286-317.

mediators and co-chairmen of the International Conference on the former Yugoslavia, David Owen and Thorvald Stoltenberg, reject this name, calling it instead "the Union of Three Republics." This plan would create a *de facto* confederacy of three mini-States, with Sarayevo and Mostar placed under U.N. and E.C. administration respectively.

Ironically, one provision of the agreement (Section 7, Article 2) provided that "none of the Constituent Republics may withdraw from the Union of Republics without the prior agreement of all of the Republics," repeating the provision of the SFRY Constitution that was ignored by its republics and by the international community. Such "constitutional fraud" was essential, according to Hayden, because the Serbs and Croats "would not accept inclusion in a real state."[104] Indeed, both the Serbs and the Croats readily accepted the "Owen-Stoltenberg Plan" while the Bosnian Muslims rejected it.[105]

Interestingly, the Bosnian Muslim leader, Alija Izetbegovic, at the time officially accepted an eventual secession of the Bosnian Croats and Serbs, provided that the Bosnian Muslims "were satisfied on territory,"[106] which most clearly underscores that territory rather than some other value was the primary goal of at least one of the warring parties. In September 1994, Izetbegovic even signed a Muslim-Serb Declaration allowing for the three republics in the union to hold referenda after two years on whether their citizens wished to remain in the union or leave the union, on the condition that there was an agreement on territorial division between the republics.[107] Balancing their interests, the Croats remained mute on this issue. In the view of Owen, they were "apprehensive that it might establish a precedent for the Krajina."[108] Finally, the Bosnian Muslims, despite U.S. support for the peace proposal, turned it down.[109] They preferred to continue the war,

---

[104] Hayden, *Blueprints for a House Divided*, 108.

[105] Woodward, *Balkan Tragedy*, 310; Laura Silber and Alan Little, *Yugoslavia: Death of a Nation*, revised and updated edition (New York: Penguin Books, 1997), 338.

[106] Owen, *Balkan Odyssey*, 215.

[107] Ibid., 215-6.

[108] Ibid., 216.

[109] Having opposed the VOPP on the grounds that it partitioned Bosnia and thereby sanctioned ethnic cleansing, the United States changed its policy. On August 19, 1994, Secretary of State Warren Christopher sent a letter to the Bosnian Muslim leader Alija Izetbegovic urging him to endorse the Owen-Stoltenberg Plan. For more, *see* David Binder, "U.S. Policymakers on Bosnia Admit Errors in Opposing Partition in 1992," *New York Times*, August 29, 1993, 8.

having made significant military gains during that period.[110] Double standards were again at play, with the United States reiterating that "they could not pressurize the Muslims, who were the victims."[111]

6.4.4. European Union Action Plan and the Contact Group Plan

The European Union Action Plan and the Contact Group Plan represented variations on the Joint Action Plan. Neither was publicly released, but an unofficial translation of a draft of the Contact Group Plan was published in the Serbian newspaper *Borba* on August 24, 1994; the Americans claimed that this was a Russian draft.[112] Significantly, the Contact Group Plan called for the creation of two rather than three entities. Bosnian Muslims and Croats would jointly govern one of the two entities, the Muslim-Croat Federation, established on a basis of a renewed military alliance between these two groups in March 1994, the Washington Agreement.[113] As in other proposals, the competence of the central government was restricted. This time there was no provision on possible secession, but entities had the right to "enter into arrangements in the realm of association, such as confederation, under condition that such an arrangement would not change the international personality or legal subjectivity of the entity or be contrary to the interests of the Union of the other Entity."[114] Analyzing the proposed Contact Group plan, the legal historian Milan St. Protich points to the absurdity of separate constitutions for Bosnia's federal units, recalling that "this particular invention of jurisprudence . . . existed in the 1974 communist Constitution of SFRY [and] was essentially the major cause of the tragic disintegration of Yugoslavia."[115] Furthermore, the Contact Group plan allowed the entities to have separate armies that could "under no circumstances . . . enter into or stay within the territory of the other Entity."[116]

---

[110] *See* Owen, *Balkan Odyssey*, 242.

[111] Ibid., 232.

[112] *See* Hayden, *Blueprints for a House Divided*, 108-9. For texts of declarations and principles relating to the European Union Action Plan and the Contact Group Plan, *see* Ramcharan, *The International Conference on the Former Yugoslavia*, 330-341.

[113] The Washington Agreement provided that the Federation be divided into several cantons that would be dominated by either Bosnian Croats or Muslims and this model was later used in the Dayton Peace Accords for Bosnia.

[114] Washington Agreement; Article 13 (c), Elements for a Constitution of the Union of Bosnia and Herzegovina (Working Paper).

[115] Milan St. Protic, *Misconceptions about Bosnia-Herzegovina; Contradiction in terms* (Belgrade: Center for Serbian Studies, 1994), 9.

[116] Article 6, Elements for a Constitution of the Union of Bosnia and Herzegovina (Working Paper).

Finally, the Contact Group Plan established the principle that the territorial division would follow the 51-49 percentage split. This was the main reason for the Bosnian Serbs to initially reject the plan, at the time holding about 70 percent of Bosnian territory.[117] The parliament of the Muslim-Croat Federation accepted the Contact Group Plan on July 18, 1995. Faced with intense NATO bombing and sanctions imposed by the FRY on August 4, 1995, the Bosnian Serbs also endorsed the Contact Group Plan on September 7, 1995, as a basis for further negotiations, which led to a new peace proposal accepted by all parties.

6.4.5. Dayton Peace Accords

Brokered by the United States on November 22, 1995, at the Wright-Patterson Air Force Base in Dayton, Ohio, the Dayton General Framework Agreement for Peace in Bosnia-Herzegovina[118] created two administrative units ("entities") within Bosnia and Herzegovina: the Republika Srpska and the (Muslim-Croat) Federation of Bosnia and Herzegovina (Article I.3), on the basis of the 49-51 territorial split. Dayton Accords relegated the status of the strategic town of Brchko (Brčko) in northeast Bosnia and Herzegovina to international arbitration, which in March 1999 rendered Brchko "a neutral district," under direct jurisdiction of the Bosnian federal authorities and an international supervisor.[119] The legal arrangement for the Brchko district represented another legal innovation. According to the presiding arbitrator, Roberts Owen, "control of the region [would be] placed in the hands of a new multiethnic district government under intensified international supervision and beyond the control of either entity."[120]

Once again, the crux of the negotiations had involved the appearance of maps. To arrive at a solution, the U.S. mediators employed "PowerScene," a highly classified $400,000 imaging system that the U.S. Department of Defense first used during

---

[117] At a popular referendum, held on August 27, 1995, the Contact Group Plan was rejected by 96.06 percent of the vote.

[118] General Framework Agreement for Peace in Bosnia and Herzegovina, December 14, 1995, U.N. Doc A/50/750, reprinted in (1996) 35 ILM 75.

[119] Brcko Arbitration Arbitral Tribunal for Dispute over Inter-Entity Boundary in Brcko Area, Final Award, March 5, 1999 (accessed October 6, 2004); available from http://www.ohr.int/ohr-offices/brcko/default.asp?content_id=5358#2.

[120] Statement by Roberts B. Owen, Presiding Arbitrator for the Brcko Arbitral Tribunal Sarayevo, Bosnia and Herzegovina, March 5, 1999 (accessed October 6, 2004); available from http://www.ohr.int/ohr-offices/brcko/arbitration/default.asp?content_id=5353.

Desert Storm, which filmed Bosnia in three dimensions, accurate down to two yards.[121] Strategic corridors were drawn with the aid of high technology.

Nevertheless, the constitutional issues were not unimportant. Holbrooke describes how even the prefix in the country's name mattered. Bosnian Muslims requested "a republic" as a prefix, the Serbs insisted that it be "union" or "confederation" but the two parties settled on no prefix.[122] The Dayton-established Constitution of Bosnia and Herzegovina bestowed on each of the country's two entities the institutions of the president and the parliament. In addition, each of the three major ethnic groups (Croats, Muslims, and Serbs) is represented by a member of the joint Presidency, each of whom calls himself or herself a President of the Presidency. This system resulted in five different Bosnian presidents, all of whom could be overruled by a sixth, international president of Bosnia—the High Commissioner, the "final authority in theatre regarding the interpretation of this Agreement on the civilian implementation of the peace settlement."[123]

Bosnia and Herzegovina nominally became an independent state and an international protectorate in practice, with the country's constitution representing "the unique case of a constitution never officially published in the official languages of the country concerned but agreed and published in a foreign language, English."[124] According to the Dayton Peace Accords, the European Court of Human Rights Council appoints three members of the Bosnian Constitutional Court, while the Council of Europe assigns eight of fourteen members of a new Human Rights Chamber, and the Organization for Security and Cooperation in Europe (OSCE) appoints an Ombudsman. Bosnia's High Commissioner responds to the "international community," an amorphous body that had in the past included members of the Contact Group or a wider "Steering Board," which the former United Kingdom Ambassador to Bosnia and Herzegovina, Charles Crawford, described as "a self-selected group of about twenty countries . . . the big obvious ones."[125]

---

[121] Holbrooke, *To End a War*, 283.

[122] Ibid., 129-131.

[123] Annex X, General Framework Agreement for Peace in Bosnia and Herzegovina 1995, U.N. Doc A/50/750, reprinted in (1996) 35 ILM 75.

[124] European Commission for Democracy through Law (Venice Commission), Opinion on the Constitutional Situation in Bosnia and Herzegovina and the Powers of the High Representative, based on Comments by Mr. J. Helgesen (Member, Norway), Mr. J. Jowell (Member, United Kingdom), Mr. G. Malinverni (Member, Switzerland), Mr. J.-C. Scholsem (Member, Belgium), Mr. K. Tuori (Member, Finland), adopted by the Venice Commission at its 62nd plenary session, Venice, March 11-12, 2005, paragraph 6.

[125] Author's Interview with Ambassador Charles Crawford, Boston, March 5, 1999.

This "self-selection" took place at the Peace Implementation Conference, held in London on December 8-9, 1995, with the aim of mobilizing international support for the Dayton Peace Agreement. In 2002, a Board of Principals was established, under the chairmanship of the High Representative, to serve as the main coordinating body of International Community activity in Bosnia and Herzegovina. Permanent members of the Board of Principles are the Office of the High Representative (OHR), European Union Force in Bosnia and Herzegovina (EUFOR), OSCE, UNHCR, the European Union Police Mission (EUPM), and the European Commission. International financial institutions such as the World Bank, the International Monetary Fund, and the U.N. Development Program are also regular participants on the Board of Principals.[126] As of 2002, the High Representative has also been dubbed the "European Union Special Representative" (EUSR) for Bosnia and Herzegovina, representing the Council of the European Union and reporting to the Council through the Secretary-General and the High Representative for the Common Foreign and Security Policy.

Over time, the position of the High Representative, created by the Dayton Peace Agreement, Annex 10: "Agreement on Civilian Implementation," arguably evolved beyond the authority intended in the agreement, which uses words like "monitor," "coordinate," and "facilitate," but not "impose." Moreover, the High Commissioner has used an ambiguous provision of the Dayton Peace Agreement to change the letter or at least the spirit of tBosnia and Herzegovina's and its two entities' constitutions. This is Article III 5 of the Constitution of Bosnia and Herzegovina, which could be interpreted as granting unlimited authority to otherwise restricted central government:

> Bosnia and Herzegovina shall assume responsibility for other matters as . . . are provided for in Annexes 5 through 8 of the General Framework Agreement; or necessary to preserve the sovereignty, territorial integrity, political independence and international personality of Bosnia and Herzegovina. Additional institutions may be established as necessary to carry out such responsibilities.

Concurrently, another vague Dayton formulation that permits entities to establish "special parallel relationships with neighboring states"[127] has been applied most restrictively in practice.

---

[126] OHR Press Release, July 29, 2002.
[127] Article III2, Constitution of Bosnia and Herzegovina.

Following signature, more transfers of population occurred, notably in Sarayevo (Sarajevo). Thousands of Serbs deserted the town,[128] primarily leaving the Grbavitsa district that they occupied throughout the war and that represents the only significant area in Bosnia-Herzegovina that changed hands after the Dayton Peace Accords. Subsequently, there has been some success with refugee return, but generally the return was either temporary, made for the purpose of retrieving and selling property, or directed to the area where the returnee's ethnic group was a majority.

The Dayton Peace Accords have in some ways legitimized the policy of "ethnic cleansing," to which the Clinton administration had objected with regard to the VOPP[129] but later accepted as inevitable, to be countered with the work of the War Crimes Tribunal[130] and subsequent attempts to centralize the Bosnian state. The Dayton Peace Accord also failed to address the wider issues such as the status of Kosovo and Metohia, and it conferred moral authority on Slobodan Miloshevich, prolonging his rule over Serbia for another five years. Its main shortcoming, however, was that it was a short-term solution, failing to provide for the long-term viability of Bosnia as an independent state or offer another framework for regional stability. Nonetheless, the Dayton Agreement is invaluable as it brought peace to the peoples of Bosnia and Herzegovina and ensured broad rights for its three principal ethnic groups, albeit within an international protectorate.

6.5. International Military Intervention in Bosnia and Herzegovina (1995)

In the first two years of the Yugoslav conflict, the international community, led by the European Union and the United States, was reluctant to impose a settlement

---

128 See Louis Sell, "The Serb Flight from Sarajevo: Dayton's First Failure," *East European Politics and Societies* 14 (2000), 179-202.

129 Glenny, *Fall of Yugoslavia*, 228.

130 The International Criminal Tribunal for the Former Yugoslavia has indicted key Serb political and military leaders on charges of war crimes, including several presidents, and a lower number of Croat and Bosnian Muslim military figures. In total, the tribunal has indicted 161 persons for serious violations of international humanitarian law committed in the territory of the former Yugoslavia (*see* http://www.un.org/icty/glance/index.htm). The Hague's Chief Prosecutor Carla del Ponte stated that ICTY had investigated both the Bosnian Muslim leader Alija Izetbegovic and the Croat leader Franjo Tudjman's role in war crimes [*see* "Late Bosnian Leader Was Being Investigated," *Associated Press,* October 23, 2003]. When asked why the indictment against Tudjman was not published prior to his death in 1999, del Ponte responded that it was difficult to collect necessary evidence but that he nonetheless received a different kind of justice [Carla del Ponte, Lecture at the Fletcher School, Boston, USA, October 27, 2005].

on the parties to the conflict, particularly if it involved the use of force. This is reflected in a statement made by Douglas Hurd, British Foreign Secretary, in 1993:

> The first priority in the conflicts affecting the former Yugoslav republics including Croatia must be a lasting political settlement which respects the legitimate concerns of all those involved. But solutions cannot be imposed from outside: they must be agreed by the parties themselves.[131]

Similarly, in 1991 the British Prime Minister John Major opposed what eventually took place in Bosnia and Herzegovina:

> What we cannot sensibly undertake is an operation which would begin with an ultimatum but might lead to a commitment to some form of international protectorate in Bosnia-Herzegovina, sustained indefinitely by military force.[132]

However, as sanctions failed to produce effect on their own and the death toll increased,[133] the pressure for international military intervention mounted. According to Babic and Jokic:

---

[131] Letter from Douglas Hurd to Vlada Vjestica (representative of the Krayina government in London, March 4, 1993. Reproduced in Slobodan Yarchevich, *Република Српска Крајина; државна документа* [Republic of Serb Krayina; State Documents] (Belgrade: Miroslav, 2005), 337-338.

[132] Letter from John Major to David Owen, August 1991, reproduced in Owen, *Balkan Odyssey*, 17-18: 18.

[133] During the war, the number of fatalities in the Bosnian war was often exploited for political reasons, having been arbitrarily set at 200,000 by the Bosnian Muslim leadership. Holbrooke has claimed that between 1991 and 1995, "close to three hundred thousand people were killed in the former Yugoslavia" (xv), whilst quoting U.S. President Clinton in the same book as asserting "two hundred and fifty thousand people killed" in same time period (309). [Holbrooke, *To End a War*] George Kenny, former State Department Yugoslavia officer who resigned in protest to U.S. failure to do more for the Bosnian Muslims, questioned these figures [George Kenney, "How many have died?" *New York Times Magazine*, April 22, 1995]. The first scientific estimate arrived only in November 2005. Investigation and Documentation Center based in Sarayevo and funded by the Noreweigan government, set the toll at close to 100,000 war casualties with 93,000 names verified. About 70 percent are Bosnian Muslims, 25 percent Bosnian Serbs, 5 percent Bosnian Croats and about one percent others. [Nedim Dervisbegovic, "Research Halves Bosnia War Death Toll to 100,000," *Reuters*, November 23, 2005]. ICTY has also concluded that genocide was committed against Bosnian Muslims in Srebrenitsa, a verdict that was later corroborated by the International Court of Justice, which simultaneously cleared the Serbian government of responsibility for committing this crime but not of the responsibility for preventing it: International Court of Justice, *Case concerning the application of the Convention on the Prevention and Punishment of the Crime of Genocide (Bosnia and Herzegovina v. Serbia and Montenegro)*, February 26, 2007.

The international sanctions against Yugoslavia illustrate very clearly how the process of escalating demands on a target country, inherent to the very process of sanctioning, can lead ultimately to overt aggression.[134]

Yet engagement in the form of peacekeeping troops had also created an obstacle to military intervention:

> Countries contributing troops to UNPROFOR in Yugoslavia—particularly France and Britain, both of which had initiated U.N. involvement and lobbied for more humanitarian action—now had an interest in preventing decisive military engagement in the war because they had troops on the ground that would be at risk.[135]

Unlike the politicians in power, David Owen had consistently defended the position that force had to back diplomatic efforts to achieve a settlement:

> I have always believed that successful diplomacy needs muscle behind it, and throughout my tenure as Co-Chairman I was arguing for applying force selectively, sensibly but in support of a specific settlement.[136]

NATO's first engagement in the former Yugoslavia was not a military but a humanitarian action. In an operation titled "Sarajevo airlift," lasting almost two years (July 3, 1992–February 9, 1994), NATO helped deliver humanitarian aid to Bosnia's capital. In 1993, NATO forces were used for another humanitarian action. "Operation Provide Promise" involved delivery of food to enclaves in Eastern Bosnia, Gorazhde, Srebrenitsa, and Zhepa over a one-year period.

An additional NATO engagement was to enforce the naval blockade on the Adriatic together with Western European Union with the aim of tightening the economic sanctions against the FRY, in an action initiated on July 16, 1992. Toward the end of 1992, the U.N. Security Council called on NATO to undertake an operation, "Deny Flight," ensuring the respect of the ban of military flights.[137]

---

[134] Jovan Babic and Aleksandar Jokic, "The Ethics of International Sanctions: The Case of Yugoslavia," *The Fletcher Forum of World Affairs* 24, no. I (Spring 2000), 87-102: 100.

[135] Woodward, *Balkan Tragedy*, 297.

[136] Owen, *Balkan Odyssey*, 284.

[137] U.N. Security Council Resolution 781, October 9, 1992; U.N. Security Council Resolution 786 of November 10, 1992.

A subsequent U.N. Security Council Resolution 816 of March 31, 1993, recalling Chapter VIII of the U.N. Charter and acting under Chapter to VII, "authorizing member states . . . to take, under the authority of the Security Council and subject to close coordination with the Secretary-General and the Force, *all necessary measures* in the airspace of Bosnia and Herzegovina, in the event of further violations" (emphasis added), turned the operation from a peacekeeping to a peace enforcement action. U.N. Security Council Resolution 836 of June 4, 1993 further widened NATO's scope of action "to deter attacks against the safe areas" (paragraph 5), using "the necessary measures, including the use of force" (paragraphs 9 and 10).[138] Importantly, the same resolution also asked NATO "to promote the withdrawal of military and paramilitary units *other than those of the Government of the Republic of Bosnia and Herzegovina*" (emphasis added), reflecting the bias toward the military of the recognized authorities.

NATO had generally restrained itself in using force until February 28, 1994,[139] when it undertook the first military action in its history. Notably, on April 10 and 11, 1994, NATO bombarded the Bosnian Serb army around the protected area of Gorazde and forced its withdrawal from the area.[140] On a much larger scale, in September 1995, NATO intensely bombed the Bosnian Serb positions for 21 days, changing the military balance on the ground:

> NATO had flown 3,400 air sorties. . . . Not only had Serb military rely systems been destroyed, their civilian telephone network had also been incapacitated. Instead of the Serbs having the capacity to redeploy rapidly and reinforce at will, it was the Croatian and Bosnian Muslim forces with indirect access to U.S. satellite intelligence who now had the over-the-horizon capacity and the ability to react quickly.[141]

The NATO bombing allowed the Muslim and Croat forces to gain significant territory, which according to Holbrooke, who brokered the Dayton Peace Agreement,

---

[138] This resolution was based on the U.N. Security Council Resolution 824 of May 6, 1993, which designates certain towns of Bosnia as "safe areas."

[139] Vladimir Bilandžić, "Angažovanje Evropske unije i NATO u rešavanju jugoslovenske krize" [Engagement of the European Union and NATO in resolving the Yugoslav Crisis"], *Medjunarodno pravo i jugoslovenska kriza* [International Law and the Yugoslav Crisis], ed. Milan Šahović (Belgrade: Institute for International Politics and Economy, 1995), 165-207: 197.

[140] Ibid., 200.

[141] Owen, *Balkan Odyssey*, 336.

was not intended[142] but took place "in a manner beneficial to the map."[143] Whether the Muslim-Croat gains could be deemed beneficial is a subjective question,[144] but also one based on an agreement reached a year earlier during negotiations over the Contact Group Plan that Bosnia would be divided according to 51-49 percent of the territory for the Muslim-Croat Federation and Republika Srpska, respectively.

Yet, while the Muslim-Croat gains against the Serbs were perhaps not intended, the bombing, titled "Operation Deliberate Force" did intend to pressure the Bosnian Serbs to comply first with a negotiated cease-fire agreement for Sarayevo and later with a full peace settlement. The goal of the bombing had clearly changed, as the action was initiated for the purpose of punishing the alleged Bosnian Serb shelling of the Sarayevo market on August 28, 1995.[145] In line with the new goal, U.S. President Clinton stressed: "Let me emphasize that if the Bosnian Serbs do not comply with their commitments, the air strikes will resume."[146]

Holbrooke explains how he convinced his government and the other NATO powers that continued bombing was necessary to maintain the credibility of NATO and the international mediation efforts in Bosnia. Addressing the NATO Council at the beginning of the NATO bombing of Bosnian Serb positions in September 1995, Holbrooke stated: "The NATO decision to bomb was necessary, given the provocation. It is now essential to establish that we are negotiating from a position of strength. . . . "[147] When NATO again considered a pause in the bombing, Holbrooke forcefully argued that this would make NATO look like "a paper tiger."[148] Holbrooke further recounts how he pushed for a continuation of the bombing "to allow the Federation offensive to continue" and thus close "the gap

---

[142]   Holbrooke, *To End a War*, 144.

[143]   Ibid, 168.

[144]   Holbrooke does not hide his partiality. He recalls telling the Bosnian Serb leader Radovan Karadzich *"with a certain pleasure*—that the bombing, even though it was not coordinated with the Federation ground troops, had the effect of helping the Muslims and Croats." Holbrooke, *To End a War*, 147-8 [Emphasis mine]. The choice of effectively assisting the non-Serbs in the Bosnian war is also subjective. As argued by Thomas:

[145]   The Serbs were blamed for the attack based on evidence that someone "heard the shell being fired from a Serb position. Later, Russian, British, French, and Canadian investigators cast strong doubt on the certainty of the U.N. report." Zeljan E. Suster, *Historical Dictionary of the Federal Republic of Yugoslavia; European Historical Dictionaries No. 29* (Lanham, MD/London: Scarecrow Press, 1999), lxiii.

[146]   Cited in Holbrooke, *To End a War*, 156.

[147]   Ibid., 119.

[148]   Ibid., 132.

among the three sides," when Anthony Lake, U.S. National Security Advisor, suggested that a peace conference be convened.[149] At the same time, Holbrooke refused to go beyond the 51-49 percentage agreement, which the Bosnian Muslim side favored, willing to sacrifice a negotiated ceasefire for Sarayevo to this end.[150] Holbrooke recalls having told the Bosnian Muslim leader Izetbegovic the following:

> If you want to let the fighting go on, that is your right, but Washington does not want you to expect the United States to be your air force. If you continue the war, you will be shooting craps with your nation's destiny.[151]

A more even treatment of the warring parties is necessary for a lasting peace, according to General Charles G. Boyd, deputy commander in chief of U.S. forces in Europe:

> [U]ntil the U.S. government can come to grips with the essential similarities between Serb, Croat and Muslim and recognize that the fears and aspirations of all are equally important, no effective policy can possibly be drafted that would help produce an enduring peace.[152]

Another lesson that the policy-makers took from the military intervention in Bosnia is that it should take place early in the conflict. According to Warren Zimmerman, the last U.S. Ambassador to Yugoslavia:

> The refusal of the Bush Administration to commit American power early was our greatest mistake of the entire Yugoslav crisis. It made an unjust outcome inevitable and wasted the opportunity to save over a hundred thousand lives.[153]

---

[149]   Ibid., 144.

[150]   Ibid., 155.

[151]   Ibid., 195. David Owen also recounts how the Bosnian Muslims resisted his attempts to enforce a demilitarization of Sarayevo since this "would remove the most powerful weapon in [their] propaganda armoury for involving the U.S." Owen further stresses the importance of public relations in waging modern war, indicating that the Croats and Muslims had engaged a Washington-based PR firm, Ruder Finn Global Public Affairs. Owen, *Balkan Odyssey*, 85.

[152]   Charles Boyd, "Making Peace with the Guilty," *Foreign Affairs* (September/October 1995), 22-38: 34.

[153]   Warren Zimmerman, *Origins of a Catastrophe: Yugoslavia and Its Destroyers* (New York: Times Books, 1996), 22.

Richard Holbrooke agrees with Zimmerman's assessment:

> The best chance to prevent war would have been to present the Yugoslavs with a clear warning that NATO airpower would be used against any party that tried to deal with the ethnic tensions of Yugoslavia by force. The United States and the Europeans could then have worked with the Yugoslav parties to mediate peaceful (although certainly contentious and complicated) divorce agreements between the republics.[154]

This appears to be an oversimplified conclusion as it is not easy to set the criteria for intervening militarily in an intrastate conflict, where all parties use force. Intervention would therefore be based on a political choice. Moreover, history has shown that foreign military interventions often contribute to escalation rather than suppression of violence.

At the same time, I fully endorse the position that the international community should have been more diplomatically engaged in the Yugoslav conflict before the parties become entrenched in their radicalized demands. As one of Bosnia's mediators, Lord David Owen has argued:

> It is in the first few days and weeks of a conflict development that conflict resolution has its greatest chance of success. In July 1991 there was such an opportunity; once missed, it took until 1995 for war exhaustion to become the determining factor.[155]

The controversy of how the conflict should have been resolved at its onset still remains. Analysts such as Hayden claim that an early, internationally mediated partition of Yugoslavia would have resulted in significantly fewer victims and less destruction of property.[156] Owen agrees with this assessment:

> The unwarranted insistence on ruling out changes to what had been internal administrative boundaries within a sovereign state was a fatal flaw in the attempted peacemaking in Yugoslavia.[157]

---

[154] Holbrooke, *To End a War*, 28.

[155] Owen, *Balkan Odyssey*, 342.

[156] "This is not to say that a partition agreed to beforehand would have been bloodless, but rather that the process would almost certainly have cost fewer lives and produced less destruction of property." Hayden, *Blueprints for a House Divided*, 163.

[157] Owen, *Balkan Odyssey*, 342-343.

However, states have generally found this endeavour to be too complicated and too risky in terms of international legal order and global security. Precisely for this reason, eleven out of twelve E.C. members rejected the Dutch proposal to this effect, made on July 13, 1991, less than three weeks after the Slovene and Croat proclamation of independence: "a voluntary redrawing of internal borders." The Dutch officials failed to convince their colleagues that the principle of self-determination had to be applied consistently:

> The principle of self-determination e.g. cannot exclusively apply to the existing republics while being deemed inapplicable to national minorities within those republics.[158]

Instead, the international intervention in Bosnia and Herzegovina, initiated by recognition and escalating into a bombardment of one of the warring parties, ended the war in this former Yugoslav republic with a settlement that produced a *de facto* partition, but further committed the international community to the preservation Bosnia's territorial integrity, in a struggle against the wishes of many of its citizens. As Holbrooke has declared: "The greater the effort we expend to impose a settlement, the greater our responsibility to see the settlement through."[159]

6.6. International Military Intervention in Serbia and Montenegro (1999)

In 1999, this time without a U.N. Security Council endorsement, NATO under-took another military intervention in the former Yugoslavia, targeting military and infrastructure sites in the Federal Republic of Yugoslavia (FRY—Serbia and Montenegro).[160] NATO Member States refused to call their intervention "a war."[161] Cynical realists would argue that this is because the Yugoslav military and police were left almost unscathed. Idealists, on the other hand, would perceive the use of

---

[158] Letter from the Dutch Government to E.C. member states, July 13, 1991, reproduced in David Owen, *Balkan Odyssey* (London: Indigo, 1996), 31-33: 32-33.

[159] Holbrooke, *To End a War*, 82.

[160] Note: NATO did not target solely the province of Kosovo and Metohia but sites throughout FRY (Serbia and Montenegro).

[161] "This was not, strictly speaking, a war." General Wesley K. Clark, "Press Briefing on the Kosovo Strike Assessment," Brussels, NATO Headquarters, September 16, 1999.

ambiguous terms like "action" or "operation" as a path to the creation of a new legal rule supporting "a humanitarian intervention" to stem massive violations of human rights. The following analysis of the so-called Kosovo intervention, militarily termed Operation Allied Force, studies its legality and morality, in order to assess whether it has influenced the application of the right to self-determination and changed its symbiotic relationship with the right to sovereignty, itself encapsulated in the right to territorial integrity.

6.6.1. *Ius ad Bellum*—The Law

Modern international law, based on the Westphalian principles of sovereignty of states, is embodied in the most important source of public international law—the U.N. Charter, which guarantees the territorial integrity of states and the inviolability of their borders.[162] The U.N. Charter permits military interventions in the domestic affairs of other countries exclusively in the case of self-defense, "if an armed attack occurs against a Member of the United Nations" (Article 51) and/or when explicitly authorized by the Security Council, assessing the crisis as a threat to international peace and security (Chapter VII, Article 39[163]). NATO had not satisfied either one of the two requirements, although the Security Council had been actively involved in the Kosovo crisis.

The Security Council adopted three resolutions under the Charter's Chapter VII in the year prior to the NATO bombing campaign. Resolution 1160 of March 31, 1998, called for negotiations; imposed an arms embargo on the FRY, including Kosovo and Metohia; and approved "a substantially greater degree of autonomy and meaningful self-determination" for Serbia's southern province. Subsequently, in Resolution 1199 of September 23, 1998, the Security Council specifically identified the escalated conflict in Kosovo as a threat to peace and security in the

---

[162] Art 2 (4): "All Members shall refrain in their international relations from the threat or use of force against the territorial integrity or political independence of any State, or in any other manner inconsistent with the Purposes of the United Nations."

This Charter provision is additionally supported by the General Assembly Resolution 2131 (XX) of December 21, 1965, "Declaration on the Inadmissibility of Intervention into the Domestic Affairs of States and the Protection of their Independence and Sovereignty," and many other international law documents. For more, *see* Chapter 1: *Legal Context of Yugoslavia's Disintegration: Sovereignty and Self-Determination of Peoples.*

[163] "The Security Council shall determine the existence of any threat to the peace, breach of the peace, or act of aggression and shall make recommendations, or decide what measures shall be taken in accordance with Articles 41 and 42, to maintain or restore international peace and security."

region and endorsed the European Community Monitoring Mission and the Kosovo Diplomatic Observer Mission in Kosovo. In its third resolution on Kosovo in 1998 (resolution 1203, adopted on October 24, 1998), the Security Council reiterated the first two resolutions and permitted the OSCE Kosovo Verification Mission (KVM) and NATO to monitor compliance (on the ground and from the air, respectively) of the agreement concluded by the U.S. Special Envoy Richard Holbrooke and the President of FR Yugoslavia Slobodan Miloshevich on October 12, 1998 (Holbrooke-Miloshevich Agreement).

Finally, Security Council Resolution 1203 "insists that the Kosovo Albanian leadership condemn all terrorist actions, demands that such actions cease immediately and emphasizes that all elements in the Kosovo Albanian community should pursue their goals by peaceful means only" (paragraph 10). Such insistence is in line with the Holbrooke-Miloshevich agreement, which mandated a partial withdrawal of the Serbian military and police forces in return for assurances that the so-called Kosovo Liberation Army (KLA) would cease its insurgency operations.

While the details of the Holbrooke-Miloshevich agreement have not been disclosed, U.S. Secretary of State Madeleine K. Albright publicly stated at the time:

> To support these negotiations, we have also delivered a clear message to the leadership of the KLA: there should be no attempt to take military advantage of the Serb pull-back. Neither side can achieve military victory in Kosovo.[164]

Serbia withdrew its forces according to the agreement[165] and with the end of the fighting most of the internally displaced people returned home.[166] However, the KLA acted against the "clear message" delivered by the U.S. government and took advantage of the Serbian withdrawal to occupy roughly half of Kosovo,[167] causing renewed counterinsurgency actions by the FRY authorities.

---

[164] U.S. Secretary of State Madeleine K. Albright, "Remarks on Kosovo," Washington, DC, October 27, 1998.

[165] Report of the Secretary-General Prepared Pursuant to Resolution 1160 (1998), 1199 (1998) and 1203 (1998) of the Security Council, U.N. Doc. S/1998/1221, December 24, 1998, 3.

[166] Independent International Commission on Kosovo, *The Kosovo Report* (Oxford: Oxford University Press, 2000), 2.

[167] "Kosovo Albanian paramilitary units have taken advantage of the lull on the fighting to re-establish their control over many villages in Kosovo as well as over some areas near urban center and highways. These actions... have only served to provoke the Serbian authorities, leading to statements that if the Kosovo Verification mission cannot control these units the Government would." U.N. Inter-Agency Report, *Update on Humanitarian Situation in Kosovo*, December 24, 1998.

The resolution adopted by the Security Council prior to the Holbrooke-Miloshevich agreement explicitly stated that "should the concrete measures demanded in this resolution and resolution 1160 (1998) not be taken . . . the Security Council [would] consider further action and additional measures" (paragraph 16), indicating the possibility of authorizing the use of force. However, the resolution endorsing the Holbrooke-Miloshevich agreement did not feature the same provision. In conclusion, although the Security Council clearly characterized the situation in Kosovo as threatening to international security and alluded to the possibility of prospectively authorizing the use of force on this basis, it ultimately did not grant such authorization. At the same time, the Security Council had constantly reiterated the U.N. Member States' commitment to Yugoslavia's territorial integrity. Following the bombing, the Security Council did not retroactively legalize the NATO attack but only prospectively authorized foreign states to intervene in the FRY to maintain peace, with Kosovo remaining an integral part of FR Yugoslavia.[168] Two permanent members of the U.N. Security Council, Russia and China, were staunchly opposed to interference in another state, partly due to their domestic considerations.[169] NATO Member States were also troubled by their action's disrespect for the U.N. Charter, inciting the Italian Foreign Minister Dini to state on May 28, 1999, that Italy would be forced to "disassociate" itself from any ground operations undertaken in Kosovo without U.N. approval.[170]

In bypassing U.N. approval for undertaking the bombing campaign, the NATO countries also violated their own North Atlantic Treaty.[171] By bombing a sovereign

---

[168] U.N. Security Council Resolution 1244, June 10, 1999.

[169] *See* Michael J. Glennon, "The New Interventionism: The Search for a Just International Law," *Foreign Affairs*, May/June 1999 and Thomas M. Franck, "The United Nations' Demise has been exaggerated; Break It, Don't Fake It," *Foreign Affairs*, July/August 1999.

[170] Kosovo Situation Reports: May 1999, Library of Congress Kosovo Task Force, CRS Report #RL30156.

[171] North Atlantic Treaty; Entered into force on August 24, 1949 (accessed March 6, 2000); available from http://www.nato.int/docu/basictxt/treaty.htm#FN2. Note: The North Atlantic Treaty pledges its signatories "to refrain in their international relations from the threat or use of force in any manner inconsistent with the purposes of the United Nations" (Article 1), explicitly recognizing "the primary responsibility of the Security Council (of the United Nations) for the maintenance of international peace and security" (Article 7). Furthermore, the NATO Charter specifically requires force to be used only when a member of NATO is attacked (Article 5). Nevertheless, Jamie Shea, the NATO spokesperson during the Kosovo intervention, claimed that NATO had not violated the latter provision because the treaty does not explicitly forbid NATO members to act as an offensive alliance (Jamie Shea, "Nato answers your questions," *BBC News*, April 20, 1999 (accessed November 24, 2004); available from http://nucnews.net/2000/du/99du/990520bb.dunato.htm.

state, NATO members breached other important international laws as well. They violated the Helsinki Accords Final Act of 1975 (Clause IV, Declaration of Principles Guiding Relations Between Participating States), which guarantees the territorial inviolability of European states,[172] and arguably also the Vienna Convention on the Law of Treaties, forbidding the use of coercion and force to compel any state to sign a treaty or agreement (Articles 51 and 52).[173] By participating in NATO's bombing of FRY, the United States government appears to have also circumvented its domestic law.[174]

Finally, the Kosovo intervention is not legally justifiable by the vague corpus of "international humanitarian law." Notably, NATO could not purport to have been stopping genocide. The act of genocide, as defined by the 1948 Convention on the Prevention and Punishment of the Crime of Genocide,[175] did not occur in Kosovo

---

[172] Conference on Security and Co-Operation in Europe, Final Act, Helsinki, August 1, 1975 (accessed September 5, 2005); available from Internet at http://www.hri.org/docs/Helsinki75.html

[173] The Vienna Convention on the Law of Treaties, adopted on May 22, 1969, and entered into force on January 27, 1980. Published as Treaty Series No.058 (1980): Cmnd 7964 / United Nations, *Treaty Series*, vol. 1155, 331 (accessed August 9, 2005); available from http://www.un.org/law/ilc/texts/treaties.htm.

[174] The Clinton administration did not comply with the War Powers Act of 1973, which stipulates that the President submits a report to the Congress within 48 hours of U.S. military involvement abroad, and that the President terminate such involvement within 60 days upon the submission of the report unless (a) the Congress declares war or enacts specific authorization for such use of U.S. Armed Forces, (b) extends by law such sixty-day period, or (3) is physically unable to meet as a result of an armed attack upon the United States [Public Law 93-148, 50 U.S.C. 1541-1548]. The U.S. legislature has questioned the Clinton administration regarding this probable breach of American law and the U.S. Constitution, as the War Powers Act is based on Article I, Section 8, of the U.S. Constitution, which states that Congress, not the president, holds the power to declare war and to punish offenses against the "law of nations." The Congress' attempt to cut funds for the Kosovo operation sent a strong signal of dissatisfaction with the administration's policy [Note: On April 28, 1999, the House failed to approve a resolution supporting NATO air strikes on Yugoslavia, with the vote tied at 213-213. Yet, on March 23, 1999, one day before the bombing, the United States Senate approved a resolution supporting NATO military operations by a vote of 58 to 41]. Nevertheless, the House Committee on International Relations did not approve the resolution (H. Con. Res. 82) directing the President, pursuant to section 5(c) of the War Powers Resolution, to remove United States Armed Forces from their positions in connection with the operations against the Federal Republic of Yugoslavia [House Of Representatives, 106th congress, 1st Session, 106-116, Adverse Report, submitted by Mr. Gilman, from the Committee on International Relations, to accompany H. Con. Res. 82: Directing the President, pursuant to Section 5(C) of the War Powers Resolution, to remove United States Armed Forces from their Positions in Connection with the Present Operations against the Federal Republic of Yugoslavia, April 27, 1999 (accessed April 7, 2000); available from http://thomas.loc.gov/cgi-bin/cpquery/T?&report=hr116&dbname=cp106&.

[175] "In the present Convention, genocide means any of the following acts committed with intent to destroy, in whole or in part, a national, ethnical, racial or religious group, as such:

(a)   Killing members of the group;

(b)   Causing serious bodily or mental harm to members of the group;

prior to or during the NATO bombing campaign. Moreover, only the U.N. Security Council could invoke this Convention as a basis for the use of force.

On April 29, 1999, Yugoslavia filed an Application instituting proceedings against ten NATO member states. On the same day, it submitted a request for the indication of provisional measures, asking the Court to order NATO members to "cease immediately its acts of use of force" and to "refrain from any act of threat or use of force" against the FRY. Delivering its decision by twelve votes to four on June 2, 1999, the International Court of Justice did not grant Yugoslavia's plea for a halt to the bombing, claiming lack of jurisdiction.[176] However, the Court hinted that NATO's use of force was illegal, declaring itself "profoundly concerned with the use of force in Yugoslavia," which "under the present circumstances . . . raises very serious issues of international law."[177] Most jurists concur with this conclusion; Pomerance vividly describes any legal justifications for NATO's bombing of FRY as "a Polo mint—a circular confection of 'connections' around a hole where the law should be."[178]

(c)   Deliberately inflicting on the group conditions of life calculated to bring about its physical destruction in whole or in part;

(d)   Imposing measures intended to prevent births within the group;

(e)   Forcibly transferring children of the group to another group."

Article 2, Convention on the Prevention and Punishment of the Crime of Genocide, approved and proposed for signature and ratification or accession by General Assembly resolution 260 A (III) of December 9, 1948 and entered into force on January 12, 1951, in accordance with article XIII (accessed April 7, 2000); available from http://www.unhchr.ch/html/menu3/b/p_genoci.htm.

[176]   The court found that it did not have jurisdiction on the basis of the declarations by which the states accepted the compulsory jurisdiction of the Court (Article 36, paragraph 2 of the ICJ Statute) because the FRY limited its consent to "disputes arising or which may arise after the signature of the present Declaration" on April 25, 1999, while the NATO intervention started prior to this date, on March 24, 1999. Secondly, Article IX of the Convention on the Prevention and Punishment of the Crime of Genocide, which provides that disputes between the contracting parties relating to the interpretation, application or fulfillment of the Convention shall be submitted to the International Court of Justice, while deemed applicable to all states, could not constitute the basis for the proceedings because the threat or use of force against a state cannot in itself constitute an act of genocide within the meaning of Article II of the Genocide Convention, which defines genocide as the intended destruction of a national, ethnical, racial or religious group as such. It did not appear to the Court at the present stage of the proceedings that the NATO bombings "entail[ed] the element of intent, towards a group as such, required by the relevant provisions of the Genocide Convention."

[177]   On December 15, 2004, the International Court of Justice dismissed the cases as injusticiable.

[178]   Patrick Thornberry, "'Come, friendly bombs . . . ': International Law in Kosovo," *Kosovo: The Politics of Delusion*, eds. Michael Waller, Kyril Drezov and Bülent Gökay (London, Portland OR: Frank Cass, 2001), 48.

6.6.2. *Ius ad Bellum*—The Morality

6.6.2a. *Exhaustion of Diplomatic Remedies*

Although the Serbian province of Kosovo and Metohia had been a volatile area for almost two decades, the international community paid it little attention. The Rugova-led Albanian peaceful resistance[179] was not used as a means to prevent a violent conflict and reach a settlement. The international community generally disregarded the non-governmental organizations and research institutes, which pleaded for preventive diplomacy.[180] The Clinton administration slighted the attempts by the Serbian opposition to change the regime and peacefully resolve the conflict in Kosovo and Metohia, including a proposal presented by Bishop Artemije, the Serbian Orthodox prelate of Kosovo, to the U.S. Secretary of State Madeleine Albright "that would have strengthened moderate forces on both sides, begun genuine negotiations . . . and weakened Milosevic."[181] Significantly, it was not until the onset of a more violent conflict, instigated by the KLA, a terrorist insurgency group[182] that the international community started dealing seriously with Kosovo.

The Rambouillet Conference in France was a start of these negotiations. However, the talks provided "a textbook example of how not to practice diplomacy."[183] Their goal was not framed as a compromise, but as a dictate, offering carrots to the Kosovo Albanians (possible independence for Kosovo in three years; no threat of military action) and sticks to the Yugoslav government (bombing). The Yugoslav

---

[179]   *See* pages 235–6 of this book.

[180]   *See*, for instance, Thanos Veremis and Evangelos Kofos, *Kosovo; Avoiding Another Balkan War* (Athens: Hellenic Foundation for European and Foreign Policy, 1998). This book, a set of policy papers, is a result of a three-year research of "non-violent ways that would prevent conflict and would facilitate a solution in Kosovo."

[181]   James George Jatras, "NATO's Myths and Bogus Justifications for Intervention," *NATO's Empty Victory; A Postmortem on the Balkan War*, ed. Ted Galen Carpenter (Washington, D.C.: CATO Institute, 2000), 21-29: 26.

[182]   United States Senate Republican Policy Committee, "The Kosovo Liberation Army: Does Clinton Policy Support Group with Terror, Drug Ties? From 'Terrorists' to 'Partners,'" March 31, 1999 (accessed March 7, 2000); available from http://www.senate.gov/~rpc/releases/1999/fr033199.htm. *See* also "KLA Finances Fight with Heroin Sales; Terror Group is Linked to Crime Network," *Washington Times*, May 3, 1999, A1; "KLA Rebels Train in Terrorist Camps; Bin Laden Offers Financing, Too," *Washington Times*, May 4, 1999, A1.

[183]   Christopher Layne, "Miscalculations and Blunders Lead to War," *NATO's Empty Victory; A Postmortem on the Balkan War*, ed. Ted Galen Carpenter (Washington, D.C.: CATO Institute, 2000), 11-20: 15.

government found the Rambouillet agreement's provision for possible independence impossible to accept even after the NATO bombing and it was excluded from the agreement leading to the U.N. administration of the province as of June 10, 1999. The FRY representatives had also rejected Appendix B of the Rambouillet agreement, entitled "Status of Multi-National Military Implementation Force." This appendix provided the NATO personnel with immunity, with "cost-free use of all Yugoslav airports, ports, roads, rails, and streets"—and, most importantly—with "free and unrestricted passage and unimpeded access throughout the FRY, including associated airspace and territorial waters."[184]

The military annex (Appendix B) was given to the parties on the last day of the conference. When the U.S. negotiator, Christopher Hill, told the press that there had been a "very full discussion of the military aspects," Boris Mayorski, the Russian representative, retorted that "there was no official presentation of any military annexes to the delegations [up to that point]" and that Russians did not take part in any discussions on military aspects of the agreement.[185] Hill later stated that he believed that Miloshevich was open to a political deal but feared that "the true intention of the force was to eliminate him—and/or detach Kosovo from Serbia."[186] This is corroborated by the *New York Times* reporting after the first of the two rounds of Rambouillet negotiations that "Mr. Milosevic has shown himself at least as reasonable as the ethnic Albanians about a political settlement for Kosovo," and further noting how the chief Serbian negotiator and president of Serbia, Milan Milutinovich, stated that Serbs are ready to discuss "an international presence in Kosovo" to implement the agreement when negotiations resume on March 15, 1999.[187] Finally, Ratko Markovich, one of the key members of the Serb negotiating team at Rambouillet, erstwhile Constitutional Judge, and one of the authors of the 1990 Serbian Constitution, has averred to the author that the "Serbian side was politically ready for compromise" and that most issues had been resolved when the U.S. mediators introduced the military annex the night before the final day of scheduled negotiations. Markovich further comments how "the Serb negotiating team felt to have been treated with disdain at Rambouillet, being given almost non-negotiable and legally incoherent texts and having as

---

184   Interim Agreement for Peace and Self-Government in Kosovo—Rambouillet Agreement, February 23, 1999 (accessed March 6, 2000); available from http://jurist.law.pitt.edu/ramb.htm.

185   Press Briefing by the Contact Group negotiators, February 18, 1999.

186   Cited in Tim Judah, *Kosovo; War and Revenge* (New Haven and London: Yale University Press, 2000), 220.

187   Steven Erlanger, "Serb View: A Victory," *New York Times*, February 24, 1999, A10.

interlocutors junior legal experts like [James C.] O'Brien and [Jonathan] Levitsky from the U.S. State Department, while the chief mediator Christopher Hill fell asleep twice during the meetings."[188]

Considering further that the Miloshevich regime eventually accepted an agreement allowing a *de facto* Kosovo and Metohia autonomy but reaffirming the territorial integrity of Yugoslavia, while restricting NATO-led peacekeeping force to the province of Kosovo and designating the U.N. as the primary administrative authority, one could argue that the bombing of and the subsequent crimes against Albanians and then Serbs and other minorities could have been avoided by granting the same provisions to the FRY government at Rambouillet. Although one could also argue that negotiations could theoretically have been conducted *ad infinitum*, it is clear that this non-violent manner of conflict resolution had been exhausted in the case of Kosovo and Metohia, where there was but one serious attempt to arrive at a political solution to the problem.

The KLA also initially refused to sign the Rambouillet agreement, demanding a clear statement that independence would be granted in three years. Nevertheless, they accepted the agreement under strong pressure by the U.S. government reminding them that their signature would lead to air strikes against the Serbs.[189] Such U.S. policy led many analysts to conclude that the 1999 bombing of the FR Yugoslavia took place to affirm NATO's credibility and grant a new mission to a Cold War organization.[190] Joseph S. Nye, Jr., former dean of Harvard University's Kennedy School of Government, has argued that NATO should have taken advantage of the initial refusal by the Albanian representatives to sign the Rambouillet agreement to step back.[191] It is not easy to explain why NATO had not done that, while it is equally difficult to believe that NATO members, namely the U.S. government, maliciously desired to bomb Yugoslavia, pressuring the KLA to accept

---

[188] Author's Interview with Dr Ratko Markovic, Professor of Constitutional Law at the University of Belgrade and one of key authors of the 1990 Serbian Constitution, Zlatibor, Serbia, July 24, 2005.

[189] Jane Perlez, "Kosovo Albanians, in Reversal, Say They Will Sign Peace Pact," *New York Times*, February 24, 1999, A1.

[190] Diana Johnstone, for instance, argues that "Nato's problem was to find a new *raison d'être* in the absence of the 'Soviet threat.' " Diana Johnstone, "Nato and the New World Order: Ideals and Self-Interest," *Degraded Capability; The Media and the Kosovo Crisis*, ed. Philip Hammond and Edward S. Herman (London, Sterling, VA: Pluto Press, 2000), 7-18:8. *See* also Craig R. Whitney, "In New Talks on Kosovo, NATO's Credibility Is at Stake," *New York Times*, March 14, 1999, A14.

[191] Cited in "The Joyless Victory," *The Wilson Quarterly* 23, No. 4 (Autumn 1999).

the agreement in order to provide them with the pretext.[192] Whatever the true reason for the initiation of the bombing campaign, it is undisputable that NATO's credibility represented a major concern for the policymakers. U.S. President William Clinton had stated on the eve of the campaign that the Alliance's failure to act "would discredit NATO,"[193] while the United Kingdom Prime Minister Tony Blair insisted: "On its 50th birthday NATO must prevail."[194]

6.6.2b. *Ius in Bello as Casus Belli—*

The Yugoslav Army and the KLA Prior to NATO Bombing

Prior to NATO's attack, in the two years of fighting between the Yugoslav forces and the KLA in Kosovo and Metohia, around 2,000 fatalities were recorded on both sides. One alleged massacre of Kosovo Albanians in the town of Rachak (Racak) was reported, but not corroborated by international forensic experts.[195]

---

[192] A high-level U.S. official reportedly told journalists at Rambouillet "We intentionally set the bar too high for the Serbs to comply. They need some bombing, and that's what they are going to get." James George Jatras, "NATO's Myths and Bogus Justifications for Intervention," *NATO's Empty Victory; A Postmortem on the Balkan War*, ed. Ted Galen Carpenter (Washington, D.C.: CATO Institute, 2000), 21-29: 24.

Former Assistant Secretary of State James Rubin has also publicly claimed: "Our internal goal was not to get a peace agreement at Rambouillet. . . . [Rambouillet] was never intended to be another Dayton." *See* Assistant Secretary of State James Rubin Interview on the Charlie Rose show, aired on April 18, 2000, transcript #2663. Note: Some analysts have also claimed that the true intention of NATO's attack on the FRY was to divert attention from the Monica Lewinski scandal and the attempted impeachment of U.S. President Clinton.

[193] "Remarks by the President [William Jefferson Clinton] to AFSCME Biennial Convention," White House, Office of the Press Secretary, March 23, 1999, 7.

[194] Anthony Blair, "Doctrine of the International Community," Speech to the Economic Club, Chicago, April 22, 1999.

[195] The Rachak massacre allegedly took place on January 15, 1999. That day the Serbian press center reported on police fighting the KLA terrorists in Rachak, allowing the Associated Press to film the course of the fighting and a French journalist to visit the site later in the afternoon. The following morning, more than fifteen hours after the fighting occurred, the U.S. Ambassador, William Walker, arrived with foreign journalists who immediately reported forty-five Albanians shot or mutilated. The KLA and the Kosovo Verification Mission (KVM) both forbade the Serbian forensic team to investigate the site. Five days later, the French press [Christophe Chatelot, "Were the dead in Racak really massacred in cold blood?" *Le Monde*, January 21, 1999] and television featured available evidence, which suggested that the Rachak "massacre" was a set-up, mounted by the KLA during the night. The *Los Angeles Times* reported on this story on January 23, 1999 [Paul Watson, "Cloud of Controversy Obscures Truth About Kosovo Killings," *Los Angeles Times*, January 23, 1999, 4]. International forensic experts could not conclude that Rachak was a massacre, witnessing extensive tampering with evidence. Helena Ranta, Finnish forensic expert and head of the international team investigating allegations over the Rachak massacre asserted that the team found several Serb victims in addition to Albanian victims on the site and complained that ICTY had not

Media generally paid scant attention to the investigation of the massacre's authenticity or to alleged KLA war crimes against Serbs in Klechka (ten people, including two children and three women) and Glodiane (at least twelve people) and the shooting of fourteen Serbian teenagers in downtown Pech, all taking place before the bombing.[196]

Yet even if the Rachak event was a massacre and if one were to disregard the Albanian war crimes against Serbs, the figure of 2,000 dead in total, especially when compared to other ethnic struggles around the globe incurring a significantly higher death toll and humanitarian crises such as those in Sierra Leone and Sri Lanka, does not appear to constitute "massive ethnic cleansing" warranting international intervention. While each human life is invaluable, the fighting in Kosovo did not present a case when the violations of *ius in bello* are so grave to justify external use of force.

In addition, one must reiterate that the KLA had been recognized as a terrorist organization by the United States officials[197] and by most of the international community, fully aware that KLA funding is derived from drug trade, human trafficking, and other illegal commerce. The U.S. intelligence community had warned the Clinton administration that the KLA acted deliberately to provoke harsh Serbian reprisals in an attempt to draw the United States and NATO into the conflict.[198] The Hague War Crimes Tribunal has indicted several Kosovo Albanians, including the first Kosovo "prime minister" Ramush Haradinaj for participating in "joint criminal enterprise" and committing crimes against humanity and war crimes in 1998.[199]

A final factor to be examined is the so-called "horseshoe plan" of premeditated ethnic cleansing allegedly prepared by the Yugoslav government. In mid-April

---

sufficiently investigated the evidence pointing to armed conflict occurring the night before the discovery of dead bodies in Rachak (*Berliner Zeitung*, January 18, 2004).

[196] The European, and especially Italian press, gave these events more notice. For more, *see* Vojin Joksimovich, *Kosovo Crisis: A Study in Foreign Policy Mismanagement* (Los Angeles: Graphics Management Press, 1999), 155, 162.

[197] Robert Gelbard, "We condemn very strongly terrorist actions in Kosovo. The UCK (KLA) is, without any question, a terrorist group." Cited in *Agence France-Presse*, February 23, 1998.

[198] Bartom Gellman, "How We Went to War," *Washington Post*, national weekly edition, April 26, 1999, 6-9. See also R. Jeffrey Smith and William Drozdiak, "A Blueprint for War: The Serbs' Military Campaign Was Meticulously Planned Months Ago," *Washington Post*, national weekly edition, April 19, 1999, A6.

[199] The International Criminal Tribunal for the Former Yugoslavia, Case No: IT-04-84-I, The Prosecutor of the Tribunal against Ramush Haradinaj, Idriz Balaj, Lahi Brahimaj, First Indictment, March 4, 2005.

1999, the German government revealed this information as a justification for the bombing, and NATO supported the claim.[200] The allegation has since been widely questioned. For instance, Jan Oberg from the Swedish Transnational Foundation for Freedom doubts the veracity of NATO's "horseshoe" claim based on the following line of argument:

(1) nobody had advanced this allegation before the bombs started falling,
(2) the bombing was directly related to Yugoslavia's refusal to sign the Rambouillet diktat,
(3) why would a regime known to be planning to ethnically cleanse the Albanians be invited to a peace conference?,
(4) perhaps worst of all—if the ethnic cleansing plan was known in advance, was it not immoral to prepare for the ensuing humanitarian emergency of hundreds of thousands of refugees?,
(5) If Milosevic planned to expel the Albanians, why would he allow Dr. Rugova and his followers to hold elections, set up a government, travel unrestrictedly in and out of the country, and to build parallel institutions?
(6) how is it that neither the OSCE mission nor the many humanitarian organizations heard of such a massive action, and
(7) if NATO planners and intelligence services knew of such a plan, why was the air campaign not more effectively planned and coordinated?"[201]

The primary NATO evidence for the "horseshoe operation" is the Yugoslav army build-up at the boundary between Central Serbia and the province of Kosovo and Metohia. Yet, the Yugoslav forces also gathered on the border with Macedonia, all in a very logical response to a NATO build-up led by 12,000 British, French, and German troops, which was reported in the international media.[202] Several days before the bombing, the U.S. National Public Radio assured its listeners that NATO was committed to implementing its threat and that planes were gathering in Aviano, Italy. The Yugoslav military strategists were certainly aware of it.

---

[200]   Javier Solana, "NATO's Success in Kosovo," *Foreign Affairs* 78, no. 6 (November-December 1999).
[201]   Jan Oberg, "The West is in Moral Trouble if there is an Ethnic Cleansing Plan—and if There isn't," *TFF Pressinfo*, April 27, 1999.
[202]   *Agence France-Presse*, March 13, 1999.

The Independent International Commission on Kosovo arrived at a similar assessment:

> The composition and placement of the Yugoslav army task force in Kosovo clearly suggests that it used the early months of 1999 to build up a territorial defense capacity in Kosovo sufficient to deter the threat of a NATO ground invasion.[203]

One year after the bombing, the retired German General Heinz Loquai, who represented Germany at the OSCE during the Kosovo operation, asserted that Operation Horseshoe "was fabricated by the German Defense Ministry."[204] Loquai's declaration initiated yet another European parliamentary inquiry into the honesty of NATO governments' statements related to the bombing.

At the same time, a vast majority (68 percent) of Kosovo Albanian refugees interviewed by Physicians for Human Rights reported that they left their homes because they were forcibly expelled by Yugoslav regular or paramilitary forces.[205] Patrick Ball, from the American Association for the Advancement on Science, on the basis of these refugee interviews and statistical patters of the exodus, deduced that "Only a small fraction of Kosovo Albanians fled Kosovo as a direct result of NATO bombing raids" and that:

> Mass migration on this scale and in this pattern could only have been driven by a centralized policy, not by individual decisions or

---

203 Independent International Commission on Kosovo, *The Kosovo Report* (Oxford: Oxford University Press, 2000), 87.

204 Cited in T. Haymes, "Germany Looking for an Out," *ABCNEWS.com*, May 3, 2000. *See* Heinz Loquai, *Der Kosovo-Konflikt; Wege in einen vermeidbaren Krieg* [The Kosovo Conflict: A War that Could Be Avoided] (Durchschnittliche Kundenwertung, 2000). Note: In his book, Loquai reports on the decision of the German higher court in Münster, adjudicating the plea of a Kosovo Albanian asylum seeker, which concluded on March 11, 1999: "Ethnic Albanians in Kosovo have neither been nor are now exposed to regional or countrywide group persecution in the Federal Republic of Yugoslavia" [Case Az: 13A 3894/94.A; court decisions also reproduced in German daily *Junge Welt*, April 24, 1999). Similarly, on March 17, 1999, a week before the bombing, the OSCE report on Kosovo asserted that the "humanitarian situation is hard, but under control. For now there is no so called humanitarian catastrophe, nor is it expected."

205 *War Crimes in Kosovo: a Population-Based Assessment of Human Rights Violations against Kosovar Albanians* (Boston/Washington, DC: Physicians for Human Rights and Program on Forced Migration and Health, Center for Population and Family Health, The Joseph L. Mailman School of Public Health, Columbia University, August 1999), 42.

emotions of either Kosovar Albanians or local Yugoslav military or police officials.[206]

In conclusion, while the exodus of Kosovo Albanians may not have been premeditated, it appears to have been systematically executed after the onslaught of the NATO bombing campaign.

6.6.2c Ius in Bello as Casus Belli—

Yugoslav forces and the KLA during the NATO bombing

At the onset of the NATO bombing of FR Yugoslavia, the conflict escalated in Kosovo. As the KLA continued its attacks on Yugoslav police and civilians, the Yugoslav forces undertook an intensified counterinsurgency operation, also targeting indiscriminately. Without any international observers on the ground, who deserted the area prior to the bombing campaign, and a chaotic situation created by the bombing, the extremist elements thrived, leading to the killings of thousands of people, including numerous civilians, the majority of whom were ethnic Albanians.[207]

While any loss of human life is tragic, the authority of NATO and the legitimacy of its intervention in FRY were undermined by exaggerated allegations of the death toll during the bombing: "500,000 ethnic Albanians missing and feared

---

[206] Patrick Ball, *Policy or Panic? The Flight of Ethnic Albanians from Kosovo, March-May 1999* (New York: American Association for the Advancement of Science, 2000), 31.

[207] The number of murdered Albanians and other ethnicities from Kosovo in Spring 1999 still has not been determined. A total of 5,882 bodies of all ethnicities but predominantly Albanian have been found in Kosovo, but this does not include all possible gravesites. Additional 798 bodies (mainly of Kosovo Albanians) were discovered in Serbia proper in 2001 and 2002, bringing the total to 6,680. An unofficial ICTY estimate today stands at "around 7,500 victims of all nationalities but mainly of Albanian origin" (Author's interview with ICTY official, November 28, 2005). It is difficult to assess the number with certainty because, as stressed by Spanish pathologist Emilio Perez Pujol, the final figure of dead would include "a lot of strange deaths that cannot be blamed on anyone in particular." [J. Lucier and K. O' Meara "Tribunal Can't Substantiate Kosovo Genocide Charges," *Insight on the News*, December 6, 1999, 15.45]. In addition, forensic experts identified many fatalities to be a result of armed conflict rather than war crimes. ICTY indicted Miloshevich for ordering the deaths of "hundreds of Albanian civilians" [The International Criminal Tribunal For The Former Yugoslavia, Case No. IT-99-37-PT, The Prosecutor of the Tribunal against Slobodan Milosevic, Milan Milutinovic, Nikola Sainovic, Dragoljub Ojdanic,Vlajko Stojiljkovic; Second Amended Indictment, October 29, 2001].

dead in Kosovo."[208] Furthermore, although the Clinton administration lowered its estimates with time, it continued to purport the existence of genocide,[209] despite the fact that the internal estimates did not corroborate this assertion.[210] Immediately after the bombing ceased, the estimate was reduced to 10,000.[211] Allegations of genocide have undermined the notion of this heinous crime and reduced the importance of recognizing the wrongfulness and tragedy of crimes that are lower in numbers. They have also sown distrust with the general public, which will be even harder to convince of the legitimacy of alleged humanitarian interventions, and generally of the legitimacy of the intervening governments' motives. This was indeed the case with the intervention in Iraq in 2003, when the media and the public were more suspicious of motives and when a serious investigation ensued, producing a great scandal in the United Kingdom.

Finally, one must remember that NATO changed the purported goals of the military intervention one week into the bombing. The original goal was to force the Miloshevich regime to sign the Rambouillet agreement. The U.S. administration publicly portrayed the Serbian authorities and specifically Slobodan Miloshevich as the party that had instigated the violent conflict in Kosovo and Metohia. In an address to the U.S. Institute for Peace, delivered three weeks before the initiation

---

[208] Cited in Charles A. Radin and Louise D. Palmer, "Number of missing Kosovars is challenged," *The Boston Globe*, April 21, 1999. Furthermore, Department spokesperson James Rubin, among others, had claimed that some 100,000 Albanian men had been herded into the Prishtina sports stadium was proven to be unsubstantiated when a reporter actually went to the stadium and found it empty. [*See* James George Jatras, "NATO's Myths and Bogus Justifications for Intervention," *NATO's Empty Victory; A Postmortem on the Balkan War*, ed. Ted Galen Carpenter (Washington, D.C.: CATO Institute, 2000), 21-29: 25.]

[209] At the end of April, Secretary of Defense William Cohen asserted that Serbs were "perpetrating genocide, killing as many as 100,000 Albanians." CBS, May 16, 1999. *New York Times*, November 11, 1999. Note: Many Jews, including the late Nobel laureate Elie Wiesel, found the frequent comparisons of events in Kosovo to genocide and the Holocaust offensive. *See Newsweek*, April 12, 1999.

[210] On November 5, 1999, the *Wall Street Journal* reported in a paragraph on its front page that an unnamed American in the region had confirmed the estimate of 2,500 killed, calling the earlier figures "a disinformation campaign." Corroborating this story, Reed Irvine, Chairman of Accuracy in Media, stated that he "found a source at the State Department who admitted that their best estimate actually was only 5,000" during the bombing [Reed Irvine, "Was Serbian 'Genocide' in Kosovo Just Propaganda to Start an Air War?" *Insight on the News*, December 6, 1999, 15.45]. The British press criticized its government more openly, accusing the Blair administration of misleading the public about the scale of deaths among Kosovo civilians to justify the NATO bombing of Yugoslavia [*London Sunday Times*, October 31, 1999].

[211] Associated Press, June 18, 1999; *New York Times*, June 18, 1999. David Binder, "Balkan balance sheet doesn't add up," MSNBC (US), July 29, 1999; Independent International Commission on Kosovo, *The Kosovo Report* (Oxford: Oxford University Press, 2000), 2. *See* footnote 207.

of the war against Yugoslavia, U.S. Secretary of State Madeleine Albright thus recounted a distorted version of the events leading to violence in 1998:

> [A]bout one year ago, President Milosevic upped the ante by launching a brutal crackdown. Police and military forces were sent in to terrorize civilians, killing hundreds and driving hundreds of thousands from their homes. Under these conditions, many Kosovars abandoned non-violence and their support to the Kosovo Liberation Army, although its tactics too were sometimes brutal and indiscriminate.[212]

Reversing the sequence of events, Secretary Albright explained how the KLA reacted to Miloshevich rather than Miloshevich taking counterinsurgency measures, which is what actually occurred and could be verified simply by following the chronology of events compiled, among others, by the *New York Times*. If one looks even deeper into the archives of the same newspaper, one is reminded of the irony that Miloshevich was brought to power by the oppressive character of the local Albanian rule.[213]

In his address regarding the bombing of Yugoslavia on March 24, 1999, U.S. President Clinton also erroneously claimed that the Serbian authorities had "stripped Kosovo of the constitutional autonomy its people enjoyed, thus denying them the right to speak their language, run their schools, shape their daily lives." Yet, the amended Serbian Constitution had continued to guarantee the Albanian ethnic minority in Serbia the rights to education, culture, freedom of religion, and public expression (Articles 32, 41, 45). Albanians had the right to express their ethnic identity, use their language and script, and be educated in their native language in the areas in which they live (Article 49); they had the right to preserve, develop, and express their ethnic, cultural, linguistic, and other specific attributes (Articles 10, 11). They also, like all citizens, had the right to organize politically and have political parties, which they did.[214]

---

212 Madeleine Albright, *Remarks at the U.S. Institute for Peace*, February 4, 1999.

213 Marvin Howe, "Exodus of Serbs Stirs Province of Yugoslavia," *New York Times*, July 12, 1982, pointing out that 57,000 Serbs had left the region during the previous decade; David Binder, "In Yugoslavia, Rising Ethnic Strife Brings Fears of Worse Civil Conflict," *New York Times*, November 1, 1987, 14.

214 An ethnic Albanian party, "Democratic League of Kosovo/a," was established in 1989, when the multiparty system was instituted in Yugoslavia.

U.S. President Clinton further postulated that the NATO military intervention was directed against "a vicious campaign of ethnic cleansing,"[215] which, as explained above, did not take place prior to NATO's decision to launch airstrikes. Even the U.S. State Department report stresses that the violence had "dramatically escalated" in Kosovo and Metohia "*since* the withdrawal of the KVM [Kosovo Verification Mission] on March 19, 1999."[216] Moreover, the U.S. government was aware that a NATO military action could aggravate the crisis:

> For weeks before the NATO air campaign against Yugoslavia . . . CIA Director George J. Tenet had been forecasting that Serb-led Yugoslav forces might respond by accelerating their campaign of ethnic cleansing in the province of Kosovo—precisely the outcome that has unfolded over the past week.[217]

Journalists had warned of this danger before the onset of the NATO campaign:

> International peace monitors began an exodus from Yugoslavia on Friday, raising Kosovo Albanian fears of a blood bath if NATO bombs start falling and Serbs seek revenge. . . .
> Without the monitors around, ethnic Albanians said, they are all the more scared that Serbs will retaliate against them if NATO delivers on its threat to strike military targets in Yugoslavia.[218]

Ethnic cleansing did occur during the seventy-eight days of NATO bombing, and even though it did not take place on the massive scale propagated by NATO governments and most Western press, it caused a grave human tragedy that continued after the airstrikes ended, now directed at the non-Albanian population of Kosovo and Metohia. However, the act of ethnic cleansing, no matter what the scale, cannot retroactively justify NATO's bombing of Yugoslavia, since we do not

---

215   William Jefferson Clinton, "A Just and Necessary War," *New York Times*, May 23, 1999, WK 17.

216   U.S. Department of State, "Erasing History: Ethnic Cleansing in Kosovo," May 10, 1999 (accessed March 10, 2000); available from http://www.state.gov/www/regions/eur/rpt_9905_ethnic_ksvo_toc.html [emphasis mine]. Department of State Press Releases describe violence as limited and focused on the suppression of the insurrectionist KLA prior to NATO bombing. *See* U.S. Department of State, Kosovo Update (March 2, 1999) (accessed March 11, 2000); available from http://www.state.gov/www/regions/eur/rpt_790312 kdom.html; U.S. Department of State, Kosovo Humanitarian Situation Report, March 31, 1999.

217   *Washington Post*, April 1, 1999.

218   Paul Watson, "Monitors' Exit from Kosovo Brings Fears of Blood Bath," *Los Angeles Times*, March 20, 1999, 9.

know whether it would have occurred if the bombing had not started. Available evidence points to the opposite conclusion. Finally, the fact that NATO could not stop ethnic cleansing against the non-Albanians following the airstrikes further undermines the legitimacy of its intervention.

Several days into the bombing campaign, when it became evident that Milosevic would not budge and sign on to the Rambouillet Agreement, the fleeing Kosovo Albanians provided a new, now critical argument for the intervention, allowing Albright to claim "We are fighting to get the refugees home, safe under our protection."[219] NATO now purported to be bombing Yugoslavia to get the Kosovo refugees home—the refugees who started fleeing Kosovo in significant numbers two days after the bombing started, chased out by the Yugoslav army and NATO bombs.[220] According to a senior NATO official: "Following the fiasco of lightning strikes, the refugees provided [NATO] with a new objective for the war. That was crucial."[221]

More specifically, in the FR Yugoslavia NATO singled out the Kosovo Albanian refugees. Almost 550,000 Serbian refugees from Croatia and Bosnia residing in Serbia[222] and over 200,000 internally displaced Serbs and other non-Albanians fleeing Kosovo in the wake of NATO bombing and later Albanian ethnic cleansing[223] apparently did not merit the same protection. Yet even NATO's alleged protection of Albanian refugees is compromised by the way they led the campaign and by the fact that the bombing appears to have provoked the fierce

---

[219] Madeleine Albright and Robin Cook, "Our Campaign Is Working," *Washington Post*, May 16, 1999, B7; *See* also "Where's Any Sign of Outrage?" *The Washington Times*, April 7, 1999, A16.

[220] *See Washington Times*, March 31, 1999; Steven Erlanger, "Fleeing Kosovars Dread Danger or NATO Above and Serb Below," *New York Times*, May 4, 1999, A1. Although one tends to refer to "refugees," many Kosovo Albanians were in fact internally displaced, taking refuge in Serbia proper and Montenegro rather than outside the country, indicating that they were not all forcibly expelled.

[221] Cited in Vincent Jauvert in *Le Nouvel Observateur*, July 1, 1999.

[222] UNHCR and the Serbian Commission for Refugees registered 537,939 refugees from Bosnia and Herzegovina and Croatia in 1996.

[223] In total, an estimated 250,000 have fled and only 13,000 returned by 2005 according to UNHCR, which reported 230,000 Serbs, Roma and other IDPs in 2005 [UNHCR, "The Balkans After the War was over," *Refugees*, Vol. 3, No. 140, 2005]. As reported by the European Commission, as of August 31, 2006, 3,236 people returned voluntarily in 2005 and 2006, bringing the total number of minority returnees since 1999 to 15,615. Out of approximately 515 families that were displaced in March 2004, 154 have returned to their homes permanently. Commission of the European Communities, *Commission Staff Working Document: Kosovo (under UNSCR 1244) 2006 Progress Report* [COM (2006) 649 final], Brussels, November 8, 2006, 16.

campaign of the FRY authorities against the Kosovo Albanians. According to Ted Galen Carpenter of the CATO Institute:

> There is little doubt that, at least in the short-term, NATO's decision to launch a military campaign to help the Albanian Kosovars had exactly the opposite effect, turning an already bad situation into a humanitarian crisis.[224]

Finally, NATO's claims to have been instigating a change of the Miloshevich regime also appear to be empty. Serbian democrats vehemently opposed the NATO action and most analysts indicated that NATO bombing would produce exactly the opposite result: "With every NATO missile that hits Yugoslav targets, Slobodan Milosevic stands to gain more power at home."[225] Indeed, Miloshevich succeeding in holding onto power for another year and a half despite dire economic conditions in the country.[226]

6.6.2d. *Ius in Bello—NATO and Moral De-legitimization*

6.6.2d (i) The Targets

In 1999, NATO claimed that it had destroyed 120 tanks, 220 armored personnel carriers and 450 artillery pieces in 744 "confirmed" air strikes. In Washington, Secretary of Defense William Cohen said these attacks had "severely crippled [Serbian] military forces in Kosovo by destroying more than 50 percent of [their] artillery and one-third of the armored vehicles." The reality, according to the 2000 Air Force report, is that NATO destroyed 14 tanks, 18 armored personnel carriers and 20 artillery pieces—more or less what the Serbian government said at the time, which was dismissed by NATO as Serbian "disinformation."[227] The revealed

---

[224] Ted Galen Carpenter, "Introduction: A Great Victory?," *NATO's Empty Victory; A Postmortem on the Balkan War*, ed. Ted Galen Carpenter (Washington, D.C.: CATO Institute, 2000), 1-10: 3.

Furthermore, according to a May 21 Fox News/Opinion Dynamics poll, 49 percent of Americans believed air strikes had made the situation "worse" and 28 percent said "better." Kosovo Situation Reports: May 1999, Library of Congress Kosovo Task Force, CRS Report #RL30156.

[225] Dusan Stojanovic, *Associated Press*, March 27, 1999.

[226] As articulated by Vojin Dimitrijevic, Serb human rights lawyer, "In one night, the NATO air strikes have wiped out ten years of hard work of groups of courageous people in the non-governmental sector and democratic opposition," "The Collateral Damage is Democracy," *Institute for War and Peace Reporting*, March 30, 1999 (accessed October 15, 2003); available from http://www.iwpr.net/index.pl?archive/bcr/bcr_19990402_5_eng.txt.

[227] *See* William Pfaff, "After NATO's Lies About Kosovo, It's Time to Come Clean," *International Herald Tribune*, May 11, 2000.

lack of NATO's efficacy in destroying the Yugoslav military calls for an investigation of the legitimacy of NATO's targets.

An analysis of NATO's military strategy demonstrates that NATO initiated the bombing as a modest effort based on a political calculation that Miloshevich would back down as soon as he realized that NATO was serious about its bombing threats. Retired British Air Vice Marshal Tony Mason, speaking at an Air Force Association symposium on Allied Force, stated:

> The fact that [General Clark] said that he was destroying the Yugoslav military—and then had to ask for triple the number of aircraft to do it weeks into the war—suggests a lack of preparation.[228]

A different outcome resulted in a shift to a greater number of targets, many of which were civilian,[229] almost leading to an open clash between the French and the American Air Force. Various NATO governments became increasingly reluctant to support the bombing operation as the targets appeared less and less legitimate. Although NATO used precision-bombing techniques, it often chose targets at great risk to the civilian surroundings. NATO hit many schools and hospitals in addition to the civilian infrastructure and industry. Non-military targets ostensibly include the Chinese embassy in Belgrade, a passenger train in Grdelitsa, an old-age home in Surdulitsa, an open-air market in Varvarin,[230] and a refugee convoy incarcerated by NATO bombs.[231] When the international press organizations protested when the Serbian Radio and Television Studios were bombed, British Prime Minister Tony Blair claimed that this was a legitimate target.

---

228 Cited in James Kitfield, "Command and Control the Messenger," *National Journal, 31.37*, September 11, 1999. *Le Nouvel Observateur* of Paris on July 1, 1999, also reported that policymakers expected Miloshevich to capitulate quickly.

229 The Human Rights Watch documented "as few as 488 and as many as 527 Yugoslav civilians killed as a result of NATO bombing" [Human Rights Watch, "Civilian Deaths in the NATO Air Campaign," 1999.]

230 *See* Steven Erlanger, "NATO Bombs Reported to Kill 20 Civilians in Southern Serbia," *New York Times*, April 28, 1999, 14; "NATO's Other Attack Blunders Tallied," *Chicago Sun-Times*, May 23, 1999, 6; "The Growing List of Allied Blunders," *New York Post*, May 23, 1999, 2; Richard Bourdreaux, "Civilian Deaths in Airstrikes Erode NATO Credibility in the Balkans; Nine People Are Killed in Bridge Attack," *Los Angeles Times*, May 31, 1999, A1; Julijana Mojsilovic and Stephen Bates, "Planes Buzzed Overhead and Then Death Came: Bridge Carnage Eyewitnesses Describe the NATO Attack on Their Town," *Guardian* (London), May 31, 1999, 5.

231 Paul Watson, "NATO Bomb Kills 17 More Civilians," *Los Angeles Times*, May 4, 1999, A16. "NATO Today Admitted That Its Warplanes Bombed Convoy in Kosovo," *Associated Press*, April 15, 1999, William Goldschlag, "Bombing Kills 79; Refugees' Deaths Blamed on NATO," *New York Daily News*, May 15, 1999, 2.

The murder of civilians continues indirectly, through the grave pollution of the environment, endangering the health of the citizens of Serbia and Montenegro and the entire region for years to come. Reportedly, "children with chemical-singed lungs find it painful to breathe and an unusual number of women suffered miscarriages following the bombing."[232]

Insufficient legitimacy of NATO targets led many to accuse NATO member countries and their leaders of war crimes. Highly respected international lawyers filed claims with the International Criminal Tribunal for the Former Yugoslavia, the Court of Human Rights in Strasbourg, and their domestic courts,[233] all of which were deemed injusticiable. Indictments listed breaches of general international law and violations of laws of war such as the Geneva Convention On the Protection of Civilian Persons in Time of War, and in particular its Article 18, providing for protection of civilian hospitals, as well as the Protocol II (June 8, 1977) to the Geneva Convention of August 12, 1949, Article 14, which provides:

> It is therefore prohibited to attack, destroy, remove or render useless . . . objects indispensable to the survival for the civilian population, such as foodstuffs . . . drinking water installations . . . [and] works or installations containing dangerous forces . . . even where these objects are military objectives.

In June 2000, the Committee established to review Operation Allied Force sub-mitted its report to the Prosecutor of the International Criminal Tribunal for the Former Yugoslavia, which did not recommend an investigation.[234] On June 2, 2000 the Prosecutor informed the U.N. Security Council of her decision not to open an investigation.[235] This decision appears to have been made under certain political influence, since it would be difficult for ICTY to investigate states that

---

232 P. Frazer, "What NATO's Bombs Did to the Environment," *Earth Island Journal*, 14.4, Winter 1999.

233 *See* for instance Bankovic and Others v. Belgium and 16 Other Contracting States, Application No. 52207/99.

234 Final Report to the Prosecutor by the Committee Established to Review the NATO Bombing Campaign Against the Federal Republic of Yugoslavia, June 13, 2000 (accessed April 7, 2005); available from http://www.un.org/icty/pressreal/nato061300.htm.

235 Press Release SC/6870, Prosecutor for International Tribunals briefs Security Council, June 2, 2000 (accessed May 10, 2004); available from http://www.un.org/News/Press/docs/2000/20000602.sc6870.doc.html.

provide it with financial support. As stressed by Jamie Shea, the NATO spokes-person during the 1999 intervention:

> As you know, without NATO countries there would be no International Court of Justice, nor would there be any International Criminal Tribunal for the former Yugoslavia, because NATO countries are in the forefront of those who have established these two tribunals, who fund these tribunals and who support on a daily basis their activities.[236]

Nonetheless, the U.S. government agreed to compensate the Chinese government and the victims of that single bombing incident.[237]

In the meantime, moral condemnation came from respected international figures such as Mary Robinson, the U.N. High Commissioner for Human Rights, who stated that "NATO's humanitarian objectives have failed because its air strikes have led to civilian deaths and injuries."[238] Walter J. Rockler, a Washington lawyer who served as a prosecutor at the Nuremberg War Crimes Trial, also insisted that justice should be universal:

> The notion that humanitarian violations can be redressed with random destruction and killing by advanced technological means is inherently sus-pect. This is mere pretext for our arrogant assertion of dominance and power in defiance of international law. We make the non-negotiable demands and rules, and implement them by military force.[239]

Sadly, the only lesson drawn by NATO military strategists was that since the destruction of the civilian infrastructure led to Miloshevich's surrender, the attacks should be more vicious in the future:

> There were probably 30 or 40 good targets in Belgrade. . . . The whole war could reasonably have been done in less than 10 days—with fewer

---

[236] Jamie Shea, *NATO Press Briefing*, May 17, 1999 (accessed February 4, 2000); available from http://www.nato.int/kosovo/press/p990517b.htm.

[237] Elisabeth Rosenthal, "U.S. Agrees To Pay China $28 Million For Bombing," *New York Times*, December 16, 1999, A6.

[238] "The U.N. High Commissioner for Human Rights, Mary Robinson, has sharply criticised Nato over its air campaign against Yugoslavia," *BBC News*, May 9, 1999, (accessed April 7, 2000); available from http://news.bbc.co.uk/hi/english/world/europe/newsid_339000/339562.stm.

[239] Walter J. Rockler, "War Crimes Law Applies to U.S. Too," *Chicago Tribune*, May 23, 1999.

sorties, fewer attacks, fewer targets. The refugee flow never would have happened.[240]

Importantly, this analysis is further evidence of NATO's awareness that the suffering of Albanian refugees would not have occurred had it not been for the poorly planned NATO bombing campaign.

6.6.2.d (ii). The Means

First, NATO conducted most of the bombing from elevations above 15,000 feet, increasing the likelihood of unintended civilian casualties.[241] Simultaneously, ground troops were ruled out, a policy that was reconsidered only after the campaign failed to bring results after two months of intense bombing despite the refugee crisis. According to a *Washington Post* report of April 5, 1999:

> Privately even the staunchest advocates of air power amongst the four star commanders doubted that air power alone could do much to budge Milosevic in the near term. They noted the challenges of sending planes against widely dispersed ground forces that were carrying out door to door terror.

Second, NATO deployed radioactive shells—depleted uranium (DU) munitions and cluster bombs. While NATO did not deny the use of depleted uranium,[242] it rejected the claims that DU produces harmful effects. Even though there is no consensus on the negative effects of depleted uranium, respected environmentalist have claimed that "just one DU 'hot particle' in the lungs is equivalent to receiving a chest X-ray every hour" for the rest of your life.[243] In practice, the NATO

---

[240] Cited in R. Newman, "Vietnam's Forgotten Lessons," U.S. *News & World Report*, 128, May 1, 2000, 17.

[241] Amnesty International concluded that "the requirement that NATO aircraft fly above 15,000 feet, made full adherence to international humanitarian law virtually impossible." Amnesty International, "NATO/Federal Republic of Yugoslavia 'Collateral Damage' or Unlawful Killings? Violations of the Laws of War by NATO during Operation Allied Force" (London: Amnesty International Publications, June 6, 2000).

[242] Letter by Lord Robertson, NATO Secretary General to Mr. Kofi Annan, U.N. Secretary General, February 7, 2000, reproduced in *Facts on Consequences of the use of Depleted Uranium in the NATO Aggression against the Federal Republic of Yugoslavia in 1999* (Belgrade: Federal Ministry of Foreign Affairs of the Federal Republic of Yugoslavia, 2000), 22.

[243] P. Frazer, "What NATO's Bombs Did to the Environment," *Earth Island Journal*, 14.4, Winter 1999.

The erstwhile Finnish Minister of Environment, Satu Hassi, in a letter to his E.U. colleagues appeals for a ban on the use of DU "as uranium dust in the respiratory tract will expose both soldiers and civilians to

countries protected their soldiers later serving in the peacekeeping forces in Kosovo and Metohia with special clothing and imported food and water.[244]

Unlike the effects of DU ammunition, the immense harm of cluster bombs to the civilian population is overt. During the bombing, one horrific incident reminded many of the marketplace bombings in Sarayevo, when NATO cluster bombs went astray above the Serbian city of Nish, killing fifteen civilians and wounding seventy in a marketplace. Unexploded cluster bombs continue to kill and maim dozens of victims today in Kosovo. According to the World Health Organization, in the first four weeks after the bombing ended, "about 150 Kosovars were killed or injured by 'land mines and unexploded ordnance,'" including bomblets.[245] Despite a strong movement against the use of cluster bombs, NATO military personnel insist on using them because they are relatively inexpensive.

Arguably, NATO bombing of chemical plants, fuel storage facilities and refineries also violated the 1976 Convention on the Prohibition of Military or Other Hostile Use of Environmental Modification Techniques and other conventions relating to environmental protection,[246] as well as the 1977 Protocol I Additional to the Geneva Conventions (Article 55), prohibiting "the use of methods or means of warfare which are intended or may be expected to cause such damage to the natural environment and thereby to prejudice the health or survival of the population." In brief, even if the use of depleted uranium and cluster bombs has not yet

---

strong radioactive radiation, [...] and permanently contaminate the areas where it is used with toxic heavy metal" [Letter by Mr. Satu Hassi to E.U. Ministers of environment, reproduced in *Facts on Consequences of the use of Depleted Uranium in the NATO Aggression against the Federal Republic of Yugoslavia in 1999* (Belgrade: Federal Ministry of Foreign Affairs of the Federal Republic of Yugoslavia, 2000), 27]. Siegwart-Horst Gunther, a German epidemiologist and president of Yellow Cross International, set up to protect children's health, said his studies in Iraq since 1991 had led him to believe that contact with DU weapon debris was linked to sharp increases in infectious diseases and immune deficiencies, Aids-like syndromes, kidney disorders and congenital deformities [Richard Norton-Taylor, "Nato bombing may hit future generations, scientists tell conference," *The Guardian*, July 31, 1999 (accessed February 10, 2000); available from http://www.guardian.co.uk/Iraq/Story/0,2763,206510,00.html.

244 For instance, "German soldiers . . . have been told not to eat local produce. . . . The orders to German soldiers come a week after a seven-page document warning of the dangers of depleted uranium was put into the mail boxes of all personnel working from the U.N. building in Pristina." Felicity Arbuthnot, "U.N. troops in Nato uranium food scare," *Sunday Herald*, June 4, 2000, 4.

245 *See* Dan Eggen, "In Kosovo, Death Comes in Clusters," *Washington Post*, July 19, 1999, A1.

246 Vienna Convention for the Protection of the Ozone Layer (1985, UNEP), the Montreal Protocol on Substances that Deplete the Ozone Layer (1987), and the United Nations Framework Convention on Climate Change (1992).

been banned, the indiscriminate grave injuries to the civilians caused by their use stand as a compelling witness to their immorality.

6.6.3. Final Analysis: Was NATO Bombing of FRY a Humanitarian Intervention? Has It Affected the Application of the Right to Self-Determination?

For 78 days, NATO relentlessly dropped bombs and missiles on a small "sovereign" nation. After undertaking 38,400 sorties,[247] the world's strongest military alliance stands accused of killing 500 civilians, wounding several hundred and imperilling the immediate and long-term public health of the region by poisoning the environment. NATO also destroyed tens of billions of dollars worth of property, including by and large the civilian infrastructure, industry, and housing. Triggered by the bombing, the intensified Yugoslav counterinsurgency actions led to the flight of almost a million Kosovo citizens[248] and the deaths of thousands.

NATO did not intervene to stop the widespread grave violations of international criminal law. Instead, by removing the observers and later by not providing a more robust enforcement,[249] NATO allowed first the FRY and then the KLA to commit such violations. The halt of the subsequent ethnic cleansing by the Yugoslav forces cannot retroactively provide a justification for the intervention because its occurrence without the intervention cannot be proven. Moreover, while NATO succeeded in forcing the Yugoslav troops out of Kosovo and returning the Albanian refugees home, it failed in its original mission of ensuring a democratic and multiethnic Kosovo.

---

[247] Figure from NATO, cited in ICTY, Final Report to the Prosecutor by the Committee Established to Review the NATO Bombing Campaign Against the Federal Republic of Yugoslavia, June 13, 2000, 17 (accessed April 7, 2005); available from http://www.un.org/icty/pressreal/nato061300.htm.

[248] OSCE estimates 862,979 ethnic Albanian refugees and more than 100,000 Serb internally displaced persons to have left Kosovo during the Operation Allied Force and to have been registered in Serbia and Montenegro. OSCE does not provide an estimate for other ethnic groups. OSCE, "Kosovo/Kosova: As Seen, As Told; Analysis of the Human Rights Findings of the OSCE Kosovo Verification Mission," 1999; (accessed April 7, 2000); available from http://www.osce.org/documents/mik/1999/11/1620_en.pdf.

[249] States have failed to provide enough troops or funds for the peace-building efforts. For example, "by March 2000, 45 countries had contributed a total of 2,361 police officers to UNMIK [United Nations Mission in Kosovo]– less than half its authorized strength of 4,718." See W.D. Hartung, "Billions for bombs; pennies for peacekeeping," Bulletin of the Atomic Scientists, 55.5, September 1999; SC/6873, Security Council hears Briefing by Head of U.N. Interim Administration Mission in Kosovo, June 9, 2000.

The preceding analysis deduces that NATO intervention was illegal. A careful study of the Rambouillet negotiations, the choice of targets, and the means of intervention also place the morality of the intervention in doubt, de-legitimizing any alleged humanitarian purpose for the intervention. Yet most troubling is the lack of clarity in the final aim of this or any other alleged humanitarian intervention. Is the aim to enforce democratic governance in a state that is object of intervention or to support a right to secession by selected "oppressed peoples"? In this dilemma lies the development of the application of the right to self-determination.

In the case of Kosovo, ethnic Albanians appear to be the Pyrrhic victors of NATO's bombing campaign. Having suffered the fate of refugees and losing thousands, they are closer to desired independence. While publicly rejecting the secessionist efforts of the KLA, the NATO governments have supported its goal by helping create a *de facto* independent Kosovo. The KLA had never really disarmed, but cloaked itself in the local police force uniforms, continuing to thrive on illegal trade and terrorize Kosovo Serbs while awaiting independence. Next to the KLA, Miloshevich was the other winner, using anti-NATO rhetoric to cling to power until October 2000, when he miscalculated his ability to win in regular elections.

The Kosovo non-Albanian ethnic groups (Serbs, Roma, Gorani, Turks and others) and the moderate Albanians are the losers of this war. Since the end of the bombing, over 2,200 people, mostly Serbs, have been murdered or kidnapped by the KLA/ethnic Albanians, receiving little protection from NATO-led peacekeepers. Most have fled their homes, with little hope of returning.[250] Ethnic cleansing *by* ethnic Albanians still rages on in Kosovo. Most notably, in March 2004, according to U.N. statistics, 50,000 Kosovo Albanians—in the presence of 18,000 NATO "peacekeepers"—drove 4,500 Serbs and other non-Albanians from their homes, injuring 900, including 150 peacekeepers, and killing 19 persons. Over 8,000 homes were looted and demolished and over 20 Serb Orthodox churches and monasteries destroyed[251] in this systematically planned pogrom.[252] Since 1999, NATO-brokered international "peace" has witnessed "a sustained attempt at

---

[250] *See* footnote 223.

[251] Rev. Irinej Dobrijevic (Coordinator, Kosovo and Metohia Committee Office, Holy Assembly of Bishops of the Serbian Orthodox Church), "Kosovo: Current and Future Status," Testimony Before the Committee on Foreign Relations, U.S. House of Representatives, Washington, DC, May 18, 2005.

[252] U.N. and NATO officials described the March 2004 attacks as planned, amounting to "ethnic cleansing." *See* Ian King and Whit Mason, *Peace at Any Price; How the World Failed Kosovo* (Ithaca, NY: Cornell

expunging the sacerdotal Serbian presence: of the original 1,657 churches, monasteries and monuments, over 150 were destroyed; 211 Orthodox cemeteries desecrated and 5,177 monuments smashed."[253] Kosovo remained a volatile area thereafter, with violence limited to banishing the minorities that live in its enclaves.[254]

NATO-led peacekeepers have struggled to keep peace in Kosovo and Metohia, fearing KLA reprisals if *de jure* independence of Kosovo were not achieved. According to one author:

> So far the KLA has played along with the United States, largely because it is winning on substance (mechanisms to establish *de facto* sovereignty) what it has yet to win on style (*de jure* independence).[255]

University Press, 2006), 5-16; Harry De Quetteville, "Kosovo in Flames as Albanians renew War on Serbs," *Telegraph* (U.K.), March 18, 2004; Matt Robinson and Christina Jennings, "Kosovo Clashes were Planned, says U.N. Official," *Scotsman*, March 18, 2004; Bill Hayton, "'Sinister Purpose' to Kosovo Clashes?," BBC, March 19, 2004; "Kosovo Clashes 'Ethnic Cleansing.'" BBC News, March 20, 2004; Kim Sengupta, "Burnt-Out Serbs Driven Into Exodus From Kosovo," *The Independent* (London), March 19, 2004; Shaban Buza, "NATO Sees Specter of Ethnic Cleansing in Kosovo," *Reuters*, March 19, 2004, etc.

[253] Rev. Irinej Dobrijevic (Coordinator, Kosovo and Metohia Committee Office, Holy Assembly of Bishops of the Serbian Orthodox Church), "Kosovo: Current and Future Status," Testimony Before the Committee on Foreign Relations, U.S. House of Representatives, Washington, DC, May 18, 2005. See also Human Rights Watch, *Failure to Protect: Anti-Minority Violence in Kosovo, March 2004*, July 2004 (accessed October 25, 2005); available from http://hrw.org/reports/2004/kosovo0704/; OSCE Mission in Kosovo, Human Rights Challenges following the March Riots (accessed October 25, 2005); available from http://www.osce.org/documents/mik/2004/05/2939_en.pdf; International Helsinki Federation for Human Rights, *Human Rights in the OSCE Region: Europe, Central Asisa and North America, Report 2005—Serbia and Montenegro (Kosovo)*, June 27, 2005 (accessed on October 25, 2005); available from http://www.ihf-hr.org/viewbinary/viewdocument.php?download=1&doc_id=6456.

[254] *See* UNHCR Position on the Continued International Protection Needs of Individuals from Kosovo," August 2004. Assessment made by UNHCR/OSCE in late 1999 remains relatively unchanged:

"The overall situation of ethnic minorities in Kosovo remains precarious. While the crime statistics released by the United Nations Mission in Kosovo (UNMIK) in mid-October indicate a decline in the overall number of violent incidents as far as minorities are concerned, this may be due in part to the fact that there has been a significant decrease in the overall non-Albanian population over the past four months. Informed observers agree that there is a climate of violence and impunity, as well as widespread discrimination, harassment and intimidation directed against non-Albanians. The combination of security concerns, restricted movement, lack of access to public services (especially education, medical/health care and pensions) are the determining factors in the departure of Serbs, primarily, and other non-Albanian groups from Kosovo to date. The widespread disrespect for human rights has increasingly also affected moderate Albanians and those who are openly critical of the current violent environment. UNHCR / OSCE, *Overview of the Situation of Ethnic Minorities in Kosovo*, November 3, 1999.

[255] John C. Hulsman, "Kosovo: Where Do We Go From Here?" *World and I*, 14.12, December 1999.

See also Peter Finn, "Kosovo Hostility Aimed at NATO," *Washington Post*, August 14, 1999, A1; Carlotta Gall, "NATO-Led Forces Begin Crackdown on Kosovar Army," *New York Times*, August 15, 1999, A1.

The first warning came during the March 2004 riots when "Albanian mobs [ultimately] turned their collective fury on their international overlords, throwing rocks at U.N. buildings, burning U.N. flags and destroying more than 100 of the administration's ubiquitous white Toyota 4Runner 4x4s."[256] To avoid the Albanian rage, Germany had initially pressured the Alliance to exit Kosovo more rapidly and partition it between North and South,[257] while other nations began clamoring for Kosovo's independence toward late 2006.[258] If Serbia's Southern province ultimately becomes independent, this would create a dangerous precedent by which foreign interventions enable insurgency groups to secede, encouraging more groups to draw an international response by provoking the government to crack down on their violence. Indeed, as Hoffmann has asserted:

> Given a small number of democracies, and the fog that surrounds the claims to an application of the principle of self-determination, to allow military interventions on behalf of either is a formula for generalized war and hypocrisy.[259]

Although NATO leaders refuse to officially acknowledge the failure of their "action" in Kosovo, they have recognized their failure in practice by not hailing Kosovo as a model for future "humanitarian interventions." Following NATO's bombing of Serbia and Montenegro, NATO General Wesley Clark faced early retirement while the political influence of U.S. Secretary of State Albright had significantly diminished.[260] Seven years later, the Prime Minister of Israel, Ehud Olmert, recalled the NATO Kosovo intervention to defend Israeli's military operations in Lebanon that led to a heavy civilian toll, concluding: "Where do they [European Union member states] get the right to preach to Israel?"[261]

Nonetheless, NATO's bombing of Serbia and Montenegro in 1999 could eventually be used to establish a pattern of state practice contributing to the development of "a right to humanitarian intervention" that would permit—and oblige—nations to violate the sanctity of sovereign borders in order to halt

---

[256] King and Mason, *Peace at Any Price*, 5-6.

[257] T. Haymes, "Germany Looking for an Out," *ABCNEWS.com*, May 3, 2000.

[258] *See* Chapter 7: *Conclusion: Former Yugoslavia's European Integration*.

[259] Stanley Hoffmann, "The Use of Force: Taming the Untamable," *Duties Beyond Borders: On the Limits and Possibilities of Ethical International Politics* (Syracuse, NY: Syracuse University Press, 1981), 69.

[260] *See* Jane Perlez, "With Berger in Catbird Seat, Albright's Star Dims," *New York Times*, December 14, 1999, A14.

[261] "Olmert to Europe: Stop 'Preaching.'" *Reuters*, August 8, 2006.

widespread human rights abuses and aid oppressed nations.[262] If this dangerously vague principle is to become a carefully defined legal rule, the present U.N. Charter would need to be amended. Alternatively, states would need to reach a consensus regarding a different interpretation of the existing U.N. Charter to support humanitarian interventions in certain cases. Otherwise the U.N. Charter, as the primary source of public international law, would clearly override any invoked right to humanitarian intervention.

Indeed, the evolution of international law in this direction can come about only if supported by state practice. Past "humanitarian interventions" constitute insufficient evidence. In fact the examples of Cuba, Vietnam, Nicaragua, Chile, Grenada, Sudan, Afghanistan, and Panama, as well as the numerous bombings of Iraq, seriously call into question the humanitarian purposes of intervening countries, while the example of Rwanda, where a horrendous genocide occurred just months before NATO decided to intervene in a relatively small conflict in Kosovo, is a shocking witness of great power indifference to a true humanitarian catastrophe.

Furthermore, great powers are not likely to intervene against their Allies or other great powers, as illustrated by the cases of Turkey (Kurds/Cyprus) and Russia (Chechnya). Instead, Russia is generally courted by the United Kingdom and other states, while the United States continues to export arms to Turkey and praise its progress towards democracy. In December 2004, the European Union ruled that Turkey was ready for negotiations on full E.U. membership and only partially suspended these negotiations in December 2006 due to lack of progress on the Cyprus issue.

If states do arrive at a consensus regarding "humanitarian interventions," the law has to be clearly formulated in order to avoid its abuses for disguised non-humanitarian purposes. Professor Jonathan Charney suggests that the International Criminal Court definition of grave war crimes be used for establishing *ius ad bellum* once all other remedies are exhausted (diplomatic means and U.N. Security Council resolution attempted). If the U.N. forum has been exhausted, regional

---

[262] As defined by one author, humanitarian intervention means "the threat or use of force by a state, group of states, or international organization primarily for the purpose of protecting the nationals of the target state from widespread deprivations of internationally recognized human rights, whether or not the intervention is authorized by the target state or the international community." Sean D. Murphy, *Humanitarian Intervention: The United Nations in an Evolving World Order* (1996), 3-4.

organizations ought to (a) warn the target state; (b) consent to ICJ jurisdiction; (c) use limited targets, minimize collateral damage, avoid unrelated effects on the target state's legitimate functions, and observe all other requirements of international humanitarian law; (d) withdraw once securing objectives unless the target state consents to their remaining or Security Council authorizes such presence.[263] Other legal scholars have suggested additional formulae, such as reforming the U.N. structure so that a two-thirds majority of the Security Council could authorize "a humanitarian intervention," without the possibility of a veto by the five permanent members,[264] or giving the necessary military and logistical resources to the U.N. to create special forces trained for "humanitarian interventions."

An abundance of possible legal solutions indicates that creating a legal rule permitting and defining humanitarian interventions is not unfeasible. It appears that only the political will is lacking, with more powerful states wishing to reserve the right to intervene on a case-by-case "selective consciousness" basis, and to escape the purported universal justice of the international courts. The Clinton doctrine also shows a lack of true political will, proclaiming that the United States will forcefully intervene to prevent human rights abuses—when it can do so.[265] One of the top U.S. political analysts, Charles Krauthammer, called the Clinton doctrine "impossibly moralistic and universal," claiming that even "Clinton people . . . cannot believe it . . . because they remember Krajina," which is "Kosovo writ large."[266] The staggering hypocrisy of international interventions was illustrated immediately after the Kosovo intervention, when an August 1999 bombing raid by the Sudanese military backing Congo's government reportedly killed 524 people, mostly civilians,[267] exploiting this "forgotten war."[268] Non-intervention in

---

263 Outlined in James I. Charney, "Anticipatory Humanitarian Intervention in Kosovo," *Vanderbilt Journal of Transnational Law* 32, no.5 (November 1999).

264 Drew Christiansen, "What We Must Learn From Kosovo: Military Intervention and Humanitarian Aid," *America*, 181.5, August 29, 1999.

265 "While there may well be a great deal of ethnic and religious conflict in the world, . . . whether within or beyond the borders of a country, if the world community has the power to stop it, we ought to stop genocide and ethnic cleansing." William Jefferson Clinton, Press Conference, June 20, 1999.

266 Charles Krauthammer, "The Clinton Doctrine," *Time*, March 29, 1999.

267 "Bombing Clouds Peace Prospects, Rebels Say," *Washington Times*, August 6, 1999, A13.

268 "Unlike the refugees of Kosovo, the four million people driven from their homes in Sudan receive only marginal world attention. The deaths of 1.9 million southern Sudanese since 1983 remain a little-known statistic." Chris Tomlinson, "The Forgotten War," *New York Times*, October 31, 1999, 28.

Sudan proved Secretary Albright right in repudiating the Clinton doctrine days after it was pronounced:

> Some hope, and others fear, that Kosovo will be a precedent for similar interventions around the globe. I would caution against any such sweeping conclusions. Every circumstance is unique. Decisions on the use of force will be made by any President on a case-by-case basis after weighing a host of factors.[269]

Finally, one should note that state practice since Kosovo, notably the Australian-led multinational mission to bring peace to East Timor, featured a regular Chapter VII intervention. Fully endorsed by a Security Council resolution,[270] this intervention demonstrated that the current international system, centered on territorial integrity, could be functional provided there was sufficient political will.

Nonetheless, NATO states have instead opted for a regional NATO consensus on international interventions, stating in its 1999 Strategic Concept:

> The combined military forces of the alliance must be prepared to contribute to conflict prevention and to conduct non-Article V [offensive] crisis response operations.[271]

U.S. President Clinton described this commitment as purely political and not legally binding.[272] Since that time, however, the NATO Alliance has pursued several "crisis response operations," most notably in Afghanistan and Iraq.

---

[269] U.S. Secretary of State Madeleine K. Albright, Speech at the Council for Foreign Relations, cited in Ivo H. Daalder, "And Now, A Clinton Doctrine?" *Haagsche Courant*, July 10, 1999.

[270] U.N. Security Council Resolution 1264, September 15, 1999.

[271] The Alliance's Strategic Concept, Approved by the Heads of State and Government participating in the meeting of the North Atlantic Council in Washington D.C. on April 23 and 24, 1999, paragraph 41 (accessed December 21, 2005); available from http://www.nato.int/docu/pr/1999/p99-065e.htm.

[272] "In order to avoid any confusion among our allies or elsewhere regarding the new NATO strategic concept, I feel compelled to make clear that the document is a political, not a legal document. As such, the strategic concept does not create any new commitment or obligation within any understanding of Section 1221 (1) to the act and therefore will not be submitted to the Senate for advice and consent." William Jefferson Clinton, "The Alliance's Strategic Concept," April 24, 1999, cited in the Hearing of the Senate Armed Services Committee: National Security Implications of the 1999 NATO Strategic Concept, *Federal News Service*, October 28, 1999.

Considering the non-humanitarian interests in the Middle East, where international interventions have focused since Kosovo, the U.N. Secretary General's remarks on the emergence of "an international norm against the violent repression of minorities"[273] appears superbly idealistic. In Kosovo, NATO's intervention merely replaced the repression of one minority by others. Put more bluntly, "the U.S. and NATO, though it was the opposite of their declared intentions, have succeeded in cleansing Kosovo of one ethnic group in favor of the other."[274] Dramatized calls to arms by activists like Michael Ignatieff, renowned journalist and lecturer on human rights, reflect a genuine misapprehension of the Kosovo conflict[275] and fail to foresee the immense harm that misguided international interventions could create. The final resolution of the status of Kosovo, coupled with the level of human rights standards enjoyed by the province's various ethnicities, will demonstrate whether purported humanitarian interventions can ultimately achieve democratic governance or whether they just arbitrarily select a holder of self determination, interpreting this right in its most extreme form, secession.[276]

---

[273] "Emerging slowly, but I believe surely, is an international norm against the violent repression of minorities that will and must take precedence over concerns of state sovereignty. . . . No government has the right to hide behind national sovereignty in order to violate the human rights or fundamental freedoms of its peoples. . . . This developing international norm will pose fundamental challenges to the United Nations." U.N. Secretary-General Kofi Annan, addressing the Commission on Human Rights in Geneva, SG/SM/6949 HR/CN/898, April 7, 1999.

[274] David Binder, "Seeking to stop ethnic cleansing, NATO finds it has accomplished it," *MSNBC*, March 19, 2000 (accessed June 7, 2004); available from http://www.msnbc.com/news/382058.asp.

[275] "The conflict in Kosovo was radical and unbridgeable: between a state bent on maintaining control of a territory by any means whatever and an ethnic majority determined to fight for self-determination. Central commitments of the world since Auschwitz, since the Universal Declaration of Human Rights— that nation states do not have the right to massacre their citizens—would have meant nothing if we had not been prepared to use force in their defense." Michael Ignatieff, *Virtual War: Kosovo and Beyond* (New York: Metropolitan Books, 2000), 213. For a comprehensive scholarly critique of the NATO bombing of Serbia and Montenegro in 1999, see Andrew J. Bacevich and Eliot A. Cohen, eds. *War over Kosovo* (New York: Columbia University Press, 2001).

[276] More in Chapter 7: *Conclusion: Former Yugoslavia's European Integration.*

Conclusion: Former Yugoslavia's European Integration

7.1. Stabilization and Association—A New Approach?

The aura of European integration has strongly impacted the development of the right to self-determination within the Yugoslav scenario. In the early 1990s, seemingly paradoxically, the European integration process adversely affected the Yugoslav constitutional crisis, fuelling the country's disintegration:

> Nations such as the Slovenes and the Croats have struggled to detach themselves from the region and recast themselves as lost sheep of the West, returning to the European flock.[1]

International policies toward (the former) Yugoslavia, beginning with international recognition of the country's largest federal units within their formerly internal, administrative boundaries, were generally applied on a selective, case-by-case basis. In contrast, toward the late 1990s the Western governments adopted a *regional* policy approach. Moreover, the policies toward the former Yugoslavia centered on the Euro-Atlantic integration as the most effective framework for resolving the remaining sources of unrest in the Balkans, stemming from conflicting expressions of self-determination.

The European Union and the United States transformed their policies toward the former Yugoslavia when two key war leaders left the political scene—the Croat

---

[1] Benn Steil and Susan L. Woodward, "A European 'New Deal' for the Balkans," *Foreign Affairs* 78, no. 6 (November-December 1999): 95. Accessed December 25, 2005. Available from Expanded Academic ASAP.

president Franjo Tudjman died in December 1999[2] and the Serbian president Slobodan Miloshevich was ousted in "a democratic revolution" in October 2000.[3] Focusing on European integration, the international community in the early 2000s granted a clear preference to the internal application of the right to self-determination, reflected in effective provision of human rights and democratic governance. The key policy-makers regarded any forceful redrawing of external boundaries as anachronistic to the post-World War II and post-colonial era. To them, the recognition of former Yugoslav republics was analogous to a delayed case of decolonization and represented a legal peculiarity rather than a precedent for legalized secession. Various jurists, such as Craven and Radan, have strongly disagreed with this view, leaving legal relevance of the recognition of the former Yugoslav republics to be clarified by future state practice.[4]

Yugoslav disintegration stood in sharp contrast to the concurrent European integration and progressive development of human rights, processes that strengthened the European as well as international preference for internal rather than external solutions to ethnic conflicts. In practice, the internal solution translated to enhanced versions of minority rights, rather than any meaningful recognition of a sub-state, territorial right of self-determination. Such a solution mirrored the Opinion of the Badinter Arbitration Commission on self-determination, an opinion that the Commission considered inapplicable to a "dissolved" Yugoslavia, but applicable to its successor states.[5]

The E.U. marked its policy shift by giving a new name to the region —"the Western Balkans."[6] This new term of political geography comprises all the former Yugoslav republics except Slovenia, while adding Albania to the group. The gradual integration of the region into Europe was titled "the Stabilization and Association Process" in 1999[7] and given impetus with the E.U. Zagreb Summit in

---

2   David Binder, "Franjo Tudmjan: Ex-Communist General Who Led Croatia's Secession, Is Dead at 77," *New York Times*, December 11, 1999.

3   Ana S. Trbovich, "Underground Movement, Above-Board Candidate Proved Right Mix against Milosevic" *The World Paper* [an international-affairs supplement], May/June 2001.

4   For more, *see* Chapter 5: *International Recognition of the (Former) Yugoslav Republics*.

5   Ibid.

6   This term first appears in the Presidency Conclusions of the Vienna European Council, December 11-12, 1998.

7   Communication from the Commission to the Council and the European Parliament on the stabilization and association process for countries of South-Eastern Europe—Bosnia and Herzegovina, Croatia, Federal Republic of Yugoslavia, former Yugoslav Republic of Macedonia and Albania, COM/99/0235, May 26, 1999; Conclusions of the E.U. General Affairs Council, 2192nd Council meeting, Luxembourg, June 21-22, 1999.

November 2000.[8] The Stabilization and Association Process (SAP) was conceived as a progressive partnership, in which the E.U. offers an aspiring member a mixture of trade concessions (Autonomous Trade Measures),[9] economic and financial assistance[10] and a contractual relationship (Stabilization and Association Agreement—SAA).

At the Thessaloniki Summit in June 2003, the E.U. pronounced "its unequivocal support to the European perspective of the Western Balkan countries"[11] and enriched the SAP with an array of new instruments, including the drafting of a joint framework for accession titled "European Partnership."[12] By reassuring the citizens of the Western Balkans of their European prospect, the E.U. bolstered the region's democratic forces. Arguably even more important was to remind the regional leaders of their obligations en route to united Europe. As postulated by the erstwhile Commissioner for External Relations, Christopher Patten:

> Thessaloniki will send two important messages to the Western Balkans: The prospect of membership of the E.U. is real, and we will not regard the map of the Union as complete until you have joined us. We in the European Commission will do all we can to help you succeed. But membership must be earned. It will take the sheer hard work and applied political will of those in power in the region. How far you proceed along the road towards European Integration, and how fast, will be up to you.[13]

---

8   Declaration of the Zagreb Summit, November 24, 2000 (accessed December 4, 2005); available from http://www.eu.int/comm/enlargement/intro/sap/summit_zagreb.htm.

9   The E.U. extended exceptional trade preferences to the Western Balkan countries in order to facilitate access to the Community market for their industrial and agricultural products and thereby revitalize their economies. *See* Council Regulation No. 2007/2000 introducing exceptional trade measures for countries and territories participating in or linked to the E.U.'s Stabilization and Association process, September 18, 2000. In November 2005, these trade preferentials were extended to the end of year 2010: Council Regulation (EC) No. 1946/2005, November 14, 2005.

10 Since 1991, the European Union has committed, through various assistance programs, € 6.8 billion to the Western Balkans. In 2000 aid to the region was streamlined through a new program called CARDS (Community Assistance for Reconstruction, Development and Stabilization) adopted with the Council Regulation (EC) No 2666/2000 of December 5, 2000. For more, *see* http://www.eu.int/comm/enlargement/cards/index_en.htm.

11 EU-Western Balkans Summit—Declaration, Thessaloniki, June 21, 2003, Press release 10229/03 (Presse 163).

12 The first European Partnerships, identifying short and mid-term priorities for reform, were approved in 2004.

13 Cited on official E.U. presentation, http://www.eu.int/comm/enlargement/see/milestone.htm (accessed December 19, 2005).

The E.U. members' chief policy interest in the Western Balkans has not been economic but political: attaining stability at Europe's Southeastern flank. Significantly, the E.U. had not used the term "stabilization" in reference to the accession of other Central and Eastern European countries, even though the integration of those countries into Europe also entailed democratic consolidation. The volatility still existing in the Western Balkans underscored the pressing need for the region to institute effective security and human right guarantees in addition to economic reforms. Any expressions of self-determination have therefore also been viewed in terms of wider security considerations.

The major international players, notably the United States, have fully endorsed the E.U's strategy toward the Western Balkans. Interwoven with this strategy is what is now known as a policy of conditionality—a policy based on "reinforcement by reward."[14] The E.U. launched its conditionality policy toward the former Yugoslav countries (with the exception of Slovenia) in October 1995 and elaborated concrete policy instruments in April 1997, in essence conditioning its political and financial assistance with the partner country's progress in areas of democracy, rule of law, higher human rights and minority rights standards, transition to a market economy, and greater interregional cooperation.[15] The conditionality policy is an integral part of the European Partnership, signed by each potential candidate[16] and a critical element of the 2005 Enlargement Strategy Paper.[17]

---

[14] Frank Schimmelfenning and Ulrich Sedelmeier, "Governance by Conditionality: E.U. rule transfer to the candidate countries of Central and Eastern Europe," *Journal of European Public Policy* 11, no. 4 (2004): 669-687: 671.

[15] General Affairs Council, Conclusions on the application of conditionality with a view to developing a coherent E.U. strategy for its relations with the countries in the region, April 29, 1997, *Bulletin of the EU*, No 4-1997.

[16] *See*, for instance, Council Decision of June 14, 2004 on the principles, priorities and conditions contained in the European Partnership with Serbia and Montenegro including Kosovo as defined by the United Nations Security Council Resolution 1244 of June 10, 1999, *Official Journal of the European Union* L 227/21, June 26, 2004, Paragraph 5, Conditionality: "Community assistance under the Stabilisation and Association process to the Western Balkan countries is conditional on further progress in satisfying the Copenhagen political criteria. Failure to respect these general conditions could lead the Council to take appropriate measures on the basis of Article 5 of Council Regulation (EC) No 2666/2000. Community assistance shall also be subject to the conditions defined by the Council in its Conclusions of April 29, 1997, in particular as regards the recipients' undertaking to carry out democratic, economic and institutional reforms, taking account the priorities set out in this European Partnership."

[17] *2005 Enlargement Strategy Paper*, 3.

The international powers have set specific and in many cases onerous conditions for the integration of the former Yugoslav countries into the Euro-Atlantic community. Most pressing is the requirement for full cooperation with the International Criminal Tribunal for the former Yugoslavia in the Hague (ICTY), a condition intended to help these countries overcome the legacy of their recent violent past.[18] The E.U. political—and economic—criteria for membership have been broadly defined at the Copenhagen European Council in June 1993:

> Membership requires that the candidate country has achieved stability of institutions guaranteeing democracy, the rule of law, human rights and respect for and protection of minorities, the existence of a functioning market economy as well as the capacity to cope with competitive pressure and market forces within the Union. Membership presupposes the candidate's ability to take on the obligations of membership including adherence to the aims of political, economic and monetary union.[19]

The Madrid E.U. Summit held in December 1995 further emphasized the need for adequate administrative capacity, deemed crucial in effective implementation of E.U. standards and legislation, collectively termed *acquis communautaire*.[20] In a similar vein, members of the North Atlantic Treaty Organization (NATO) are pressing for reforms of the local armed forces in addition to the fulfillment of political criteria such as cooperation with the ICTY. Both the E.U. and NATO have made their membership contingent upon the Western Balkan countries' regional cooperation. In official E.U. jargon, "enhanced regional co-operation is recognised as a qualifying indicator of the Western Balkan countries' readiness to integrate into the European Union."[21] Regional integration is perceived as a precursor to wider European integration.

---

[18]   For a critical view of ICTY, *see* Alfred P. Rubin, "Dayton, Bosnia, and the Limits of Law," *The National Interest*, no. 46 (Winter 1996): 41(6). Accessed December 25, 2005. Available from Expanded Academic ASAP.

[19]   European Council in Copenhagen, June 21-22, 1993: Conclusions of the Presidency, SN 180/1/93, 12.

[20]   "[I]nstitutions, as well as their functioning, and procedures have to be improved in order to preserve [EU's] capacity for action, while maintaining the 'acquis communautaire' and developing it and also respecting the balance between the institutions." Madrid European Council, December 16, 1995.

[21]   Official Internet Presentation of the European Union (accessed on December 16, 2005), http://www.eu.int/comm/enlargement/intro/sap.htm.

Notably, the 2005 Enlargement Strategy Paper added a new enlargement condition: "the EU's absorption capacity." As expounded in this document:

> Enlargement is about sharing a project based on common principles, policies and institutions. The Union has to ensure it can maintain its capacity to act and decide according to a fair balance within its institutions; respect budgetary limits; and implement common policies that function well and achieve their objectives.[22]

The so-called enlargement fatigue had almost endangered the European prospect of one Western Balkan country, the Former Yugoslav Republic of Macedonia (FYROM), when squabbles over the 2006-2013 E.U. budget threatened to result in a negative opinion on Macedonia's candidacy for accession negotiations in December 2005.[23] In the end, proponents of enlargement prevailed but a mixed message was sent to the region, undoing some of the achievements of the Thessaloniki summit. The E.U.'s failure to adopt the European Constitution, marked by the document's rejections in the popular referenda in France and the Netherlands in 2005, will remain an obstacle to enlargement since the E.U. can effectively widen only by streamlining its own decision-making structures. Furthermore, one should not overlook the fact that France changed its own constitution in March 2005, mandating that all new accession treaties, following Bulgaria and Romania, be put to a national referendum.[24]

Overall, the Stabilization and Association Process in the Western Balkans has been relatively successful, thanks to the enticing carrots available to the international community, such as preferential trade agreements. The European Union became the region's largest trading partner in early 2000s, with over half of all exports going to the European market. The trade preferentials allowed for more than 80 percent of all goods from the Western Balkan region to enter Europe without customs restrictions.[25] Equally enticing is the political appeal of E.U. accession. Most parties in the region, including those on the right, have not dared

---

[22] *2005 Enlargement Strategy Paper*, 3.

[23] "Macedonia's candidacy may suffer delay," *Euractiv*, December 12, 2005 (accessed December 15, 2005); available from http://www.euractiv.com/Article?tcmuri=tcm:29-150823-16&type=News.

[24] For more, *see* Breffni O'Rourke, "E.U.: After French Referendum, Europe Seen as Changed Forever," *RFE/RL*, May 30, 2005; "Dutch referendum; Dead and buried," *The Guardian*, June 2, 2005.

[25] Official Internet Presentation of the European Union (accessed December 16, 2005); available from http://www.eu.int/comm/enlargement/see/milestone.htm.

to voice disagreement, given that the population generally views the E.U. as an economic panacea. Membership in NATO has been more controversial for the citizens of the former Yugoslavia, particularly Serbia, which NATO bombed in 1999.[26]

One should stress, however, that conditionality has not always yielded the intended results. For instance, when the E.U. conditioned a positive answer to Serbia's feasibility study on preparedness for SAA negotiations with further compliance with ICTY, the Serbian government encouraged voluntary surrender of indictees, hailing them as national heroes. A Canadian scholar, Nikolas Rajkovic, thus urges caution: "if the fundamental purpose of political conditionality is the socialization of target states in 'democratic values,' then more attention has to be paid to how the means impact upon the ends."[27]

Social costs, including transitory unemployment, are the unavoidable consequence of reforms geared toward European integration. The pain of transition is especially great in the former Yugoslav countries, where the criteria for attaining market functionality and a high degree of democracy often conflict with the countries' intricate constitutional arrangements, initially created to bring peace to the region and stem further disintegration.

In an asymmetric partnership, the international community, led by the E.U. and the United States, has been actively involved in creating the constitutional frameworks for most of the former Yugoslav countries.[28] Today, it continues to assist with the adjustment of these frameworks, intending to enhance their functionality and thereby facilitate the region's integration into the Euro-Atlantic community.

---

[26]   In Serbia, support for NATO membership is low but slowly growing. In April 2004 it stood at 28 percent, in April 2005 at 37 percent and in March 2006 at 40 percent. Notably, although the support for NATO membership is growing, lack of trust in NATO is constantly high in Serbia—at around 80 percent with 4-5 percent population trusting NATO. In contrast, the support for the Partnership for Peace Program is relatively high (around 70 percent). Source: Strategic Marketing and Media Research Institute, Belgrade, Serbia.

[27]   Nikolas Milan Rajkovic, "Conditionality and the Public Sphere: A Synthetic Explanation of Hague Conditionality and (Non)Compliance in Serbia," Master Thesis, Central European University, June 2, 2005, 1-72: 66.

[28]   Constitution of the Federation of Bosnia and Herzegovina (1994); Constitution of Bosnia and Herzegovina (1995); Amendments to the Constitution of the Republika Srpska (1996); Constitutional Framework for Kosovo (2001); Macedonia's Constitutional Arrangement: Ohrid Agreement (2001); Constitutional Charter of Serbia and Montenegro (2003).

Simultaneously, certain ethnic groups continue to claim an external right to self-determination, preferring to first secede from their home state and then rejoin that state in a different framework—within a common E.U. structure—a step first taken by Slovenia in 1991.[29] An analysis of Montenegro's separation from Serbia in 2006 and issues currently at stake in Croatia, Bosnia and Herzegovina, Serbia and Macedonia will seek to demonstrate why secession remains a popular option, impeding a more progressive evolution of the internal interpretation of the right to self-determination.

7.2. European Integration as Leverage for Enhancing Minority Rights in Croatia

Croatia became a member of the Council of Europe in 1996, an associate E.U. member in 2001, and an official candidate for E.U. membership in June 2004,[30] initiating negotiations on full membership in October 2005. It reached these steps despite its varied cooperation with the War Crimes Tribunal and a rather dismal record in the area of refugee return[31] and minority rights. As Woodward underscores:

> Continuing discrimination against employment of Serbs, an official campaign during 1994 to evict all Serbs from publicly owned apartments without due process, and the failure to set up the promised human rights court did not bring condemnation by European human rights institutions such as the Council of Europe or its patrons Germany and the United States.[32]

---

[29] According to the last U.S. Ambassador to Yugoslavia, Warren Zimmerman, Slovenes "bear considerable responsibility for the bloodbath that followed their secession." Warren Zimmerman, *Origins of a Catastrophe, Yugoslavia and Its Destroyers—America's Last Ambassador Tells What Happened and Why* (New York: Times Books, 1996), 70-71.

[30] Commission of the European Communities, Opinion on Croatia's Application for Membership of the European Union, Brussels, April 20, 2004, COM (2004) 257; Council of the European Union, Presidency Conclusions, June 17 and 18, 2004.

[31] Between 300,000 and 350,000 ethnic Serbs left their homes in Croatia during the 1991-1995 war in the former Yugoslavia. Organization for Security and Co-Operation in Europe (OSCE), Mission to Croatia, "Report on Croatia's Progress in Meeting International Commitments Since 2001," June 9, 2006, 13. *See also* Human Rights Watch, *Croatia: A Decade of Disappointment; Continuing Obstacles to the Reintegration of Serb Returnees*, Vol. 18, No. 7, September 2006 (accessed December 11, 2006); available from http://hrw.org/reports/2006/croatia0906/croatia0906webwcover.pdf.

[32] Susan L. Woodward, *Balkan Tragedy; Chaos and Dissolution after the Cold War* (Washington, D.C.: The Brookings Institution, 1995), 392.

The first and the only time that the conditionality policy was strictly applied in the case of Croatia was in March 2005, when the E.U. stalled Croatia's negotiations on full membership in the Union for six months, that is, until the Croatian government demonstrated that it was fully cooperative with the Hague War Crimes Tribunal.

In the last few years Croatia has taken some steps to improve refugee return but its minority rights system has remained poorly implemented. In the 2005 Enlargement Strategy Paper, the European Commission has emphasized that, in Croatia, "important efforts are still needed" in areas such as "unbiased prosecution of war crimes[,] ... situation of minorities[,] and ... refugees' return."[33] The Strategy Paper further noted "an ethnic bias against Serb defendants" in the judiciary, that "the implementation of the Constitutional Law on National Minorities ... has been slow" and that generally "Serbs and Roma face discrimination."[34]

Nonetheless, the European Commission concluded that present-day Croatia "faces no difficulties in meeting the political requirements for membership."[35] In a similar vein, the European Commission officially branded Turkey as a country that "continues to sufficiently fulfil the Copenhagen political criteria," although "human rights violations ... continue to occur."[36] Higher political considerations appear to have prevailed, with Austria strongly lobbying on behalf of Croatia[37] and the United States on behalf of Turkey.[38]

While Croatia's progress toward E.U. membership furnishes a good model to other countries in the region, its record on minority rights and refugee return and the international attitude in this respect set a poor example. Ominously, the behavior of Croatia may have strengthened the belief that group rights could

---

[33]   *2005 Enlargement Strategy Paper*, 5.

[34]   Ibid., 21.

[35]   Ibid., 5.

[36]   Ibid., 29.

[37]   "Croatia Thanks Austria for E.U. Talks," *Associated Press*, October 4, 2005; "E.U. Opens Turkey Membership Talks," *BBC News*, October 4, 2005.

[38]   "At one point the Bush Administration, which wants to tie Turkey firmly to the West, became so concerned that it risked the charge of interference in E.U. affairs by intervening directly." Anthony Browne, "Path to E.U. opens for Turkey after last-minute deal," *The Times* (London), October 4, 2005.

be attained exclusively through secession. As deduced by the International Commission on the Balkans in 1996:

> In the Balkans, minorities do not trust legal guarantees if they are not accompanied by territorial autonomy, while the major national groups fear that granting collective rights and autonomy will encourage disintegration and irredentism.[39]

Although this statement could be applied to many other minority discords internationally, the fate of Krayina has certainly reinforced the negative image of the Balkans as a place where violence is the only means to resolve conflicts.[40]

For a long time, the international community had refused to link the resolution of the "Bosnian Problem" with the "Krayina Problem." Nonetheless, the connectedness of the two was obvious to diplomats on the ground such as Ian Oliver, diplomat at the Office of the High Representative (OHR) and the European Community Monitoring Mission in Bosnia from 1995 through 1998:

> In essence, the Bosnian Serbs were always going to be reluctant to enter in to a two-way 'return process' with the Federation when no one was addressing the issue of one hundred and fifty thousand Serbs who had been ethnically cleansed from Croatia. In their eyes, the 'return process' had always been a three-way process involving Tudjman's Croatia.[41]

Finally, in January 2005, the regional approach to refugee return was firmly embraced. Bosnia and Herzegovina, Croatia and Serbia and Montenegro, helped by UNHCR, the European Union and the Organization for Security and Cooperation in Europe (OSCE), then agreed to resolve all outstanding refugee and internal displacement issues by the end of 2006.[42] This was a promising

---

[39] *Unfinished Peace; Report of the International Commission on the Balkans* (Washington: Carnegie Endowment for International Peace, 1996), xviii.

[40] "A startling response to the outbreak of war in Yugoslavia was the reissue in 1993 of the report of the Carnegie Commission on the Balkan Wars of 1912-13, the view being offered in all seriousness that it would illuminate the current conflict—'the same Balkan world.'" John B. Allcock, *Explaining Yugoslavia* (New York: Columbia University Press, 2000), 2.

[41] Ian Oliver, *War and Peace in The Balkans; The Diplomacy of Conflict in the Former Yugoslavia* (London: I.B. Tauris, 2005), 89.

[42] Declaration, Regional Ministerial Conference on Refugee Returns, Sarajevo, January 2005 (accessed December 27, 2005); available from http://www.mhrr.gov.ba/PDF/engleski.pdf; E.U. Statement on the

development, particularly with regard to Croatia, which had previously entertained a concerted policy of impeding refugee return, described as "quiet ethnic cleansing" by Human Rights Watch in 1999.[43] Unfortunately, the Declaration became another moot point.

A more concrete development in Serb-Croat relations in Croatia was embodied in the agreement concluded in late 2003 between Croatia's government and the Independent Serbian Democratic Party—SDSS. According to SDSS president Voyislav Stanimirovich, the agreement was achieved precisely "because [Serb] demands corresponded to those of the European Union, which primarily demand refugee return, restoration of returnees' property, respect for minority rights and cooperation with Hague (Tribunal)."[44] The agreement provided the Serbian minority with eight Assistant Ministers in the Croatian government and specific pledges concerning property return, rebuilding of returnees' houses, and application of Constitutional law on national minorities at the local level. Although the Croatian government has not fully implemented the agreement, and numerous incidents and hate speech against Serbs continue in Croatia,[45] the three Serb minority representatives in the Croatian Parliament still consider it as their best recourse to cooperate with the government and exert due political pressure. "They need our hands when it comes to voting in the parliament," Stanimirovich elucidated,[46] demonstrating how a democratic process, when encouraged and monitored by the international community, could lead to improvements in minority rights.

In a most significant achievement since the war and in full accordance with the law, the Serb representatives established the National coordination of Serb

---

Regional Ministerial Conference on Refugee Returns held in Sarajevo on January 31, 2005, Permanent Council No 543, February 3, 2005.

[43] Human Rights Watch, *Croatia, Second class citizens, the Serbs of Croatia* 11, No. 3 (D) (March 1999) (accessed April 19, 2001); available from http://www.hrw.org/reports/1999/croatia/.

[44] Voyislav Stanimirovich, Interview published in *Glas yavnosti* (Belgrade), December 31, 2003–January 2, 2004, 14 [Translation mine].

[45] OSCE Press release: OSCE Mission and international community in Croatia call for urgent action to stop returnee from losing home, December 16, 2005; OSCE, Status report No. 17 on Croatia's progress in meeting international commitments, July 2005; R. Arsenich "Hate from TV screens," *Politika* (Belgrade), May 24, 2005, 2. Organization for Security and Co-operation in Europe, OSCE Mission to Croatia, *Status Report No. 17 on Croatia's Progress in Meeting International Commitments since July 2005*, November 10, 2005.

[46] Author's interview with Voyislav Stanimirovich, Belgrade, December 8, 2005 [Translation mine].

minority councils in Croatia on April 9, 2005. Interestingly, that same month the Croat government resisted a Croat-initiated administrative redivision of the country by means of the creation of a Slavonia-Baranya region,[47] and generally continues to resist the concept of territorial autonomy, afraid of potential secessionism. Although some Krayina Serb human rights activists, such as the Director of the Veritas Documentation Center, Savo Shtrbats, advocate the revival of the 1995 Z-4 Peace Plan, enshrining territorial autonomy for a part of Krayina,[48] Serb political representatives in Croatia, such as Voyislav Stanimirovich, consider this to be a futile effort, due to the fact that Krayina's population mainly remains exiled and that returnees tend to be aged people, pointing to a trend of a decreasing demographic presence of Serbs in Croatia.[49]

The international community could and should use the prospect of acceding to the E.U. and NATO as a means of inducing Croatian and other regional governments to apply minority rights and thus contribute to regional and wider integration, undoing a credo once cynically coined by a Macedonian analyst, Vladimir Gligorov: "Why should I be a minority in your state when you can be a minority in mine?"[50] The European Commission's Proposal for a Council Decision on the Principles, Priorities, and Conditions contained in the Accession Partnership with Croatia appears to have espoused this approach, identifying implementation

---

47 The ruling Croatian party (HDZ) expelled one of its highest ranking members Branimir Glavaš in April 2005 for attempting to create a Slavonia-Baranya region. Glavas explained this move by saying that the region was becoming poorer and falling into an ever deeper economic, political and social crisis. He went ahead and established the "Croatian democratic parliament of Slavonia and Baranya" on April 23, 2005, with two proclaimed aims: "regionalization and awaking the original spirit of HDZ." In local elections of June 2005, Glavaš' list of independent candidates won relative majority in Osijek and Osijek-Baranya county. In July 2005, Croatian press implicated Glavaš in the 1991 murders of Serbian civilians in Osijek, and the judiciary announced an investigation. The timing does not appear to be coincidental since such allegations had been voiced earlier but never seriously discussed in the Croatian public sphere. One example is Crnobrnja's account of Branimir Glavaš as a man who "gained fame by ethnically cleansing Serb villages in the vicinity of the front-line town of Osijek [... and ...] did not hesitate to murder Croat policemen who maintained good relations with Serbs or just happened to step in his way. Today he is the mayor of Osijek." Mihailo Crnobrnja, *The Yugoslav Drama*, 2nd edition (Montreal: McGill-Queen's University Press, 1996), 170. *See* also R. Arsenich, "Branimir Glavas expelled from the party," *Politika* (Belgrade), April 23, 2005, 2; "Glavaš' Slavonic Uprising," *Globus* (Zagreb), No. 751, April 29, 2005.

48 Author's interview with Savo Shtrbats, Belgrade, November 28, 2005.

49 Author's interview with Voyislav Stanimirovich, Belgrade, December 8, 2005.

50 Vladimir Gligorov, "Is What is Left Right? (The Yugoslav Heritage)," in János Matyás Kovacs, ed., *Transition to Capitalism? The Communist Legacy in Eastern Europe* (New Brunswick, NJ: Transaction Publishers, 1994), 158. Further explored in Vladimir Gligorov, *Why Do Countries Break Up? The Case of Yugoslavia* (Uppsala: Acta Universitatis Upsaliensis, 1994).

of minority rights and completion of refugee return as "key short term priorities" for Croatia, which in the medium term needs to "ensure full implementation of the Constitutional Law on National Minorities, particularly as regards proportional representation of minorities" and "improve economic and social conditions to improve the climate for returnees' reintegration and the acceptance of returnees by receiving communities."[51]

7.3. Rendering Bosnia and Herzegovina a Functional State

On the road to E.U. membership, Bosnia and Herzegovina, a state that could be most aptly depicted as an international protectorate, has encountered a number of hurdles. These were outlined in the E.U.'s Feasibility Study on Bosnia and Herzegovina's Readiness for Negotiating and Implementing a Stability and Association Agreement,[52] and translated into a plan of action by Bosnia's High Representative. The particular weakness of the Bosnian state required that the E.U. draft a "road map" for the country, which the Bosnian Presidency endorsed on April 6, 2000. Green light for negotiations on E.U. associate status arrived, not coincidentally, on the tenth anniversary of the Dayton Peace Accords (November 2005),[53] reminding everyone that European integration was about peace and stability.

In its state-building efforts in Bosnia, the international community committed vast sums of aid and an engaged diplomatic and security corps, reaping many successes:

> Five billion dollars of aid poured into the country in the early peace years. Around half of Bosnia's 500,000 destroyed homes were rebuilt or replaced. Some 200,000 property disputes were resolved peacefully. . . . The number

---

51 Commission of the European Communities, *Proposal for a Council Decision on the Principles, Priorities, and Conditions contained in the Accession Partnership with Croatia*, COM (2005) 556, Brussels, November 9, 2005, 7, 13.

52 Commission of the European Communities, *Report from the Commission to the Council on the Preparedness of Bosnia and Herzegovina to Negotiate a Stabilisation and Association Agreement with the European Union*, COM (2003) 692, Brussels, November 18, 2003.

53 Conclusions of the Council of the European Union, 2691st Council Meeting: General Affairs and External Relations, Brussels, November 21-22, 2005, 8.

of international peacekeeping troops in Bosnia dropped from a high of 69,000 to 7,000 in the absence of any major security incidents.[54]

Nonetheless, Bosnia's political representatives have resisted the High Representative's strategy for transforming the country into a functional state when they perceived the strategy as removing the guarantees that the Dayton Peace Agreement provided for Bosnia's principal ethnic groups. For instance, when the international community attempted to direct the reform of Bosnia and Herzegovina's police forces, the Bosnian Serbs voted down the proposed reform because it would have entailed the creation of new police districts that would cross the inter-entity borderline. Bosnian Serbs appeared willing to jeopardize the country's associate E.U. membership, conditioned by proposed police reform,[55] in order to safeguard the autonomy bequeathed to the Republika Srpska under the 1995 Dayton Peace Agreement.

One month later, in October 2005, the Republika Srpska Parliament endorsed the "Agreement on the Restructuring of Police Structures," transferring policing functions to the state level over a phased five-year period, but leaving the shape of the police districts to be determined in future negotiations. As explained by the erstwhile High Commissioner, Lord Paddy Ashdown:

> Within five years, Bosnia will have a single integrated police service at the state level, and local police areas which will cross the inter-entity border line *in the limited areas where it is technically necessary.*[56]

The agreement represented a compromise that would allow Bosnia and Herzegovina to move forward on its path to the European Union while preserving, in the main, the inter-ethnic boundary. This example has shown both that Bosnia could reform and that many of the Dayton safeguards could be maintained once the country joins the E.U. without causing inefficiency. Yet for political reasons the agony over police reform has continued.[57] It appears that the

---

54   UNHCR, "The Balkans After the War was over," *Refugees* 3, No. 140 (2005), 10.

55   European Union Special Representative in Bosnia and Herzegovina Press Release: E.U. Conditions Start of SAA on Reform Process, June 29, 2005.

56   Cited in Patrick Moore, "Bosnia-Herzegovina: Finally On The Path To The EU?" *RFE/RL*, October 6, 2005 [Emphasis added].

57   "Stalled reforms holding up BiH's E.U. integration progress," *Southeast European Times*, March 16, 2007.

pull of the E.U. membership has been exploited by the High Representative, that is, by the international community led by the United States, to render Bosnia and Herzegovina a more unitary state not for the sake of efficiency but for the sake of the unwritten principle that Bosnia's internal partition, necessary to end the war, should be reversed in peace:

> The best way to make the Bosnian state more coherent and legitimate is to make borders less relevant between the two entities.[58]

The international community in Bosnia is overtly engaged not just in state-building in Bosnia but also in "nation-building." Since 1997, the High Representative has imposed a number of "laws," which included constitutional amendments, ousting of elected officials and deciding the country's very insignia—flag, coat of arms, and anthem. To do this, the High Representative invoked the so-called Bonn Powers, granted to him by the Peace Implementation Council at the December 1997 meeting in Bonn, which welcomed the High Representative's "intention to use his final authority . . . regarding interpretation of the [Dayton] Agreement . . . in order to facilitate the resolution of difficulties by making binding decisions, as he judges necessary," including "interim measures to take effect when parties are unable to reach agreement" and "other measures," which might "include actions against persons holding public office."[59]

The Bonn powers were deemed necessary to further reform and stem reconciliation efforts. Cooperation among Bosnia's three major ethnic groups was manifestly lacking. Most pointedly, in June 1998, the United States had decided to "suspended part of a military aid program [for a Muslim-Croat Federation] because its Muslims and Croats refused to cooperate on issues of joint security."[60] With the help of the High Representative, unconstitutionally and not most democratically, Bosnia gained a unified defense and intelligence services, an indirect taxation system, and a single prosecutorial service. The unified town of Mostar is hailed as another achievement, made despite the fact that Mostar's Muslims and Croats, separated by the famous bridge, held two separate referenda with different

---

58   Patrice C. McMahon, "Rebuilding Bosnia: A Model to Emulate or to Avoid?" *Political Science Quarterly* 119, no. 4 (Winter 2004).

59   Bonn Peace Implementation Conference 1997; Bosnia and Herzegovina 1998: Self-sustaining Structures, Summary of Conclusions, December 10, 1997 (accessed December 27, 2005); available from http://www. oscebih.org/documents/61-eng.pdf.

60   *New York Times*, June 5, 1998, A4.

outcomes regarding the administrative division of the town. The Office of the High Representative did not heed these expressions of self-determination.[61]

Polls indicate that "most Serbs and Croats in Bosnia do not even consider Bosnia and Herzegovina to be their homeland" while Bosnian Muslims identify themselves principally as Bosniaks or Muslims rather than Bosnians.[62] Despite unification of ethnic militaries and an oath dedicated to Bosnia and Herzegovina, military conscripts in Republika Srpska spontaneously swear duty to Republika Srpska[63] and Croat conscripts play Croatia's national anthem.[64] The refugee return has contributed little to Bosnia's multiethnic character. On the surface the policy has been a complete success:

> More than a million people have returned to their pre-war homes in Bosnia and Herzegovina, with, remarkably, nearly half of those returning to areas where they find themselves an ethnic minority.[65]

However, these figures are based on applications for identity cards and other documents that "returnees" had to obtain to retrieve their property. The fact that many quickly sold their property and deserted the municipality in which they were a minority is duly disregarded. The real figure of returnees is nearer 300,000, with the vast majority returning to the area dominated by their ethnic group.[66]

---

61   "Unified Town," *Tanjug*, January 27, 2004; "Three pre-dominantly Croat municipalities in Mostar decide to call for referendum on the future of Mostar," *Dnevni list* (Bosnia), January 10, 2004; "Approximately 99 percent of the citizens of three Mostar municipalities who participated in a referendum voted for Mostar to be organised as a single city with one electoral unit. HR Ashdown stated earlier that he would make his decision on the organization of Mostar without taking into consideration the results of either the Bosniac or Croat referendum that were conducted in Mostar municipalities." "Results of referendum in Mostar," *BiH Radio 1*, SFOR Main News Summary, January 26, 2004 (accessed December 27, 2005); available from http://www.nato.int/sfor/media/2004/ms040126.htm. Note: Mostar Croats preferred one electoral unit because such a system would give them more political leverage and not because they desired a greater unification of the town.

62   Laura Silber, "Dayton, Ten Years After," *New York Times*, November 21, 2005, A1; Mirko Kapor, "Bosnians as Yugoslavs," *Politika* (Belgrade), June 8, 2005, 4.

63   On June 3, 2005, the commanders of EUFOR and NATO Headquarters in Sarajevo ordered the dismissal of General Novak Djukic, Republika Srpska Army chief of staff, for not reacting to this "incident." Antonio Prlenda, "RS Army Chief of Staff Sacked Over Oath-Taking Incidents," *Southeast European Times*, June 6, 2005.

64   *Dan* (Podgoritsa), April 30, 2005, 25.

65   Remarks as Prepared, Undersecretary for Political Affairs R. Nicholas Burns, "Bosnia Ten Years Later: Successes and Challenges," *United States Institute of Peace*, Washington, D.C., November 21, 2005.

66   Vesna Peric Zimonjic, "Bosnian Poll to Finish Job of Ethnic Cleansing," *The Independent*, September 30, 2006.

A case in point is Bosnia and Herzegovina's capital Sarayevo, whose cantonal government had 92.2 percent Bosniak (Bosnian Muslim) employees in August 2004.[67] As summarized by Laura Silber:

> Bosnia's ethnic groups now mostly live apart, and even in towns and villages where they reside in close proximity, they lead virtually segregated lives, sometimes going so far as to send their children to separate classes within the same school building.[68]

Eleven years after the end of the war and the signing of the Dayton Peace Accords, people in Bosnia and Herzegovina continue to vote along ethnic lines and share the same preferences with regard to the constitutional set up of the country. According to Vesna Peric Zimonjic:

> Muslim Bosniaks insist on greater central authority for Sarajevo. The Catholic Croats, the smallest group, claim their existence is threatened without an entity of their own. And Orthodox Serbs continue to eye closer ties with Serbia proper, disregarding that they live in Bosnia-Herzegovina. The international officials' optimism and the reality on the ground continue to differ profoundly.[69]

Sumantra Bose agrees with this assessment:

> Among the three communities in BiH, the Bosniacs alone associate their collective identity and interests—indeed, their very future as a people—with the development of a functional Bosnian state.[70]

However, as pointed out by Bose,

> The shrill protests of many (not all) Bosnian and foreign integrationist revisionists against the Dayton settlement are inspired, in fact, not by a value-based commitment to a multinational, civic *society* but by a desire

---

67 Mirko Kapor, "Forgotten Decisions," *Politika* (Belgrade), August 17, 2004, 5.

68 Laura Silber, "Dayton, Ten Years After," *New York Times*, November 21, 2005, A1.

69 Vesna Peric Zimonjic, "Bosnian Poll to Finish Job of Ethnic Cleansing," *The Independent*, September 30, 2006.

70 Sumantra Bose, *Bosnia after Dayton* (New York: Oxford University Press, 2002), 27.

for a less decentralized, more unitary *state* which will put the disobedient and disloyal Bosnian Serbs (and to a lesser degree, the intransigent BiH Croats) in their place.[71]

Bosnian Muslim leaders, such as Haris Silajdzic, Bosnian Muslim member of the joint Presidency, have repeatedly called for the abolishment of the Republika Srpska entity in order to transform Bosnia into a unitary, centralized state.[72] In March 2007, the Bosnian Muslims also became the first ethnic group in Bosnia to officially request a change in boundaries, proposing that the municipality of Srebrenitsa, presently a majority Serb area, be given the status of a special district similar to Brchko and removed from the jurisdiction of Republika Srpska.[73] The Bosnian Croat member of the Bosnian Presidency seconded this motion although it was clear that it could not be implemented in practice.[74] The key argument of the Bosnian Muslims, particularly since the International Court of Justice confirmed that genocide occurred in Srebrenitsa,[75] was that "boundaries established based on genocide" were not "legitimate."[76] The High Representative responded by stating that the initiative of the Srebrenitsa Municipal Assembly "clearly exceeded its constitutional authority," describing the action as part of "a spate of political maneuvers that have taken up a great deal of time and energy (and in some cases public funds) but produced no positive dividends for citizens."[77]

In contrast to the Bosnian Muslims, Bosnian Serbs strongly cling to the Dayton Peace Accords. With time, the Bosnian Serbs have become comfortable with the idea of a Dayton Bosnia. A separate entity within Bosnia allows them to preserve

---

[71] Ibid, 200.

[72] Ibid, 27. *See also* Zdravko Ljubas, "Bosnia's Presidency may bring new ethnic split," *dpa German Press Agency,* October 2, 2006.

[73] Bosnian Muslim members of the Municipal Assembly of Srebrenitsa adopted a resolution requesting special status and removal from the jurisdiction of Republika Srpska after the Bosnian Serb members of the Municipal Assembly left the session in protest that such a resolution would impair the constitutional order of Republika Srpska and infringe on Dayton Peace Accords. The Bosnian Serbs form a minority in the town assembly although they form a majority of the inhabitants. "Bosniaks seek separation of Srebrenitsa from RS," *Politika,* March 25, 2007.

[74] Nedim Dervisbegovic, "Bosnia split on Srebrenica request for self rule," *Reuters,* March 12, 2007.

[75] International Court of Justice, *Case concerning the application of the Convention on the Prevention and Punishment of the Crime of Genocide (Bosnia and Herzegovina v Serbia and Montenegro),* February 26, 2007.

[76] Voice of America (VOA) News, March 16, 2007.

[77] OHR, "Gesture politics delivers nothing," March 30, 2007 (accessed April 1, 2007), available from http://www.ohr.int/ohr-dept/presso/pressr/default.asp?content_id=39452.

their identity and culture, while the international presence ensures peace, stability, and certain economic progress. The former president of Republika Srpska, Bilyana Plavshich,[78] was the first among Bosnian Serb leaders to recognize the importance of full compliance with Dayton Peace Accords and the Constitution of Republika Srpska. To this end, in 1997 she spoke against the adoption of the Agreement on special relations between Republika Srpska and the Federal Republic of Yugoslavia (FRY—Serbia and Montenegro) if the adoption procedure were not fully constitutional and in line with the Dayton Accord.[79] She warned that if the Bosnian Serbs were to disrespect the Dayton Accords and their Constitution, others could do the same, endangering their rights. Plavshich proceeded to give an example of the erstwhile president of the Federal Republic of Yugoslavia, Slobodan Miloshevich, signing a document on behalf of Republika Srpska on August 26, 1996, agreeing that the issue of Brchko be settled without the concurrence of at least one other arbitrator. The international community at the time sought and accepted the authority of another country's president, overlooking the legal ramifications.

Today, all Bosnian Serb politicians are unified in demanding that the Republika Srpska entity not be abolished in any future constitutional reforms, embracing the autonomy guarantees stipulated by the Dayton Peace Accords.[80] Nonetheless, since the Montenegrin referendum on independence and increased possibility of Kosovo's independence, Bosnian Serbs have also reopened the issue of Republika Srpska's referendum on independence and possible joining with Serbia.

The international community appeared to have accepted that any constitutional reform in Bosnia and Herzegovina had to be negotiated to be legitimate. Instead of forcing a new constitution, on the occasion of Dayton's tenth anniversary on November 22, 2005, Bosnia celebrated the "Commitment to Pursue Constitutional reform by March 2006," pledged by the state's leading politicians.[81] Particular sensitivity shown in this case, however, may have been the result of the opening of

---

[78] Often spelled "Biljana Plavsic" in the international press.

[79] "Address of Bilyana Plavshich, President of Republika Srpska, March 15, 1997, regarding the recently signed agreement on parallel relations between RS and FRY."

[80] "Bosnian Serbs defend Dayton and Republika Srpska in Washington," *Serbian Unity Congress News* (Washington, DC), November 30, 2005 (accessed November 30, 2005); available from http://news.serbianunity.net/bydate/2005/November_30/18.html.

[81] "Commitment to Pursue Constitutional reform," published at the Official Internet Presentation of the U.S. Embassy in Bosnia and Herzegovina, (accessed December 29, 2005); available from http://www.bhembassy.org/pdf/constreform%20statement%20english.pdf.

negotiations on Kosovo's future status. If Kosovo were granted independence, effectively partitioning Serbia, it would be difficult to deny the same right to Republika Srpska. The regional balance would then be shifted toward seeking external accommodation of self-determination:

> Serbs in Bosnia no longer dream of secession or union with Serbia because . . . their autonomy as a Serb Republic within Bosnia is secure. . . . But if that position is threatened they could seek independence using the same argument as ethnic Albanians in Serbia's breakaway province of Kosovo, who are pushing for formal independence on the basis of the right of self-determination.[82]

Indeed, as various international governments announced possible independence for Kosovo in spring 2007, a Bosnian-Serb non-governmental organization symbolically called "The Choice is ours" collected more than 50,000 signatures in support of an independence referendum for Republika Srpska. It presented the petition to the Parliament of Republika Srpska on March 29, 2007, at the height of the U.N. Security Council debate on the future status of Kosovo.[83] As elucidated by the Prime Minister of Republika Srpska, Milorad Dodik, any imposition of a unitary state-system instead of the federation that Dayton provides for Bosnia would push the Bosnian Serbs to seek independence:

> Sarayevo politicians want a unitary Bosnia and Herzegovina, and that is not disputed, but it should also not be disputed that we are requesting a federation or an end [to Bosnia]. That is a legitimate position.[84]

Similarly, although Bosnian Croats "would like nothing more than to join Croatia,"[85] they appeared to have given up claims to independence from Bosnia, resurrected on several occasions in the post-Dayton period.[86] The key factor that

---

[82] Interview with Milorad Dodik [main Serb opposition leader in Republika Srpska], *Reuters*, December 2, 2005.

[83] Onasa News Agency (Sarayevo), March 29, 2007.

[84] "Dodik: Either a Federalization of B&H or—the End!" *Srna News Agency*, March 17, 2007.

[85] Jeffrey T. Kuhne, "Redrawing Bosnian borders," *Washington Times*, September 30, 2003. *See also* Bose, *Bosnia after Dayton*, 28-29.

[86] *See*, for instance, Robert Fox, "Croat Mini-State Threatens to Undermine Dayton Election Plan," *Daily (Electronic) Telegraph* (London), June 17, 1996. As late as October 1999, Croatian President Franjo Tudman called for the formal creation of a separate Croat entity in Bosnia-Hercegovina: "Croatian

altered the Bosnian Croat stance was Croatia's commitment, wrested under international pressure, to respect Bosnian territorial integrity.[87] The other factor that contributed to change in the Bosnian Croat position, aside from actions by the Office of the High Representative to dismantle the Bosnian Croat para-state of Herzeg-Bosna,[88] was the high level of economic emigration:

> Of Bosnia's pre-war Croat population of some 830,000, only half remain. Many, especially the young, have gone to Croatia, which, since independence, has offered them automatic citizenship.[89]

However, Montenegrin independence in 2006 and increased international support for the potential independence of Kosovo have refueled demands for a separate Croat entity in Bosnia, summarized in the Declaration of the constitutional-law position of Croats in Bosnia and Herzegovina promulgated at the October 2005 conference organized by the University of Mostar and the Croatian Society of Arts and Science.[90] Since the conference, thousands of Bosnian Croats have signed a petition to this effect.[91] The Prime Minister of Republika Srpska, Milorad Dodik, has even proposed in 2006 that Bosnia and Herzegovina be reorganized into three entities. However this option is not acceptable to the Bosnian Muslims or to many members of the international community. The U.S. Ambassador to Bosnia,

---

President Talks to Foreign Reporters About Domestic International Issues," *BBC Worldwide Monitoring*, October 19, 1999.

[87] "Croatia Ends Bosnia Croat Separatist Dreams," *Reuters*, March 31, 2000. Note: In unwritten, realpolitik considerations Croatia was permitted to "recuperate" Krayina by force in return for supporting a Muslim-Croat Federation in Bosnia.

[88] *See*, for instance, 12th Report of the High Representative for Implementation of the Peace Agreement to the Secretary-General of the United Nations, February 12, 1999, particularly paragraph 35 (accessed December 30, 2005); available from http://www.ohr.int/other-doc/hr-reports/default.asp?content_id=3675.

[89] "Bosnia Ten Years on; Peaceful, Rebuilt But Still Divided," *The Economist*, November 24, 2005.

[90] "Starting from the scientific cognitions and practical experiences, we think, that in consultation with the representatives of Serbian and Bosniak people and International Community, we should organize Bosnia and Herzegovina as the compound federal state, composed of three federal units and with three levels of government. Since only the republic, as a democratic form of the rule of nations, includes and guarantees the highest level of democracy, political, cultural and every other autonomy, we pledge for the establishment of three republics for three sovereign nations, which is in full accordance with the provisions of the United Nations Pact on the civil, social and cultural rights to the equality of all nations regardless of their numerousness." *Declaration of the constitutional-law position of Croats in Bosnia and Herzegovina*; Neum, Bosnia and Herzegovina, October 27-28, 2005.

[91] "Bosnia's Croats Step up Calls for Their Own Entity," *DTT-Net.com*, February 21, 2007.

Douglas L. McElhaney, expressed this country's staunch objections to Bosnia's decentralization:

> There will be no third entity. We are trying to create a state and not another entity. We wish to have a situation in which a state is more centralized.[92]

The European Commissioner for Enlargement, Olli Rehn, did not comment specifically on the creation of a third entity but criticized calls for referendum on Republika Srpska's independence, stressing that Bosnia deserved reform "through constitutional evolution, not through constitutional revolution."[93]

Notably, most analysts have not questioned the legitimacy of intervening in a state to create a (Bosnian) nation, instead pondering how the process could be improved.[94] At the same time, while continuing to insist on Bosnia's unity, the international community has acknowledged the need to allow the Bosnian people to make more decisions for themselves by "phasing out" the legal and political interventions of the High Representative. In June 2004, the Parliamentary Assembly of the Council of Europe openly criticized the authority vested with the High Representative (OHR), considering as "irreconcilable with democratic principles that the OHR should be able to take enforceable decisions without being accountable for them or obliged to justify their validity and without there being a legal remedy."[95]

In evaluating the acts of the High Representative one is faced with the dilemma of a Bosnian peacemaker. Should the international community permit the people of Bosnia to separate into two or three different entities or force the

---

[92] Sead Numanović, Interview with U.S. Ambassador Douglas L. McElhaney: "Bosnia and Herzegovina is not and will not disintegrate!" *Dnevni Avaz*, March 21, 2007 [Translation mine].

[93] "International officials rebuff calls for RS independence referendum," *Southeast European Times*, May 31, 2006.

[94] *See, for instance*, Patrice C. McMahon, "Rebuilding Bosnia: A Model to Emulate or to Avoid?" *Political Science Quarterly* 119, No.4 (Winter 2004).

[95] Parliamentary Assembly of the Council of Europe Resolution 1384: "Strengthening of democratic institutions in Bosnia and Herzegovina," June 2004, Paragraph 13. Council of Europe's Venice Commission concurred. *See* European Commission for Democracy through Law (Venice Commission), Opinion on the Constitutional Situation in Bosnia and Herzegovina and the Powers of the High Representative, based on Comments by Mr. J. Helgesen (Member, Norway), Mr. J. Jowell (Member, United Kingdom), Mr. G. Malinverni (Member, Switzerland), Mr. J.-C. Scholsem (Member, Belgium), Mr. K. Tuori (Member, Finland), adopted by the Venice Commission at its 62nd plenary session, Venice, March 11-12, 2005, particularly paragraphs 86-100.

country's unification? Memories of recent violence are still fresh. As stressed by Lord Ashdown: "Anyone who thinks that the Bosnia's E.U. accession process will be the same as say, Lithuania, should visit Sarajevo and Srebrenica."[96] Bosnian partition into three entities is generally considered to be anathema and is seldom voiced. Yet, as pinpointed by Friedman, this may be the only sustainable solution:

> Bosnia can be democratic and self-sustaining, but only if the country gives up being unified and multi-ethnic. Or Bosnia can be multi-ethnic, democratic and unified, but not self-sustaining.[97]

In the words of the most famous American real-politician, Henry Kissinger:

> Should American casualties be incurred to force the various ethnic groups into a multinational state that the majority of them do not want? Why should we violate our own principle of self-determination in pursuit of such goals?[98]

The Dayton Peace Accords, while bringing peace, put the international community in the somewhat anachronistic position of a colonial power, a trustee. When Austria-Hungary annexed Bosnia and Herzegovina in 1908, Emperor Franz Joseph proclaimed, in full hypocrisy: "We estimate that time is ripe for granting the inhabitants of two countries [Bosnia and Herzegovina] a new proof of our confidence in their political maturity."[99] The reason given for the Dual Empire's administration of Bosnia and Herzegovina after the Congress of Vienna was also not dissimilar to the current arguments of the international community with regard to Bosnia:

> The Emperor and King could no longer remain a passive spectator of the violence and discord which reigned in the neighbourhood of

---

96 High Representative's remarks to the OSCE Permanent Council, December 15, 2005 (accessed December 28, 2005); available from http://www.ohr.int/ohr-dept/presso/presssp/default.asp?content_id=36276.

97 Thomas L. Friedman, "Foreign Affairs; Not Happening," *New York Times*, January 23, 2001, A 21; *see also* Gary T. Dempsey, "Rethinking the Dayton Agreement: Bosnia Three Years Later," *Cato Policy Analysis* No. 327, December 14, 1998.

98 Henry Kissinger, "Limits to What the U.S. Can Do in Bosnia," *Washington Post*, September 22, 1997.

99 Proclamation of the annexation of Bosnia and Herzegovina by the Emperor Franz Joseph, Vienna, October 3, 1908, reproduced in Pierre Albin, *Les Grands Traités Politiques* (Paris, 1912), 231. Original text: " . . . nous estimons que le moment est venu pour donner aux habitants des deux pays une nouvelle preuve de notre confiance en leur maturité politique" [Translation mine].

his provinces. . . . No violent change shall be introduced without your desires having been maturely considered. . . . Place yourselves with confidence under the protection of the glorious standard of Austria-Hungary. Receive our soldiers as friends, obey the authorities, resume your work, and you will obtain protection for the fruit of your labours.[100]

As elaborated by the first British Ambassador to a Dayton Bosnia, Charles Crawford, "normally a foreign diplomat is forbidden from any intervention in the host country's internal affairs" but "in Bosnia we were required to give internal affairs and then interfere in them." This created an enormous problem of democratic deficit:

> Neither the government nor the public thought that the government was there for the public—there was no link between action and responsibility to the public.[101]

The international community's zeal to build the Bosnian nation has paradoxically weakened the Bosnian state. As deduced by Maurizio Massari, Italian diplomat and OSCE Ambassador to Serbia:

> In a perfect paradox, the OHR has had to impose its rule in order to strengthen the Bosnian state, but the more it has used such powers, the more it has reinforced passivity and irresponsibility on the part of BiH's political elites, thereby undermining the goal of creating an independent and self-sustaining Bosnian state.[102]

In its 2005 Progress Report on Bosnia and Herzegovina, the E.U. notes with satisfaction that the number of decisions adopted by the High Representative is diminishing and that "in the reporting period, the High Representative has not

---

[100] Austrian proclamation on the entrance of Austro-Hungarian troops into Bosnia and Herzegovina, July 28, 1878, reproduced in Snezana Trifunovska, ed. *Yugoslavia through Documents: from Its Creation to Its Dissolution* (Dordrecht, The Netherlands: Martinus Nijhoff Publishers, 1994), 97.

[101] Author's Interview with Ambassador Charles Crawford, Boston, March 5, 1999.

[102] Maurizio Massari, "Do All Roads Lead to Brussels? Analysis of the Different Trajectories of Croatia, Serbia-Montenegro and Bosnia-Herzegovina," *Cambridge Review of International Affairs* 18, no. 2 (July 2005), 262. Note: The Venice Commission has also concluded that wide powers of the High Representative lead to insufficient accountability of the country's political representatives. Venice Commission, Opinion on the Constitutional Situation in Bosnia and Herzegovina and the Powers of the High Representative, 2005, paragraph 90.

imposed laws or decisions directly related to the Feasibility Study priorities."[103] Subsequently, the E.U.'s High Representative for Foreign and Security Policy, Javier Solana, announced that "the Peace Implementation Council has said it is ready to phase out the Bonn Powers and move to a mission led by an E.U. Special Representative, perhaps as early as the 2006 elections."[104] Since the High Representative is now also the E.U. Special Representative, one can only assume that this would imply a softer version of external guidance for Bosnia and Herzegovina than the dictate presented by the Deputy High Representative, Hanns Schumacher of Germany, as necessary for the implementation of Dayton Peace Accords:

> We dictate what will be done . . . we simply do not pay attention to those who obstruct! I think we have already proved that we can use the authorities that Dayton gives us and all those who resist will have to face the consequences.[105]

Nonetheless, as late as March 2007 Bonn Powers were still used by the High Representative, this time by High Representative Christian Schwarz-Schilling, who suspended the newly-appointed government of the Bosnian-Croat Federation because it did not respect "the vetting process," which allows the High Representative to scrutinize ministerial candidates. At the time, Schwarz-Schilling stated: "I have deliberately stayed out of the government-formation process, believing that this is a core function of any normal democracy."[106] One could argue that the choice of ministerial candidates is also a core function of a normal democracy, vested to the politicians by the voters. In another decision, also promulgated in March 2007, the High Representative officially proclaimed himself to

---

[103] "The number of decisions adopted by the High Representative is down in 2005 (52 by the end of September) compared with 2004, when there were 158 (including the dismissal of 59 officials in June 2004 for non-cooperation with the ICTY)." European Commission, *Bosnia and Herzegovina 2005 Progress Report*, COM (2005) 561, Brussels, November 9, 2005, 13.

[104] Speech by Javier Solana, E.U. High Representative for the CFSP, at the Policy Dialogue "Dayton at Ten: Drawing Lessons from the Past," organized by the European Policy Centre and King Baudouin Foundation," Brussels, November 25, 2005, S382/05.

[105] Interview with Hanns H. Schumacher by Emir Suljagic, *Dani* (Sarajevo), April 11, 1998, published on the Internet presentation of the Office of the High Representative (accessed May 24, 2005); available from http://www.ohr.int/ohr-dept/presso/pressi/default.asp?content_id=3416.

[106] OHR, Statement by the High Representative for B&H, Christian Schwarz-Schilling at the Press Conference, March 23, 2007 (accessed March 25, 2007); available from http://www.ohr.int/ohr-dept/presso/pressb/default.asp?content_id=39395.

be above law, nullifying the proceedings in the Bosnian courts that repeal his decisions:

> Notwithstanding any contrary provision in any legislation in Bosnia and Herzegovina, any proceeding instituted before any court in Bosnia and Herzegovina, which challenges or takes issue in any way whatsoever with one or more decisions of the High Representative, shall be declared inadmissible unless the High Representative expressly gives his prior consent.[107]

The exercise of the Bonn Powers hardly contributes to the expectation of the international community that Bosnia and Herzegovina should gradually take ownership of its reform process and establish a "democratic governance" that is mandated by (internal) self-determination.

While endorsing the Bonn Powers, the European Union and the United States also continue to exert strong pressure for constitutional reform in Bosnia and Herzegovina. As Solana has explained,

> To integrate itself progressively with the European Union, Bosnia and Herzegovina needs stronger state-institutions. To deliver the benefits that its citizens deserve, it needs to cut the cost of government.[108]

Yet constitutional reform could be accomplished in different ways. In reviewing the possibilities for reform, the Venice Commission finds both the option of abolishing entities and the option of eliminating the cantons to be unfeasible, and calls for "concentration of legislative tasks" at the level of the entity in the case of the Federation of Bosnia and Herzegovina and for a simultaneous transfer of competence from the entities to the state level, to be accompanied by the streamlining of decision-making procedures within the country,[109] *de facto* creating a (more)

---

[107] OHR, Order on the Implementation of the Decision of the Constitutional Court of Bosnia and Herzegovina in the Appeal of Milorad Bilbija et al, No. AP-953/05, March 23, 2007 (accessed March 25, 2007); available from http://www.ohr.int/decisions/statemattersdec/default.asp?content_id=39397.

[108] Solana, "Dayton at Ten: Drawing Lessons from the Past"; High U.S. officials, such as the Undersecretary of State Nicholas Burns, have also made strong statements to this effect. *See* Remarks as Prepared, Undersecretary for Political Affairs R. Nicholas Burns, "Bosnia Ten Years Later: Successes and Challenges," *United States Institute of Peace*, Washington, D.C., November 21, 2005.

[109] Venice Commission, Opinion on the Constitutional Situation in Bosnia and Herzegovina and the Powers of the High Representative, 2005, particularly paragraphs 46, 51, 53, 55, 56, 101-104.

unitary state. The European Stability Initiative (ESI), an international non-governmental institute based in Berlin, Brussels, and Sarayevo, has instead creatively proposed that Bosnia be transformed into "functionally equivalent federal units," equalizing the existing cantons with the Republika Srpska entity and the Brchko district, while eliminating the Muslim-Croat entity. The strongest Bosnian Croat party, the Croat Democratic Community of Bosnia and Herzegovina, espoused the ESI proposal but left Republika Srpska the option to remain "an entity" rather than "a canton,"[110] which is more in tune with the Bosnian Serb demands. If this is how reform is directed, aiming for a more effective decision-making procedure rather unifying the country for the sake of principle, an agreement among the key stakeholders should be possible, provided Bosnian Muslims also aim at a more effective state. The latter could also be achieved by creating three ethnic-based entities that would render Bosnia a more functional federal state, as proposed by the Prime Minister of Republika Srpska, Milorad Dodik.

One could further argue that the international community in fact contributed to the complexity and cost of Bosnian government by awarding the town of Brchko the status of "a district" to be "held 'in condominium' by both entities [which would not] exercise any authority,"[111] despite the fact that this act also infringed on the negotiating principles for the Dayton Peace Accords that defined entities as continuous and specified the territorial percentage division as 49 percent for Republika Srpska. Moreover, to ensure equal rights for the three main ethnic groups throughout the country, the High Representative enacted amendments to the Entities' Constitutions in line with the Bosnia and Herzegovina Constitutional Court ruling in the "Constituent peoples' case,"[112] with a side effect of complicating the decision-making procedure at various government levels. As summarized by the Venice Commission:

> Power-sharing provisions, including a vital interest veto, similar to the provisions at State level were introduced in both Entities and the Cantons, and rules allocating the most important positions equally among the three constituent peoples were included in the respective Constitutions. As a result

---

[110] European Stability Initiative, "Making Federalism Work—A Radical Proposal for Practical Reform," January 8, 2004.

[111] Brcko Arbitration Arbitral Tribunal for Dispute over Inter-Entity Boundary in Brcko Area, Final Award, March 5, 1999, paragraph 11. (accessed October 6, 2004); available from http://www.ohr.int/ohr-offices/brcko/default.asp?content_id=5358#2.

[112] The full text of the decision appears in document CDL (2000)81.

of these historical developments, BiH now on the one hand continues to be divided into different units—two Entities, one of which is subdivided into 10 Cantons—originally set up to ensure the control of the respective territories by one (or in the case of the FBiH and the two mixed Cantons, two) constituent people(s). On the other hand, the representatives of the three constituent peoples now constitutionally have in these various units a strong blocking position, even where they represent only a very limited number of voters.[113]

Constituent peoples have abused the vital interest veto due to its broad definition, which the Venice Commission proposes be narrowed to facilitate more effective decision-making.[114] While praising the role of ethnic safeguards in preserving peace, the Venice Commission nonetheless advocates "further constitutional reforms, changing the emphasis from a state based on the equality of three constituent peoples to a state based on the equality of citizens."[115]

Professor Robert Hayden disagrees, arguing that constitutional ethnic safeguards represent the only framework for a sustainable Bosnia:

> A constitution linking Bosnia's peoples while not pretending to dissolve them would seem most suitable to the social constructions used by the Bosnian peoples themselves.[116]

Hayden further recalls that U.N. Secretary General Kofi Annan's proposal for a constitutional structure for Cyprus, a partitioned country that enjoys full E.U. membership, "resembled very closely the Dayton constitution for Bosnia: a weak union of two almost completely self-governing component states."[117] In other words, Bosnia is not a constitutional anomaly. As shown by the European Union's annual review of the accession countries, Bosnia and Herzegovina shares the problems of other countries in the region, including Croatia, such as an inefficient

---

[113] Venice Commission, Opinion on the Constitutional Situation in Bosnia and Herzegovina and the Powers of the High Representative, 2005, paragraph 10.

[114] Ibid., paragraphs 30-32.

[115] Ibid., paragraph 104.

[116] Robert M. Hayden, "Constitutional Structures in a Nationless State," Paper presented at the conference on "The Tenth Anniversary of the Dayton Accords: Reflections on Post-Conflict state- and Nation-Building," Woodrow Wilson International Center for Scholars, Washington, DC, December 7, 2005.

[117] Ibid.

judiciary or corruption. Yet unlike Croatia, Bosnia and Herzegovina has whole-heartedly implemented the policy of refugee return as requested by the European Union. Some Bosnian officials such as Mario Nenadić, Assistant Minister for Human Rights and Refugees, therefore consider the two countries' position vis-à-vis the E.U. to be unfair: "We've done everything by the book and we're the ones who are behind in the European integration process."[118]

Nonetheless, one significant difference between Croatia and Bosnia is that Bosnia is inherently unstable. As postulated by Major General David Leakey, commander of a 7,000-strong European Union military force that replaced NATO's peace-keeping mission in Bosnia in 2004, without sustained international pressure, including a military presence, "a cocktail of destabilising factors could unlock instability."[119] Burg and Shoup have pointed out the paradox that it is now the Bosnian Serbs who are the principal beneficiaries of the international military presence on the ground, with the Bosnian Muslims having a greater interest in restarting the war, "in pursuit of the Muslim leadership's claims to authority over all of Bosnia."[120]

The only way out of this vicious cycle in Bosnia is to confer greater democratic accountability to its ethnic representatives, facilitating a constitutional solution that may not be perfectly multiethnic on the surface but that would eventually lead to democratic governance, including high human rights standards. European integration is a key factor in this process, not only because of its promise of eco-nomic prosperity but also because it will permit stronger ties to Bosnia's two unwilling partners, Bosnian Serbs and the Bosnian Croats, with the neighboring Croatia and Serbia, further reducing the allure of secessionism, provided the international community stems similar movements in the region. Recognizing such possibilities, the Council of Ministers of Bosnia and Herzegovina in December 2005 legalized a standing practice of conferring dual citizenship to citizens of Bosnia and Croatia, but also providing the non-Croat Bosnians with the same opportunity.[121] Sumantra Bose also concludes that the future of the

---

[118]   Mario Nenadić, speaking at the Harvard Club of Serbia and Montenegro conference: "The Rights of Displaced Serbs in Light of European Integration," OSCE, Belgrade, December 8, 2005.

[119]   Eric Jansson, "Stability Eludes Bosnia Ten Years after Dayton," *Financial Times*, November 21, 2005.

[120]   Steven L. Burg and Paul S. Shoup, *The War in Bosnia-Herzegovina: Ethnic Conflict and International Intervention* (New York: M. E. Sharp Inc., 1999), 386-387.

[121]   Bosnian Muslims/Bosniaks have an interest in obtaining Croatian citizenship in order to become eligible for visa-free travel to E.U. member states that the Croat citizens enjoy.

Bosnian state lies in greater inter-entity and regional cooperation rather than "classical" integration:

> 'Integration' in the classic sense is unlikely, but growing cooperation between Bosnia's fragments is likely, as it is likely between the successor-states to former Yugoslavia as a whole, including Bosnia.[122]

One should stress, however, that the potential independence of Kosovo would encourage the external rather than internal options to self-determination in Bosnia and Herzegovina. Unfortunately, High Representative Miroslav Lajčàk's measures to single-handedly change Bosnia's Law on the Council of Ministers in October 2007, and thereby indirectly amend Bosnia's Constitution by curtailing ethnic safeguards in the decision-making process, have also contributed to Bosnia's ethnic rife rather interethnic cooperation.

7.4. Macedonia's Decentralization as a Means of Fulfilling "Internal" Self-Determination

The Former Yugoslav Republic of Macedonia was the first country in the region to be invited to start negotiations on the Stabilization and Association Agreement (SAA) with the EU. The invitation, not incidentally, arrived in the aftermath of NATO's bombing of Yugoslavia (Serbia and Montenegro), on June 16, 1999.[123] Macedonian stability, shaken by a large influx of refugees,[124] needed to be bolstered by a strong signal that the integrative forces in the country would be rewarded by greater national prosperity.

Macedonia was also the first in the Western Balkans to sign an SAA and thereby become associate E.U. member on April 9, 1999. Presently, it closely follows Croatia on the road to full E.U. membership, becoming an official candidate on December 17, 2005,[125] but without a set date for accession

---

[122] Bose, *Bosnia after Dayton*, 32.

[123] Com (99) 300, June 16, 1999. European Council (heads of E.U. states) accepted the Commission's proposals on June 19, 1999.

[124] "The majority of the Slav electorate was seething with discontent against its Albanian compatriots and felt alienated from a ruling coalition that had won an absolute majority in parliamentary elections less than six months previously." Kyril Drezov, "Collateral Damage: The Impact on Macedonia of the Kosovo War," *Kosovo: The Politics of Delusion*, eds. Michael Waller, Kyril Drezov and Bülent Gökay (London, Portland OR: Frank Cass, 2001), 65.

[125] Commission of the European Communities, Commission Opinion on the Application from the Former Yugoslav Republic of Macedonia for Membership of the European Union, Brussels, November 9, 2005, COM (2005) 562; Council of the European Union, Presidency Conclusions 15914/05, Brussels, December 17, 2005, 7.

negotiations.[126] Although Greece still has not consented to Macedonia's name, tensions over this issue have largely been diffused, with Greece becoming the largest investor in Macedonia by 1998, and its second-largest trading partner.[127]

A Macedonian analyst, Kyril Drezov, considers three factors to be critical for Macedonian stability: "state monopoly in the means of violence, Slav domination of the state and Western support for this state."[128] Drezov stresses that "in some respects Macedonian policies were even more draconian than Serbian policies in Kosovo,"[129] but that the international community tolerated such actions and praised Macedonia's treatment of minorities, providing this weak country with the security and economic and diplomatic support that were essential for its survival.[130] As one commentator, Simon Jenkins, has cynically remarked:

> So it was OK to bomb Belgrade in 1999, but not the Macedonian capital of Skopje in 2001. Kosovo has good Albanians, Macedonia has bad ones. That is the joy of dabbling in other people's conflicts. You can treat right and wrong as black and white. One gets a million dollars, the other gets cluster bombs.

Jenkins deduces that the Macedonian Albanians and Albanians of Serbia's Preshevo valley close to Kosovo both learned a negative lesson from the NATO's 1999 bombing of Serbia and Montenegro by rebelling in 2001:

> These Albanians know from experience how to win friends in the West. They terrorize the ruling power and provoke it into retaliatory suppression and atrocity. They raise the tempo of this atrocity until it is noticed by the Western media, which is the catalyst to panicking politicians into "something must be done". Then they sit tight and await the bombs and aid.[131]

---

[126] Olli Rehn, E.U. Enlargement Commissioner, "Making the European Perspective real in the Balkans," Keynote address at the Conference "Bringing the Balkans into Mainstream Europe" by Friends of Europe, Brussels, December 8, 2005, SPEECH/05/770.

[127] Richard Holbrooke, *To End a War* (New York: Random House, 1998), 127.

[128] Drezov, "Collateral Damage: The Impact on Macedonia of the Kosovo War," 60.

[129] "For example, throughout the 1990s the Serbs tolerated Albanian higher education in private houses, but in 1995 Macedonian police bulldozed a private building earmarked for an Albanian university in Tetovo and imprisoned its first rector." Ibid., 60.

[130] Ibid., 61.

[131] Simon Jenkins, "Nato prepares to reap the Balkan whirlwind," *The Times* (London), March 21, 2001.

Nonetheless, the international community, led by the United States and the European Union, rejected the irredentism of Preshevo Albanians.[132] In Macedonia, the U.S. and the E.U. negotiated the end of the 2001 conflict between the Macedonian Slav authorities and the Albanian insurgents by giving in to Albanian demands—short of secession. The Western governments forced the Macedonian leadership to introduce far-reaching amendments to the constitution, significantly enhancing the rights of the Macedonian Albanians.[133] The Agreement of Ohrid of August 13, 2001 ["The Framework Agreement"] embodied these changes, translated to fifteen amendments to the Macedonian constitution, approved by a large majority of ninety-four against fourteen votes on November 15, 2001. Interestingly, as in the case of Dayton Peace Accords: "The English language version of this Agreement is the only authentic version."[134]

The Preamble to the Macedonian Constitution was changed to declare the Republic of Macedonia "a state of all its citizens." In line with this change, the new wording of the constitution has replaced the terms "Macedonian people," "nationalities," and "minorities" with more politically correct terms: "majority population," "communities," and "communities not in the majority." A positive side effect of this change was that other Macedonian minorities, namely Serbs, who previously were not recognized by the country's Constitution, attained a more equal treatment.

The Ohrid Agreement also met long-standing Albanian demands with regard to establishing the official status of the Albanian language. While Macedonian remains the main official language, to be exclusively used in foreign relations,[135] "any other language spoken by at least 20 percent of the population is also an official language, written using its alphabet, as specified below" (Article 7 of the Macedonian Constitution). The percentage formula conformed to the civic approach of not mentioning ethnic groups but in reality corresponded only to the Albanians, who may now use Albanian in communication with the central government, as well as with regional and local authorities in those areas where they constitute more than 20 percent, and enjoy a right to government-paid translation in criminal and judicial proceedings. Furthermore, the government

---

132 Nebi Qena, "USA Does Not Support UCPMB, Says Dell," *Koha Ditore* (Pristina), December 7, 2001 (accessed October 25, 2005); available from http://pristina.usmission.gov/dells/dell2.htm.

133 Raymond Detrez, "The Right to Self-Determination and Secession in Yugoslavia: A Hornets' Nest of Inconsistencies," in *Contextualizing Secession: Normative Studies in Comparative Perspective*, eds. Bruno Coppieters **and Richard Sakwa** (Oxford: Oxford University Press, 2003), 112-132: 126.

134 Framework Agreement (Ohrid Agreement), August 13, 2001, Article 10.2.

135 Ibid., Article 6.4.

has been obligated to provide university education for language communities that speak an official language other than Macedonian,[136] with the Albanian-language Tetovo University receiving legal recognition in February 2004.[137]

Radmila Shekerinska, the Deputy Prime Minister of Macedonia, has recently praised the implementation of these provisions:

> Minority languages could be used in parliament, Albanian-speaking citizens could address the central government and courts in their own language, and the state television channel offered Albanian programming.[138]

Pursuant to the Ohrid Agreement, a constitutional amendment was adopted that requires a "double majority" for laws related to ethnic minorities: the majority of all parliamentary deputies and the majority of all deputies representing ethnic minorities must support such a law in order for it to be adopted. This concerns laws "that directly affect culture, use of language, education, personal documentation, and use of symbols," as well as certain laws in the area of local self-government, including boundaries of municipalities, and certain amendments to the Constitution.[139] The same provision applies to the election of a third of the judges of the Constitutional Court, the members of the Republican Judicial Council, and the Ombudsman. Yet, unlike in Bosnia, ethnic safeguards, complicating the decision-making procedure, are not considered as an obstacle but a bridge to European integration.

Finally, the new constitutional framework prescribes "equitable representation of communities in all central and local public bodies and at all levels of employment within such bodies."[140] As a result, from 2001 to 2005, there has been an 80 percent increase in the employment of minorities, allowing Albanians to obtain a level of representation in the state administration, army, and police that is closer to their share of the overall population.[141]

---

[136] "State funding will be provided for university level education in languages spoken by at least 20 percent of the population of Macedonia, on the basis of specific agreements." Ibid., Article 6.2.

[137] *See* Human Rights Watch, World Report 2005; Human Rights Overview: Macedonia (accessed December 26, 2005); available from http://hrw.org/english/docs/2005/01/13/macedo9875.htm.

[138] European Policy Centre, Communication to Members S48 /05: Macedonia—Preparing for the European Union; Breakfast Policy Briefing, September 26, 2005.

[139] Framework Agreement, 2001, 5.2; Macedonian Constitution, Articles 69 (2), 78, 109, 114 and 131.

[140] Framework Agreement, 2001, Article 4.

[141] In September 2005, 20 percent of the army and police force was composed of ethnic Albanians and more than 20 percent of public service positions were staffed by "non -majority" citizens.

On July 15, 2005, the Macedonian government formally fulfilled all the stipulations of the Ohrid Agreement by adopting the Law on Community Symbols. The key provision, relating to the decentralization of powers, was fully accomplished, thanks to an agreement negotiated by the ruling Macedonian Slav and Albanian parties in mid-2004 on new local government boundaries. The role of decentralization in curbing violent separatism appears to have been fully recognized by the Macedonian population, reflected in insufficient voter turnout at a November 2004 referendum that aimed to overturn the new territorial division. Government officials, such as Prime Minister Vlado Buckovski, formerly Macedonia' s defense minister, described the outcome as "a strong message to the European Union and NATO that the citizens know the way ahead and they are counting on international support for (the country's) integration."[142]

The new territorial organization had particularly disturbed the inhabitants of Struga municipality with a slim Macedonian Slav majority, which was to become a part of an Albanian-dominated district. In protest, Struga's citizens demonstrated and local parties announced that they would seek independence for the municipality, hoping to enjoy a status similar to that of San Marino or Monaco.[143] The government acted swiftly, arresting the Struga demonstrators. In March 2005, local elections paved the way for full implementation of the government decentralization. These elections were peaceful and deemed sufficiently democratic despite numerous irregularities.

Nonetheless, Human Rights Watch warns that, in practice "discrimination against national minorities, including in particular ethnic Albanians and Roma, and police violence continue to be problems in the country."[144] The authorities continue to discriminate against the Serbian Orthodox Church as well, imprisoning the head of the Serbian Orthodox Church in Macedonia in July 2005 for "inciting national, racial and religious hatred, schism and intolerance" for performing a baptism in a church building belonging to the rival Macedonian Orthodox Church.[145]

---

[142] Only 26 percent of 1.7 million voters showed up, while more than half was required. Boris Babic, "Macedonians nervous and divided over poll," *Diplomacy and Trade* (Hungary's International Monthly), January 2005.

[143] Ibid. *See also* M. Tomovski, "War between Struga and the State," *Politika* (Belgrade), August 11, 2004, 2.

[144] Human Rights Watch, World Report 2005; Human Rights Overview: Macedonia (accessed December 26, 2005); available from http://hrw.org/english/docs/2005/01/13/macedo9875.htm.

[145] "Forum 18," an international NGO based in Oslo, Norway and agitating for a right to belief has reported that the Macedonian authorities have, since independence, among other things, repeatedly refused to

In brief, the Ohrid Agreement, as pointed out by Nicholas Whyte, brought Macedonia "as close as you can get to the ideal of a civic democracy in an ethnically divided society."[146] Time will show whether granting extensive minority rights through a decentralization process and benefits of membership in the Euro-Atlantic community will successfully dissuade violent secessionism in Macedonia of the type that occurred in 2001.

7.5. Montenegro's Separation from Serbia: Success or Failure of European Integration?

Stabilization and Association Process opened for the Federal Republic of Yugoslavia (Serbia and Montenegro) once Serbia's citizens ousted Slobodan Miloshevich in October 2000. The E.U. granted Serbia and Montenegro trade preferentials in November 2000 and initiated expert ("Consultative Task Force") meetings in July 2001 with a view to preparing for negotiations on associate membership—Stabilization and Association Agreement (SAA). However, the process was prolonged, with official SAA negotiations commencing only five years after democratic changes in Serbia, in October 2005. The key reason for the delay was the unresolved status of the country.

The Montenegrin leadership, discontent with the country's federal arrangement, demanded that the state be reorganized into a loose union of states, also considering secession. Proponents of Montenegrin secession considered the state arrangement of 2000 to be a barrier to the prosperity of both republics:

> The Federation of Montenegro and Serbia is a relic of Yugoslavia. It is the very barrier to the prosperity of both Serbia and Montenegro. These two republics are not connected by capital, or the structure of the industrial future or by the responsibility towards adjusting to the European Union.[147]

---

give state registration to the Serbian Orthodox Church, staged police raids with priests of the rival Macedonian Orthodox Church to "persuade" members of the Serbian Church in Macedonia to join the Macedonian Church, and demolished a monastery after a paramilitary "state security unit" attacked it with machine guns. For more, see http://www.forum18.org.

146 Nicholas Whyte, "The Macedonian Framework Document and European Standards," *CEPS—Europa South-East Monitor* 26 (Brussels) August 2001, 2.

147 Ljubisav Marković, *Kapital, ekonomija i socijalizacija* [Capital, Economy and Socialization] (Belgrade: Faculty of Political Science, 2004), 319 [Translation mine]. Original text: "Federacija Crne Gore i Srbije je krhotina Jugoslavije. Upravo barijera za prosperitet i Srbije i Crne Gore. Ove dve republike ne povezuje niti kapital, niti struktura privredne budućnosti, niti odgovornost prema prilagodjavanju Evropskoj uniji."

Agitating for independence, Montenegrin Foreign Minister Miodrag Vlahovic further argued that Montenegro did not wish to remain a "hostage" of Serbia's reluctance to cooperate with the Hague-based war crimes tribunal,[148] overlooking the frequently voiced suspicion that one of the most wanted ICTY fugitives may be hiding in Montenegro, not Serbia. In March 2004, the Montenegrin separatists, enjoying a majority in government structures, changed the language in the school curricula from "Serbian" to "mother tongue" without specifying what the "mother tongue" was.[149] The separatists also demonstrated support for the Montenegrin Orthodox Church, which, unlike the Serb Orthodox Church, has a minor following in Montenegro. Both of these actions were taken with a goal of strengthening the non-Serb Montenegrin identity. Such acts have disturbed many Montenegrins,[150] enhancing the concern that violence could erupt in Montenegro if the procedure for realizing independence were not considered democratic by key political representatives.[151]

The E.U. intervened in the dispute over the Serb-Montenegrin state structure. In March 2002, Javier Solana, E.U. High Representative for Foreign and Security Policy mediated an agreement titled "Proceeding Points for the Restructuring of Relations between Serbia and Montenegro," which became better known as "the Belgrade Agreement."[152] Due to different interpretations of the agreement, the Constitutional Charter of Serbia and Montenegro was adopted almost one year later, on February 4, 2003.[153] Various constitutional lawyers have criticized the procedure by which the new constitution was adopted, stressing that it was illegal and therefore not a sound basis for a state.[154]

---

[148] RFE/RL Balkan Report 9, No. 6, February 11, 2005.

[149] Rajko Cerovic, "Too frightened to call the language Montenegrin," *Monitor* (Podgoritsa), March 26, 2004.

[150] *See* Declaration: In Defense Of The Name Of The Serbian Language, December 5, 2004 (accessed December 31, 2005); available from http://www.spc.yu/Vesti-2004/12/07-12-04-e.html.

[151] Other analysts had foreseen political instability but not violence in this case. *See* U.K. House of Commons Foreign Affairs Committee, Foreign Affairs—Third Report, February 1, 2005, particularly paragraph 89 (accessed December 31, 2005); available from http://www.publications.parliament.uk/pa/cm200405/cmselect/cmfaff/87/8707.htm#n117.

[152] Proceeding Points for the Restructuring of Relations between Serbia and Montenegro (Belgrade Agreement), March 2002 (accessed November 19, 2005); available from http://www.mfa.gov.yu/Bilteni/Engleski/b150302_e.html#N2.

[153] Constitutional Charter of Serbia and Montenegro, February 4, 2003 (accessed November 14, 2005); available from http://www.mfa.gov.yu/Facts/const_scg.pdf.

[154] The procedure for amending the constitution did not conform to the 1992 Constitution of the Federal Republic of Yugoslavia or the constitutions of the member republics. For more, *see* Oliver Nikolic,

The Belgrade agreement gave Yugoslavia a new name—"Serbia and Montenegro" and preserved important federal institutions such as the parliament, the president, the Council of Ministers, and the Constitutional Court. Yet it also narrowed the competence of federal authorities to five areas, the only exclusive areas being defense and human rights. Foreign affairs became a shared competence since Montenegro had an independent Minister of Foreign Affairs at the republic level and independent missions abroad in addition to participating in the common diplomatic corps. The state union government was also in charge of *coordinating* internal and external foreign relations, which translated to a minimal function in practice. The Parliament of Serbia and Montenegro consisted of 126 members, 91 from Serbia and 35 from Montenegro. Although the Charter did not provide for a specific formula, Nikolic deduced the following:

> It is clear that the substantially greater number of electors in Serbia was taken into account, but positive discrimination concerning the number of members from Montenegro is also visible.[155]

To adopt legislation, the parliament required a double majority—the majority of delegates present and the majority of delegates from each state. The Constitutional Charter of Serbia and Montenegro embodied other safeguards as well, such as a rule that the Minister of Defense and the Minister of Foreign Affairs could not be from the same republic. However, this provision was twice rebutted, unconstitutionally but upon agreement of both member republics. In 2003, Serbia and Montenegro thus became a "state union," and as such neither a federation nor a confederation, but a structure dependant on the political compromise of its two members. Significantly, both the Belgrade Agreement and the Constitutional Charter stipulated that "integration into the European structures and in particular the European Union" represented one of the primary objectives of the joint state (Article 3). The European Union participated in the drafting of the Constitutional Charter. Nonetheless, the final version of the Charter was a much diffused version of E.U.-proposed "Draft elements for possible inclusion in the Constitutional Charter," to the detriment of the functionality of the state union. For instance, the Minister for internal economic relations came to be charged

---

"Constitutional Charter of Serbia and Montenegro," *Constitution; Lex Superior*, ed. Srdjan Djordjevic (Belgrade: Association de droit constitutionnel de Serbie, 2004), 391-400: 392.

[155] Oliver Nikolic, "Constitutional Charter of Serbia and Montenegro," 395. Note: Serbian population numbered more than ten times that of Montenegro and Serbia contributed more than 95 percent to the country's gross domestic product.

with coordinating internal economic relations instead of establishing a common market as the E.U. suggested.[156]

The vagueness and the limited scope of the Constitutional Charter led to problems in its implementation, often creating obstacles to the country's E.U. accession, a process that requires clear institutional competences. Having failed to convince Serbia and Montenegro to converge their economies, the E.U. eventually accepted that the country would essentially accede to the Union with two distinct economic markets, under a "twin-track" mechanism:

> The Council expressed its support for the twin-track approach, which would imply a single Stabilisation and Association Agreement with distinct negotiations with the Republics on trade, economic and possibly on other relevant sectoral policies.[157]

Upon pronouncing this decision, the E.U. foreign ministers reaffirmed their "commitment to a strengthened State Union of Serbia and Montenegro based on the Constitutional Charter,"[158] clarifying that the twin-track approach does not imply endorsement of full separatism.

Serbia and Montenegro's constitutional inadequacies were compounded by the lack of clarity in the will of the Montenegrin citizens to live in a joint state with Serbia. Opinion polls showed a polarized population,[159] and the procedure for holding a referendum became highly politicized. The ad-hoc Contact Group countries (France, Germany, Russia, the United Kingdom, and the United States) took a firm stand on the issue, warning Montenegro in April 2000 that a unilateral declaration on independence would lead to the loss of political and financial support from the international community.[160]

---

[156] E.U. non-paper "Draft elements for possible inclusion in the Constitutional Charter" in author's possession.

[157] Council of the European Union, Press Release 12770/04, 2609th Council Meeting: General Affairs and External Relations, Luxembourg, October 11, 2004, 23.

[158] Ibid.

[159] The most recent research by Marten Board International finds 39 percent of the citizens in favor and 34 percent opposed to Montenegrin independence. Cited in *Inet News*, December 8, 2005 (accessed December 9, 2005); available from http://www.inet.co.yu/index.php?date=20051208.

[160] *Financial Times*, April 26, 2001.

The Constitutional Charter recognized the possibility of a member state seceding from the state union, initiated with a public referendum in that state. Significantly, the Charter also delineated the succession procedure, underscoring that Montenegro's potential secession would not impair Serbia's right to territorial integrity with regard to the province of Kosovo:

> Upon the expiry of a three-year period the member state shall have the right to initiate the procedure for a change of the state status, i.e. for withdrawal from the State Union of Serbia and Montenegro.
>
> A decision to withdraw from the State Union of Serbia and Montenegro shall be made after a referendum has been held. The Law on Referendum shall be passed by a member state, taking into account recognised democratic standards.
>
> If Montenegro withdraws from the State Union of Serbia and Montenegro, the international documents related to the Federal Republic of Yugoslavia, particularly United Nations Security Council Resolution 1244, shall pertain and apply fully to Serbia as its successor.
>
> The member state that exercises the right of withdrawal shall not inherit the right to international legal personality and all outstanding issues shall be regulated separately between the successor state and the state that has become independent.
>
> If both member states declare in a referendum that they are in favour of changing the state status, i.e. in favour of independence, all outstanding issues shall be resolved in the succession procedure, as was the case with the former Socialist Federal Republic of Yugoslavia.[161]

The Agreement amending the Constitutional Charter, signed on April 7, 2005 and negotiated primarily to regulate elections of state union parliament deputies, also included a reference regarding the referendum:

> Regulations on a potential referendum, in accordance with Article 60 of the Constitutional Charter, must be founded on *internationally recognized democratic standards*. The member state organizing a referendum will cooperate with the European Union on respecting international democratic standards, as envisaged by the Constitutional Charter (Point 3).[162]

---

[161] Constitutional Charter of Serbia and Montenegro, 2003, Article 60.

[162] Reproduced in *Politika* (Belgrade), April 8, 2005, 7 [Translation and emphasis mine]. Note: As in the case of the Belgrade Agreement, E.U. High Representative Javier Solana was a signatory to this agreement in

According to Montenegrin legislation, a referendum on independence, to be successful, required "a majority vote of the citizens who have voted, provided that the majority of citizens with voting rights had voted."[163] The United States government declared that it found this threshold for participation and approval in the referendum on independence to be too low, not because it did not meet minimal standards but because it regarded "a momentous decision."[164] The European Union insisted that Montenegro follow the highest international standards in this area, calling on the Council of Europe Venice Commission to make a legal pronouncement. The Venice Commission concluded that "no clear and binding internationally recognised standards exist concerning the level of participation in referendums in general" and that comparative review shows Montenegrin legislation on referenda to be "consistent with international standards."[165] At the same time, the Commission strongly recommended that more stringent and precise criteria be legislated concerning the required voter majority in order to "ensure greater legitimacy for the outcome."[166] Similarly, the Venice Commission found the voter twenty-four-month residency requirement "justified in principle" but "excessive."[167] In a final assessment, reminiscent of the 1998 Canadian Supreme Court ruling that Quebec's secession entailed a duty to negotiate:[168]

> The Commission strongly recommends that serious negotiations should take place between the majority and opposition within Montenegro in order to achieve a consensus on matters of principle concerning the conduct and implementation of the proposed referendum, in particular as regards the specific majority that should be required to ensure that the outcome of the referendum is accepted by all major political groups in Montenegro.

---

addition to the presidents and prime ministers of the member republics and the president of the state union of Serbia and Montenegro.

163 The Law on Referendum of the Republic of Montenegro, February 19, 2001, Article 37.

164 United States Mission to the OSCE, Statement on Montenegro Delivered by Ambassador David T. Johnson to the (OSCE) Permanent Council, Vienna, November 8, 2001.

165 European Commission for Democracy through Law (Venice Commission), Opinion on the Compatibility of the Existing Legislation in Montenegro concerning the Organisation of Referendums with Applicable International Standards, adopted by the Venice Commission at its 65th Plenary Session, Venice, December 16-17, 2005, on the basis of comments by Mr. Anthony Bradley (Substitute Member, United Kingdom) Mr. Carlos Closa Montero (Member, Spain), Mr. Kaarlo Tuori (Member, Finland), Strasbourg, December 19, 2005 [Opinion no. 343 / 2005, CDL-AD(2005)041Or.Engl.], paragraph 22.

166 Ibid., paragraph 40.

167 Ibid., paragraph 49.

168 Reference re: Secession of Quebec (1998) 161 DLR (4th) 426, paragraph 92.

The European Union, which by virtue of the agreement on amending the Constitutional Charter of the State Union of 7 April 2005 plays a specific role in this respect, could facilitate such negotiations.[169]

The European Union envoy, Miroslav Lajčák, took the role of mediator between the ruling parties in Montenegro that favored a simple majority referendum approval and the opposition parties that favored a two-thirds super majority, concluding the negotiations with a 55 percent supermajority of votes if at least 50 percent of votes were cast. The Council of Europe unanimously agreed with this proposal that was ultimately also endorsed by the Montenegrin government, albeit with a subsequent political comment that independence would be sought even if only a simple majority referendum approval were reached.[170]

The international attitude toward potential Montenegrin secession was reflective of its general policy shift toward stronger support for the country's integrity since Serbia's change to a democratic regime in October 2000. At the same time, the international community, including the Serbian government, was ready to accept Montenegrin independence, provided it was a result of a democratic process.[171] Both marked a radical change from the approach taken in the early 1990s, now contributing to the application of an external right to self-determination in a peaceful manner.

Exercising its constitutional right, the Montenegrin government organized a referendum on May 21, 2006, with a turnout of 86.5 percent of registered voters. A total of 55.5 percent voted in favor and 44.5 percent against separating from the state union with Serbia. International recognition followed since the result met the threshold requirement of 55 percent approval set by the EU. The Montenegrin Parliament adopted a formal Declaration of Independence on June 3, 2006. The Serbian government accepted the result of the referendum and recognized Montenegro on June 15, 2006.

In legal terms, Montenegro's independence was not a case of secession but an agreed separation as in the case of the Czechoslovakia and the Soviet Union. The peaceful separation of Montenegro from the state union of Serbia and

---

[169] Venice Commission, Opinion on the Compatibility of the Existing Legislation in Montenegro concerning the Organisation of Referendums with Applicable International Standards, 2005, paragraph 64.

[170] "E.U. Wins Montenegro's Support for its Referendum Formula," *E.U. Observer*, February 27, 2006.

[171] *See* U.K. House of Commons Foreign Affairs Committee, Foreign Affairs—Third Report, February 1, 2005, particularly paragraph 90; "Solana: Consensus of Authorities, Opposition for Referendum," *Beta* (Belgrade), November 30, 2005.

Montenegro is an immense and insufficiently recognized foreign policy success of the European Union. Nonetheless, this success could only be temporary if the rights of Serbs and other non-Montenegrins in an independent Montenegro are not respected. Serb political parties in Montenegro, namely the Serbian List, have attempted to attract attention to this issue, both from the international community and the Serb community in Montenegro, emphasizing that the new Montenegrin state is a multicultural, non-majority state where the rights of the Serbs and other large ethnic communities need to be safeguarded.[172] In its Progress Report on Montenegro's Stabilization and Association Process, the European Commission did underscore that the new Montenegrin Constitution "needed to be developed and adopted in line with European values, standards and practices, especially in the area of human and minority rights,"[173] but the SAA negotiations were concluded and the Stabilization and Association Agreement initialed in March 2007 and signed in September 2007, prior to the adoption of the new Montenegrin Constitution, thereby leaving the European Union with less leverage to seek from Montenegro a progressive Constitution that would embody all the notions of democratic governance in full application of the (internal) right to self-determination.

7.6. Self-Determination and Kosovo and Metohia's Future Status[174]

NATO's 1999 bombing of the Federal Republic of Yugoslavia (Serbia and Montenegro) raised expectations harbored by Kosovo Albanians that the

---

[172] *See* Misa Djurkovic, "Montenegro: Headed for new Divisions?" *Conflict Studies Research Centre: Balkan Series* 07/11, (Watchfield: Defence Academy of the United Kingdom, March 2007). Zhelidrag Nikchevich, *Rights of Serbs in Montenegro* [Права Срба у Црној Гори] (Belgrade: Igam, 2006). In 2007, the locus of the political discourse in Montenegro centered on the Draft text of the Constitution of the Republic of Montenegro, adopted on April 3, 2007, as draft text that included proposed amendments by opposition parties. The Draft Constitution, as proposed by the ruling parties, referred to "the Montenegrin nation and other autochthonous nations," but without defining these "other nations" or providing any specific protection of their rights. The Draft Constitution did provide for use of other languages in municipalities "with significant minority presence" but again without defining the minorities [text in author's possession]. Briefly, Montenegrins, who constitute 43 percent of the population of Montenegro, were favored over Serbs (32 percent), Bosniaks (7.8 percent) and Albanians (7 percent). The preference given to the Montenegrin language is most evident of this discrimination since 63.5 percent of Montenegrin citizens stated that they speak Serbian and only 22 percent stated that they speak the Montenegrin language (data from 2003 Population Census in Montenegro).

[173] Commission of the European Communities, *Commission Staff Working Document: Montenegro 2006 Progress Report* [COM (2006) 649 final], Brussels, November 8, 2006, 6.

[174] As throughout this book, the term "Kosovo" will be used as shorthand for "Kosovo and Metohia."

province would be recognized as an independent state. However, the key international actors, such as the U.S. Deputy Secretary of State, Strobe Talbott, then rebutted such aspirations, expressing fear that Kosovo's "secession would give heart to separatists and irredentists of every stripe in the region."[175] The international community urged patience and delayed the resolution of the Kosovo status, defined by the U.N. Security Council Resolution 1244 (1999) as "substantial autonomy within the Federal Republic of Yugoslavia," administered by the United Nations. As postulated by U.S. diplomat Christopher Hill in 2000:

> Kosovo status cannot be solved now. It has to be solved peacefully, and this is a long-term process. Kosovo will be under U.N. mandate for many years.[176]

Although the United Nations Interim Administration Mission in Kosovo (UNMIK) in its first enactment stated, "All legislative and executive authority with respect to Kosovo, including the administration of the judiciary, is vested in UNMIK and is exercised by the Special Representative of the Secretary-General [SRSG],"[177] some of the authority was later devolved to local authorities. In 2001, a Constitutional Framework for Provisional Self-Government[178] was adopted, dividing responsibilities between UNMIK and the Provisional Institutions of Self-Government (PISG) to develop self-government in Kosovo pending a final settlement, as provided by UNSCR 1244. UNMIK retained control of the most sensitive areas, including security, most economic policy, and "external relations." Moreover, UNMIK was always careful to note when adopting regulations in the international arena, such as issuing travel documents, that these acts had no implications for the international status of the territory.[179] The Constitutional Framework equally reasserted the primacy of UNSCR 1244, affirming that "the exercise of the responsibilities of Provisional Institutions of Self-Government in Kosovo shall not in any way affect or diminish the ultimate authority of the SRSG for the implementation of UNSCR 1244." To obtain Serbia's support for Serb participation in the ensuing elections for the Kosovo Assembly, UNMIK signed

---

[175] U.S. Deputy Secretary of State Strobe Talbott, Address at the Aspen Institute: *The Balkan Question and the European Answer*, August 24, 1999 (accessed December 15, 2005); available from http://www.state.gov/www/policy_remarks/1999/990824_talbott_aspen.html.

[176] Christopher Hill, speaking at the Fletcher School, Boston, USA, February 28, 2000.

[177] UNMIK/REG/1999/1, July 25, 1999, S/1999/987, 14.

[178] Constitutional Framework for Provisional Self-Government, UNMIK/REG/2001/9, May 15, 2001.

[179] *See* House of Lords Debates 610, WA 139-40, March 8, 2000, (2000) 71 British Yearbook of International Law, 556.

"the Common Document" with the Government of Serbia that affirmed that the new institutions would have no authority to take any steps towards resolving Kosovo's final status, additionally establishing "a High Level Working Group" as a form under the auspices of the SRSG that would bring together officials from Belgrade, UNMIK and PISG to discuss minority issues.[180]

However, the fear felt by Kosovo Serbs that any support lent to provisional institutions would bolster Kosovo's independence was not placated by this document. The subsequent marginalization of other ethnic groups by the Kosovo Albanians in the Assembly and other institutions solidified their decision not to participate in local self-government. As related by international peacekeepers, a multiethnic Kosovo did not feature even symbolically in the Assembly that the Constitutional Framework established:

> The official opening of the Assembly's refurbished hall was marred by Kosovo Serbs' understandable complaints about murals depicting scenes that reflected only the Albanians' view of history—effectively erasing that of the other ethnic groups who have inhabited Kosovo for centuries.[181]

Another factor that instigated the atmosphere of mistrust and prevented interethnic reconciliation in Kosovo was the "reverse" ethnic cleansing which occurred immediately after the Yugoslav forces withdrew and international troops took over the security role in the province. As portrayed by U.S. diplomat Christopher Hill: "War was hell but peace could at least be called purgatory."[182] UNMIK's inability to take control was so apparent that by May 2003, the Kosovo Protection Corps, established to enforce the rule of law, had direct links to the Albanian National Army, "a terrorist group bent on ethnically cleansing Kosovo of non-Albanians," leading the Kosovo International Security Force (KFOR) commander to assert that "all members of the KPC were criminals."[183] As a result, the international community demanded that Kosovo and Metohia achieve a certain level of international standards before undertaking negotiations on the status and the

---

[180] Ian King and Whit Mason, *Peace at Any Price; How the World Failed Kosovo* (Ithaca, NY: Cornell University Press, 2006), 122-123.

[181] Ibid., 7.

[182] Christopher Hill, speaking at the Fletcher School, Boston, USA, February 28, 2000. For more information, *see* Chapter 6: *Changing Borders by Force*, particularly pages 355-6.

[183] King and Mason, *Peace at Any Price*, 149.

policy of "Standards before Status" was formally adopted in December 2003.[184] Sadly, this policy was ultimately abandoned, once the March 2004 pogrom of the Serb minority convinced the international community that the situation in the province was "unsustainable"[185] and that the policy needed to be reversed, in hopes that a clear status would lead to enhanced human and minority rights. The international peacekeepers on the ground were bitterly disappointed after the March riots:

> They all came to Pristina bright-eyed and ready to help the poor down-trodden Albanians. Now they gripe more than anyone, frustrated because they feel the Kosovo Albanians aren't even trying to make a democratic state for themselves.[186]

The new policy became one of "standards and status," as pronounced by U.S. Undersecretary of State Nicholas Burns.[187] In December 2005, the Norwegian Permanent Representative to NATO Council Kai Aide, appointed by U.N. Secretary-General Kofi Annan to assess the situation on the ground, effectively concluded that, despite progress, standards had not been met in most areas:

> The main findings are mixed. What I found were significant achievements in some areas, such as building of institutions and establishment of legal framework. We must remember that back in 1999 there was, in fact, nothing and there was a need to start from the very ground. So I think in this respect there have been some very significant achievements. And then there are some very, very important shortcomings. The justice system is very weak; the question of respect for rule of law is weak too. There is no

---

184 The Standards for Kosovo, presented by the United Nations Interim Administration Mission in Kosovo on December 10, 2003, covered eight broad categories of democratization to be met before addressing the question of Kosovo's future status: 1) Functioning Democratic Institutions, including elections the Provisional Institutions of Self-Government and media and civil society; 2) Rule of Law (police/judiciary); 3) Freedom of Movement, including free use of language, 4) Returns and Integration; 5) Economy (Legislation, Balanced Budget, Privatization); 6) Respect for Property Rights (Clear Title, Restitution), including preservation of cultural heritage; 7) Dialogue, including Prishtina-Belgrade dialogue and regional dialogue; and 8) Kosovo Protection Corps (Size, Compliance with Mandate, Minority Participation).

185 International Commission on the Balkans, *The Balkans in Europe's Future*, April 2005, 10. For more information on the March 2004 pogrom, *see* Chapter 6: *Changing Borders by Force*, particularly page 355.

186 King and Mason, *Peace at Any Price*, 18.

187 Nicholas Burns, cited in Jonathan Steele, "U.S. Pushes for Decision on Kosovo Status," *Guardian* (London), June 8, 2005.

doubt about that. *Regarding interethnic problems, I believe very little has happened and the reconciliation process has not yet started.*[188]

Aide nonetheless recommending that negotiations begin and the U.N. Secretary-General adopted the Ambassador's recommendation,[189] despite the fact that he had personally concluded several months prior, on February 14, 2005, that "none of the eight standards has yet been fulfilled" and that "there must be 'real progress on the standards' before Kosovo's final status can be determined."[190] In line with the new political decision, the European Commission officially described the political situation in Kosovo in November 2005 as "stable" and relations between Serbs and Albanians as simply "strained."[191] In January 2006, the European Commission integrated the eight chapters of the "UN Standards for Kosovo" into the document that serves as a roadmap for the region's European integration process—the European Partnership. In November 2006, the E.C. for the first time produced a separate "Progress Report on Kosovo (under UNSCR 1244)" in terms of the Stabilization and Process, having previously merged its reporting on Kosovo with the wider report on Serbia.[192] At the same time, the E.C. officially announced that "the E.U. will have a major role to play in the status settlement and its imple-mentation, once it is agreed by the United Nations Security Council."[193] Once again it was recognized that "the European perspective is crucial to provide all involved with a vision of a common future in the European Union."[194] Yet to make that perspective more real for the people of Kosovo, the E.U.'s twenty-seven member states would be asked to provide at least 1.5 billion euros to finance the

---

[188] *See* "Kosovo: RFE/RL Speaks with U.N. Special Envoy Kai Aide" (accessed December 31, 2005); available from http://www.rferl.org/featuresarticle/2005/10/b8f625da-0b53-4b62-b9a2-21cd562f63db.html [Emphasis added].

[189] "Kosovo: Annan Recommends Starting Future Status Talks Now" (accessed December 31, 2005); available from http://www.un.org/apps/news/story.asp?NewsID=16322&Cr=kosovo&Cr1=.

[190] Report of the Secretary-General on the United Nations Interim Administration Mission in Kosovo, S/2005/88, February 14, 2005, paragraphs 2, 17; "Progress in Kosovo Insufficient for Final Status Review," *Southeastern European Times*, February 16, 2005. For a brief outline of the standards, *see* footnote 184 above.

[191] *2005 Enlargement Strategy Paper*, 26.

[192] Commission of the European Communities, Communication from the Commission to the European Parliament and the Council, "Enlargement Strategy and Main Challenges 2006—2007, including annexed-special report on the EU's capacity to integrate new members" [COM (2006) 649 final], Brussels, November 8, 2006.

[193] Commission of the European Communities, *Commission Staff Working Document: Kosovo (under UNSCR 1244) 2006 Progress Report* [COM (2006) 649 final], Brussels, November 8, 2006, 15.

[194] Ibid.

development of Kosovo as soon as its status is settled by the United Nations Security Council, according to Olli Rehn, the E.U. enlargement commissioner:[195]

> An injection of money will be needed to protect the Serb minority and its cultural monuments, end widespread corruption and find ways to attract investment in an area where unemployment is running at 40 percent, according to the European Bank for Reconstruction and Development. While NATO will maintain a large military presence, the E.U. will need money to send 2,000 police and judicial experts.[196]

On November 14, 2005, former Finnish President Martti Ahtisaari was appointed the special envoy of the U.N. Secretary-General for the negotiations on Kosovo's future status, initiated on February 20, 2006. Several meetings of the Prishtina and Belgrade delegations, organized under the auspices of Mr. Ahtisaari, were held between February 2006 and March 2007, focusing on decentralization, community rights, religious and cultural heritage, and economic issues.

The negotiating parties had different goals. Kosovo Albanian leaders demanded nothing short of independence. In contrast, the Serbian government, while rejecting independence, has offered a compromising "substantial autonomy" translating to *de facto* but not *de jure* independence, albeit with extensive self-rule for certain areas within Kosovo and Metohia with strong links to Belgrade.[197]

Ethnic Albanian claims for independence have generally been based on demographics and past oppression. As suggested by one Albanian jurist, who intentionally ignores the Albanian oppression of the Serbs that occurred in both the recent and the more distant past, and the terrorist nature of the Albanian revolt in late 1990s:

> The international community should reward Kosovars [ethnic Albanians] for their patience in seeking self-determination, and their use of force only as a last resort, by allowing them, in pursuance with international law, to

---

[195] The E.U. has already spent €2 billion in the province since 1999.

[196] Judy Dempsey, "€1.5 Billion Expected from E.U. for Kosovo Development," *International Herald Tribune*, April 1, 2007.

[197] *See* Interview, Sanda Raskovic-Ivic, More Than Autonomy, Less Than Independence—A Fair Offer (accessed October 18, 2005); available from http://www.kosovo.net/news/archive/2005/October_17/3.html. For more, see below.

secede from their long-time oppressor and obtain the status of a fully independent country.[198]

Both of these arguments could easily be reversed. First, while the majority of the Kosovo and Metohia province is ethnic Albanian, the majority of the state is Serbian. Second and as previously noted, the oppressors and the victims in the province have not been of one nationality.[199] It is of particular concern that Kosovo Albanians may have taken cues from the international non-response to Croat ethnic cleansing of Krayina as an effective means of ending the "minority problem," when undertaking systematic violence in March 2004. As revealed by an anonymous Western diplomat:

> Albanians are trying to cleanse the Serbs and create a fait accompli before any talks. . . . Anyone with political experience can see that.[200]

The Serbian stance on Kosovo is derived from both romantic and practical concerns. The province of Kosovo and Metohia has both a material and non-material value for the Serbian people. The Serbs' emotional and spiritual attachment to this region is comparable to that of Jews to Israel. As relayed by one of the famous Serb poets, Matiya Bechkovich:

> [N]othing is more critical for the Serb people than the present struggle in Kosovo and for Kosovo. . . . Kosovo is the most precious of Serb words. It has been paid for with the blood of the whole nation. Because of that price it is entrenched at the throne of the Serb language. Without blood it could not be bought, without blood it cannot be sold.[201]

---

[198] Korab R. Sejdiu, "The Revival of a Forgotten Dispute: Deciding Kosova's Future," *Rutgers University Journal of Law and Urban Policy* 3, no. 1, 117.

[199] *See* Chapter 2: *Pre-1914 Administrative Boundaries and the Birth of Yugoslavia*, Chapter 3: *Yugoslavias' Administrative Boundaries (1918-1991)*, Chapter 6: *Changing Borders by Force*.

[200] Shaban Buza, "NATO sees specter of ethnic cleansing in Kosovo," *Reuters*, March 19, 2004. Note: Similarly, the OSCE described the 1999 incidents as organized: "although many incidents were disparate, individual acts of revenge, others have assumed a more systematic pattern and appear to have been organized. The evidence in part points to a careful targeting of victims and an underlying intention to expel." Report on Human Rights Findings of the OSCE Mission in Kosovo, OSCE, December 1999.

[201] Matiya Bechkovich, Косово—најскупља српска реч [Kosovo—the most precious Serb word] (Valyevo: Biblioteka Glas Crkve, 1989), 7-8.

The non-material value of territory is not unimportant. On the contrary, as pin-pointed by Monica Duffy Toft: "Recognizing this double meaning of territory is the first step toward a better understanding of the origins, character, and duration of ethnic violence."[202] Moreover, Serbian insistence on an institutional link with Kosovo is not exclusively non-material. It is based on well-defined interests, including legal protection of Serbs and other non-Albanians, access to Serb religious and cultural sites, and avoidance of negative precedents for other parts of Serbia, such as the Preshevo Valley or Sandjak.

On April 29, 2004, the democratic Serbian government adopted a Plan for Kosovo, which envisaged five "territorial autonomies" for Serbs in Kosovo, "based on the principle of subsidiarity" in areas where Serbs constituted majority in 1999 and without prejudging the final resolution of the province's status.[203] In conformity with this plan, during an official visit to Russia in November 2005, Serbian President Boris Tadich proposed that two entities be created in Kosovo, one Serb and one Albanian, which need not be territorially cohesive, and with the Serbian entity "institutionally linked to Belgrade."[204] This solution would cater to different needs of the two communities relating to language, religion or education—needs that are at the core of human rights. The 2004 Serb Plan for Kosovo resembled the model of the Jura canton in Switzerland that enabled internal partition based on local plebiscites while safeguarding the state's territorial integrity. President Tadich insisted that Serbia was ready "to recognize all the possible rights of ethnic Albanians and their maximum possible independence from Belgrade, while at the same time preserving the sovereignty and territorial integrity of Serbia over Kosovo."[205] On April 4, 2007, at the U.N. Security Council debate on the future status of Kosovo, the Serb Prime Minister Voyislav Koshtunitsa[206] reiterated the position that Serbia would provide Kosovo with "the highest degree of autonomy" but not independence.[207]

---

[202] Monica Duffy Toft, *The Geography of Ethnic Violence* (Princeton and Oxford: Princeton University Press, 2003), 148.

[203] Serbian President Boris Tadich's Plan for Kosovo presented in *Politika* (Belgrade), April 30, 2004, A5. *See* Figure 21.

[204] Katarina Subasic, "Kosovo can be Independent within Serbia: Serbian President," *Agence-France Presse* (AFP), December 15, 2005.

[205] Ibid.

[206] Often spelled as "Vojislav Kostunica" in the international press.

[207] Nikola Krastev, "Kosovo: U.N. Security Council Begins Final-Status Debate," *Radio Free Europe/Radio Liberty*, April 4, 2007.

After one year of negotiations, the U.N. mediator, Martti Ahtisaari, concluded that "the parties [were] not able to reach an agreement on Kosovo's future status," and that "the negotiations' potential to produce any mutually agreeable outcome on Kosovo's status [was] exhausted."[208] In his report to the Security Council, delivered on March 29, 2007, Ahtisaari recommended "independence, to be supervised for an initial period by the international community."[209] The Special Envoy asked the United Nations to encourage the dismemberment of one of its member states for the first time in history, claiming that Kosovo's secession, guided by the advised "Comprehensive Proposal for the Kosovo Status Settlement"[210] would bring prosperity to the region:

> Concluding this last episode in the dissolution of the former Yugoslavia will allow the region to begin a new chapter in its history — one that is based upon peace, stability and prosperity for all.[211]

In contrast to Ahtisaari's optimism, the international human rights organization Amnesty International expressed concern "that an imposed solution would exacerbate the already heightened tensions within Kosovo, and may lead to further violations of human rights." The organization continues to urge that any final agreement must be arrived at in consultation with, and address the rights of, all communities in Kosovo—including Albanians, Serbs, Roma, Ashkali, Egyptians, Bosniaks, Gorani, and Turks—as well as women, even if that consultation requires further time.[212]

Supervised independence for Kosovo proposed by Special Envoy Ahtisaari is analogous to conditional recognition, defined by Lauterpacht as "recognition the grant or continuance of which is made dependent upon the fulfillment of stipulations other than the normal requirements of statehood."[213] In the past, states generally have not adhered to the imposed conditions, leading James Crawford, who specialized in international public law relating to the creation of states, to

---

208   Report of the Special Envoy of the Secretary-General on Kosovo's future status, S/2007/168, March 26, 2007, 2.

209   Ibid.

210   Comprehensive Proposal for the Kosovo Status Settlement, S/2007/168/Add.1, March 26, 2007.

211   Report of the Special Envoy of the Secretary-General on Kosovo's future status, S/2007/168, March 26, 2007, 5.

212   Amnesty International Public Statement, "Kosovo (Serbia): Need to Consult Civil Society and Ensure Effective Protection of Human Rights," AI Index: EUR 70/014/2006 (Public) News Service No: 249, September 22, 2006.

213   Hans Lauterpacht, *Recognition in International Law* (Cambridge: Cambridge University Press, 1947), 358.

conclude: "Collective conditional recognition is thus of limited value in qualifying the authority or conduct of new states."[214] As a guarantee that "Comprehensive Proposal for the Kosovo Status Settlement" would be implemented, the document provides for "an International Civilian Representative," who would essentially be a carbon copy of the High Representative in Bosnia, exercising power to annul laws or decisions by Kosovo authorities and the right "to sanction or remove from office any public official *or take other measures, as necessary*, to ensure full respect for this Settlement and its implementation."[215] The U.N. Special Envoy proposed the very model that the Parliamentary Assembly of the Council of Europe berated as "irreconcilable with democratic principles."[216] The Serbian government immediately rejected Ahtisaari's proposal for the Kosovo Status Settlement, recalling the amendments that the Serb negotiating team suggested to the Envoy's draft proposal during the final two rounds of talks in February and March 2007.[217] These amendments essentially transform the Ahtisaari-advised "supervised independence" into a "supervised autonomy."[218] Importantly, the Serbian government has criticized the document's provisions that relate to group rights of Kosovo's non-Albanian ethnicities, the largest of which are Serbs. While the U.N. Special Envoy reported to have "incorporated 11 pages of amendments into his final package,"[219] a member of the Serb negotiating team and long-standing Kosovo expert Dushan Batakovich has asserted that Ahtisaari's final proposal instead "ignored various agreements achieved during the negotiation process, namely in relation to decentralization and the protection of Serb cultural and spiritual heritage in Kosovo."[220] The key Serbian amendment, in addition to changes that relate to province's ability to conduct foreign relations, refers to the right of the majority

---

[214] James Crawford, *The Creation of States in International Law*, 2nd ed. (Oxford: Clarendon Press, 2006), 546.

[215] Article 2, Comprehensive Proposal for the Kosovo Status Settlement, S/2007/168/Add.1, March 26, 2007, 52.

[216] *See* footnote 95 above.

[217] Government of Serbia Press Release: Belgrade Team submits new Amendments to Ahtisaari's Proposal, February 24, 2007.

[218] The text of the amendments, including Annex I, was published in the Serbian daily newspaper, *Politika* on February 25 and 26, 2007. The entire body of the amendments was distributed to the members of the Security Council.

[219] Security Council Report, April 2007 (accessed April 11, 2007); available from http://www.securitycouncilreport. org/site/c.glKWLeMTIsG/b.2620595/k.8BAE/April_2007BRKosovo.htm.

[220] Author's Interview with Dushan T. Batakovich, Belgrade, Serbia, April 12, 2007. Note: Ahtisaari became an unacceptable mediator to the Serbian government at this point as he was considered to be biased and unfair. Soon after, Ahtisaari's personal reputation was further marred by news reports alleging that he was paid by Albanian lobbyists and that this was documented by German intelligence. Oliver Dulich, the speaker of the Parliament of Serbia called for a formal inquiry into these allegations, while Ahtisaari refuted the reports.

Serb municipalities to "form a Serbian entity in order to secure efficient application of their authority and competences."[221]

After a debate held on April 3, 2004, the Security Council members could not
come to an agreement on the future status of Kosovo, with Russia taking the lead
among states that refuted Ahtisaari's proposal. The United States officially supported Kosovo's independence, as did many European states, including the United
Kingdom, Germany, and France. In contrast, other European Union members,
notably Slovakia, Greece, and Romania, declared their preference for a high level
of autonomy for the province.[222] Even the E.U. states that endorsed Ahtisaari's
proposal did so with anxiety, having earlier suggested solutions that mirrored
the Serb proposal. Italian President Carlo Ciampi, for instance, had suggested
that Kosovo be resolved according to the model of South Tyrol.[223] As a result of
discord, the European Union also failed to endorse Ahtisaari's proposal.[224]

After several draft U.N. Security Council resolutions failed to receive Russia's support during summer 2007 because they opened a possibility of Kosovo's independence, new negotiations between Albanians and Serbs over the future status of
Kosovo were initiated on August 30, 2007. This time the mediators were a troika
made up of European, Russian and American envoys.

However, one cannot say that the new negotiations were conducted "in good
faith" since the Kosovo Albanians had no interest to consider alternative solutions
to independence, with the U.S. officials stating that the United States would recognize the province's independence if unilaterally declared at the end of the envisaged 120-day negotiating process.[225] As discussed earlier, secession is neither legal
nor illegal, but it could be rendered successful by international recognition,
especially if heralded by important states such as the United States. The only two

---

[221] Amendments proposed by the Negotiating Team of the Republic of Serbia to the Draft Comprehensive
Proposal for the Kosovo Status Settlement, February 24, 2007, Article 6.3 (provision elaborated in amendments proposed to Annex III).

[222] See Mark Beunderman, "EU Divided over Future Status of Kosovo," E.U. Observer (Brussels), November
29, 2005 (accessed November 30, 2005); available from http://euobserver.com/9/20437. "E.U. Fails to
Endorse Kosovo Independence Plan," Associated Press, March 30, 2007 (accessed April 3, 2007); available
from http://www.iht.com/articles/ap/2007/03/30/europe/EU-GEN-EU-Kosovo.php.

[223] Milan Yakshich, "Kosovo to be resolved like South Tyrol," Politika (Belgrade), June 8, 2005, 2.

[224] "E.U. Fails to Endorse Kosovo Independence Plan," Associated Press, March 30, 2007. .

[225] See AFP, September 8, 2007; Daniel Dombey and Neil MacDonald, "Europe, US try to maintain united on
Kosovo," The Financial Times, August 12, 2007.

examples of successful secession by separatist groups are Bangladesh and the former Yugoslav republics.[226] However, these are not clear legal precedents. In Bangladesh, the majority of the state "seceded," while secession of the former Yugoslav republics was never publicly avowed. It was excused by dubious legal opinions of the Badinter Arbitration Commission, which pronounced Yugoslavia dead ("dissolved").[227]

If Kosovo were granted independence, such a policy would affirm the Badinter rulings that granted the most extreme form of the right to self-determination, secession, to select federal units (republics) rather than peoples. If provinces, namely Kosovo, were extended international recognition in a context that could not even evasively be construed as a case of state dissolution despite Ahtisaari's allusions, "a right of a federal unit to secession" would be more firmly instituted. All separatists enjoying some type of a territorial autonomy, including Spain's Basques or Canada's Quebec, would be in a position to invoke the right to secession. As claimed by one analyst:

> The situation in Kosovo makes an intriguing precedent in the world: it shows a mechanism of making unrecognized states legitimate; this can be also applied to the unrecognized states in the post-soviet territory—Transdnestr, South Ossetia, Abkhazia, Nagorno Karabakh.[228]

To counter such alarms, the Contact Group countries, in a document endorsed by the United Nations in November 2005, asserted:

> The territorial integrity and internal stability of regional neighbors will be fully respected.[229]

The European Union has supported this position, officially stating in the European Commission's 2006 Kosovo Progress Report that "Kosovo's status question is

---

[226] Note: Czechoslovakia and the Soviet Union disintegrated by consent while Ethiopia agreed to Eritrea's separation and the case of East Timor is linked to decolonization policy.

[227] The term secession was never used by the United Nations or individual states with respect to Yugoslavia's disintegration. Hurst Hannum, *Autonomy, Sovereignty, and Self-Determination: The Accommodation of Conflicting Rights*, Rev. ed. (Philadelphia: University of Pennsylvania Press, 1996), 498.

[228] "Expert: 'Kosovo scenario gives the best fit for Transdnestr,'" *Regnum News Agency* (Moscow), November 29, 2005 (accessed November 30, 2005); available from http://www.regnum.ru/english/polit/548254.html.

[229] Contact Group Guiding Principles for a Settlement of Kosovo's Status (Point 6); integral text provided as Annex to the Letter from the President of the Security Council addressed to the Secretary-General, S/2005/709, November 10, 2005.

sui generis, and hence sets no precedent."[230] U.N. Special Envoy Martti Ahtisaari reiterated this stance in his letter to the Security Council, "Kosovo is a unique case that demands a unique solution. It does not create a precedent for other unresolved conflicts."[231] Ahtisaari attempted to explain Kosovo's uniqueness by the very UNSCR 1244 that underscores Serbia's territorial integrity, choosing to focus exclusively on the Resolution's provision relating to the promotion of "meaningful self-administration for Kosovo," a concept that could also be interpreted as a high degree of autonomy:

> In unanimously adopting resolution 1244 (1999), the Security Council responded to Milosevic's actions in Kosovo by denying Serbia a role in its governance, placing Kosovo under temporary United Nations administration and envisaging a political process designed to determine Kosovo's future. The combination of these factors makes Kosovo's circumstances extraordinary.[232]

In brief, the position that Kosovo's secession would not be a precedent is impossible to uphold. Russian President Vladimir Putin has made plain that if the Albanian-dominated province were given sovereignty, it would be difficult to explain to people in Georgia's breakaway regions of Abkhazia and South Ossetia why they could not secede from Georgia:

> When we hear that one approach is possible in one place [but] is unacceptable in another, it is difficult to understand and is even more difficult to explain to people.[233]

Statements to the effect that other secessions are not possible out of respect for the home states' territorial integrity automatically lose credibility if the territorial integrity of another state, Serbia, were to be simultaneously discarded. Sergey Bagapsh, the leader of Georgia's break-away province of Abhazia, has already announced that they expect Russia's international recognition if Kosovo secedes

---

[230] Commission of the European Communities, *Commission Staff Working Document: Kosovo (under UNSCR 1244) 2006 Progress Report* [COM (2006) 649 final], Brussels, November 8, 2006, 15.

[231] Report of the Special Envoy of the Secretary-General on Kosovo's future status, S/2007/168, March 26, 2007, 4.

[232] Ibid.

[233] "Putin urges uniform regional-conflict approaches," *RIA Novosti News Agency* (Moscow), June 2, 2006.

from Serbia,[234] while the Azerbaijani government expressed fear "that any decision granting independence to Kosovo could set a precedent for Nagorno-Karabakh, which has a mainly Armenian population."[235] Eduard Kokoity, president of the unrecognized Republic of South Ossetia, has also hailed Putin's call for the application of universal principles, asserting that this position signals a break with "double standards" that ignore the universally accepted right of peoples to self-determination and divide peoples into "good and bad," of whom the "good" are considered "more equal."[236] Indeed, while the independence for one group does not automatically grant the same to another even if they evoke it unilaterally, the precedent that the secession of Kosovo would set in public international law would enable supportive states to grant recognition to break-away territories and even allow these new states to request membership in the United Nations.

An arbitrary territorial reading of self-determination that permits secession of a state's administrative unit dominated by a separatist majority is certain to stall development of minority rights and stimulate separatism worldwide. To prevent this, self-determination should be applied in the context of democratic governance, complementing the right to territorial integrity. In Kosovo, this would translate into a carefully drafted autonomy for the province's two main ethnic groups, Albanians and Serbs, legally woven into Serbia's constitutional system, with continued international monitoring of human rights.

Formerly, the Albanian politicians such as the erstwhile Prime Minister of Albania, Fatos Nano, have voiced their understanding for a compromise solution on the Kosovo status:

> This crisis could be more easily settled if Kosovo were recognized as a republic within the Federal Yugoslav Republic, like Montenegro, but a republic without the right of secession. This is the status of the Republika Srpska in Bosnia, for example.[237]

---

234 "Председник Абхазије: Решење за Косово биће светски преседан" [President of Abkhazia: Solution to Kosovo will be a World Precedent], *Tanjug* (Moscow), March 28, 2007.

235 "Azerbaijan: Baku Urges E.U. To Reject Kosovo Precedent," *Radio Free Europe/Radio Liberty*, March 20, 2007.

236 "Russia: Putin Calls For 'Universal Principles' to Settle Frozen Conflicts," Radio Free Europe/Radio Liberty, February 1, 2006.

237 Interview with Albanian Prime Minister Fatos Nano by Marc Semo, "Turn Kosovo Into a Republic without Right of Secession," *Liberation* (Paris), April 3, 1998, 13.

Today, such voices are mute. Instead, the Kosovo Albanians have hired prominent American diplomats, such as Hon. Frank Carlucci, former U.S. Secretary of Defense, gathered around the "Alliance for a New Kosovo" to represent their quest for independence internationally:

> At a time when a prospective "clash of civilizations" between the West and Islam is widely feared, the creation of a Muslim-majority secular state, tolerant of all ethnic peoples regardless of personal creed, would be viewed as a victory for the national values espoused by the United States and the nations of the European Union.[238]

The presented romantic view of Kosovo is countered by evidence on the ground, not only in terms of ethnic intolerance,[239] but also organized crime and corruption that led academic researchers such as Svante Cornell and Michael Jonsson to warn that an independent Kosovo "looks set to become a heavily criminalized state in the heart of Europe, with far-reaching implications."[240]

Other international experts, mainly gathered around the International Commission on Kosovo established in 2000, attempted to assuage concerns of current and possible future deficiencies in human and minority rights in Kosovo by proposing "conditional independence" for the province, which the U.N. Special Envoy, Martti Ahtisaari, has since endorsed.[241] Yet the critical feature of independence as an irreversible process refutes proposals for "conditional independence" as unfeasible. Independence cannot be conditioned. Previous attempts at "conditional

---

[238] Alliance for a New Kosovo, *Independence for Kosovo* (accessed on November 26, 2005); available from http://www.newkosovo.org/Independence percent20for percent20Kosovo.pdf.

[239] According to two international peacekeepers who served as UNMIK officials, the 2004 March riots "exemplified UNMIK's failure to control the levers of 'soft power'—education and the media—and KFOR's and the police's failure to marshal the 'hard power' necessary to maintain physical security. Without commanding these heights of security and social change, UNMIK's domination of the middle ground of administrative authority counted for very little when violent national chauvinists decided to test its resolve." King and Mason, *Peace at Any Price*, 6. A 124-report commissioned by the German army and released by the Institute for European Politics in Berlin in March 2007 has also concluded that the planned "construction of a multi-ethnic society" has "failed" in Kosovo and that it does not exist "outside the bureaucratic statements of the international community," further noting that the European Union's security strategy for a future mission in Kosovo is "neither analytically nor conceptually sustainable." *See* "The Failure of the West's 'Ostrich' Policy," *SMD/Spiegel/Reuters/AP*, March 12, 2007. *See also* Chapter 6: *Changing Borders by Force*, particularly pages 355-357.

[240] Svante E. Cornell and Michael Jonsson, "Creating a State of Denial," *International Herald Tribune*, March 22, 2007.

[241] Independent International Commission on Kosovo, *The Kosovo Report* (Oxford: Oxford University Press, 2000).

recognition" have not yielded results even in the former Yugoslav republics, which the U.S. and the European Union had obligated to safeguard minority and human rights upon independence. In Croatia, the Serbian minority has been reduced to a third of its 1990 level, human rights abuses continue to this day, and refugee return remains unsatisfactory. Bosnia and Herzegovina was partitioned following an atrocious civil war in which close to 100,000 people perished. Both Bosnia and Macedonia remain fledgling states, despite significant international presence.[242]

Yet, unlike independence, the European Union accession process can be and is conditioned. Gains of Euro-Atlantic integration should be used for balancing nationalist aims and not for blackmailing one nation, as the former U.S. Assistant Secretary of State Richard Holbrooke suggests: "The Serbs will have to choose between trying to join the European Union and trying to regain Kosovo."[243]

If the international community hopes to impose high human rights standards on a state, it appears more logical—and practical—that it apply such a policy to the original country rather than recognize one of its parts, where the same problems are simply reproduced. As Horowitz correctly asks, "If, after all, conditions on the exercise of an international-law right to secede can be enforced, why not enforce those conditions in the undivided state so as to forestall the need to secede?"[244] One could further argue that, since the ousting of Miloshevich in 2000, Serbia has proved itself more worthy of this proposition than Kosovo's local government. As highlighted by former Minister for Human and Minority Rights, Rasim Lyayich, himself a Bosniak:

> Since democratic changes in 2000, Serbia and Montenegro accomplished greatest progress precisely in the area of human and minority rights, not only in terms of legislation but also in creating the appropriate environment. . . . International standards in the area of minority rights tend to be low and the ones that Serbia built into its state structure are far higher. . . . Our Law on minorities grants collective rights to minorities and the electoral law has abolished the census for minorities.[245]

---

[242] *See* above.

[243] Richard Holbrooke, "New Course For Kosovo; Rice Makes Her Presence Felt," *Washington Post*, April 20, 2005, A25.

[244] Donald L. Horowitz, "A Right to Secede?" *Secession and Self-Determination*, eds. Stephen Macedo and Allen Buchanan, Nomos XLV: Yearbook of the American Society for Political and Legal Philosophy (New York, London: New York University Press, 2003), 50-76: 54.

[245] Rasim Ljajic, Minister of Human and Minority Rights, "The Rule of Law and European Standards for Human Rights Protection," International Conference: Serbia—Five Years After, organized by the Belgrade

In October 2006, the Parliament of Serbia adopted a new Constitution of the Republic of Serbia that features extensive human and minority rights, granting a form of self-rule to the autonomous republic of Voivodina and defining the province of Kosovo and Metohia in the preamble as an "integral part of the territory of Serbia" with "the status of a substantial autonomy."[246] In this manner, Serbia officially committed itself to granting Kosovo a high degree of autonomy.

By supporting a substantial autonomy for Kosovo short of independence, choosing to supervise autonomy under the auspices of the European integration process instead of supervising independence, the members of the U.N. Security Council would uphold the international legal order and promote further development of the internal application of the right to self-determination. In contrast, an externally endorsed independence for Kosovo, resisted by the home state, would seriously undermine the founding principle of international law, the right to territorial integrity.

The only other possible solution to the Kosovo question would be an agreed adjustment of the province's boundaries that would permit a legal separation of the Albanian-majority areas in Kosovo. The Contact Group countries had initially ruled out this option:

> There will be no changes in the current territory of Kosovo, i.e. no partition of Kosovo and no union of Kosovo with any country or part of any country. [247]

Human rights professor Hurst Hannum has instead suggested that change in boundaries represents "the one alternative that might actually help bring peace to the region":

> Changing borders does not guarantee that human rights will be better protected in the new states than they were in the old. In Kosovo, however, it

---

Fund for Political Excellence and the Balkan Trust for Democracy/German Marshall Fund, Belgrade, October 4-5, 2005.

[246] Organization for Security and Cooperation in Europe and the European Union positively assessed the adoption of the 2006 Serbian Constitution, which was approved by the popular referendum. One should note, nonetheless, that several Serb parties and non-governmental organizations criticized the Constitution's content in areas such as appointment of judiciary. The text of the Constitution in English version is available online, at the Internet presentation of Serbia's Ministry of Foreign Affairs, http://www.mfa.gov.yu/Facts/UstavRS_pdf.pdf (accessed March 6, 2007).

[247] Contact Group Guiding Principles for a Settlement of Kosovo's Status (Point 6); integral text provided as Annex to the Letter from the President of the Security Council addressed to the Secretary-General, S/2005/709, November 10, 2005.

offers the only possibility of a solution, ceding the primarily Serb areas to Serbia and allowing full independence to the remainder of the territory. This option would offer a chance for both peoples to take charge of their destinies.[248]

Policy-makers who support this stance, such as the prime minister of the Czech Republic, have been rare.[249] Yet in refuting the possibility of a negotiated change of boundaries, while simultaneously advocating an imposed change of Serbia's boundaries by the secession of Kosovo, the United States and other proponents of Kosovo's secession are clearly engaged in hypocrisy.[250] In line with this position, the U.S. Assistant Secretary of State has warned of danger posed by Serb irredentism, omitting to assess the danger posed by Albanian irredentism that exploded into violence not only in Serbia (in Kosovo and the Preshevo Valley), but also in the neighboring Macedonia.[251] In August 2006, a senior Albanian official Koco Danaj, political adviser to Albania's prime minister, Sali Berisha, told the

---

[248] Hurst Hannum, "Beware Balkans' Border Solutions," *Los Angeles Times*, February 4, 2007. Hannum's proposal was later seconded by other American scholars from National Defense University and George Washington University in Washington, DC. See "Analysis—Kosovo Solution May Mean Partition," *Reuters*, April 13, 2007.

[249] *See also* Charles A. Kupchan, "Independence for Kosovo," *Foreign Affairs* 84.6 (November-December 2005).

[250] "It's a perilous exercise . . . for foreigners to begin to draw lines," Burns told reporters when asked about the possibility of partitioning Kosovo into separate ethnic enclaves. "It's the view of all of our European allies that it would be a mistake to say that one of the options for the final-status talks in Kosovo would simply to be redefine the borders." On-the-Record Briefing, Under Secretary of State for Political Affairs R. Nicholas Burnson U.S. Strategy For Kosovo, November 8, 2005, Washington, D.C., USA.

In June 2005, the E.U. heads of states and governments unequivocally concluded, "there will be no partition of Kosovo." Council of the European Union, Brussels European Council—Presidency Conclusions, Brussels, June 18, 2005, 10255/05, Annex III, 35. They made a similar declaration with regards to Bosnia thirteen years later, where, ironically, Ambassador Marti Ahttisaari also had a role to mediate a settlement:

"The European Council [. . . will not] accept the partition of Bosnia and Herzegovina. The European Council strongly supports the efforts of the Co-Chairmen to arrive at a constitutional settlement based on the proposals made by Ambassador Ahtisaari and on a mutual recognition of the multi-ethnic character of Bosnia and Herzegovina." European Council Declaration on Former Yugoslavia, European Council, Conclusions of the Presidency (Annex D.1), Edinburgh, December 11-12, 1992, SN456/92 (accessed September 15, 2005); available from http://www.europarl.eu.int/summits/edinburgh/d1_en.pdf.

[251] "We also have some work to do to try to still the forces of irredentism and of violence that unfortunately are part of the fabric of Balkan political life in our time. There are still some Serbs who believe that the Serbs should unite themselves -- the Serbs in Serbia, in Kosovo, and in Bosnia, and that kind of irredentist force which was so destructive when Yugoslavia broke up 10 or 15 years ago cannot be allowed to return to be a political force in the Balkans." R. Nicholas Burns, Under Secretary for Political Affairs Remarks to the Atlantic Council, February 21, 2007 (accessed April 9, 2007); available from http://podgorica.usembassy.gov/embassy/press/2007/070221.html.

Prishtina-based Albanian language daily *Epoka e Re* that that, following Montenegro's referendum on independence, "ethnic Albanians in Macedonia and Montenegro should also have the right to choose with whom to live. Instead of having Albanians participate in those countries' governments, it would be more natural that they had one government in the Albanian capital, Tirana."[252]

The diplomatic inconsistencies are even more apparent when viewed in a wider international setting. Evelyn Farkas, who analyzed the U.S. interventions in Iraq, Ethiopia, and Bosnia, concluded that the largest world power approached these crises on a case-by-case basis:

> There is no evidence that decisions were made based on one set of firm principles or with an interest in maintaining rigid consistency. Indeed, the outcome in all three situations varied—Iraq and Bosnia were *de facto* partitioned, while Ethiopia was partitioned to create, or recreate, Eritrea."[253]

Susan Woodward has suggested that, by recognizing republic borders in 1991, "the major powers were applying not the sovereignty norm but Occam's razor— that it was simply more prudent to stick with the existing borders than to complicate the diplomatic process manifold."[254] The same analogy could be applied to Kosovo today. However, if a more complicated diplomatic process would lead to a solution that would be peaceful and that would minimize displacement of population, it should be considered. Woodward, as an internationally recognized scholarly expert on the former Yugoslavia, supports this position:

> In light of the subsequent wars of Yugoslav succession, it is clear that a method to negotiate the borders in 1991 and to confirm popular preferences would have saved much later diplomatic complication, huge loss of life, and massive military and financial commitments to restore peace and stability. . . . Border commissions set up at the time and discussions among members of the Yugoslav collective presidency in 1990-1991 also suggest

---

[252] "Balkans: Official Calls for a 'Natural Albania,'" AKI (Tirana), August 22, 2006.

[253] Evelyn Farkas, *Fractured States and U.S. Foreign Policy: Iraq, Ethiopia, and Bosnia in the 1990s* (New York: Palgrave Macmillan, 2003), 3.

[254] Susan L. Woodward, "Compromised Sovereignty to Create Sovereignty: Is Dayton Bosnia a Futile Exercise or an Emerging Model?," *Problematic Sovereignty; Contested Rules and Political Possibilities*, ed. Stephen D. Krasner (New York: Columbia University Press, 2001), 268.

that there were solutions that might have been debated without violence had the Dutch proposal been accepted.[255]

The first sign that a negotiated partition could be a politically acceptable solution came from the E.U. member of the troika charged with mediating Kosovo status talks, Wolfgang Ischinger in August 2007.[256] However, the E.U. foreign ministers soon declared themselves against such a solution, as have the Albanian and Serb representatives. Consequently, Ischinger also reverted to the position that partition would be perilous.[257]

7.7. Returning to Slovenia

To fully assess the role of European integration with regard to the application of the right to self-determination in the former Yugoslavia, one should also analyze the case of Slovenia, a former Yugoslav republic that became a full member of the European Union in 2004. Nominally an exemplary democratic state, Slovenia has been discriminatory to its citizens in practice.

Ethnic discrimination in Slovenia is rooted in its legal distinction between autochthonous and non-autochthonous minorities. When the Council of Europe analyzed the application of the Framework Convention for the Protection of National Minorities (Framework Convention) in Slovenia in 2002, it principally limited itself to the situation of those ethnic groups that Slovenes officially defined as (autochthonous) minorities: Italians, Hungarians and Roma. The Advisory Committee on the Framework Convention for the Protection of National Minorities noted that, upon depositing its instrument of ratification of the Framework Convention, the Slovene authorities invoked the absence of a definition of the notion of national minorities.[258] In 2005, the Advisory Committee instead opinioned that it "considers that the distinction based on the concept of 'autochthonous' should not be retained as the determining criterion to define the

---

[255] Ibid. For more on Dutch proposal, *see* Chapter 5: *International Recognition of the Former Yugoslav Republics*, 319.

[256] Note: The French Foreign Minister Bernard Kouchner, and the British Ambassador to Serbia Steven Wordsworth had also alluded to this possibility in July 2007. See Douglas Hamilton "Major power nudge Serbs, Kosovo toward partition," *Reuters*, July 12, 2007.

[257] Dan Bilefsky, "Top E.U. Mediator warns against Partition," *International Herald Tribune*, September 15, 2007.

[258] Advisory Committee on the Framework Convention for the Protection of National Minorities, Opinion on Slovenia, adopted on September 12, 2002, paragraph 12.

personal scope of application of the Framework Convention."[259] The Committee recalled "the presence in Slovenia of a significant number of former citizens of other republics of former Yugoslavia (SFRY)—of Albanian, Bosniac, Croatian, Macedonian, Montenegrin, Serbian and other ethnic origins—who do not enjoy a recognition or protection comparable to that afforded to the Hungarian and Italian minorities, or even to the Roma," although most possess Slovene citizenship and jointly represent a significant proportion of Slovene population.[260]

Notably, several thousand of such disenfranchised Slovene citizens still lack permanent residence and/or citizenship, as a result of a government decree that deleted these persons from the registers of permanent residents on February 26, 1992, transferring them automatically to the registers of foreigners. The Slovene government has been slow to implement its Constitutional Court's decision to restore their rights without further delay and retrospectively, considering that the authorities had illegally removed them from the register of permanent residents. As a consequence of their irregular legal status, the "deleted" Slovene citizens have incurred "violations of their economic and social rights, with some of them having lost their homes, employment or retirement pension entitlements, and [they have been] seriously hindered [in] the exercise of their rights to family life and freedom of movement."[261] The Advisory Committee is particularly aware of the "social climate in Slovenia," noting that in the referendum held in April 2004 on the Act on the Implementation of Item number 8 of Constitutional Court Decision no. U-I-246/02 (the so-called "Technical Act on Erased Persons"), 94.7 percent of participants (representing 31.45 percent of voters) expressed their opposition to this Act."[262] The referendum was organized by opposition parties and boycotted by the Slovene president and Prime Minister who called on other Slovene citizens to join the boycott. Even though there was a low turnout, this has been the usual turnout for referendums in Slovenia, where four of five taken referendums aver-

---

259 Advisory Committee on the Framework Convention for the Protection of National Minorities, Second Opinion on Slovenia, adopted on May 26, 2005, ACFC/INF/OP/II(2005)005, paragraphs 14-15.

260 Ibid., paragraph 33. Note: According to non-governmental estimates, such persons account for 10 percent of the total population. According to the results of the population census held in 2002, the ethnic composition of the population of Slovenia (a total of 1,964,036) is as follows: 1,631,363 (83.06 percent) Slovenes; 38,964 Serbs (1.98 percent); 35,642 Croats (1.81 percent); 21,542 Bosniacs (1.10 percent); 10,467 Muslims (0.53 percent); 6,243 Hungarians (0.32 percent); 6,186 Albanians (0.31 percent); 3,972 Macedonians (0.20 percent); 3,246 Roma (0.17 percent); 2,667 Montenegrins (0.14 percent); 2,258 Italians (0.11 percent), 499 Germans (0.03 percent), 181 Austrians (0.01 percent), etc.

261 Ibid., paragraph 57.

262 Ibid., paragraph 58.

aged 30 percent. The referendum will have no recourse on the Constitutional Court decision to restore rights to "the deleted citizens," but it legitimizes their disenfranchisement. However, as late as March 2007, the Serbian government was not able to resolve issues such as outstanding pension payments with the Slovene government.[263]

When the Slovenes seceded from Yugoslavia, their leader and current Minister of Foreign Affairs declared Slovenia to be "willing to 'renounce' its sovereignty to Brussels and Strasbourg, but not Belgrade. . . . In order for Slovenia to become a democratic and European country, [Yugoslavia] needed to be ruthlessly destroyed."[264] Yet, Slovenia still clings to its "sovereignty." In addition to circumventing full application of minority rights with regard to its obligations toward the Council of Europe, in 2004 it joined the opposition to the reference to federalism in the draft European Constitution (Article 1), invoking "a bad experience of Slovenia in the former federal state (of Yugoslavia)."[265]

Ivan Kristan, former judge of the Yugoslav Constitutional Court of Slovene ethnicity, disagrees with this assessment, insisting that the flexibilities of the Yugoslav Constitution allowed for the autonomous development for each republic, including Slovenia. He stresses that Slovenia had a bad experience only in the late 1980s, albeit with the Milosevic regime rather than the country's federal model.[266]

The Slovene example reveals that European Union is not necessarily a haven for people's self-determination in a sense of human and minority rights extending to self-government. Nonetheless, this is what the European Union continues to represent to its aspiring members, as a corpus of states with the highest standards in this arena. For them, the internal right to self-determination has been equated to membership in the European Union, itself hailed as a model for democratic governance. In this respect, self-determination appears to have gained a new, regional dimension. Perhaps this is the legal translation of Europeanization, otherwise defined by political scientists as "a process reorienting the direction and shape of

---

263 "Slovenia deleted about 17,000 Serbian retirees from its pension records in 1991. Only 700 of these people [. . .] managed to secure pensions," *Beta News Agency* (Belgrade), March 2, 2007.

264 Dimitrij Rupel, "Slovenia in Post-Modern Europe," *Nationalities Papers* 21 (1993), 51-9: 57-58.

265 Ivan Kristan, «Европски устав и федерализам» [The European Constitution and Federalism], *Constitution; Lex Superior*, ed. Srdjan Djordjevich (Belgrade, Association for Constitutional Law of Serbia, 2004), 257-268: 258.

266 Ibid., 257-268: 264-267.

politics to the degree that E.U. political and economic dynamics become part of the organizational logic of national politics and policy making."[267] Certainly, Europeanization should also apply to the existing E.U. members, defeating warranted criticism of human rights activists such a Žarko Puhovski, head of Croatian Helsinki Committee for Human Rights:

> We are entering Europe because Europe is worse and not because we are better . . . . Cyprus is more divided than Bosnia . . . . and Baltic states entertain a catastrophic policy toward minorities.[268]

In the ideal scenario, Europe shall jointly advance toward relations such as those currently entertained between Norway and Finland. In 2002, Norway passed ownership over the previously disputed "Island Where Mathis, the Son of Samuel, Does the Mowing," an uninhabited stretch of barren land in the Inarijoki River, which marks the border between the two countries. This territorial transfer produced little practical difference and passed almost unnoticed.[269]

7.8. Toward a Conclusion

Since the year 2000, the European Union and the United States have principally attempted to reconstruct democracy in the former Yugoslav countries and otherwise facilitate the peoples' expression of self-determination within the bounds of the Euro-Atlantic community. As explained by Antoaneta Dimitrova:

> The European Union focused the aspirations of post-communist elites and populations by providing a model of prosperity and democracy to be emulated and thus became the closest thing to an external guiding power.[270]

---

[267] Robert Ladrech, "Europeanization of domestic politics and institutions: the case of France," *Journal of Common Market Studies* 32:1 (1984): 69-88, cited in Kevin Featherstone and Georgios Kazamias, eds. *Europeanisation and the Southern Periphery* (London: Frank Cass, 2001), 13.

[268] Žarko Puhovski, speaking at the International Conference: Serbia—Five Years After, organized by the Belgrade Fund for Political Excellence and the Balkan Trust for Democracy/German Marshall Fund, Belgrade, October 4-5, 2005.

[269] Cited in Sam Coates, "The land that time almost forgot," *The Times* (London), January 22, 2002.

[270] Antoaneta L. Dimitrova, ed., "Enlargement-driven change and post-communist transformations: a new perspective," *Driven to change; the European Union's Enlargement Viewed from the East* (Manchester and New York: Manchester University Press, 2004), 3.

The policies applied with this aim have contributed both to regional stability and international order and security, but have not yet settled all claims relating to both internal and external right to self-determination, as shown by different but very much related disputes on the territory of the former Yugoslavia. The reason for this is that even the principally supranational European Union structure reaches its most important decisions in an intergovernmental forum, underscoring the supremacy of nation-states, since:

> For a nation to mean something normally means it needs a state, or a share in one. And for a state to mean something it needs a border.[271]

Nonetheless, resolving self-determination issues in a wider, regional framework demonstrates strong potential for success, as demonstrated by a cautious approach to Montenegrin referendum question and Macedonian decentralization process. Momir Bulatovich, one of the republican leaders at the time of Yugoslavia's break-up, then the president of Montenegro, expressed regret that this approach was not espoused a decade earlier:

> Almost a decade after the end of conflicts on the territory of the Second [Communist] Yugoslavia, we have occurring what should have occurred at the beginning in order to avoid the conflict. The region received a new name (Western Balkans), all states are encouraged (diplomatic expression for forced) to cooperate with one another, conditions for free flow of people, goods and capital have been created. Everyone is adopting modern, European laws, which are in essence one and the same, since all have the same goal—membership in the European Union.[272]

---

[271] "Good Fences," *The Economist*, December 19, 1998, 22.

[272] Momir Bulatović, *Pravila ćutanja* [Rules of Silence] (Belgrade: Narodna knjiga—Alfa, 2004), 21 [Translation mine]. Original: "Gotovo deceniju nakon prestanka sukoba na prostorima druge Jugoslavije, dešava se ono što je trebalo da se uradi na početku, pa da ne bude sukoba. Region je dobio novo ime (Zapadni Balkan), sve države bivaju ohrabrene (diplomatski izraz za primorane) da medjusobno saradjuju, kreiraju se uslovi za slobodan protok ljudi, dobara i kapitala. Svi donose moderne, evropske zakone, koji su u osnovi isti, budući da je svima isti cilj—članstvo u Evropskoj uniji."

Note: Steil and Woodward also underscore benefits of economic integration in curbing violent conflicts: "Early staged entry into liberal European economic regimes will encourage private-sector development, reduce the state's economic role, underpin the rule of law, and increase the benefits of forswearing violent conflict over resources and national boundaries." Benn Steil and Susan L. Woodward, "A European 'New Deal' For The Balkans," *Foreign Affairs* 78, no. 6 (November-December 1999): 95. Accessed December 25, 2005. Available from Expanded Academic ASAP.

In a practical and symbolic move, the countries of the Western Balkans have since 2000 created a free trade area in the form of an enlarged Central European Free Trade Area (CEFTA), and established a wider, South East Europe Energy Community, slashing regulations on cross-border electricity trading among Romania, Bulgaria, Croatia, Serbia (including Kosovo and Metohia), Montenegro, Bosnia and Herzegovina, Macedonia, and Albania. These regional integrations are reminiscent of the foundation of the European Union, first as the European Steel and Coal Community in 1951 and as a European Economic Community in 1957.[273]

In addition to a belated use of "Europeanization" in resolving the former Yugoslav crisis, Louis Sell singles out as "the single greatest overall conceptual fault" of the international community "the failure to address on an equal basis the claims to self-determination of all the peoples that inhabited the former Yugoslavia," elaborating:

> By insisting that the internal borders of the republics that constituted Yugoslavia must be maintained as the external borders of the new states emerging from the rubble of Yugoslavia's collapse, the international community denied to Serbs and Albanians—the peoples of Yugoslavia whose ethnic borders most deviated from the political ones—the independent nation-states that it granted to Slovenes, Croats, Macedonians, and Bosnians.[274]

Susan Woodward convincingly argues that double standards are derived from "the way that outsiders redefined events in terms of categories familiar to them":

> The constraining role of the norm of sovereignty is particularly strong in the way in which the history of the Yugoslav crisis has already been rewritten to conform to international decisions of recognition. It is now accepted without demur that the "Serbian army" "invaded" Slovenia, then Croatia, and then Bosnia and Herzegovina; that Serbian aggression was and still is the cause of the war; that the issue in Kosovo was Albanian human rights. . . . The consequence of this revisionist history is to obscure

---

[273] For more, *see* the Internet presentation of the Stability Pact for South Eastern Europe, http://www.stabilitypact.org/.

[274] Louis Sell, *Slobodan Milosevic and the Destruction of Yugoslavia* (Durham and London: Duke University Press, 2002), 6.

another significant effect of the sovereignty norm: in selecting winners and losers from among the alternatives at the time.[275]

Double standards are still present, illustrated by proposals to use the European framework for substituting independence with a promise of prosperity in the case of Republika Srpska, but for facilitating secession in the case of Kosovo and Metohia. The International Commission on the Balkans thus contradictorily argues in the same document that "the E.U. accession process is the only framework that gives Serbia real incentives if not to endorse then at least to consent to such a fundamental change in the status of Kosovo as independence represents" but that this framework would "provide the requisite incentives for the strengthening of the state's federal structures"[276] in Bosnia.

Instead, the European Union should be used as a model for the successful coexistence of romantic and civic nationalism, allowing "Bosnians" to accept the cosmopolitan alternative to the same extent as "Belgians," and encouraging Kosovo Albanians to seek a wider political space in lieu of an exclusive right to territory. The Serb Prime Minister Koshtunitsa has identified the espousal of European standards and the country's integration in the European Union as a strong argument for an *internal* application of the right to self-determination with regard to Kosovo and Metohia:

> Regional cooperation based on the European principles of democracy, human rights and good neighborly relations will constitute a strong incentive for the Western Balkans in their efforts toward a timely accession to the European Union. This is also the only way to solve all disputes, and to find a durable and stable solution for Kosovo and Metohia. A solution that would be a compromise.[277]

Two key lessons to be drawn from the Yugoslav disintegration are that the European integration process offers more opportunities for integrative solutions to conflicting claims of self-determination, and that development of the right of self-determination in a manner that strengthens the international legal order

---

[275] Woodward, "Compromised Sovereignty to Create Sovereignty," 268-269.

[276] International Commission on the Balkans, *The Balkans in Europe's Future*, April 2005, 23, 25.

[277] Vojislav Kostunica, Opening Speech, European Bank for Reconstruction and Development Annual Meeting and Business Forum, Belgrade, May 22, 2005.

requires an equitable approach and consistent principles. The latter is difficult to achieve in the imperfect world where political decisions tend to be based on immediate realpolitik considerations. In an ideal world we would have an "International Political Tribunal" as an institution of impartial political arbitration or significantly reformed existing agencies of great power agreement (Security Council etc.), as proposed by István Bibó three decades ago.[278] In the interim, the redrawing of boundaries, especially internal, pre-recognition boundaries should not be automatically ruled out. As discussed earlier and encapsulated by Hannum:

> Self-determination should be concerned primarily with people, not territory. . . . In most cases, the best way of determining the wishes of those within a new state would be through a series of plebiscites to redraw what were formerly internal boundaries. . . . Accepting the possibility of altering borders might be a useful precondition for recognition of a new state whenever a significant proportion of the population appears not to support the new borders.[279]

Such an approach would avoid the creation of protectorates and costly engagement in state building without the consent of the governed. It would also empower the notion of "people" and return the right to self-determination to its intended titular, ending the current arbitrary application of this noble legal principle, illustrated by Tomuschat:

> Whenever a state has come into being, the ethnic communities within that state are legally debarred from asserting themselves as people.[280]

The right to secede, if extended, should be granted to all significant ethnic groups, carefully defined and possibly constitutionalized to allow for a peaceful application of the right to self-determination. If the procedure for secession had been

---

[278] *See* István Bibó, *The Paralysis of International Institutions and the Remedies: A Study of Self Determination, Concord among the Major Powers, and Political Arbitration* (New York: John Wiley and Sons, 1976), 145-147.

[279] Hurst Hannum, "The Specter of Secession, Responding to Claims for Ethnic Self-Determination," *Foreign Affairs* 77, No. 2 (1998), 13, 17-18.

[280] Christian Tomuschat, ed., *Modern Law of Self-Determination* (Dordrecht: Martinus Nijhoff Publishers, 1993), 16.

delineated in the Constitution of the former Yugoslavia, this could have been the key factor in preventing war and perhaps even in dissuading certain republics from seceding. This is also the view taken by Koskenniemi, who maintains:

> Non-recognition by important European States of the new Balkan entities as States before a peaceful transition had been realised and minority and human rights safeguarded might have paved the way for a new, realistic and politically sensitive doctrine of self-determination.[281]

Instead, recognition of former Yugoslav republics within the formerly internal boundaries, coupled with strong insistence on respect toward a newly created international territory "made any compromise settlement vulnerable to the charge of rewarding aggression."[282] The same argument applies in reference to the proposed recognition of the Kosovo province. In fact, this argument has been accentuated by explanations provided by former U.S. diplomats such as Richard Holbrooke, who suggests that Kosovo should be recognized to avoid backlash by the disappointed Kosovo Albanians:

> A major European crisis would be assured. Bloodshed would return to the Balkans. NATO, which is pledged to keep peace in Kosovo, could find itself back in battle in Europe.[283]

Holbrooke's assertion has been seconded by Ylber Hasa, a senior member of the Kosovo Albanian negotiating team, who warned that the adoption of a watered-down version of the Special Envoy's Proposal for Kosovo settlement would lead to war: "If you want to see a new Balkan war, that is the perfect scenario."[284] These arguments threaten stability not just in the region but worldwide because they are a signal to separatists that menaces over escalation of violence could lend them more credibility. This signal would be amplified manifold if Kosovo were granted recognition. To safeguard stability, threats over the use of violence should instead be interpreted as a factor that undermines the separatists' claim to have a right to secession.

---

[281] Martti Koskenniemi, "National Self-Determination Today: Problems of Legal Theory and Practice," *International and Comparative Law Quarterly* 43, no. 2 (April 1994), 268.

[282] Robert W. Tucker and David Hendrickson, "America and Bosnia," *The National Interest* (Fall 1993), 19, cited by Koskenniemi, "National Self-Determination Today," 269.

[283] Richard Holbrooke, "Russia's Test in Kosovo," *Washington Post*, March 13, 2007, 17.

[284] John Phillips, "Kosovar warns of War if Self-Rule is denied," *The Washington Times*, February 20, 2007.

While committing a grave error in territorially interpreting the right to self-determination and arbitrarily selecting its titular, the Badinter Commission should at least be credited with attempting to link the external right to self-determination to its internal corollary of human and minority rights. Nonetheless, as experience has shown, independence cannot be conditioned. The lesson has been learnt in the case of Montenegro, where the application of the external right to self-determination has been constitutionally prescribed, but should now be closely monitored to ensure that the authorities adhere to the ultimate notion of self-determination, democratic governance. Constitutionalizing secession and conditioning membership in attractive regional and international organization minimizes violence more effectively than does conditioning independence.

Another question to be posed is: "How far should one extend human and minority rights, including territorial autonomy, without simultaneously encouraging secession?" Howse and Knopp effectively describe the dilemma faced by the federal government, which could be applied to the present day Serbian provinces Kosovo or even Voivodina (which jointly constitute about 37 percent of Serbia's territory), as well as many other places worldwide:

> Either it can exercise the powers necessary to advance effectively the common interests that justify the very existence of a federation, in which case it will be accused by the nationalists of intrusive or domineering behavior, or it can allow itself to be weakened or hamstrung, in which case the nationalists will claim that the federal government is ineffective. In sum, the nationalists will always be able to portray a strong federal government as menacing and a weak one as a superfluous annoyance.[285]

When U.S. Secretary of State James Baker visited Yugoslavia in June 1991, days before Slovenia and Croatia proclaimed independence, he understood the resolution of the crisis to be in "the devolution of additional authority and responsibility and sovereignty to the republics of Yugoslavia."[286] Yet the positions of the member republics appeared irreconcilable. Slovenia and Croatia desired *de facto* independence, while Serbia and Montenegro preferred a more centralized government but conceded to limiting federal competence to "defense, foreign affairs,

---

[285] Robert Howse and Karen Knop, "Federalism, Secession, and the Limits of Ethnic Accommodation: A Canadian Perspective," *New Europe Law* Review 1, no. 2 (1993), 269-320: 275.

[286] Thomas L. Friedman, "Baker Urges End to Yugoslav Rift," *New York Times*, June 22, 1991, A1.

human-rights protection, national rights protection and one market with one central bank."[287] Serbia and Montenegro at the time were not prepared for a formula, famously worded by the President of the Supreme Soviet of the Russian Republic, Boris Yeltsin, allowing the republics to "take as much power as they could swallow."[288] In the case of the Soviet Union, this recipe led directly to disintegration.

Intervening in the Yugoslav dispute, the international community granted independence to all the interested republics within their administrative boundaries without studying the intended purpose of these boundaries. Yet Yugoslav boundaries were sacrosanct only in terms of Communist ideology,[289] which was shattered to pieces with the fall of the Berlin Wall but resurrected by the Badinter Commission. By invoking a forgotten principle of *uti possidetis juris*, the Badinter Commission gave Yugoslav administrative boundaries the significance that their creator, Josip Broz Tito, had constantly refuted:

> Many do not yet understand what is the meaning of federative Yugoslavia. It does not mean the drawing of a borderline between this or that federative unit. . . . No! Those border lines, as I see them, must be something like white veins in a marble staircase. The lines between federated states in a federal Yugoslavia are not lines of separation, but of union.[290]

The key function of the Yugoslav internal boundaries was to counter forced unification of constituent peoples' historical, cultural, and other national characteristics, while preventing any effective division in choosing lines that were partly historical but that did not correspond to ethnic maps, with the exception of Slovenia, where the compactness of the population prevented alternate administrative division. Such an approach corresponds to a general observation made by

---

[287] Ibid.

[288] Cited in Micheal Lesage "Administration in Russia," *Administrative Transformation in Central and Eastern Europe; Towards Public Sector Reform in Post-Communist Societies* (Oxford: Blackwell Publishers, 1993), 123.

[289] "The reason for the sacrosanct nature of these borders was the view that they were the achievement of the Partisan war and revolution. As such they were part of the underpinning of the entire constitutional and legal system and thus bound all future constitution-makers." Peter Radan, *The Break-up of Yugoslavia and International Law*, Routledge Studies in International Law (London, New York: Routledge, 2002), 153. For more, *see* Chapter 2: *Pre-1914 Administrative Boundaries and the Birth of Yugoslavia* and Chapter 3: *Yugoslavias' Administrative Boundaries (1918-1991)*.

[290] Josip Broz Tito, speaking in May 1945 in Zagreb, cited in Frits W. Hondius, *The Yugoslav Community of Nations* (Hague: Mouton, 1968), 180.

Steven Ratner that "governments establish interstate boundaries to separate states and peoples, while they establish or recognize internal borders to unify and effectively govern a polity."[291] As explained earlier, the different internal administrative arrangements that marked Yugoslavia's political history, both under Communism and under monarchy, were all designed with a view to preserving Yugoslav unity, and were not ever seen as possibly becoming international borders in the event that Yugoslavia disintegrated. Interestingly, even the generally compact and economically progressive Slovenia today has an unresolved border dispute with the neighboring Croatia, prompting Andrej Ster, the Slovene State Secretary of Foreign Affairs, to assert in January 2007:

> It is a known fact that there were no borders between the republics in the former Yugoslavia.[292]

The depth of the recent ethnic conflict in Yugoslavia tragically confirmed that Yugoslav nations would not have accepted the internal division of the country if this division were intended to be permanent, drawing different repercussions for their individual and group rights. It further revealed that an attempt to regulate secession within borders that corresponded more closely to demographics and took account of other relevant factors, such as economic viability or historic heritage, be they new international frontiers or perimeters of territorial autonomies, would probably have provided for a more peaceful disintegration of Yugoslavia.[293] Instead, it was the war that changed the demographic reality as the Yugoslav peoples sought refuge within borders of their own national states. The most poignant example is the 1995 Serb exodus from the Krayina, which transformed this region into the silence of a state-sponsored map that screams of forced exclusion.[294]

---

[291] Steven R. Ratner, "Drawing a Better Line: *Uti Possidetis* and the Borders of New States," *American Journal of International Law* 90 (1996), 590-624: 602.

[292] "The Dispute between Slovenia and Crotia over the Border in the Adriatic," *STA News Agency* (Ljubljana), January 29, 2007.

[293] This view is shared by Musgrave: "Early recognition precluded the possibility of a political settlement based upon a readjustment of boundaries to reflect more closely the ethnic distribution in the region—existing territorial arrangements should be the first framework for examination, dialogue, negotiation, confidence-building and possible disposition." Thomas D. Musgrave, *Self-Determination and National Minorities* (Oxford: Clarendon Press, 1997), 236-7.

[294] State-sponsored maps may not always recognize certain natural or social and cultural realities-sometimes these silences are silences of uniformity and sometimes they are silences of exclusion and even repression that can even be reflected in a change in names of certain places." Alan Henrikson, "The Power and Politics of Maps," *Reordering the World; Geopolitical Perspectives on the 21st Century*, ed. George J. Demko and William B. Wood (Boulder: Westview Press, 1999), 105.

In addition to fostering new interpretations of the right to self-determination, the international policies toward Yugoslav disintegration have shaken the cornerstone of public international law, the right to territorial integrity. In 1991 the international community usurped the right to pronounce a country dissolved and on that basis furnish its select parts with international recognition, potentially creating a territorial right to secession and discouraging decentralization as a means of assuaging national concerns. In 1999, NATO militarily intervened in a state it assessed to have reached an intolerable level of minority oppression and took over the governance of one of its constituent units, arguably encouraging insurgency and generally failing to construct ethnic tolerance.[295] Finally, externally imposed nation-building efforts, namely in Bosnia and Herzegovina, have returned us to the colonial era deemed long over, a practice that was emulated in the subsequent international interventions in Iraq and Afghanistan.

In contrast, recently intensified insistence on fulfillment of internal aspects of self-determination, using the E.U. accession process as a carrot and a vehicle, has complemented the principle of integrity and bolstered the international legal order, permitting Western governments to at least partially mollify their past inconsistencies. It is the resolution of Kosovo's legal status, if found within Serbia, that holds the key to the ideal compromise between the provisions of territorial integrity and self-determination, one that speaks of inclusion, empowering all the peoples.

If, on the other hand, Kosovo were to be granted independence without the full consent of its home state, a right of a federal unit (republic, province, canton, etc) to secession will have been created and the right to territorial integrity practically revoked. In reaction to this, the development of the internal aspects of self-determination, such as minority rights, including decentralization and territorial autonomy, would most certainly be stalled. The only scenario in which neither the international legal order nor the internal application of the right to self-determination would be threatened is one where the right to secession is defined in precise terms, ideally as an amendment to the U.N. Charter, permitting intervention, including international recognition, in cases of extreme oppression but strictly defining the level of required oppression and mandating that a

---

[295] For mor, see Chapter 6: Changing Borders by Force.

minority created by the recognition of a new state be granted an equal right to self-determination, including secession. The challenge of this task lies in defining "oppression" and "a minority," as "a people with a right to self-determination." Lawyers and policymakers need to address this challenge to advance international peace and security, as well as the very essence of democracy. Thus far, for political reasons, "attempts to declare rules about recognition within the framework of international codification have always been rejected."[296] In Kosovo and Metohia, fear of an ethnic Albanian backlash if Kosovo is not granted independence, possibly resulting in systematic attacks on international peacekeepers may well cause the standards in the province to fall even lower, bowing to the new status.[297]

The international intervention in the former Yugoslavia since the initial recognition of Yugoslav republics as new states has rendered human and minority rights the only legitimate form of self-determination, a conclusion accepted by the current leaders of Macedonian Albanians or Bosnian Serbs—but not by Kosovo Albanians. The right of a territory to secede could have been established by the 1991 recognition policy were it not later reversed by the the staunch political refusal to call the international recognition of former Yugoslav republics a precedent, claiming that this was not the case of secession but "dissolution." Only Kosovo's international recognition now, as a clear case of endorsed secession, would imply that the exclusive international focus on the internal aspects of self-determination following the recognition of former Yugoslav republics was but a temporary aberration based on geopolitical concerns, and that secession remained a viable option for dissatisfied peoples in the twenty-first century.

---

[296] Crawford, *The Creation of States in International Law*, 2nd ed. (Oxford: Clarendon Press, 2006), 37-38.

[297] See, for instance, "Finally, final Status," *Financial Times*, 22 February 2006; Steven Woehrel, "Kosovo's Future Status and U.S. Policy," *Congressional Research Service Report for Congress*, RS21721, 9 January 2005; Peter Finn, "Kosovo Hostility Aimed at NATO," *Washington Post*, 14 August 1999; Arben Qirezi, Kosovo: UN Facing Backlash," *Institute for War and Peace Reporting*, 23 August 2002.

APPENDIX I

List of Maps

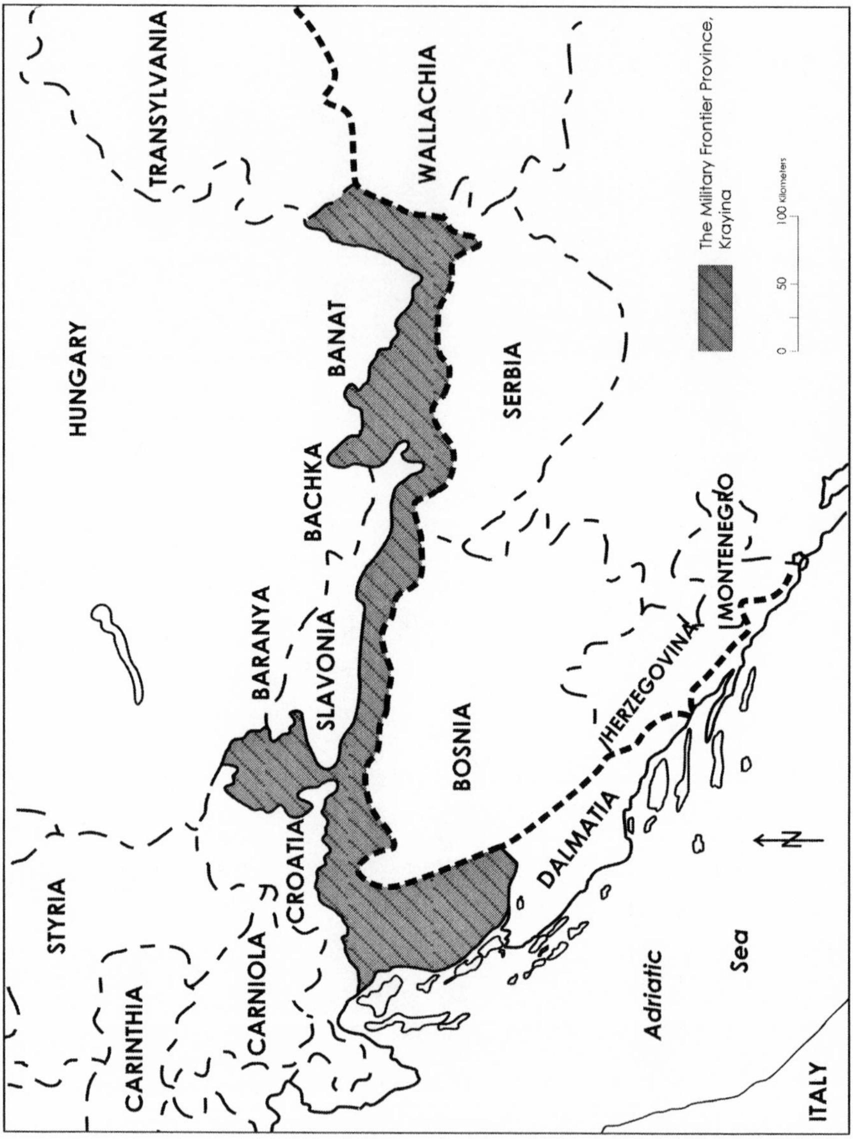

MAP 1. Military Frontier Province: Krayina

Map 2.   Yugoslavia, Administrative Division 1921-1929: 33 Districts

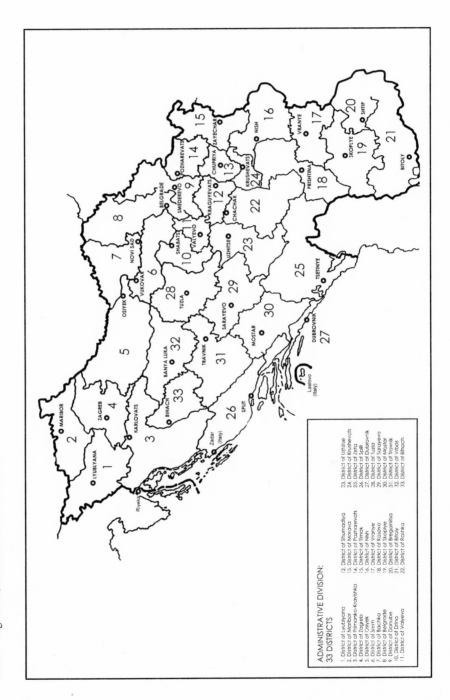

ADMINISTRATIVE DIVISION:
33 DISTRICTS

1. District of Lyublyana
2. District of Maribor
3. District of Primorsko-Kravinka
4. District of Zagreb
5. District of Osiyek
6. District of Srem
7. District of Bachka
8. District of Belgrade
9. District of Danube
10. District of Drina
11. District of Valyevo

12. District of Shumadiya
13. District of Morava
14. District of Pozharevats
15. District of Timok
16. District of Nish
17. District of Vranye
18. District of Kosovo
19. District of Skoplye
20. District of Bregalnitsa
21. District of Bitoly
22. District of Rashka

23. District of Uzhitse
24. District of Krushevats
25. District of Zeta
26. District of Split
27. District of Dubrovnik
28. District of Tuzla
29. District of Sarayevo
30. District of Mostar
31. District of Travnik
32. District of Vrbas
33. District of Bihach

MAP 3. Yugoslavia, Administrative Division 1929-1939: Banovinas

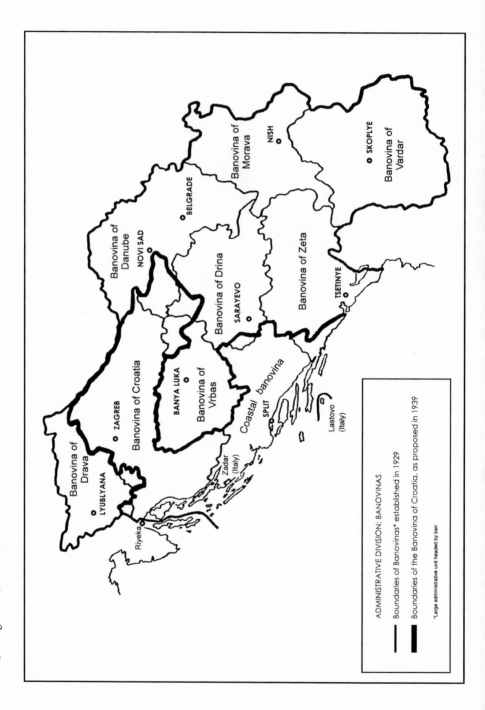

ADMINISTRATIVE DIVISION: BANOVINAS

Boundaries of Banovinas* established in 1929

Boundaries of the Banovina of Croatia, as proposed in 1939

*Large administrative unit headed by ban

MAP 4. Yugoslavia, Administrative Division 1945-1991:
Republics and Provinces

MAP 5. Yugoslavia, Ethnic Composition, 1991

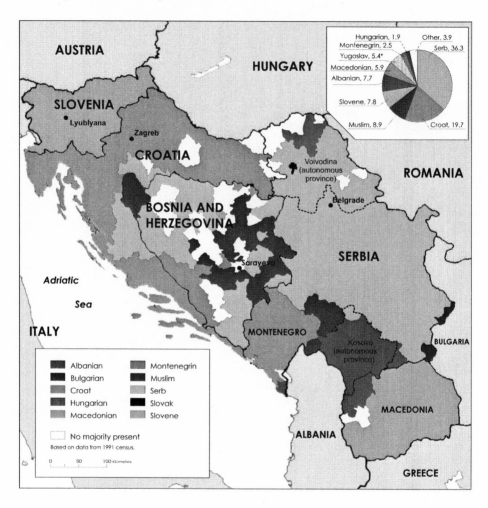

A LEGAL GEOGRAPHY OF YUGOSLAVIA'S DISINTEGRATION

Map 6. Bosnia and Herzegovina: Carrington-Cutileiro Peace Plan, March 1992

Map 7. Bosnia and Herzegovina: Vance-Owen Peace Plan, October 1992

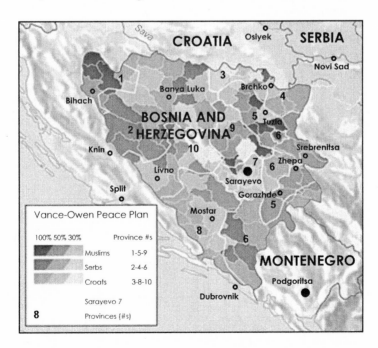

MAP 8. Bosnia and Herzegovina: Union of Three Republics Peace
Plan (Owen-Stoltenberg Peace Plan), August 1993

MAP 9. Bosnia and Herzegovina: Contact Group Peace Plan,
October 1994

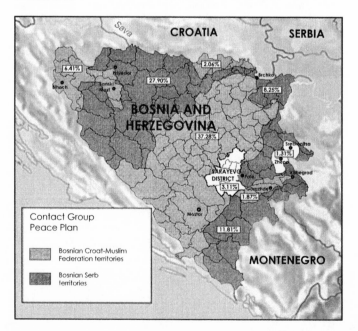

MAP 10. Bosnia and Herzegovina: Dayton Peace Accords, 1995 (juxtaposed on a map showing ethnic composition in 1991)

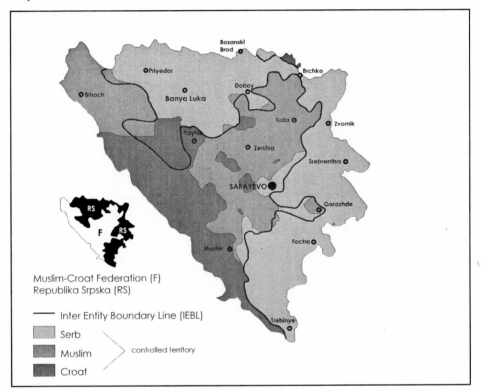

MAP 11. Bosnia and Herzegovina: Dayton Peace Accords, 1995 (juxtaposed on a map showing ethnic composition in 1995)

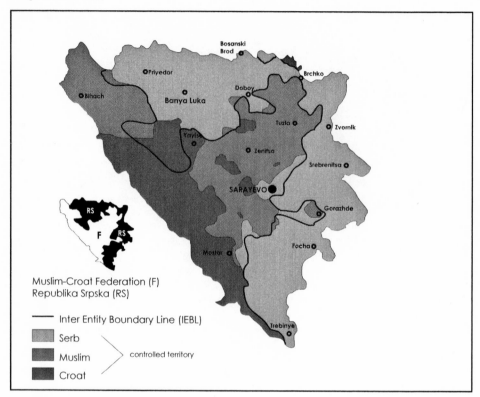

MAP 12. Bosnia and Herzegovina: Dayton Peace Accords, 1995 (juxtaposed on a map showing ethnic composition in 1998)

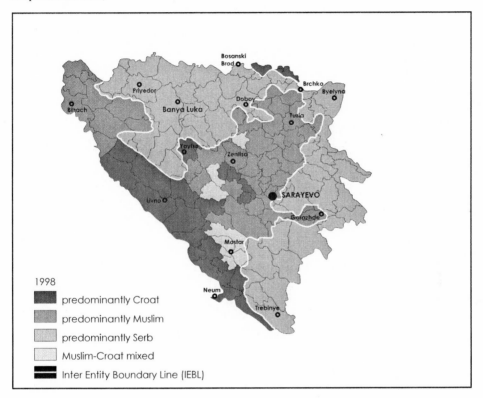

MAP 13. Kosovo and Metohia: Serbian Population 1999-2004

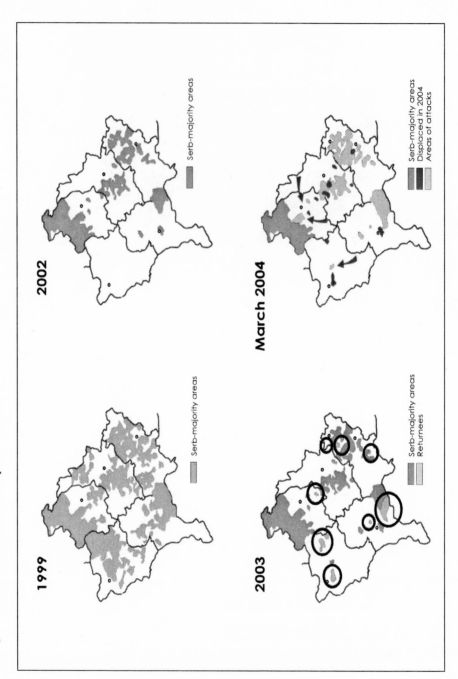

MAP 14.   Greater Albania (as perceived by Albanian nationalists)

449

Bibliography

PRIMARY SOURCES

Cases:

The Aaland Islands Question, Report presented to the Council of the League by the Commission of Rapporteurs, League of Nations Doc. B.7.21/68/106 (1921).

Advisory Opinion of the International Court of Justice on the Western Sahara (1975), icj Reports 12; Sep. Op. Dillard [16 October 1975].

Artukovich v. Boyle, in United States, Federal Supplement, vol. 107, 11, 20, note 6 (1952, District Court, Southern District, California), *Yearbook of the International Law Commission*, 1970, vol. II, 125.

Bankovic and Others v. Belgium and 16 Other Contracting States, Application No. 52207/99.

Brcko Arbitration Arbitral Tribunal for Dispute over Inter-Entity Boundary in Brcko Area, Final Award, 5 March 1999.

Case Relating to Certain Aspects of the Laws on the Use of Languages in Education in Belgium Merits, European Court of Human Rights A, No. 6, Judgment of 23 July 1968.

Constituent peoples case, Opinion of the Bosnia and Herzegovina Constitutional Court, CDL (2000)81.

Slovene Constitutional Court Decision no. U-I-246/02 ("Technical Act on Erased Persons").

Dubai-Sharjah Border Arbitration (1981) 91 ILR 543.

Frontier Dispute Case, (1986) ICJ Reports 554.

Ivanchevich v. Artukovich, in United States, Federal Reporter, second series, vol. 211 F2 nd., 565 (1954, Court of Appeals, 9th Circuit), Yearbook of the International Law Commission, 1970, vol. II, 125.

Namibia Case, Advisory Opinion, ICJ Reports 1971.

Reference re: Secession of Quebec (1998) 161 DLR (4th) 385.

Reparation for Injuries suffered in the Service of the United Nations, Advisory Opinion, ICJ Reports 1949

Report of the International Committee of Jurists entrusted by the Council of the League of Nations with the task of giving an advisory opinion upon the legal aspects of the Aaland Islands question. *League of Nations Official Journal*, Special Supplement No. 3, October 1920.

U.S. Supreme Court, Marbury v. Madison, 5 U.S. 137 (1803).

The International Criminal Tribunal For The Former Yugoslavia, Case No. IT-99-37-PT, The Prosecutor of the Tribunal against Slobodan Milosevic, Milan Milutinovic, Nikola Sainovic, Dragoljub Ojdanic,Vlajko Stojiljkovic; Second Amended Indictment, 29 October 2001.

The International Criminal Tribunal For The Former Yugoslavia, Prosecutor v. Ante Gotovina, Case No. IT-01-45, Amended Indictment, 19 February 2004.

The International Criminal Tribunal for the Former Yugoslavia, Case No: IT-04-84-I, The Prosecutor of the Tribunal against Ramush Haradinaj, Idriz Balaj, Lahi Brahimaj, First Indictment, 4 March 2005.

International Court of Justice, *Case concerning the application of the Convention on the Prevention and Punishment of the Crime of Genocide (Bosnia and Herzegovina v. Serbia and Montenegro)*, 26 February 2007.

Opinions of the Yugoslav Constitutional Court (in chronological order):

Мишљење Уставног суда Југославије о супротности амандмана IX-XC на устав СР Словеније с уставом СФРЈ [Opinion of the Yugoslav Constitutional Court on the Contradiction of Amendments IX-XC to the Slovene Constitution with SFRY Constitution], 18 January 1990, *Службени гласник СФРЈ* [Official Gazette of SFRY] 46, no. 10, 23 February 1990

Separate Opinion of Judges Ivan Kristan and Radko Mochivnik to The Opinion of the Yugoslav Constitutional Court on the Contradiction of Amendments IX-XC to the Slovene Constitution with SFRY Constitution

Одлука о оцењивању уставности одредаба чл. 4 и чл. 10 Закона о плебисциту о самосталности и независности Републике Словенија [Decision on Evaluating the Constitutionality of the Provisions of Articles 4 and 10 of the Law on Plebiscite on the Sovereignty and Independence of the Republic of Slovenia], 10 January 1991, *Службени гласник СФРЈ* [Official Gazette of SFRY], 7 November 1991.

Одлука о оцењивању уставности Уставне декларације о Косову као самосталној и равноправној јединици у оквиру федерације (конфедерације) Југославије и као равноправног субјекта са осталим јединицама у федерацији (конфедерацији) [Decision on Evaluating the Constitutionality of the Constitutional Declaration on Kosovo as a Sovereign and Equal Unit within the Federal (Confederal) Yugoslavia and an Equal Subject with other Units in the Federation (Confederation)], 19 February 1991, *Official Gazette of SFRY* 47, no. 3, 20 May 1991.

Одлука о оцењивању уставности Декларације о сувирености Социјалистичке Републике Македоније [Decision on Evaluating the Constitutionality of the Declaration on Sovereignty of the Socialist Republic of Macedonia], 28 January 1991, *Official Gazette of SFRY*, no 35/91.

Мишљење Уставног суда Југославије о супротности уставног закона за спровођење уставних амандмана XCVI и XCVII на устав Републике Словеније у области народне одбране са уставом СФРЈ [The Opinion of the Yugoslav Constitutional Court on the Contradiction of Constitutional Law for the Implementation of Constitutional Amendments XCVI and XCVII to the Slovene Constitution in the field of national defense with SFRY Constitution], 2 October 1991.

Мишљење Уставног суда Југославије о супротности уставног амандмана XCIX на устав Републике Словеније с Уставом СФРЈ [Opinion of the Yugoslav Constitutional Court on the Contradiction of Constitutional Amendment XCIX to the Slovene Constitution with SFRY Constitution], 2 October 1991.

Одлука о оцењивању уставности Уставног закона за спровођење Основне уставне повеље о самосталности и независности Републике Словеније [Decision on Evaluating the Law on Enforcement of the Constitutional Charter on the Autonomy and Independence of the Republic on Slovenia], 16 October 1991, *Official Gazette of SFRY* 47, no. 89, 13 December 1991, 1427.

Одлука о оцењивању уставности Основне уставне повеље о самосталности и независности Републике Словеније [Decision on Evaluating the Constitutional Charter on the Autonomy and Independence of the Republic of Slovenia], 16 October 1991, *Official Gazette of SFRY* 47, no. 89, 13 December 1991, 1422.

Одлука о оцењивању уставности Уставне одлуке о сувирености и самосталности Републике Хрватске [Decision on Evaluating the Constitutionality of the Constitutional Decision on the Sovereignty and Independence of the Republic of Croatia], 16 October 1991.

Одлука о оцењивању уставности Декларације о проглашењу суверене и самосталне Републике Хрватске [Decision on Evaluating the Constitutionality of the Declaration on the Establishment of the Sovereign and Independent Republic of Croatia], 13 November 1991.

Response to the question of Lord Carrington about whether Yugoslavia is facing disintegration or secession, 5 December 1991, Document no 365/91.

Opinions of the Arbitration Commission to the Peace Conference on Yugoslavia:

Opinion No. 1 of the Arbitration Commission of the Peace Conference on Yugoslavia (1992) 31 ILM 1494.

Opinion No. 2 of the Arbitration Commission of the Peace Conference on Yugoslavia (1992) 31 ILM 1497.

Opinion No. 3 of the Arbitration Commission of the Peace Conference on Yugoslavia (1992) 31 ILM 1499.

Opinion No. 4 of the Arbitration Commission of the Peace Conference on Yugoslavia (1992) 31 ILM 1501.

Opinion No. 5 of the Arbitration Commission of the Peace Conference on Yugoslavia (1992) 31 ILM 1503.
Opinion No. 6 of the Arbitration Commission of the Peace Conference on Yugoslavia (1992) 31 ILM 1507
Opinion No. 7 of the Arbitration Commission of the Peace Conference on Yugoslavia (1992) 31 ILM 1512.
The Interlocutory Decision (1992) 31 ILM 1518.
Opinion No. 8 of the Arbitration Commission of the Peace Conference on Yugoslavia (1992)
    31 ILM 1521
Opinion No. 11 of the Arbitration Commission of the Peace Conference on Yugoslavia (1992)
    31 ILM 1589.
Conference on Yugoslavia, Arbitration Commission, Observations on Croatian Constitutional Law, 4 July 1992:
    92 ILR 209.

Constitutions and constitutional framework documents of the former Yugoslavia:

Statuta Valachorum, 5 October 1630.
Amendments to the Constitution of the Republika Srpska (1996).
Amendments to the Constitution of the Republic of Serbia, *Official Gazette of the Socialist Republic of Serbia*,
    11/1989.
Amendments to the Constitution of SR Slovenia, *Uradni list Republike Slovenije* [Official Gazette of the
    Republic of Slovenia], numbers 37/90, 4/91, 10/91.
"Basic Agreement on the Region of Eastern Slavonia, Baranya and Western Sirmium," U.N. Doc. S/1995/951,
    annex.
Constitution of Bosnia and Herzegovina (1995).
Constitution of the Federal Peoples' Republic of Yugoslavia, 1946, *Official Gazette of FPRY*, 10/1946.
Constitution of the Federation of Bosnia and Herzegovina (1994).
Constitution of the Republic of Serbia, *Official Gazette of the Republic of Serbia*, 1/1990
Constitution of the Socialist Federalist Republic of Yugoslavia, 7 April 1963, *Official Gazette of
    SFRY*, 14/1963.
Constitution of the Socialist Federalist Republic of Yugoslavia, 1974, *Official Gazette of SFRY*, 9/1974.
Constitution of Socialist Autonomous Province of Kosovo, 1974.
Constitution of the Kingdom of Yugoslavia, 3 September 1931, *Official Gazette of Yugoslavia*
    no 207/1931.
Constitutional Decision on the Sovereignty and Independence of the Republic of Croatia and a Declaration on
    the Establishment of the Sovereign and Independent Republic of Croatia, published in the *Official Gazette
    of the Republic of Croatia*, no 31/91.
Ustav Republike Hrvatske [Constitution of the Republic of Croatia], Izvjesca Hrvatskoga sabora [Proceedingss
    of the Croatian Assembly, no. 15, 22 December 1990.
Vance Plan, "Concept for a United Nations Peace-Keeping Operation in Yugoslavia, as Discussed with Yugoslav
    Leaders by the Honourable Cyrus R. Vance, Personal Envoy of the Secretary-General and Marrack
    Goulding, Under-Secretary-General for Special Political Affairs," November/December 1991.
Constitutional Framework for Kosovo (2001)
Constitutional Charter of Serbia and Montenegro, 4 February 2003.
Constitutional Charter on the Autonomy and Independence of the Republic on Slovenia, 24 June 1991.
Framework Agreement (Ohrid Agreement), 13 August 2001, Article 10.2.
General Framework Agreement for Peace in Bosnia and Herzegovina 1995, U.N. Doc A/50/750, reprinted in
    (1996) 35 ILM 75.
Political compromise between Croatia and Hungary, 18 November 1868.
Proceeding Points for the Restructuring of Relations between Serbia and Montenegro (Belgrade Agreement),
    March 2002.
Constitution of the Republic of Serbia, October 2006.

Constitutional proposals:

Constitutional Agreement of the Union of Republics of Bosnia and Herzegovina; Appendix I to the Letter from
the U.N. Secretary-General addressed to the President of the Security Council, 20 August 1993,
U.N. Document S/26337.
Draft Constitution of Republic of Serbia, June 2004.
Draft Z-4 Plan for Peace in Croatia, 1995.
E.U. non-paper: "Draft elements for possible inclusion in the Constitutional Charter"
Government of Serbia Plan for Kosovo and Metohia, April 2005.
Interim Agreement for Peace and Self-Government in Kosovo – Rambouillet Agreement, 23 February 1999.
Serbian President Boris Tadic's Plan for Kosovo, November 2005.
Proposed Constitutional Structure for Bosnia and Herzegovina (Vance-Owen Peace Plan), International
Conference on the Former Yugoslavia, document STC/2/2, 27 October 1992.
Statement of Principles of 18 March 1992 for New Constitutional Arrangements for Bosnia and Herzegovina.
Ustavni nacrt Stojana Protica [Draft Constitution by Stoyan Protich], 1920.

Documents relating to Yugoslav constitutional history (in chronological order):

"Nachertaniye of Iliya Garashanin"
Saborski spisi sabora kraljevinah Dalmacije, Hrvatske i Slavonije od godine 1865-1867 [Parliamentary Acts of
the Parliament of the Kingdoms of Dalmatia, Croatia and Slavonia 1865-1857]. Zagreb, 1900.
Law regulating the activities of the Eastern Greek Church and the use of Cyrillic, adopted on 14 May 1887.
Stenografički zapisnici sabora Kraljevine Hrvatske, Slavonije i Dalmacije (1901-1906) [Stenographic Minutes
of the Parliament of the Kingdom of Croatia, Slavonia and Dalmatia]. Zagreb: Tisak kraljevske zemaljske
tiskare, 1903.
Letter of Austrian Foreign Minister Goluchowski to the Austro-Hungarian Ambassador Calice in
Constantinopolis, 31 December 1904.
Minutes of the meeting in Zadar on 14 November 1905. Printed as a document "Sporazum sa Hrvatima"
[Agreement with the Croats] by the Serb Dubrovnik printing house, kept in the Archives of the Serbian
Academy of Arts and Sciences, dr F. Nikich's fund, number 14.528.
Proclamation of the annexation of Bosnia and Herzegovina by the Emperor Franz Joseph, Vienna, 3 October
1908.
"Popis žitelja od 31.prosinca 1910. u Kraljevinama Hrvatskoj i Slavoniji" [Census of 31 December 1910 in
the Kingdoms of Croatia and Slavonia] in *Publikacije Kr.zemaljskog statistickog ureda u Zagrebu*, LXIII
(Zagreb, 1914), 50-51.
"Niška Deklaracija" [Nish Declaration], 7 December 1914.
"Zaključak tajne sednice Narodne skupštine Kraljevine Srbije" [Conclusions of the secret session of the
National Assembly of the Kingdom of Serbia], 23 December 1914.
"Krfska deklaracija" [Corfu Declaration], 20 July 1917.
"Deklaracija Crnogorskog odbora za narodno ujedinjenje" [Declaration of the Montenegrin Committee for
National Unity], 11 August 1917.
"Narodni svet za Sloveniju i Istru" [National Council for Slovenia and Istria], 17 August 1918.
Deklaracija Starčićeve stranke prava [Declaration of Starčević's Party of Rights], 5 June 1917 and Izjava vodja
slovenačkih stranaka [Statement of leaders of Slovene Parties], 15 September 1917.
"Saopštenje o osnivanju Narodnog Vijeća Slovenaca, Hrvata i Srba" [Announcement on the establishment of
the National Council of Slovenes, Croats and Serbs], 6 October 1918.
"Sastav i pravilnik Narodnog Vijeća Slovenaca, Hrvata i Srba" [Composition and Statute of the National
Council of Slovenes, Croats and Serbs]
"Objava Narodnog Vijeća SHS" [Announcement of the National Council of Serbs, Croats and Slovenes],
19 October 1918.

"Proglašenje Države Slovenaca, Hrvata i Srba" [Proclamation of the state of Slovenes, Croats and Serbs,] 29 October 1918.

Dispatch of Pashich to the accredited ministers (ambassadors) of the Kingdom of Serbia in Paris, London, Washington and Rome, Geneva, 8 November 1918.

Letter, "N Pasic - A Korosecu", 8 November 1918.

Geneva Declaration, 9 November 1918.

"Odluka Velike Narodne Skupštine Srpskog naroda u Crnoj Gori" [Decision of the Great National Assembly in Montenegro], 13 November 1918.

"Proclamation by the National Council of the Unification of the State of Slovenes, Croats and Serbs with the Kingdom of Serbia and Montenegro," 23 November 1918.

"Odluka Velike Narodne Skupštine Vojvodine" [Decision of the Great National Assembly of Voivodina], 25 November 1918.

"Narodno vijeće u Banjaluci – Vojvodi S. Stepanoviću" [National Council in Banya Luka] to Duke S. Stepanovich, 27 November 1918.

"Adresa izaslanstva Narodnog Vijeća SHS Prestolonasledniku Aleksandru i njegov odgovor" [Addressing of the delegation of the National Council of SCS to the Prince Regent Alexander and his response], 1 December 1918.

Official proclamation of the union of the Kingdom of Serbia and Montenegro with the state of the Slovenes, Croats and Serbs, adopted by the National Assembly of Serbia at its 98th ordinary sitting, Belgrade, 16 December 1918.

"Uredba o podeli zemlje na oblasti" [Decree on dividing state into districts], 26 April 1922, Official Gazette of the Kingdom of Serbs, Croats and Slovenes, no 92, 28 April 1922

"Memorandum Hrvatskog bloka medjunarodnoj konferenciji u Djenovi" [Memorandum of Croatian Bloc to the International Conference in Genoa], 25 March 1922.

Communist Party of Yugoslavia, Rezolucija o nacionalnom pitanju [Resolution on the National Question], 1924.

"Izjava S. Radića o prihvatanju monarhije i centralizma" [Statement by S. Radić on accepting monarchy and centralism], April 1925.

"Proklamacija Kralja Aleksandra" [Proclamation of King Alexander], 6 January 1929.

Zakon o nazivu i podeli Kraljevine na upravna područja" [Law on name and division of Kingdom into administrative areas], Article 2, 3 October 1929.

Decision on establishing the Yugoslav Radical Union [Odluka o stvaranju JRZ], 5 September 1935.

"Tsvetkovich-Machek (Cvetković-Maček) Agreement" (1939).

"Uredba o Banovini Hrvatskoj" [Decree on Banovina Hrvatska], Official Gazette of the Kingdom of Yugoslavia, 26 August 1939.

Decree of the Regency Council of Yugoslavia extending the Decree of 26 August 1939 regarding the Banovina of Croatia to other Banovinas, Belgrade, 27 August 1939.

Nacrt uredbe o organizaciji srpske zemlje [Draft Decree on the Organization of Serbian Land], 1940.

Ujedinjene srpske zemlje, Ravnogorski nacionalni program [United Serb lands; National program of Ravna Gora].

Croatian Appeal to the Italian Foreign Minister, June 1940 (DDI, 9, VI, number 848).

"Rezolucija o organizaciji AVNOJ" [Resolution on the organization of AVNOJ], 27 November 1942.

"Odluka o izgradnji Jugoslavije na federativnom principu, "Decision on Constructing Yugoslavia Upon a Federal Principle, 20 November 1943.

"Odluka Drugog zasedanja Antifašističkog Vijeća narodnog oslobodjenja Jugoslavije o izgradnji Jugoslavije na federativnom principu" [Decision of the Second AVNOJ Session on Constructing Yugoslavia Upon a Federal Principle], 29 November 1943.

Statement made by Milovan Djilas in the National Assembly. Belgrade: Office of Information attached to the Government of the Federative People's Republic of Yugoslavia, 1947.

"Osnovni zakon o upravljanju državnim privrednim poduzećima i višim privrednim udruženjima od strane radnih kolektiva" [Framework law on the management of public economic enterprises and higher economic associations by the work collectives], 27 June 1950.

"Ustavni zakon o osnovama društvenog i političkog uredjenja Federativne Narodne Republike Jugoslavije i saveznih organa vlasti" [Constitutional law on the foundations of social and political regulation of the Federal People's Republic of Yugoslavia and the federal authorities], 13 January 1953, *Official Gazette of FPRY*, 3/1953.

Conclusions of the Novi Sad Agreement, December 1954.

Law on territories of municipalities and districts in the People's Republic of Serbia, *Official Gazette of People's Republic of Serbia*, 56/1955.

Law on territories of municipalities and districts in the People's Republic of Serbia, *Official Gazette of People's Republic of Serbia*, 51/1959

Memorandum of the Serbian Academy of Sciences and Arts, 1986

"Contributions to the Slovenian National Program," *Nova Revija*, no. 57, February 1987.

Declaration on the Sovereignty of the Republic of Slovenia, 2 July 1990.

The transcript of talks between Franjo Tudjman and Yovan Rashkovich (Jovan Raskovic). Zagreb, July 1990.

"Discussions between the President or Presidents of the Presidencies of the Yugoslav Republics" 1990.

"A confederal model among the south Slavic states", October 1990.

"Predstavništvo SFRJ dostavilo Skupštini koncept federativnog uredjenja Jugoslavije" [The SFRY Presidency submitted a Concept of Federal Arrangement of Yugoslavia to the Assembly], October 1990.

Izetbegović-Gligorov Platform, 1991.

Resolution of the Croatian Assembly, 21 February 1991.

Resolution on the disassociation of the Republic of Croatia and SAO Krajina, 28 February 1991.

Odluka o odvajanju od Republike Hrvatske [Resolution on the disassociation of the Republic of Croatia and SAO Krajina], 18 March 1991.

Odluka o prisajedinjenju SAO Krajine Republici Srbiji [Decision on Joining of SAO Krayina with Serbia], 1 April 1991.

Declaration on the Peaceful Settlement of the Yugoslav Crisis and against Civil War and Violence, 2 April 1991.

Declaration of Sovereignty and Autonomy of the Serb People in Croatia [Deklaracija o suverenosti i autonomiji srpskog naroda u Hrvatskoj].

Slovenia's Declaration of Independence, 24 June 1991.

Memorandum on the Sovereignty of Bosnia-Herzegovina to the National Assembly, *Official Gazette of the Socialist Republic of Bosnia and Herzegovina*, 32/91.

Resolution on the Position of Socialist Republic of Bosnia and Herzegovina in Resolving the Yugoslav crisis, 1991.

Platform for the Future Yugoslav Community, June 1991.

Constitutional Declaration on Kosovo as a sovereign and equal unit within the federal (confederal) Yugoslavia and an equal subject to other units in the federation (confederation), 1991.

Decision on the Direct Insurance of the Implementation of Federal Legislation on Crossing of the State Border on the Territory of the Republic of Slovenia, *Official Gazette of the SFRY*, no 47, 1991.

Yugoslav-EC Joint Declaration, 8 July 1991.

Assessment and positions of the SFRY Presidency concerning the proclamation of the independence of the Republic of Croatia and Slovenia, Belgrade, 11 October 1991.

Party of Democratic Action, Public Declaration of Forty Party Founders.

"The right to self-determination and secession is the right of nations and not the right of republics." Letter by Yugoslav Presidency Vice-President to Chairman of the Conference on Yugoslavia, 8 December 1991.

Federal Presidency's Letter to Security Council President, 19 December 1991.

Preamble to the Declaration on Proclamation of the Republic of Serbian People in Bosnia Herzegovina, 9 January 1992.

Franjo Tudjman [President of Croatia] to Robert Badinter [President of the Arbitration Commission to the Peace Conference on Yugoslavia], letter, Zagreb, 15 January 1992.

Declaration on Proclamation of the Republic of Serbian People in Bosnia Herzegovina.

Letter from the Prime Minister of the Federal Republic of Yugoslavia [Milan Panich] addressed to the President of the Security Council, 17 August 1992, U.N. Doc. A/46/960 – S/ 24454, Annex.

Letter from Goran Hadzic, President of the Republic of Serbian Krayina, to William Clinton, President of the United States, 1993.

Letter from Franjo Tudjman, President of the Republic of Croatia to Boutros Boutros Ghali, Secretary General of the United Nations, 13 September 1993.

Agreement on Economic Issues, December 1994.

Minutes from the meeting of the Croatian Defense and National Security Council, held in Presidential palace, 30 April 1995.

Minutes from the meeting of the President of Croatia Franjo Tudjman with military officials on 31 July 1995 on the Croatian island of Brioni, Part I.

The Law on Referendum of the Republic of Montenegro, 19 February 2001.

Declaration on remaining within Serbia, adopted by the Assembly of Serbian municipalities and municipal units of Kosovo and Metohia on 25 February 2003 in Kosovska Mitrovica.

Declaration: In Defense of the Name of the Serbian Language, Montenegro, 5 December 2004.

"Commitment to Pursue Constitutional reform," 22 November 2005.

Amendments proposed by the Negotiating Team of the Republic of Serbia to the Draft Comprehensive Proposal for the Kosovo Status Settlement, 24 February 2007

CSCE/OSCE Documents:

Document of the Copenhagen Meeting of the Conference on the Human Dimension, Conference for Security and Co-Operation in Europe, Second Conference on the Human Dimension of the CSCE, Copenhagen, 5 - 29 June 1990.

Conference for Security and Co-operation in Europe, Charter of Paris for a New Europe, 1990 Summit, Paris, 21 November 1990.

Statement on the Situation in Yugoslavia, First Meeting of the CSCE Council of Ministers, Berlin 19-20 June 1991.

Report of CSCE Experts on Peaceful Settlement of Disputes, Section XII, reprinted in (1991) 30 ILM, 382-95.

Strengthening the CSCE, Budapest Decisions, Towards a Genuine Partnership in a New Era, Conference for Security and Co-operation in Europe, 1994 Summit, Budapest, 5-6 December 1994.

OSCE, "Kosovo/Kosova: As Seen, As Told; Analysis of the Human Rights Findings of the OSCE Kosovo Verification Mission," 1999.

UNHCR / OSCE, *Overview of the Situation of Ethnic Minorities in Kosovo*, 3 November 1999.

United States Mission to the OSCE, Statement on Montenegro Delivered by Ambassador David T. Johnson to the (OSCE) Permanent Council, Vienna, 8 November 2001.

OSCE Mission in Kosovo, Human Rights Challenges following the March Riots. May 2004.

OSCE Press release: OSCE Mission and international community in Croatia call for urgent action to stop returnee from losing home, 16 December 2005; OSCE, Status report No. 17 on Croatia's progress in meeting international commitments, July 2005

OSCE Mission to Croatia, Status Report No. 17 on Croatia's Progress in Meeting International Commitments since July 2005, 10 November 2005.

Council of Europe Documents:

Advisory Committee on the Framework Convention for the Protection of National Minorities, Opinion on Slovenia, adopted on 12 September 2002.

Advisory Committee on the Framework Convention for the Protection of National Minorities, Second Opinion on Slovenia, adopted on 26 May 2005, ACFC/INF/OP/II(2005)005

Charter for Protection of Regional and Minority Languages, ETS no: 148, 05/11/1992, in force 01/03/1998.

European Convention on Human Rights and Fundamental Freedoms, ETS no. 005, 04/11/1950, in force 03/09/1953

Framework Convention for the Protection of National Minorities, ETS no: 157, 01/02/1995, in force
01/02/1998.

Parliamentary Assembly of the Council of Europe Resolution 1384: "Strengthening of democratic institutions in
Bosnia and Herzegovina," June 2004.

Recommendation 1134 (1990) on the Rights of Minorities, Council of Europe, Parliamentary Assembly, 1
October 1990 (14th Sitting).

Statute of the Council of Europe, London, 5 May 1949, CETS 001.

Statute of the European Commission for Democracy through Law, Appendix to Resolution (90) 6 On a
Partial Agreement Establishing the European Commission for Democracy through Law (adopted by the
Committee of Ministers on 10 May 1990 at its 86th Session).

Statute: Resolution (2002)3: Revised Statute of the European Commission for Democracy through Law
(adopted by the Committee of Ministers on 21 February 2002 at the 784th meeting of the Ministers'
Deputies).

Opinions of the Council of Europe Venice Commission:

European Commission for Democracy through Law (Venice Commission), Opinion on the Constitutional
Situation in Bosnia and Herzegovina and the Powers of the High Representative, based on Comments by
Mr. J. Helgesen (Member, Norway), Mr. J. Jowell (Member, United Kingdom), Mr. G. Malinverni (Member,
Switzerland), Mr. J.-C. Scholsem (Member, Belgium), Mr. K. Tuori (Member, Finland), adopted by the
Venice Commission at its 62nd plenary session, Venice, 11-12 March 2005.

European Commission for Democracy through Law (Venice Commission), Opinion on the Compatibility
of the Existing Legislation in Montenegro concerning the Organisation of Referendums with Applicable
International Standards, adopted by the Venice Commission at its 65th Plenary Session, Venice, 16-
17 December 2005, on the basis of comments by Mr. Anthony Bradley (Substitute Member, United
Kingdom), Mr. Carlos Closa Montero (Member, Spain), Mr. Kaarlo Tuori (Member, Finland), Strasbourg,
19 December 2005 [Opinion no. 343 / 2005, CDL-AD(2005)041Or.Engl.]

E.U. Documents (in chronological order):

Declaration on Human Rights, Conclusions of the Luxembourg European Council, 29 June 1991.

Letter from the Dutch Government to E.C. member states, 13 July 1991.

Declaration on Yugoslavia, 20 August 1991, EC Press Release P.77/91

EC Declaration on Yugoslavia, 3 September 1991.

EC Declaration on the Occasion of the Ceremonial Opening of the Conference on Yugoslavia, The Hague, 7
September 1991.

EC Declaration on the situation in Yugoslavia, adopted at the Informal meeting of Ministers for Foreign Affairs,
Haarzuilens, 6 October 1991, UN Doc. S/23114, Annex II.

Resolution on Human Rights, Democracy and Development, Council and Member States, meeting within the
Council, 28 November 1991.

[EC] Declaration on Positive Measures, 2 December 1991.

Declaration on the Guidelines on the European Community Recognition of New States in Eastern Europe and
in the Soviet Union, 16 December 1991.

Declaration on Yugoslavia, 17 December 1991.

Treaty on European Union (Treaty of Maastricht), 7 February 1992.

US/EC Declaration on the Recognition of the Yugoslav Republics, Brussels, 10 March 1992.

European Council Declaration on Former Yugoslavia, European Council, Conclusions of the Presidency
(Annex D.1), Edinburgh, 11-12 December 1992, SN456/92.

European Council in Copenhagen, 21-22 June 1993: Conclusions of the Presidency, SN 180/1/93.

Presidency Conclusions, Madrid European Council, 16 December 1995.

General Affairs Council, Conclusions on the application of conditionality with a view to developing a coherent
EU strategy for its relations with the countries in the region, 29 April 1997, *Bulletin of the EU*, No 4-1997.

Treaty of Amsterdam amending the Treaty on European Union, the Treaties establishing the European Communities and related Acts, Official Journal C 340, 10 November 1997, entered into force on 1 May 1999.

Declaration on the occasion of the 50th anniversary of the Universal Declaration of Human Rights, Vienna, 10 December 1998.

Communication from the Commission to the Council and the European Parliament on the stabilisation and association process for countries of South-Eastern Europe - Bosnia and Herzegovina, Croatia, Federal Republic of Yugoslavia, former Yugoslav Republic of Macedonia and Albania, COM/99/0235, 26 May 1999

Conclusions of the EU General Affairs Council, 2192nd Council meeting, Luxembourg, 21-22 June 1999.

Council Regulation No. 2007/2000 introducing exceptional trade measures for countries and territories participating in or linked to the EU's Stabilization and Association process, 18 September 2000.

Declaration of the Zagreb Summit, 24 November 2000.

Council Regulation (EC) No 2666/2000 of 5 December 2000.

European Union Charter of Fundamental Rights, as signed and proclaimed by the Presidents of the European Parliament, the Council and the Commission at the European Council meeting in Nice on 7 December 2000, Official Journal of the European Communities 2000/C 364/01, 18 December 2000 (entry into force 1 November 2003).

European Union guidelines on Human rights dialogues, Council of the European Union, 13 December 2001.

Commission Staff Working Document: European Initiative For Democracy And Human Rights Programming Document 2002-2004, 20 December 2001.

Communication from the Commission to the Council and the European Parliament, "Reinvigorating EU Actions on Human Rights and Democratisation with Mediterranean Partners; Strategic Guidelines," Brussels, 21 June 2003, COM (2003) 294.

Commission of the European Communities, Report from the Commission to the Council on the Preparedness of Bosnia and Herzegovina to negotiate a Stabilisation and Association Agreement with the European Union, COM (2003) 692, Brussels, 18 November 2003.

EU-Western Balkans Summit – Declaration, Thessaloniki, 21 June 2003, Press release 10229/03 (Presse 163).

Commission of the European Communities, Opinion on Croatia's Application for Membership of the European Union, Brussels, 20 April 2004, COM (2004) 257.

Council Decision of 14 June 2004 on the principles, priorities and conditions contained in the European Partnership with Serbia and Montenegro including Kosovo as defined by the United Nations Security Council Resolution 1244 of 10 June 1999, Official Journal of the European Union L 227/21, 26 June 2004.

Council of the European Union, Presidency Conclusions, 17 and 18 June 2004.

Council of the European Union, Press Release 12770/04, 2609th Council Meeting: General Affairs and External Relations, Luxembourg, 11 October 2004.

EU Statement on the Regional Ministerial Conference on Refugee Returns held in Sarajevo on 31 January 2005, Permanent Council No 543, 3 February 2005.

Council of the European Union, Brussels European Council – Presidency Conclusions, Brussels, 18 June 2005, 10255/05, Annex III.

European Union Special Representative in Bosnia and Herzegovina Press Release: EU Conditions Start of SAA on Reform Process, 29 June 2005.

Commission of the European Communities, Proposal for a Council Decision on the Principles, Priorities, and Conditions contained in the Accession Partnership with Croatia, COM (2005) 556, Brussels, 9 November 2005.

European Commission, Bosnia and Herzegovina 2005 Progress Report, COM (2005) 561, Brussels, 9 November 2005.

Commission of the European Communities, Commission Opinion on the Application from the Former Yugoslav Republic of Macedonia for Membership of the European Union, Brussels, 9 November 2005, COM (2005) 562.

Council Regulation (EC) No. 1946/2005, 14 November 2005.

Conclusions of the Council of the European Union, 2691st Council Meeting: General Affairs and External Relations, Brussels, 21-22 November 2005.

Council of the European Union, Presidency Conclusions 15914/05, Brussels, 17 December 2005, 7.
Commission of the European Communities, *Commission Staff Working Document: Kosovo (under UNSCR 1244) 2006 Progress Report* [COM (2006) 649 final], Brussels, 8 November 2006

U.N. Documents (in chronological order):
U.N. Charter

Security Council Resolutions:

S/RES/384, 22 December 1975, S/RES/389, 22 April 1976, S/RES/713, 25 November 1991, S/RES/743, 21 February 1992, S/RES/781, 9 October 1992, S/RES/786, 10 November 1992, S/RES/802, 25 January 1993, S/RES/820, 17 April 1993, S/RES/1037, 15 January 1996, S/RES/1160, 31 March 1998, S/RES/1236, 7 May 1999, S/RES/1244, 10 June 1999, S/RES/1246, 11 June 1999, S/RES/660, 2 August 1990, S/RES/1257, 3 August 1999, S/RES/661, 6 August 1990, S/RES/1262, 27 August 1999, S/RES/1264, 15 September 1999, S/RES/1272, 22 October 1999.

General Assembly Resolutions (Declarations and Conventions):

Universal Declaration of Human Rights, U.N. General Assembly Resolution 217 A (III), 10 December 1948.

Convention on the Prevention and Punishment of the Crime of Genocide, U.N. General Assembly Resolution 260 (III), 9 December 1948, entered into force on 12 January 1951.

Declaration on the Granting of Independence to Colonial Countries and Peoples, U.N. General Assembly Resolution 1514 (XV), 14 December 1960.

International Convention on the Elimination of All Forms of Racial Discrimination, U.N. General Assembly Resolution 2106 (XX), 21 December 1965

1966 Covenant on Civil and Political Rights and Economic Rights Covenant, U.N. General Assembly Resolution 2200 (XXI), 16 December 1966. The Civil Rights Covenant entered into force on 23 March 1976

The Economic Rights Covenant entered into force on 3 January 1976.Declarations, India, U.N. General Assembly Resolution 2200 (XXI), 16 December 1966. Declarations, United Kingdom, U.N. General Assembly Resolution 2200 (XXI), 16 December 1966

Declaration on Friendly Relations and Co-operation among States in accordance with the Charter of the United Nations (Declaration on Friendly Relations, U.N. General Assembly Resolution 2625 (XXV), 24 October 1970

Declaration on the Elimination of All Forms of Intolerance and Discrimination Based on Religion or Belief, U.N. General Assembly Resolution 36/55, 25 November 1981.

1989 Convention on the Rights of the Child, U.N. General Assembly Resolution 44/25, 20 November 1989, entered into force 2 September 1990, in accordance with article 49 Declaration on the Rights of Persons belonging to National or Ethnic, Religious or Linguistic Minorities, U.N. General Assembly Resolution 47/135, 8 December 1992.

Other U.N.G.A. Resolutions:

944 (X), 15 December 1955, 1044 (XI), 13 December 1956, 1541 (XV), 14 December 1960, 1608 (XV), 21 April 1961, 1746 (XVI), 27 June 1962, 2353 (XXII), 19 December 1967, 2504 (XXIV), 20 November 1969, 3161 (XXVIII), 14 December 1973, 3288 (XXIX), 13 December 1974, 3291 (XXIX), 13 December 1974, 3314 (XXIX), 14 December 1974, 3433 (XXX), 9 December 1975, 3485 (XXX), 12 December 1975, 31/4, 21 October 1976, 31/53, 1 December 1976, 32/7, 1 November 1977, 32/34, 28 November 1977, 34/69, 33/39, 13 December 1978, 34/40, 21 November 1979, 6 December 1979, 35/43, 35/20, 11 November 1980, 35/27, 11 November 1980, 28 November 1980, 36/50, 24 November 1981, 36/105, 10 December 1981, 37/30, 23 November 1982, 37/65, 3 December 1982, 38/13, 21 November 1983, 39/48, 11 December 1984, 40/62, 9

December 1985, 41/30, 3 November 1986, 42/17, 11 November 1987, 43/14, 26 October 1988, 44/9, 18 October 1989, 45/11, 1 November 1990, 46/9, 16 October 1991; 46/236, 46/237 and 46/238, 22 May 1992, 47/9, 27 October 1992, 48/56, 13 December 1993, 940, 1994, 54/194, 17 February 2000.

U.N. Reports, Addresses, Press releases:

OR-GA, First Session, Part II, Summary Record of the Joint First and Sixth Committees, 25 November 1946.

Palley, Claire. Constitutional Law and Minorities, Minority Rights Group Report, No. 36 (1978).

Héctor Gros Espiell, Special Rapporteur, Implementation of United Nations Resolutions Relating to the Right of Peoples under Colonial and Alien Domination to Self- determination, Study for the Sub-Commission on Prevention of Discrimination and Protection of Minorities of the Commission on Human Rights, U.N. Doc. E/CNA/Sub.2/390 (and Corr. 1 and Add. 1), 22 June 1977, 17, paragraph 74); 1978 Gros Espiell Report 1 (U.N. Doc. E/CNA/Sub.2/405, 20 June 1978), 38, paragraph 85)

Jordan, art. 40 CCPR Report, U.N. Doc. CCPR/C/1/Add.55 (1981)

General Comment 12, paragraph 6, the Human Rights Committee, adopted by the Committee at its 516th meeting on 12 April 1984.

Study by the Secretary-General on Popular Participation, U.N. Doc. E/CN.4/1985/10 (1985).

Statement by the representative of U.S.S.R. to the Human Rights Committee, 42 U.N. GAOR, Supp. (No. 40), U.N. Doc. A/42/40 (1987).

Report of the Secretary General Pursuant to Security Council Resolution 743 (S/23777) of 2 April 1992.

An Agenda for Peace, Report of the Secretary-General to the Security Council, U.N. Doc. A/47/277-S/24111 (1992).

U.N. doc. E/CN.4/Sub.2/1992/6, paragraph 3(d)., U.N. Doc E/CN.4/SR.52, 9.

UNSC Docs. A/46/912-S/23884, A/46/913-S/23885, A/46/921-S23971 of 21 May 1992.

Report of the Secretary-General Pursuant to Paragraph 4 of Security Council Resolution 752 (S/24049, 30 May 1992).

Concluding Observations of the Human Rights Committee: Croatia, 28 December 1992, CCPR/C/79/Add.15.

Statement by the President of the Security Council (S/25162), 25 January 1993.

Programme of Action of the United Nations International Conference on Population and Development, Cairo, 5-13 September 1994. Office of the High Commissioner for Human Rights, General Recommendation No. 21: Right to self-determination, 23 August 1996.

UN Inter-Agency Report, Update on Humanitarian Situation in Kosovo, 24 December 1998.

Report of the Secretary-General Prepared Pursuant to Resolution 1160 (1998), 1199 (1998) and 1203 (1998) of the Security Council, UN Doc. S/1998/1221, 24 December 1998.

12th Report of the High Representative for Implementation of the Peace Agreement to the Secretary-General of the United Nations, 12 February 1999.

UN Secretary-General Kofi Annan, addressing the Commission on Human Rights in Geneva, SG/SM/6949HR/CN/898, 7 April 1999.

Press Release SC/6870, Prosecutor for International Tribunals briefs Security Council, 2 June 2000.

Security Council hears Briefing by Head of U.N. Interim Administration Mission in Kosovo, 9 June 2000, SC/6873.

Richard Garfield, Economic Sanctions, Health and Wellbeing in Yugoslavia, 1990-2000; Report published by UN OCHA and UNICEF/Belgrade. New York: UN Office for the Coordination of Humanitarian Affairs, 2001.

OHR Press Release, 29 July 2002.United Nations Interim Administration Mission in Kosovo, The Standards for Kosovo, 10 December 2003.

Report of the Secretary-General on the United Nations Interim Administration Mission in Kosovo, S/2005/88, 14 February 2005.

High Representative's remarks to the OSCE Permanent Council, 15 December 2005.OHR, Order on the Implementation of the Decision of the Constitutional Court of Bosnia and Herzegovina in the Appeal of Milorad Bilbija et al, No. AP-953/05, 23 March 2007.OHR, Statement by the High Representative for B&H, Christian Schwarz-Schilling at the Press Conference, 23 March 2007.

OHR, "Gesture politics delivers nothing," 30 March 2007.

Report of the Special Envoy of the Secretary-General on Kosovo's future status, S/2007/168, 26 March 2007.

Comprehensive Proposal for the Kosovo Status Settlement, S/2007/168/Add.1, 26 March 2007.

Other documents (in chronological order):

Treaties:

Peace Treaties of Westphalia [Peace Treaty between the Holy Roman Emperor and the King of France and their respective Allies], 24 October 1648

Holy Alliance Treaty, signed on 26 September 1815 by the sovereigns of Austria, Prussia and Russia

Treaty of San Stefano, 3 March 1878.

Treaty Between Great Britain, Austria-Hungary, France, Germany, Italy, Russia and Turkey. (Treaty of Berlin), 13 July 1878, 153 CTS 171-191.

Treaty of Bucharest, 10 August 1913, 218 CTS 322-337

Treaty of London, 26 April 1915, 221 CTS 56-63.

Treaty between the Principal Allied and Associated Powers and the Serb-Croat-Slovene State [Yugoslav Minorities Treaty] (St. Germain-en-Laye, 10 September 1919, entered into force on 16 July 1920):

The Peace Treaty of Versailles, 28 June 1919.

Treaty of Gruber-De Gasperi, September 1946.

North Atlantic Treaty; Entered into force on 24 August 1949

Treaty of Peace with Italy, Paris, 10 February 1947.

North Atlantic Treaty; Entered into force on 24 August 1949.

General Conference of the United Nations Educational, Scientific and Cultural Organization, Convention against Discrimination in Education, adopted on 14 December 1960, entered into force on 22 May 1962. Treaty of Osimo, 1975.

Other documents:

U.S. Congressional Record, 27 May 1916, Volume 53, Part 9, 8854.

President Woodrow Wilson's Fourteen Points, 8 January 1918, Delivered in Joint Session, US Congress. Charter of the United Nations.

(1923) PCIJ Reports, Series B, No. 6

Covenant of the League of Nations, including Amendments adopted to December, 1924.

Montevideo Convention on the Rights and Duties of States, adopted on 26 December 1933 and entered into force on 26 December 1934.165 League of Nations Treaty Series.

(1935) PCIJ Reports, Series A/B, No. 64

The Statute of the International Court of Justice

Constitution of the Union of Burma, 24 September 1947.

Charter of the Organization of African Unity, 479 U.N.T.S. 39, entered into force 13 September 1963.

The Durban Declaration in Tribute to the Organization of African Unity and on the Launching of the African Union, ASS/AU/Decl. 2 (I)

OAU Assembly Resolution, Border Disputes among African States, paragraph 2 [AHG/Res. 16(1), First Ordinary Session, Cairo, 17-21 July 1964.

OAU Assembly Resolution, Border Disputes among African States, AHG/Res. 51(4), Fourth Ordinary Session, Kinshasa, 11-14 September 1967.

Final Act of the Helsinki Conference on Security and Co-operation in Europe: Questions Relating to Security in Europe – Declaration on Principles Guiding Relations between Participating States, 1 August 1975, 14 ILM 1292.

Universal Declaration of the Rights of Peoples, Algiers, 4 July 1976.

The Vienna Convention on the Law of Treaties, adopted on May 22 1969 and entered into force on 27 January 1980. Published as Treaty Series No.058 (1980): Cmnd 7964 / United Nations, *Treaty Series*, vol. 1155,331

Vienna Convention for the Protection of the Ozone Layer (1985, UNEP)

African [Banjul] Charter on Human and Peoples' Rights, adopted June 27, 1981, OAU Doc. CAB/LEG/67/3 rev. 5, 21 I.L.M. 58 (1982), entered into force 21 October 1986.

Montreal Protocol on Substances that Deplete the Ozone Layer (1987)

United Nations Framework Convention on Climate Change (1992)

Vienna Declaration and Programme of Action, the World Conference on Human Rights, 25 June 1993.

Constitution of Ethiopia, 8 December 1994.

Copenhagen Declaration on Social Development, and the Programme of Action of the World Summit for Social Development, Copenhagen, March 1995.

Beijing Declaration and Platform for Action, Forth World Conference on Women, Beijing 1995.

The Alliance's Strategic Concept, Approved by the Heads of State and Government participating in the meeting of the North Atlantic Council in Washington D.C. on 23 and 24 April 1999.

The Federation of Saint Christopher and Nevis Constitutional Order of 1983.

Additional international documents specific to the former Yugoslavia:

George Bush Letter to the SFRY Prime Minister Ante Markovich of 28 March 1991.

Deutscher Bundestag: Stengraphische Protokolle [Stenographic Minutes] 12/37, 4 September 1991.

Arrangements for a General Settlement proposed by the Conference on Yugoslavia at the Hague, 18 October 1991.

White House Press release, Washington, 7 April 1992.

Statement of Principles adopted at the Peace Conference on Yugoslavia, 31 ILM (1992), 1533.

Bonn Peace Implementation Conference 1997: Bosnia and Herzegovina 1998: Self-sustaining Structures, Summary of Conclusions, 10 December 1997.

Letter by Lord Robertson, NATO Secretary General to Mr. Kofi Annan, U.N. Secretary General, 7 February 2000.

Declaration, Regional Ministerial Conference on Refugee Returns, Sarajevo, January 2005.

Contact Group Guiding Principles for a Settlement of Kosovo's Status (Point 6); integral text provided as Annex to the Letter from the President of the Security Council addressed to the Secretary-General, S/2005/709, 10 November 2005.

Interviews:

Author's Interview with Robert Badinter, Paris, 19 November 2002.

Author's Interview with Ambassador Charles Crawford, Boston, 5 March 1999.

Author's Interview with Ratko Markovich, Professor of Constitutional Law at the University of Belgrade and one of key authors of the 1990 Serbian Constitution, Zlatibor, 24 July 2005.

Author's Interview with Milovan Buzadjich, former President of Yugoslav Constitutional Court, Belgrade, 24 August 2005.

Author's Interview with Savo Shtrbats, Director of Veritas, Belgrade, 28 November 2005.

Author's Interview with ICTY official, 28 November 2005

Author's interview with Voyislav Stanimirovich, Belgrade, 8 December 2005.

Author's Interview with Ambassador Dushan T. Batakovich, Advisor to the President of Serbia for Kosovo, Belgrade, Serbia, 12 April 2007.

Public Statements/ Press Briefings / Hearings:

Albright, Madeleine K., U.S. Secretary of State. "Remarks on Kosovo," Washington, DC, 27 October 1998.

———. Remarks at the U.S. Institute for Peace, 4 February 1999.

———. Speech at the Council for Foreign Relations, cited in Ivo H. Daalder, "And Now, A Clinton Doctrine?" *Haagsche Courant*, 10 July 1999.

Blair, Anthony. "Doctrine of the International Community," Speech to the Economic Club, Chicago, 22 April '1999.

Broz Tito, Josip. Speech. (Zagreb, May 1945).

———. "Iz govora Generalnog Sekretara KPJ JB Tita na osnivackom kongresu KP Srbije" [From the speech of the General Secretary of the CPY Josip Broz Tito at the Founding Congress of the Communist Party of Serbia], 8 May 1945.

Burns, R. Nicholas. On-the-Record Briefing, Under Secretary of State for Political Affairs R. Nicholas Burns on U.S. Strategy For Kosovo, 8 November 2005, Washington, D.C. Remarks as Prepared, "Bosnia Ten Years Later: Successes and Challenges." United States Institue of Peace, Washington, D.C., 21 November 2005.

Clark, General Wesley K. "Press Briefing on the Kosovo Strike Assessment." Brussels, NATO Headquarters, 16 September 1999.

Clinton, William Jefferson. "Remarks by the President to AFSCME Biennial Convention," White House, Office of the Press Secretary, 23 March 1999, 7.

———.Press Conference, 20 June 1999.

del Ponte, Carla. Lecture at the Fletcher School, Boston, USA, 27 October 2005.

Dobrijevic Rev. Irinej, Coordinator, Kosovo and Metohia Committee Office, Holy Assembly of Bishops of the Serbian Orthodox Church. "Kosovo: Current and Future Status." Testimony Before the Committee on Foreign Relations, U.S. House of Representatives. Washington, DC, 18 May 2005.

European Policy Centre. Communication to Members S48/05: Macedonia - Preparing for the European Union; Breakfast Policy Briefing. 26 September 2005.

Hearing by the House International Relations Committee, Chaired by Representative Benjamin A Gilman, Witness: James Baker, Former Secretary of State, 12 January 1995, Federal News Service Transcript.

Hill, Christopher. Lecture at the Fletcher School, Boston, USA, 28 February 2000.

House Of Representatives, 106th congress, 1st Session, 106-116, Adverse Report, submitted by Mr. Gilman, from the Committee on International Relations, to accompany H. Con. Res. 82: Directing the President, pursuant to Section 5(C) of the War Powers Resolution, to remove United States Armed Forces from their Positions in Connection with the Present Operations against the Federal Republic of Yugoslavia, 27 April 1999.

Kardelj, Edvard. "Main Characteristics of the Constitution of the Federative People's Republic of Yugoslavia." Speech broadcast by Radio Belgrade, 5 December 1945; published by the Office of Information attached to the Government of the Federative People's Republic of Yugoslavia, Belgrade 1947.

Kostunica, Vojislav, Prime Minister of Serbia. Opening Speech, European Bank for Reconstruction and Development Annual Meeting and Business Forum. Belgrade, 22 May 2005.

Ljajic, Rasim, Minister of Human and Minority Rights. "The Rule of Law and European Standards for Human Rights Protection." International Conference: Serbia – Five Years After, organized by the Belgrade Fund for Political Excellence and the Balkan Trust for Democracy/German Marshall Fund. Belgrade, 4-5 October 2005.

Mesić, Stipe, President of Yugoslavia. Address to the Croatian Assembly, 8 December 1991.

Owen, Roberts B., Presiding Arbitrator for the Brcko Arbitral Tribunal Sarajevo, Bosnia and Herzegovina. Statement, 5 March 1999.

Plavshich, Bilyana (Plavsic, Biljana), President of Republika Srpska. "Address of 15 March 1997, regarding the recently signed agreement on parallel relations between RS and FRY."

Press Briefing by the Contact Group negotiators, 18 February 1999.

Puhovski, Zarko. Discussion, International Conference: Serbia – Five Years After, organized by the Belgrade Fund for Political Excellence and the Balkan Trust for Democracy/German Marshall Fund. Belgrade, 4-5 October 2005.

Rehn, Olli, E.U. Enlargement Commissioner. "Making the European Perspective real in the Balkans." Keynote address at the Conference "Bringing the Balkans into Mainstream Europe" by Friends of Europe. Brussels, 8 December 2005. SPEECH/05/770.

Shea, Jamie. NATO Press Briefing, 17 May 1999.

Solana, Javier, EU High Representative for the CFSP. Speech at the Policy Dialogue "Dayton at 10: drawing lessons from the past," organized by the European Policy Centre and King Baudouin Foundation." Brussels, 25 November 2005, S382/05.

Talbott, Strobe, U.S. Deputy Secretary of State. Address at the Aspen Institute: The Balkan Question and the European Answer, 24 August 1999.

Tudjman, Franjo. "We find ourselves before a great historical test," Statement at the Occasion of the Ceremonial Proclamation of the Constitution of the Republic of Croatia in the Croatian Assembly on 22 December 1990, *Izvjesca Hrvatskoga sabora* [Proceedingss of the Croatian Assembly, number 15, 22 December 1990.

Public Opinion Research:

Strategic Marketing and Media Research Institute Public Opinion Research, 2004 - 2007.

Marten Board International Public Opinion Research, cited in *Inet News*, 8 December 2005

Reports:

Alliance for a New Kosovo, *Independence for Kosovo*

Amnesty International, "NATO/Federal Republic of Yugoslavia 'Collateral Damage' or Unlawful Killings? Violations of the Laws of War by NATO during Operation Allied Force." London: Amnesty International Pubications, 6 June 2000.

———. *Slovenia, 2005.*

Amnesty International Public Statement, "Kosovo (Serbia): Need to consult civil society and ensure effective protection of human rights," AI Index: EUR 70/014/2006 (Public) News Service No: 249, 22 September 2006.

Ball, Patrick. *Policy or Panic? The Flight of Ethnic Albanians from Kosovo, March-May 1999.* New York: American Association for the Advancement of Science, 2000.

Bill 99: A Sovereign Act of Dispossession, Dishonour and Disgrace," Brief of The Grand Council of the Crees (Eeyou Istchee) to the Québec National Assembly Committee on Institutions (Summary), 1 February 2000.

European Stability Initiative. "Making Federalism Work – A Radical Proposal for Practical Reform." 8 January 2004.

Final Report to the Prosecutor by the Committee Established to Review the NATO Bombing Campaign Against the Federal Republic of Yugoslavia, 13 June 2000.

Franck, Thomas et al. *The Territorial Integrity of Quebec in the Event of the Attainment of Sovereignty* (The Quebec Report), 8 May 1992.

Human Rights Watch, *Civil and Political Rights in Croatia*, 1995.

———. *Croatia: Impunity for abuses committed during 'Operation Storm' and the denial of the right of refugees to return to the Krajina* 8, No. 13 (D), August 1996.

———.*Croatia, Second class citizens, the Serbs of Croatia* 11, No. 3 (D) (March 1999).

———.*Civilian Deaths in the NATO Air Campaign*, 1999.

———.*Failure to Protect: Anti-Minority Violence in Kosovo, March 2004*, July 2004.

———.*Human Rights Overview: Macedonia*, 2005.

Institute for War and Peace Reporting, "The Collateral Damage is Democracy," 30 March 1999.

International Commission on the Balkans, *The Balkans in Europe's Future*, April 2005

International Helsinki Federation for Human Rights, *Human Rights in the OSCE Region: Europe, Central Asisa and North America, Report 2005 – Serbia and Montenegro (Kosovo)*, 27 June 2005.

Kosovo Situation Reports: May 1999, Library of Congress Kosovo Task Force, CRS Report #RL30156.

Oberg, Jan. "The West is in Moral Trouble if there is an Ethnic Cleansing Plan – and if There isn't." *TFF Pressinfo*, 27 April 1999.

U.K. House of Commons Foreign Affairs Committee, Foreign Affairs – Third Report, 1 February 2005.

UNHCR. "The Balkans After the War was over." *Refugees* 3, No. 140 (2005).

U.S. Department of State, Kosovo Update, 2 March 1999

———.Kosovo Humanitarian Situation Report, 31 March 1999.

———.Erasing History: Ethnic Cleansing in Kosovo, 10 May 1999

United States Senate Republican Policy Committee. "The Kosovo Liberation Army: Does Clinton Policy Support Group with Terror, Drug Ties? From 'Terrorists' to 'Partners,'" 31 March 1999.

War Crimes in Kosovo: a Population-Based Assessment of Human Rights Violations against Kosovar Albanians. Boston/Washington, DC: Physicians for Human Rights and Program on Forced Migration and Health, Center for Population and Family Health, The Joseph L. Mailman School of Public Health, Columbia University, August 1999.

SECONDARY SOURCES

Books:

Albin, Pierre. *Les Grands Traités Politiques.* Paris, 1912.

Alden, Percy, ed. *Hungary of Today.* London: Fawside House, 1909.

Alexander, Stella. "Croatia: The Catholic Church and Clergy, 1919-1945." In *Catholics, the State, and the European Radical Right, 1919-1945,* ed. Richard J. Wolff and Jörg K. Hoensch. New York: Columbia University Press, 1987.

Allcock, John B. *Explaining Yugoslavia.* New York: Columbia University Press, 2000.

Ambrosio, Thomas. *Irredentism: Ethnic Conflict and International Politics.* Westport, CT: Praeger Publishers, 2001.

Anderson, Benedict R. O'G. *Imagined Communities: Reflections on the Origin and Spread of Nationalism.* London: Verso, 1983.

Anderson, M.S.   *The Eastern Question, 1774-1923.* New York: Macmillan, 1966.

Angelet, Nicolas. "Quelques observations sur le principe de l'uti possidetis a l'aune du cas hypothétique de la Belgique." In *Démembrements d'Etats et délimitations territoriales:l'uti possidetis en question(s),* eds. Olivier Corten et al. Bruxelles: Bruylant, 1999.

Atlagic, David. *Nacija, nacionalno pitanje i odnosi medju narodima Jugoslavija* [Nation, national question and relations among Yugoslav nations]. Belgrade: Radnicki univerzitet "Djuro Salaj," 1964.

Avakumovic, Ivan. *History of the Communist Party of Yugoslavia* I. Aberdeen: University of Aberdeen Press, 1964.

Babich, Ivan. "Military History." In *Croatia; Land, People, Culture* I, eds. Francis H. Eterovich and Christopher Spalatin. Toronto: University of Toronto Press, 1964.

Bacevich, Andrew J. and Cohen, Eliot A., eds. *War over Kosovo.* New York: Columbia University Press, 2001.

Baker, James A. III. *The Politics of Diplomacy, Revolution, War and Peace, 1989-1992.* New York: G. P. Putnam's Sons, 1995.

Batakovic, Dusan T.

———. *Histoire du Peuple Serbe.* Lausanne: L'Age d'Homme, 2005.

———. *The Kosovo Chronicles.* Belgrade: Plato, 1992.

———. *The Serbs of Bosnia & Herzegovina: History and Politics.* Paris: Dialogue, 1996.

———. *Yougoslavie. Nations, religions, idéologies.* Lausanne: L'Age d'Homme, 1994.

Barker, Thomas M. *The Slovene Minority in Carinthia.* East European Monographs. Boulder, 1984.

Bartl, Peter. *Albanien; Vom Mittelalter bis zur Gegenwart* [Albanians: From Middle Ages to the Present]. Regensburg, 1995, translated to Serbian by Lyubinka Milenkovich. Belgrade: Clio, 2001.

Bechkovich, Matiya. *Kosovo – Najskuplja srpska rec* [Kosovo – the most precious Serb word]. Valyevo: Biblioteka Glas Crkve, 1989.

Beloff, Nora. *Tito's Flawed Legacy: Yugoslavia and the West, 1939-84.* London: Victor Gollancz, ltd., 1985.

Berenbaum, Michael, ed. *A Mosaic of Victims, Non-Jews Persecuted and Murdered by the Nazis.* New York: New York University Press, 1990.

Berman, Harold J. and Quigley, John B., eds. *Basic Laws on the Structure of the Soviet State.* Cambridge: Harvard University Press, 1969.

Bibó, István. *The Paralysis of International Institutions and the Remedies: A Study of Self Determination, Concord among the Major Powers, and Political Arbitration*. New York: John Wiley and Sons, 1976.

Bilandžić, Vladimir. "Angažovanje Evropske unije i NATO u rešavanju jugoslovenske krize" [Engagement of the European Union and NATO in resolving the Yugoslav Crisis]. In *Medjunarodno pravo i jugoslovenska kriza* [International Law and the Yugoslav Crisis], ed. Milan Šahović, 165-207. Belgrade: Institute for International Politics and Economy, 1995.

Biberaj, Elez. *Albania, A Socialist Maverick*. Boulder: Westview Press, 1990.

—— "Kosova: The Balkan Powder Keg." In *Ethnic and Religious Conflicts: Europe and Asia*, ed. P. Janke. Dartmouth: Aldershot, 1994.

Bilbija, Zarko. "The Serbs and Yugoslavia." In *The Serbs and their National Interest*, eds. Norma von Ragenfeld-Feldman and Dusan T. Batakovic. San Francisko: Serbian Unity Congress, 1997.

Binns, Christopher. "Federalism, Nationalism and Socialism in Yugoslavia." In *Federalism and Nationalism*, ed. Murray Forsyth, 115-146. Leicester: Leicester University Press, 1989.

Biondich, Mark "'We were defending the state': Nationalism, Myth, and Memory in Twentieth-Century Croatia." In *Ideologies and National Identities; The Case of Twentieth Century Southeastern Europe*, eds. John R. Lampe and Mark Mazower, 54-82. Budapest, New York: Central European University Press, 2004.

Blagojevic, Marina. "The Migration of Serbs from Kosovo during the 1970s and 1980s: Trauma and/or Catharsis." In *The Road to War in Serbia: Trauma and Catharsis*, ed. Nebojsa Popov, 224-230. Budapest: Central European University Press, 2000.

Bloomfield, Louis M. *The British Honduras/Guatemala Dispute*. Toronto: The Carswell Company Limited, 1953.

Bobetko, Janko. *Sve moje bitke* [All my battles]. Zagreb: Vlastita naklada, 1996.

Boillat, Pierre. *Jura naissance d'un etat – Aux sources du droit et des institutions jurassiennes* [Jura, Birth of a State – At the Source of Jurassian Law and Institutions]. Lausanne: Editions Payot, 1989.

Bojović, Jovan R., ed. *Podgorička Skupština 1918* [Podgoritsa Assembly 1918]. Gornji Milanovac: Dečje novine, 1989.

Bougarel, Xavier. *Bosnie; Anatomie d'un conflit*. Paris: La Découverte, 1996.

Brockett, L.P. *The Bogomils of Bulgaria and Bosnia; The Early Protestants of the East*. 1879.

Brownlie, Ian. "The Rights of Peoples in Modern International Law." In *The Rights of Peoples*, ed. James Crawford, x, 236. Oxford, England; New York: Clarendon Press; Oxford University Press, 1988.

Broz Tito, Josip. "The National Question in Yugoslavia in the Light of the National Liberation War." In *The National Liberation War and Revolution in Yugoslavia (1941-1945); Selected Documents*, ed. Fabijan Trgo, 394-402. Belgrade: Military History Institute of the Yugoslav People's Army, 1982.

Bubalo, Ratko. "Stanje ljudskih i drzavljanskih prava u Hrvatskoj" [The State of Human Rights and Citizenship Rights in Croatia]. In *Srbi u Hrvatskoj* [Serbs in Croatia], ed. Ivo Banac. Zagreb: Helsinki Committee for Human Rights in Croatia, 1998.

Buchanan, Allen. "The Morality of Secession." In *The Rights of Minority Cultures*, ed. Will Kymlicka, 350-74. Oxford, New York: Oxford University Press, 1995.

Buchar, Vekoslav. *Политичка историја Словеначке* [The Political History of Slovenia]. Belgrade: Politika AD, 1939.

Buchheit, Lee C. *Secession: The Legitimacy of Self-Determination*. New Haven, Conn.: Yale University Press, 1978.

Buisson, Jean-Christophe. *Héros trahi par les alliés; le général Mihailović 1893-1946* [Hero betrayed by his allies; General Mihailovich]. Paris: Perrin, 1999.

Bulatović, Momir. *Pravila ćutanja; istiniti politički triler sa poznatim završetkom* [Rules of Silence; A True Political Thriller with a Familiar Ending]. Belgrade: Narodna knjiga, 2004.

Burg, Steven L. *Conflict and Cohesion in Socialist Yugoslavia, Political Decision Making Since 1966*. Princeton University Press, 1983.

Burg, Steven L. and Shoup, Paul S. *The War in Bosnia-Herzegovina: Ethnic Conflict and International Intervention*. New York: M. E. Sharp Inc., 1999.

Buzadjich, Milovan. *Сецесија бивших југословенских републике у светлости одлука Уставног суда Југославије; Збирка докумената с уводном расправом* [Secession of former Yugoslav republics in light of decisions of the Yugoslav Constitutional Court; Collection of Documents with Introductory Discussion]. Belgrade: Official Gazette of SRY, 1994.

Carpenter, Ted Galen. "Introduction: A Great Victory?" In *NATO's Empty Victory; A Postmortem on the Balkan War*, ed. Ted Galen Carpenter, 1-10. Washington, D.C.: CATO Institute, 2000.

Cassese, Antonio. "The Helsinki Declaration and Self-Determination." In *Human Rights, International Law and the Helsinki Accord*, ed. Thomas Buergenthal. New York: Universe Books, 1977.

——. "The Self-Determination of Peoples." In *The International Bill of Rights: the Covenant on Civil and Political Rights*, ed. Louis Henkin. New York: Columbia University Press, 1981.

——. *Self-Determination of Peoples: A Legal Reappraisal*. Cambridge: Cambridge University Press, 1995.

Castellan, Georges. *Histoire des Balkans XIVᵉ-XXᵉ siècle*. Paris: Fayard, 1991.

Castellino, Joshua and Allen, Steve. *Title to Territory in International Law; A Temporal Analysis*. Law, Social Change and Development Series. Aldershot: Ashgate, 2003.

Cavoski, Kosta [Chavoshki, Kosta / Чавошки, Коста]. *Half a Century of Distorted Constitutionality in Yugoslavia*. Belgrade: Centre for Serbian Studies, 1997.

——. *Na rubovima srpstva; Srpsko pitanje danas* [On the edges of Serbdom; Serbian question today]. Belgrade: Tersit, 1995.

Cesarich, George W. "Yugoslavia was Created against the Will of the Croatian People." In *The Croatian Nation in its Struggle for Freedom and Independence*, eds. Antun F Bonifacic and Clement S Mihanovich. Chicago: "Croatia" Cultural Publishing Center, 1955.

Chorovich, Vladimir. *Политичке прилике у Босни и Херцеговини* [Political situation in Bosnia and Herzegovina]. Belgrade: Politika AD, 1939.

Churchill, Winston. *The Second World War*. London: Cassell, 1959.

Claude, Inis L. *National Minorities; an International Problem*. New York: Greenwood Press, 1969.

Clayer, Natalie. *Aux origins du nationalisme albanais; la naissance d'une nation majoritairement musulmane en Europe*. Paris: Editions Karthala, 2007.

Clinton, Bill. *My Life*. New York: Vintage Books, 2005.

Cobban, Alfred. *The Nation State and National Self-Determination*. Rev. ed. London: Collins, 1969.

Cohen, Lenard J. *Broken Bonds; Yugoslavia's Disintegration and Balkan Politics in Transition*. 2nd ed. Boulder: Westview Press, 1995.

The Columbia Electronic Encyclopedia, 6th ed. New York: Columbia University Press, 2005.

Connor, Walker. *The National Question in Marxist-Leninist Theory and Strategy*. Princeton: Princeton University Press, 1984.

Corten, Olivier. "Droit des peuples à disposer d'eux-mêmes et uti possidetis: deux faces d'une même médaille?" In *Démembrements d'Etats et délimitations territoriales: l'uti possidetis en question(s)*, eds. Olivier Corten et al. Bruxelles: Bruylant, 1999.

Corwell, John. *Hitler's Pope; The Secret History of Pius XII*. New York: Penguin Group, 1999.

Crawford, James. *The Creation of States in International Law*. Oxford, New York: Clarendon Press; Oxford University Press, 1979.

——. *The Creation of States in International Law*, 2ⁿᵈ ed. Oxford, New York: Clarendon Press; Oxford University Press, 2006.

——. "Outside the Colonial Context." In *Self-Determination in the Commonwealth*, ed. William J. Macartney. Aberdeen: Aberdeen University Press, 1998.

——. "The Right to Self-Determination in International Law: Its Development and Future." In *People's Rights*, ed. Philip Alston, 7-68. New York: Oxford University Press, 2001.

Crnobrnja, Mihailo. *The Yugoslav Drama*. Montreal: McGill-Queen's University Press, 1992; rev. ed 1996.

Cuvalo, Ante. *The Croatian National Movement, 1966-1972*, East European Monographs. New York, 1990.

Dabich, Vojin S. *Војна крајина; Карловачки генералат (1530-1746)* [Military Frontierland; The Karlovats generalcy (1530-1746)]. Belgrade: Holy Synod of the Serbian Orthodox Church, 2000.

Dakic, Mile. *Srpska Krajina; Istorijski temelji i nastanak* [Serbian Krayina: Historical Foundations and Creation]. Knin: Iskra, 1994.

Danforth, Loring M. *The Macedonian Conflict; Ethnic Nationalism in a Transnational World*. Princeton, NJ: Princeton University Press, 1997.

A LEGAL GEOGRAPHY OF YUGOSLAVIA'S DISINTEGRATION

Dedijer, Vladimir. *The Yugoslav Auschwitz and the Vatican.* Prometheus, 1988.

Deroc, M. *British Special Operations Explored, Yugoslavia in Turmoil 1941-1943 and the British Response.* East European Monographs. Boulder: 1988.

Detrez, Raymond. "The Right to Self-Determination and Secession in Yugoslavia: A Hornets' Nest of Inconsistencies." In *Contextualizing secession: normative studies in comparative perspective,* eds. Bruno Coppieters and Richard Sakwa, 112-132. Oxford: Oxford University Press, 2003.

Dimitrijevic, Vojin and Pejic, Jelena. "Ucinci sankcija protiv SR Jugoslavije" ["The Effects of Sanctions against the SFRY"]. In *Medjunarodno pravo i jugoslovenska kriza* [International Law and the Yugoslav Crisis], ed. Milan Shahovich, 245-274. Belgrade: Institute for International Politics and Economy, 1995.

Dimitrova, Antoaneta L., ed. "Enlargement-driven change and post-communist transformations: a new perspective" In *Driven to change; the European Union's Enlargement Viewed from the East.* Manchester and New York: Manchester University Press, 2004.

Djekich, Mirko. *Upotreba Srbije; optuzbe i priznanje Draze Markovica* [Making Use of Serbia; Accusations and Avowal of Drazha Markovich]. Belgrade: Beseda 1990.

Djilas, Aleksa. *The Contested Country; Yugoslav Unity and Communist Revolution, 1919-1953.* Cambridge: Harvard University Press, 1991.

Djilas, Milovan. *Wartime.* London: Martin Secker & Warburg, 1977.

Djukich, Slavoljub. *Kako se dogodio vodja* [How a Leader was Born]. (Belgrade: Filip Visnjic, 1992.

———. *Izmedju slave i anateme: Politicka biografija Slobodana Milosevica* [Between Glory and Anathema: Political Biography of Slobodan Milosevic].Belgrade, 1994.

Djordjevic, Dimitrije. *Les revolutions nationales des peoples balkaniques.* Belgrade: Institut d'Histoire, 1965.

———.ed. *The Creation of Yugoslavia 1914-1918.* Santa Barbara: Clio Books, 1980.

Donia, Robert J. and Fine, John V.A. Jr. *Bosnia and Herzegovina; A Tradition Betrayed.* New York: Columbia University Press, 1994.

Dorich, William. "Epilogue." In *Kosovo,* ed. Basil W.R. Jenkins. Alhambra, CA: Kosovo Charity Fund, 1992.

Dragic-Kijuk, Predrag R.. "A Land Laid Waste," *Krajina; Tragedy of a People.* Hamilton, ON: Canadian-Serbian Council, 1998.

Dragnich, Alex N. *Serbia, Nikola Pasic and Yugoslavia.* New Brunswick: Rutgers University Press, 1974.

———.*The First Yugoslavia, Search For a Viable Political System.* Hoover Institution Press, Stanford, 1983.

———."Nikola Pasic." In *The Serbs and their Leaders in the Twentieth Century,* eds. Peter Radan and Aleksandar Pavkovic. Aldershot: Ashgate, 1997.

———. "The Serbian Government, the Army, and the Unification of Yugoslavs,." In *Creation of Yugoslavia 1914-1918,* ed. Dimitrije Djordjevic. Santa Barbara: Clio Books, 1980.

Draskovic, Milivoj. "Specifičnost ustavnog položaja SR Srbije" [Specificity of the constitutional position of SR Serbia]. In *Osnovi novog ustavnog uredjenja Jugoslavije* [Foundations of the new constitutional regulation of Yugoslavia], ed. Miodrag Jovicic. Belgrade: SANU, 1990.

Drezov, Kyril. "Collateral Damage: The Impact on Macedonia of the Kosovo War." In *Kosovo: The Politics of Delusion,* eds. Michael Waller, Kyril Drezov and Bülent Gökay. London, Portland OR: Frank Cass, 2001.

Eide, Asbjørn. "In Search of Constructive Alternatives to Secession." In *Modern Law of Self-Determination,* ed. Christian Tomuschat, 139-76. Dordrecht; Boston: M. Nijhoff Publishers, 1993.

Ekmečić, Milorad. *Stvaranje Jugoslavije 1790-1918* [Creation of Yugoslavia 1790-1918], Vol 2. Belgrade: Prosveta, 1989.

———.*Bosanski ustanak 1875-1878* [Bosnian Uprising 1875-1878]. Sarajevo: Veselin Masleša, 1973.

Ekwall-Uebelhart, Barbara and Raevsky, Andrei. *Managing Arms in Peace Processes: Croatia and Bosnia-Herzegovina.* Geneva: United Nations Institute for Disarmament Research, 1996.

Emmert, Thomas A. "The Kosovo Legacy" in *Kosovo,* ed. Basil W.R. Jenkins. Alahambra, CA: The Kosovo Charity Fund, 1992.

Engels, Friedrich. "Hungary and Panslavism." In *Marx and Engels, the Russian Menace in Europe,* ed. Paul Blackstock and Bert Hoselitz. Glencoe: Free Press, 1952.

Eterovich, Francis H. and Spalatin, Christopher, eds. *Croatia; Land, People, Culture.* Toronto: University of Toronto Press, 1970.

Etinski, Rodoljub. "Has the SFR of Yugoslavia Ceased to Exist as a Subject of International Law?" In *International Law and the Changed Yugoslavia*, ed. Radovan Petkovich. Belgrade: Institute of International Politics and Economics, 1995.

Farkas, Evelyn. *Fractured States and U.S. Foreign Policy: Iraq, Ethiopia, and Bosnia in the 1990s*. New York: Palgrave Macmillan, 2003.

Featherstone, Kevin and Kazamias, Georgios, eds. *Europeanisation and the Southern Periphery*. London: Frank Cass, 2001.

Federal Ministry of Foreign Affairs of the Federal Republic of Yugoslavia, *Facts on Consequences of the use of Depleted Uranium in the NATO Aggression against the Federal Republic of Yugoslavia in 1999*. Belgrade: Federal Ministry of Foreign Affairs of the Federal Republic of Yugoslavia, 2000.

"Federation, Defederation and Refederation: from the Soviet Union to Russian Statehood." In *Federalism: The Multiethnic Challenge*. London: Longman Group, 1995.

Feldman, Andrea, Stipetić, Vladimir and Zenko, Franjo. *Liberalna misao u Hrvatskoj* [Liberal Idea in Croatia]. Zagreb: Friedrich Naumann Stiftung, 2000.

Fisk, Robert. "Foreward." In *Crisis at Bihac; Bosnia's Bloody Collapse*, Brendan O' Shea. Phoenix Mill: Sutton Publishing Limited, 1998.

Franck, Thomas M. *The Power of Legitimacy Among Nations*. New York, Oxford: Oxford University Press, 1990.

———. "Postmodern Tribalism and the Right to Secession." In *Peoples and Minorities in International Law*, eds. Catherine Brölmann, René Lefeber, and Marjoleine Zieck. Dodrecht: M. Nijhoff, 1993.

Gagnon, Valhre P. Jr. *The Myth of Ethnic War: Serbia and Croatia in the 1990s*. Ithaca, N.Y.: Cornell University Press, 2004.

Gamser, Dušan, Graovac, Igor and Milosavljević, Olivera, eds., *Dijalog povjesničara-istoričara 4* [Dialogue of historians 4]. Zagreb: Friedrich Naumann Stiftung, 2001.

Gazi, Stephen. *A History of Croatia*. New York: Barnes & Noble Books, 1993.

Gellner, Ernest. *Culture, Identity, and Politics*. Cambridge: Cambridge University Press, 1987.

Genscher, Hans-Dietrich. *Rebuilding a House Divided: A Memoir by the Architect of Germany's Reunification*. New York: Broadway Books, 1998.

Glenny, Misha. *The Fall of Yugoslavia; The Third Balkan War*. 3rd rev. ed. New York: Penguin Books, 1996.

———. *The Balkans; Nationalism, War, and the Great Powers, 1804-1999*. New York: Penguin Books, 1999.

Gligorov, Vladimir. "Is What is Left Right? (The Yugoslav Heritage)." In *Transition to Capitalism? The Communist Legacy in Eastern Europe*, ed. János Matyás Kovacs. New Brunswick, NJ: Transaction Publishers, 1994.

———. *Why Do Countries Break Up? The Case of Yugoslavia*. Uppsala: Acta Universitatis Upsaliensis, 1994.

Green, Leslie. "Internal Minorities and Their Rights." In *The Rights of Minority Cultures*, ed. Will Kymlicka, 257-72. Oxford, New York: Oxford University Press, 1995.

Gross, Mirjana and Szabo, Agneza. *Prema hrvatskome gradjanskom društvu. Društveni razvoj u civilnoj Hrvatskoj i Slavoniji šezdesetih i sedamdesetih godina 19. stoljeća* [Towards a Croat Civil Society. Social Development in Civil Croatia and Slavonia in 1860s and 1870s]. Zagreb, 1992.

Hall, Derek. *Albania and the Albanians*. London: Pinter Reference, 1994.

Hall, William Edward. *A Treatise on International Law*, 8th ed. Oxford: Oxford University Press, 1924.

Halperin, Morton H., Scheffer, David J. and Small, Patricia L., eds., *Self-Determination in the New World Order*. Washington, DC: Carnegie Endowment for International Peace, 1992.

Hannikainen, Lauri and Horn, Frank, eds. *Autonomy and Demilitarisation: The Aaland Islands in a Changing Europe*. The Hague: Kluwer Law International, 1997.

Hannum, Hurst. *Autonomy, Sovereignty, and Self-Determination: The Accommodation of Conflicting Rights*. Rev. ed. Philadelphia: University of Pennsylvania Press, 1996.

———. *Documents on Autonomy and Minority Rights*. Dordrecht; Boston: M. Nijhoff, 1993.

Haus Hof und Staats Archiv, Wien, Politisches Archiv XII, k. 272 Nationaliteten und Religionskarte der Vilajete Kosovo, Salonika, Scutari Janina und Monastir, 1903.

Hayden, Robert M. *Blueprints for a House Divided; The Constitutional Logic of the Yugoslav Conflicts*. Ann Arbor: The University of Michigan Press, 2000.

Henrikson, Alan. "The Power and Politics of Maps." In *Reordering the World; Geopolitical Perspectives on the 21st Century*, ed. George J. Demko and William B. Wood. Boulder: Westview Press, 1999.

Heraclides, Alexis. *The Self-Determination of Minorities in International Politics*. London; Portland, Or.: F. Cass, 1991.

Hertslet, Edward Cecil. *The Map of Europe by Treaty*. 1875.

Higgins, Rosalyn. *The Development of International Law through the Political Organs of the United Nations*. London, New York, Toronto: Oxford University Press, 1963.

———. *Problems and Process, International Law and How We Use It*. Oxford: Clarendon Press, 1994.

Hilling, C. "Les frontières du Québec dans l'hypothèse de son accession à l'indépendance: pour une interprétation contémporaine de l'uti possidetis juris." In *Démembrements d'Etats et délimitations territoriales:l'uti possidetis en question(s)*, eds. O. Corten et al. Bruxelles: Bruylant, 1999.

Hinsley, Francis Harry. *Sovereignty*. New York: Basic Books, 1966.

Hobsbawm, E. J. *Nations and Nationalism since 1780: Programme, Myth, Reality*. Cambridge, England; New York: Cambridge University Press, 1990

Hodgkinson, Harry. *Scanderbeg: From Ottoman Captive to Albanian Hero*, 2nd ed. I.B. Tauris/Centre for Albanian Studies, 2005.

Hoffmann, Stanley. "The Use of Force: Taming the Untamable." In *Duties Beyond Borders: On the Limits and Possibilities of Ethical International Politics*. Syracuse, NY: Syracuse University Press, 1981.

Holbrooke, Richard. *To End a War*. New York: Random House, 1998.

Hondius, Frits W. *The Yugoslav Community of Nations/* Hague: Mouton, 1968.

Hoptner, Jacob B. *Yugoslavia in Crisis, 1934-1941*. New York: Columbia University Press, 1962.

Horowitz, Donald L. "A Right to Secede?" In *Secession and Self-Determination*, eds. Stephen Macedo and Allen Buchanan, 50-76. Nomos XLV: Yearbook of the American Society for Political and Legal Philosophy. New York, London: New York University Press, 2003.

Horvat, Branko. *Kosovsko pitanje* [The Kosovo Question]. Zagreb: Globus, 1988.

Ignatieff, Michael. *Virtual War: Kosovo and Beyond*. New York: Metropolitan Books, 2000), 213.

Ilic, Jovan. "The Serbs in the Former SR Croatia." In *The Serbian Question in the Balkans; Geographical and Historical Aspects*, ed. Bratislav Atanackovic, 307-348. Belgrade: Faculty of Geography, University of Belgrade, 1995.

Independent International Commission on Kosovo. *The Kosovo Report*. Oxford: Oxford University Press, 2000.

Ivankovic, Nenad. *Bonn: druga Hrvatska fronta* [Bonn: The Second Croatian Front]. Zagreb: Mladost, 1993.

Izetbegović, Alija. *Odabrani govori, pisma, izjave, intervjui* [Selected speeches, letters, statements, interviews]. Zagreb: Prvo muslimansko Dioničko društvo, 1995.

—. *Sjecanja; autobiografski zapis* [Memoirs; autobiographic script]. Sarajevo: TKD Sahinpasic, 2001.

Jakovljević, Boško. "Humanitarna pomoc u jugoslovenskoj krizi" [Humanitarian Assistance in the Yugoslav Crisis]. In *Medjunarodno pravo i jugoslovenska kriza* [International Law and the Yugoslav Crisis], ed. Milan Šahović, 275-315. Belgrade: Institute for International Politics and Economy, 1995.

Janša, Janez. *The Making of the Slovenian State 1988-1992; The Collapse of Yugoslavia*. Ljubljana: Mladinska knjiga, 1994.

Jatras, James George. "NATO's Myths and Bogus Justifications for Intervention." In *NATO's Empty Victory; A Postmortem on the Balkan War*, ed. Ted Galen Carpenter, 21-29. Washington, D.C.: CATO Institute, 2000.

Jelavich, Charles and Barbara. *The Establishment of the Balkan National States, 1804-1920*. 2nd ed. Seattle, London: University of Washington Press, 1993; 1st edition 1986.

Jennings, Ivor W. *The Approach to Self-Government*. Cambridge: Cambridge University Press, 1956.

Jennings, Robert Y. *The Acquisition of Territory in International Law*. Manchester: Manchester University Press, 1963.

———. "Closing Address." In *Peoples and Minorities in International Law*, eds. Catherine Brölmann, René Lefeber, and Marjoleine Zieck. Dodrecht: M. Nijhoff, 1993.

Diana. Johnstone. "Nato and the New World Order: Ideals and Self-Interest." In *Degraded Capability; The Media and the Kosovo Crisis*, ed. Philip Hammond and Edward S. Herman, 7-18. London, Sterling, VA: Pluto Press, 2000.

Joksimovich, Vojin. *Kosovo Crisis: A Study in Foreign Policy Mismanagement*. Los Angeles: Graphics Management Press, 1999.

Jovicic, Miodrag, ed. *Osnovi novog ustavnog uredjenja Jugoslavije* [Foundations of the constitutional regulation of Yugoslavia. Belgrade: SANU, 1990.

Judah, Tim. *Kosovo; War and Revenge*. New Haven and London: Yale University Press, 2000.

Kadijević, Veljko [Kadiyevich, Velyko]. *Moje vidjenje raspada: vojska bez države* [My Views of the Break-Up: Army without the Country]. Belgrade: Politika, 1993.

Kapidžić, Hamdija. *Hercegovački ustanak 1882. godine* [The Herzegovinian Uprising of 1882]. Sarajevo, 1973.

Kardelj, Edvard. *The New Yugoslav Federal Assembly*. Belgrade: Mladost, 1964.

Kellas, James G. *The Politics of Nationalism and Ethnicity*. New York: St. Martin's Press, 1991.

Kesar, Jovan, Bilbija, Djuro and Stefanović, Nenad. *Geneza maspoka u Hrvatskoj* [Genesis of Maspok in Croatia]. Belgrade: Književne novine, 1990.

Kimminich, Otto. "The Issue of a Right of Secession." In *Modern Law of Self-Determination*, ed. Christian Tomuschat, 83-100. Dordrecht; Boston: M. Nijhoff Publishers, 1993.

King, Ian and Mason, Whit. *Peace at Any Price; How the World failed Kosovo*. Ithaca, NY: Cornell University Press, 2006.

Klaić, Vjekoslav. *Povijest Hrvata; od najstarijih vremena do svršetka XIX stoljeća* [History of Croats from the earliest times to end of XIX century]. Zagreb: Nakladni Zavod Matice Hrvatske, 1975.

Kočović, Bogoljub. *Žrtve Drugog svetskog rata u Jugoslaviji* [Victims of World War II in Yugoslavia]. Sarajevo: Svjetlost, 1990.

Kofos, Evangelos. *Nationalism and Communism in Macedonia*. Thessaloniki: Institute for Balkan Studies, 1964.

Kosancic, Ivan. *Novopazarski sandzak* [Sanjak of Novi Pazar]. Belgrade, 1912.

Kostunica, Vojislav. "The Constitution and the Federal States." In *Yugoslavia, A Fractured Federalism*, ed. Dennison Rusinow. Washington, DC: The Wilson Center Press, 1988.

Kosović, Momčilo. "Srpske političke, privredne i kulturne ustanove poslije Drugog svetskog rata" [Serbian Political, Business and Cultural Institutions After WWII]. In *Republika Srpska Krajina* [Republic of Serbian Krayina], 367-377. Belgrade: Radnička štampa, 1996.

Knight, David B. "Rethinking Territory, Sovereignty, and Identities." In *Reordering the World: Geopolitical Perspectives on the Twenty-First Century*, ed. George J. Demko and William B. Wood. Boulder, Colo.: Westview Press, 1999.

Kostich, Lazo M. *Католички Срби* [Catholic Serbs]. Toronto: St. Sava Serb Cultural Club, 1963.

Kraljačić, Tomislav. *Kalajev rezim u Bosni i Hercegovini (1882-1903)* [The Kállay Regime in Bosnia and Hercegovina (1882-1903)]. Sarajevo: Veselin Masleša, 1987.

Krestich, Vasiliye Dj. *History of the Serbs in Croatia and Slavonia 1848-1914*, transl. Margot and Boško Milosavljević. Belgrade: BIGZ, 1997.*Из историје Срба и српско-хрватских* односа [From the History of Serbs and Serb-Croat Relations]. Belgrade: BIGZ, 1994.

———. *Грађа о Србима у Хрватској и Славонији (1848-1914)* [Documents on Serbs in Croatia and Slavonia (1848-1914)]. Belgrade: BIGZ, 1995.

———. *Знаменити Срби о Хрватима* [Eminent Serbs on Croats]. Novi Sad: Prometey, 1999.

Kristan, Ivan. «Европски устав и федерализам» [The European Constitution and Federalism]. In *Constitution; Lex Superior*, ed. Srdjan Djordjevich, 257-268. Belgrade, Association for Constitutional Law of Serbia, 2004.

Krizman, Bogdan. *Korespondencija Stjepana Radića 1885-1918* [Correspondence of Stjepan Radić 1885-1918]. Zagreb, 1972.

Kruševac, Todor. "Društvene promene kod bosanskih jevreja za austrijskog vremena" [Social change among Bosnian Jews in Austrian times] In *Spomenica, 400 godina od dolaska Jevreja u Bosnu i Hercegovinu* [Commemoration of the four-hundredth anniversary of the arrival of the Jews to Bosnia-Herzegovina], ed. Samuel Kamhi. Sarajevo, 1966.

Kukathas, Chandran. "Are There Any Cultural Rights?" In *The Rights of Minority Cultures*, ed. Will Kymlicka. Oxford, New York: Oxford University Press, 1995.

Kymlicka, Will. "Introduction." In *The Rights of Minority Cultures*, ed. Will Kymlicka, 1-27. Oxford, New York: Oxford University Press, 1995.

———, ed. *The Rights of Minority Cultures*. Oxford, New York: Oxford University Press, 1995.

Lalonde, Suzanne. *Determining Boundaries in a Conflicting World; The Role of Uti Possidetis*. Montreal: McGill University Press, 2002.

Lampe, John R. *Yugoslavia as History. Twice there was a country*. Cambridge, New York: Cambridge University Press, 1996.

Lansing, Robert. *The Peace Negotiations: A Personal Narrative*, 1921.

Larrabee, Stephen. "US Policy in the Balkans: From Containment to Strategic Reengagement." In *Crises in the Balkans, Views from the Participants*, eds. Constantine P. Danopoulos and Kostas G. Messas, 275-295. Boulder: Westview Press, 1997.

Lauterpacht, Hersch. *Recognition in International Law*. Cambridge: Cambridge University. Press, 1947.

Layne, Christopher. "Miscalculations and Blunders Lead to War." In *NATO's Empty Victory; A Postmortem on the Balkan War*, ed. Ted Galen Carpenter11-20. Washington, D.C.: CATO Institute, 2000.

Lederer, Ivo. *Yugoslavia at the Paris Peace Conference; A Study in Frontiermaking*. New Haven: Yale University Press, 1963.

Lee McBain, Howard and Rogers, Lindsay. *The New Constitutions of Europe*. New York: Page & Co, 1922.

Lenin, Vladimir Ilyich. "The Right of Nations to Self-Determination." In *The Nationalism Reader*. ed. Omar Dahbour and Micheline R. Ishay. New Jersey: Humanities Press, 1995.

Lepre, George. *Himmler's Bosnian Division; The Waffen-SS Handschar Division 1943-1945*. Atlgen, PA:Schiffer, 1997.

Lesage Micheal. "Administration in Russia." In *Administrative Transformation in Central and Eastern Europe; Towards Public Sector Reform in Post-Communist Societies*. Oxford: Blackwell Publishers, 1993.

Libal, Michael. *Limits of Persuasion; Germany and the Yugoslav Crisis, 1991-1992*. Westport, CT: Praeger Publishers, 1997.

Liebich, André. *Les Minorités Nationales en Europe Centrale et Orientale* [National Minorities in Central and Eastern Europe]. Geneva: Georg Editeur, 1999.

Lijphart, Arend. "Self-Determination Versus Pre-Determination of Ethnic Minorities in Power-Sharing Systems." In *The Rights of Minority Cultures*, ed. Will Kymlicka, 275-87. Oxford, New York: Oxford University Press, 1995.

Lyushich, Radosh. «Илија Гарашанин о српској државности» [Iliya Garashanin on Serb Statehood]. In *Гарашанин; сусрети и виђења 2001* [Garashanin; meetings and perceptions 2001], ed. Zoran Konstantinovich and Slobodan Pavichevich. Kragujevac: Jefimija, 2002.

Lukic, Reneo and Lynch, Allen. *Europe from the Balkans to the Urals; The Disintegration of Yugoslavia and the Soviet Union*. New York: Sipri, Oxford University Press, 1996.

Macartney, Carlile A. *National States and National Minorities, Royal Institute of International Affairs*. London: Oxford University Press H. Milford, 1934.

Macek, Vladko. *In the Struggle for Freedom*. University Park: State University Press, 1957.

Mackenzie Wallace, Sir Donald, Prince Kropotkin, Mijatovich, C and Bourchier, J.D. *A Short History of Russia and the Balkan States*; reproduced from the 11th edition of the Encyclopaedia Britannica. London: The Encyclopaedia Britannica Company, 1914.

Makinson, David. "Rights of Peoples: Point of View of a Logician." In *The Rights of Peoples*, ed. James Crawford. Oxford, England; New York: Clarendon Press; Oxford University Press, 1988.

Mandić, Ante. *Fragmenti za historiju ujedinjenja* [Fragments for the History of Unification]. Zagreb: JAZU, 1956.

Margalit, Avishai, and Raz, Joseph. "National Self-Determination." In *The Rights of Minority Cultures*, ed. Will Kymlicka, 79-92. Oxford, New York: Oxford University Press, 1995.

Marjanović, Milan. *Londonski ugovor iz godine 1915*. [The 1915 Treaty of London]. Zagreb: JAZU, 1960.

Marković, Laza. *Jugoslovenska drzava i hrvatsko pitanje (1914-1929)* [The Yugoslav state and the Croatian question (1914-1929)]. Zagreb: Komisiona naklada, 1935.

Marković, Ljubisav. *Kapital, ekonomija i socijalizacija* [Capital, Economy and Socialization]. Belgrade: Faculty of Political Science, 2004.

Markovich, Slobodan G. "Two Centuries of Convergence or Divergence between Serbia and Western Europe." In *Challenges to New Democracies in the Balkans*, eds. S. G. Markovich, E. B. Weaver and V. Pavlovic. Belgrade: Cigoja Press, 2004, 114.

Marriott, John. *The Eastern Question*. Oxford: Clarendon Press, 1917.

Mayall, James. *Nationalism and International Society*, Cambridge Studies in International Relations 10. Cambridge, England; New York: Cambridge University Press, 1990.

McEvedy, Colin. *The Penguin Atlas of Recent History (Europe since 1815)*. Penguin, 1982.

Melanson, Richard A. *American Foreign Policy since the Vietnam War; The Search for Consensus from Nixon to Clinton*. New York: M.E. Sharpe, 1996.

Mesić, Stipe. *Kako smo srušili Jugoslaviju: politički memoari posljednjeg predsjednika Predsjedništva SFRJ* [How We Destroyed Yugoslavia: Political Memoirs of the Last President of the Yugoslav Presidency]. Zagreb: Globus International, 1992.

Mihailovic, Kosta and Krestic, Vasilije. *Memorandum of the Serbian Academy of Sciences and Arts; Answers to Criticisms*. Belgrade: Serbian Academy of Arts and Sciences, 1995.

Miladinovich, Zharko. *Тумач повластица, закона, уредаба и других наређења српске народне црквене автономије у Угарској, Хрватској и Славонији* [Interpretation of privileges, laws, decrees and other orders of the Serb national church autonomy in Hungary, Croatia and Slavonia]. Novi Sad, 1897.

Milak, Enes. *Italija i Jugoslavija 1931-1937* [Italy and Yugoslavia 1931-1937]. Belgrade: Institut za savremenu istoriju, 1987.

Mill, John Stewart. "Considerations on Representative Government." In *Utilitarianism, on Liberty, Considerations on Representative Government*, ed. H.B. Acton. London: J.M. Dent and Sons, 1972.

Miller, Nicholas J. *Between Nation and State*. Pittsburgh: University of Pittsburgh Press, 1997.

Miloshevich, Slobodan. *Godine raspleta* [Years of Unraveling]. Belgrade: BIGZ, 1989.

Mishina, Veljko Djurich, ed. *Република Српска Крајина; Десет година послије* [Republic of Serbian Krayina; Ten years later]. Belgrade, Dobra volja, 2005.

Missirkov, Krste P. *On Macedonian Matters*, translated by Alan McConnell. Skopje: Macedonian Review Editions, 1974, orig. 1903.

Mitrović, Andrej. *Prodor na Balkan. Srbija u planovima Nemačke i Austro-Ugarske 1908-1918* [A Foray to the Balkans; Serbia in the plans of Germany and Austria-Hungary]. Belgrade: Nolit, 1983.

Mostov, Julie. "Democracy and Decisionmaking." In *Yugoslavia, A Fractured Federation*, ed. Dennison Rusinow, 105-119. Washington, DC: The Wilson Center Press, 1988.

Mojzes, Paul. "The Camouflaged Role of Religion in the War in Bosnia and Herzegovina." In *Religion and the War in Bosnia*, ed. Paul Mojzes. Atlanta: Scholars Press, 1998.

Mrdjenovic, Dusan, ed. *Ustavi i Vlade Knezevine Srbije, Kraljevine Srbije, Kraljevine SHS i Kraljevine Jugoslavije (1835-1941)* [Constitutions and Governments of the Duchy of Serbia, Kingdom of Serbia, Kingdom of Serbs, Croats and Slovenes and Kingdom of Yugoslavia (1835-1941)]. Belgrade: Nova Knjiga, 1988.

Murphy, Sean D. *Humanitarian Intervention: The United Nations in an Evolving World Order*, 1996.

Murswiek, Dietrich. "The Issue of a Right of Secession." In *Modern Law of Self-Determination*, ed. Christian Tomuschat, 21-39. Dordrecht; Boston: M. Nijhoff Publishers, 1993.

Musgrave, Thomas D. *Self-Determination and National Minorities*. Oxford Monographs in International Law. Oxford, New York: Clarendon Press; Oxford University Press, 1997.

Navaratna-Bandara, Abeysinghe M. *The Management of Ethnic Secessionist Conflict; the Big Neighbor Syndrome*. Aldershot: Dartmouth Publishing Company, 1995.

Necatigil, Zaim M. *The Cyprus Question and Turkish Position in International Law*, 2nd ed. Oxford: Oxford University Press, 1993.

Nikchevich, Zhelidrag. *Rights of Serbs in Montenegro* [Права Срба у Црној Гори]. Belgrade: Igam, 2006.

Nikolic, Oliver. "Constitutional Charter of Serbia and Montenegro." In *Constitution; Lex Superior*, ed. Srdjan Djordjevich, 391-400. Belgrade: Association de droit constitutionnel de Serbie, 2004.

Nikolić, Pavle. "Socijalističke autonomne pokrajine i novi ustav" [Socialist autonomous provinces and the new Constitution]. In *Osnovi novog ustavnog uredjenja Jugoslavije* [Foundations of the new Yugoslav constitutional order], ed. Miodrag Jovičić. Belgrade: SANU, 1990.

Nimni, Ephraim, ed., *National Cultural Autonomy and its Contemporary Critics*. New York: Routledge, 2005.

————. "Marx, Engels, and the National Question." In *The Rights of Minority Cultures*, ed. Will Kymlicka, 57-75. Oxford, New York: Oxford University Press, 1995.

Norman, Wayne. "Domesticating Secession." In *Secession and Self-Determination*, eds. Stephen Macedo and Allen Buchanan. Nomos XLV: Yearbook of the American Society for Political and Legal Philosophy. New York, London: New York University Press, 2003.

Obradović, Konstantin. "Problemi vezani za sukcesiju SFRJ" [Problems relating to the SFRY Succession]. In *Medjunarodno pravo i jugoslovenska kriza* [International Law and the Yugoslav Crisis], ed. Milan Šahović, 275-315. Belgrade: Institute for International Politics and Economy, 1995.

Oppenheim, Lassa F.L. *International Law, A Treatise*, 4th edition, London, A.D. Mc. Nair, 1928.

O'Shea, Brendan. *Crisis at Bihac: Bosnia's Bloody Battlefield*. Phoenix Mill: Sutton Publishing, 1998.

Oliver, Ian. *War and Peace in The Balkans; The Diplomacy of Conflict in the Former Yugoslavia*. London: I.B. Tauris, 2005.

Owen, David. *Balkan Odyssey*. London: Indigo, 1996.

Palmer, Stephen E. Jr. and King, Robert R. *Yugoslav Communism and the Macedonian Question*. Hamden: Archon Books, 1971.

Paris, Edmond. *Genocide in Satellite Croatia; A Record of Racial and Religious Prosecutions and Massacres*. Chicago: American Institute for Balkan Affairs, 1961.

Patton, Kenneth S. *Kingdom of Serbs, Croats and Slovenes (Yugoslavia): A Commercial and Industrial Handbook*. Washington, DC: U. S. Government Printing Office, 1928.

Paulova, Milada. *Jugoslavenski odbor; povijest jugoslavenske emigracije za Svjetskog rata od 1914.-1915.* [Yugoslav Committee; the History of the Yugoslav Emigration during the World War, 1914-1915]. Zagreb: Prosvjeta, 1925.

Pavkovic, Aleksandar. *Fragmentation of Yugoslavia; Nationalism and War in the Balkans*, 2nd ed. London: Palgrave Macmillan, 2000.

Pavlovich, Voyislav G. *Од монархије до републике; САД и Југославија (1941-1945)* [From Monarchy to a Republic; USA and Yugoslavia (1941-1945)]. Belgrade: Clio/Glas srpski, 1998.

Pavlowitch, Stevan K. *A History of the Balkans 1804-1945*. London and New York: Longman, 1999.

————. *Serbia; The History behind the Name*. London: Hurst & Company, 2002.

Pegan, Sergije. "Politicki system" [Political System]. In *Jugosloveni o drustvenoj krizi (istrazivanje javnog mnjenja, 1985. godine)* [Yugoslavs on Societal Crisis (Public Opinion Research in 1985)], ed. Drasko Grbic. Belgrade: Komunist, 1989.

Petranović, Branko. *Balkanska Federacija 1943-1948* [Balkan Federation 1943-1948]. Sabac: IKP Zaslon, 1991.

————. *Istoričar i savremena epoha* [Historian and the Contemporary Period]. Belgrade: Vojska, 1994.

————. *Srbija u drugom svetskom ratu, 1939-1945* [Serbia in the Second World War]. Belgrade: Vojna štamparija, 1992.

Petranović, Branko and Štrbac, Čedomir, eds., *Istorija socialističke Jugoslavije* [History of Socialist Yugoslavia] Documents I, Vol. 2. Belgrade: Radnička štampa, 1977.

Petranović, Branko and Zečević, Momčilo, eds. *Jugoslavija 1918-1984, Zbirka dokumenata* [Yugoslavia 1918-1984; Collection of documents]. Belgrade: Rad, 1985.

————. *Jugoslovenski federalizam, ideje i stvarnost, Tematska zbirka dokumenata I, 1914-1943* [Yugoslav federalism, ideas and reality; Thematic collection of documents I, 1914-1943]. Belgrade: Prosveta, 1987.

Petrovich, Michael Boro. *A History of Modern Serbia, 1804-1918*. New York: Harcourt Brace Jovanovich, 1976.

Petrović, Rade. *Nacionalno pitanje u Dalmaciji u XIX stoljecu* [National question in Dalmatia in XIX Century]. Sarajevo: Svjetlost, and Zagreb: Prosvjeta, 1982.

Pipa, Arshi and Repishti, Sami, eds., *Studies on Kosova*. Boulder, CO: East European Monographs, 1984.

Plavshich, Bilyana [Биљана Плавшић/Biljana Plavsic]. "Witnessing" [Сведочим]. Banya Luka: Trioprint, 2005.

Pomerance, Michla. *Self-Determination in Law and Practice: The New Doctrine in the United Nations*. The Hague; Boston: M. Nijhoff, 1982.

Popovic, Dragoljub. *Short Essays on Serbian Constitutional Problems*. Belgrade: Center for Serbian Studies, 1997.

Popovski, Vesna. "Yugoslavia: Politics, Federation, Nation." In *Public Policy and Administration in the Soviet Union*, ed. Smith, Gordon B. New York: Praeger Publishers, 1980.

Pribichevich, Stojan. *Macedonia, Its People and History*. University Park: Pennsylvania State University Press, 1982.

Pribichevich, Svetozar. "Misao vodilja Srba i Hrvata" [Guiding Thought of Serbs and Croats]. In *Narodna misao*, eds. Jovan Banjanin et al. Zagreb: Dionicka tiskara, 1897.

Protich, Milan St. *Успон и пад српске идеје* [Rise and Fall of the Serbian Idea]. Belgrade: Cigoja stampa, 1995.

———. *Misconceptions about Bosnia-Herzegovina; Contradiction in terms*. Belgrade: Center for Serbian Studies, 1994.

Protich, Stoyan. *Nacrt Ustava* [Draft Constitution] (Belgrade: Dositeja Obradovica, 1920).

Przhich, Iliya. *Спољашња политика Србије (1804-1914)* [Serbia's Foreign Policy (1804-1914)]. Belgrade: Politika AD, 1939.

Račić, Obrad. "Mirno rešavanje sporova i traženje rešenja za jugoslovensku krizu" [Peaceful Conflict Resolution and Seeking Solutions to the Yugoslav Crisis]. In *Medjunarodno pravo i jugoslovenska kriza* [International Law and the Yugoslav Crisis], ed. Milan Šahović, 89-119. Belgrade: Institute for International Politics and Economy, 1995.

Radan, Peter. *The Break-up of Yugoslavia and International Law*. Routledge Studies in International Law. London; New York: Routledge, 2002.

Radulovic, Srdjan. *Sudbina Krajine* [The Fate of Krayina]. Belgrade: Dan Graf, 1996.

Ramcharan, Bertrand B., ed. *The International Conference on the Former Yugoslavia: Official Papers*. Kluwer Law International, 1997.

Rashkovich, Yovan [Raskovic, Jovan / Рашковић, Јован]. *Luda Zemlja* [An Insane Country]. Belgrade: Akvarijus, 1990.

Rivelli, Marco Aurelio. *L'Arcivescovo del genocidio* [Archbishop of Genocide]. Milano: Kaos Edizioni, 1999.

Roberts, Walter R. *Tito, Mihailović, and the Allies, 1941-1945*. New Brunswick, NJ: Rutgers University Press, 1973. Reprint. Durham, NC: Duke University Press, 1987.

Rodolphe, François. *Les Constitutions Modernes-Recueil des constitutions en vigueur dans les divers Etats d'Europe, d'Amérique et du monde civilisé*. Paris: Challamel, 1910.

Roksandić, Drago. *Srbi u Hrvatskoj* [Serbs in Croatia]. Zagreb: Vjesnik, 1991.

Rothenberg, Gunther E. *The Military Border in Croatia, 1740-1881*. Chicago: University of Chicago Press, 1966.

Ridley, Jasper. *Tito, A Biography*. London: Constable, 1994.

Rogel, Carole. "In the Beginning: the Slovenes from the Seventh Century to 1945." In *Independent Slovenia; Origins, Movements, Prospects*, eds. Jill Benderly and Evan Kraft, 3-21. London: Macmillan Press, 1994.

Rozett, Robert and Spector, Shmuel, eds. *The Encyclopedia of the Holocaust* 2. Yad Vashem and The Jerusalem Publishing House and Facts On File, 2000.

Rubin, Alfred P. *Ethics and Authority in International Law*. Edited by James Crawford, Cambridge Studies in International and Comparative Law. Cambridge: Cambridge University Press, 1997.

Rusinow, Dennison. *The Yugoslav Experiment 1948-1974*. London: C.Hurst and company, 1977.

Salmon, Jean. "Internal Aspects of the Right to Self-Determination: Towards a Democratic Legitimacy Principle?" In *Modern Law of Self-Determination*, ed. Christian Tomuschat, 253-82. Dordrecht; Boston: M. Nijhoff Publishers, 1993.

Samardjitch, Radovan. *Mehmed Sokolovitch*. Lausanne: L'Age d'Homme, 1994.

Schwadner-Seivers, Stephanie and Fischer, Bernd J., eds. *Albanian identities: Myth and history*. London: Hurst & Company, 2002.

Sell, Louis. *Slobodan Milosevic and the Destruction of Yugoslavia*. Durham and London: Duke University Press, 2002.

Shoup, Paul. *Communism and the Yugoslav National Question* (New York: Columbia University Press, 1968).

Silber, Laura and Little, Alan. *Yugoslavia: Death of a Nation*, rev. ed. New York: Penguin Books, 1997.

Singleton, Fred. *A Short History of the Yugoslav Peoples*. Cambridge: Cambridge University Press, 1985.

Sisic, Ferdo. *Abridged Political History of Rieka (Fiume)*. Paris, 1919.

———. *Dokumenti o postanku Kraljevine Srba, Hrvata i Slovenaca, 1914-1919* [Documents on the Creation of Kingdom of Serbs, Croats and Slovenes]. Zagreb, 1920.

Skendi, Stavro. *The Albanian National Awakening 1878-1912*. Princeton, NJ: Princeton University Press, 1967.

Sliyepchevich, Dyoko [Ђоко Слијепчевић]. *Историја српске православне цркве* [History of the Serbian Orthodox Church], vol. 1. Belgrade: BIGZ, 1991.

Smilyanich, Ilya. *Dalmatian Kosovo*. Belgrade: Serbian Cultural Society "Zora" and Association of Serbs from Croatia, 2006.

Smith, Gordon B., ed. *Public Policy and Administration in the Soviet Union*. New York: Praeger Publishers, 1980.

Spasovski, Milena, Zivkovich, Dragica and Stepich, Milomir. "The Ethnic Structure of the Population in Bosnia and Herzegovina." In *The Serbian Question in the Balkans; Geographical and Historical Aspects*, ed. Bratislav Atanackovic. Belgrade: Faculty of Geography, University of Belgrade, 1995.

Spomenica Nikole P. Pašića [In memory of Nikola P. Pashich]. Belgrade, 1926.

Statistical Yearbook of Yugoslavia 1991. Belgrade: Federal statistics bureau, 1992.

Stefanovski, Mirjana. "Pitanje pravne valjanosti Uredbe o Banovini Hrvatskoj" [Question of legal validity of the Decree on Banovina Hrvatska]. In *Pravna i politička misao Mihaila Ilića* [Legal and political thought of Mihailo Ilich], eds. Dragaš Denković and Jovica Trkulja, 306-317. Belgrade: Pravni fakultet Univerziteta u Beogradu, 1995.

Steinberg, Jonathan. "The Roman Catholic Church and Genocide in Croatia, 1941-1945." In *Christianity and Judaism*, ed. Diana Wood. London: Blackwell Publishers, 1992.

Stoyadinovitch, Dr Milan. *La Yougoslavie entre les deux guerres; ni le pacte, ni la guerre*. Paris: Nouvelles Editions Latines, 1979.

Stojanović, Ivan. *Povjest Dubrovačke Republike* [The History of the Republic of Dubrovnik], orig. written in German by Ivan Hristijan v. Engel. Dubrovnik: Srpske Dubrovačke Štamparije A. Pasarića, 1903.

Stoyanovich, Nikola. *Србија и југословенско уједињење* [Serbia and the Yugoslav Union]. Belgrade: Politika AD, 1939.

Stokes, Gale. "The Role of the Yugoslav Committee in the Formation of Yugoslavia." In Dimitrije Djordjevic, ed., *The Creation of Yugoslavia 1914-1918*, 51-71. Santa Barbara: Clio Books, 1980.

Sunstein, Cass R. *Designing Democracy, What Constitutions Do*. New York: Oxford University Press, 2001.

Sureda, A. Rigo. *The Evolution of the Right of Self-Determination: A Study of United Nations Practice*. Leiden, AW Sijthoff, 1973,

Susmel, Edoardo and Susmel, Duilio eds. "Il patto di Corfu." In *Opera omnia di Benito Mussolini* IX. Florence, La Fenice, 1951.

Suster, Zeljan E. *Historical Dictionary of the Federal Republic of Yugoslavia*. European Historical Dictionaries No. 29. Lanham, MD/London: Scarecrow Press, 1999.

Šehić, Nusret. *Autonomni pokret Muslimana za vrijeme austrougarske uprave u Bosni i Hercegovini* [The Autonomy Movement of Muslims during Austro-Hungarian Administration in Bosnia-Herzegovina]. Sarajevo, 1980.

Šepić, Dragovan. *Italija, saveznici i jugoslavensko pitanje 1914-1918* [Italy, the Allies and the Yugoslav Question, 1914-1918]. Zagreb: Školska knjiga, 1970.

Tanner, Marcus. *Croatia; A Nation forged in War*. New Haven and London: Yale University Press, 1997.

Terrett, Steve. *The Dissolution of Yugoslavia and the Badinter Arbitration Commission; A Contextual Study of Peace-Making Efforts in the Post-Cold War World*. Aldershot: Ashgate Dartmouth Publishing, 2000.

Terzic, Slavenko. "The Right to Self-Determination and the Serbian Question." In *The Serbian Question in the Balkans; Geographical and Historical Aspects*, ed. Bratislav Atanackovic. Belgrade: Faculty of Geography, University of Belgrade, 1995.

Thornberry, Patrick. "The Democratic or Internal Aspects of Self-Determination with Some Remarks on Federalism." In *Modern Law of Self-Determination*, ed. Christian Tomuschat, 101-38. Dordrecht; Boston: M. Nijhoff Publishers, 1993.

―――. *International Law and the Rights of Minorities*. Oxford, England; New York: Clarendon Press; Oxford University Press, 1991.

Todorova, Maria N. *Imagining the Balkans*. Oxford, New York: Oxford University Press, 1997.

Toft, Monica Duffy. *The Geography of Ethnic Violence*. Princeton and Oxford: Princeton University Press, 2003.

Tomasevich, Jozo. *War and Revolution in Yugoslavia, 1941-1945; Occupation and Collaboration*. Stanford: Stanford University Press, 1975.

Tomuschat, Christian. "Self-Determination in a Post-Colonial World." In *Modern Law of Self-Determination*, ed. Christian Tomuschat, 1-20. Dordrecht; Boston: M. Nijhoff Publishers, 1993.

——, ed. *Modern Law of Self-Determination*. Developments in International Law 16. Dordrecht; Boston: M. Nijhoff Publishers, 1993.

Treadway, John D. *The Falcon and the Eagle, Montenegro and Austria-Hungary, 1908-1914*. West Lafayette: Purdue University Press, 1983.

Trifkovic, Srdja. *Ustasha; Croatian Separatism and European Politics, 1929-1945*. London: The Lord Byron Foundation for Balkan Studies, 1998.

Trifunovska, Snezana. *Yugoslavia Through Documents From Its Creation to its Dissolution*. Dordrecht: Martinus Nijhoff, 1994.

Tripalo, Miko. *Hrvatsko proljece* [Croatian Spring]. Zagreb: Globus, 1990.

Tudjman, Franjo. *Bespuća povijesne zbilnosti: Rasprava o povijesti i filosofiji zlosilje* [Impasses of historical reality: A discussion of the history and philosophy of malevolent power), 2nd ed. Zagreb: Matica Hrvatska, 1989.

——, *Nacionalno pitanje u suvremenoj Evropi* [National Question in Contemporary Europe), 2nd ed. Munchen-Barcelona: Knjizica Hrvatske Revije, 1982.

Unfinished Peace; Report of the International Commission on the Balkans. Washington: Carnegie Endowment for International Peace, 1996.

Veremis, Thanos and Kofos, Evangelos. *Kosovo; Avoiding Another Balkan War*. Athens: Hellenic Foundation for European and Foreign Policy, 1998.

Vickers, Miranda. *Between Serb and Albanian; A History of Kosovo*. New York: Columbia University Press, 1998.

Vincic, Branko. "History of Serbs in Croatia." In *Krayina; Tragedy of a People*. Hamilton, ON: Canadian-Serbian Council, 1998.

Vladisavljević, Milan. *Hrvatska autonomija pod Austro-Ugarskom* [Croat autonomy under Austria-Hungary]. Belgrade: Politika AD, 1939.

Vodopivec, Peter. "Seven Decades of Unconfronted Incongruities: The Slovenes and Yugoslavia." In *Independent Slovenia; Origins, Movements, Prospects*, eds. Jill Benderly and Evan Kraft. ondon: Macmillan Press, 1994.

von Ranke, Leopold. *History of Servia and the Servian Revolution*. London: Benn, 1848,

Vucinich, Wayne. "The Formation of Yugoslavia." In In *Creation of Yugoslavia 1914-1918*, ed. Dimitrije Djordjevic. Santa Barbara: Clio Books, 1980.

————ed. *The First Serbian Uprising 1804-1813*. Boulder, New York: Columbia University Press, 1982.

Vujović, Dimitrije Dimo. *Podgorička Skupština 1918* [Podgorica Assembly 1918]. Zagreb: Školska knjiga, 1989.

Vukichevich, Milenko M. *Знаменити Срби муслимани* [Eminent Serb Muslims], 2nd ed. Belgrade: NNK, 1998; orig. 1906.

Vuynovich, Andrey «Одржавање елемената државности и покушаји обнове српске државе од XVI до XIX столећа» [Preserving elements of statehood and attempts to renew Serb state from the XVI to the XIX century]. In *Први српски устанак и обнова српске државе* [The First Serbian Insurrection and Renewal of Serb State]. Belgrade: Historical Museum of Serbia, 2004.

Yosipovich, Dushan. *Принципи политичко-територијалне поделе у Југославији* [Principles of political-territorial division in Yugoslavia]. Belgrade: Rad, 1963.

Yovanovich, Slobodan [Jovanovic, Slobodan / Јовановић, Слободан]. *Политичке и правне расправе* I-III [Political and legal discussions I-III]. Belgrade: BIGZ, 1990, orig. 1908.

——. *Влада Александра Обреновића* [The Government of Alexander Obrenovich] Vol. 2 (1897-1903). Belgrade, BIGZ, 1990, 1st ed. 1931.

Yarchevich, Slobodan [Jarcevic, Slobodan / Јарчевић, Слободан]. *Република Српска Крајина; државна документа* [Republic of Serb Krayina; State Documents]. Belgrade: Miroslav, 2005.

Yovich, Spyridon [Јовић, Сприридон]. *Ethnographic Picture of the Military Border in Slavonia*, 2nd ed., orig. 1835 [Етнографска слика Славонске војне границе] Belgrade:Chigoya shtampa, 2004.

Wachtel, Andrew Baruch. *Making a Nation, Breaking a Nation: Literature and Cultural Politics in Yugoslavia*. Stanford: Stanford University Press, 1998.

Waldron, Jeremy. "Minority Cultures and the Cosmopolitan Alternative." In *The Rights of Minority Cultures*, ed. Will Kymlicka, 93-119. Oxford, New York: Oxford University Press, 1995.

A LEGAL GEOGRAPHY OF YUGOSLAVIA'S DISINTEGRATION

Wheeler, Mark C. *Britain and the War for Yugoslavia, 1940-1943*. East European Monographs. Boulder, 1980.
Webster, Charles K. and Herbert, Syndey. *The League of Nations in Theory and Practice*. London: G. Allen & Unwin, 1933.

Weiss, Thomas G. "Collective Spinelessness: U.N. Actions in the Former Yugoslavia." In *The World and Yugoslavia's Wars*, ed. Richard H. Ullman. New York: Council on Foreign Relations, 1996.

West, Richard. *Tito and the Rise and Fall of Yugoslavia*. London: Sinclair-Stevenson, 1994.

Whiteman, Marjorie M. *Digest of International Law*. 2. 1963.

Williams, John. *Legitimacy in International Relations and the Rise and Fall of Yugoslavia*. London: Macmillan Press, 1998.

Williamson, Samuel R. Jr. *Austria-Hungary and the Origins of the First World War*. London: Macmillan, 1991.

Wilson, Woodrow. *The Messages and Papers of Woodrow Wilson*, ed. Albert Shaw. New York: The Review of Reviews Corporation, 1924.

Woodward, Susan L. *Balkan Tragedy; Chaos and Dissolution after the Cold War*. Washington, D.C.: The Brookings Institution, 1995.

——. "Redrawing Borders in a Period of Systemic Transition." In *International Organizations and Ethnic Conflict*, eds. Milton J. Esman and Shibley Telhani. Ithaca, NY: Cornell University Press, 1995.

——. "Compromised Sovereignty to Create Sovereignty: Is Dayton Bosnia a Futile Exercise or an Emerging Model?" In *Problematic Sovereignty; Contested Rules and Political Possibilities*, ed. Stephen D. Krasner. New York: Columbia University Press, 2001.

Zecevic, Miodrag and Lekic, Bogdan. *Frontiers and Internal Territorial Division of Yugoslavia*. Belgrade: Ministry of Information of the Republic of Serbia, 1991.

Zimmermann, Warren. *Origins of a Catastrophe, Yugoslavia and Its Destroyers - America's Last Ambassador Tells What Happened and Why*. New York: Times Books, 1996.

Zivojinovic, Dragoljub R. *America, Italy, and the Birth of Yugoslavia 1917-19*. Boulder CO: East European Quarterly, 1972.

Journal Articles and Academic Presentations:

Antonopoulos, Constantine. "The Principle of Uti Possidetis Juris in Contemporary International Law." *Revue hellénique de droit international* 49 (1996): 29-88.

Babic, Jovan and Jokic, Aleksandar. "The Ethics of International Sanctions: The Case of Yugoslavia." *The Fletcher Forum of World Affairs* 24, no. I (Spring 2000): 87-102.

Bagwell, Ben. "Yugoslavian Constitutional Questions: Self-Determination and Secession of Member Republics." *Georgia Journal of International and Comparative Law* 21, No. 3 (1991).

Bartos, Tomas. "Uti Possidetis. Quo Vadis?" *Australian Year Book of International Law*, 18 (1997): 37-96.

Batakovic, Dusan T.

—— "A Balkan-Style French Revolution? The 1804 Serbian Uprising in European Perspective." *Balcanica XXXVI*. Belgrade: Institute for Balkan Studies, 2006, 113-129.

"Twentieth-Century Kosovo-Metohija: Migrations, Nationalism, and Communism," *Journal of the North American Society for Serbian Studies* 13(2): 1-23, 1999

Beran, Harry. "A Liberal Theory of Secession." *Political Studies* 78 (1984): 21-31.

Biondich, Mark. "Religion and Nation in Wartime Croatia: Reflections on the Ustasha Policy of Forced Religious Conversions, 1941-192." *Slavonic and East European Review* 83, No. 1 (January 2005): 71-116.

Boyd, Charles. "Making Peace with the Guilty." *Foreign Affairs* (September/October 1995): 22-38.

Buchar, Bojko. "Medjunarodni aspekti jugoslovenske reforme i osamostaljenja Slovenije" [International aspects of the Yugoslav reform and the Autonomy of Slovenia]. *Medjunarodna Politika*, no. 988 (June 1991).

Burg, Steven L. "Ethnic Conflict and the Federalization of Socialist Yugoslavia: The Serbo-Croat Conflict." *Publius: The Journal of Federalism* 7 (1977): 119-143.

——."Republican and Provincial Constitution Making in Yugoslav Politics." *Publius: The Journal of Federalism* 12 (1982).

Castellino, Joshua and Allen, Steve. "The Doctrine of *Uti Possidetis*: Crystallization of Modern Post-Colonial Identity." *German Yearbook of International Law* 43 (2000): 205-226.

Charney, James I. "Anticipatory Humanitarian Intervention in Kosovo." *Vanderbilt Journal of Transnational Law* 32, no.5 (November 1999).

Christiansen, Drew. "What We Must Learn From Kosovo: Military Intervention and Humanitarian Aid." *America*, 181.5, 29 August 1999.

Cohen, Lenard J. "Russia and the Balkans: pan-Slavism, partnership and Power." *International Journal* XLIX, no. 1 (Canadian Institute of International Affairs, Autumn 1994): 814-845.

Connor, Walker. "From Tribe to Nation." *History of European Ideas* 13 (1991).

Conversi, Daniele. "German-Bashing and the Breakup of Yugoslavia." The Donald W. Treadgold Papers (Jackson School of International Studies, University of Washington, 1998).

Craven, Matthew. "The European Community Arbitration Commission on Yugoslavia." *The British Yearbook of International Law* 66 (1995).

Beverly Crawford, "Explaining Defection from International Cooperation: Germany's Unilateral Recognition of Croatia." *World Politics* 48, No. 4 (July 1996): 482-521.

Crawford, James. "State Practice and International Law in relation to Secession." *The British Yearbook of International Law* 69 (1998): 85-117.

Cvijic, Jovan. "The Geographical Distribution of the Balkan Peoples." *The Geographical Review* V, No. 5 (May 1918): 345-361.

Delcourt, Barbara. "L'application de l'uti possidetis juris au démembrement de la Yougoslavie: règle coutumière ou impératif politique?" *Revue Belge de Droit International* (Bruxelles: Bruylant, 1998/1).

Dedijer, Jevto. "Stara Srbija; geografska i etnografska slika" [Old Serbia; Geographic and Ethnographic Picture]. *Srpski knjizevni glasnik* XXIX (1912), 674-699.

Dempsey, Gary T. "Rethinking the Dayton Agreement: Bosnia Three Years Later." *Cato Policy Analysis* No. 327, 14 December 1998.

Dimić, Ljubodrag. "Nekoliko dokumenata o privremenoj administrativnoj granici izmedju jugoslovenskih republika Srbije i Hrvatske" [Several documents on the temporary administrative border between the Yugoslav republics Serbia and Croatia]. *History of 20th Century* X, no 1-2 (1992).

Dinstein, Yoram. "Collective Human Rights of Peoples and Minorities." *International and Comparative Law Quarterly*, no. 102 (1976).

Djordjevich, Dimitrije. "The Serbs as an Integrating and Disintegrating Factor." *Austrian History Yearbook* 3, No. 2 (1967): 48-82.

Djurić, Mihailo. "Smišljene smutnje" [Devised confusions]. *Anali pravnog fakulteta u Beogradu* XIX, No. 3 (1971): 230-233.

Djurkovic, Misa. "Montenegro: Headed for new Divisions?" *Conflict Studies Research Centre: Balkan Series* 07/11. Watchfield: Defence Academy of the United Kingdom, March 2007.

Donia, Robert J. "Fin-de-Siecle Sarajevo: the Habsburg transformation of an Ottoman town." *Austrian History Yearbook* (January 2002).

Draper, Stark. "The Conceptualization of an Albanian Nation." *Ethnic and Racial Studies* 20, no. 1 (January 1997)

Drew, Catriona. "Independence through Devolution - Scotland, Self-determination and the Badinter Paradox." *Juridical Review*, no. 2 (1996): 161-4.

Dugard, John. "Secession: Is the Case of Yugoslavia a Precedent for Africa?" *African Journal of International and Comparative Law* 5 (1993): 163-75.

Ewin, Robert. "Peoples and Political Obligation." *Macquarie Law Journal* 3 (2003).

Gligorijevic, Branislav. "Unutrasnje (administrativne) granice Jugoslavije izmedju dva svetska rata 1918-1941" [Internal (administrative] borders of Yugoslavia between two world wars 1918-1941]. *The History of 20th Century X*, no 1-2 (1992).

Gordon, Philip. *Die Deutsch-Französische Partnerschaft und die Atlantische Allianz* [The German-French Partnership and the Atlantic Alliance]. (Bonn: Arbeitspapiere zur Internationalen Politik, no. 82, 1993).

Gow, James. "After the Flood: Literature on the Context, Causes and Course of the Yugoslav War - Reflections and Refractions." *Slavonic & East European Review* 75 (1997): 446-484.

Hannum, Hurst. "Self-Determination, Yugoslavia, and Europe: Old Wine in New Bottles?" 3 *Transnational Law and Contemporary Problems* 57 (1993).

Hannum, Hurst "Rethinking Self-Determination," Virginia Journal of International Law 34 (1993),

———. "The Specter of Secession, Responding to Claims for Ethnic Self-Determination," *Foreign Affairs* 77, no. 2 (1998).

Hayden, Robert M. "Constitutional Nationalism in the Formerly Yugoslav Republics," *Slavic Review* 51 (1992).

———. "Constitutional Nationalism and the Logic of the Wars in Yugoslavia." *Problems of Post-Communism* 43, no. 5 (1996)

———. "Bosnia's Internal War and the International Criminal Tribunal." *Fletcher Forum of World Affairs* 22, no. 1 (1998): 45-63.

———. "Constitutional Structures in a Nationless State." Paper presented at the conference on "The Tenth Anniversary of the Dayton Accords: Reflections on Post-Conflict state- and Nation-Building." Woodrow Wilson International Center for Scholars. Washington, DC, 7 December 2005.

Hoare, Attila. "The People's Liberation Movement in Bosnia and Hercegovina, 1941-45: What Did it Mean to fight for a Multi-National State?" *Nationalism & Ethnic Politics* 2 (1996): 415-445.

Hoppe, Hans-Joachim "Moscow and the Conflicts in Former Yugoslavia." *Aussenpolitik*, no. 3 (1997): 267-277.

Howse, Robert and Knop, Karen. "Federalism, Secession, and the Limits of Ethnic Accommodation: A Canadian Perspective." *New Europe Law* Review 1, no. 2 (1993): 269-320.

Janjatović, Bosiljka. "Progoni triju političkih grupacija u Hrvatskoj (1918-1921)" [Persecution of three political groupings in Croatia]. *Historijski zbornik* XLV, No. 1 (Zagreb, 1992): 1-374.

Jelavich, Charles. "The Croatian Problem in the Habsburg Empire in the Nineteenth Century." *Austrian History Yearbook* 3, No. 2 (1967): 83-115.

Jovanovich, Vladislav "The Status of the Federal Republic of Yugoslavia in the United Nations." *Fordham International Law Journal* 21 (1998).

"The Joyless Victory." *The Wilson Quarterly* 23, No. 4 (Autumn 1999).

Kalić, Nada. "Pacta conventa ili tobožnji ugovor između plemstva dvanaestoro plemena i kralja Kolomana 1102. godine" [*Pacta conventa* or the alleged contract between twelve tribes and king Koloman of 1102]. *Historijski pregled* 2 (1960).

Kardelj, Edvard. "Prednacrt Ustava FSRL" [Draft Constitution of SFRY]. *Komunist* (1962).

Kofman, Daniel. "Secession, Law and Rights: The Case of the Former Yugoslavia." *Human Rights Review* I, No. 2 (2000): 9-26.

Kohen, Marcelo G. "Le problème des frontières en cas de dissolution et de séparation d'états: quelles alternatives?" *Revue Belge de Droit International* (1998/1).

Kostrenčić, Marko. "Pacta conventa", *Enciklopedija Jugoslavije*. Zagreb, 1955.

Knapp, Viktor. "Socialist Federation - A Legal Means to the Solution of the Nationality Problem: A Comparative Study." *Michigan Law Review* 82 (1984): 1213-1228.

Kolar-Dimitrijević, Mira. "Privredne veze izmedju Austrije i sjeverne Hrvatske od 1918. do 1925" [Economic ties between Austria and North Croatia].*Historijski zbornik* XLV, No. 1 (Zagreb, 1992): 1-374.

Koskenniemi, Martti. "National Self-Determination Today: Problems of Legal Theory and Practice." *International and Comparative Law Quarterly* 43, no. 2 (April 1994).

Kreća, Milenko. "Badinterova Arbitražna komisija; kritički osvrt" [Badinter's Arbitration Commission; A Critical Commentary]. *Jugoslovenski pregled [Yugoslav Review]* (Belgrade, 1993).

Kupchan, Charles A. "Independence for Kosovo." *Foreign Affairs* 84, no. 6 (November-December 2005).

Ladrech, Robert. "Europeanization of domestic politics and institutions: the case of France." *Journal of Common Market Studies* 32, no. 1 (1984): 69-88.

Lalonde, Suzanne. "The Role of *Uti Possidetis* in Determining Boundaries: From Kosovo to Quebec." Paper presented at the International conference on Legal and Political Solutions to Disputes over Sovereignty – From Kosovo to Quebec. Belgrade University, 7-10 July 2005.

Last, Major D.M. "Reflections from the Field: Ethical Challenges in Peacekeeping and Humanitarian Interventions." *The Fletcher Forum of World Affairs* 24, no. 1 (Spring 2000): 73-86.

Lencek, Rado L. "The Enlightenment's Interest in Languages and the National Revival of the South Slavs." *Canadian Revue of Studies in Nationalism* 10 (1983): 111-134.

Lloyd, David O. "Succession, Secession, and State Membership in the United Nations." *New York University Journal of International Law and Politics* 26 (1994).

Lewis, Flora. "Bavarian TV and the Balkan War." *New Perspectives Quarterly*, Vol. II, No. 3 (Summer 1994).

Macleod, Alex. "French policy toward the war in the former Yugoslavia: a bid for international leadership." *International Journal* LII, no. 2 (Spring 1997).

Marković, Slobodan G. "Communist 'Liberation' and new Order in Belgrade." *The South Slav Journal* 24, No. 3-4 (Autumn-Winter 2003).

Massari, Maurizio. "Do All Roads Lead to Brussels? Analysis of the Different Trajectories of Croatia, Serbia-Montenegro and Bosnia-Herzegovina." *Cambridge Review of International Affairs* 18, no. 2 (July 2005).

Maull, Hanns W. "Germany in the Yugoslav Crisis." *Survival* 37, no.4 (Winter 1995-96): 99-130.

McMahon, Patrice C. "Rebuilding Bosnia: A Model to Emulate or to Avoid?" *Political Science Quarterly*, 119.4 (Winter 2004).

Milojevic, "Branko Z. "The Kingdom of Serbs, Croats, and Slovenes: Administrative Divisions in Relation to Natural Regions." *Geographical Review* 15 (1925).

Mullerson, Rein. "The Continuity and Succession of States By Reference to the Former Soviet USSR and Yugoslavia." *International and Comparative Law Quarterly* 42 (1993).

Naldi, Gino J. "Separatism in the Comoros: Some Legal Aspects." *Leiden Journal of International Law* 11 (1998).

Nenadic, Mario. "Rights of Displaced Serbs in Bosnia and Herzegovina." Paper Presented at the Harvard Club of Serbia and Montenegro conference: "The Rights of Displaced Serbs in Light of European Integration." OSCE, Belgrade, 8 December 2005.

Nesi, G. "L'uti possidetis hors du contexte de la décolonisation: le cas de l'Europe." *AFDI* 44 (1998).

Pallua, Emilio. "A Survey of the Constitutional History of the Kingdom of Dalmatia, Croatia, and Slavonia." *Canadian-American Slavic Studies* 24 (1990): 129-154.

Paunovic, Milan. "Serbia's Borders are Inviolable." *Review of International Affairs* 4, no. 1067 (15 April 1998): 1-4.

Pavkovic, Aleksandar. "Multiculturalism as a prelude to state fragmentation: the case of Yugoslavia." *Journal of Southern Europe and the Balkans* 3, No. 2 (2001).

———. "Review Article: The Origins of Contemporary Serb Nationalism: Yet Another Case of trahison des clercs?" *The Slavonic and East European Review* 82, no. 1 (January 2004).

Pecelj, Branko M. "Constitutional Characteristics of the Socialist Republic of Bosnia and Herzegovina." *Review of the Study Centre for Jugoslav Affairs* 5 (1965): 328-338.

Pellet, Alain. "The Opinions of the Badinter Arbitration Committee; A Second Breath for the Self-Determination of Peoples." *European Journal of International Law* 3 (1992).

Petrovich, Michael B. "The Rise of Modern Slovenian Historiography." *Journal of Central European Affairs* 22 (1963).

———. "The Central Government of Yugoslavia." *Political Science Quarterly* 62, No. 4 (1947): 504-530.

Petrovic, Nenad V. "The Fall of Aleksandar Rankovic." *Review of the Study Centre for Yugoslav Affairs* I, No 6 (1967): 533-551.

Pierre-Caps, Stéphane. "Karl Renner et l'Etat Multinationale: Contribution Juridique á la Solution d'Imbroglios Politiques Contemporains." *Droit et Société* 27 (1994): 421-441.

Pipa, Arishi. "The Political Situation of the Albanians in Yugoslavia, With Particular Attention to the Kosovo Problem: A Critical Approach." 23 *East European Quarterly* (1989): 159-181.

Porter, Kirsten. "Realisation of National Minority Rights." *Macquarie Law Journal* 3 (2003): 51-72.

Radan, Peter. "The Legal Regulation of Secession: Lessons from Yugoslavia." Paper presented at the International conference on Legal and Political Solutions to Disputes over Sovereignty – From Kosovo to Quebec. Belgrade University, 7-10 July 2005.

Rady, Martyn. "Self Determination and the Dissolution of Yugoslavia." *Ethnic and Racial Studies* 19 (1996).

Ramet, Pedro. "Kosovo and the Limits of Yugoslav Socialist Patriotism." *Canadian Review of Studies in Nationalism* 16. (1989): 227-250.

Ratner, Steven R. "Drawing a Better Line: *Uti Possidetis* and the Borders of New States." *American Journal of International Law* 90 (1996): 590-624.

Rossos, Andrew. "The British Foreign Office and Macedonian National Identity, 1918-1941." *Slavic Review* 53, No. 2 (Summer, 1994): 369-394.

Rubin, Alfred P. "Dayton, Bosnia, and the limits of law." *The National Interest*, no. 46 (Winter 1996): 41(6).

Rupel, Dimitrij. "Slovenia and the World." *Review of International Affairs* XLII (Belgrade, 5 February 1991).

Schell, Jonathan. "The Unconquerable World." *Harper's Magazine* 306 (2003). Schimmelfenning, Frank and Sedelmeier, Ulrich. "Governance by Conditionality: EU rule transfer to the candidate countries of Central and Eastern Europe." *Journal of European Public Policy* 11, no. 4 (2004): 669-687

Sejdiu, Korab R. "The Revival of a Forgotten Dispute: Deciding Kosova's Future," *Rutgers University Journal of Law and Urban Policy* 3, no. 1.

Sell, Louis. "The Serb Flight from Sarajevo: Dayton's First Failure." *East European Politics and Societies* 14 (2000): 179-202.

Shaw, N. "Peoples, Territorialism and Boundaries." *European Journal of International Law* 3 (1997).

Shelah, Menachem. "The Catholic Church in Croatia, the Vatican and the Murder of the Croatian Jews." *Holocaust and Genocide Studies* 4, No. 3 (1990): 323-339.

Solana, Javier. "NATO's Success in Kosovo." *Foreign Affairs* 78, no. 6 (November-December 1999).

Spence, Richard B. "General Stephan Freiherr Sarkotić von Lovčen and Croatian Nationalism." *Canadian Review of Studies in Nationalism* 17, 1-2 (1990): 147-55.

Stefanovic, Djordje, "Seeing the Albanians through Serbian eyes: The inventors of the tradition of intolerance and their critics." *European History Quarterly* 35, no 3 (1995): 465-492.

Steil, Benn and Woodward, Susan L. "A European 'New Deal' For The Balkans." *Foreign Affairs* 78, no. 6 (November-December 1999).

Sunstein, Cass R. "Should Constitutions Protect the Right to Secede? A Reply to Weinstock." *Journal of Political Philosophy* 9, No. 3 (2001): 350-355.

Szasz, Paul C. "The Fragmentation of Yugoslavia." The American Society of International Law: Proceedings of the 88th Annual Meeting (6-9 April 1994).

Thornberry, Cedric. "Saving the War Crimes Tribunal." *Foreign Policy*, no 104 (Fall 1996).

Thumann, Michael. "Between Ambition and Paralysis: Germany's Balkan Policy, 1991-1994." *The Balkans and CFSP; The Views of Greece and Germany.* CEPS Paper No. 59 (Brussels, July 1994).

Tiersky, Ronald. "France in New Europe." *Foreign Affairs* (Spring 1992).

Trifkovic, Srdjan. "The First Yugoslavia and Origins of Croatian Separatism." *East European Quarterly* 26 (1992): 345-370.

Tubilewicz, Czeslaw. "China and the Yugoslav Crisis, 1990-94: Beijing's Exercise in Dialectics." *Issues & Studies* 33, no. 4 (April 1997): 94-112.

Tucker, Robert W. and Hendrickson, David. "America and Bosnia." *The National Interest* (Fall 1993).

Valentić, Mirko, "Koncepcija Garašaninovog 'Načertanija' (1844)." *Historijski pregled* VII (1961).

Várady, Tibor. "Collective Minority Rights and Problems in their Legal Protection: The Example of Yugoslavia." *East European Politics and Societies* 6 (1992).

Weinstock, Daniel. "Constitutionalizing the Right to Secede." *Journal of Political Philosophy* 9, No. 2 (2001): 182-203.

Weller, Marc. "International Law and Chaos." *Cambridge Law Journal* 52, no. 8 (1993).

Wildhaber. "Territorial Modifications and Breakups in Federal States." *Canadian Yearbook of International Law* (1995).

Zečević, Momčilo. "Ideološke osnove jugoslovenskih unutrašnjih razgraničenja" [The ideological basis for the internal border delimitation]. *The History of 20th Century* X, no 1-2 (1992).

Zwitter, Fran. "The Slovenes and the Habsburg Monarchy." *Austrian History Yearbook* 3, No. 2 (1967): 159-188.

Doctoral Dissertations:

Godtfredsen, Lawrence R. *Federalism and Yugoslav Political Integration*. Unpublished Doctoral Dissertation. Tufts University, 1973.

Radan, Peter. *Self-Determination, Uti Possidetis and Post-Secession International Borders: The Case of Yugoslavia*. Unpublished Doctoral Dissertation. University of Sydney, 1998.

Masters Theses:

Rajkovic, Nikolas M. "Conditionality and the Public Sphere: A Synthetic Explanation of Hague Conditionality and (Non)Compliance in Serbia." Master Thesis. Central European University, 2005.

Index

A

A LEGAL GEOGRAPHY OF YUGOSLAVIA'S DISINTEGRATION

E